DCN
Designing
Cisco®
Networks

Thomas M. Thomas II,
Erik Freeland, Michael Coker,
Donald A. Stoddard

McGraw-Hill
New York   San Francisco   Washington, D.C.
Auckland   Bogotá   Caracas   Lisbon   London
Madrid   Mexico City   Milan   Montreal   New Delhi
San Juan   Singapore   Sydney   Tokyo   Toronto

McGraw-Hill

A Division of The **McGraw·Hill** *Companies*

Copyright © 2001 by The McGraw-Hill Companies, Inc. All rights reserved.
Printed in the United States of America. Except as permitted under the United
States Copyright Act of 1976, no part of this publication may be reproduced or
distributed in any form or by any means, or stored in a data base or retrieval
system, without the prior written permission of the publisher.

1 2 3 4 5 6 7 8 9 0   PBT/PBT   0 5 4 3 2 1 0

P/N 0-07-212571-3
PART OF ISBN 0-07-212573-X

The executive editor for this book was Steven Elliot, the associate development
editor was Franny Kelly, and the production supervisor was Daina Penikas. It was
set in Century Schoolbook by D&G Limited, LLC.

Printed and bound by Phoenix Book Technology.

This study guide and/or material is not sponsored by, endorsed by or affiliated with
Cisco Systems, Inc., Cisco®, Cisco Systems®, CCDA™, CCNA™, CCDP™, CCNP™,
CCIE™, CCSI™, the Cisco Systems logo and the CCIE logo are trademarks or registered trademarks of Cisco Systems, Inc. in the United States and certain other countries. All other trademarks are trademarks of their respective owners. Rather than put
a trademark symbol after every occurrence of a trademarked name, we use names in
an editorial fashion only, and to the benefit of the trademark owner, with no intention
of infringement of the trademark. Where such designations appear in this book, they
have been printed with initial caps.

Information contained in this work has been obtained by The McGraw-Hill
Companies, Inc. ("McGraw-Hill") from sources believed to be reliable. However,
neither McGraw-Hill nor its authors guarantees the accuracy or completeness
of any information published herein and neither McGraw-Hill nor its authors
shall be responsible for any errors, omissions, or damages arising out of use of
this information. This work is published with the understanding that McGraw-
Hill and its authors are supplying information but are not attempting to render engineering or other professional services. If such services are required, the
assistance of an appropriate professional should be sought.

 This book is printed on recycled, acid-free paper containing a minimum of 50
percent recycled de-inked fiber.

This book is dedicated to my wonderful wife Rose, through her support and love I have been able to accomplish many things in my life. I have always been amazed and impressed by her ability to support our family; she is a miracle in so many ways that only in my mind can I truly express the feelings I have for her. I am grateful for the wonderful things that we have experienced together, and there is no doubt that we were brought together for a reason; simple words are all I have . . . Thank you.

—THOMAS M. THOMAS, II

This book is dedicated to my wife, Angela, and son, Alex. Angela, thank you for all your support and help during these last few months. Without you, I could have never finished this book. Alex, daddy can play now.

—ERIK FREELAND

I'd like to dedicate this book to my loving parents for raising me with solid values and a strong belief in God.

—MICHAEL COKER

This book is dedicated to my wife, Denise. Without her constant encouragement, love, and understanding nothing in my life would be as it is, and to my children, Megan (seven) and Cameron (two), for making me take time out to play.

—DONALD STODDARD

CONTENTS

Acknowledgements   xvii

About the Authors   xix

About the Reviewers   xxi

Chapter 1   Introduction to Designing Cisco Networks   1

Introduction   2

Who Should Read This Book?   3

   CCDA Candidates   3

   Network Professionals Who Are Interested in Design   3

Standards Used throughout the Book   4

   Configurations   4

Author's Notes   4

Case Studies   5

Overview of Chapters   5

   Chapter 2—Internetworking Overview   5

   Chapter 3—Cisco Product Line Overview   5

   Chapter 4—Cisco Design Fundamentals   6

   Chapter 5—Documenting the Existing Network   6

   Chapter 6—Documenting New Requirements   6

   Chapter 7—Network Topology   6

   Chapter 8—LAN Design   7

   Chapter 9—WAN Design   7

   Chapter 10—Addressing Design   7

   Chapter 11—Routing Design   7

   Chapter 12—The Finishing Touches   7

   Chapter 13—Proving the Design   8

   Chapter 14—Testing the Design   8

Cisco CCDA Requirements   8

   Test Objectives   8

   How to Study for the Exam   8

   How to Take the Exam   13

Summary   13

Chapter 2   Internetworking Technology Overview   15

Objectives Covered in This Chapter   16

The OSI Model   17

Protocols   19

LAN Protocols	19
WAN Protocols	20
Routed versus Routing Protocols	22
Upper Layer Protocols	23
Network Topology Overviews	33
Basic Ethernet	34
Basic Token Ring	41
Fiber Distributed Data Interface (FDDI)	42
Summary	43
Frequently Asked Questions (FAQ)	44
Questions	47
Answers	51
Chapter 3 Choosing Cisco Hardware and Software	**55**
Objectives Covered in This Chapter	56
Introduction	56
Routers	57
Small-Office Routers	57
Mid-Range Routers	59
High-End Routers	60
LAN Switches	61
Fixed-Port Switches	61
Modular Switches	62
Specialized Hardware	64
ISDN and DSL Routers	64
Remote Access Routers	65
Firewalls	65
ATM Switches	66
SwitchProbes	67
LocalDirector	67
Software	67
IOS Software	68
CiscoSecure	68
CiscoWorks 2000	69
Netsys	69
Summary	69
Frequently Asked Questions (FAQ)	70
Questions	71
Answers	75

Contents

Chapter 4   Cisco Design Fundamentals   79

Objectives Covered in This Chapter   80
Cisco's Framework Triangle   80
   Protocols   81
   Media   82
   Transport   83
Hierarchical Design Principles   84
   The Three-Layer Approach   84
   The Hierarchical Model   85
Hierarchical Design Examples   89
Summary   93
Questions   94
Answers   99

Chapter 5   Documenting the Existing Network   101

Objectives Covered in This Chapter   102
Documentation Checklist   102
Network Maps   103
   Topology Maps   104
   Server/User Maps   106
Usage Documentation   107
   Application Usage   107
   Protocol Usage   109
Documentation Tools   110
   Protocol Analyzers   110
   NETSYS   111
   CiscoWorks   111
   Multi-Router Traffic Grapher (MRTG)   111
State of the Network   111
   Utilization   112
   Availability   114
   Reliability   115
   Performance   116
   Router and Switch Loads   117
   Network Management   118
   Potential Growth   118
Summary   119
Case Study   120
   Widget Manufacturing   120

Questions	124
Case Study: Limbo Medical Group	124
Case Study: Global Supplies Corporation	125
Case Study: Bank of Pompeii	127
Case Study: G&S Productions	128
Answers	131

Chapter 6	**Documenting the New Network**	**135**

Objectives Covered in This Chapter	136
Introduction	136
Documentation Checklist	136
Business Issues	137
What Problem Are You Trying to Solve?	138
Business Goals	140
Business Constraints	141
Company Policies	142
Project Scope	143
Exact Requirements	144
Acceptance Criteria	144
Design Requirements	145
Security Requirements	145
Manageability Requirements	145
Application Requirements	146
Performance Requirements	146
Usage Requirements	147
Traffic-Pattern Prediction	147
Case Study: Widget Manufacturing	148
Step 1: Business Issues—Problem Identification	148
Step 2: Business Issues—Goals and Objectives	149
Step 3: Business Issues—Constraints	150
Step 4: Scope of Work	150
Project Requirements	150
Project Timeline	151
Customer Deliverables	151
Acceptance Criteria	151
Step 5: Design Requirements	152
Security Requirements	152
Manageability Requirements	152
Application Requirements	152
Performance Requirements	153
Usage Requirements	153

Contents

Step 6: Traffic Pattern Determination 153
Summary 153
Questions 154
  Case Study: Limbo Medical Group 154
  Case Study: Global Supplies Corporation 156
  Case Study: Bank of Pompeii 158
  Case Study: G&S Productions 160
Answers 163

Chapter 7   Network Topology   167

Objectives Covered in this Chapter 168
Introduction 168
Hierarchical Model 169
  Router-Hub Network Model 170
  Virtual Local Area Network (VLAN) Model 172
  Multiprotocol over ATM (MPOA) Model 174
Redundant Network Model 177
  Physical Redundancy 177
  Router/Switch Redundancy 179
  Host Redundancy 182
Secure Network Model 183
  Basic Firewalls 186
  Virtual Private Network (VPN) Technology 189
Summary 191
Questions 193
Answers 197

Chapter 8   Local Area Network (LAN) Design   199

Objectives Covered in This Chapter 200
Introduction 200
  Network Media 201
  Route or Switch 217
  Case Studies: Widget Manufacturing 224
Summary 226
Questions 228
  Case Study: The Bank of Pompeii 231
Answers 233
LAN Terms Defined 236
  Cyclic Redundancy Check (CRC) 236
  Multistation Access Unit (MAU) 236

Routing Information Field (RIF)	236
Twisted Pair	236
Unshielded Twisted Pair (UTP)	236
Shielded Twisted Pair (STP)	237
Ethernet	237
Fast Ethernet	237
Token Ring	237
Gigabit Ethernet	237
Fiber Distributed Data Interface (FDDI)	237
Copper Distributed Data Interface (CDDI)	238
10Base2	238
10Base5	238
10BaseT	238
10BaseF	238
Fiber-Optic Inter-Repeater Link (FOIRL)	238
100BaseT	239
100BaseFX	239
100Base-T4	239
100BaseTX	239
Source Route Bridging (SRB)	239
Source Route/Translational Bridging (SR/TLB)	239
Inter-Switch Link (ISL)	240
American National Standards Institute (ANSI)	240
High-Speed Token Ring (HSTR)	240
Broadcast Domain	240
Collision Domain	240
Data Terminal Equipment (DTE)	241
Remote Monitoring (RMON)	241
Webliography	241
Bibliographic Chapter References	242

Chapter 9	**Designing Wide Area Networks (WANs)**	**243**

Objectives Covered in This Chapter	244
Introduction	244
WAN Circuits	244
Switched Circuits	245
Platform Selection	260
Case Study	261
Summary	263
Questions	264

Contents

Case Study: Limbo Medical Group 264
Case Study: Global Supplies Corporation 266
Case Study: G&S Productions 267
Answers 270

Chapter 10   Designing Network Addressing **271**

Objectives Covered in This Chapter 272
Introduction 272
Network Addressing Principles 272
    IP Addressing 273
    NAT 275
    Variable-Length Subnet Masks (VLSMs) 278
    Address Summarization 280
    IPX Addressing 282
    Selecting Addresses 284
    Case Study 285
Summary 289
Questions 290
    Case Study: Limbo Medical Group 290
    Case Study: Global Supplies Corporation 291
    Case Study: G&S Productions 293
Answers 294

Chapter 11   Designing Routing Architecture **297**

Objectives Covered in This Chapter 298
Introduction 298
    Static Routes 298
    Distance-Vector Protocols 300
    Link-State Protocols 310
    Overhead 315
    Design Notes 315
    Hybrid Protocols 316
    Convergence and Overhead 318
    Design Notes 318
    Bridging Protocols 318
    Operation 319
    Transparent Bridging 319
    Source-Route Bridging 320
    Overhead 323
    Design Notes 323

Case Study   323

Summary   324

Questions   326

   Case Study: Limbo Medical Group   326

   Case Study: Global Supplies Corporation   327

   Case Study: G&S Productions   329

Answers   331

Chapter 12 The Finishing Touches   333

Objectives Covered in This Chapter   334

Introduction   334

Router Software Features   334

   Access Lists   334

   Proxy Services   340

Encryption   341

   Encryption Key and Peer Router Configuration 342

   Peer Router Authentication   342

   Actual Data Encryption   343

   Queuing   346

   Case Study   350

Summary   352

Questions   353

   Case Study: Limbo Medical Group   353

   Case Study: Global Supplies Corporation   354

   Case Study: The Bank of Pompeii   356

Answers   359

Chapter 13 Proving the Design   361

Objectives Covered in This Chapter   362

Introduction   362

   Prototype versus Pilot   362

   Case Study: Widget Manufacturing   366

Summary   370

Questions   371

   Case Study: Limbo Medical Group   371

   Case Study: Global Supplies Corporation   372

   Case Study: The Bank of Pompeii   373

   Case Study: G&S Productions   375

Answers   377

Chapter 14   Testing the Design   379

   Objectives Covered in This Chapter   380
   Introduction   380
   Designing Testing Resources   380
     Showing Commands   380
     Protocol Analyzers   381
     Capturing Network Traffic   382
     Generating Network Traffic   382
     Customer Presentation   382
     Requirements   382
     Cost   383
     Risk   383
     Customer Presentation Template   383
     Case Study: Widget Manufacturing   385
   Summary   387
   Questions   388
     Case Study: Limbo Medical Group   388
     Case Study: Global Supplies Corporation   389
     Case Study: The Bank of Pompeii   390
   Answers   393

Appendix A   Glossary   395

Appendix B   Firewalls and DMZ Design   493

Appendix C   Desktop Protocol Design   535

Appendix D   Windows NT Networks   601

Appendix E   OSI Model   667

Bibliography   701

Webliography   703

Index   705

ACKNOWLEDGMENTS

I would like to acknowledge the abilities and support of the authors, Erik, Mike, and Don for their assistance in getting this book accomplished. There should be a book on how to design a successful team as I am sure you all would be in it.

Thomas M. Thomas, II

First, I'd like to thank Tom for asking me to participate in this project. Next, thanks to Mike and Don for all their help in bringing this book to completion. Finally, thanks to McGraw-Hill for the constant pestering to meet deadlines. Without all of these people, this book would never had happened.

Erik Freeland

I would like to acknowledge Tom Thomas and the rest of the coauthors for putting together such a valuable book. I'd also like to thank my tech reviewers whom are all teammates and good friends: Chuck Cummiskey, Richard Corley, and Robert Melis. Thanks to the entire Netigy team for the continued support. Lastly, I'd like to thank my wife for "continuing" to put up with the long and strenuous hours of writing.

Michael Coker

I'd like to thank Thomas M. Thomas for the opportunity to contribute to this book and the people at McGraw-Hill for accepting his recommendation. Also, the individuals that spent hours reviewing the book; you are the truly dedicated. Thank You.

Donald Stoddard

ABOUT THE AUTHORS

Thomas M. Thomas, II is a *Certified Cisco Systems Instructor* (CCSI), CCNP, CCDP, CCDA, and CCNA as well as the founder of NetCerts.com (www.netcerts.com) and the *Cisco Professional Association—Worldwide* (CPAW) for short (www.cpaw.org), an organization designed to bring together the users of Cisco equipment to learn and network. He was previously a course developer for Cisco Systems and an instructor for Chesapeake Computer Consultants. He has also authored *OSPF Network Design Solutions* and *Thomas' Concise Telecom & Networking Dictionary*. Tom is currently working as a Senior Principle Consultant and as the Assistant Director of CCPrep.com.

Erik Freeland is the Vice President/Director of Technology for Pinnacle Networking and Technology. Pinnacle is a full-service networking and systems consulting/integration company in Los Angeles. Erik is currently studying for his lab and expects to make his first attempt in early 2001. Currently, Erik holds CCNP, CCDP, CNX, and MSCE certifications.

Michael Coker, CCNP, MCSE, MCP+I, CNA, is a consultant at Netigy Corporation (Sacramento, CA), a Strategic Alliance Partner with Cisco, where he provides e-business infrastructure planning, design, and implementation. Michael is a member of Netigy's Global Security Practice, focusing on VPN design solutions as well as vulnerability assessments and facilitated risk analysis of customers' e-business architectures.

Michael is also a list moderator and an active member in many Cisco study groups assisting others in their pursuit for knowledge and careers in the Cisco networking industry. In addition, Michael has co-authored *Interconnecting Cisco Network Devices* published by McGraw-Hill.

Donald A. Stoddard, CCNA, CCDA, and MCP is a Windows NT Infrastructure Administrator for a leading consulting firm in Colorado. He has several years experience in the networking field. Prior to his career in the private sector, he served in the United States Air Force from 1988–1998 as a Personnel Specialist.

ABOUT THE CONTRIBUTOR

Gaurav Sabharwal is a Senior Systems Engineer for Hughes Software Systems (http://www.hssworld.com), India's #1 communication software company. At HSS Gaurav assists the IT team in designing, planning, and implementing the corporate network. He has spent the last eight years as a systems/network administrator. Gaurav holds a B.E. in Electronics and Communication. He is currently responsible for network and system administration support at Thuraya (http://www.thuraya.com), a satellite telecommunications company for Hughes Network Systems (http://www.hns.com), a Hughes Electronics Corporation company, a world leader in telecommunications technology, satellite, digital cellular, frame relay, ATM, and IP switching.

ABOUT THE REVIEWERS

A the leading publisher of technical books for more than 100 years, McGraw-Hill prides itself on bringing you the most authoritative and up-to-date information available. To ensure that our books meet the highest standards of accuracy, we have asked a number of top professionals and technical experts to review the accuracy of the material you are about to read.

We take great pleasure in thanking the following technical reviewers for their insights:

John C. Meggers, CCNP, CCDP, MCSE, MCP+I is a Network Support Engineer with Cisco Systems, supporting dial services for a major telecommunications client in the Washington, D.C. area. Prior to that, John worked for Sprint Enterprise Network Services in Fairfax, VA, where he was assigned to a project designing and implementing networks for a major financial organization, involving such issues and technologies as IP address design, Frame Relay, ISDN PRI and BRI, DLSw, STUN, hardware-based encryption, HSRP, EIGRP, OSPF, and network management. With more than 20 years' experience working with computers ranging from mainframes to minis to desktops, he has spent the last six years in NOS and networking support, implementation, design, and troubleshooting. When not working or with his family, John can generally be found studying for the CCIE lab exam.

Chuck Cummiskey, CISSP, has been involved with security for 30 years. Most recently, he has been a consultant in the electrical utility industry, providing guidance and input on *Secure Network Architecture* (SNA). He also has extensive security experience in the semiconductor industry, as well as government agencies. Specific areas of expertise include security policies, security team building and positioning, and forensics.

Richard Corley is a Senior Consultant with Netigy Corporation specializing in Network Architecture and Design. During the past seven years he has constructed and supported many large enterprise networks for California State Agencies and the first deregulated utility organization to use commercial-based communication as its sole form of local and wide area networking. He can be reached at `Richard.Corley@Netigy.com`.

Robert Melis is a Senior Consultant with Netigy Corporation in Sacramento, CA. In addition to his B.S. Degree in Electrical and Electronic Engineering, Robert has more than four years' experience in telecommunications and internetworking. Robert's telecommunication experience includes Project Engineering and Project Management for a large telecommunications carrier. His internetworking experience includes network design, implementation, and support for large enterprise networks in the utilities, telecommunications, and health care industries. Robert has experience with ATM, IP routing, switching, network management, and network security.

Don Sautter's career in the data communications field spans nearly 20 years doing many different jobs. He is currently employed at Cisco Systems as an NSA Engineer in the Research Triangle Park. Prior to Cisco, he was employed by MCI WorldCom for three years in two positions—the last as a Senior Network Design Engineer in the Customer Network Delivery division. His first position was on the McCoy's United States Postal Service Network as the 2nd level group leader.

CHAPTER 1

Introduction to Designing Cisco Networks

Introduction

There is no single book or manual that can teach you how to properly design computer networks. Many items contribute to the final design. For the perfect design, the designer would have to be a hardware guru, a cabling expert, a protocol master, and a routing genius. There is not a book on the market today that can fulfill these four requirements, nor can this book fulfill all of these requirements. This book, however, will assist fledgling designers with learning the basic foundations of network design.

Learning how to design networks is comprised of four basic areas: hardware, cabling, protocols, and routing. Few people will ever be experts in all of these fields, and few will ever be experts in all areas of a single field. For example, someone might be well acquainted with the *Transmission Control Protocol/Internet Protocol* (TCP/IP), but he or she might have never used IPX/SPX.

A designer can gain hardware knowledge in several ways. One method is to constantly surf the Cisco Systems Web site and closely examine every product. Another way might be to have the local Cisco account team explain the newer products on the market. The best way to gain hardware experience, however, is to actually see and use the equipment. Perhaps one of the most confusing aspects of hardware is building a modular router or switch. After the designer has completed one or two of them, much of the mystery is solved.

Cabling is an integral part of any network. Even a wireless network requires some type of physical connection to the rest of the network. Because cables come in many forms—*Unshielded Twisted Pair* (UTP), coaxial, or even fiber optic—learning the specifics of each can be time consuming. Again, the best knowledge comes from doing. A designer will forever remember the difference between fiber-optic connects if the equipment ordered comes with SC connectors and the cables have ST connectors.

NOTE: *When explaining networks to laymen, I often ask the question, "What three things make up a network?" I get many answers, ranging from a hub and routers to servers and users. But I believe that all networks are made up of zeros, ones, and a little*

bit of wire. In its most basic form, a network is simply binary communication over some type of cable.

A designer can gain protocol and routing knowledge simply by reading and studying. While experience helps, this experience is almost always based on a good understanding of the technology. For example, if a designer does not know anything about the *Open Shortest Path First* (OSPF) routing protocol, he or she cannot troubleshoot it. If he or she knows something about the protocol, however, then he or she can troubleshoot only up to that level.

Who Should Read This Book?

Any networking professional at any point in his or her professional development can read this book. This text covers the basic foundations of designing a network for a small- to medium-sized business. In general, no technology is covered in depth; rather, only the basics are presented. The book is best suited for two different individuals: *Cisco Certified Design Associate* (CCDA) candidates and networking professionals who are interested in network design.

CCDA Candidates

CCDA is the first step in the design track of Cisco career certifications. The CCDA title is the equivalent of the *Cisco Certified Network Associate* (CCNA) certification. This book will familiarize the reader with the Designing Cisco Networks course and prepare him or her for the CCDA test.

Network Professionals Who Are Interested in Design

Networking professionals who are interested in network design or who are faced with an impending design project can also use this book. If the design project seems more complex and in depth than some of the examples presented in this text, then the design might be beyond the abilities of a fledgling designer.

Standards Used throughout the Book

Throughout the book, there are several recurring items that we need to explain: router configurations, notes, and the case studies.

Configurations

Router configurations are a part of a later chapter that focuses on designing specific portions of the network. Router configurations are depicted in the following manner:

```
Midway Router Config
hostname Midway
!
ipx routing
!
interface Ethernet0
 ip address 172.16.4.1 255.255.255.0
 ipx network DD
```

These configurations are used to provide a deeper understanding of the examples provided. There are no configuration or command questions on the CCDA exam.

Author's Notes

Throughout the book, there will be times when special attention or explanation is required. In this case, a special note is indicated. These notes range from design tips to lessons learned.

NOTE: *This is an example of a note.*

Case Studies

Finally, the core of the CCDA exam is the case studies. There will be five case studies that we will follow throughout the book. One of these case studies will be used as an example that illustrates the topics covered in each chapter. The best way to approach case studies for the exam is to read the entire case study, then refer to the appropriate section in order to answer a question. But you should always read the case study first.

Overview of Chapters

The chapters begin by covering the basics of technology and design, followed by several chapters that cover the preliminary design requirements and the actual design process. Finally, we present the procedure for validating the design.

Chapter 2—Internetworking Overview

One of the keys to understanding design is understanding technology. It is impossible to design an IPX network if the fundamentals of IPX are nebulous. This chapter presents the basic of internetworking technologies and lays a foundation for later design topics.

Chapter 3—Cisco Product Line Overview

One of the requirements for designing a network is to understand the hardware that is available for the design. Hardware should not drive the design itself; however, some facets of the hardware itself might alter portions of the design. For example, if two requirements were for a low-cost *Asynchronous Transfer Mode* (ATM) network, then knowing about hardware would enable the designer to see the contradiction in these requirements.

Chapter 4—Cisco Design Fundamentals

The last fundamentals of design are the design fundamentals themselves. There are several rules for network design that enable the designer to ensure a quality design. The most important thing to remember is that these design fundamentals are common to not only basic designs but also to complex designs.

Chapter 5—Documenting the Existing Network

The first step of any network design is to document the existing network. This step includes baselining traffic and drawing network diagrams for existing servers, users, and traffic flows.

Chapter 6—Documenting New Requirements

The next step in the design process is to document the requirements of the new network. These requirements include the customer(s) requirements and other factors such as budget and political considerations.

Chapter 7—Network Topology

Before we address the specifics of network design, we will cover various network topologies in order to ensure that the designer has the necessary foundations. All network designs are based on these networking topologies.

Chapter 8—LAN Design

This chapter deals with the specific design requirements for *Local Area Networks* (LANs). In addition to LAN design, we provide a short description and explanation of various LAN technologies.

Chapter 9—WAN Design

This chapter deals with the specific design requirements for *Wide Area Networks* (WANs). In addition to WAN design, we provide a short description and explanation of various WAN technologies.

Chapter 10—Addressing Design

This chapter will provide the budding network designer with a basic understanding of network addressing and addressing design. TCP/IP and IPX addressing are covered. In addition, we will briefly cover several addressing concepts, such as summarization and *Variable Length Subnet Masks* (VLSMs).

Chapter 11—Routing Design

This chapter will provide an initial look at the design of routing protocols. We will provide a general overview of each protocol in order to enable the designer to select the appropriate protocols for his or her environment.

Chapter 12—The Finishing Touches

This chapter will cover various design elements that we have yet to address. These topics range from access lists to queuing and encryption. These finishing touches are important in order to ensure that the design is 100 percent complete.

Chapter 13—Proving the Design

Before any design is complete, it must be tested. There are several ways to test a network design. This chapter covers the selection of a pilot or prototype in order to test the network design.

Chapter 14—Testing the Design

Again, before any design is complete, it must be tested. Because the type of test has been determined, this chapter covers how to perform the test itself. This test is the final step in the design process, because it will validate the network design.

Cisco CCDA Requirements

The only requirement to achieve the CCDA certification is to pass the DCN exam, 640–441. This exam is based on the material covered in this book. The CCDA certification is the same level as the CCNA exam; however, the CCDA certification is part of the design track.

Test Objectives

Before taking the CCDA exam, 640–441, it is advisable for you to carefully review the objectives of the exam. All Cisco exams follow the objectives religiously. All questions fall within the boundary of one of these objectives. For example, there is no mention of DLSW in the objectives for the CCDA exam. Therefore, there is no need to study this technology for the CCDA exam. Table 1-1 shows the objectives for the CCDA exam and the chapter in which we cover this objective.

How to Study for the Exam

The best way to classify this exam is to compare it to an exam that is familiar to the candidate. This exam—specifically, the case study

Table 1-1	Number	Objective	Chapter(s)
CCDA exam objectives and their chapter locations	1.	Identify data to gather to characterize the customer's network	5, 6
	2.	Applications, protocols, topology, users, peak usage, security, and network management	5, 6
	3.	Business issues in a network-design project	6
	4.	Health of the existing network	5
	5.	Diagram the flow of information	5
	6.	Tools to characterize new network traffic	5, 6
	7.	Amount and type of traffic and its causes	5, 6
	8.	Advantages, disadvantages, scalability issues, and applicability of standard topologies	2, 7–12
	9.	Topology map of high-level view of devices and media	5
	10.	Scalability constraints and issues for standard technologies	2, 7–12
	11.	Scalability constraints and issues for standard WAN technologies and performance budgets	2, 9
	12.	Products to meet the requirements for performance, capacity, and scalability in an enterprise network	3
	13.	Addressing model for networks, subnetworks, and end stations that meet scalability requirements	10
	14.	Configuring addresses	10
	15.	Naming scheme for servers, routers, and user stations	10
	16.	Scalability constraints and issues for IGRP, Enhanced IGRP, IP RIP, IPX RIP/SAP, NLSP, AppleTalk RTMP and AURP, static routing, and bridging protocols	11
	17.	Routing and bridging protocols that meet a customer's requirements for performance, security, and capacity	11
	18.	Scalability issues for various Cisco IOS software features, access lists, proxy services, encryption, compression, and queuing	12
	19.	Cisco IOS software features for performance, security, capacity, and scalability	12
	20.	Proving that the network design meets the customer's needs	13, 14

(continues)

Table 1-1

Continued.

Number	Objective	Chapter(s)
21.	Tasks required to build a prototype that demonstrates the functionality of the network design	13, 14
22.	Cisco IOS software commands that you should use to determine whether a network structure meets the customer's performance and scalability goals	13, 14
23.	Demonstrate how the prototype meets the requirements for performance, security, capacity, and scalability and that the costs and risks are acceptable	13, 14
24.	Identify and describe the functions and process of communication by the seven layers of the OSI reference model	2
25.	Describe the basic process of information exchange between two applications across a network	2
26.	Distinguish between basic protocol information formats and describe their uses in data communications	2
27.	Identify and describe the elements of a hierarchical network, as specified by ISO	2, 4
28.	Define the term *protocol* and describe the difference between network architecture, such as the OSI model, and a protocol	2
29.	Describe connection-oriented network service and connectionless network service and identify the key differences between them	2
30.	Describe data-link addresses and network addresses and identify the key differences between them	2
31.	Define and describe the function of a MAC address	2
32.	Identify the three most commonly used methods to learn the MAC address of a network device and describe their basic operation	2
33.	Describe a flat address space and a hierarchical address space and identify the key differences between them	2, 10
34.	Identify the difference between static address assignment, dynamic address assignment, and server address assignment	10
35.	Identify the key differences between names and addresses in an internetwork	10
36.	Define flow control and describe the three basic methods used in networking	2

	Number	Objective	Chapter(s)
Table 1-1 *Continued.*	37.	Define error checking and describe the basic operation of the CRC	2
	38.	Define multiplexing and describe its function in internetworking	2
	39.	Identify the major standards organizations and bodies that specify internetworking standards	2
	40.	Identify the layers of the OSI model at which the LAN protocols operate	2, 7, 8
	41.	Briefly describe the two media access schemes most commonly used by LAN protocols	2, 7, 8
	42.	Define and describe the operation of unicast, multicast, and broadcast transmissions	2, 7, 8
	43.	Describe and compare the most common LAN topologies	2, 7, 8
	44.	Identify and describe the basic functions of the devices commonly found in LAN environments	2, 7, 8
	45.	Define WAN and identify the layers of the OSI reference model at which the WAN technologies operate	2, 9
	46.	Define and describe the operation of point-to-point, circuit-switched, and packet-switched links through a WAN	2, 9
	47.	Define PVC and SVC and identify the key differences between them	2, 9
	48.	Describe the operation of the DDR and dial-backup WAN implementations	9
	49.	Identify and describe the basic function of the devices commonly found in WANs	2, 9
	50.	Identify the layer of the OSI reference model at which bridging and switching technologies operate	2, 11
	51.	Identify and describe the hardware devices used in bridging and switching environments	2, 11
	52.	Identify the key differences between bridging and switching technologies	2, 11
	53.	Briefly describe the function of the routed protocols	2, 11
	54.	Identify the layers of the OSI model at which routed protocols operate	2, 11

(continues)

Table 1-1	**Number**	**Objective**	**Chapter(s)**
Continued.	55.	Describe the two fundamental functions served by routing protocols: path determination and path switching	2, 11
	55.	Describe the two fundamental functions served by routing protocols: path determination and path switching	2, 11
	56.	Define the term *routing metric* and describe how specific routing metrics operate	11
	57.	Describe the function of a routing table	11
	58.	Describe the function of routing updates	11
	59.	Describe the operation of link-state and distance vector routing protocols and identify the key differences between them	11
	60.	Describe the key features of routers	2, 11
	61.	Describe how hold-downs and the split-horizon rule help prevent routing loops	11
	62.	Identify the key difference between *interdomain* and *intradomain* routing	11
	63.	Identify the difference between the distributed and centralized routing strategies	11
	64.	Identify the difference between the host-based and router-based routing strategies	11
	65.	Describe the difference between static and dynamic routing and identify situations in which each would be appropriate to use	11
	66.	Describe both the *ships in the night* and the integrated solutions for multi-protocol routing and identify the key differences between them	11
	67.	Describe the function of routing firewalls in an internetwork environment	11

portion—is equivalent to reading the comprehension portion of the *Scholastic Aptitude Test* (SAT) exams that are used for college entrance exams in the United States.

The first study step is to read this book once from start to finish. Even if some of the material seems familiar, it is important that all the material is covered initially. Next, reread any section that still seems unfamiliar. Finally, reread all of the chapters that cover the foundations of technologies (especially Chapter 2, "Internetworking Technology Overview," and Chapter 7, "Network Topology").

Now, passing the exam should be within the candidate's grasp. The CCDA exam, 640–441, can be scheduled by calling Sylvan Prometric at 1-800-829-6387 within the United States. Outside the United States, call your local testing center for registration information.

How to Take the Exam

Unlike other Cisco exams, this test is focused on two types of questions: technology-based and case study-based questions. You should tackle each type of question in a different manner.

For the technology-based question, the best way to answer the question is to simply know the answer; however, you will not know some items. Therefore, the next solution is to try to eliminate answers that are known to be incorrect. Finally, look at questions later or earlier in the exam that might offer insight as to the answer to this mysterious question.

For the case study-based questions, the best way to attack the question is to completely read and reread the introductory case study material. Next, examine the first case study question. See whether the question is answered explicitly in the case study. If the answer does not appear in the text, examine the answers that are provided for the question. See which answer best fits the question based on the implied information in the case study material. This approach might sound basic and elementary, but most failures are caused by rushing through the test and assuming that the correct answer was located.

SUMMARY ▪ ▪ ▪ ▪ ▪ ▪ ▪ ▪

The key to understanding this book and the CCDA exam is that this material is for the beginning designer. All of the topics that are covered as part of the CCNP certification are generally beyond the scope of this exam. The exam focuses on three key areas:

- Basic networking technologies
- Basic design fundamentals
- Understanding and analyzing case studies

Probably the best suggestion for understanding design and for passing the exam is to closely review the chapters on design fundamentals and networking technologies. These two items, along with close reading, will simplify the third area: understanding case studies.

Internetworking Technology Overview

Objectives Covered in This Chapter

■ Review internetworking technology

The connecting of one computer or device to another, called *internetworking*, has been in use for many years. Understanding the technologies behind internetworking is a key principle in network design.

All network designs are based on a specific technology or a spectrum of networking technologies. Without knowing the basis tenets of networking technology, designing any network would be impossible.

Since the early days of internetworking, when terminals communicate with mainframes, a technology has always controlled the communication. The technologies that determine the rules and regulations for communication are called *protocols*. A protocol is much like an everyday communication. When someone starts a conversation with "Hello," they expect a greeting in return. A protocol dictates that saying "Goodbye" cannot start a conversation.

Local Area Networks (LANs) enable users within a building to share files and other information via a central file server. Future evolution of the file server has allowed database sharing and e-mail.

Wide Area Networks (WANs) are used to connect multiple LANs together into an internetwork. Traditionally, WANs were slower in speed than LANs.

NOTE: *The speed of modern WANs has finally surpassed LAN speeds. The fastest LAN protocol is Gigabit Ethernet, which has a speed of one Gbps. The fastest WAN protocol is OC-196, which has a speed of approximately 10 Gbps.*

The information presented in this chapter is intended to build upon the *Internetworking Technology Multimedia CD-ROM* developed by Cisco Systems. It is assumed that you are familiar with the topics and technologies presented in this CD-ROM.

The OSI Model

The reference point for all discussions of LAN and WAN protocols is the *Open Systems Interconnect* (OSI) model. This model was developed by the *International Organization for Standardization* (ISO). The model has seven layers. Each layer is intended to represent all the functions that must occur for an internetwork to operate. Figure 2-1 depicts the seven layers of the OSI model.

Each layer has a specific function and responsibility. According to the model, each layer is responsible for encapsulating the data received from an upper layer and passing it to a lower layer. The reverse happens upon receiving data from a lower layer. The data is de-encapsulated and is passed to the upper layer. This encapsulation process can be seen in Figure 2-2.

The layers from the bottom to the top are as follows: physical, data link, network, transport, session, presentation, and application. Each layer has a specific function and definition. More information regarding the OSI models and the specific layer functions can be found in Appendix C. The layers are outlined here:

■ *Physical*   This layer defines the electrical, mechanical, procedural, and functional specifications for activating, maintaining, and deactivating the physical link between end systems.

■ *Data link*   This provides a reliable transit of data across a physical link. The data link layer is concerned with physical

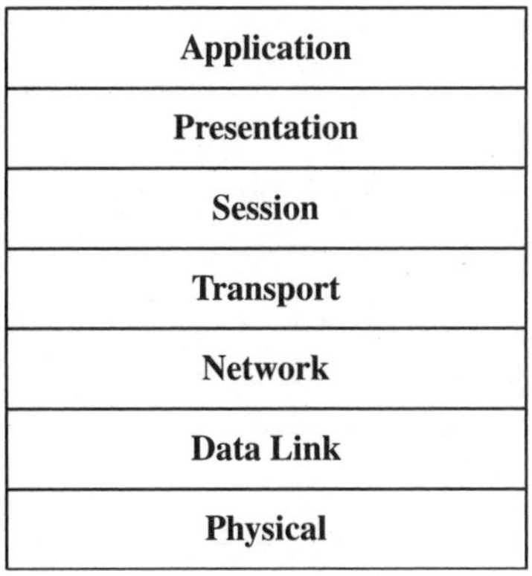

Figure 2-1
The seven-layer
OSI model

| Application |
| Presentation |
| Session |
| Transport |
| Network |
| Data Link |
| Physical |

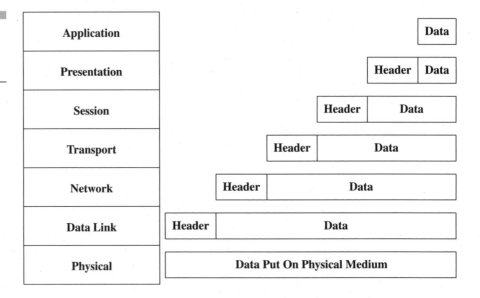

Figure 2-2
The encapsulation process of the OSI model

addressing, network topology, line discipline, error notification, the ordered delivery of frames, and flow control.

■ *Network*   This layer provides connectivity and path selection between two end systems. The network layer is the layer at which routing occurs.

■ *Transport*   This layer is responsible for reliable network communication between end nodes. The transport layer provides mechanisms for the establishment, maintenance, and termination of virtual circuits, transport fault detection and recovery, and information flow control.

■ *Session*   This layer establishes, manages, and terminates sessions between applications and manages the data exchange between presentation layer entities.

■ *Presentation*   This layer provides network resource management, session presentation services, and some application management. Encryption and decryption take place at this layer.

■ *Application*   This layer provides services to application processes (such as e-mail, file transfers, and terminal emulation) that are outside of the OSI model.

NOTE: *Except for exam purposes, do not take the OSI model as the absolute truth. For many protocols like ATM, it is impossible to classify them and their components according to the OSI model.*

Protocols

The types of protocols used depend on the OSI layer referenced as well as the type of network, LAN or WAN. For instance, TCP/IP, a layer 3 and above protocol, can be implemented on a LAN or WAN. The Ethernet protocol, a layer 1 and 2 protocol, is for LANs only.

LAN Protocols

LAN protocols operate at layers 1 and 2 of the OSI model. Of the many various LAN protocols, the most commonly used are Ethernet, in many speeds, Token Ring and *Fiber Distributed Data Interface* (FDDI).

As of 1999, Ethernet and its derivatives, Fast Ethernet and Gigabit Ethernet, are the most common LAN protocols. They use a contention-based method, *Carrier Sense Multiple Access / Collision Detection* (CSMA/CD) to access the physical medium. CSMA/CD means that the device tests the media to ensure it is free of traffic before sending data, using its "carrier sense." The multiple access portion of the name means that multiple devices can access the same physical medium. Finally, the collision detection means that devices will detect when a packet collision happens on the physical media.

In the '90s, Ethernet, with a speed of 10 Mbps, was tuned to allow for higher traffic speeds. Fast Ethernet operates at speeds of 100 Mbps over copper and fiber. Gigabit Ethernet operates at speeds of 1000 Mbps over copper and fiber.

NOTE: *In June 1999, the IEEE 802.3ab committee announced the formal ratification of the Gigabit Ethernet Over Copper standard.*

The second most common protocol in use is Token Ring. Token Ring uses a deterministic method of access. A token is passed along the ring to each station. The station with the token is allowed to send traffic. Unlike CSMA/CD environments, token-passing networks never have collisions. Token Ring operates at speeds of four Mbps and 16 Mbps.

FDDI is also a token-passing protocol. It operates at speeds of 100 Mbps. Depending on the FDDI configuration, the ring itself can be self-healing in the event of cable breaks.

WAN Protocols

WAN protocols, just like LAN protocols, operate at layers 1 and 2 of the OSI model. The most commonly used WAN protocols are *High Level Data Link Control* (HDLC), Frame Relay, *Asynchronous Transfer Mode* (ATM), and *Integrated Services Digital Network* (ISDN).

HDLC is the primary protocol used for point-to-point serial lines. Point-to-point lines provide a single circuit from one location to another. Here fixed circuits are always in operation.

Layer 2 addressing is not required in an HDLC environment. Since all links are point-to-point, the destination for any traffic is the other end of the link.

NOTE: *Cisco's implementation of HDLC is proprietary. You cannot use it to communicate with another vendor's equipment on the opposite end.*

Frame Relay is an example of a packet-switched service. Packets sent by the end nodes are switched within the provider's network until the destination is reached. Frame Relay is one of the most common types of WAN protocols in use today. It is less expensive to install a frame circuit over a long-distance link than a point-to-point serial link. Packet-switched networks can use either *permanent virtual circuits* (PVCs) or they can dynamically set up the circuit. PVCs are specified in the networking equipment. Dynamic circuits, or *switched virtual circuits* (SVCs), are created by the networking equipment when a call needs to be placed. SVCs are then torn down upon completion of the call.

The basis for all Frame Relay traffic is the *Data Link Connection Identifier* (DLCI). The DLCI is the Layer-2 address that identifies the PVC to use in order to reach a specific destination. The DLCI is locally significant. This means that for the edge device connected to the Frame Relay cloud, this DLCI identifies a local path. That same DLCI number can be used in another location to indicate another path.

NOTE: *SVCs are normally not provided by most telephone service providers. They only provide PVC circuits.*

ATM is another packet-switched network. Like Frame Relay, it can use either PVCs or SVCs. However, unlike Frame Relay, all ATM packets, called *cells*, are always 53 bytes long. This fixed size enables ATM switches to quickly switch cells from source port to destination port.

ATM addresses use 20 bytes or 160-bit addresses. These long addresses enable ATM to use a hierarchical method for routing calls through the network.

NOTE: *It may seem unusual for a 53-byte packet to have a 20-byte address, but in ATM the address is only used to set up the call. After that, it is no longer used. The actual addressing information in an ATM cell is only five bytes.*

ISDN is simply a digital dial-up. Using a digital connection, a remote location is called. This call setup request is passed through the service provider network to the destination number. This call is a circuit-switched service. All circuits are switched through the provider's network on a temporary basis. When the circuit is finished carrying traffic, it is disconnected.

ISDN addressing is similar to both ATM and HDLC addressing. In the first phase, the circuit is established. This is done by calling the destination phone number. This is identical to an ATM network setting up a SVC. After the circuit is established, all traffic follows the point-to-point model of HDLC.

Routed versus Routing Protocols

LAN and WAN protocols generally end at Layer 2 of the OSI model. Protocols that exist above layer 2 can usually be classified as routing protocols or routed protocols.

NOTE: *Several protocols, such as SNA and NetBIOS, cannot be routed because they do not have Layer-3 addresses. Though they are neither routed nor routing protocols, these protocols still exist above Layer 2.*

The standard definitions for routed and routing protocols are as follows:

- A routed protocol contains network, Layer 3, and addressing information. This Layer-3 information enables the protocol to be directed from one network to another. End user traffic is carried on routed protocols.
- A routing protocol provides support to a routed protocol by sharing routing information. The routing protocol information is distributed among routers. These protocols enable routers to update their route tables. Routing protocols do not carry end user data.

A router directs packets of a routed protocol from network to network. The router learns about these networks from routing protocols. Table 2-1 gives a short list of routed and routing protocols.

Table 2-1

Routed and routing protocols

Routed Protocols	Routing Protocols
TCP/IP	RIP, OSPF, EIGRP, BGP
IPX/SPX	RIP, EIGRP, NLSP
AppleTalk	RTMP, EIGRP

Upper Layer Protocols

Upper layer protocols occupy Layers 3 to 7 on the OSI model. They include routed, non-routed, and routing protocols including TCP/IP, *Internetwork Packet Exchange/Sequenced Packet Exchange* (IPX/ SPX), *Routing Internet Protocol* (RIP), and NetBIOS.

Transmission Control Protocol/Internet Protocol (TCP/IP)
TCP/IP is the most commonly used protocol in the world, and it is used on the Internet exclusively. TCP/IP is more than just the TCP and IP protocols; it is actually a suite of protocols that operate at all levels of the OSI model. Figure 2-3 details the TCP/IP protocols and how they match with the OSI model.

TCP/IP Network Layer This portion of the TCP/IP protocol suite deals with IP addressing and communication with the data link layer. The routing protocols of TCP/IP will be at the end of this section, even though they lie at Layer 3. The network layer consists of the following:

■ The *Internet Protocol* (IP) is the foundation for all the other TCP/IP protocols. It handles addressing information and

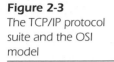

Figure 2-3
The TCP/IP protocol
suite and the OSI
model

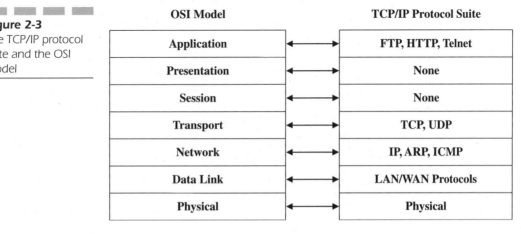

OSI Model		TCP/IP Protocol Suite
Application	←→	FTP, HTTP, Telnet
Presentation	←→	None
Session	←→	None
Transport	←→	TCP, UDP
Network	←→	IP, ARP, ICMP
Data Link	←→	LAN/WAN Protocols
Physical	←→	Physical

provides a best-effort, connectionless packet delivery service. It fragments and reassembles fragments caused by datagrams that are too large for the next network.

- The *Address Resolution Protocol* (ARP) is the protocol that discovers the data link address, or *media access control* (MAC) address, of the destination address. An ARP table is a listing of IP addresses on the local network and their corresponding MAC addresses.

- The *Internet Control Message Protocol* (ICMP) is used to report network errors. It is the basis for the ping command.

TCP/IP Transport layer   The following two protocols, the *Transmission Control Protocol* (TCP) and the *User Datagram Protocol* (UDP), form the basis for all user data traffic. All application protocols use one of these underlying protocols. Both protocols communicate with the upper layers based on port numbers. Each application layer protocol communicates over a transport layer protocol using a specific port number.

- TCP is a connection-oriented, reliable protocol. Every TCP session begins in the same manner. Host A requests a session setup from the destination. Host B acknowledges Host A's request and asks to set up a session on Host A. Finally, Host A acknowledges Host B's request. Now both sides can transmit any data required. When the conversation is finished, this session is disconnected. The reliable portion of the description means that all TCP packets are sequenced. If the packets arrive out of sequence, they can be easily reassembled. Also, if a packet is missed, the destination can request a specific packet from the source be resent.

- UDP is a connectionless protocol. It is not reliable. It simply sends datagrams to a destination IP address.

TCP/IP Application Layer   The application layer is home to the majority of the TCP/IP protocols. Each of the application-layer protocols uses one of the underlying transport protocols as well as IP for communication. The application-layer protocols are as follows:

■ The *File Transfer Protocol* (FTP) is used to transfer files between hosts.

■ The *Hypertext Transfer Protocol* (HTTP) is used across the Web to view Web pages.

■ Telnet is a terminal emulation application.

TCP/IP Routing Protocols   These routing protocols are responsible for passing network information from router to router. They do not carry user data:

■ RIP is the first TCP/IP routing protocol developed. It is a distance vector protocol and uses a hop count metric. It is limited, however, to a network of at most 15 hops. RIP does not support multiple subnet masks. It is a classful protocol. This means that RIP is constrained by the class of the IP address. The classes of IP addresses will be discussed in the next section. RIP version 2 is an enhancement to RIP. It enables multiple subnet masks as well as for 255 hops. Unlike RIP version 1, version 2 is not constrained by the IP class boundary. Therefore, RIP version 2 is a classless protocol.

■ The *Interior Gateway Routing Protocol* (IGRP) is a Cisco proprietary, distance vector, routing protocol. It does not support multiple subnet masks and is a classful protocol like RIP version 1. It uses a combination of metrics including bandwidth, delay, reliability, load, and *Maximum Transmission Unit* (MTU).

■ The *Enhanced IGRP* (EIGRP) is also a Cisco proprietary routing protocol. It is a hybrid routing protocol that integrates several link-state capabilities with several distance vector capabilities. It supports multiple subnet masks and is a classless protocol. Like IGRP, it uses a combination of metrics including bandwidth, delay, reliability, load, and MTU.

■ *Open Shortest Path First* (OSPF) is a link-state routing protocol. It is standards-based and supports multiple subnet masks. It is a classless protocol and supports an unlimited number of hops.

■ The *Border Gateway Protocol* (BGP) is the routing protocol of the Internet. It performs routing between multiple *autonomous systems* (ASs). It is also a classless protocol.

IP Addressing   IP addresses have two distinct parts: a network portion and a host portion. The network portion is always listed first. Devices on the same LAN will have the network portion but a unique host portion. An IP address is composed of 32 bits. These bits are divided into four sections, each with eight bits. These four sections are also called *octets*. The division between the host and network portions falls within these 32 bits. Sometimes it ends evenly on an octet boundary, but it does not have to end on a boundary.

These addresses can be written in their native form, which is binary, but this is difficult to read. The standard notation for IP addresses is the dotted decimal. Each octet is converted to a decimal number from 0 to 255. The octets are divided with a period. The dotted decimal address and its binary equivalent are shown in Figure 2-4.

Address Classes   All IP addresses can be classified depending on the range in which they fall. The five classes are A, B, C, D, and E. However, only Classes A through C can be used for production networks. Class D is used for multicast addresses and Class E addresses are reserved. In addition, all IP address classes are associated with a specific range of IP addresses. These IP address ranges are created by the first four digits of the first octet of the IP address. Table 2-2 lists the classes of addresses and the IP address ranges within these classes.

The IP address 127.0.0.1 is reserved for use as a loopback address and therefore the network is not included in the Class A range.

IP Subnets   Each class of addresses also has a default subnet mask. The subnet mask is used to indicate the division between the network and host portion of the address. According to the default subnet mask, all IP networks by default are only used in one LAN. Table 2-3 lists the default subnet masks for each class and the default number of hosts available.

Figure 2-4
IP addressing in binary and dotted decimal

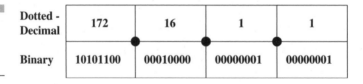

Dotted-Decimal	172	16	1	1
Binary	10101100	00010000	00000001	00000001

Table 2-2

IP addresses classes
and ranges

Class	First Four Bits of the First Octet	Address Range
Class A	0000	1.0.0.0–126.255.255.255*
Class B	1000	128.0.0.0–191.255.255.255
Class C	1100	192.0.0.0–223.255.255.255
Class D	1110	224.0.0.0–239.255.255.255
Class E	1111	240.0.0.0–247.255.255.255

Table 2-3

IP address classes
and default subnet
masks

Class	Default Subnet Mask	Sample Network	Available Hosts
Class A	255.0.0.0	10.0.0.0	> 16 million
Class B	255.255.0.0	172.16.0.0	65,534
Class C	255.255.255.0	192.168.1.0	254

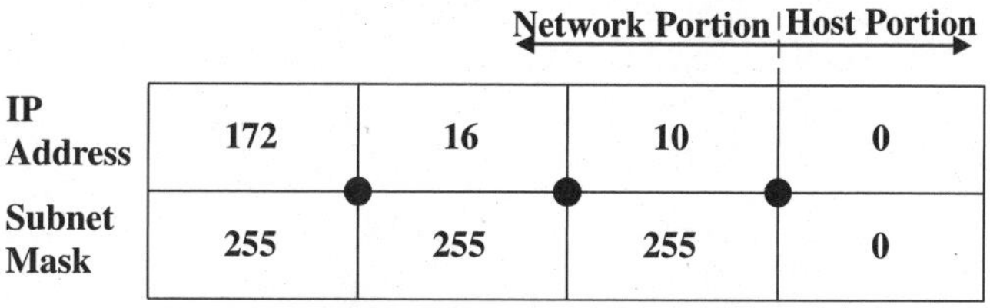

Figure 2-5
IP address with a
subnet applied

Some of the IP networks can have users on many LANs. However, in no network will you find 65,000 users on a single LAN. A method is required to further subdivide the host portion of the address into a subnet and host portion. Figure 2-5 shows a subnet applied to a network.

In essence, a subnet borrows bits from the host portion of the address. These borrowed bits enable a large network to be subdivided into smaller networks. When a portion of the address represents the network portion of an address, the binary bit of the subnet mask is set to 1. A bit set to zero in the subnet mask represents the host portion of the network. For instance, the subnet mask 255.255.255.0 represents the default mask of a class C network. It also could be a class B network with eight bits of subnetting and eight bits representing the hosts. The number of hosts or subnets available is calculated by raising to the power represented by the number of bits and then subtracting 2 ($2^8 - 2$).

Two is subtracted from the possible number of hosts and subnets because the binary equivalent of "all zeros" and "all ones" cannot be used. In the host portion of the address, "all zeros" represents the network itself. "All ones" represents the broadcast address of the network. For an eight-bit mask and an eight-bit host portion, this would result in 254 possible subnets and 254 possible hosts.

The same method is used for subnet masks that do not fall within the octet boundaries. Table 2-4 lists the possible values in a subnet mask and their binary representations.

The key to IP subnetting is remembering that the network portion of the network is always represented by a binary 1 in the subnet mask. For example, Figure 2-6 presents a class B network with a subnet mask of 255.255.254.0

First, convert the mask to binary and divide the network and host portion. Count the ones in the subnet portion of the address. In this case, we have seven ones. Count the zeros in the host portion of the address, which adds up to nine. The number of subnets available will be $2^7 - 2$, or 126. The number of hosts available will be $2^9 - 2$, or 510.

Table 2-4	Decimal Value of Subnet	Binary Equivalent
Subnet values and the binary equivalents	0	00000000
	128	10000000
	192	11000000
	224	11100000
	240	11110000
	248	11111000
	252	11111100
	254	11111110
	255	11111111

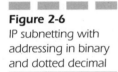

Figure 2-6

IP subnetting with addressing in binary and dotted decimal

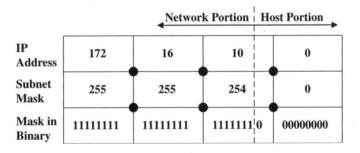

	Network Portion →			Host Portion
IP Address	172	16	10	0
Subnet Mask	255	255	254	0
Mask in Binary	11111111	11111111	11111110	00000000

Figure 2-7

The IPX protocol suite and the OSI model

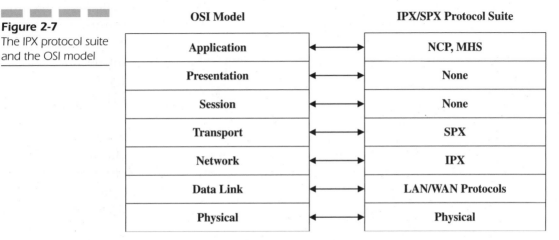

OSI Model		IPX/SPX Protocol Suite
Application	↔	NCP, MHS
Presentation	↔	None
Session	↔	None
Transport	↔	SPX
Network	↔	IPX
Data Link	↔	LAN/WAN Protocols
Physical	↔	Physical

Internetwork Packet Exchange/Sequenced Packet Exchange
Novell, Inc. developed the IPX/SPX protocol suite for use in their NetWare network operating system. When this suite was developed, TCP/IP had not become the *de facto* standard for addressing. TCP/IP was one of the various protocol suites of the era. Novell patterned their IPX suite after the *Xerox Network System* (XNS) protocol of Xerox. Just like TCP/IP, the IPX protocol suite can also be broken down by the accompanying OSI layer. Figure 2-7 shows the relationship between the OSI model and the IPX protocol suite.

IPX Network Layer This portion of the IPX protocol suite deals with IPX addressing and communication with the data link layer.

IPX is the foundation for all the other IPX/SPX protocols. It handles addressing information and provides a best-effort, connectionless packet delivery service. This service makes it similar to IP.

IPX Transport layer   In IPX, only one main protocol is used for the basis for all user data traffic. All application protocols use this protocol for communication. Each application layer protocol communicates over a transport layer protocol using a specific socket number. Like TCP, SPX is also aconnection-oriented, reliable protocol. All conversations are set up by the source and torn down when the conversation is finished. In addition, all packets are sequenced to ensure delivery.

IPX/SPX Application Layer   The application layer is home to the majority of the IPX/SPX protocols. Each of the application layer protocols use SPX for their underlying transport protocols as well as IPX for communication:

■ *NetWare Core Protocols* (NCPs) are the server-based protocols that provide file and print management for a NetWare operating system.

■ The *NetWare Message Handling System* (MHS) is a messaging system.

IPX Routing Protocols   These routing protocols are responsible for passing network information from router to router. They do not carry user data. The protocols include the following:

■ IPX RIP is modeled after IP RIP. The basic metrics are hop count and ticks, which are 1/18th of a second.

NOTE: *IPX RIP uses a completely different routing table and routing process than IP RIP.*

- EIGRP is a Cisco proprietary routing protocol that uses the same routing algorithm as both AppleTalk and IP EIGRP routing protocols. In addition, the packet formats and protocol specifics are the same for all three variants.

- The *Service Advertisement Protocol* (SAP) enables NetWare resources to advertise their existence to other devices on the network, for instance, whether a server is connected to the network. All SAP tables of servers and routers would be updated with this new resource.

- The *NetWare Link-Service Protocol* (NLSP) is a link-state protocol, similar to OSPF and *Intermediate System-to-Intermediate System* (IS-IS). It was developed to overcome many of the issues associated with IPX RIP and SAP.

IPX Addressing   IPX addressing, in comparison to IP addressing, is simple. The IPX network is assigned at the server and router interfaces. These network numbers must match on all devices on the network. If they do not match, the communication between them is inhibited. The IPX network number is a 32-bit number.

Clients have an IPX network layer address that is comprised of two parts. The first part or network portion is identical to all devices on the same LAN. The second portion of the network layer address is the host portion. The host portion of the address is identical to the client's MAC address. Since MAC addresses are unique, each IPX address is unique without any settings.

AppleTalk   Apple Computer Inc. developed the AppleTalk protocol suite in the early '80s for use with their Macintosh computers. AppleTalk has two distinct versions, Phase I and Phase II. Figure 2-8 shows the relationship between the OSI model and the AppleTalk protocol suite.

NOTE: *AppleTalk Phase 1 and Phase 2 are not compatible. This can cause issues when attempting to upgrade a network.*

Figure 2-8
The AppleTalk
protocol suite and
the OSI model

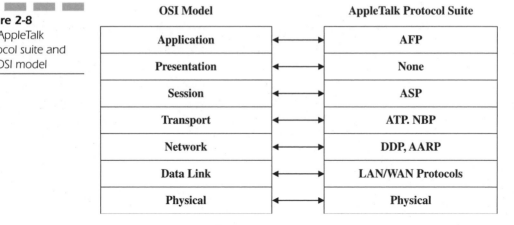

OSI Model		AppleTalk Protocol Suite
Application	←→	AFP
Presentation	←→	None
Session	←→	ASP
Transport	←→	ATP. NBP
Network	←→	DDP, AARP
Data Link	←→	LAN/WAN Protocols
Physical	←→	Physical

AppleTalk Network Layer This portion of the AppleTalk protocol suite deals with AppleTalk addressing and communication with the data link layer. It is composed of the following protocols:

- The *Datagram Delivery Protocol* (DDP) is the foundation for all the other AppleTalk protocols. It handles addressing information and provides a best-effort, connectionless packet delivery service. This service makes it similar to IP.

- The *AppleTalk Address-Resolution Protocol* (AARP) is the protocol that maps network-layer AppleTalk addresses to data-link MAC addresses. It is similar to the TCP/IP protocol ARP.

AppleTalk Transport Layer In AppleTalk, two important protocols operate at this layer. One is the basis for all user data traffic, while the other handles AppleTalk name-to-address resolution:

- The *AppleTalk Transaction Protocol* (ATP) is responsible for the transactions between AppleTalk nodes.

- The *Name Binding Protocol* (NBP) maps AppleTalk node names to network layer addresses. It is similar to the TCP/IP protocol DNS.

AppleTalk Session Layer AppleTalk is the first protocol covered that has a true session layer. The responsibilities of the protocols in this layer are to establish and maintain communications between nodes.

AppleTalk Application Layer   The application layer is home to a single protocol. This protocol, the *AppleTalk Filing Protocol* (AFP), is responsible for file sharing between clients and servers.

AppleTalk Routing Protocols   These routing protocols are responsible for passing network information from router to router and they do not carry user data:

■ The *Route Table Maintenance Protocol* (RTMP) is modeled after IP RIP. The basic metric is the hop count. RTMP broadcasts updates every 10 seconds.

■ EIGRP is a Cisco proprietary protocol that uses the same routing algorithm as both IPX and IP EIGRP routing protocols. In addition, the packet formats and protocol specifics are the same for all three variants.

AppleTalk Addressing   AppleTalk addressing is a little more complex than IPX addressing. Every network has a number assigned to it. This is configured on the router as the cable range. Each node communicates with the router upon startup to retrieve this network number. Then the node attempts to select its own node number. If the number chosen is already in use, another node number is chosen.

This process results in an address that is comprised of two portions, the network and node sections. The network section is a 16-bit value that identifies the AppleTalk network. The node portion is an 8-bit value. The length of the node portion restricts the number of nodes on a specific network to 256. For networks larger than this, a range of network numbers is assigned to the network.

Network Topology Overviews

Now that protocols have been covered in depth, it is time to examine the basics of networking equipment and network topologies. Since the middle of the '80s, networking equipment has changed dramatically. Modular chassis switches with backplane speeds of 256 Gbps have replaced the hubs that were once clustered throughout the data center.

Basic Ethernet

Ethernet was developed in the late '70s at the *Palo Alto Research Center* (PARC) of Xerox. Over the next 20 years, the speed of the original has been increased 100 times. However, the principles of Gigabit and Fast Ethernet are essentially the same as basic 10 Mbps Ethernet.

Ethernet is simply a group of devices that access a common shared medium, a cable, to exchange information. In the earliest days, the same cable was shared among all the users. One cable was physically connected to each device. After time, the size of LANs grew too large for one cable to suffice. From this need and other limitations of LANs, networking equipment was developed. The main pieces of network equipment for an Ethernet network are hubs, bridges/switches, and routers.

Many types of Ethernet exist. These types, like 10BaseT, are comprised of three separate parts. Figure 2-9 details the three parts.

The first part of any Ethernet type is always the speed in Mbps of the technology. For example, 100BaseT, or Fast Ethernet, runs at 100 Mbps. Likewise, 10BaseFL runs at 10 Mbps.

The second portion of the type is the signaling type. Here you have only two options. The most common option is Base. This means that the signaling method is *baseband*. A baseband signal enables only one signal to be transmitted at one time. The other method is *broadband*. The only type of Ethernet that uses broadband communications is 10Broad36. In this type of cable, multiple signals are multiplexed onto the media.

The final portion of the Ethernet type is the media type. This part can be one of the following descriptions:

Figure 2-9
Ethernet name
compositions

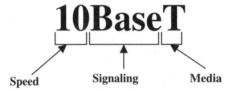

Speed   Signaling   Media

- *T*   This is *unshielded twisted pair* (UTP) cable. The maximum transmission distance is 100 meters or 328 feet.

- *F*   This is fiber-optic cable. The maximum transmission distance depends of the specific subtype:

  - *FB*   This provides backbone synchronous cabling. It enables additional segments and repeaters to be connected. The maximum transmission distance is 2000 meters or 1.2 miles.

  - *FL*   This is used to connect two fiber-optic repeaters. No additional segments or repeaters can be added. The maximum transmission distance is 2000 meters or 1.2 miles.

  - *FP*   This is used to connect computers into a star topology without the use of repeaters. The maximum transmission distance is 500 meters or 1,640 feet.

- *2*   This is coaxial cable. The cable type is RG58 or thinnet. The maximum transmission distance is 185 meters or 606 feet.

- *5*   This is coaxial cable. The cable type is RG8 or thicknet. The maximum transmission distance is 500 meters or 1,640 feet.

- *36*   This is coaxial cable. The cable type is broadband coaxial cable. The maximum transmission distance is 3,600 meters or 2.2 miles.

- *TX*   This is UTP wiring. The first pair of wires is used to receive data; the second is used to transmit. The maximum transmission distance is also 100 meters or 328 feet.

- *FX*   This is fiber-optic wiring. Two strands of fiber are used, one each for transmission and receiving. The maximum transmission distance is 400 meters or 1,312 feet.

- *T4*   Similar to TX, but all four pairs of wire are used to transmit and receive data. The maximum transmission distance is 100 meters or 328 feet.

- *LX*   This is fiber-optic cable. It is also called long-haul fiber. It uses long-wave lasers to transmit the signal. The maximum transmission distance is 550 meters or 1,804 feet.

- *SX*   This is also fiber-optic cable. It is also called short-haul fiber. It uses short-wave lasers to transmit the signal. The maximum transmission distance is 550 meters or 1,804 feet. Though the maximum transmission distance is equal to LX, most SX implementations are limited to 250 meters or 820 feet.

- *CX*   This is *shielded twisted pair* (STP). This is a special cable; it is not the same as IBM Type I or II STP. The maximum transmission distance is 25 meters or 82 feet.

Hubs   Hubs were one of the first pieces of networking equipment. They are also known as repeaters since they just repeat what they receive. They are simple devices. Figure 2-10 is a simple diagram of a network connected with a hub. When Host A communicates with Host D, the packet is also sent to Host B, Host C, and Host D. The packet is addressed to Host D, so Hosts B and C simply drop the packet.

As the size of these LANs grew, the number of hubs grew. Suddenly, what was once a basic network became a large complex network that was prone to broadcast storms and collisions.

For an Ethernet LAN of any size to operate, it must follow the 5-4-3 rule with regard to hubs. There can be a maximum of five segments between two hosts in a network, and there can be at most four hubs between these stations. Finally, only three of the segments can have users. Figure 2-11 depicts a hub network that has grown too large.

Figure 2-10
A basic network
with one hub

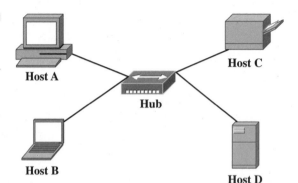

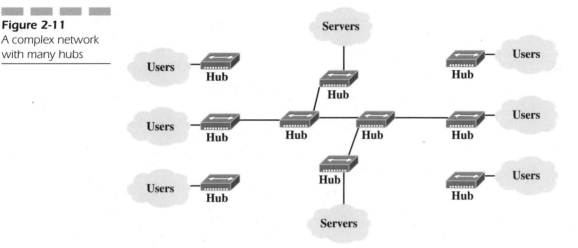

Figure 2-11
A complex network with many hubs

NOTE: *The 5-4-3 rule is for 10-Mbps hub networks only. A bridge, switch, or router negates this rule.*

Bridges/Switches   As networks grew larger and more complex, the traffic increased. Hubs kept propagating more and more user traffic. Large networks slowed as all the users contended for the same shared media. One answer was to segment users into *collision domains*. A collision domain is a group of users that share the same media.

In a pure hub environment, all users share the same media and therefore they are all in the same collision domain. The more users in a collision domain, the more collisions on the network. In order to reduce the number of users in a shared segment, the bridge was developed. Bridges and switches operate at layer 2 of the OSI model and segment traffic based on layer-2 or MAC addresses.

Bridges simply segment a network into several collision domains. Each of these collision domains is still considered part of the same LAN. In Figure 2-12, a basic bridge configuration has been depicted. If Host A is communicating with Host B, no packets are sent across the bridge. However, if host A wants to communicate with Host D,

Figure 2-12
A basic bridged
internetwork

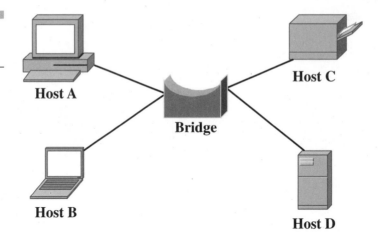

Figure 2-12
A basic bridged
internetwork

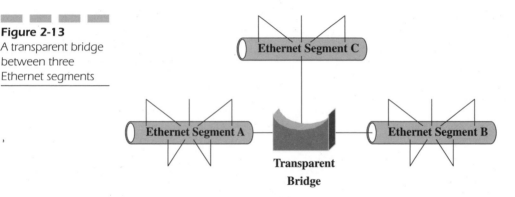

Figure 2-13
A transparent bridge
between three
Ethernet segments

the packets are sent through the bridge. This entire process is transparent to the end user.

Switches behave exactly like bridges. Switches are actually evolved bridges. They generally have more network ports as well as faster processing speeds. Switches use hardware devices to make forwarding decisions. Bridges use software to make these same decisions. As switches and bridges have grown in networks, a series of protocols has been created to enable intercommunication. The following are a few of the types of bridges:

■ *Transparent*   Bridging in an Ethernet environment. Figure 2-13 shows the placement and function of a transparent bridge.

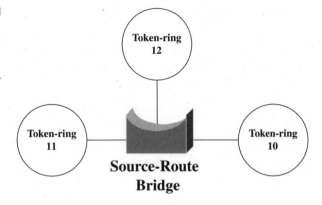

Figure 2-14
A source-route bridge
linking Token Ring
environments

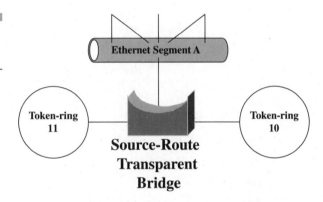

Figure 2-15
A source-route
translational bridge

- *Source-Route*   Bridging in a Token Ring environment. Figure 2-14 shows the placement and function of a source-route bridge.

- *Source-Route Translational*   This enables a bridge to support both Ethernet and Token Ring bridging. In addition, it can translate frames from the Ethernet network to the Token Ring network. Figure 2-15 shows the placement and function of a source-route translational bridge.

NOTE: *Source-Route Translational bridging is rarely used. The preferred device for this function is a router.*

As switched networks have grown, more attention has been devoted to another limitation of switched Ethernet: redundancy. A loop in a switched Ethernet network of any type can quickly bring the network to a halt with broadcast storms. This can be solved, however, with the Spanning Tree Protocol, IEEE 802.1d. This protocol is negotiated between switches and bridges upon startup. It can detect loops in the network and block all activity on these ports. As a network change occurs, the bridges and switches reevaluate the Spanning Tree Protocol. If the loop is removed, the port resumes normal forwarding mode.

Routers   Although bridges and switches segment collision domains, routers segment broadcast domains. Because switches will not propagate a collision, routers will never propagate a broadcast. A router is also the boundary of a LAN. It either connects two LANs or it connects a LAN with a WAN. A device that provides a network boundary operates at layer 3 of the OSI model. Of all the devices covered, a router is the most intelligent. Figure 2-16 depicts a basic router configuration for a WAN. If Host A sends a packet to Host B, Router A looks up the destination network in its route table. Then Router A sends the packet to Router B, which performs the same lookup. It then sends the packet to Host B.

The routing protocols that routers use can be classified in many ways. The most basic classification is distance vector versus link-state protocols.

Distance vector routing is often called routing by rumor. A distance vector protocol updates its routing table based on what it hears from its neighbor, a rumor. It always assumes that this information

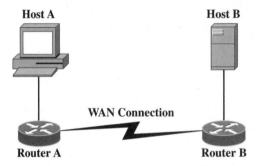

Figure 2-16
A basic routed
network

is accurate and timely. This assumption is one of the major limitations of distance vector protocols.

Link state routing creates a more consistent view of the network than distance vector protocols. A link state protocol develops a formal relationship with its neighbors. As this formal relationship grows, the router becomes aware of all the other devices in the same area. By monitoring the state of its neighbor's link, a router can quickly fail over to a redundant link if necessary.

Table 2-5 lists the most common routing protocols and the classifications they fall under.

NOTE: *EIGRP is a hybrid protocol that exhibits both traits of distance vector protocols and link state protocols.*

Basic Token Ring

IBM developed Token Ring in the late '70s. It is a deterministic, token-passing topology based on a logical ring. The ring is logical because generally the stations are connected in a star topology via a *MultiStation Access Unit* (MSAU). Figure 2-17 shows both the logical and physical layouts of a Token Ring network.

In a Token Ring network, end nodes are connected via MSAUs. A MSAU essentially operates like an Ethernet hub. It simply provides connectivity. Unlike Ethernet, the Token Ring specification includes several special fault-management functions to ensure smooth operation.

Table 2-5	Distance Vector	Link State
Routing protocols and their classifications	RIP	OSPF
	IGRP	NLSP
	IPX RIP	IS-IS

Figure 2-17
The logical and
physical views of a
Token Ring network

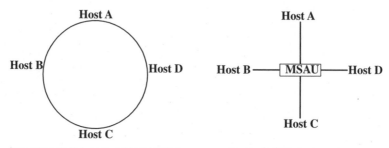

TOKEN RING - LOGICAL VIEW   TOKEN RING - PHYSICAL

MSAUs are connected to each other to form larger and larger rings. Simple patch cables connect MSAUs to each other. Token Ring also enables the automatic insertion and removal of devices from the ring. As a device drops its connectivity, a bypass relay inside the MSAU removes that port from the ring. The reverse happens as a device comes onto the ring.

One of the stations attached to the ring is the active monitor. The active monitor controls all timing-related functions on the ring. The active monitor is also responsible for ensuring that continuously circling tokens are removed from the ring. A station is supposed to remove its data token once the information has been copied.

The operation of a Token Ring is pretty straightforward. The token is passed along the ring. Devices can only send data if it has the token. However, like any network, cable faults can occur. When a cable fault is detected, a special algorithm called beaconing begins. Beaconing enables the nodes to route traffic around the failed node in the ring.

Bridges, switches, and routers behave almost identically to their Ethernet counterparts. Bridges and switches divide the networks into smaller rings. Routers connect Token Ring LANs with other LANs and WANs.

Fiber Distributed Data Interface (FDDI)

FDDI is a 100 Mbps, token-passing LAN technology that uses dual fiber-optic rings. FDDI is often used as a high-speed backbone.

It uses a two-ring design. Traffic flows over each ring in opposite directions. One ring is the primary and the other is the secondary.

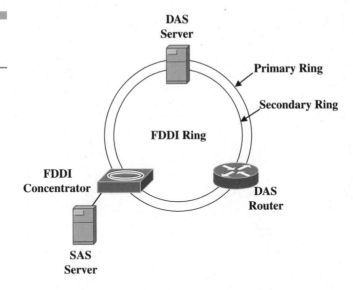

Figure 2-18
Components of a
FDDI LAN

DAS
Server

Primary Ring

Secondary Ring

FDDI Ring

FDDI
Concentrator

DAS
Router

SAS
Server

The primary is used for all data transmissions in normal operations, while the secondary ring is not used. Traffic flows in opposite directions on each of these rings. This is called *counter-rotating*.

FDDI stations are connected to either both rings through a *dual attached station* (DASs) or one ring through a *single attached station* (SAS). Stations can also connect to concentrators. Concentrators are similar in operation to MSAUs and hubs. They provide entry points for devices onto the ring. Figure 2-18 shows the components of a FDDI network.

The secondary ring is used for redundancy. In the event of a cable break, traffic can be passed along the secondary ring. Remember, the secondary ring passes data in the opposite direction from the primary ring. Therefore, when a failure is detected, the device before the break transmits the data on the secondary ring. This use of the secondary ring now bypasses the break and enables normal operations.

SUMMARY

The foundations of internetworking technology have not changed for many years. Ethernet has been in use for almost 30 years, while RIP

Figure 2-19
FDDI LAN
redundancy example

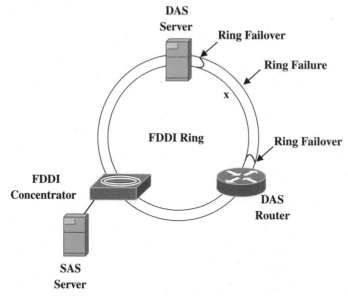

has been in use since the early '80s. Though the information technology arena has changed rapidly during the mid to late '90s with the evolution of the Web, the underlying foundations have remained relatively static.

To design a good network, it is necessary to know the options available. All technologies that are being developed have their roots in these technologies and protocols. By building a strong foundation in protocols like TCP/IP and technologies like Ethernet, newer technologies like IPv6 or 10-Gigabit Ethernet do not seem extraordinary.

FREQUENTLY ASKED QUESTIONS (FAQ)

Question: Which is faster: Ethernet or Token Ring?

Answer: It depends. The speed of Ethernet is 10 Mbps, while the speed of Token Ring is four Mbps. From this number, Ethernet appears to be faster, but this is the top speed of the technology. As more stations are added to an Ethernet LAN, the true speed of the LAN is greatly reduced. For instance, 10 users on an Ethernet LAN have approximately 1 Mbps throughput. The same 10 users on a Token Ring LAN would still have a top speed of four Mbps. The contention access system of Ethernet slows the throughput as more nodes are placed on a network.

Switches, however, change this equation. The limiting factor of Ethernet is collisions. Since switches segment nodes into separate collision domains, the average throughput increases. The same 10 users all connected to separate switch ports would have an average throughput near 10 Mbps.

NOTE: Faster versions of Ethernet, 100 Mbps and 1000 Mbps, are available. In addition, faster speeds of Token Ring, 16 Mbps and 32 Mbps, are available.

Many of the answers to networking questions can be answered, "It depends." The problems are usually multi-faceted and therefore a simple answer will not suffice.

Question: What type of routing protocol is best: distance-vector or link-state?

Answer: It depends. Because link-state protocols tend to converge faster and usually portray a more accurate depiction of the network topology, they seem like the best choice. However, link-state protocols can be difficult to configure. Also, it takes practice to learn how to troubleshoot these protocols. Distance vector protocols are quite simple in configuration, operation, and troubleshooting. Generally, smaller networks run distance vector protocols.

Question: Is it better to use a router or a switch?

Answer: It depends. In the past, the general principle was route where you can, bridge where you must. It was easier then to interconnect a network with routers than bridges. Currently, another principle is used: Switch where you can and route where you must. Newer networks generally demand greater speeds. Routers are inherently slower devices than switches. Routers perform all operations via software calculations. Switches use hardware to perform their functions. These hardware calculations are much faster than software calculations. Another option to consider is the evolution of wire-speed routers. These are routers that perform all calculations in hardware. With this evolution, the principle may soon again be route where you can, switch where you must.

QUESTIONS ▪ ▪ ▪ ▪ ▪ ▪ ▪ ▪

1. Which layer of the OSI model is responsible for the reliable network communication between end nodes?

    a. Data link
    b. Network
    c. Transport
    d. Session

2. Which layer of the OSI model is responsible for the path selection between two end nodes?

    a. Data link
    b. Network
    c. Transport
    d. Session

3. Which layer of the OSI model is responsible for the fault detection and information flow control?

    a. Network
    b. Transport
    c. Session
    d. Presentation

4. Which layer of the OSI model is responsible for the reliable transit of data across a physical link?

    a. Physical
    b. Data link
    c. Transport
    d. Session

5. Which of the following is a deterministic networking topology?

    a. Ethernet
    b. Fast Ethernet
    c. TCP/IP
    d. Token Ring

6. Which of the following is a packet-switching WAN service that uses fixed-length cells?

    a. ATM
    b. Frame Relay

    c. ISDN

    d. HDLC

7. Which of the following WAN services are considered dial-ups?

    a. ATM

    b. Frame Relay

    c. ISDN

    d. HDLC

8. Which part of the TCP/IP protocol suite is responsible for resolving IP addresses to MAC addresses?

    a. IP

    b. INARP

    c. RARP

    d. ARP

9. Which part of the TCP/IP protocol suite is responsible for sending datagrams via a connectionless service?

    a. TCP

    b. IP

    c. UDP

    d. DNS

10. What is the foundation protocol of the Novell NetWare proprietary protocol suite?

    a. IPX

    b. SPX

    c. IP

    d. CPX

11. Which AppleTalk protocol is responsible for resolving names to network addresses?

    a. DNS

    b. NBP

    c. ANP

    d. AFP

12. Which of the following is/are routing protocols?

    a. IPX

    b. RIP

    c. TCP

    d. SMTP

13. Which of the following is/are routed protocols?

   a. NetBios

   b. OSPF

   c. IGRP

   d. IPX

14. Which networking device connects LANs to WANs?

   a. Hub

   b. Switch

   c. Router

   d. MSAU

15. Which type of bridging is most commonly used in Ethernet environments?

   a. Source Route

   b. Transparent

   c. Translational

   d. Source Route Translational

16. Which technology is used to detect and remove loops in a bridged network?

   a. Spanning Tree

   b. Loop Free

   c. Looping Tree

   d. 802.1 Protocol

17. Which of the following routing protocols is based on a link-state algorithm?

   a. RIP

   b. RTMP

   c. IGRP

   d. NLSP

18. Which rule must be followed when designing a basic Ethernet network?

   a. 6-5-4 Rule

   b. 4-3-2 Rule

   c. 5-4-3 Rule

   d. 3-2-1 Rule

19. Which Token Ring device is responsible for removing errant tokens from the ring?

    a. Passive monitor

    b. Active monitor

    c. Ring monitor

    d. Beacon monitor

20. Which of the following IP addresses are matched correctly with their class?

    a. Class A - 128.0.0.1

    b. Class B - 191.0.0.1

    c. Class B - 192.0.0.1

    d. Class C - 191.0.0.1

ANSWERS

1. **c.** Transport

   The transport is responsible for reliable network communication between end nodes. The transport layer provides mechanisms for the establishment, maintenance, and termination of virtual circuits, transport fault detection and recovery, and information flow control.

2. **b.** Network

   The network layer provides connectivity and path selection between two end systems. The network layer is the layer at which routing occurs.

3. **b.** Transport

   The transport is responsible for reliable network communication between end nodes. The transport layer provides mechanisms for the establishment, maintenance, and termination of virtual circuits, transport fault detection and recovery, and information flow control.

4. **b.** Data Link

   The Data link layer provides the reliable transit of data across a physical link. The data-link layer is concerned with physical addressing, network topology, line discipline, error notification, the ordered delivery of frames, and flow control.

5. **d.** Token Ring

   Token Ring is the only deterministic protocol. Ethernet and Fast Ethernet are contention-based. TCP/IP is not a network topology, but a protocol.

6. **a.** ATM

   ATM is a WAN, packet-switched service that uses a fixed-length 53-byte cell. Frame Relay does not have fixed-length cells. ISDN is circuit-switched. HDLC is for leased lines only.

7. c. ISDN

ISDN is a circuit-switched service like standard dial-up. ATM is a WAN, packet-switched service that uses a fixed-length 53-byte cell. Frame Relay does not have fixed-length cells. HDLC is for leased lines only.

8. d. ARP

ARP is the protocol that discovers the data link address, or the MAC address, of the destination address. An ARP table is a listing of all remote IP addresses and their corresponding MAC addresses.

9. c. UDP

UDP is responsible for sending connectionless datagrams. IP is also a connectionless service, but it sends packets not datagrams.

10. a. IPX

The *Internet Packet Exchange* (IPX) is the core protocol of the NetWare suite. It is similar to IP in its responsibilities as a network layer protocol.

11. b. NBP

The *Name Binding Protocol* (NBP) is responsible for resolving AppleTalk node names into network layer addresses. DNS is a similar service but for the TCP/IP suite.

12. b. RIP

The *Routing Internet Protocol* (RIP) is the only routing protocol of the list. IPX and TCP are routed protocols. SMTP is a member of the TCP/IP suite.

13. d. IPX

NetBIOS is not a routing protocol or a router. The others are routing protocols.

14. c. Router

A router connects LANs to LANs or LANs to WANs.

15. b. Transparent

Transparent bridges are used in Ethernet environments. Source route bridges are used in Token Ring environments. Translational bridges connect Token Ring LANs to Ethernet LANs.

16. **a.** Spanning Tree

    Spanning Tree, 802.1d, is the technology that enables bridges and switches to detect and remove loops from the network.

17. **d.** NLSP

    The *Novell Link State Protocol* (NLSP) is based on a link state algorithm. Other link-state protocols are OSPF and IS-IS.

18. **c.** 5-4-3 Rule

    For an Ethernet LAN of any size to operate, it must follow the 5-4-3 rule with regard to hubs. There can be a maximum of five segments between two hosts in a network and there can be at most four hubs between these stations. Finally, only three of the segments can have users.

19. **b.** Active monitor

    The active monitor is responsible for ensuring that continuously circling tokens are removed from the ring.

20. **b.** Class B - 191.0.0.1

    The Class B network range starts at 128.0.0.0 and ends at 191.255.255.255.

Choosing Cisco Hardware and Software

Objectives Covered in This Chapter

■ Assemble Cisco product lines in an end-to-end solution.

Introduction

One of the foundations of network design is internetworking technology. Another foundation is the knowledge of networking hardware and software. As important as technology is in network design, a network without equipment is simply a mass of cables. The key to specifying the equipment required in a network is knowing the various types of equipment that can be used and where to use them.

One of the principle elements of a final design is the equipment that will be used in the new network. This equipment could be a redistribution of existing equipment or a purchase of new networking equipment. The capabilities of this old and new equipment can make portions of a design impractical or costly.

Several classifications of networking equipment make up network design. Routers are used for *Local Area Network* (LAN) to *LAN/Wide Area Network* (WAN) connectivity. Ethernet/Token Ring switches are used for user connectivity to the LAN. Specialized products like access servers and firewalls are also used. Finally, the other IOS software ties them all together.

The classifications and information provided are only guidelines for provisioning equipment. The final determination is a mix of requirements, budget, and vision.

NOTE: *The actual specification and selection of networking equipment is the last step of actual network design. Networking equipment should never dictate the complete network design. However, knowing the equipment characteristics in general is useful in completing the network design.*

Routers

Routers as a whole can be quickly divided into their performance capabilities. Some routers are more suited to remote office locations than the network core. Routers have always fallen into three general classifications: small-office, mid-range, and high-end routers.

Small-Office Routers

Small-office routers can be classified as such by the amount of traffic they can accommodate as well as their limited protocol choices. Small-office routers, for instance, will not support the *Fiber Distributed Data Interface* (FDDI) or *Asynchronous Transfer Mode* (ATM).

The most common small-office router in use today is the Cisco 2500 series router. The 2500 series is comprised of 25 variations. They range from a 2501, which has two serial ports and one Ethernet port, to the 2525, which has one Token Ring port and three slots for WAN modules. The Cisco 2524 and 2525 are unusual in that they enable various WAN modules. The rest of the 2500 series has fixed ports that are not interchangeable.

NOTE: *The 2501 is one of the most prevalent routers in use today. Remember that 70 percent of all networks are Ethernet. They are a good choice for a small remote office that uses Ethernet topology and needs WAN connectivity. In addition, they are perfect for the home lab.*

The 2500 series with all its variation provides a number of LAN and WAN connectivity options. In addition, several varieties of the 2500 provide LAN-to-LAN connectivity. The 2513 router provides Token Ring-to-Ethernet routing.

Cisco 2500 routers come with Flash *Erasable Programmable Read-Only Memory* (EPROM) technology for simplified software maintenance. These systems support a variety of Cisco IOS software feature sets. A feature set that supports your specific protocol environment can be selected. Mission-specific models contain less memory and less hardware functionality to support a subset of protocols. Each mission-specific model can be upgraded to full-router capability by downloading a new Cisco IOS software feature set and adding memory if required.

NOTE: *Many routers in the 2500 series use an* Attachment Unit Interface *(AUI) connector for the Ethernet port. Ensure that you have the appropriate transceiver to connect an AUI port to your network.*

Although the 2500 series is still in use today, the 1600 and 2600 series routers are supplanting them. The 1600 series routers are known as *desktop modular access routers.* The 1600 series routers are intended for small offices and branches. They support *Integrated Services Digital Networks* (ISDN) as well as standard serial connections. They also can provide *Virtual Private Networks* (VPNs) and firewall software services. The key feature for the 1600 series is its use of modular *WAN Interface Cards* (WICs) in addition to fixed ports.

The Cisco 1600 series also offers a range of features specifically designed for branch and small-office applications. These are a modular design for WAN flexibility, security and firewall options, and integrated *Channel Service Unit* (CSU)/*Data Service Unit* (DSU) support.

The 1600 is not a rack-mountable device.

The 2600 series routers build upon the modular WAN connections of the 1600. It has a faster processor and more memory than the 1600 series. It is intended for use in branch and remote offices. The 2600 series, like the 2500 series, is capable of routing traffic between LANs. In addition to their fixed ports, all 2600 series routers can hold two WICs.

The Cisco 2600 series modular architecture offers a branch office solution that provides the versatility needed to adapt to changes in network technology as new services and applications become available. The Cisco 2600 series shares modular interfaces with the Cisco 1600, 1700, and 3600 series.

Mid-Range Routers

The main dividing point between a mid-range router and a small-office router is the capability to be both modular and provide a high port density. The 2600 series, while modular, does not provide a high port density. This modularity and high density are required to support the breadth of operations at a regional office or small headquarters. In addition, this class of router has a much faster processor and more memory than the small-office router.

The currently installed mid-range router is the 4000 series. This series is comprised of various chassis, each with a backplane and processor. A Cisco 4000 chassis does not have any fixed ports. It does have three modular slots. Each slot holds a *Network Processing Module* (NPM). Each NPM holds one or more ports. The ports range from Ethernet to DS3 ATM.

A limit exists on the number and type of interfaces supported. The limit is the number of high-speed interfaces in the chassis. A maximum of two high-speed interfaces is supported on the Cisco 4000 series routers. This includes Fast Ethernet, FDDI, and ATM OC-3 or DS-3. However, only one ATM OC-3 can be on a single router.

The 4000 series is still in production, but Cisco has released another mid-range router, the 3600 series. These routers are in the same family as both the 1600 and 2600 series routers. The largest router in the 3600 series is the 3660. The 3600 series is versatile. It supports not only LAN and WAN technologies, but also many voice applications including *Voice over IP* (VoIP). The 3600 series can also be configured as an access server for dial-up users.

The Cisco 3600 series includes the Cisco 3660, Cisco 3640, and Cisco 3620 access servers/routers. These routers/access servers are modular solutions. The Cisco 3660 has six network module slots, the Cisco 3640 has four network module slots, and the Cisco 3620 has two slots. Each network module slot accepts a variety of network module interface cards, including LAN and WAN mixed media cards. These cards provide the foundation for LAN and WAN connectivity on a single network module. Additional applications are supported with a series of network module cards offering digital modems, asynchronous and synchronous serials, ISDN *Primary Rate Interface* (PRI), and ISDN *Basic Rate Interface* (BRI). The Cisco 3600 series shares network modules, WICs, and Voice Interface Cards with the Cisco 2600 Series.

High-End Routers

High-end routers are generally used at the core of your network as a backbone router. They are also used to route packets across the Internet. These routers have sophisticated backplanes and route-switch processors. Most high-end routers today are members of either the 7000 series or the 7500 series. These series are similar in composition. They each hold the same types of cards and both can use *Versatile Interface Processors* (VIPs). A VIP is a card that holds two *Port Adapter Modules* (PAMs). Each PAM holds one or more ports. This is the reason that the port naming in a 7000 or 7500 series is complex. Ethernet 0/0/0 means the Ethernet port located in the first slot, first PAM, and first port. In addition to VIP *line cards* (LCs), the 7500 and 7000 series can also hold interface cards that provide connectivity to ATM networks, Frame Relay clouds, and mainframe computers.

NOTE: *Several types of VIP cards exist. The actual model of the VIP card required depends on the PAMs that will be supported.*

The 7500 series has a faster processor and, more importantly, a faster bus than the 7000 series. The 7500 series is comprised of the Cisco Extended Bus, CyBus. Each specific model of the 7500 series has at least one bus. The 7505 has one CyBus, while the 7507 and 7513 have two CyBuses. The 7576 has four CyBuses. Each router can hold up to two *Route Switch Processors* (RSPs) and a series of *line cards* (LCs) for connectivity. These LCs range from simple Ethernet interfaces to ATM interfaces.

Another high-end router series is the Cisco 12000 *Gigabit Switch Router* (GSR) series. The GSR series was designed and developed for the core of service provider and enterprise IP backbones. The GSR family includes two models: the Cisco 12008 and 12012. The 12008 model provides a 40 Gbps switch fabric and has eight slots, and the 12012 model provides a 60 Gbps switch fabric and has 12 slots. Each chassis can support interfaces ranging from DS3 to OC-48.

The GSR is based on a high-speed distributed routing architecture combined with a switching core that delivers Layer-3 routing at gigabit speeds. The GSR is optimized for routing and forwarding IP datagrams across a network. The routing function is performed in the *Gigabit Route Processors* (GRPs). It is responsible for running the routing protocols and building the routing tables. This routing information is then used to build the forwarding tables distributed to the LCs. In addition, the GRP is also responsible for the system control and administrative functions.

The packet-forwarding functions are performed by each of the LCs. A copy of the forwarding tables computed by the GRP is distributed to each of the LCs in the system. Each LC performs an independent lookup of a destination address for each datagram received on a local copy of the forwarding table, and the datagram is switched across a crossbar switch fabric to the destination LC.

LAN Switches

Switches are used to connect end users to the network. Switches come in a variety of sizes, but their application is generally uniform. Switches provide large quantities of ports. Some switches provide these ports in a fixed manner, while other switches are more modular.

Fixed-Port Switches

Fixed-port switches are also called workgroup or stackable switches. These switches have a fixed number of ports for end users or for connections to hubs or other switches. The switches may have an uplink port that provides a faster speed to a core network device. For example, a 24-port Ethernet switch may have a Fast Ethernet uplink. This faster uplink to ensure user traffic is not blocked. The Cisco 2900XL and 3500XL series of switches are examples of fixed-port switches. The 2924XL provides 24 Fast Ethernet switched ports and two 100 MB-FX fiber uplinks. The 3524XL provides 24 Fast Ethernet ports and two slots for *Gigabit Interface Cards* (GBICs). A GBIC is a special card that provides either 1000Base-SX or 1000Base-LX gigabit fiber connections.

Cisco Catalyst 3500 XL, 2900 XL, and 1900 switches also use Cisco switch clustering technology. In Cisco switch clustering, users can manage over 380 ports from a single IP address and connect up to 16 switches, regardless of physical location, with a broad range of Ethernet, Fast Ethernet, and Gigabit Ethernet media.

NOTE: *1000Base-SX Gigabit Ethernet (GE) is also called short-haul fiber, and 1000Base-LX GE is also called long-haul fiber. The distance limitation of LX is greater than SX.*

Modular Switches

Modular switches are comprised of the same parts that also comprise mid-range and high-end routers. They are also based on a chassis. Each chassis can hold a specific number of line cards, and each LC can hold a specific number of ports. A chassis is not required to hold the same type of LCs in each slot. For instance, if you require Fast Ethernet and regular Ethernet ports, a modular switch can hold both types of cards.

NOTE: *The port cost of modular switches is generally higher than the port cost of a fixer-port switch. However, the greater density of the modular switches means that only one modular switch would be required, instead of multiple fixed-port switches.*

Modular switches can be of various sizes and can perform various functions. The Catalyst 5000 is a small member of the Catalyst family. It only holds four LCs.

The Catalyst 5000 family has integrated frame and cell switching, full support for Cisco IOS-based routing, and full support for Fast EtherChannel, Gigabit EtherChannel, and ATM. The media-independent architecture supports all legacy LAN and ATM switching technologies through a wide range of Ethernet, Fast Ethernet, GE, FDDI, Token Ring, and ATM switch modules.

The next generation of Catalyst switches, the 6000 series, has several models as well. The largest of the Catalyst 6000 series is the 6509. The 6509 switch can hold eight LCs. Each LC can accommodate 48 Fast Ethernet ports. This means that the 6509 switch can support up to 384 users.

The Catalyst 6000 family consists of the Catalyst 6000 series and the Catalyst 6500 series. Both series support six- and nine-slot versions, providing a wide range of configuration and price/performance options. Both Catalyst 6000 and 6500 series switches support a wide range of interface types and densities. The architecture of the Catalyst 6500 series supports switching bandwidth up to 256 Gbps and multilayer switching up to 150 Mpps. The Catalyst 6000 series provides a backplane bandwidth of 32 Gbps and multilayer switching to 30 Mpps.

All Catalyst 5000 family switches support NetFlow switching as part of the architecture. NetFlow switching combines the simplicity and speed of switching with the intelligence and scalability of routing. This feature enables *multilayer switching* (MLS) scalability. A *route-switch module* (RSM) delivers integrated support for Cisco IOS-based multiprotocol routing. New supervisor engines integrated with Netflow II functionality that have optional full-multiprotocol routing deliver wirespeed IP and IPX switching at multimillion-packet-per-second rates.

The next generation of switches is moving from simply switching frames at the data link layer to making intelligent routing decisions at the network layer. These devices are called *wire speed routers*, *switching routers*, or *Layer-3 switches*. These devices can route packets, but they perform their routing functions in hardware not software. This enables them to quickly route packets to their destination. The Catalyst 8540CSR routes almost 24 million packets per second.

The Catalyst 8500 family can also support multiservice ATM switching and routing or Layer-2/Layer-3 switching for GE. The Catalyst 8500 family delivers campus and metropolitan network solutions with scalable performance.

Two versions of the 8500 series can be used: the *Campus Switch Router* (CSR) and the *Multiprotocol Switch Router* (MSR). The CSR provides Layer-3 switching and routing on a variety of media. The MSR version supports ATM switching as well as standard layer-3 switching and routing.

Specialized Hardware

Although routers and switches are the most commonly seen pieces of networking equipment, several pieces of hardware perform specialized functions that are not found in routers and switches. This specialized hardware ranges from simplistic ISDN routers to complex ATM switches.

ISDN and DSL Routers

ISDN/DSL routers are smaller versions of the Cisco 1600 series. They are comprised of an ISDN port and an Ethernet port. ISDN/DSL routers are intended for home use. The Cisco 700 and 800 series are comprised of ISDN and DSL routers. The various models reflect the type of interface provided. Some models require a *Network Termination 1* (NT1) device. Other models have a NT1 built into the router. Some models provide analog ports for use with non-ISDN equipment.

An NT1 is a required device for all ISDN communication. The NT1 must be connected between the ISDN device and the central office. All ISDN devices have either an S/T or U type interface. The S/T type interface requires a NT1. The NT1 then provides a U interface for connection to the central office. If the ISDN device has a U interface, the NT1 is internal to the device and it can be directly connected to the central office.

NOTE: *An ISDN circuit must be provisioned by the service provider to support both voice, analog, and data or digital services simultaneously for the analog ports to work.*

Remote Access Routers

Remote access routers provide both analog and ISDN dial-up access to a network. They connect to the network and act as a gateway for all incoming calls. The access server product from Cisco is the AS5xxx series. This series is comprised of the AS5100, AS5200, AS5300, and the AS5800. The products are the same in operation, but the products with the higher numbers support more simultaneous users and have faster processors. The devices are connected to the service provider by ISDN PRI circuits. These PRI circuits enable inbound digital or analog calls. Analog and digital calls are received on the same line, but a modem must be installed in the access server to terminate analog calls. These modems are installed into the access server slots just like the digital PRI cards.

In addition to digital PRI circuits, standard analog circuits can also be used. Individual analog lines can be connected to analog modem modules in the AS5xxx series. In addition, external analog modems can be used with a Cisco 2509 access server.

Firewalls

A firewall is a specialized piece of equipment that protects an internal network from users on an exterior network, like the Internet. The Cisco firewall solution is called the PIX. The PIX is an integrated hardware/software appliance, and no underlying operating system can be penetrated. A PIX firewall can support over 250,000 simultaneous connections. Also, the PIX supports a variety of *network interface cards* (NICs) for integration into diverse networks.

The key to the underlying security of the PIX is the lack of a penetrable operating system like Unix or Windows NT. The core of the PIX firewall is the *adaptive security algorithm* (ASA). This algorithm maintains the secure perimeters between the networks controlled by the firewall. The PIX firewall also has a failover option that ensures high availability and eliminates a single point of failure.

ATM Switches

An ATM switch is used at the core of an ATM network. Its responsibility is to switch ATM cells from one port to another. Cisco has a range of ATM switches. The smaller capacity switch, intended for use at the workgroup or campus level, is the LightStream 1010. The LightStream 1010 uses a five-slot, modular chassis featuring the option of dual, fault-tolerant, load-sharing power supplies.

The central slot in the LightStream 1010 is dedicated to a single ATM switch processor module, the ASP. The LightStream 1010 has a five Gbps, shared-memory, fully nonblocking switch fabric. The remaining slots support up to four hot-swappable *carrier modules* (CAMs), each of which in turn can support up to two hot-swappable PAMs.

The LightStream 1010 has advanced traffic management mechanisms that enable the support of bursty, data traffic while also delivering the *quality of service* (QoS) guarantees for applications. The LightStream 1010 supports all ATM Forum *Private Network Node Interface* (PNNI) protocols.

The larger ATM WAN switches, the IGX, MGX, and BPX series, are intended for use at the service provider level to aggregate voice, data, and video traffic across high-speed ATM circuits. They support a wide range of technologies and interfaces. These switches cannot only switch ATM cells; they can also act as Frame Relay switches.

NOTE: *These WAN switches are not covered in the Routing and Switching track of the Cisco Career Certifications. They are covered in the WAN Switching track. WAN switches are specialized devices that do not run Cisco IOS software and are different from routing or LAN switching.*

SwitchProbes

The SwitchProbe products provide a powerful distributed management tool for traffic analysis, troubleshooting, and proactive network management. SwitchProbes provide the capability to determine network behavior and incorporate that into long term planning. Also, the SwitchProbe enables you to troubleshoot network errors from the data link layer to the application layer.

The SwitchProbe series is a complete family of dedicated, enhanced LAN, WAN, and ATM remote monitoring probes for comprehensive seven-layer monitoring. SwitchProbes provide real-time traffic analysis and trend-reporting capabilities. They provide the diagnostic information needed for troubleshooting the data-link, network, or application-layer problems before they can affect the network.

LocalDirector

LocalDirector is a load-balancing solution for the TCP/IP protocol suite. It provides a high availability that provides continual access for end users to application servers. LocalDirector enables administrators to direct TCP traffic to different servers based on the service requested, the distribution method, and the server availability. For example, all FTP requests can be sent to one server, while Web requests are sent to another server.

LocalDirector uses an algorithm called the *Session Distribution Algorithm* (SDA). SDA enables the forwarding of traffic based on weight and the number of open connections. This ensures that servers do not fail from traffic overload. LocalDirector can also probe the server to determine availability.

Software

Without software, routers and switches are large doorstops. Although *Internetworking Operating System* (IOS) software is inherent to

Cisco routers and switches, several other Cisco software products can add value to any network.

IOS Software

This is the software that makes the routing decisions on a router. It is also the software that adds feature sets to routers and switches. IOS software comes in many forms. For routers, the software is based on the feature set used. For example, a feature set may consist of only the features associated with the IP protocol suite. Another set may include the IP set plus the features sets for IPX/SPX, AppleTalk, and DEC. Each software version requires a specific amount of RAM and flash memory for operation.

The Cisco IOS is what sets it apart from many other hardware manufactures. This IOS is common among almost all Cisco products. The IOS has extensive help information imbedded into the software. In addition to the IOS, many Cisco switches use the Catalyst version of the IOS. This software is similar to the IOS, but it has subtle differences. Not all Catalyst switches use this version. The Catalyst 2900XL and 3500XL series use the same IOS that is present in Cisco routers.

CiscoSecure

CiscoSecure is an *Authentication, Authorization, and Accounting* (AAA) program that controls the access of users throughout the network. It provides user authentication via *Terminal Access Controller Access Control System Plus* (TACACS+) or *Remote Dial-In User Service* (RADIUS). It can integrate with an existing user database for easy maintenance. CiscoSecure used in conjunction with an AS5X00 access server can provide simple and secure dial-up access for many users.

CiscoSecure can also be configured to use token-based authentication methods. These methods are one of the most secure methods of authentication. These tokens contain codes that frequently change. Authentication is provided by using this code and a secret number as a password.

CiscoWorks 2000

CiscoWorks 2000 is comprised of two products. The first, *CiscoWorks for Switched Internetworks* (CWSI), provides network performance management, configuration, and monitoring. The second portion, *Resource Manager Essentials* (RME), provides a Web-based platform for archiving configuration files and software images and managing system logs. RME provides device management tools to streamline the tasks of managing network inventory and device changes, archiving and searching configuration files, and rapidly deploying new software images. Essentials also helps troubleshoot the basic connectivity status of critical network devices and provides information needed for hardware capacity planning. CiscoWorks 2000 provides an efficient user interface for management applications and enables other Cisco, third-party, or user-developed, Web-based tools to be integrated.

Netsys

Netsys enables the management of all aspects of network connectivity and performance. It provides a single, service-level management solution. In addition, Netsys can provide invaluable network modeling when you are considering network design changes.

SUMMARY ▬ ▬ ▬ ▬ ▬ ▬ ▬ ▬ ▬

To design a good network, it is necessary to know both the technologies available and the equipment that will enable these technologies. After the designer has selected a specific technology, like ISDN, they must ensure that all the devices can accommodate that technology. However, the equipment listed in the chapter will undergo continuous change. Hardware will continue to get faster and more adaptable. Like technology, things will always be in a state of change. But routers will always route and switches will always switch.

FREQUENTLY ASKED QUESTIONS (FAQ) ▨▨ ▨ ▨

Question: Which is better to use: routers or switches?

Answer: It depends. There is no rule that says you must route traffic in one instance and switch traffic in another. Also, with the evolution of routing switches, like the Catalyst 6500, and switching routers, like the Catalyst 8500, the distinction is further fading. The amount of traffic, unicast and broadcast, is also a variable that plays an important part in the decision. Later, the suggested user limits for various protocols will be addressed. However, in an IP network, more than 500 users in the same LAN or broadcast domain can cause performance issues.

Question: Do I have to have a firewall to connect to the Internet?

Answer: No, a firewall is not required. All that is truly required to connect to the Internet is a router and an ISP connection. A firewall protects your network from intruders. However, firewall and Internet connectivity design is a complex topic. Also, a firewall type of service can be implemented with a router by using access lists. Finally, Cisco is shipping a special IOS feature set that implements firewall functionality and intrusion detection on a router.

Question: Are digital PRI circuits better than analog circuits?

Answer: Not necessarily, but they are more compact. A PRI circuit is comprised of 24 individual channels. Each channel is the same as an individual analog line. A PRI is given a number that enables inbound dialing. This number enables 24 simultaneous users to connect. An analog circuit will only enable one user to be connected at one time. In addition, without special configuration, a separate number is required for each analog circuit.

QUESTIONS ▪▪▪ ▪▪▪ ▪▪▪ ▪▪▪ ▪▪▪ ▪▪▪ ▪▪▪

1. Which series of Cisco equipment would most likely be used in the backbone of a network?

   a. Cisco 2500
   b. Cisco 1600
   c. Catalyst 3500
   d. Cisco 7500

2. Which series of Cisco equipment would most likely be used to interconnect two ATM networks?

   a. Cisco 7500
   b. LightStream 1010
   c. Catalyst 6500
   d. Cisco 3600

3. Which series of Cisco equipment would most likely be used in the wiring closet for 300 users?

   a. Cisco 2500
   b. Catalyst 3500XL
   c. Catalyst 5000
   d. Cisco 12000

4. Which series of Cisco equipment would most likely be used to protect an network from intruders on the Internet?

   a. PIX
   b. Cisco 1600
   c. Cisco 700
   d. CiscoSecure

5. Which series of Cisco equipment would most likely be used to connect a home telecommuter to the central office via an ISDN line?

   a. AS5x00 access server
   b. Cisco 700
   c. Cisco 2600
   d. Catalyst 2900XL

6. Which series of Cisco equipment would most likely be used to route traffic on the Internet?

   a. PIX
   b. Catalyst 6500
   c. Cisco 2500
   d. Cisco 12000

7. Which series of Cisco equipment would most likely be used to load-balance traffic to a series of Web servers?

   a. PIX
   b. Catalyst 6500
   c. Local Director
   d. LightStream 1010

8. Which series of Cisco equipment would most likely be used at a branch office to route traffic across a Frame Relay network?

   a. Cisco 7500
   b. Cisco 800
   c. Cisco 5000
   d. Cisco 2600

9. Which series of Cisco equipment would most likely be used at a branch office of 25 users for access to the network?

   a. Catalyst 5000
   b. Catalyst 3500
   c. Cisco 1600
   d. Cisco 2500

10. Which series of Cisco equipment would most likely be used to provide detailed management information?

    a. CiscoSecure
    b. PIX
    c. Switch Probe
    d. Local Director

11. Which series of Cisco equipment would most likely be used at a central office to provide dial-in access to a large number of users?

    a. Cisco 7500
    b. Catalyst 2500
    c. Cisco 2500
    d. AS 5200

12. Which series of Cisco equipment would most likely be used as a backbone router to perform all the following functions: route traffic, switch traffic, and switch ATM traffic.

    a. Catalyst 8500 MSR
    b. Catalyst 6500
    c. Catalyst 8500 CSR
    d. Catalyst 4000

13. Which equipment pair listed below is the most similar in use?

    a. Cisco 7500 - Cisco 8500
    b. Cisco 2600 - Cisco 3600
    c. PIX - CiscoSecure
    d. Catalyst 5000 - Catalyst 6000

14. Which equipment pair listed below is the most similar in use?

    a. Cisco 4500 - Cisco 4700
    b. Cisco 2500 - Cisco 2600
    c. Catalyst 5000 - Catalyst 3500XL
    d. Catalyst 2900XL - Catalyst 3000

15. What is the name of the line card that can support multiple port adapter modules in the Cisco 7500 series?

    a. Various Interface Processor
    b. Versatile Interface Plane
    c. Versatile Interface Processor
    d. Versatile Input Processor

16. A small office requires protection from external connections on the Internet. Which of the following solutions will satisfy this requirement?

    a. Cisco 2600 with firewall feature set
    b. Catalyst 3500XL
    c. Cisco 2500 with IP feature set
    d. Cisco Secure

17. Which Cisco software product enables network administrators to manage remote users with a centralized database?

    a. Cisco Secure
    b. Cisco Works 2000
    c. IOS Software
    d. NetSys

18. Which Cisco software product enables network designers to characterize network changes without affecting their production environment?

    a. Cisco Secure

    b. Cisco Works 2000

    c. IOS Software

    d. NetSys

19. Which Cisco software product is the foundation for the many Cisco hardware products?

    a. Cisco Secure

    b. Cisco Works 2000

    c. IOS Software

    d. NetSys

20. Which Cisco software product is capable of managing and monitoring all the Cisco devices on a network?

    a. Cisco Secure

    b. Cisco Works 2000

    c. IOS Software

    d. NetSys

ANSWERS

1. **d.** Cisco 7500

   The Cisco 7500 series is composed of high-end routers that are generally used at the core of your network as a backbone router.

2. **b.** LightStream 1010

   The LS1010 is the primary series of equipment that can connect ATM networks. The IGX, BGX, and MGX WAN switches could also fulfill this requirement.

3. **c.** Catalyst 5000

   For user connectivity, a switch is required. The Catalyst 3500XL series is a workgroup switch that can only support 48 users per device. For 300 users, the Catalyst 5000 is a better selection.

4. **a.** PIX

   A PIX firewall is a specialized piece of equipment that protects an internal network from users on the exterior network. This exterior network could be a vendor's network or the Internet.

5. **b.** Cisco 700

   The Cisco 700 is an ISDN router that will enable telecommuters to connect with the central office. A Cisco 2600 could also be used, but it is an expensive solution for a home user.

6. **d.** Cisco 12000

   A catalyst cannot route traffic. A Cisco 2500 can be used to connect to the Internet, but it is not capable of routing traffic across the Internet. However, the Cisco 12000 has the capability to route Internet traffic.

7. **c.** Local Director

   LocalDirector enables administrators to direct TCP traffic to different servers based on the service requested, distribution method, and server availability.

8. d. Cisco 2600

The 2600 series is the best answer. The 7500 is a core router, and the 800 is a home-office router. Finally, the Cisco 5000 is not an actual router series. The 2600 series is intended for use in branch and remote offices.

9. b. Catalyst 3500

Due to the small number of users, a Catalyst 5000 is a costly solution. The Catalyst 3500XL would provide a cost-effective solution for network access.

10. c. Switch Probe

The SwitchProbe products provide a powerful distributed management tool for traffic analysis, troubleshooting, and proactive network management.

11. d. AS 5200

Remote access routers like the AS 5200 provide both analog and ISDN dial-up access to a network. The Cisco 2500 series would be an acceptable solution for a small number of dial-in users but is not acceptable for a large number of users.

12. a. Catalyst 8540 MSR

The MSR is the only candidate that can fulfill all of the requirements. A 6500 cannot route traffic nor switch ATM traffic. A Catalyst 8540 CSR cannot switch ATM traffic. A Catalyst 4000 is a small version of the 6500 with the same limitations.

13. d. Catalyst 5000 - Catalyst 6000

The next generation of the Catalyst 5000 platform is the Catalyst 6000 platform. The Catalyst 6000 expands the capabilities of the 5000 series by adding enhancements like IP phone support.

14. b. Cisco 2500 - Cisco 2600

The Cisco 2600 is the next-generation remote office router series that began with the 2500. It expands the flexibility of the 2500 series by using modular *WAN Interface Cards* (WICs).

15. c. Versatile Interface Processor

VIPs are the foundation for many of the routing interfaces on the 7500 series. They support the *Port Adapter Modules* (PAMs) that are the actual interfaces for the router.

16. a. Cisco 2600 with Firewall feature set

In many instances, a complete PIX firewall solution is not justified, but protection is still required. This protection can be derived from a router running a feature set of the IOS that provides firewall functionality.

17. a. Cisco Secure

CiscoSecure provides user authentication via TACACS+ or RADIUS. It uses a central database for easy administration.

18. d. NetSys

Netsys enables the management of all aspects of network connectivity and performance. It provides a single, service-level management solution. In addition, Netsys can provide invaluable network modeling when you are considering network design changes.

19. c. IOS Software

The IOS software is at the heart of all Cisco products. This common front end gives almost all Cisco devices that same look and feel.

20. b. Cisco Works 2000

CiscoWorks provides network performance management, configuration, and monitoring. In addition, it also provides a Web-based platform for archiving configuration files and software images and managing system logs.

Cisco Design Fundamentals

Objectives Covered in This Chapter

■ Review the Cisco design theory and fundamentals

The final foundation for network design is the fundamentals of design. These fundamentals depend not only on the networking technology used, but also the hardware used. The fundamentals of design are the basis for any size or type of network design.

Without knowledge of networking technologies, a network designer will not be able to choose the best design solution. Without knowledge of networking equipment, a network designer will not be able to choose the best equipment for the solution. The final requirement for a network design is to bring the equipment and the technology together to form a complete design. By following two main design principles, assembling the complete design can be accomplished. These principles are the Cisco framework triangle and the hierarchical design approach.

Cisco's Framework Triangle

As networks have grown over time, the design methodologies have changed and grown as well. Early *Local Area Networks* (LANs) were generally comprised of 10-Mbps Ethernet and Novell servers running the IPX/SPX protocol. Most current designs have to deal with additional concerns, such as multiprotocol support, or the use of voice traffic over a LAN. With the facets of design changing, Cisco created the small- to medium-sized business solution framework.

The Cisco framework triangle can be used to identify possible solutions for network problems. These problems revolve around Layers two and three of the OSI model. The triangle, shown in Figure 4-1, is composed of three problem areas:

■ Protocol problems

■ Media problems

■ Transport problems

Each problem area covers a discrete set of design issues. However, accompanying these problems is a general set of solutions or

Figure 4-1
The framework
triangle

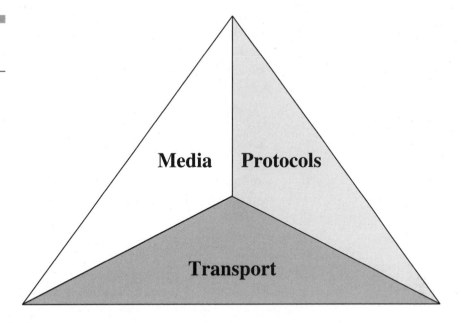

directions that will assist the network designer in eliminating the problem.

Protocols

Protocols problems are the result of implementations that do not scale. For example, the need for *Variable Length Subnet Masks* (VLSMs) in a RIP environment is a protocol problem. The excessive amount of Spanning Tree traffic in a large switched environment is a result of the protocol's operation. These problems occur when a specific protocol that is used for smaller networks is implemented in a larger environment. For example, NetBIOS is an excellent protocol for a small workgroup. However, because it cannot be routed, it is not suitable for a large internetwork.

The solutions for protocol problems almost always involve routing. Installing a router and creating multiple subnets can curb the excessive Spanning Tree activity. The VLSM implementation in a RIP network requires that another routing protocol be chosen for all the routers.

NOTE: *A protocol problem even exists on the Internet. IP Version 4 and the restricted number of IP addresses caused the develop of a new protocol, IP Version 6, and a way to better use IP addresses,* Network Address Translation *(NAT).*

Protocol problems are not limited to the TCP/IP protocol stack. For instance, one of the limiting factors of any Novell Netware LAN are RIP/SAP broadcasts. IPX's *Routing Information Protocol* (RIP) is used to exchange information about remote networks between servers, routers, and clients. The *Service Advertisement Protocol* (SAP) is used to exchange information about the services present on a particular network. These include file servers, printers, and other services. These RIP/SAP broadcasts are distributed every 60 seconds.

RIP/SAP broadcasts grow as the number of resources and networks on the network grows. A slow *Wide Area Network* (WAN) link could easily get congested as these RIP/SAP broadcasts increase. This can be solved by using access lists to restrict updates or to implement IPX's *Enhanced Interior Gateway Routing Protocol* (EIGRP). IPX EIGRP will only communicate changes to neighboring routers. This will keep slow WAN links from being overburdened by excessive RIP/SAP traffic.

Media

Media problems are always layer two-related. Specifically, they are related to the lack of a layer-two device, a bridge, or a switch. A layer-two device segments the collision domains of end stations. If 10 devices are connected to a hub, which is then connected to a switch, all 10 hosts are in the same collision domain. If these 10 end stations are each connected to the switch, then they each reside in their own collision domain. Connecting devices to a switch is often called *microsegmenting* because many Ethernet segments are created on each switch port. The presence or absence of collisions in an Ethernet segment is crucial to the operation and throughput of the segment. Too many collisions will render the segment useless. However, an end station that is directly attached to a switch will have speeds approaching the maximum possible.

Token Ring and *Fiber Distributed Data Interface* (FDDI) environments can also have media problems. Too many end stations on a ring increase the wait time for a free token and the capability to transmit data. Installing a Layer-two device will reduce the number of end stations on the ring as well as the wait time.

Media problems can also exist on WAN circuits. If a Frame Relay circuit has a *Committed Information Rate* (CIR) of 64 Kbps and 100 Kbps of traffic is usually sent over the circuit, then some of that excess traffic may be dropped by the Frame Relay service provider. This is a limitation of the medium. The possible solutions are to reduce the amount of traffic sent or to increase the speed of the Frame Relay circuit.

NOTE: *Media problems are some of the most common issues on networks today. However, the rapid evolution and installation of switches is reducing the frequency of these problems.*

Transport

Transport problems represent the technology's inability to carry either enough or specific types of traffic. For example, Ethernet will not transport native voice traffic. For this application, an *Asynchronous Transport Mode* (ATM) transport is required. Another transport issue is the requirement of the transmission of large amounts of data. Ethernet may not be the best transport for this requirement, but FDDI or Fast Ethernet is an acceptable alternative.

The solution for transport problems is usually more speed. In a pure Ethernet environment, the access to central resources may be slow. By moving the resources to a faster transport, like Fast Ethernet, the problem is solved. Another transport issue related to network design is the inclusion of voice traffic on a WAN circuit. In this case, the traffic may dictate the transport protocol to be used. The only transport that can support voice and data traffic across the WAN while providing specific *Quality of Service* (QoS) parameters is ATM.

> **NOTE:**   *Packetized Voice, or* Voice over IP *(VoIP), enables both voice and data traffic to be carried across transports other than ATM, like Gigabit Ethernet. However, depending on the implementation, some signaling information may be lost.*

Hierarchical Design Principles

These principles enable a network designer to design three specific layers of a network. When the three layers are combined, the whole will be much more than the individual parts. Each layer has specific functions and responsibilities within this hierarchy.

The Three-Layer Approach

Having three specific layers in a network is beneficial in several aspects. The reasons are as follows:

- Easier to understand
- Easier to troubleshoot
- Easier to failover
- Easier to grow

First, the network is easier to understand. Even the most complex network can be broken down into these three components. This enables each component to be examined individually. The most complex ATM network, after being broken down into three parts, is not as complex as the network as a whole.

Next, the three-layer approach makes a network easier to troubleshoot. If the problem can be isolated to a specific area, more time can be devoted to fixing the issue than determining the scope of the issue. Generally, network problems will affect discrete areas that fall within one of the three layers.

If a network has three distinct layers, each layer can be connected to various components in another layer. This will create multiple paths through the network and create less downtime due to equipment failures. Each layer should be redundantly connected to multiple devices in the other layers.

Finally, all networks change over time. They may grow or shrink, but they always change. By implementing a three-layer model, pieces can be added into a specific layer without altering the design of the entire network. Only the specific layer affected needs to be altered.

NOTE: *It is important to remember that these layers are logical divisions of a network. It is possible that a single device will contain two or more of these layers.*

The Hierarchical Model

The three parts of the model, pictured in Figure 4-2, are the core layer, the distribution layer, and the access layer. The core layer provides the backbone transport services. The distribution layer provides policy-based connectivity. Finally, the access layer provides end-user access to the network.

Figure 4-2
The three-layer
hierarchical model

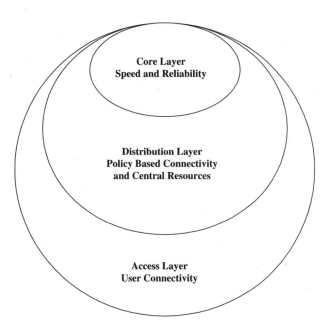

The Core Layer   This is the backbone of the network. It provides reliable, high-speed communications to all distribution layers of the network. The backbone can encompass both WAN and LAN technologies. The core layer exhibits the following characteristics:

- High reliability
- Redundancy and fault tolerance
- Adaptability
- Limited size or diameter
- Low latency and fast processing
- Manageability

High reliability is crucial to the success of this layer and the network design as a whole. The core cannot have unexpected downtime. All possible efforts must be dedicated to ensuring the core itself is always available. This means that the hardware must have physically redundant parts, and all communication links must be redundant as well.

Redundancy is also a key feature of the core layer. Redundancy enables the devices and the core itself to be highly reliable. All core devices should be connected to two or more other core devices. This will allow the complete redundancy of the entire backbone. The connections to the distribution-layer services should also be redundant. The most reliable and redundant backbone is made useless if the distribution layer loses connectivity.

The core must also be adaptable. This adaptability enables new locations to be added without disrupting core traffic. Also, the core must be adaptable enough to support multiple types of traffic.

In addition, limiting the diameter of the core provides predictable performances at end stations. A network that has a diameter of three hops will behave the same for all distribution layers connected to it. The core should include devices that can process traffic quickly and have a low latency. For instance, using a Cisco 1600 router to pass traffic throughout the core would not be advisable. This router does not have the processing capability to quickly pass large amounts of traffic through the core. In addition, if all your links are high-speed, the presence of lower speed links could cause an increased amount of latency in the WAN.

The manageability of this layer is critical. The utilization of the links and devices is critical to the operation of the backbone. If fully redundant fast devices become overutilized, resources will be unavailable. By constantly managing the state of the core layer, problems can be proactively avoided or reactively solved without a tremendous loss of productivity.

The core layer is generally comprised of equipment that can operate at high speeds and be adaptable to numerous technologies. A Cisco 75xx router is an example of core-layer equipment. It has a fast backplane as well as the capability to support almost any type of network technology from basic Ethernet to ATM. However, many switches can also operate at the core layer. The Catalyst 8540 MSR is an ATM switch that can be deployed in the core.

The keys to the core layer are reliability and speed. No overhead processing like filtering and security should take place in the core layer. Traffic should never be slowed or restricted through the core layer. Users should not be given direct access to the core layer. All user access should come through the distribution layer.

NOTE: *The most important points to remember about the core layer are speed and reliability.*

The Distribution Layer This is the interface between the core and the access layers. It provides policy-based connectivity between the two layers. The distribution layer can perform the following tasks:

- Route redistribution and address summarization
- Media translations
- *Network Address Translation* (NAT)
- QoS
- Access-list filtering
- Encryption

The key to the distribution layer is connectivity that follows a particular set of rules or policies. All overhead processing should be handled at this level. Any access lists should be implemented at this level. Traffic that should not be carried on the core must be restricted here. By nature, the core will not restrict any traffic; it will forward it as fast as possible to the destination.

Other overhead processes that the distribution layer is responsible for are route distribution and summarization. If various routing protocols are in use across a network, then all redistribution happens in the distribution layer. Likewise, NAT also happens on the distribution layer.

Encryption should always be handled at the distribution layer since it is a processor-intensive operation. If these processes are running on the core layer, then an unacceptable amount of latency could be introduced. If the encryption process is installed on the access layer, the multiple encryption processes would be required for each access layer.

The equipment that is used at this layer should be fast enough so that the many policy and access restrictions can be implemented without affecting the speed of the network. The Cisco 4000 and 3600 series of routers can be used at this layer. Catalyst 5500 and 6500 switches can also provide some access restrictions at this layer.

NOTE: *Current design thought believes that the distribution layer should be composed of devices that operate at layer three of the OSI model. Traditionally, this meant routers. However, new Layer-three switches provide the same policy capabilities as traditional routers and provide throughput speeds equal to layer-two switches.*

The Access Layer   This layer provides network access for all end stations. In LANs, this layer is generally implemented with hubs and switches. Switches are used to divide the network into separate collision domains, or microsegmenting. For WANs, this layer is for home or small office users that connect via an *Integrated Services Digital Network* (ISDN) or a *Digital Subscriber Line* (DSL).

The key to the access layer is raw network connectivity. For a user to access any network resources, they must first access the network itself. The access layer provides a connection point for all devices. In order to access any resources, the traffic must pass from the access layer through the distribution layer to the network resources.

New networks should never be added to the access layer. If more devices are required for user connectivity, they should always be connected to the distribution layer devices.

The equipment that is used at this layer is hubs and switches. Any hub or switch can be used to provide this raw connectivity. The Catalyst 2924XL switch and the Catalyst 6500, thought considerably different in price and capacity, provide the same type of raw access.

Hierarchical Design Examples

The following three examples show how the hierarchical model can be applied to various types of networks. The first network, pictured in Figure 4-3, is comprised of a central office with remote offices connected via a hub and spoke Frame Relay WAN. This model is a common implementation for many companies. The WAN may be composed of Frame Relay, ATM, leased line, or DSL circuits, but the central hub office surrounded by spoke offices is identical.

The core layer is the WAN itself with all the attached routers, 7507 and 2500s. The network diameter is identical for each remote

Figure 4-3
Central office WAN hierarchical model example

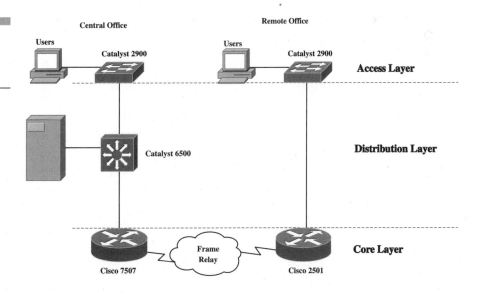

office. All central resources connect to this core area. No traffic restrictions take place on this backbone area, and all traffic will pass as quickly as possible through the core layer.

The distribution layer is comprised of the Ethernet ports of the WAN routers as well as the backbone switches, the Catalyst 6500s, of the central network. All security policies are implemented at this layer. For instance, if one set of access users is in an accounting *Virtual Local Area Network* (VLAN) and another set of users is in a sales VLAN, access between the VLANs would be controlled at this point. In addition, any bandwidth restrictions would be implemented at this layer.

The access layer is comprised of the switches, the Catalyst 2900s, which provide connectivity to all users. At this point, user access to the network is not restricted. Connectivity is provided to any device or host that is attached to the Catalyst 2900.

The second network, pictured in Figure 4-4, is a campus environment. Two large office towers are connected via a Gigabit Ethernet backbone. This campus environment is radically different in many ways from the central office example, but the campus design still exhibits the three-layer model.

Figure 4-4
Campus LAN
hierarchical model
example

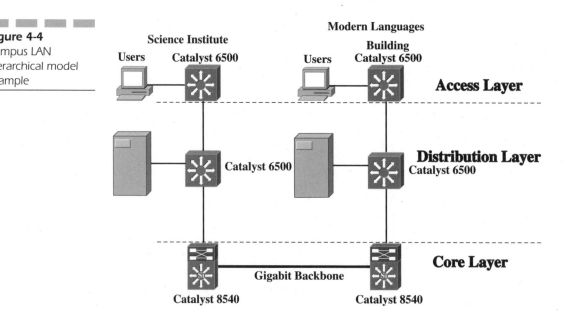

The core layer is the Gigabit backbone and the two attached wire-speed routers, the Catalyst 8540s. The core in the campus model is much faster that the central office model. Generally, the backbone in a campus model runs at LAN speeds approaching Gigabit Ethernet. This backbone is a high-speed network that will move traffic from point to point with no inhabitations.

NOTE: *Though the campus model generally uses high-speed LAN technologies like Gigabit Ethernet, it is not always faster than WANs. Currently, the highest theoretical speed possible over a WAN is over nine Gbps, which is made possible using OC-192 fiber-optic links. This top WAN speed is more that quadruple the top LAN speed of Gigabit Ethernet.*

The distribution layer is comprised of the uplink ports in the Catalyst 8540 routers as well as the uplink modules of the Catalyst 6500s. At this point, any policy and security restrictions are implemented. For example, if no users are permitted to access departmental resources except members of that department, a security restriction would be placed at this layer. If members of the audit department are an exception to this rule, then this exception would also be implemented at this layer.

The access layer is comprised of the Catalyst 6500 switches that provide user connectivity. Though the Catalyst series of switches enables you to implement many security features, it is not advisable to use these features on the access level.

NOTE: *The main reason for not using security features on the access layer is that these features are usually used on a port-by-port basis. Imagine 2,000 users on a campus network. The average move or churn rate for these users is 25 percent. That means that in a given year, 500 users will move throughout the campus. Each move requires two configuration changes, for a total of 1,000 changes. One change is required to remove the existing access-layer security and another change is required to implement access-layer security in the new location. It would take a large staff and intricate notes to ensure this happened smoothly.*

Figure 4-5

A single-chassis
hierarchical model
example

CATALYST 5500

Slot 1 - Supervisor Module	Distribution Layer
Slot 2 - Route/Switch Module	
Slot 3 - 10/100 Module	
Slot 4 - 10/100 Module	Access Layer
Slot 5 - 100B Fiber Module	
Slot 9 - ATM Switch Processor	
Slot 10 - DS3 ATM Ports	Core Layer

The last network, pictured in Figure 4-5, is a single piece of equipment, a Catalyst 5500. However, this single device provides all three layers in a single chassis.

NOTE: *Only the Catalyst 5500 is capable of providing this type of solution. Neither the members of the Catalyst 5000 family nor the Catalyst 6000 family can provide this complete three-layer solution.*

The core layer is the ATM backbone and the LightStream 1010 modules installed in the lower slots of the chassis. Another member of the core layer is the ATM uplink port in the Catalyst 5000. This port is the ATM edge device. The bottom five slots of the Catalyst 5000, when comprised of ATM lines cards, are identical to the mid-range ATM switch, the LightStream 1010. These cards operate on a separate bus from the remaining cards in the chassis. No direct communication takes place between the Catalyst portion and Light-Stream portion of the switch. The ATM uplink port on the Catalyst 5000 must be connected to the LightStream portion of the switch.

The distribution layer is comprised of the route/switch module in slot 2. The *Route Switch Model* (RSM) routes traffic between the respective VLANs. The RSM is a device that gives the Catalyst 5500, a Layer-two device, the capability to route traffic and enforce policies similar to a router.

The access layer is comprised of the Ethernet line cards in the remaining slots. These ports can be divided into several VLANs as required, and no direct communication goes on between the VLANs. All traffic destined for another VLAN will be directed to the RSMs at the distribution layer.

NOTE: *Though the access and distribution layers are pictured in opposite positions in Figure 4-5, all users communicate with the access layer. This layer then communicates with the distribution layer. This layer then passes traffic to the core layer.*

SUMMARY

In this chapter, two design fundamentals were covered. The first, the framework triangle, is a starting point for determining the requirements of the design project. The framework triangle is an invaluable tool that enables all facets and implications of a design to be considered. The second fundamental, the three-layer hierarchy, is a model for designing reliable and scalable networks. The three-layer model enables all designs to retain the same basic foundations.

The fundamentals of technology, equipment, and design principles are the core precepts of network design. Without any one of these items, designing a robust and complete network that fulfills the requirements of a customer would be near impossible. As technology changes, it is more important than ever for the network designer to stay abreast of change in technology, products, and design principles.

QUESTIONS ▬ ▬ ▬ ▬ ▬ ▬ ▬ ▬

1. Which layer of the hierarchical model is responsible for user connectivity?

    a. Core
    b. Distribution
    c. Access

2. Which layer of the hierarchical model is responsible for fast and reliable transports?

    a. Core
    b. Distribution
    c. Access

3. Which layer of the hierarchical model is responsible for restricting access to resources?

    a. Core
    b. Distribution
    c. Access

4. What is the term for using switches to limit the number of users in a collision domain?

    a. Bridging
    b. Tight switching
    c. Spanning Tree
    d. Microsegmenting

5. What type of problem does using *Network Address Translation* (NAT) solve?

    a. Hierarchy
    b. Media
    c. Protocol
    d. Transport

6. Examine Figure 4-6. Which layer of the hierarchical model is the Catalyst 2900 a member of?

    a. Core
    b. Distribution
    c. Access

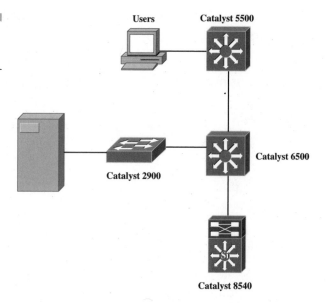

Figure 4-6
Hierarchical model
example 1

7. Refer to Figure 4-6. Which layer of the hierarchical model is the Catalyst 5500 a member of?

   a. Core

   b. Distribution

   c. Access

8. A router that connects your network to another location via a VPN connection would be a member of which layer?

   a. Core

   b. Distribution

   c. Access

9. The majority of all network issues are located in which segment of the framework triangle?

   a. Media

   b. Protocol

   c. Transport

10. The requirement to upgrade from Ethernet to Gigabit Ethernet is a result of issues in which segment of the framework triangle?

    a. Media

    b. Protocol

    c. Transport

11. Examine Figure 4-7. Which layer of the hierarchical model is the Cisco 2502 a member of?

    a. Core
    b. Distribution
    c. Access

12. Refer to Figure 4-7. Which layer of the hierarchical model is the MSAU a member of?

    a. Core
    b. Distribution
    c. Access

13. Examine Figure 4-8. Which layer of the hierarchical model is the Cisco 1600 a member of?

    a. Core
    b. Distribution
    c. Access

14. Refer to Figure 4-8. Which layer of the hierarchical model is the Cisco AS5200 a member of?

    a. Core
    b. Distribution
    c. Access

Figure 4-7
Hierarchical model
example 2

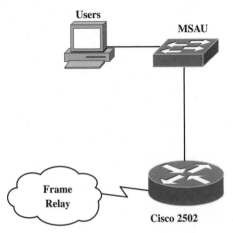

Figure 4-8
Hierarchical model
example 3

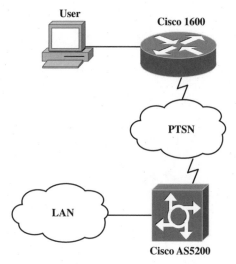

15. Which type of problem is a result of using RIP for routing?

    a. Hierarchy
    b. Media
    c. Protocol
    d. Transport

16. Which layer of the hierarchical model requires extensive manageability?

    a. Core
    b. Distribution
    c. Access

17. Router A is connecting two separate EIGRP ASs. In which layer of the hierarchical model would Router A lie?

    a. Core
    b. Distribution
    c. Access

18. The requirement to change the routing on a WAN link from RTMP to EIGRP is a result of issues in which segment of the framework triangle?

    a. Media
    b. Protocol
    c. Transport

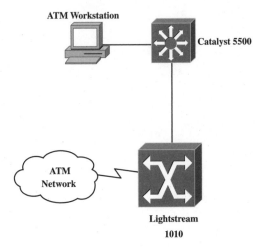

Figure 4-9
Hierarchical model
example 4

19. Examine Figure 4-9. Which layer of the hierarchical model is the LightStream 1010 a member of?

   a. Core
   b. Distribution
   c. Access

20. Refer to Figure 4-8. Which layer of the hierarchical model is the Catalyst 5500 a member of?

   a. Core
   b. Distribution
   c. Access

ANSWERS

1. **c.** Access

   This layer provides network access for all end stations.

2. **a.** Core

   This is the backbone of the network. It provides reliable, high-speed communications to all distribution layers of the network.

3. **b.** Distribution

   This is the interface between the core and the access layers. It provides for policy-based connectivity and security between the two layers.

4. **d.** Microsegmenting

   Switches are used to divide the network into separate collision domains. This is also called microsegmenting.

5. **c.** Protocol

   Protocols problems are the result of implementations that do not scale. A limitation of the TCP/IP protocol is that there are not enough public IP addresses. Therefore, NAT is used to translate a private IP range into a public IP range.

6. **b.** Distribution

   Any device connected to central resources would be part of the distribution layer. Security would be applied to this device.

7. **c.** Access

   The Catalyst 5500 forms the central connection point for all the users.

8. **b.** Distribution

   All encryption and decryption processes take place at the distribution level.

9. **a.** Media

   Physical layer or media problems are the most common cause of network problems.

10. **c.** Transport

    Changing Ethernet for Gigabit Ethernet changes the transport for the network.

11. a. Core

The 2502 router is connected to the Frame Relay WAN. This is the backbone for the entire network. This means that the 2502 is part of the core layer.

12. c. Access

An MSAU is a Token Ring hub that provides user connectivity. A device that provides user connectivity is a member of the access layer.

13. c. Access

Though it is a router, it is the device that is providing user connectivity. Therefore, it is in the access layer.

14. b. Distribution

All security mechanisms for connecting to resources are part of the distribution layer. Since the AS5200 is responsible for authenticating users to the network, it is also part of the distribution layer.

15. c. Protocol

Protocol problems are the result of implementations that do not scale. A limitation of the RIP protocol is that multiple subnet masks cannot be used.

16. a. Core

By constantly managing the state of the core layer, problems can be proactively avoided or reactively solved without a tremendous loss of productivity.

17. b. Distribution

The distribution layer performs all routing redistribution and summarization. Therefore, RouterA is a part of the distribution layer.

18. b. Protocol

RTMP is a distance vector routing protocol that updates its neighbors frequently. This may cause a slow WAN connection to become congested. By changing protocols, the congestion can be alleviated.

19. a. Core

The ATM switch is part of the core network backbone. In this case, the backbone is an ATM internetwork.

20. c. Access

Here the Catalyst 5500 is providing *LAN emulation* (LANE) access for several end users. All devices that are providing network access are part of the access layer.

Documenting the Existing Network

Objectives Covered in This Chapter

- Identify all the data you should gather to characterize the customer's existing network.

- Document the customer's current applications, protocols, topology, and number of users.

- Assess the health of the customer's existing network and make conclusions about the network's capability to support growth.

- Diagram the flow of information for new applications.

- List some tools that will help you characterize new network traffic.

- Predict the amount of traffic and the type of traffic caused by the applications, given charts that characterize typical network traffic.

Before embarking on a network design, a tremendous amount of information must be gathered. The first step in this process is documenting the existing network and traffic. This step is central to the design process. Without knowing the existing environment and applications, designing a network would be impossible.

The status of a client's existing network is an integral part in completing the final design. Regardless of the final network design, the client's applications will be a major consideration. For example, designing a low-speed *Wide Area Network* (WAN) connection may impair the communication between users at the remote offices and the centralized mainframe resources.

In addition to the technical details of the current infrastructure, the business and administrative details of the current infrastructure must also be determined. In some instances, these details may be more important than the technical details. The business and administrative details will be covered in Chapter 6.

Documentation Checklist

Determining the status of the existing network is a series of tasks instead of a single task. It is important that all these tasks be completed. For instance, if a bandwidth utilization study has not been completed, then a network designer may be upgrading backbone links that are barely utilized. The following checklist can be used as a documentation starting point.

NOTE: *This checklist is a guideline to follow when determining the technical information that will be required for a complete design. This list is not exhaustive and is meant to be a guideline only.*

Network Maps
    1. *Topology map*
    2. *User map*
    3. *Server / resource map*

Usage Documentation
    1. *Application usage*
    2. *Protocol usage*

State of the Network
    1. *Bandwidth utilization*
    2. *Availability*
    3. *Performance*
    4. *Reliability*
    5. *Router / switch load*
    6. *Network management system*
    7. *Growth Potential*

Network Maps

Maps of the network and network communication patterns are the first logical step in any documentation process. Maps enable the designer to make more informed decisions about possible bottlenecks in the existing network. Without a network map, it would be difficult to determine the optimum places to gather more data.

Maps of a network should communicate not only the physical layout of the network, but also the logical layout of the network. The most important information should always be prominently placed on the drawing. For instance, on a Frame Relay map, the *Data Link Connection Identifier* (DLCI) and *Internet Protocol* (IP) addresses of the link should always be noted. Note, however, that including all the service provider circuit numbers could quickly make the map unreadable.

NOTE: *Visio 2000 Enterprise provides the network designer's method for mapping a network automatically. It uses the* Simple Network Management Protocol *(SNMP) to acquire detailed information and statistics from all the network devices.*

NOTE: *In my experience, necessary but seldom-used details like service provider circuit numbers or* Media Access Control *(MAC) addresses should be listed on a spreadsheet for easier reference.*

Two additional types of maps will enable the designer to ascertain many features and aspects of the existing network. The maps are topology maps and server/user location maps.

Topology Maps

Topology maps range from the simple to the complex. Depending on the size of the network, a single page map may provide all the information required (see Figure 5-1). However, a more complex or large network may require several maps to capture the entire network topology. The first page of a complex network is shown in Figure 5-2.

NOTE: *The complex map shows only a general overview of the network. Further details like IP addressing, remote offices, and firewall configurations would be on separate pages.*

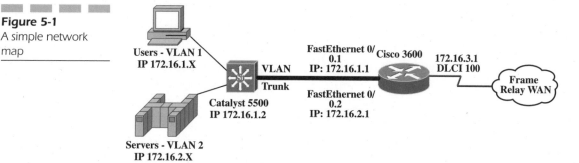

Figure 5-1
A simple network map

Users - VLAN 1
IP 172.16.1.X

VLAN Trunk

Catalyst 5500
IP 172.16.1.2

Servers - VLAN 2
IP 172.16.2.X

FastEthernet 0/0.1
IP: 172.16.1.1

FastEthernet 0/0.2
IP: 172.16.2.1

Cisco 3600

172.16.3.1
DLCI 100

Frame Relay WAN

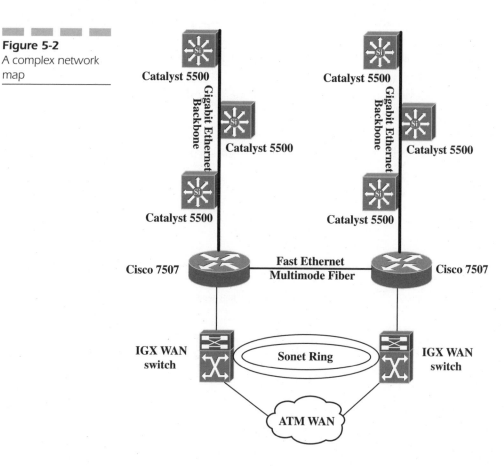

Figure 5-2
A complex network map

Server/User Maps

The number of users on a network and their location in relation to network devices must be noted. Are the users located on a remote *Local Area Network* (LAN) that is connected via a DS3 *Asynchronous Transfer Mode* (ATM) circuit or a 64-Kbps leased line circuit? Figure 5-3 is an example of a server/user map. In this figure, approximately 100 users are located across a 256-Kbps Frame Relay connection. The remaining 500 users are located within the campus network.

Just like user maps, server maps are used to locate and quantify the server resources on the network. Are all the servers located on server farms? Are there any types of firewall devices that may block or restrict traffic?

One of the most important details to examine on this map is the location of the users and servers in relation to each other. The next section will cover this in more detail. As shown in Figure 5-3, however, all users must cross the Cisco 7507 router in order to access the mainframe and the enterprise servers. In addition, no servers are located at the remote office. All traffic must cross the 128-Kbps WAN circuit in order to reach a resource. If a large number of users are on the remote network, this low-speed WAN pipe may become overloaded.

Figure 5-3
Network user/
server map

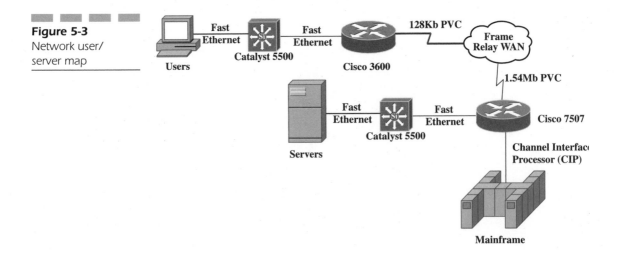

Usage Documentation

The topology, user, and server maps when combined will form the basis for the usage documentation. Usage documentation is the gathering of application traffic and information between users and servers. In addition, the protocol distribution of the traffic must be determined.

Application Usage

The purpose of a network infrastructure is to transport application traffic from the source to the destination. This traffic and the impact upon the network are the key considerations in a network design. Remember to consider the bidirectional flow of traffic. Users request data from servers. This request is generally a small packet. Then generally a larger data packet is sent from the server to the user. The type of application data sent is also important. For example, many small packets are sent during a Telnet session. During a Web session, the packets are generally large packets.

NOTE: *Application changes can also have drastic impacts upon the network infrastructure. If a text-based Telnet program is upgraded to a Web-based, graphic-intensive program, then almost all network segments will have more traffic.*

The key facets of application usage that must be examined are as follows:

- *Application name* The common name of the application
- *Application type* World Wide Web, database, file server, and so on
- *Number of users* The total number of users throughout the network
- *Number of servers* The total number of servers throughout the network
- *Additional information* Other application information relevant to network design

Application Name	Application Type	Number of Users	Number of Servers	Additional Information

In addition to the raw data gathered, the application traffic flows need to be identified. Traffic that flows over slow links needs to be identified and quantified. Since the location of the users and servers has been identified, this map will now be used to identify traffic flows.

In Figure 5-4, the traffic flow for a mainframe application is depicted. All mainframe traffic from the users goes to the mainframe. This traffic passes through two routers and passes over a slow Frame Relay circuit.

Figure 5-5 shows the traffic flow for an e-mail application on the same network. Notice that for a portion of the trip, the traffic pattern is the same as the mainframe traffic flow. Although one traffic flow over the slow Frame Relay link may not be a concern, both traffic flows may cause the circuit to become saturated.

Figure 5-4

Mainframe traffic flow

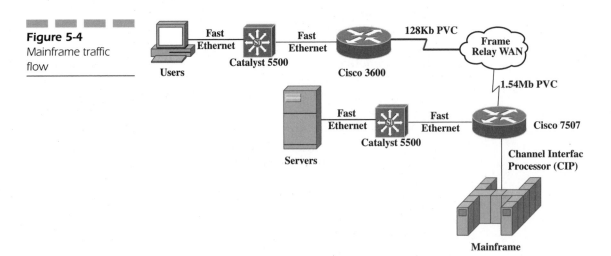

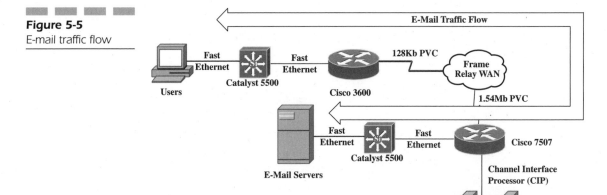

Figure 5-5
E-mail traffic flow

Protocol Usage

Just like application usage documentation, protocol usage is another variable that must be documented. Although applications have to use a protocol to communicate across the network, this protocol traffic must be listed. For example, if IPX/SPX traffic is predominate in a network, the designer must know where this protocol is in use. The added overhead traffic of this protocol is a key to determining the bandwidth. In addition, if offices do not share these resources, then this overhead RIP/SAP traffic can be safely eliminated from the network.

The following facets of protocol usage should be documented:

- *Protocol Name*   The common name of the protocol
- *Protocol Type*   Client/server, connectionless, and so on
- *Number of Users*   The total number of protocol users throughout the network
- *Number of Servers*   The total number of protocol servers throughout the network
- *Additional Information*   Other protocol information relevant to network design

Protocol Name	Protocol Type	Number of Users	Number of Servers	Additional Information

As a next step, the traffic can be further refined, such as the percentage of user IP traffic that is Web traffic. If the only business-related IP traffic on a network is Telnet, and Web traffic accounts for 95 percent, then security policies may need to be implemented on the Internet connection.

Documentation Tools

After the initial network maps and usage has been documented, the next phase is to determine the state of the network itself. In order to complete this documentation, the designer can use a number of tools and resources. These tools enable the designer to quantify the exact state of the network.

Protocol Analyzers

Protocol analyzers allow one to determine the exact protocols and amount of traffic on a segment at any given time. A protocol analyzer can determine the sizes, sources, destinations, and errors present in the traffic. These devices can also be used to capture small amounts of traffic for detailed analysis. A protocol analyzer can also be used to capture data on WAN circuits. This enables the designer to accurately quantify existing circuit utilization.

NOTE: *Protocol analyzers are one of the powerful tools available to a network designer. The most important tip to remember is that generally they will not provide a direct answer to a question, but they will provide small clues as to the nature of the network. These clues that are collected over time can then be analyzed as a whole to determine the probable state of the network.*

NETSYS

NETSYS tools is a Cisco product that enables complex models to take place without impacting a production network. NETSYS first takes a snapshot of the existing network and changes are subsequently made to the computer model. The resulting traffic patterns can then be analyzed. This entire analysis takes place in a computer model and therefore does not affect the existing network in any manner.

CiscoWorks

CiscoWorks is another Cisco product. It has a set of SNMP-based tools for documenting a customer's existing network. CiscoWorks enables the designer to monitor devices, maintain device configurations, and troubleshoot various network problems.

Multi-Router Traffic Grapher (MRTG)

The *Multi-Router Traffic Grapher* (MRTG) is a software package that is a freeware program. It enables network designers to gather interface statistics from remote routers and other network devices using SNMP. These statistics are then stored in the program's database. This data can be viewed in graphical format using any Web browser.

 NOTE:　*MRTG can be used to gather and present any data from any device that is capable of using SNMP. This includes not only networking devices, but also printers and servers.*

State of the Network

Now the basic network maps are complete, and the application traffic flows have been identified. The documentation tools have also been identified. Next, the various statistics of the network can be gathered. These statistics will enable the maps to have real meaning. Instead of being 64-Kb Frame Relay links, they will be 64-Kb Frame Relay links that are 95 percent utilized. Gathering this final bit of information is critical when determining the true nature of the network. The statistics and information that should be gathered are as follows:

- Utilization
- Availability
- Reliability
- Performance
- Router/switch loads
- Network management
- Growth potential

Utilization

The key in determining network utilization is identifying problem areas in advance. It is impossible and impractical to determine the utilization of the entire network in a complex environment. By using the topology maps as well as the application traffic flows, the possible bottlenecks can be identified. For example, in Figure 5-6, two separate user segments connect to a Frame Relay backbone via a 128-Kbps *Permanent Virtual Circuit* (PVC). This slow circuit could be a bottleneck, but the determining factor is the actual traffic flow across the circuit. If all resources are located on the LAN and not across the WAN circuit, the PVC is probably not a bottleneck.

Another utilization characteristic that should be determined at this time is the source and destination of this traffic. The traffic

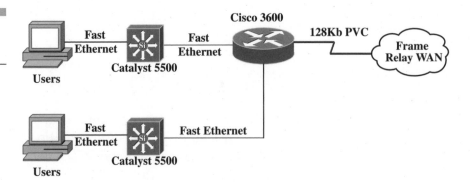

Figure 5-6
Network utilization over Frame Relay

should be separated in four categories depending on the locality of the source and destination traffic.

Network Segment	Source and Destination Are Local	Source Is Remote, Destination Is Local	Source Is Local, Destination Is Remote	Source and Destination Are Remote

The next step in utilization analysis is determining the protocol distribution for the network. The information required for this is as follows:

- *Protocol*   The name of the protocol
- *Average Utilization*   The average utilization of each protocol
- *Peak Utilization*   The top utilization of each protocol
- *Average Frame Size*   The average size of all the protocol frames
- *Broadcasts*   The total number of the broadcast and multicast frames

Protocol	Average Utilization	Peak Utilization	Average Frame Size	Broadcasts/ Multicasts per Second
TCP/IP				
IPX/SPX				
AppleTalk				
Other				

NOTE: *For protocols with many component parts like TCP/IP, it may be advisable to track specific application utilization, such as Web or Telnet traffic.*

Availability

The effects of downtime on a network can be tremendous. In addition, some portions of a network may have more frequent outages than other segments. Documenting these outages and the average time between them will enable the designer to alleviate the effects of these outages on the new design. The key requirement for this network component is the cost of possible downtime. This cost should be not only on a departmental basis, but also on a corporate basis. For many companies, the cost of a WAN outage affecting all business units can be astronomical.

NOTE: *This specific calculation is one of the most important for network design. At times, the high cost of these implementations can be prohibitive. By understanding the costs of not changing less reliable systems, the actual cost may be dramatically less.*

Several statistics are required for this analysis. They are as follows:

- *Network / Segment*   The specific network or segment
- Mean Time Between Failure *(MTBF)*   MTBF is the average time between each failure
- *Last Downtime*   The date of last downtime
- *Duration of Last Downtime*   The length of the downtime
- *Cause of Last Downtime*   The specific root cause of the downtime

Network/ Segment	MTBF	Last Downtime	Duration of Last Downtime	Cause of Last Downtime

Reliability

As stated earlier, the affects of downtime on a network can be tremendous. For many companies, the cost of a WAN outage affecting all business units can be astronomical.

Several statistics are required for this analysis. They are as follows:

- *Average Utilization* The average utilization of each protocol
- *Peak Utilization* The top utilization of each protocol
- *Average Frame Size* The average size of all the protocol frames
- *Total Number of CRC Errors* The errors in the *Cyclical Redundancy Check* (CRC)
- *Total Number of Layer 2 Errors* The number of Ethernet collisions, Token Ring soft errors, and FDDI ring operation errors
- *Broadcasts* The total number of broadcast and multicast frames

Network/ Segment	Average. Network Utilization	Peak Network Utilization	Average Frame Size	CRC Error Rate	MAC Layer Error Rate	Broadcasts/ Multicasts

The key reliability statistic to examine is the relationship between the errors and bytes. To calculate the CRC error rate, the number of CRC errors is divided by the total amount of traffic in megabytes. The MAC layer error rate is calculated by dividing the number of MAC layer errors by the total number of frames. Finally, for the broadcasts/multicast rate, the total number of broadcasts/multicasts is divided by the total number of frames.

The following data can be used as an example for the reliability calculations:

- Total MB Transferred: 100 MB
- Total Number of Frames: 250,000
- Total Number of CRC Errors: 5
- Total Number of MAC Layer Errors: 100
- Total Number of Broadcasts: 10,000

Using the previous statistics, the following error rates can be derived:

- The CRC error rate is five errors in 100 MB (5/100 = 5%).
- The MAC layer error rate is 100 errors divided by 250,000 frames (100/250,000 = .04%).
- The broadcast rate is 10,000 frames divided by 250,000 frames (10,000/250,000 = 4%).

Performance

The network performance is a metric that will enable a designer to quantify the affects of a network change. First, the average throughput between several hosts is determined. For best results, the hosts should be located at varying points in the network. This data can be analyzed for what the client characterizes as a *slow* response time and a *normal* response time. Next, the network change is made. Finally, the same hosts are reexamined to see if there is a difference in network performance. The following table will assist the designer in completing the performance analysis.

	Host A	Host B	Host C	Host D
Host A				
Host B				
Host C				
Host D				

NOTE: *Often, I have seen many remarks about slow networks or about applications performing poorly because of the network. The network is always blamed first, because it places the burden of proof on the network infrastructure itself. However, by learning about the network baselines and how the network behaves, network problems can be quickly proved or disproved. Many times, the network problem turned out to be a poorly performing application. Remember, a router will not decide to route some packets slower than others.*

Router and Switch Loads

Another metric that can be gathered to document the network is the router and switch utilization statistics. These statistics provide a health check of all the network devices in an infrastructure. On a Cisco router or another device that runs the Cisco IOS, the following commands can be used to gather the necessary statistics:

- *Show interface*   This command is used for the dropped, missed, and ignored packets.

- *Show processes*   This command is used to gather the five-minute CPU utilization.

The following table will assist the designer in gathering the necessary router data.

Router Name	Five-Minute CPU Util.	Output Queue Drops per Hour	Input Queue Drops per Hour	Missed Packets per Hour	Ignored Packets per Hour	Additional Information
Router A						
Router B						
Router C						
Router D						

This data is crucial for identifying any overloaded network devices. If a core router is constantly running at 95 percent utilization, it may not be wise to add BGP routing to that device. On the other hand, if a Catalyst 5000 switch is only running at two percent utilization, it may not wise to upgrade solely for increased backplane capacity.

Network Management

The network management requirements of any design are another factor that must be considered. The first consideration is whether or not network management is required. If network management is required and currently exists, the new device must be able to communicate with the management station. In addition, the management station may have to be patched or upgraded in order to recognize the new devices.

If network management is required but not currently installed, a management system must be installed. This will be an additional step in the design process. The installation and configuration of network management systems like Cisco Works 2000 and HP Openview take careful planning to ensure that the desired management results are obtained.

Potential Growth

The final component of a network design is the growth potential of the existing network. If a network cannot grow in a specific area, then the new design may involve replacing that component. If a wiring closet is filled to capacity, then a portion of the new design may be a device with an greater capacity than that closet. The following growth considerations should all be taken into account:

- *Port capacity* The quantity of free ports available for growth is an important aspect. If more ports are required, a determination must be made about how to increase the quantity.

■ *Congested uplinks* If the uplinks are congested, then no more hosts should be added to that uplink segment.

■ *Overloaded backplane* In this case, the switch equipment must be upgraded to a device with a faster backplane. If the device cannot be upgraded, then a portion of the traffic must be moved to another device.

■ *Slot capacity* Like the quantity of free ports, the remaining slots in a router or switch is an important factor. A Cisco 7505 that has no remaining slots is a limiting factor in redesigning an existing network.

A network that is operating at maximum port capacity demands a different solution than a network that is operating with congested uplinks or overloaded backplanes. Determining the existing issues with a network will help ensure the new design does not have the same faults or limitations. It will also allow the designer to provide solutions to issues the client may not even realize exist.

SUMMARY

The beginning considerations of design have now been introduced. These considerations document the existing network and its various utilization statistics. These maps and statistics are critical for determining which parts of the network design need special consideration. By analyzing the network statistics, a designer can ensure that existing network issues will not compromise the integrity of the new network.

Network design is not a magical process. It is simply a long period of data gathering and analysis followed by a relatively short design phase. The most difficult part of designing a network is becoming familiar with the existing network and all of its unique features.

Case Study

Case studies provide a way for network designers to practice what they have learned. Case Study 1 deals with a medium-sized manufacturing company, Widget Manufacturing.

NOTE: *Case Study 1 will be developed by the authors as part of each chapter. The remaining four case studies will be developed by the reader as part of the chapter questions.*

Widget Manufacturing

Widget Manufacturing has recently decided to upgrade its network infrastructure. The existing network has had performance and availability problems, as it has grown over the past two years. The network is comprised of 1,500 users who are located across a large manufacturing facility. Their current network infrastructure has been in place for almost seven years.

Step 1: Network Topology and Server/User Topology   The network is comprised of 10-MB Ethernet that runs both Thinnet and Thicknet coaxial cable. The Thinnet cable is used to connect the users to hubs and repeaters. The Thicknet cable is used to connect the repeaters and hubs together to form a routed internetwork. Figure 5-7 depicts the existing network.

The network map also details the location of the users and the servers. One key to the existing network design is that all user traffic must cross the Cisco 7000 router. Also, because all the network segments are shared segments, there may be utilization problems on the segments.

Step 2: Usage Documentation   The network has two main applications in use. The first is a Telnet-based manufacturing and accounting package that is hosted on a mini-computer in the server

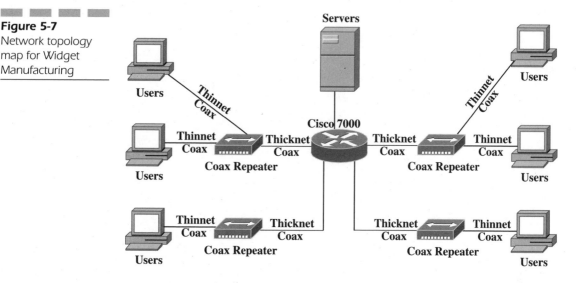

Figure 5-7
Network topology map for Widget Manufacturing

farm. The second application is the file and print services that are in use. The file and print services are five Novell 3.12 servers. One server is used as a departmental file and print server. Figure 5-8 depicts the application usage across the network.

All traffic flows across the router to the server farm. Because the server farm is on a shared segment, it is quite likely that all the user traffic will create bandwidth problems on the server segment.

Next, the protocol usage for the network needs to be analyzed. Only two protocols are in use: TCP/IP is used for the Telnet application, while IPX/SPX is used for communication between the users and the departmental file servers. Approximately, 500 people use the file servers only, and 500 people use the Telnet application only. A thousand users have access to both systems. The following table is the next step in the documentation gathering process.

Protocol Name	Protocol Type	Number of Users	Number of Servers	Additional Information
TCP/IP	Client/Server	1000	1	
IPX/SPX	Client/Server	1000	5	

Figure 5-8
The application traffic
flow for Widget
Manufacturing

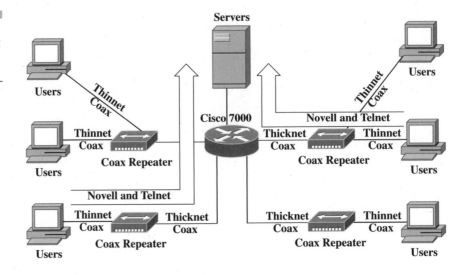

Step 3: State of the Network   Next, the state of the existing network must be examined. The bandwidth utilization can be measured using protocol analyzers. Looking at the application traffic flows, all traffic is destined for a remote network. Further analysis of the server segment results in the following protocol distribution:

Protocol	Average Utilization	Peak Utilization	Average Frame Size	Broadcasts/ Multicasts per Second
TCP/IP	25%	80%	100 Bytes	4000
IPX/SPX	45%	100%	1,000 Bytes	7000

The availability of the network is a problem. On occasion, broadcast storms will render portions of the network unusable. The router will contain these storms on particular segments. The root cause of these broadcast storms is network card errors taking place on user machines. The network performance is also affected by these broadcast storms. The performance and response time for the Telnet application varies throughout the day as the load on the network increases.

The reliability of the network is as questionable as the availability and performance statistics. This lack of reliability is the driving force for the upgrade and replacement of the aged infrastructure.

The load of the Cisco 7000 is also a possible bottleneck. When the router CPU was examined, the average five-minute CPU utilization was 50 percent. Though the router does not seem to be overutilized, the specific Ethernet interfaces should also be examined. Upon examining the Ethernet interfaces, all interfaces except the server segment seen to be operating normally. However, the server segment has a high utilization that has resulted in a large number of collisions.

Currently, no network management system is in place at Widget Manufacturing. Part of the new design requirement will be the installation and configuration of an *Network Management System* (NMS).

The growth potential of this network is suspect. As more users require network access, more repeaters are added. As repeaters are added, more traffic is added to the shared segments. Since all servers are located on the same segment, more users mean more traffic on the server segment. As more users are added, the traffic problems increase.

NOTE: *Four additional case studies will be examined as part of the study questions for each chapter.*

QUESTIONS ▆▆ ▆▆ ▆▆ ▆▆ ▆▆ ▆▆ ▆▆

The following section contains four case studies with accompanying questions to test your knowledge.

Case Study: Limbo Medical Group

The Limbo Medical Group was on the cutting edge of network technology 10 years ago. They decided to implement a centralized computer system for all their day-to-day operations. This system consisted of an X.25 WAN that connects 50 small offices to a central hospital facility. This X.25 WAN carried legacy *Systems Network Architecture* (SNA) traffic between the hosts and a mainframe.

They now are developing a new client/server application to replace this mainframe application. In addition, the legacy X.25 network will be replaced with a Frame Relay network. The operations of the medical group run throughout the day. Any network downtime would be detrimental to these operations. Therefore, the new network must be reliable and fault-tolerant.

The new client/server application will be an IP-based application that is housed in an Oracle database. In order to keep client upgrades to a minimum, all client interaction will be though a Web browser.

1. Why is a map of the existing network not required in this case study?

   a. The existing network is old, so documentation is not required.

   b. Because it carries only SNA traffic.

   c. Because it is an X.25 network.

   d. Because the old network will be replaced by the new network.

2. Which of the following characteristics are most important to the IT department at Limbo Medical?

   a. Speed

   b. Availability

   c. Low Latency

   d. Flexibility

3. Which protocol will run over the Frame Relay network?

   a. SNA

   b. IPX

   c. IP

   d. Oracle

4. What role will the mainframe play in the new network?

   a. It will be the central data repository.

   b. It will perform conversion functions for the new client/server application.

   c. None

   d. It will become a router.

5. Which application layer protocol will account for a majority of the traffic on the Frame Relay network?

   a. HTTP

   b. FTP

   c. IP

   d. Oracle

Case Study: Global Supplies Corporation

Global Supplies is a multinational corporation that is comprised of approximately 15 separate facilities throughout North America. Each facility has an existing LAN that has been upgraded according to the needs of the specific facility. The LANs range from small 10-Mb Ethernet networks to large Fast Ethernet networks with Gigabit backbones.

The concern of Global Supplies' corporate IT group is the WAN. The existing WAN is comprised of only leased lines. At least two leased lines connect each office to another office. In some cases, an individual is connected via leased lines to three of four other offices. The multiple links ensure that the quickest path to the destination is selected with the best redundancy.

Figure 5-9 is an example of a portion of the network. Multiple T1 lines are set up from location to location. These lines support not only data, but also voice communications. It is crucial that the new

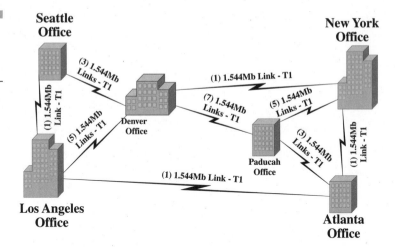

Figure 5-9
Global Supplies'
network topology
map

WAN infrastructure continue to support both voice and data traffic, but the existing voice equipment cannot be changed at this time.

The data portion of the leased-line circuits is currently running at 90 percent capacity. The financial and operational applications reside at each site and they work independently of each other. The traffic across the WAN is Novell server traffic, e-mail traffic, Internet traffic, and a special distance learning application. Global Suppliers has determined that distance learning is the key to their company's continued success. This training is delivered in the form of intranet-based streaming media presentations. It is imperative that this training be delivered in a timely manner.

6. Since it is required that both voice and data need to traverse the WAN at the same time, what technology can best accommodate this?

a. Frame Relay

b. X.25

c. ISDN

d. ATM

7. Where are the server resources primarily located?

a. Local to each network

b. Both local and remote

c. Remote to each network

8. Which protocols will run over the ATM network? Choose as many as apply.

   a. SNA

   b. IPX

   c. IP

   d. AppleTalk

9. According to the information provided, which network characteristic seems to be most important to the IT staff of Global Supplies.

   a. Speed

   b. Redundancy

   c. Reliability

   d. Low latency

10. Which technology can be used to reduce the amount of IPX broadcast traffic, RIPs, and SAPs that traverses the WAN?

    a. IPX EIGRP

    b. OSPF

    c. Offset lists

    d. ATM

Case Study: Bank of Pompeii

The Bank of Pompeii has just completed a new corporate office tower in a prime downtown location. This will enable the bank to consolidate six small offices into the new corporate tower. In addition to this move, all the SNA traffic will be removed from the WAN.

All the offices are connected via a Frame Relay WAN in a hub and spoke configuration. The hub of the Frame Relay network will be the new corporate tower. The remainder of the offices will remain on the Frame Relay network.

After the new offices are moved to the corporate tower, they will be connected to the newly designed Gigabit backbone. The existing branch networks are shared 10-Mb Ethernet. They will be converted to a switched 100-Mb Fast Ethernet LAN.

After the conversion, all network traffic will be IP-based protocols. The only applications in use are e-mail and a Telnet-based bank application.

11. Why is a map of the existing network WAN not required in this case study?

    a. The existing network is old, so documentation is not required.

    b. Because it carries traffic the branches that are moving.

    c. Because it is a Frame Relay network.

    d. Because the existing network is not being drastically altered.

12. Which new technology will enable the new backbone to handle the increased capacity of six more branches?

    a. Frame Relay

    b. ATM

    c. Gigabit Ethernet

    d. Ethernet

Case Study: G&S Productions

Gimball Productions and Shapiro Productions have recently merged. The new company, G&S Productions, has become a major commercial production company. Two main sites have been created, each with about 250 users. In addition to this, each company has three to five smaller offices throughout the United Sates. Figure 5-10 depicts the current environment of G&S Productions.

The two companies currently use an ISDN dialup connection to pass only e-mail traffic between the sites. The e-mail server is a Windows NT-based system. The main sites each use leased lines to connect to their remote offices. The leased lines are only 56-KB circuits.

The requirement from the newly formed IT department is to build a reliable, cost-effective WAN that will start the integration of the new network. Eventually, the financial and operational applications of both companies will be combined.

Both companies are using Windows NT and AppleShare servers. The protocols in use on the network are TCP/IP for Windows NT and

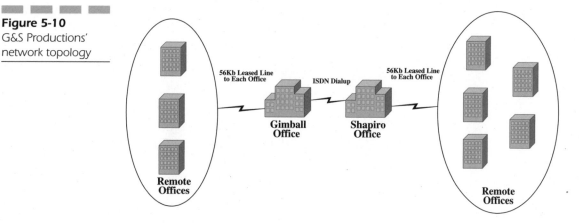

Figure 5-10
G&S Productions'
network topology

AppleTalk for the AppleShare servers. The existing networks accommodate both Ethernet and Fast Ethernet switched traffic.

13. Which protocol will run over the ISDN dialup link?

  a. AppleTalk

  b. IP

  c. Frame Relay

  d. Voice

14. Which WAN solution would fulfill the requirements of the IT department?

  a. ISDN

  b. Leased lines

  c. ATM

  d. Frame Relay

15. Why is the ISDN link not sufficient as an interoffice link?

  a. It will not support the maximum bandwidth that can be sent from the remote offices.

  b. It is a dial-up circuit.

  c. It is a low-speed circuit.

  d. It is based on X.25.

16. If a Cisco 7507 router has two route/switch processors and five VIP-2 cards, what growth-potential factor has been reached?

   a. Port Capacity

   b. Congested Uplink

   c. Overloaded Backplane

   d. Slot Capacity

17. If a 24-port switch currently has 23 users resident, what growth-potential factor has been reached?

   a. Port Capacity

   b. Congested Uplink

   c. Overloaded Backplane

   d. Slot Capacity

18. What "state of the network" measurement is closely associated with HP Openview?

   a. Availability

   b. Router/switch load

   c. Network management

   d. Utilization

19. Which command is used to show the number of dropped packets on an interface?

   a. show errors

   b. show interface

   c. show drops

   d. show packets

20. Which command is used to show the CPU utilization of a router?

   a. show version

   b. show interface

   c. show cpu

   d. show processes

ANSWERS

1. d. Because the old network will be replaced by the new network.

Because the old network will not be reused, there is no reason to document this network. However, you will have to design and document the new Frame Relay network.

2. b. Availability

Remember this network operates 24 hours a day. Reliability, uptime, and fault-tolerance are critical.

3. c. IP

The only protocol that will traverse the new network is IP. IP is the base foundation protocol for the Oracle traffic. All SNA traffic will remain on the old X.25 network.

4. c. None

The new network will make the mainframe and X.25 network obsolete.

5. a. HTTP

Though the back-end server is Oracle-based, the transport method between the clients and the server is used via a Web browser. This means that the protocol in use is HTTP.

6. d. ATM

Only ATM can support both voice and data traffic simultaneously over the same circuit.

7. b. Both local and remote

All financial and operational applications are local, while all distance-learning applications are remote.

8. b. IP and **c.** IPX

IPX will run across the network for the Novell server communication. The distance-learning application is intranet-based and therefore IP-based. The e-mail protocol has not been identified at this time.

9. **d.** Low latency

The key component to the network design is the timely delivery of the training material. This requires a network that has low latency and passes traffic. Speed, while a possible answer, does not necessarily satisfy the requirement. A network can be fast and still have problems passing traffic through fast but clogged circuits.

10. **a.** IPX EIGRP

IPX EIGRP communicates only topology changes across the WAN circuits. The near continuous RIP/SAPs are not sent across the WAN.

11. **d.** Because the existing WAN is not being drastically altered.

The WAN will not be changed and several sites will be removed. This will not alter the traffic characteristics of the WAN. In addition, the removal of SNA will not have adverse effects on the WAN traffic.

12. **c.** Gigabit Ethernet

Gigabit Ethernet is the backbone technology of choice for the corporate towers.

13. **b.** IP

Only e-mail traffic is passed across the ISDN circuit. E-mail is on a Windows NT-based system. All Windows NT systems use the TCP/IP protocol.

14. **d.** Frame Relay

Their requirements are a reliable and cost-effective WAN. ISDN is circuit-switched and not reliable. ATM and leased lines are not cost-effective.

15. **a.** It will not support the maximum bandwidth that can be sent from the remote offices.

The remote offices' combined bandwidth ranges from 168 KB to 280 KB. The maximum throughput on any ISDN circuit is only 128 KB.

16. d. Slot Capacity

A 7507 has seven slots. Each RSP occupies one slot. The remaining five VIP2 cards fill the router completely.

17. a. Port Capacity

The quantity of free ports available for growth is an important aspect. If more ports are required, a determination must be made about how to increase the quantity.

18. c. Network Management

HP Openview is a network management platform that integrates with CiscoWorks 2000.

19. b. show interface

This command is used for the dropped, missed, and ignored packets.

20. d. show processes

This command is used to gather the five-minute CPU utilization.

6

Documenting the New Network

Objectives Covered in This Chapter

1. Documenting the customer's business issues that are relevant to a network-design project
2. Diagramming the flow of information for new applications
3. Listing some tools that will help you characterize new network traffic

Introduction

Now that the existing network has been documented, it is time to identify the new needs and requirements of the customer. This process includes not only the performance characteristics, but also the management and security characteristics.

In addition to the technical details and requirements of the new infrastructure, you must also determine the business and administrative details of the project. In some instances, these details might be more important than the technical details. Finally, you must introduce the task of project scoping and new traffic analysis.

Documentation Checklist

Determining the actual requirements of the new network is a series of tasks instead of a single task. You must complete all of these tasks. For instance, if the budget has not been determined, then a network designer might be specifying a solution that does not meet the customer's fiscal expectations. You can use the following checklist as a starting point:

Business issues

1. Problem identification
2. Goals
3. Constraints

Project scope

1. Expectations
2. Deadlines
3. Deliverables
4. Acceptance criteria

Design requirements

1. Security requirements
2. Manageability requirements
3. Application requirements
4. Performance requirements
5. Usage requirements

Traffic-pattern prediction

1. Tools
2. Type
3. Direction
4. Amount

Business Issues

The network designer should examine the business issues first. Someone once said that business issues occupy the "eighth layer" of the *Open Systems Interconnectivity* (OSI) model (the political layer). Figure 6-1 depicts the importance of this eighth layer.

The political layer is the most problematic for most network designers. Resolving issues with protocol stacks and routing tables is easy compared to navigating the political minefields in some corporations. Imagine a project as simple as upgrading a network backbone. While this project might be straightforward, there could be many varied political issues that arise:

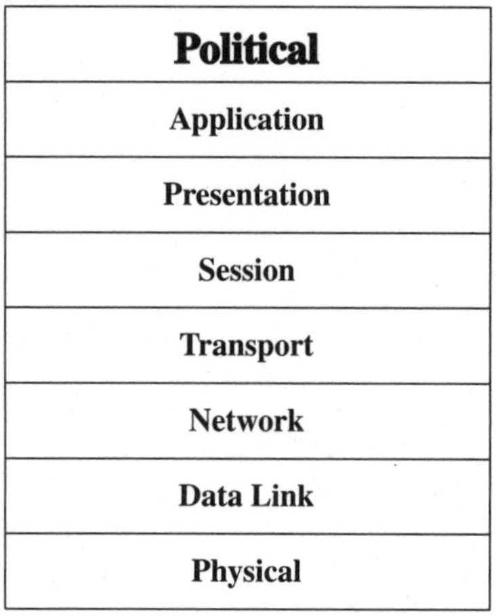

Figure 6-1

The eighth layer of
the OSI model

Political
Application
Presentation
Session
Transport
Network
Data Link
Physical

1. The original network architect, now the *chief information officer* (CIO), feels that the current network is acceptable.

2. The existing network must be moved to a new location. A vendor that will soon become obsolete, however, is running the existing network. This situation will make gathering information a challenge.

3. Budgets are being cut significantly. What impact will this cut have on the project?

4. Midway through the project-scope creation, the company undergoes a merger. What impact will this merger have on the project?

Dealing with the business and political issues surrounding a problem might seem unimportant or trivial. The true success of the project, however, will almost always lie in understanding these political details and business issues as well as the raw, technical details of the implementation. The first step in assessing the business issues surrounding a project is to determine the specific problem that needs to be solved. Next, you need to establish the goals and constraints.

What Problem Are You Trying to Solve?

This question is one that designers do not frequently ask. The question itself is simple, but the answer might be hidden. For example, a company decides to upgrade its backbone from FDDI to Gigabit Ethernet. When asked the reason for this change, a technician replies, "Because it's faster." In essence, Gigabit Ethernet is 10 times as fast as FDDI. What problem will increasing the throughput of the backplane alleviate, however? The answer might now be that the company's applications will run faster. Unless a traffic analysis was done on the existing backbone to suggest that it was oversubscribed, however, this statement might not be accurate. One possible answer is that the company is about to launch some streaming media application that is bandwidth intensive. The organization's studies have shown that while its existing backbone is acceptable for its current applications, this new application will increase the organization's backbone needs by 200 percent.

Often, finding the root reason for the design is a daunting challenge. For example, a company decided to convert 100 remote offices that were recently acquired in a merger from Token Ring to Fast Ethernet. The reason is for speed. A survey showed that a significant amount of the properties were operating within the bandwidth limitations of Token Ring. The root cause for the change was that the existing staff had no operating experience with Token Ring and was more comfortable supporting an Ethernet environment. Although this concern might be valid, it might not be worth the cost of converting 100 properties. Remember, not only do routers and switches have to be converted, but workstations and servers also must be converted.

By searching for this root cause and for the actual business problem, the network designer can ensure that a solution is provided. Imagine that a complete backbone redesign is done in order to make application transactions faster. A 100Mb Fast Ethernet fiber backbone is upgraded to Gigabit Ethernet. The company purchases new switches in order to support this backbone. After the upgrade is complete, the application response times do not change. Here, the client has spent thousands of dollars for no visible return.

Had the designer conducted an initial traffic study, he or she might have seen no traffic issues and advised against such an upgrade because it would not solve the problem. The upgrade would make the network faster, but it would not make application transactions occur more quickly.

NOTE: *We cannot stress the importance of this section and this concept. If you take nothing else away from this book, please remember to always look for the root problem.*

You could also use this same approach in any *information technology* (IT) decision-making process. In this example, in order to achieve faster transactions, the network designer determined that the bottleneck was the server. Then, the designer could analyze the server to determine the root cause of the slow transactions.

Business Goals

The goals of the business follow closely with problem identification. In general, a company will have a specific result in mind when it begins a project. If these goals and expectations are met, the customer will generally consider the project a success.

These goals need to be ascertained from all levels of management and operation within a company. For example, the CIO might have a goal of the new infrastructure supporting the new application in development. The network manager might have the goal of the network being 100 percent managed. The network engineering team might expect it will get to participate in the project.

NOTE: *These goals will become part of the project scope that the network designer will be developing in the next section.*

All of these needs and goals are important in order to recognize, evaluate, and communicate back to the customer. For example, the role of the network-engineering staff should be clearly detailed at the beginning of the project. The manageability of the new network also needs to be clearly delineated. In addition, the actual turnover of this managed network needs to be detailed to the customer. Without this turnover, the customer might be handed software with which he or she is completely unfamiliar.

Another goal of the company is the project completion date, deliverables, and acceptance. For example, with most network installations, network documentation is required. What form should this documentation take? The project completion is also something that must be ascertained early in the project. If 100 remote offices are having their *Wide Area Network* (WAN) circuits upgraded from 64Kb leased-line circuits to 128Kb Frame Relay circuits, what is the project length? If the expectation is that the project will be complete in one month, is this expectation feasible? When will the design be required? In this scenario, what design steps will you have to accelerate or forego in the interest of time?

Business Constraints

In addition to the business goals and objectives, you must also investigate the constraints of the business. These constraints can be almost anything. In general, however, there are three major constraints: budgets, corporate policies, and time.

Budget   In most corporations across the globe, the budget truly drives and shapes the project. If the budget for a project is fixed, then any network design that carries an excessively high cost will not be considered. Likewise, a solution that is under budget might be regarded as not meeting the expectations.

Several facets to budgets exist. Some costs are visible, and others are hidden. The first budget cost that you should examine is the capital cost of the project. The capital cost is almost always visible to the clients. This cost represents the majority of the visible costs and is basically the cost of the project implementation. This cost should include all of the hardware required to complete the project. The software and labor for a project might or might not be a part of the capital cost, but it is an appreciable cost nonetheless.

Another cost that is present in almost any network-design project is staffing. This cost can be visible or hidden, depending on the client. For example, if a company is implementing new WAN-based Cisco routers, it will need to add staff in order to administrate this WAN. Depending on the size of the project, the human cost can be astronomical. Staffing can also refer to the cost of implementing the project. Imagine the staffing cost in the Token Ring-to-Ethernet conversion. If there are 100 remote offices and each office has 50 users, then there are approximately 5,000 Token Ring nodes. If the human cost to replace one node is $150, then this portion of the project alone would cost $750,000.

NOTE: *In the conversion example, existing staff could be used for this type of conversion. What repercussions would happen to the day-to-day operations that these individuals were currently handling, however?*

The last cost is hidden and often forgotten: the cost of maintaining the new network. These costs fall within several areas, but two key areas are new employees and training. One option for maintaining a newly designed network is to hire people who have the skills necessary to maintain these networks. This solution might be easy, but often it is impractical to add employees simply to support every new IT project.

Instead, the existing staff will have to be trained on the new technologies. For example, a company is estimating the cost of replacing 500 3Com routers with Cisco routers. The hardware costs and labor costs have been fully estimated and budgeted. Because existing hardware was being replaced, no staff additions were budgeted. The existing staff members have no knowledge of the Cisco IOS, however, and cannot perform their jobs without this knowledge. A team of 10 people taking several courses each in order to perform their jobs could easily cost $100,000.

Company Policies

Company policies can impose many constraints on network design. Company policies range from limited access to production equipment to audit requirements for new equipment. For example, a large financial company has a lengthy audit and change-control process.

Physically touching any networking equipment is almost impossible. If a requirement of the project is to produce network-performance metrics, what information must you retrieve from the equipment, and does this procedure fall within the policies of the company?

Other policies such as the inability to *File Transfer Protocol* (FTP) files through the company firewall can cause unforeseen time delays. Imagine that a project is underway to make a design change. As part of the change, the code on a router is being upgraded to a new revision. By disallowing FTP through the company firewall, the designer will have to spend several hours dialing up to the Internet and retrieving the information in that manner.

Another example of company policies and the constraints that they apply is in Internet security designs. Most companies have specific policies about what content users can access from the Internet. A network designer should not get deeply embroiled in company policies and procedures. Rather, he or she should simply ensure that the design can support the required policy or procedure. The designer also needs to ensure that the policy is clearly delineated. This procedure will enable the designer to ensure that he or she can satisfy this requirement.

Time   The project completion date can be a constraint as well as a project requirement. If a complete network redesign is required and the designer is given two weeks to complete the assignment, then what steps are time-critical to the completion of the job? For instance, how long should the traffic analysis and data-gathering tasks take? Is one week's worth of data enough on which to base a network design? Will all of the necessary customer goals be obtained in this short time? A design in such a short time is not impossible. Actually, it is quite possible as long as the network designer ensures that the scope of work for the project completely identifies these constraints.

Project Scope

The scope of the project consists of the following items:

1. The actual work that the designer will perform
2. The project deadline

3. The items that will be delivered to the customer upon completion of the project

4. The acceptance criteria for the designer's work

This process might seem like a redundant effort based on the data gathering that has occurred. In some instances, however, this document will ensure that both the designer and the customer have the same goals, objectives, and constraints.

Exact Requirements

This section should contain the various requirements that we have gathered from the customer. You do not have to meet all the objectives; however, it is advisable that you should at least address any requirement (for example, if the new design must run on the existing fiber-optic cable plant).

Deadline   You should note the deadline for the project in the scope of work. This way, deadlines cannot be moved. You might also find it a good idea to note milestones for specific phases of the project.

Deliverables   This area should document what items you will deliver to the customer. The following items are examples of deliverables:

1. A network drawing in Visio 2000 format

2. Traffic-analysis documentation

3. Router-performance documentation

4. The manufacturer's documentation from all hardware and software

5. Router and switch configuration documentation

Acceptance Criteria

This area of the document will ensure that the scope of the project does not grow beyond recognition. For instance, the acceptance criteria for a Frame Relay WAN circuit would be the successful LMI negotiation with the Frame Relay switch. A successful router conversion from

Token Ring to Ethernet might be as simple as a successful ping. Regardless of the complexity or simplicity of the acceptance criteria, the designer and the customer must mutually agree upon these details.

Design Requirements

There are many possible requirements for a network design. By examining some of the specific requirements of each of the following areas, a network designer can ensure that important information is not missed.

Security Requirements

The security requirements of any design project are always of concern—not simply when the project deals with Internet connectivity. You can put various security precautions in place throughout a network. Security involves more than just firewalls and anti-virus protection. In some cases, you must install network equipment so that passwords are unique for users. In other words, users could not use the standard access and enable passwords on a router or on a switch. You would either have to create usernames or use an authentication protocol (such as RADIUS or TACACS+).

Manageability Requirements

The management requirements of any design project should always be a concern. Although some projects will focus specifically on the installation of network-management platforms, such as CiscoWorks 2000, manageability should always be in the designer's mind. For instance, should unmanageable devices be used in the access layer of a network? On average, this idea is poor. These devices are invisible to management stations, and this situation would make faults harder to locate. You can put various management functions in place throughout a network as it is designed. For instance, by creating SNMP community strings as new equipment is installed, a network-management system can be more easily implemented in the future.

Application Requirements

Do the current or proposed applications have specific requirements? For example, an application might only run on Novell 3.x servers. This situation would require IPX to be transported on the network. In addition, it would require Novell IPX *Router Information Protocol* (RIP) and *Service Access Protocol* (SAP) communication between the clients and servers at every site. If the number of servers is high and the speed of the WAN links is low, then the low-speed WAN links could become saturated with these Novell updates. This situation might require the design of access lists to inhibit the distribution of these servers and networks.

Performance Requirements

This requirement is the bandwidth metric and is based generally on speed or lack of speed. In many minds, the speed of a network transaction is based solely on the bandwidth of the link. Given that the bandwidth constraint is the network, however, there is a point of no return when the speed of the link is increased. At some point, the bandwidth is greater than the traffic. At this point, more bandwidth offers no value.

Performance requirements can also be a result of the application itself. Many SNA applications, for instance, are in tolerant of response time delays. These constraints might force the use of queuing strategies to prioritize traffic or access lists to remove overhead traffic.

Another performance requirement that would drive a specific design response could be in the networking hardware. For instance, if a customer desires to load-balance his or her Internet connection between two different *Internet Service Providers* (ISPs), he or she would have to run *Border Gateway Protocol* (BGP) routing. Only a router that has a large amount of *Random Access Memory* (RAM) and a fast processor will be capable of holding this type of routing table. Therefore, this requirement would necessitate a powerful router with a lot of memory, such as a Cisco 7500 series router.

NOTE: *Bandwidth latency is the delay in processing a transaction due to low-speed lines. You can overcome bandwidth latency by increasing the bandwidth. Distance latency is the delay that is introduced into the transaction because the two devices are separated by hundreds of miles. This latency cannot be avoided with the exception of moving the devices closer together.*

Usage Requirements

This topic ties in closely with performance and application requirements. What requirements will the number of users attaching to the application demand of the network? This question ties in closely with the performance requirements section of this book.

In a shared network, are too many users on the same segment? Are they all contending with each other for the same shared medium? Performance on shared networks tends to degrade as the number of users increases.

In switched networks, the usage requirements of the backbone links are the most critical. Each desktop, in an Ethernet environment, has 10Mbps available for use. If 100 of these 10Mbps connections are uplinked over a 100Mbps backbone to the server farm, then there might be delays at peak traffic times. The delay is from trying to pass a maximum of 1000Mbps over a link that is only 100Mbps, or 10 percent of the maximum load.

NOTE: *In many texts, authors insert copious tables in order to detail the boot process and the traffic on the network. In the year 2000, the majority of networks are switched. This switching relieves any stress that simultaneous login traffic would have on network performance.*

Traffic-Pattern Prediction

The final part of documenting a new network is estimating the performance impact and traffic patterns. The majority of this work was completed with the characterization of the existing network. If a designer knows the existing traffic and the new network, then he or she can probably identify traffic flows. The traffic-pattern prediction should contain the following three types of information:

1. *Type*   The type of traffic. The type should be separated by protocol and by application (for instance, *World Wide Web* (WWW) traffic and Oracle database traffic).

2. *Direction*   The directional flow of traffic. The direction is determined by application traffic flows as well by noting the traffic that is sent to remote subnets and traffic that is kept on the local subnet.

3. *Amount*   The quantity of these types and directions of traffic

Case Study: Widget Manufacturing

Widget Manufacturing recently decided to upgrade its network infrastructure. The existing network has had performance and availability problems as it has grown over the past two years. The network is comprised of 1,500 users who are located across a large manufacturing facility. The industry's current network infrastructure has been in place for almost seven years.

In this phase of the case study, we need to examine the business goals and constraints. The information provided in the previous chapter is included to make the case study as whole as possible.

Step 1: Business Issues—Problem Identification

The network consists of 10Mb Ethernet that runs both Thinnet and Thicknet coaxial cable. The Thinnet cable is used to connect users to hubs and repeaters. The Thicknet cable is used to connect the repeaters and hubs together to form a routed internetwork. Figure 6-2 depicts the existing network.

The problem that the Widget IT group is trying to solve is the performance and availability problems of the existing network. These

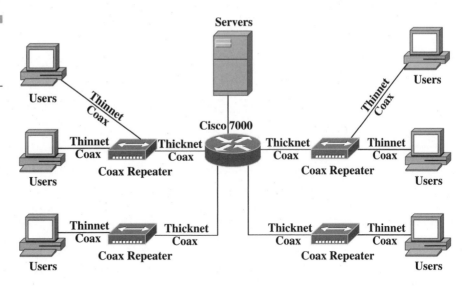

Figure 6-2
The existing Widget
Manufacturing
network

problems are associated with the existing cable plant and network infrastructure. Over the past few months, they have documented the performance of the network. This documentation shows that there is an above average number of collisions and that collisions are almost 10 percent of all traffic at peak times. Additional analysis shows that several of the uplink 10Base5 cables have an unusually large number of CRC errors. The only solution to these types of errors is to recable the plant and install new networking equipment.

Step 2: Business Issues—Goals and Objectives

Various members of the IT and executive team desire several objectives:

1. *Finance*   A cost-effective solution with a life cycle of five years

2. *Operations*   24-hour-a-day, seven-days-a-week operations. When the network is down, products are not being assembled.

3. *IT management*   Modern equipment that enables the staff to be more proactive in problem resolution

4. *IT engineers*   Anything faster and newer

Step 3: Business Issues—Constraints

The constraints on the implementation are as follows:

1. *Budget*   Management realizes that it has been an eternity since any equipment was upgraded. There is no specific budget in mind.

2. *Management approval*   All levels of management are open to this redesign.

3. *Operations*   The existing network must remain in place until the upgrade is complete. No down time is permitted unless it is scheduled one week in advance.

4. *Deadline*   The manufacturing facility has a three-week production halt over the Christmas holiday. This situation would be the opportune time to make this change. This break begins in one month, however.

NOTE: *The following scope of work is an example of using information gathered in the earlier tasks and in the network characterization tasks in the previous chapter.*

Step 4: Scope of Work

The existing network infrastructure of Widget Manufacturing has reached the end of its life span. In addition, the existing cable plant has also reached the end of its life span. The infrastructure needs to be rebuilt in order to improve both performance and availability.

Project Requirements

1. The new network will have the capability to support 24-hour-a-day, seven-day-a-week operation.

2. The network will have numerous fault-tolerant design points in order to ensure high availability.

3. The network will support management from one or more central stations. The level of management and integration with existing software has yet to be determined.

NOTE: *The designer might be able to add more details in this section if he or she has a basic idea of the design layout. For example, you can state that the new network equipment must support category 5 cable and fiber-optic cable.*

Project Timeline

1. Start project: November 15
2. Milestone: design complete—December 1
3. Milestone: upgrade start—December 21
4. Milestone: upgrade complete and in production—January 7
5. Project finished—January 14

Customer Deliverables

1. Network drawing in Visio 2000 format
2. Backbone traffic analysis documentation
3. Router performance documentation
4. Manufacturer's documentation from all hardware and software

Acceptance Criteria

When the following items have been completed, the project will be considered officially accepted and complete:

1. All network devices can ping one another.
2. A central management station can successfully get SNMP statistics.
3. A central management station receives SNMP traps from all devices.
4. All deliverables have been given to the customer.

Step 5: Design Requirements

After the scope of work is complete (or, in some cases, as the scope of work is being finished), you can examine the specific requirements of the project. Not all of these requirements might be applicable to all designs.

Security Requirements

At this time, no security requirements have been specified.

Manageability Requirements

Management requirements have not been spelled out; however, from the goals of the management of Widget Manufacturing, we can infer that management is a key concern. Therefore, the design should include and allow for the future implementation of a network-management system.

Application Requirements

The applications are not changing in the foreseeable future. Because the major problem with the existing network is performance and availability, a faster, high-availability network will meet the application requirements.

Performance Requirements

The existing network is thought to have performance problems. The new network must not inhibit performance in any way.

Usage Requirements

The usage requirements are that the network must be available on a 24-hour-a-day, seven-day-a-week basis.

Step 6: Traffic Pattern Determination

At this point, the application location and client locations are not changing. The network components will change around them. Therefore, the application traffic flow will remain the same. The equipment in the network will simply change in order to support the new requirements.

SUMMARY

This step of network design is the least concrete of all of the steps. This procedure usually involves many meetings with various representatives of the company and involves repeating the network-design strategy to many people and departments.

With all of the meetings and repetition, this step in the project—if completed correctly—will ensure that the project is completed to the customer's satisfaction. The majority of projects do not fail because of the technical limitations of the design consultant. These projects fail, rather, because the designer did not understand the customer, the requirements, or the constraints.

QUESTIONS

Case Study: Limbo Medical Group

The Limbo Medical Group was on the cutting edge of network technology 10 years ago. The company decided to implement a centralized computer system for all of its day-to-day operations. This system consisted of an X.25 WAN that connected 50 small offices to a central hospital facility. This X.25 WAN carries legacy SNA traffic between hosts and a mainframe. Figure 6-3 is a representation of the existing network design.

The medical group is now developing a new client/server application to replace this mainframe application. In addition, a Frame Relay network will replace the legacy X.25 network. The operations of the medical group run throughout the day. Any network down time would be detrimental to these operations. Therefore, the new network must be reliable and fault tolerant.

The new client/server application will be an *Internet Protocol* (IP)-based application that is housed in an Oracle database. In order to keep client upgrades to a minimum, all client interaction will occur though a Web browser.

The IT group of Limbo Medical realizes the need for the new application. Its focus, however, is on the new application. The IT group is

Figure 6-3
The existing Limbo Medical Group network

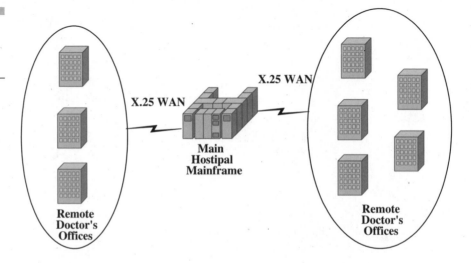

unsure of the network requirements. The idea for the new WAN was brought forward by a member of the Limbo LAN administration team. This project and concept has not yet been introduced to the executive management of Limbo Medical.

Performance of the new application is important to the Limbo IT group. The SNA application was sensitive to delays, and therefore, the application response time was excellent. The LAN administrator is also concerned about security and manageability; however, he does not have any specific requirements.

After meeting with the IT management and executive management, the developers have many questions about the funding for the project. Currently, the application migration is funded and is a highly visible project for the company.

1. What constraint could cause this project to fail?

   a. No budget

   b. Requirement for manageability

   c. Application response time requirements

   d. No visibility to upper management

2. Which of the following characteristics are most important to the IT department at Limbo Medical?

   a. Security

   b. Availability

   c. Manageability

   d. Throughput

3. Why will traffic patterns change during the upgrade?

   a. The application is changing.

   b. The WAN is changing.

   c. The LAN is changing.

   d. The WAN is being outsourced.

4. Which of the following would be part of the acceptance criteria?

   a. IPX server visibility

   b. Frame Relay packets observed

   c. A faster network

   d. IP connectivity between remote and main offices

5. Which of the following important network concepts have not even been discussed by the Limbo Medical Group's IT department?

    a. Security

    b. Management

    c. Routing

    d. WAN Protocols

Case Study: Global Supplies Corporation

Global Supplies is a multi-national corporation that consists of approximately 15 separate facilities throughout North America. Each facility has an existing LAN that has been upgraded according to the needs of the specific facility. The LANs range from small 10Mb Ethernet networks to large Fast Ethernet networks with Gigabit backbones. Each LAN is administered by a department that does not normally interact with the corporate IT group.

The concern of the corporate IT group of Global Supplies is the WAN. The existing WAN is comprised of only leased lines. At least two leased lines connect each office to another office. In some cases, an individual office is connected via leased lines to three or four other offices. The multiple links ensure that the quickest path to the destination is selected (as well as ensure redundancy). The new WAN infrastructure must continue to support both voice and data traffic. The existing voice equipment cannot be changed at this time, however. Figure 6-4 is a depiction of the existing network.

Currently, the only protocols that are in use across the WAN are IP, IPX, and SNA. Some of the organizations use SNA for legacy mainframe connectivity. The existing leased lines are configured to use half of the bandwidth for voice and the other half of the bandwidth for data. A multiplexer performs the split of the channels.

This project is being led by the corporate IT department. The executive management is aware of this project and supports it as well. The budget has yet to be defined, however. By removing the numerous leased lines, the company expects that the monthly access costs will drop significantly and that this situation will offset any initial hardware costs in several months.

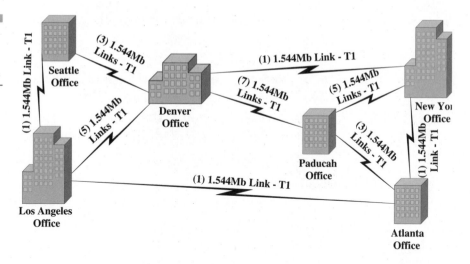

Figure 6-4
The existing Global
Supplies Corporation
network

The IT department is concerned about monitoring the health and state of the network at all times. Because its responsibility is inter-company communication, the IT department must set up a WAN that is error-free.

A new application—a distance-learning application—has the most bandwidth requirements. This training is delivered in the form of intranet-based streaming media presentations. This training must be delivered in a timely manner.

6. What constraints are present in the Global Supplies case study?
   a. Budget
   b. Management
   c. Bandwidth
   d. Training

7. What is the problem that this new design is attempting to solve?
   a. Cost
   b. Speed
   c. Manageability
   d. Security

8. How will the application traffic flow change after the leased lines are removed?
   a. Not at all
   b. Voice will be added to the list of applications that are conveyed across the WAN.
   c. It will flow towards the corporate office.
   d. It will flow away from the corporate office.

9. Which of the following tasks are not addressed in this case study and must still be determined?
   a. Project requirements
   b. Project deliverables
   c. Project timelines
   d. Project constraints

10. Which of the following constraints could make data gathering at the remote locations difficult?
    a. Lack of a WAN
    b. Budget
    c. Leased lines
    d. Independent LAN administrators

Case Study: Bank of Pompeii

The Bank of Pompeii has just completed a new corporate office tower in a prime downtown location. This location will enable the bank to consolidate six of 20 small offices into the new corporate tower. In addition to this move, all of the SNA traffic will be removed from the WAN.

All of the offices are connected via a Frame Relay WAN in a hub-and-spoke configuration. The hub of the Frame Relay network will be the new corporate tower. The remainder of the offices will remain on the Frame Relay network. Figure 6-5 depicts the network of the Bank of Pompeii.

As the new offices are moved to the corporate tower, they will be connected to the newly designed Gigabit backbone. The existing branch networks are shared 10Mb Ethernet. They will be converted to a switched 100Mb Fast Ethernet LAN. After the conversion, all

Figure 6-5

The existing Bank of Pompeii network

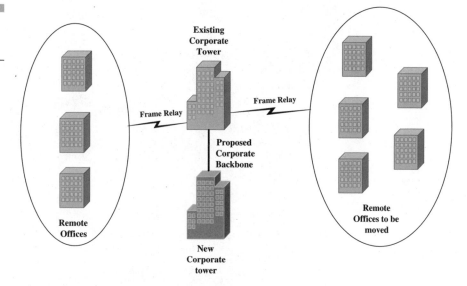

network traffic will be IP-based protocols. The only applications in use are e-mail and a Telnet-based bank application.

One expectation for the IT department of the bank is that the design will be completed in time for budget reviews in one month. Another deadline is that the project must be in place and completed before the offices move in three months. This network expansion is a necessary part of the relocation project and is supported by all levels of management.

As part of the customer requirements, the following items are needed for the upgrade: an IP addressing scheme, a routing plan, a network diagram, and complete specifications of all required equipment. Currently, the customer is using a public IP scheme. At the initial implementation of the network, the original designer used a Class B address of 172.32.0.0. This address was believed to be a private IP address range, but the actual private IP address ranges begins at 172.16.0.0 and end at 172.31.255.255. A portion of this project will also include readdressing the network to fit within a private IP address range.

One of the most important requirements for any installation at the Bank of Pompeii is security. A complete audit trail is required for all of the equipment that is placed in the network. This audit material is routinely scanned for any unusual activity.

11. What is the problem that this new design will solve?
    a. Security issues
    b. Bandwidth issues
    c. Office relocation
    d. High WAN costs

12. How long does the network designer have to complete the network design?
    a. One week
    b. One month
    c. Three months
    d. One year

13. Which of the following items is *not* a customer deliverable?
    a. A network diagram
    b. A routing design
    c. IOS software documentation
    d. IP addressing scheme

14. What impact will the existing applications have on the new network?
    a. None
    b. They will severely degrade performance.
    c. They will slightly inhibit performance.
    d. You cannot determine the result from the information given.

15. Which of the following design requirements has been addressed?
    a. Security
    b. Management
    c. Usage
    d. Application

Case Study: G&S Productions

Gimball Productions and Shapiro Productions recently merged. The new company, G&S Productions, has become a major commercial production company. There are two main sites, each having about 250 users. In addition, each company has three to five smaller offices throughout the United States.

The two companies currently use an ISDN dialup connection to pass only e-mail traffic between each other. The e-mail server is a Windows NT-based system. The main company sites each use leased lines to connect to their remote offices. The leased lines are only 56Kb circuits. Figure 6-6 depicts the G&S Productions network after the merger.

The requirement for the newly formed IT department is to build a reliable, cost-effective WAN that will start the integration of the new network. Eventually, the financial and operational applications of both companies will be combined.

Although the IT departments have been combined, they are still separate in their goals and requirements. The IT department from Gimball is interested in quickly linking the two main sites. The Shapiro IT department is more interested in a consolidated WAN between all of the offices. The Gimball department is interested in a simple configuration where both IP and AppleTalk protocols are sent across the WAN. The Shapiro IT group would prefer to see a more complex environment with IP as the only backbone protocol.

There are no budget issues with this network design. Both companies need to communicate regardless of the cost. The existing staffs are currently operating the current WANs and will be able to easily administer this new WAN.

Figure 6-6

The existing G&S Productions network

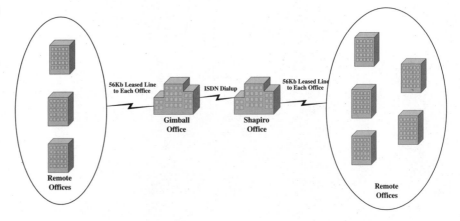

56Kb Leased Line to Each Office

ISDN Dialup

56Kb Leased Line to Each Office

Gimball Office

Shapiro Office

Remote Offices

Remote Offices

16. What problem is this design intended to solve?

    a. Lack of a WAN circuit

    b. Increased bandwidth demand

    c. A company merger

    d. Slow leased lines to the remote offices

17. What possible constraint has been alleviated because the existing staff can manage the WAN?

    a. Budget

    b. Training

    c. Staffing

    d. Time

18. What should be the primary concern of the network designer?

    a. Budget

    b. Internal IT conflict

    c. Staff shortage

    d. Old infrastructure

19. What are the management requirements for this new design?

    a. Integration with the existing system

    b. New implementation

    c. SNMP configuration

    d. None

20. Because both IP and AppleTalk information must be exchanged between the sites, can the backbone protocol recommendation of the Shapiro group work?

    a. Yes

    b. No

    c. Not enough information to determine the result

ANSWERS

1. **d.** No visibility to upper management

   Remember, the LAN administrator introduced this project. The remainder of the IT staff is focused on the application migration and is somewhat oblivious to the WAN infrastructure.

2. **b.** Availability

   Remember, this network operates 24 hours a day. Reliability, up time, and fault tolerance are critical.

3. **a.** The application is changing.

   Although the WAN is also changing, the applications truly drive the traffic flows. Because the application is changing, the traffic flows will also change.

4. **d.** IP connectivity between the remote and main offices

   IP connectivity will mean that the clients can communicate with the servers. If this communication path has been proven, then any issues would reside in the client or in the server.

5. **c.** Routing protocols

   Security and management are a concern. In addition, the WAN protocol will be Frame Relay. We have not discussed the routing protocol.

6. **d.** Training

   While training is not specifically listed in the case study, the new network will require a lot of training for the existing staff. They will have to learn new operational processes and troubleshooting procedures.

7. **b.** Speed

   While the cost will be reduced, the real need is for increased speed. This speed will be used to support the new application.

8. **d.** It will flow away from the corporate office.

   Voice is a part of the current network and will operate in the same manner. The new distance-learning application, however, will increase the amount of traffic that flows from the corporate office to the remote sites.

9. b. and **c.** Project timeline and project deliverables

Neither item has been addressed yet. Before the scope of work can be completed, both tasks need to be completed.

10. d. Independent LAN administrators

Because each LAN has independent administrators, cooperation with the corporate IT group is not guaranteed.

11. c. Office relocation

The issue driving the design change is the new office building being built.

12. b. One month

The design is due in one month for budget review.

13. c. IOS software documentation

The other items are specifically spelled out in the case study requirements.

14. d. It cannot be determined from the information given.

While it should not have any impact, there is no traffic data to verify this assertion.

15. a. and **d.** Security, application

Only these two design requirements have been addressed. Usage and management have not yet been addressed.

16. c. Company merger

The merger has prompted the need for network redesign.

17. b. Training

Extensive training would probably not be required for the existing IT staff in order to support the new environment.

18. b. Internal IT conflict

The existing IT department has not learned how to communicate effectively. The designer might have to become a referee as well as a designer.

19. d. None

At this point, no management requirements have been identified.

20. a. Yes

Although only IP will be used across the backbone, AppleTalk can be tunneled over the *Transmission Control Protocol / Internet Protocol* (TCP/IP) protocol stack. This situation would enable an IP-only backbone to transport AppleTalk packets.

Network Topology

Objectives Covered in this Chapter

- To draw a topology map that meets the customer's needs and includes a high-level view of internetworking devices and interconnecting media with hardware and media
- To recognize scalability constraints and issues for standard *Wide Area Network* (WAN) technologies

One of the prerequisites for a Cisco Certified Design Associate is to be able to provide your customer with the most viable solution, keeping his existing setup in mind. This can be achieved if and only if one has a good understanding of the various network topologies followed in practical internetworking using Cisco devices.

The network topology needs to be planned while keeping in mind the customer's existing network, budget, and requirements. The various network topologies described in this chapter can help you determine which scenario is the best for your client as well as how easily one can deploy it either in the existing network or in a new network.

The chapter is divided broadly into three different sections:

- The hierarchical model section
- The redundant network model section
- The secure network model section

The hierarchical model discusses the traditional router-hub network model, which is being used most widely, but with the rapidly changing network requirements, enterprises today are moving out of this model and moving on to *Virtual Local Area Network* (VLAN) or *Multiprotocol over ATM* (MPOA) model. By using the three models, one can use various permutations and combinations and hence provide your customer with one that suits his needs in the best way.

Introduction

One of the foremost prerequisites for a Cisco Certified Design Associate is to have a thorough knowledge of the various possible network models. Understanding them is of utmost importance and we shall be covering the same in this chapter. Having a command over the network models while designing a network for your client helps you better understand the existing network and incorporate new changes without disturbing the existing network to a large extent.

This chapter starts off with a discussion of the hierarchical model that is the most widely used model when designing inter-networks. Whether implemented with an Ethernet or an *Asynchronous Transfer Mode* (ATM) backbone, the hierarchical model has many advantages. The model is highly deterministic and makes it easier to expand, manage, and troubleshoot as it scales. The models that we are going to discuss support all common campus protocols. The chapter also covers redundant network design and secure network models.

Hierarchical Model

Scalable and reliable networks are logically hierarchical. These models are one of the most widely used models in networking. These are mostly specific to *Local Area Networks* (LANs) where the enterprise likes to maintain a hierarchy of the various routers and switches in the network, depending upon the needs. Hierarchical network models help us achieve lower operation costs, higher understandability of the network, and hence an ease in fault isolation and troubleshooting. Campus network designs typically consist of three logical levels:

- *Core layer* This layer is generally known as the high-speed backbone of the network. The core layer takes care of the interconnectivity and hence is the most critical part of a hierarchical network and should be highly reliable. It is generally designed with redundant components. Speed is of most importance at the core layer and hence any kind of packet filtering should be avoided. Appropriate routing features should be considered for faster convergence and optimizing packet throughput. The core layer should be designed within a set diameter and it should be realized that the diameter does not increase whenever distribution-layer routers or switches are added to the network.

- *Distribution layer*   The "jam in the sandwich" or the layer that lies between the core and the access layers of the network is what is the distribution layer. Packet filtering, security policies, *Quality of Service* (QoS), and other network policy implementations are part of the distribution layer. Address translation is one of the other functions that happen on the distribution layer. This is generally done to keep the CPU loads on the backbone routers low. Routing between VLANs, broadcasts, and collision domain definitions are part of the distribution layer in the network.

- *Access layer*   This layer is generally comprised of the switches that are in turn connected to the distribution layer and provide the end-network devices access to the network. Access layers can help form bandwidth or broadcast domains.

We shall discuss the following models to better understand the core, distribution, and access models:

- Router-hub network model
- VLAN model
- Multiprotocol over ATM model

Router-Hub Network Model

The most primitive network design is the flat network design in which the network devices are added on a single LAN. This typical model can be named as a hub-only model where all the network devices share a half-duplex 10-Mbps network. As explained in Chapter 2, "Internetworking Technology Overview," the contention-based method, the *Carrier Sense Multiple Access/Collision Detection* (CSMA/CD) scheme, is used on the Ethernet. In the flat network scenario, the LAN can be considered as a collision domain where the device or carrier senses the media to ensure it is free of traffic before it sends data. Collisions are common in this kind of scenario. In a congested LAN, a bridge working with the *Media Access Control* (MAC) addresses can be inserted and can act as a store-and-forward switch. Bridges can also restrict the collision domains. The Spanning

Tree Protocol has come into the picture to avoid routing loops and redundancy on the networks.

Troubleshooting and management becomes more and more difficult as the number of active network devices increase on the network. Any misconfigured or malfunctioning network device can cause serious problems leading to long downtimes that are never acceptable for any network.

Bridges can be replaced by routers, which work on the network layer (layer 3 of the OSI model) and forward the packets based on network addresses rather than the MAC addresses. Routers fit very well in the internetworking scenarios and make use of protocols such as the *Routing Internet Protocol* (RIP) and *Open Shortest Path First* (OSPF) besides controlling broadcasts. Cisco routers are useful in scenarios where value-added features are required.

Figure 7-1 shows a typical router- and hub-based network where the core layer contains concentrators or repeaters for faster links between the core servers and the adjacent routers. Routers in the distribution layer use routing protocols for network information updates, segmentation of the network, and broadcast control. The hubs are placed in the wiring closet and can be homed to arouter port or several hubs can be cascaded together to form one logical subnet.

Figure 7-1
Typical router-
hub network

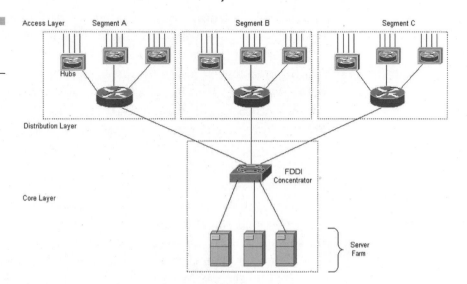

This model maps well in a multiprotocol scenario where TCP/IP, Novell *Internetwork Packet Exchange/Sequenced Packet Exchange* (IPX/SPX), DECnet, AppleTalk, and so on are being used. The modularity of this model makes it easier to manage, troubleshoot, and upgrade it according to the needs of the enterprise.

The major disadvantage in this model is that the bandwidth is shared between the network devices that are connected to the same hub. The movement of network devices is restricted and is only possible by reconfiguring its TCP/IP properties.

 NOTE: *It can be argued that by using the* Dynamic Host Configuration Protocol *(DHCP) the need to reconfigure is eliminated. It should be noted that DHCP has its own overheads and would not necessarily fit in every network design.*

Virtual Local Area Network (VLAN) Model

One of the prominent technological models used in campus-wide networks is the VLAN. A VLAN is a Layer-2 logical network that enables the network administrator to connect network devices, even if they are physically dispersed. Each VLAN functions as a separate broadcast domain. A VLAN is somewhat similar to an extended, bridged network in that they share the same characteristics. A network designer can form a VLAN on a Cisco switch by grouping according to the switch ports, based on the Layer-2 addresses of the network devices, that is, by using the MAC address or by using the Layer-3 protocols. MAC address-based VLANs are common only in areas where security is of prime importance. The administrative overhead is quite high, as the ability to move network devices freely is restricted. VLANs that are based upon Layer-3 protocols are used in networks where the protocols can be easily differentiated.

Let's say the finance and administration departments of a company use only the IPX protocol, whereas the engineering uses only IP. In this scenario, a network designer/administrator would form VLANs based upon the protocol in use. VLANs based on a switched port are still the most widely used models and are quite successful in enterprise networks where one can see a variety of protocols and network devices moving quite often.

Figure 7-2 shows a conventional campus-wide VLAN model. Layer-2 switching is used in the access, distribution, and core layers. Multiple workgroups are distributed across several access-layer switches and the connectivity across them is via a router or a *Route Switch Module* (RSM). The VLAN model provides multilayer services, including flexibility and scalability, which is the need of most organizations. With the help of the VLAN model, one can move statically configured end stations to a different floor or building within the campus by using Cisco's *VLAN Membership Policy Server* (VMPS) and the *VLAN Trunking Protocol* (VTP). With this, a notebook user could simply work on different floors or in another building by plugging his notebook into the network. The Cisco Catalyst switches send a query to the VMPS and come to know the access policy and VLAN membership for the user. Then the Catalyst switch adds the user's port to the appropriate VLAN.

In the Cisco switch family, VLANs can be implemented using one of three methods:

- IEEE 802.10
- *Inter-Switch Links* (ISL)
- LAN emulation

Figure 7-2
VLAN model

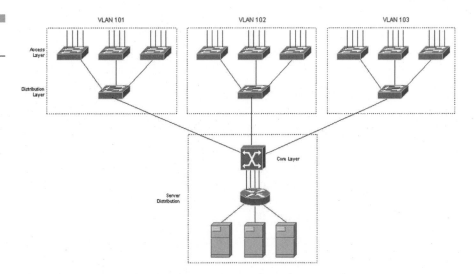

VLAN trunking is used to implement campus-wide VLANs. A VLAN trunk is used between two or more Layer-2 switches to enable traffic from several logical networks to be multiplexed. Trunking between routers and switches is used to connect to several logical networks over a single physical interface. ISL, 802.10, and 802.1q are VLAN tagging protocols that are used to enable VLAN trunking. Depending upon the type of tagging protocol in use, an integer is incorporated into the header of frames passing between the two devices. This tag value enables the data from multiple VLANs to be multiplexed and de-multiplexed.

ATM's *Local Area Network Emulation* (LANE) permits logical LANs to exist over a single switched ATM infrastructure. Integer indices similar to ISL, 802.10, and 802.1q are used by ATM *Emulated LANs* (ELANs) and are compatible with Ethernet VLANs from end to end. As shown earlier in Figure 7-2, LANE cards in Catalyst switches act as *LANE clients* (LECs) that connect the Ethernet VLANs across the ATM backbone. Cisco IOS supports *LANE Configuration Servers* (LECS), *LANE Server* (LES), and *Broadcast and Unknown Server* (BUS) functions that are required to make ATM work like Ethernet. The Cisco LightStream 1010 switch, the Cisco Catalyst 5000 series with a LANE card, or a Cisco router with an ATM interface are popular examples of devices that can support these functions. In these scenarios, the routing is taken care of by the RSM, which is an IOS router with the same *Reduced Instruction Set Computing* (RISC) processor as the RSP2 engine in the high-end Cisco 7500 series routers. Cisco RSMs give full multiprotocol routing support.

Multiprotocol over ATM (MPOA) Model

The initial ATM network models were IP over ATM, which focused only upon the IP and was not able to take care of other protocols that are widely used in campus networks. MPOA standards were put in by the ATM Forum to end the "IP only" problem. MPOA has support for protocols that include IP, DECnet, AppleTalk, and IPX to name a few. RFC 2684 defines multiprotocol encapsulation over *ATM Adaptation Layer* (AAL) 5. AAL is used to perform the necessary mapping between the ATM layer and the higher layers. The classes of service are general concepts, but they are mapped onto the following different specific AAL types:

- Class A: AAL 1
- Class B: AAL 2
- Class C & D: AAL 3/4
- Class C & D: AAL 5

  - *AAL Type 1* AAL Type 1 or Class A is a connection-oriented service that was designed to support video signal transports, voice-band signal transports, and high-quality audio transports. It supports both synchronous and asynchronous circuits.

  - *AAL Type 2* AAL Type 2 or Class B is currently not defined. It is supposed to be a connection-oriented service that will

- Transfer service data units with a variable source bit rate.
- Transfer timing information between the source and destination.

  - *AAL Type 3/4* AAL Type 3/4 was originally two distinct AALs in themselves. Down the line they were merged together to form Class C AAL. AAL 3 was designed for connection-oriented data, and AAL 4 for connectionless-oriented data.

  - *AAL Type 5* AAL Type 5 or Class D is designed for the same class of service as AAL 3/4 but contains less overheads. Unlike AAL 3/4 , it enables the full 48 bytes of payload to be used for transportation.

ATM adaptation layers insert and extract information into the 48-byte payload and are divided into four classes. AAL 5 is designed for data traffic and has less overheads than AAL 3/4. RFC 2684 describes in depth the two-encapsulation models used to carry network traffic over AAL type 5 over ATM:

- Multiple protocols share the same *virtual connection* (VC).
- Each protocol has its own VC.

MPOA operates at both Layer 2 and Layer 3 and is capable of handling non-routable as well as routable protocols. LANE, discussed in

Figure 17-3
A MPOA model

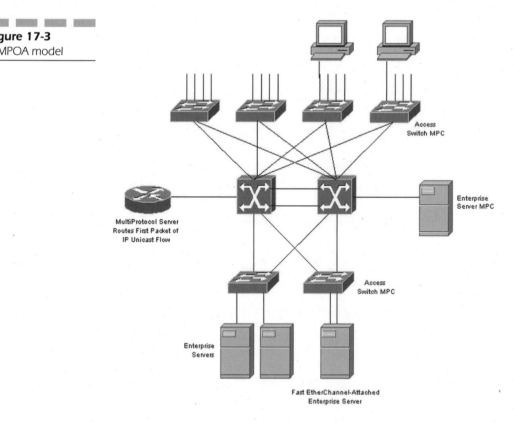

Figure 17-3
A MPOA model

the previous section, operates at Layer 2 of the OSI model. Figure 7-3 describes a MPOA model. With MPOA, one gets Layer-3, cut-through switching to ATM LANE, while the ATM infrastructure is the same as ATM LANE and LECS, and the LES/BUS for each The new elements in the MPOA model are the *multiprotocol client* (MPC) hardware and software on the access switches as well as *multiprotocol server* (MPS), which is implemented in the IOS of the router in Figure 7-3. When a client in a VLAN requests data from any enterprise server, the first packet goes from the MPC in the access switch to the MPS using LANE. The MPS in turn forwards the packet to the destination MPC using LANE. MPS tells the two MPCs to establish a direct *switched virtual circuit* (SVC) path between the source ELAN and the server farm subnet. Once the SVC is established, the IP unicast traffic takes the cut-through SVC as indicated. Multicast packets are sent to the BUS to be flooded in the originating ELAN.

Other than IP packets, the rest follow the LANE-to-router-to-LANE path without establishing a direct cut-through SVC. MPOA design is considered by the amount of broadcast, multicast, and non-IP traffic. MPOA is considered for networks with predominately IP unicast traffic and ATM trunks to the wiring closet switch.

It must be kept in mind that ATM is not a simple technology and is rather highly complex in nature. However, in an enterprise network, ATM can be effectively used for the core layer or for WAN links to provide greater bandwidth, flexibility, and QoS support. We shall be taking an in-depth look into ATM when it comes to WAN in Chapter 9.

Redundant Network Model

The key aspects of any enterprise network are flexibility, scalability, reliability, QoS, security, and management. Which services are required and how they need to be deployed depends upon the function and the location of the equipment in the network. With the network-based applications growing quickly every day, there is a need for maintaining high-service availability. We shall discuss redundancy in this section of the book. One of the best means to achieve reliability is by using a redundant network model. Depending upon the network and the nature of requirements, redundancy can be either at the access layer, distribution layer, or the core layers. We shall discuss the same topics in three ways:

- Physical redundancy
- Router/switch redundancy
- Host redundancy

Physical Redundancy

Cisco networks can be designed with varying degrees of redundancy. Network devices may support redundant common equipment, such as redundant power supplies and supervisor modules. Figure 7-4 shows a Cisco Catalyst 5000 series with dual power supplies to provide redundancy.

Consider the case of a distribution switch that caters to more than a thousand users in one building. A power supply failure in this scenario would lead to users losing connections and hence

Figure 7-4
Cisco Catalyst 5000
with dual power
supplies

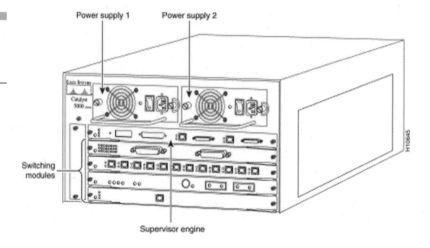

Figure 7-5
High-availability
network design

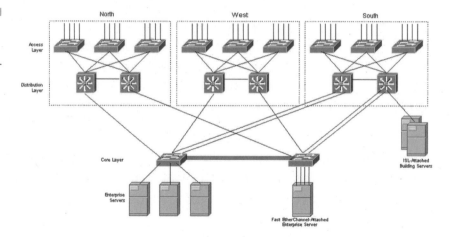

work getting hampered. Connections by users to the backbone
would be lost if a physical link between the wiring closet switch
and the distribution layer switch goes bad due to unforeseen reasons. Figure 7-5 shows a high-network design that addresses these
issues.

Two or four Ethernet links can be concatenated to create a single logical link. This capability is known as EtherChannel and is
available for 10-Mbps Ethernet and 100-Mbps (Fast) Ethernet. In
a campus-wide network, EtherChannel technology is used to pro-

vide improved reliability and greater throughput by balancing the load across multiple links. If one of the links that compromise an EtherChannel goes down, the remaining links will carry the load. For example, four Fast Ethernet links can be used to connect a server to the backbone over a single 400-Mbps, full-duplex logical channel. On the server end, a quad network interface card is concatenated into a single logical link and used. Products from Intel, Hewlett Packard, Compaq, Sun Microsystems, Adaptec, Silicon Graphics, Xircom, and NetFrame support the EtherChannel technology.

Multilayer switches with redundant power supplies and redundant physical links provide redundant connectivity to the network. These redundant links from each access-layer switch connect to distribution-layer switches. Two or more Catalyst switches in the core layer with redundant physical connectivity take care of the core layer. This kind of model not only provides physical redundancy, but also helps in load balancing the various connectivity paths available on the network.

Router/Switch Redundancy

In the previous section, we discussed how physical router/switch redundancy is achieved. Along with the redundant hardware option, redundant links can be implemented using *Inter-Switch Link* (ISL) at Layer 2 or using *Hot Standby Routing Protocol / Multiple Hot Standby Routing Protocol* (HSRP/MHSRP) at Layer 3. HSRP/MHSRP is used for fault-tolerant IP routing across VLANs in a campus-wide network. HSRP provides automatic router backups and is compatible with Novell's IPX, AppleTalk, and Banyan VINES. It is also compatible with DECnet and *Xerox Network Systems* (XNS) when certain configurations are used. Network devices such as user workstations are configured with a single default gateway, which in turn points to the router. The need of HSRP comes in a network where multiple routers are used not only for load-balancing, but act as a hot standby in case one fails. In an HSRP scenario, the routers are configured to use the MAC address and IP network address of a virtual router, which physically does not exist. The end user workstation is configured in such a way that it uses the virtual router's IP address as the default gateway. Convergence in case of any router failure with HSRP is fast enough and the end user is not aware of any router downtime. This ensures high availability of the network for the users.

NOTE: *HSRP is supported on any Cisco router that is running Cisco IOS Software Release 10.0 or later. Cisco IOS Software Release 11.0(3)(1) and above provide improved support for the use of secondary IP addresses with HSRP.*

High-availability networks are designed with multiple paths between two points. The spanning tree algorithm is used to ensure that the lowest cost path is always used. With the help of this algorithm, a new path is selected in case the lowest cost path fails. It is always ensured that there is never more than one path connecting two points. Convergence in the spanning tree domain and the selection of a new path can take about 50 seconds. A delay of 50 seconds might not be acceptable in high-availability networks, as sessions might terminate. In this scenario, Cisco features PortFast, Uplink-Fast, and BackboneFast. These features help spanning trees to converge within five seconds after a fault. BackboneFast, UplinkFast, and PortFast features are available on the Catalyst 5500 product family.

Inter-Switch Link (ISL) is generally used to provide Layer-2 link redundancy and load-sharing between two layers of the hierarchical network model. When using ISL VLAN trunks, traffic is divided into two different VLANs for redundant load-sharing uplinks. As shown later in Figure 7-7, 250 users are assigned to VLAN 1 and 250 users to VLAN 2. Two ISL ports can be found on the access switch. One of the ISL trunks provides a primary path for traffic originating from VLAN 1 and a secondary path for the traffic originating from VLAN 2. The other ISL trunk provides a primary path for traffic originating from VLAN 2 and a secondary path for the traffic originating from VLAN 1. If either trunk fails, all the traffic is carried on a single ISL trunk. Separate spanning tree domains make this link redundancy possible.

Redundancy on Layer 3 is achieved by using routing protocols like OSPF, the *Enhanced Interior Gateway Routing Protocol* (EIGRP), or the *Border Gateway Protocol* (BGP) on the LAN or WAN. OSPF is a link-state routing protocol with two primary characteristics. First, the specifications of this protocol are in the public domain with the specifications published as *Request for Comments* (RFC) 1247. The second characteristic is that OSPF is based on the *Shortest Path First* (SPF) algorithm, designed by the *Internet Engineering Task Force* (IETF). Cisco's implementation of OSPF conforms to the OSPF Version 2 specifications detailed in the RFC 1583. EIGRP supports load-sharing across up to six paths with different route metric values.

Redundancy in terms of links, that is, connectivity, can also be incorporated for a high-availability network by using the *Dial-on-Demand Routing* (DDR) solutions that are the most popular way of providing backups for WAN links. With DDR, one can provide redundant network connections over *Public Switch Telephone Networks* (PSTN). Asynchronous modems can be used for DDR on the AUX port of the router. Synchronous modems or ISDN TAs can be used on serial ports, and integrated ISDN ports (BRI, MBRI, or PRI) can be used. DDR can be used either in a link failure scenario or can act as a backup in case the load on the dedicated link exceeds a certain permitted level. The primary or dedicated link is configured in such a way that if the primary link fails or the primary link exceeds the specified load threshold, the backup interface is activated and a connection is established using the same. In order to filter traffic on a backup link, dialer list and dialer groups are used. This is similar to *Access Lists* (ACLs). With the help of dialer filtering, you can define what kind of traffic can flow through in case of link failure. You can specify that only *Simple Mail Transfer Protocol* (SMTP) traffic should be able to flow on the backup link. These dialer lists can be for routing or routed protocols. Routing protocols are generally blocked on the backup links. DDR is generally used in scenarios where the traffic is low and periodic. Depending upon the traffic pattern of the network, three topologies can be used:

- *Point-to-point* This is the most common scenario for small- to medium-sized networks in which two sites are connected to each other.

- *Fully meshed topology*   In a fully meshed topology, each and every site can establish a connection to any site. This topology scales well in small networks only. As the network grows, maintaining this kind of setup is highly difficult and the topology itself is not highly scalable.

- *Hub-and-spoke topology*   This topology is essentially used for larger enterprise networks where all the "spokes" (the remote and branch offices) call up the "hub" (a central office). This topology is highly scalable. Remote offices call up the central office directly and do not call any of the other remote offices.

Host Redundancy

The crucial parts of the networks are the servers themselves. Packets are more or less useless without the servers, which acknowledge and process them. As a network designer, one should not show any kind of leniency on this part of the network. Physical redundancy and load-balancing play a crucial part in this scenario. Consider an example of a news site or an online trading Web site. A data center for, say, an online stock trading Web site would require multiple servers and Cisco LocalDirector for load-balancing across various servers. These kind of network designs are generally used by Web-hosting service providers, mission-critical server environments, and high-volume Web sites. Multiple servers are used to take loads from various users with the help of the Cisco LocalDirector. The LocalDirector uses adaptive load-balancing algorithms to distribute TCP/IP connections sent to a single address across a set of servers. The Local or Distributed Director calculates network proximity by querying routers for BGP and IGP route info, and then combines the round-trip latency, server up/down status, and administrative input to select the "best" server. Cisco LocalDirector is an ideal choice for high-traffic Internet sites requiring up to 200 Mbps of throughput. Cisco LocalDirector 416 is priced higher than 430 and is a high-availability solution for all TCP applications. Figure 7-6 illustrates LocalDirector catering to a server farm.

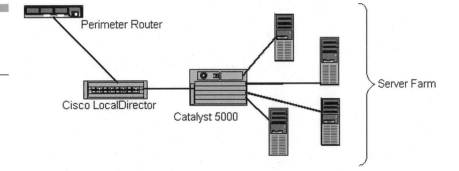

Figure 7-6
LocalDirector
catering to a server
farm

Cisco's DistributedDirectors are used in geographically distributed data centers that require host as well as network redundancy. Cisco DistributedDirector supports Ethernet, Fast Ethernet, Token Ring and FDDI mode LAN interfaces only. The Cisco Distributed Director uses *Director Response Protocol* (DRP), which is a *User Datagram Protocol* (UDP)-based application to query Cisco routers as to which topologically dispersed servers are connected on the Internet. With the help of DRP, users are transparently and automatically assigned a server anywhere on the Internet.

Taking into consideration the exact needs of the client, as a network designer you should select the best possible network architecture, which stands not only to the existing needs of the client, but is also highly scalable for future expansion.

Secure Network Model

With the explosion in network applications as businesses depend upon network services and availability, the need to protect not only network and data, but also the network from the *denial of services* (DoS) is emerging fast. Access control policies are formed by corporate policies that define the type of access that is allowed across an organization. A secure network model should not only take into account the border network perimeter, but the entire organization's network perimeter.

A firewall is one of the objects of a secure network model. A firewall is a system or a group of systems that enforces an access control policy depending upon the requirement of a network. If two offices have a private leased line connecting them, the use of a firewall is bleak. But in the same place, a firewall can be used for a dial-in modem pool to control access from a dial-in modem pool or between departments.

The other objects in a secure network model include the routers, switches, network access server, and the enterprise servers. In an enterprise network, it is important to control access to Cisco routers, switches, and network access servers. To protect Cisco devices from unauthorized access, control policies should be applied to them. Console access, telnet access, and *Simple Network Management Protocol* (SNMP) access can be implemented within the router software. Organizations use a *Terminal Access Controller Access Control System* (TACACS) or a *Remote Access Dial-In User Service* (RADIUS) to provide *Authentication, Authorization, and Accounting* (AAA) to verify the user, grant appropriate access to them, and keep a track of user's action.

For Internet and intranet security, Cisco has two solutions to offer:

- Cisco Secure Integrated Software
- *Cisco Secure Private Internet Exchange* (PIX) Firewall

Apart from the basic security provided by the Cisco IOS, Cisco Secure Integrated Software is an all-in-one security option that sits on top of the Cisco IOS. No new hardware upgrades are required and it provides rich application support and DoS protection. Cisco Secure Integrated Software is an excellent choice for small- to medium-sized businesses that want cost-effective, high-performance security solutions. Security policies can be applied to any of the interfaces, hence providing security for the entire perimeter covering Internet, intranet, or extranet services. The Cisco Secure Integrated Software provides a complete *virtual private network* (VPN) solution based on Cisco IOS IPSec, L2TP tunneling, and QoS. Figure 7-7 shows a small- to medium-sized facility connected to the Internet via a Cisco 1600 or Cisco 2500 router and the network perimeter being protected by the Cisco IOS Firewall Feature Set.

Figure 7-7
Network perimeter
security with Cisco
IOS Firewall Feature
Set

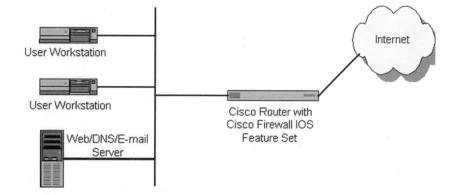

Figure 7-7
Network perimeter security with Cisco IOS Firewall Feature Set

The key features of the Cisco IOS Firewall Feature Set are as follows:

- Java blocking
- Context-based access control
- Attack detection and prevention
- Real-time alerts
- VPN support

Cisco Secure PIX firewall is a dedicated firewall that works in conjunction with the perimeter routers to provide high-performance security for the network. The feature set of PIX is advanced and has extensive support for the applications used in internetworking. The real-time embedded system makes the Cisco Secure PIX firewall handle up to 256,000 simultaneous connections. The PIX firewall uses the *Adaptive Security Algorithm* (ASA), which is much more robust than packet filtering and offers higher performance. The stateful, connection-oriented ASA design creates session flows based on source and destination addresses.

NOTE: *Cisco Centri Firewall is not discussed here as the product has been discontinued by Cisco.*

Basic Firewalls

Having discussed the Cisco solutions, this section discusses the basic firewall architecture prevailing in the industry today. Theoretically, firewalls are divided into two types:

- Application-layer firewalls
- Stateful inspection firewalls

Application-level firewalls permit no traffic directly between a protected network and the Internet, but rather act as hosts running proxies that audit the traffic passing through them. Application-layer firewalls work in both transparent as well as proxy mode. Application-layer firewalls start processing the packet at the application layer, which means that the packet can make a connection to the firewall in the first place. In this scenario, a vulnerable operating system could be dangerous for networks where security is a prime concern.

Stateful inspection firewalls, better known as network-layer firewalls, make decisions based on the source, destination addresses, and ports in individual IP packets. People term a normal packet-filtering router as a network-layer firewall. Security experts consider stateful inspection firewalls to be unable to provide very secure protection. With stateful inspection firewalls, the firewall doesn't act as a mediator between the internal network and the Internet, but passes the packets according to the policy list on the firewall. Another disadvantage is the extensity of logging by help of stateful inspection firewalls. The logging level is a bit lower than the application-level firewall.

As times change, newer technologies are coming up. As a network designer, you should keep in mind the objectives and requirements of the customer. The following are some issues that one should keep in mind while designing secure networks:

- Protecting the network and the data
- The total cost of ownership
- Manageability of the entire secure perimeter

- Protecting mobile and remote employees, partners, customers, and so on
- Maintaining the network performance, reliability, and availability

Figure 7-8 discusses the most widely used firewall network design. The primary components of a three-part firewall network design are

- The external network
- The internal network
- The *demilitarized zone* (DMZ)

Broadly speaking, an alien or external network is a network that is not trusted by an enterprise. This is one of the biggest threats for any enterprise network. With the help of the rule base on the firewall, it has to be ensured that the incoming packets are screened appropriately and are rejected, dropped, or accepted accordingly.

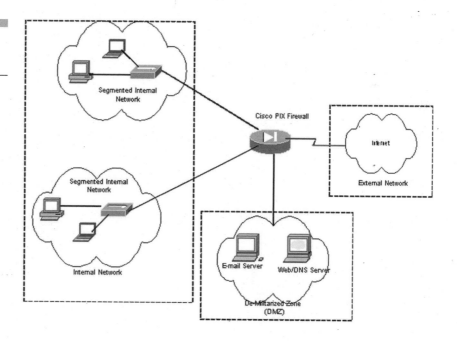

Figure 7-8
Three-part firewall
network design

The internal network consists of a network(s) that comes within the trusted networks and is known to the network administrator/designer. An internal network could also be treated as one of the threats to the integrity and security of the network. Generally, network designers do not pay much attention to this aspect of network security. Depending upon the needs or goals of the business, one must take care of the security of the internal network.

A DMZ should never be directly part of the exterior network or the internal network. This is a separate network area between the exterior network and the internal network. Servers and machines placed on the DMZ are known as *bastion hosts*. The DMZ is the main point of contact for incoming packets. It is generally used to host the following:

- Incoming and outgoing SMTP sessions
- Web servers are placed on the DMZ to take care of all the Web requests that are generated from the alien or exterior network
- To host *Domain Name Service* (DNS) servers
- To host FTP servers to make it possible for customers, vendors, and so on to download data from them in a secured manner
- *Network Access Servers* (NAS) and modem pools can be placed in the DMZ while placing the authenticating server inside the internal network

The addition of a perimeter network, shown in Figure 7-9, can further tighten a firewall design. In a perimeter network design, two packet-filtering routers separate the external and internal networks. This firewall network design is quite secure when the threat is perceived from the external network. The external router takes care of the packets coming in from the external network and forwards them appropriately to the firewall. The internal router protects the internal network from both the Internet and the perimeter network. The perimeter network is also sometimes termed as DMZ.

A Cisco Secure PIX firewall is the interface between the internal and the external networks, which are also known as the trusted and not-trusted networks respectively. With the network technologies and topologies changing every now and then, as a network designer,

Figure 7-9
The perimeter
network using
two routers

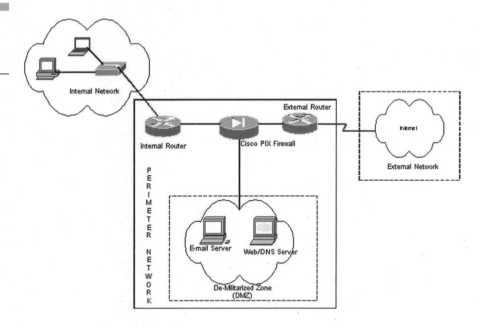

one must keep the design highly scalable, while not forgetting the major task at hand, securing the network. A higher level of security might have a trade-off in terms of speed. Based upon the business requirements, security policies, staff constraints, costs, and the perceived threat of attacks (internal or external), the network designer must make the appropriate design decision.

Virtual Private Network (VPN) Technology

VPN is the technology that enables the existing public network infrastructure to form a private network enabling two remote sites to get connected via a secure medium or a tunnel. The most popular way to extend the classical WAN is through the VPNs. Earlier, inter-office connectivity used to be possible through traditional, dedicated leased lines and public Frame Relay circuits. The costs were higher, and manageability and scalability used to be low. These reasons by themselves were quite motivating to the invention of the VPN technology, which is highly scalable and the total cost of ownership is highly reduced. With the emerging technology, not only data is supported over VPNs, but also voice and video services are consolidated onto a single network, reducing operational and capital expenses. A VPN enables one to send data between two networks across a shared or public Internet in a manner that emulates the properties of a point-to-point private link. To emulate a private link, data is encapsulated, or encrypted, with a header that provides routing information, enabling it to traverse the shared or public Internet and reach its final destination. VPN connections enable an organization to trade in long-distance, dial-up, or leased lines for local dial-up or leased lines to an *Internet Service Provider* (ISP). With enterprises moving out of the in-house *Network Access Server* (NAS) setup and outsourcing to ISPs, VPNs would provide the same reliability, manageability, and performance and still lower the total cost of ownership.

Figure 7-10 illustrates two networks connected over the Internet via the help of a VPN. The enterprise connects to the Internet using local dedicated WAN links, instead of using an expensive, long-distance, dedicated WAN link between offices.

A router-to-router VPN or a PIX-to-PIX VPN is initiated in the previous case and routers forward the traffic to each other using the VPN connection. The same scenario can apply to connecting branch offices using the dial-up WAN links. The branch office router calls a

Figure 7-10

A VPN connecting two remote networks across the Internet

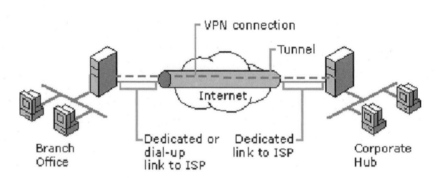

local ISP instead of making a long-distance call or calling the corporate NAS and initiates a VPN connection over the Internet to the corporate office router. The corporate office router acts as a VPN server and the branch office router acts as a client. The VPN connection takes care of the encapsulation, authentication, and data encryption. With the help of the VPNs, the IP addressing scheme of an enterprise remains the same and private IP addresses can be transported over the tunnel. Cisco Systems follows a comprehensive five-element strategy for VPN solutions:

1. Scalable platforms
2. Extensive data, packet, and user security
3. Robust VPN services, including QoS and VPN routing services
4. High-performance VPN appliances
5. End-to-end, policy-based management with service monitoring and auditing capabilities

The Cisco 1000, 1600, 2500, 4500, and 4700 series are appropriate for VPNs with moderate encryption and tunneling requirements. These are better known as VPN-enabled routers. Cisco Systems has another series of routers better known as VPN-optimized routers that consist of the Cisco 800, 1720, 2600, 2600, 7200, and 7500 series routers. These are capable of addressing more scalable security requirements as well as VPN-centric WAN topologies.

SUMMARY

The hierarchical, redundant, and secure network models covered in this chapter will help you design a network that best suits your customers' needs. Traffic volumes are growing dramatically and traffic patterns are becoming highly unpredictable as the Internet applications and Web technology are being deployed throughout enterprise networks. In order to develop a strong network design, one must analyze traffic patterns, paying attention to bandwidth requirements, protocol traffic, and the applications in use. Multilayer services are necessary to support emerging applications, to allow networks to grow as the bandwidth requirements increase, and to cost-effectively maintain a network to provide the security necessary to protect corporate resources.

By appropriately using the three network models (the hierarchical model, the redundant model, and the secure model), you can easily achieve a customer's goal and provide her with a scalable, adaptive, and high-performance network design.

QUESTIONS

1. Which of the following layers are parts of the hierarchical network model?

   a. Access layer

   b. Network layer

   c. Access point layer

   d. Core layer

   e. Distribution layer

   f. Distributed layer

2. Which of the following is true for the hierarchical network model?

   a. Hierarchical network models are easier to troubleshoot and scalable internetworks can be achieved.

   b. Hierarchical network models are adequate only for small- to medium-sized networks.

   c. Hierarchical network models are easier to design.

   d. In hierarchical network models, it is advisable to filter packets in the core layer.

3. Which of the following are not parts of the core layer of the hierarchical model?

   a. Packet filtering

   b. High-speed switching

   c. Extranet connectivity

   d. Redundant network paths

   e. *Network Address Translation* (NAT)

4. How many layers should one place after the distribution layer in the three-layer hierarchical model?

   a. Two

   b. One

   c. None

   d. Three

5. The Cisco *Virtual Membership Policy Server* (VMPS) is used for

  a. Routing between VLANs

  b. Enabling statically placed network devices to work across various VLANs

  c. Providing redundancy between two switches

  d. It is used only in the ATM VLAN model.

6. Which of the following protocols can be used to implement VLANs using a Cisco Catalyst 5500 family switch?

  a. *Inter-Switch Link* (ISL)

  b. Cut-through switching

  c. 802.10

  d. 801.11

  e. LAN emulation

7. Which of the following components are required to make ATM work like Ethernet?

  a. *LANE Configuration Server* (LECS)

  b. *LANE Server* (LES)

  c. *Bridge Relay Function* (BRF)

  d. *Broadcast and Unknown Server* (BUS)

8. What does DDR stand for?

  a. Dial-Demand Routing

  b. Demand-on-Dial Routing

  c. Dial-on-Demand Routing

  d. Distributed Demand Routing

9. Which of the following topologies is scalable for large enterprise networks when implementing a DDR solution?

  a. Hub-and-spoke topology

  b. Point-to-point topology

  c. Partially meshed topology

  d. Fully meshed topology

10. On which of the following OSI layers does Multiprotocol over ATM operate?

   a. Layer 3

   b. Layer 1

   c. Layer 5

   d. Layer 4

   e. Layer 2

11. Which of the following holds true for ATM?

   a. Voice applications cannot be implemented over ATM.

   b. ATM is complex and extremely difficult to implement, especially on the desktop.

   c. It can be used easily at the access layer.

   d. It is not a globally accepted standard.

12. At which layer do the *Hot Standby Routing Protocol* (HSRP) and the *Multiple Hot Standby Routing Protocol* (MHSRP) work?

   a. Network layer

   b. Data link layer

   c. Session layer

   d. Transport layer

13. Cisco LocalDirector is an ideal choice for high-traffic Internet sites requiring up to ____ Mbps of throughput.

   a. 200 Mbps

   b. 300 Mbps

   c. 100 Mbps

   d. 250 Mbps

14. How many load-sharing paths does EIGRP support with different route metric values?

   a. Two

   b. Four

   c. Six

   d. Ten

15. Which of the following is used by the Cisco Secure PIX Firewall?

    a. Stateful inspection

    b. Application layer filtering

    c. Adaptive state algorithm

    d. Packet filtering

16. Which of the following is part of the firewall network?

    a. External network

    b. Internal network

    c. HSRP

    d. DMZ

17. You are supposed to place an FTP server for your client. The distributors who have a username and password for them will use the FTP server to download pricing and product information. Where will you place the FTP server? An anonymous FTP is disabled on the server.

    a. In the internal network

    b. In the DMZ

    c. In the data center of your ISP

    d. All of the above

18. Which of the following are true in the case of VPNs?

    a. They reduce the total cost of ownership.

    b. They always provide much better QoS than the traditional medium.

    c. They protect the network and the data.

    d. They provide redundancy.

    e. They provide data, packet, and user security.

ANSWERS

1. a., d., and **e.**

Core, distribution, and access layers form a hierarchical network.

2. a.

With the help of the three-layer hierarchical network model, it is easier to design scalable and reliable internetworks, and fault isolation and troubleshooting is easier.

3. a. and **e.**

Packet filtering and NAT are part of the distribution layer and not the core layer. This is generally done so that the routers and switches at the core layer are not overloaded and could lead to choking on the backbone.

4. b.

In the three-layer hierarchical network model, one can place only one layer after the distribution layer. The three layers of a hierarchical model are core, distribution, and access layers.

5. c.

To allow statically placed network devices to work across various VLANs, a *Virtual Membership Policy Server* (VMPS) placed on a campus-wide network enables statically placed network devices to be moved across various VLANs with no configuration changes required on the switches.

6. a., d., and **e.**

ISL, 802.10, and LAN emulation are the protocols used to implement VLAN on Cisco Catalyst 5500 family switches.

7. a., b., and **d.**

LECS, LES, and BUS are required to make ATM work like Ethernet. The *Bridge Relay Function* (BRF) is used in a Token Ring network to form a single bridge-hop-across switch.

8. c.

DDR stands for Dial-on-Demand Routing and is used for backup connectivity purposes.

9. a.

Hub-and-Spoke topology is highly scalable and flexible when it comes to implementing DDR solutions for large solutions. The overall manageability for this kind of network is much lower than a fully meshed topology.

10. a. and **e.**

MPOA can function over Layer 2 and Layer 3 of the OSI model and can use non-routable as well as routable protocols.

11. b.

ATM networks are one of the most complex networks today and it can be a highly trivial task to implement them successfully.

12. a.

HSRP and MHSRP work on the Layer 3, the network layer of the OSI model.

13. a.

14. c.

15. b.

Cisco Secure PIX Firewall uses the *Adaptive State Algorithm* (ASA). The stateful, connection-oriented ASA design creates session flows based on source and destination addresses.

16. a., b., and **d.**

The exterior network, internal network, and the *demilitarized zone* (DMZ) are part of a three-part firewall.

17. b.

The DMZ is the best place to place the FTP server. Although anonymous ftp has been disabled, it is not advisable to place the FTP server in the internal network.

18. a., c., and, **e.**

Local Area Network (LAN) Design

We have completed all of the preliminary network-design steps. Now, the actual work of designing network components and topologies can begin. The first portion of a network design is the *Local Area Network* (LAN) design. LANs enable various workstations in a location to exchange data and to share resources across the network. A portion of LAN design will cover various data-link layer technologies, including Ethernet, Fast Ethernet, Token Ring, FDDI, and Gigabit Ethernet.

Next, we will investigate the broadcast domain, collision domain, and the 80-20 design rule. Furthermore, we will discuss the scenarios in which we should use a router and where we should use a switch. The basic motive of discussing these technologies is to ensure that the network designer is well versed with the various technologies used for LAN implementation. This discussion also provides criteria for a designer when implementing campus LANs. Keep in mind, however, that there is no single solution to all of the types of LAN implementations.

Objectives Covered in This Chapter

- Recognizing scalability constraints and issues for standard LAN technologies
- Recommending Cisco Systems products and LAN technologies that will meet a customer's requirements for performance, capacity, and scalability in small-to-medium-sized networks

Introduction

LANs are accelerating at a phenomenal speed. The computer generation has changed rapidly from the large mainframes of the 1960s with terminals attached directly to the mainframe to almost every computer having some type of connection to a LAN. During the dark ages of local area networking, end-user terminals were dumb terminals—and the environment was known as centralized computing. IBM developed the first *personal computer* (PC) in 1981, which was the start of the user-computing environment. The demand for high network availability, reliability, scalability, and performance has increased drastically over the years. Just as PCs have changed over the years, network LAN technologies have changed as well.

Network Media

The number of ways to configure LAN access is quite large. From arcane Arcnet and little-used 100VG-AnyLAN to the more common-place Ethernet and Token Ring, there are too many methods for us to cover them all. Instead, we will describe the five most common methods:

- 10Mbps Ethernet
- 100Mbps (Fast Ethernet)
- Gigabit Ethernet
- Token Ring
- *Fiber-Distributed Data Interface* (FDDI)

10Mbps Ethernet   In an Ethernet LAN system, *Carrier Sense Multiple Access and Collision Detection* (CSMA/CD) is the access method. This method ensures that multiple stations can share the resources on a shared cabling network equally by using the control mechanism provided by CSMA/CD. A workstation will sense the wire to detect whether it can freely send data. Ethernet working on the data-link layer performs three functions:

1. Transmitting and receiving formatted data and packets
2. Decoding the packets and checking for valid addresses before informing upper-layer software
3. Detecting errors with the packet or the network

Bob Metcalfe at the Xerox Corporation first invented Ethernet, which was later standardized by IEEE as the IEEE 802.3 standard. In 1980, *Digital Equipment Corporation* (DEC), Intel, and Xerox standardized Ethernet with the release of Ethernet Version 1. This implementation of Ethernet is called DIX Ethernet.

In 1985, the IEEE 802.3 standard came into the picture by using the same algorithm as the Ethernet. This function provided a specification for Ethernet connectivity over thin and thick coaxial cable. There are four major types of media in use today:

1. Thick coax for 10Base5 networks

2. Thin coax for 10Base2 networks

3. *Unshielded Twisted Pair* (UTP) for 10Base-T networks

4. Fiber optic for 10Base-FL or *Fiber Optic Inter-Repeater Link* (FOIRL) networks

Ethernet Operation   The current IEEE 802.3 specification includes thin coaxial cable, thick coaxial cable, twisted-pair cabling, and fiber. Figure 8-1 shows normal Ethernet operation.

A workstation that needs to send data to another node on the same cabling system listens and waits until no packet is being transmitted over the cable and waits until the cable is available for the sole use of the workstation. The workstation then forms the packet and sends it over the cabling system to which all of the other workstations are listening for incoming packets.

A collision occurs when two or more workstations send packets simultaneously over the same cabling system. As soon as a collision is detected, the collision-detection algorithm comes into the picture—and a back-off algorithm is invoked on all of the workstations. This function is popularly known as a *jam*. The jam helps to

Figure 8-1
Normal Ethernet
operation

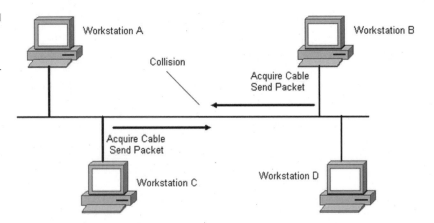

ensure that the other transmitting station recognizes that a collision has occurred on the cable system. The algorithm then generates a random delay number that is used to defer any further transmissions. This time is different for any two computers, therefore reducing the possibility of another collision. After the random delay, the stations start listening and wait until they can acquire media to retransmit the information.

Ethernet is a broadcast transmission medium; hence, all of the workstations on the network will receive the information but will only process the information that is meant for them. The receiver will also detect errors in the packet by checking the *Cyclic Redundancy Check* (CRC) field of the packet. If the receiver finds any errors in the packet, the packet is discarded. After stripping off the headers and trailers of a packet, the data is passed on to the upper layers for processing. Standard Ethernet is also known as a connectionless protocol (in other words, the packet is received or dropped by the receiver and no acknowledgment is conveyed back to the sender). Ethernet does not care about the contents of the packets and does its job of sending and receiving packets on the network. The upper layers (layer 3 to layer 7) have the responsibility of verifying that the packet has come in the proper sequence and ensuring that the data is in good condition. Figures 8-2 and 8-3 show the algorithm flow for Ethernet packet transmission and reception.

NOTE: *One type of Ethernet, LLC2, is a connection-oriented protocol. This version of Ethernet is beyond the scope of this exam. For more information, however, refer to* Interconnections *by Radia Perlman. We took the algorithms in this book from the* Network Protocol Handbook, *by Matthew G. Nagule.*

The network utilization of "healthy" Ethernet should never exceed more than 50 percent, and the collisions should always be fewer than 1 percent. According to standard beliefs, the network utilization should not exceed more than 80 percent, and the collisions should not be greater than 5 percent over a period.

Figure 8-2
Ethernet transmission
flowchart

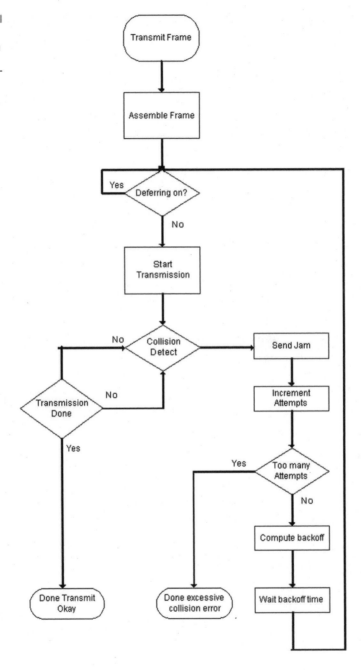

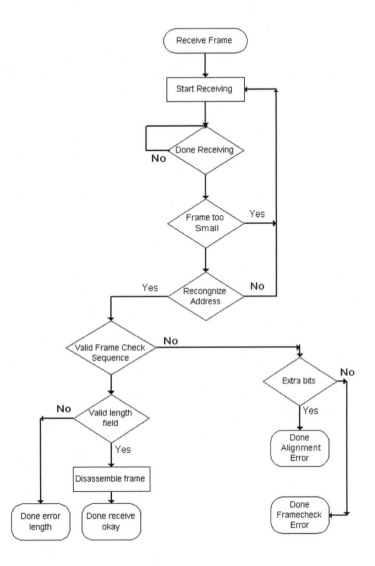

Figure 8-3
Ethernet reception
flowchart

NOTE: *These numbers might seem to be more than the normally suggested percentages. They reflect studies in the early '90s. These studies do not support the assumption that Ethernet is saturated at 37 percent. The current book,* Ethernet: The Definitive Guide *by Charles Spurgeon is an excellent reference for detailed Ethernet operations and information.*

100Mbps Ethernet (Fast Ethernet) Fast Ethernet has been standardized under the IEEE 802.3u standard and was approved in June 1995. 100Base-T Fast Ethernet is based on the same CSMA/CD protocol like 10Base-T Ethernet. With 100Mbps bandwidth, Fast Ethernet is the logical choice for most of the enterprise networks in today's world. Fast Ethernet is based on a star wiring scheme, unlike the bus wiring scheme of 10Mbps Ethernet with coaxial cable. The topology is more reliable and easier to troubleshoot. The three types of Fast Ethernet are as follows:

1. 100Base-TX for use with category 5 UTP cable
2. 100Base-FX for use with fiber-optic cable
3. 100Base-T4 that operates over four pairs of category 3 cable

100Base-TX is the most widely used standard because of its close compatibility with the 10Base-T Ethernet standard. Fast Ethernet supports the use of twisted-pair, fiber-optic, and Token Ring lobe cable. Support for Token Ring lobe cable makes it possible for Token Ring customers to continue with their existing Token Ring networks and gives them a path to easily migrate to Fast Ethernet while leaving their cabling plants intact.

For the network manager, the incorporation of Fast Ethernet into an existing configuration presents a host of decisions. Managers must determine the number of users in each site on the network that needs the higher throughput, decide which segments of the backbone need to be reconfigured specifically for 100Base-T, and then choose the necessary hardware to connect the 100Base-T segments with existing 10Base-T segments.

The 100Base-T standard enables the same device to operate at 10Mbps as well as at 100Mbps half- and full-duplex speeds. Loopback and collision detection needs to be disabled for full-duplex Ethernet operation. Although this function has been performed with 10Base-T also, it was not that successful. Another major difference between the 10Base-T and the 100Base-T standards is the auto-negotiation feature that is available only in the 100Base-T standard. These two features preserve the plug-and-play image of Ethernet.

NOTE: *Speed auto negotiation uses* Fast Link Pulse *(FLP) as its detection mechanism. An FLP burst is composed of 17 to 33 link pulses that are identical to the link pulses used in 10BASE-T to determine whether a link has a valid connection (sometimes referred to as* Normal Link Pulses *[NLPs]). FLP bursts and NLPs occur at intervals of 16.8ms. An FLP burst has a duration of 2ms. See Figure 8-4.*

Figure 8-4 illustrates a hybrid 10Mbps and 100Mbps Ethernet topology. Two switches are connected via optical fiber by using the *Inter-Switch Link* (ISL) ports. A half-duplex fiber ISL is capable of stretching to a distance of 400 m, and a full-duplex fiber ISL is capable of covering a distance of 2 km. We must note that repeaters are share-medium devices that do not operate in full-duplex mode.

A *Fast Ethernet Interface Processor* (FEIP) card for the Cisco 7000 family of high-end routers offers one or two 100Base-TX ports that

Figure 8-4
10/100 Base-T
full/half-duplex
network

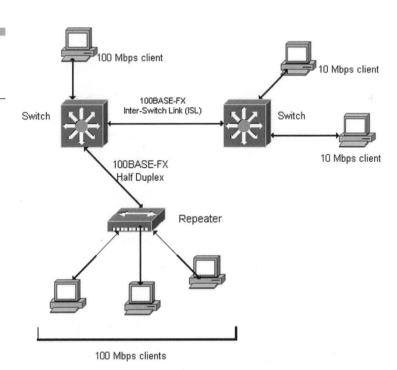

support half- and full-duplex operation. Cisco 2900 switches are widely used for providing Fast Ethernet backbone connectivity to the server farm. Modular catalyst series switches such as the Catalyst 5000 family can have Fast Ethernet modules based upon the requirements of a network. Cisco Catalyst 5500, 5509, 5505, 5000, and 5002 switches support switched 10/100 Base-Tx Fast Ethernet (24 ports) and switched 100Base-FX Fast Ethernet (12 ports) modules.

Gigabit Ethernet Also known as the future Ethernet technology, Gigabit Ethernet provides 1Gbps bandwidth for campus networks while employing the same CSMA/CD protocol, same frame format, and same frame size as its predecessors. Gigabit Ethernet is based on the IEEE 802.3z standard. At the physical layer, Gigabit Ethernet uses a mixture of the original Ethernet and the ANSI X3T11 Fiber Channel specification. Gigabit Ethernet is finally expected to support two physical media types: fiber and UTP. We will define these types in 802.3z (1000Base-X) and 802.3ab (1000Base-T).

- 1000Base-T

  This standard is based on long-haul copper UTP and is supposed to support 25 m to 100 m distances over four pairs of category 5 UTP.

- 1000Base-X

  This standard is based on the Fiber Channel physical layer. Fiber Channel has a four-layer architecture. The lowest two layers, FC-0 and FC-1, are used in Gigabit Ethernet. Three types of media are included in the 1000Base-X standard:

  - 1000Base-SX: 850 nm short-wave lasers on multi-mode fiber support a distance of 500 m.
  - 1000Base-LX: 1300 nm long-wave lasers on single-mode fiber support a distance of 3 km (and multi-mode fiber supports 550 m).
  - 1000Base-CX: Short-haul copper jumpers support 25 m two-pair shielded twinax cable in a single room or rack. This type uses 8b/10b coding.

NOTE: *These distances reflect multi-mode fiber. If single-mode fiber is used, then the distances approach a maximum distance of 2 km.*

The bandwidth needs of an end-user station are still not in the gigabits-per-second range; however, in today's world, this kind of bandwidth requirement comes into the picture in backbone technologies. *Asynchronous Transfer Mode* (ATM) has the capability of providing bandwidth of 622Mbps (OC-12) and also 2.4Gbps (OC-48), but these require frame formats to change. Frame conversion itself makes the procedure extremely expensive. Gigabit Ethernet scales in these scenarios as follows:

- Low cost of ownership
- Easy migration to higher-performance levels without disruption
- Network-design flexibility

NOTE: *Gigabit* Network Interface Cards *(NICs) are being developed for servers. In general, however, the bus speeds of servers in early 2000 cannot handle the full capacity of full-duplex Gigabit Ethernet.*

Gigabit Ethernet offers the potential to upgrade the core of the network simply and efficiently and enables network managers to leverage their existing knowledge of Ethernet in order to manage and maintain gigabit networks. Per-port cost of Gigabit Ethernet is lower than the OC-12 ATM port. The auto-negotiation scheme of Ethernet is optimized for UTP and is not suitable for fiber-optic media. Gigabit Ethernet uses 8B/10B line coding, which fiber channels also use to code signals before transmitting them over the physical layer. Multimedia, Internet access, and groupware applications are demanding higher bandwidth needs everyday. Gigabit Ethernet

Figure 8-5
Gigabit Ethernet in
the core layer of a
network

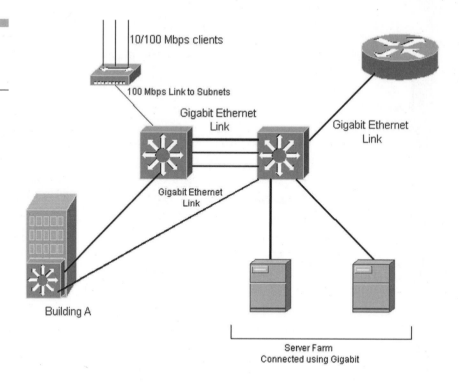

fits in as a campus technology that is used generally on the backbone in a campus-wide network. Figure 8-5 depicts a network that uses Gigabit Ethernet in the core layer of a network. Gigabit Ethernet is used to connect buildings to expand the existing campus network.

According to the Gigabit Ethernet Alliance, there are five upgrade scenarios:

- Upgrading switch-server connections
- Upgrading switch-switch connections
- Upgrading a Fast Ethernet backbone
- Upgrading a shared FDDI backbone
- Upgrading high-performance workstations

The Cisco Systems Catalyst 5000 and 6000 family offers a variety of Gigabit Ethernet products, from high-density Gigabit Ethernet switching modules for use as distribution layer and server-connectivity devices in small and medium-sized networks to Gigabit Ethernet uplink modules that aggregate traffic from high-density 10/100 Mbps wiring closets.

Token Ring According to the name, Token Ring is an IEEE 802.5 standard that connects computers in a closed ring. There are proprietary implementations for ring access, but the most popular one used is the IEEE 802.5 standard. A token, which is a 24-bit packet that is continuously transmitted on the ring, helps transmit data on a Token Ring network. The network device that wants to transmit the data must have the token with itself in order to transmit data on the ring. This situation is something like having an access card to traverse into a secure zone. All of the other network devices wait for the token. A device on the Token Ring network acts as an active monitor, whereas the rest of the devices act as standby monitors. There can only be one active monitor on the network at any given time. The active monitor provides many functions on a Token Ring network, including the following:

- Master clocking on the Token Ring network and lower-level management of the Token Ring network
- Inserting a 24-bit propagation delay to prevent the end of a frame from wrapping onto the beginning of the frame
- Confirming that a data frame or a good token is received every 10 ms. This timer sets the maximum possible frame size on a Token Ring network to 4048 bytes on a 4-megabit ring and 17,997 bytes on a 16-megabit ring.
- Removes circulating frames from the ring. As a frame passes the active monitor, a special bit called a *monitor count bit* is set. If the monitor count bit is set, the active monitor assumes that the original sender of the frame was unable to remove the frame from the ring. The active monitor purges this frame and sends a Token Error Soft Error to the Ring Error Monitor.

If the active monitor is removed from the ring or is no longer capable of performing the active monitor functions, one of the standby

Figure 8-6
Token Ring operation

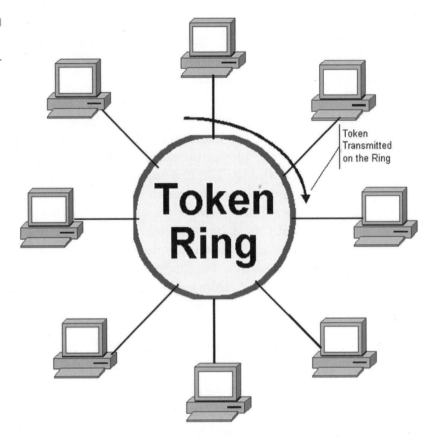

monitors on the ring will take over as active monitor. Figure 8-6 shows the normal Token Ring operation.

There can be multiple data frames on a Token Ring network, but there cannot be more than one token. This situation is made possible by the *Early Token Release* (ETR) technique. ETR is a technique used in Token Ring networks that enables a station to release a new token onto the ring immediately after transmitting, instead of waiting for the first frame to return.

A Token Ring network can operate at either 4Mbps or 16Mbps. These standards are better known as the 16/4 standards. 16Mbps Token Ring devices will not work in a ring with 4Mbps Token Ring devices. To implement a heterogeneous Token Ring network, you need to use either bridges or routers to interconnect 4Mbps and 16Mbps speed rings. Bridges and routers are also necessary when you need to enable communications between an Ethernet network and a Token Ring network.

NOTE: *You can use translational bridges to connect Token Ring and Ethernet networks; however, the advised method for connecting dissimilar networks is a router.*

You need the following physical devices to form a Token Ring network:

- *Multistation Access Unit* (MAU or MSAU)
- Token Ring lobe cable
- Token Ring adapter card

MAUs are the wiring concentrator units for Token Ring networks. All network devices connect to MAUs, and the MAU maintains a ring inside it. MAU also has a *ring in* (RI) and *ring out* (RO), which are ports that are used to interconnect MAUs. An RO port is connected to the RI port of another MAU.

The Token Ring lobe cable is used to connect the Token Ring station to the MAU. The cable can be *Shielded Twisted Pair* (STP), *Unshielded Twisted Pair* (UTP), and fiber optic. Every station in a Token Ring network uses a Token Ring adapter card to connect to a Token Ring network.

Source-Route Bridging (SRB)   SRB is used to connect two or more Token Ring networks via bridges. End network stations use the source-route algorithm to discover remote end stations, hence the name SRB. The transmitting stations are aware of all of the bridges in the network and predetermine the complete route to the destination station before transmitting.

In SRB, a route explorer frame is sent out by the end station to find the route to the destination. The bridges in the rings will forward these frames to all of the rings. The SRB adds this route information to the frame prior to forwarding it. This route information is called the *Routing Information Field* (RIF). Figure 8-7 describes diagrammatically how the source finds the path to the destination.

Figure 8-7

How Host A (source)
finds Host B
(destination)

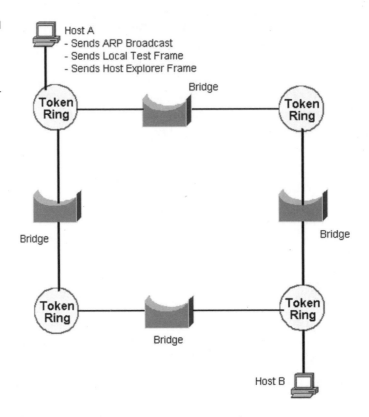

Host A
- Sends ARP Broadcast
- Sends Local Test Frame
- Sends Host Explorer Frame

Host A starts its search for Host B by sending an ARP broadcast. The ARP broadcast that travels the entire local network and the connected segments both know the MAC address of Host B. Having found the MAC address, Host A sends a local test frame that will travel in the Token Ring 5 only. With the help of this test frame, Host A ensures that Host B is not in the local segment.

Once it is confirmed that the destination is not in the local segment, a host explorer broadcast frame is sent. As the frame crosses a bridge, the bridge will place the bridge ID in the RIF. The ring places its ring identification in the RIF as the frame crosses a ring. The destination eventually receives the explorer frame and will send both of them back to the source. Host B receives two frames and will turn both of them back to Host A. Host A takes the first reply as its path to reach Host B and discards any subsequent replies.

Cisco Systems offers a dedicated Token Ring port adapter for Cisco 7200 and 7500 series routers. The dedicated Token Ring port adapter offers increased functionality, flexibility, and performance for Token Ring networks. The Token Ring adapter has four Token Ring ports that can support 4/16 /32Mbps transmission speeds. They are configurable in Token Ring concentrator mode for direct attachment of the server, switches, and stations. The Catalyst 3900 stackable Token Ring switch and the Token Ring switching module for the Catalyst 5000 series are the solutions that Cisco provides. The Cisco 3900 Series Token Ring switch offers 20 fixed ports, a stack port, and a unique FlexSlot that supports up to two feature cards that can provide additional Token Ring ports or high-speed uplinks.

By using switches to connect token rings, a network manager obtains the bridging and packet-forwarding functionality at a much faster rate than bridges. With the help of switches, you can obtain support for *Virtual LANs* (VLANs) and full-duplex mode. The Cisco 3900 and Catalyst 5000 Series switches are better known as second-generation Token Ring switches. Second-generation Token Ring switches have the following features:

- High performance
- Low port cost
- Support for auto negotiation of speeds
- Filtering capabilities
- Comprehensive network management
- Choice of uplinks (Token Ring LANE for ATM)
- VLAN support

Second-generation Token Ring switches offer these features and make it possible for a customer to reap the benefits of the switches. Or, customers can migrate effectively to Ethernet according to business requirements. By mixing Ethernet and Token Ring switches with an ATM or ISL backbone, LAN traffic shares the same backbone bandwidth. RSM or routers can be used to move traffic between Ethernet and Token Ring VLANs. When established, this design can be used to support a mixed environment indefinitely or to migrate from Token Ring to Ethernet in a phased manner. In either case, the benefits of high-performance LAN switching are available to both Token Ring and Ethernet users.

High-Speed Token Ring (HSTR) is a new Token Ring standard that promises speeds of up to 100Mbps and 1Gbps. HSTR products were first introduced in early 1999.

FDDI Work on FDDI started back in 1982 when the need for higher bandwidths on LANs was emerging. The *American National Standards Institute* (ANSI) X3T9.5 work group standardized FDDI. The operating rate of FDDI, which operates at 100Mbps, is five to 25 times faster than Token Ring and 10 times faster than 10Base-T Ethernet standards.

FDDI uses two rings that are formed in a ring-star topology. Similar to the IEEE 802.5 Token Ring standard, a rotating token is transmitted on the network, and the network device needs to have the token prior to sending data. One ring is known as the primary, which is similar to the Token Ring network. The second ring is the secondary, which acts as a backup for the primary.

This dual-ring topology and the use of optical media makes it possible for FDDI to give the highest degree of embedded fault tolerance in a standards-based technology. The control of the rings is not centralized; hence, if any component fails, other components can reorganize themselves without disrupting network services. The function of this secondary ring is to provide an alternate data path in the event of any fault occurrence on the primary ring. Because of the use of optical media, it provides higher reliability, extended transmission distances, and immunity to electromagnetic interference.

FDDI is widely used to form a campus backbone in which you can leverage the advantages of both speed and multi-protocol network integration. By using bridges and routers, you can consolidate Ethernet and Token Ring networks. Unlike IEEE 802.3, Ethernet, and IEEE 802.5, Token Ring supports asynchronous traffic only, and FDDI supports both asynchronous (time-insensitive) as well as synchronous (time-sensitive) traffic. By using the synchronous class of transmission, you can allocate guaranteed bandwidth for a particular transmission.

The time taken by the token to move around in the ring is accurately measured by each station and is used to determine the usability of the token. FDDI can be termed a high-performance, fault-tolerant networking solution. A FDDI network consists mainly of three hardware devices:

1. Concentrator: Attaches directly to the two rings
2. *Single Attached Station* (SAS): Attached to the primary ring only
3. *Dual Attached Station* (DAS): Attached to both of the rings

In an FDDI network, servers are generally DAS—whereas workstations are generally SAS.

Cisco 1400 CDDI/FDDI workgroup concentrators with hot-swappable module support come with two-slot chassis that support a variety of CDDI and FDDI environments including UTP, multimode, and single-mode fiber. A C1400 supports 32 ports CDDI, 20 ports FDDI with SC connectors, and 16 ports FDDI with MIC connectors in a single chassis. Figure 8-8 shows an FDDI network that uses C1400 concentrators for FDDI clients and connects to other switches (such as Catalyst 5000 family switches).

Route or Switch

In this section, we will examine the concepts of collision domains and broadcast domains. You must keep these key aspects in mind as you are designing networks. Next, we will cover the 80/20 network-design

Figure 8-8
An FDDI network
that uses C1400

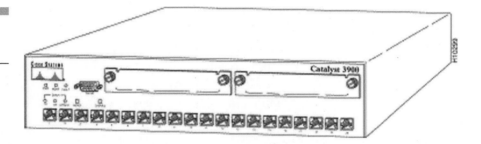

rule and some LAN design guidelines. Finally, in the end we will discuss the use of the routers and switches in a campus LAN, which will help the network designer choose appropriately between the two.

Collision Domain and the Layer 2 Barrier   A collision domain is defined as a group of Ethernet or Fast Ethernet CSMA/CD networks that are directly connected via repeaters or hubs. Only one device in the collision domain can transmit data. A collision will result if two or more computers in the domain transmit at the same time. When a device is transmitting, the rest of the devices monitor the media. The communication devices use the *Media Access Control* (MAC) protocol in order to establish access to a network. MAC resides in all of the *Data Terminal Equipment* (DTE). PCs, servers, bridges, switches, and routers are a few typical DTE devices. Repeaters or hubs do not contain a MAC and operate with a simplified set of rules. We already explained the operation of the Ethernet MAC layer in the Ethernet section of this chapter.

One of the key aspects of designing networks is the collision domain diameter. This diameter is greatly dependent upon the timing issue, where the diameter is the distance between the two farthest nodes. The maximum diameter of a collision domain is defined as the total time that it takes for the smallest packet to travel round trip between two farthest-away DTEs of that domain. The smallest packet size for Ethernet and Fast Ethernet is 64 bytes.

Whenever a packet is transmitted, all of the stations on the network hear it. A collision occurs when a station begins transmission and then receives the beginning of a frame from another station. The station will immediately stop transmission and issue a jam signal onto the wire. This signal will indicate to the other transmitting station that a collision has occurred, and both stations will back off for a random amount of time and try to retransmit after the time.

As a network designer, you must take into consideration that the collision must occur in the first 512 bit times, or 64 bytes, of transmission. If the transmission occurs later, there is no certainty that the transmission will be successful. The collision domain that limits the collision diameter to 512 bit times ensures that all collisions will occur in an acceptable time frame. You should consider that collision domains do not cross bridges or switches. Every port on a switch represents a separate collision domain.

You must use switches to build larger network systems by interconnecting individual collision domains. There is no restriction on the number of collision domains that you can link in order to form a large network. With Fast Ethernet, the distances are limited to one-tenth the distance possible by Ethernet. You must carefully plan the design and layout of such a network. Fast Ethernet collision domain diameters are limited to 412 meters over fiber and 205 meters over twisted pair. Figure 8-9 illustrates a network where switches and bridges are operating at layer 2 of the OSI model and shows how the formation of different collision domains extends LANs.

NOTE: *The distance limitations for Fast Ethernet apply to collision domains—not to the entire LAN. With most switches, each port is a separate collision domain. Therefore, the maximum size of the collision domain is the maximum length of the media type.*

Figure 8-9
Separate collision domains by switching

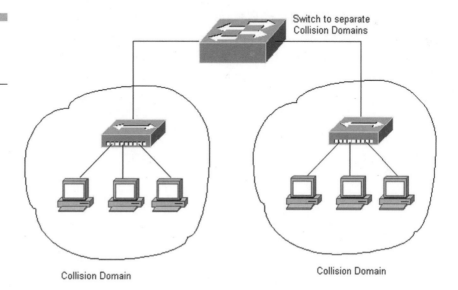

Switch to separate
Collision Domains

Collision Domain

Collision Domain

To extend the distance limitation, you can separate the collision domains by using switches and bridges in a campus network. Instead of propagating all signals between Ethernet segments, you can use LAN switches and bridges to reduce the size of collision domains while extending the Ethernet and enabling the segments to operate independently.

Bridges and switches operate at layer 2 of the OSI model. They maintain a forwarding table that matches layer 2 MAC addresses to physical ports on the bridge or switch. As a packet is received, one of three actions is performed:

1. *Forward*   If the destination MAC is in the forwarding table, the packet is sent to the appropriate port.

2. *Flood*   If the destination MAC is not in the forwarding table, the packet is sent to all ports.

3. *Drop*   If the destination MAC is in the forwarding table and is on the same port as the received packet, then the packet is dropped.

Broadcast Domain and the Layer 3 Barrier   Unlike non-broadcast networks (such as ATM or Frame Relay), every frame is visible in connectionless or medium networks (such as Ethernet and Token Ring). Every frame is visible to all of the stations on the network. Thus, any frame that is flagged as a broadcast (typically done by making the destination MAC address all ones) can reach every destination on the segment or ring at once.

Multiple network segments interconnected by bridges or switches comprise a broadcast domain. Protocols such as NetBIOS, AppleTalk, IPX, and IP require broadcasts or multicasts for resource discovery. For example, when a NetWare/IntraNetWare client is turned on, it broadcasts a Get Nearest Server packet in order to connect to the Novell server and log in. All of the stations see broadcasts from the transmitting host on the bridged network. Bridges forward broadcasts to every port, and they also forward frames with unknown destinations to every port. So, traffic that is local to a collision domain is invisible to the rest of the broadcast domain, while broadcasts and frames with unknown destinations are flooded to every other node

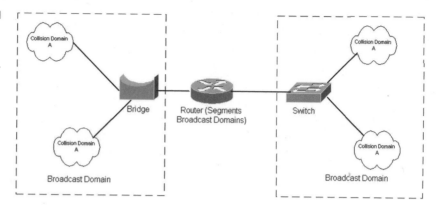

Figure 8-10
Broadcast domains
segmented by router

on the broadcast domain. Figure 8-10 shows broadcast domains. Every broadcast domain consists of a number of collision domains that are separated by either switches or bridges. Just as a switch limits collision domains, a router limits broadcast domains.

Broadcasts can degrade the performance of a networked PC. Frames that are not destined for the station are dropped by the NIC, and no *Central Processing Unit* (CPU) utilization is needed. Broadcasts contain higher-layer information, and processor interrupt is required. Large, flat networks that can be formed by connecting multiple-collision domains are not advisable, because broadcast traffic itself on the flat network can overload PCs and the network.

You should also segment networks with routers in order to fit the end user's needs. Forming a group of users that will use a particular protocol, such as IPX/SPX, is more beneficial than sending IPX/SPX broadcasts over the entire network. By segmenting networks, you relieve possible congestion and effectively use the available bandwidth. Bridges, switches, and routers are used for this network segmentation. By configuring VLANs on the switches in a given network, you can easily segment flat networks to form different broadcast domains. To route between the VLANs, you need to use either a router or an RSM that can fit into a Catalyst 5000 family series switch and provide routing functionality in the LAN. With the help of VLANs, you can segment the network depending upon the requirements.

Consider a network that consists of two groups of networked stations. One group is using AppleTalk, and the other group is using IPX/SPX. By configuring VLANs on the switch, you can segment the network in such a way that AppleTalk broadcasts remain in the AppleTalk subnet and the IPX/SPX broadcasts remain in the IPX/SPX subnet. By using VLANs, you can segment the network, and the broadcast domain has been reduced. A router or an RSM is used to route packets between the two networks. The router or the RSM does not forward any broadcasts or multicast packets; rather, it only forwards unicast packets and directed broadcasts. Each VLAN is a separate broadcast domain, and hosts use broadcasts (ARPs) to locate each other.

The 80-20 Rule   The design rule of early '90s networks was the 80-20 rule, which states that 80 percent of the traffic should be local to the LAN or VLAN, and only 20 percent of the traffic should go to a different LAN or VLAN. This rule was used in order to ensure that the majority of traffic remained in the local subnet. Thereby, you could reduce the amount of load on routers.

With the advent of wire-speed routers, however, this network-design principle is becoming obsolete. Modern networks tend to have server farms that are centrally located. In other words, the majority of the traffic is no longer local to the user subnet. While the 80/20 rule was key to network design in years past, its importance has waned.

Guidelines   When designing networks, network designers must always keep the basic 5-4-3 design rule in mind. The 5-4-3 design rule states that for an Ethernet packet to travel from its source to its destination, it must travel through the following:

- A maximum of five segments
- A maximum of four repeaters/hubs
- A maximum of three populated segments

These rules are based on traditional hub-centric Ethernet LANs. These LANs are being phased out by the continuous demand of higher bandwidth by the bandwidth-hungry applications such as *Voice over IP* (VoIP), video, and others. These trends are reversing the 80/20 design rule in such a way that 20 percent of the traffic remains in the local LAN or VLAN, and the rest of the 80 percent traverses the backbone for resources. Therefore the design of high-speed backbones is essential.

When designing networks, a network designer must keep in mind where to switch and where to route. Switches are generally referred to multi-port bridging or are implemented in hardware or ASICs (for low cost and high performance). The benefits of switches are as follows:

- High throughput and low latency
- Low price per port
- Plug-and-play system
- Simple and easy to manage
- Transparent to protocols
- Create smaller collision domains
- Share LAN bandwidth with fewer systems

Routers operate at layer 3 of the OSI model and are required to distinguish among different network-layer protocols. The router maintains a routing table for each network-layer protocol and forwards frames based on the network-layer address. Routers are mainly used to interconnect and define the edges of broadcast domains on a LAN.

Routers can slow performance in a campus LAN, where the 80/20 rule is being phased out and is being reversed by higher traffic on the backbone of the network (rather than on the local LAN or VLAN).

In the mid-1990s, people often used the following guidelines: 1) all user traffic should be switched to the local servers; 2) in general, all traffic in a particular company site can be switched; and 3) traffic between companies or offices can be routed.

With the advent of wire-speed routers, these guidelines have now blurred. Where a designer might have selected a 100 percent switched network, he or she can further segment the network with a wire-speed router. This procedure will enable the designer to add flexibility to the network design. The ability to route and filter traffic in a central area is a definite advantage.

These hybrid devices are called Layer 3 switches. They have evolved by combining the Layer 2 switching and layer 3 routing features. Layer 3 switches switch within a subnet or VLANs and route between VLANs/subnets. A Layer 3 switch does everything to a packet that a traditional router does. This switch takes care of determining the forwarding path based on the network address (Layer 3 information). This switch validates the integrity of the Layer 3 header via checksum. In addition, a Layer 3 switch also has security controls (similar to traditional routers). Layer 3 switches are becoming more and more popular on campus networks as they supercede traditional routers in the functionality, pricing, manageability, forwarding, and *Quality of Service* (QoS).

Case Studies: Widget Manufacturing

Widget Manufacturing recently decided to upgrade its network infrastructure. The existing network has had performance and availability problems as it has grown over the past two years. The network is comprised of 1,500 users who are located across a large manufacturing facility. Their current network infrastructure has been in place for almost seven years.

In this phase of the case study, we will identify the specifics of the LAN design. The information provided in the previous chapter was included to make the case study as whole as possible.

The network consists of 10Mb Ethernet that runs both Thinnet and Thicknet coaxial cable. The Thinnet cable is used to connect the users to hubs and repeaters. The Thicknet cable is used to connect the repeaters and hubs in order to form a routed internetwork. Figure 8-11 depicts the existing network.

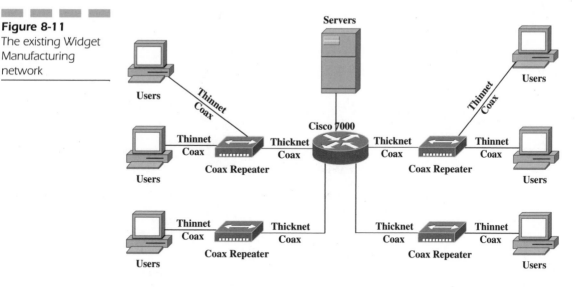

Figure 8-11
The existing Widget Manufacturing network

Remember from Chapter 5, "Documenting the Existing Network," that the total user count for the network was approximately 1,000. Also remember that Chapter 5 listed 500 users as the recommended maximum number of users in a broadcast domain. Because we have given many guidelines for network design, the design presented as follows is one of several designs that fit the customer's requirements.

The suggested design possibility is a complete overhaul of the existing cable plant, as well as the networking equipment. Figure 8-12 represents the new network design.

All of the legacy hubs are slated for replacement with 10/100 switches. Depending on the number of users at each location, these could be either high-capacity Catalyst 6000 enterprise switches or Catalyst 2900XL workgroup switches. The uplinks to the Catalyst 6000 Core switch/router are listed as 100MB fiber. Instead of 100MB fiber, however, you could use Gigabit Ethernet fiber as well.

NOTE: *The choice of backbone fiber between 100MB and Gigabit Ethernet is difficult to make. 100MB fiber tends to be less expensive (but not significantly so). Gigabit Ethernet, on the other hand, is more expensive but also 10 times the speed.*

Figure 8-12
The new Widget
Manufacturing
network design

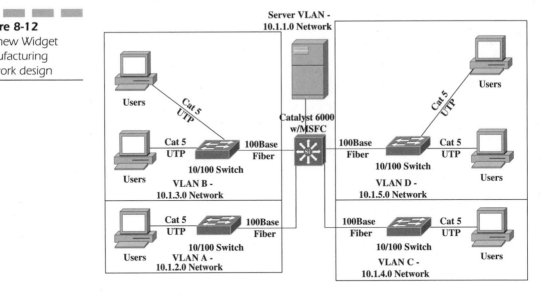

The core switch is a Catalyst 6000 with a multi-function switch card. This card is a daughter card that connects to the supervisor module of the Catalyst 6000. This card performs all routing between the VLANs. This situation is an example of using a wire-speed layer 3 device at the distribution layer in order to connect access layers. This device replaces the existing Cisco 7000 and provides the same broadcast domain separation as the Cisco 7000.

SUMMARY

This chapter covers the LAN design of a campus network. This chapter also details data-link layer technologies such as Ethernet, Fast Ethernet, Token Ring, FDDI, and Gigabit Ethernet. We also covered collision domains, broadcast domains, and the 80/20 design rule for small and medium-sized networks.

The LAN design of a network is simply a small portion of a much larger project. In the case study earlier, however, a replacement of the cable plant and the networking equipment is the complete project. Only the LAN design is required. The existing VLANs mirror the old network structure.

Next, we will discuss WAN design and other network-design topics. These remaining topics will flush out the remaining parts of a complete network-design project.

QUESTIONS

1. Which of the following statements hold true for an Ethernet repeater?

   a. Repeaters are shared-medium devices.
   b. Repeaters can operate at full duplex.
   c. Repeaters cannot operate at full duplex.
   d. Repeaters can operate at Gigabit Ethernet speeds.

2. You have recently migrated a client to Fast Ethernet from Ethernet. What is the disadvantage that could be of prime concern to the client?

   a. Manageability is difficult.
   b. Operation cost is high.
   c. Physical distances are reduced.
   d. Technology is not scalable.

3. What is the distance over which a half-duplex fiber ISL can stretch?

   a. 2500 m
   b. 200 m
   c. 400 m
   d. 100 m

4. What is the distance over which a full-duplex fiber ISL can stretch?

   a. 2000 m
   b. 500 m
   c. 1000 m
   d. 250 m

5. In a network design that has high network bandwidth requirements, on what area of network design would you focus more of your attention?

   a. Network protocols
   b. Network media
   c. Network management
   d. Network documentation

6. When is a Token Ring station allowed to transmit data?

 a. After forming a packet

 b. After it has received a token

 c. After it has received data from another Token Ring station

 d. When there are multiple tokens on the ring

7. To interconnect 4Mbps and 16Mbps Token Rings, which of the following can you use? (Choose all correct answers.)

 a. Router

 b. MSAU

 c. Hub

 d. Bridge

8. Collisions are common on the Token Ring network (True or False?).

 a. True

 b. False

9. Wiring concentrators in a Token Ring network are known as:

 a. Hub

 b. *Multistation Access Unit* (MSAU)

 c. Token Ring router

 d. Concentrators

10. What is the IEEE specification for Gigabit Ethernet?

 a. IEEE 802.3

 b. IEEE 802.5z

 c. IEEE 802.3z

 d. IEEE 802.2

11. Which of the following are FDDI devices?

 a. Dual-node station

 b. Concentrator

 c. LAN extender

 d. *Single Access Station* (SAS)

 e. *Dual Access Station* (DAS)

12. A collision is said to have occurred when:

    a. A station senses the state of the medium and determines that it is idle.

    b. Two stations in the same collision domain receive data at the same time.

    c. Two stations in different collision domains transmit data at the same time.

    d. Two stations in the same collision domain transmit data at the same time.

13. Which of the following statements hold true for routers? (Choose all that apply.)

    a. They interconnect different broadcast domains.

    b. They are necessary so that broadcasts from each broadcast domain can be flooded across VLANs or LANs.

    c. Routers operate at layer 2 and layer 3 of the OSI layer.

    d. They maintain a routing table for each routing protocol.

    e. Their forwarding architecture is hardware based.

14. Which of the following statements is true for an Ethernet network?

    a. You have a problem if the network utilization is higher than 10 percent.

    b. You have a problem if the network utilization is higher than 40 percent.

    c. The collisions should not be greater than 5 percent over a period.

    d. There is no performance hit in a network segment because of collisions.

    e. Collisions occur across bridges.

15. Which of the following statements is not true for the 5-4-3 design rule?

    a. The maximum number of segments is five.

    b. The maximum number of repeater/hubs is five.

    c. The maximum number of populated segments is three.

    d. The maximum number of repeaters is four.

NOTE: *Some of the case studies that we have covered thus far do not have any LAN components. These case studies are the Limbo Medical Group, the Global Supplies Corporation, and G & S Productions.*

Case Study: The Bank of Pompeii

The Bank of Pompeii has just completed a new corporate office tower in a prime downtown location. This location will enable the bank to consolidate six small offices into the new corporate tower. In addition to this move, all of the SNA traffic will be removed from the WAN.

All of the offices are connected via a Frame Relay WAN in a hub-and-spoke configuration. The hub of the Frame Relay network will be the new corporate tower. The remainder of the offices will remain on the Frame Relay network.

As the new offices are moved to the corporate tower, they will be connected to the newly designed Gigabit backbone. The existing branch networks are shared 10Mb Ethernet. They will be converted to a switched 100Mb Fast Ethernet LAN. After the conversion, all network traffic will involve IP-based protocols. The only applications in use are e-mail and a Telnet-based bank application.

16. The Gigabit solution that has been chosen will require what type of physical media?

   a. UTP

   b. STP

   c. Coax

   d. Fiber-optic

17. With the information given, what additional information is required to accurately design the networking components?

   a. Routing protocol

   b. User counts

   c. Protocols in use

18. Why would a Token Ring implementation not be advisable?

   a. The existing staff members are not experienced with Token Ring, but they do know Ethernet.

   b. Token Ring is slower than Ethernet.

   c. Token Ring is a collision-based technology.

   d. It is prone to errors.

19. What technology will be used for the backbone?

   a. Fast Ethernet

   b. Ethernet

   c. FDDI

   d. Gigabit Ethernet

20. What would be the most logical way to configure the networks of the six small offices that have been consolidated?

   a. A flat network with new IP addresses

   b. A flat network with existing IP addresses

   c. A routed VLAN network with new IP addresses

   d. A routed VLAN network with existing IP addresses

ANSWERS

1. a. and **c.** Repeaters are shared-medium devices, and they cannot operate at full duplex.

Repeaters simply repeat a signal along a shared medium. Repeaters cannot operate at full duplex, because full-duplex operations remove collision detection. Collision detection is required for a shared medium.

2. b. Physical distances are reduced.

Because Fast Ethernet is 10 times faster and uses the same operation, the distances are reduced tenfold.

3. c. 400 m

The maximum length for 100MB Fast Ethernet operating in half-duplex is 400m.

4. a. 2 km

The maximum length for 100MB Fast Ethernet operating in full duplex is 2 km.

5. b. Network media

The speed of the network is solely based on the media type.

6. b. After it has received a token

For any Token Ring station to transmit data, it must possess an empty token.

7. a. and **d.** Bridge and router

Of the listed devices, only bridges and routers can connect rings of various speeds.

8. b. False

Due to its deterministic nature, a Token Ring network can never have collisions.

9. b. *Multistation Access Unit* (MSAU)

An MSAU is a basic connectivity device, like a hub, for Token Ring networks.

10. c. IEEE 802.3z

IEEE 802.3 is the Ethernet Standards committee. The 802.3z is responsible for Gigabit Ethernet. IEEE 802.5 is the Token Ring committee.

11. b., d., and **e.** Concentrator, *Single Attached Station* (SAS), *Dual Attached Station* (DAS)

Concentrators are like hubs for FDDI networks. SASes are devices that connect to concentrators. DASes are connected to the main ring, not to concentrators.

12. d. Two stations in the same collision domain transmit data at the same time.

When two stations in the same collision domain transmit data at the same instance, a collision will occur and will force the stations to resend.

13. a. and **d.** To interconnect different broadcast domains, maintain a routing table for each routing protocol.

Routers connect broadcast domains and networks. In addition, in order to perform their job, routers have router tables that enable them to pass traffic from network to network.

14. c. The collisions should not be greater than 5 percent over a period.

Collisions should not be great than 1 percent on average and 5 percent over a short period.

15. b. The maximum number of repeater/hubs is five.

The rules are as follows:

Maximum of five segments

Maximum of four repeaters/hubs

Maximum of three populated segments

16. d. Fiber

The Gigabit backbone will be a fiber backbone. While copper is possible, it is preferable to use fiber for backbone links.

17. b. User counts

The user counts of the various networks is required so that the designer can appropriately size the networking equipment.

18. **c.** The existing staff members are not experienced with Token Ring, but they do know Ethernet.

    The primary reason for not implementing Token Ring in this environment would be because of the knowledge of the existing staff. The staff members are familiar with Ethernet, so changing layer 2 technologies would not be advisable.

19. **d.** Gigabit Ethernet

    The passage states that the backbone will be Gigabit Ethernet.

20. **d.** A routed VLAN network with existing IP addresses

    The most logical way to design the network is to keep the new network as similar as possible to the old network. By keeping each office on its own network and VLAN, almost no changes will take place in the end-user devices.

LAN TERMS DEFINED ▬ ▬ ▬ ▬ ▬ ▬ ▬

Cyclic Redundancy Check (CRC)

The field in the packet that the receiver checks for any errors

Multistation Access Unit (MAU)

MAUs are the wiring concentrator units for Token Ring network. MAU is responsible for the actual physical and electrical interface to and from the medium. MAU is a central hub in a Token Ring LAN.

Routing Information Field (RIF)

Part of a Token Ring frame that dictates how the frame should proceed through the Token Ring bridged network

Twisted Pair

Twisted pair is a thin-diameter wire commonly used for telephone and network cabling. The wires are twisted around each other in order to minimize interference. The following table defines the categories of twisted pair:

Category	Cable Type	Application
1	UTP	Analog Voice
2	UTP	Digital Voice, 4Mbps data
3	UTP, STP	16Mbps data
4	UTP, STP	20Mbps data
5	UTP, STP	100Mbps data

Unshielded Twisted Pair (UTP)

UTP is the most commonly used four-pair wire medium for LANs.

Shielded Twisted Pair (STP)

STP is a two-pair wiring medium that has a layer of metal sheath to eliminate external interference.

Ethernet

The most widely used LAN technology, Ethernet was originally developed by the Xerox Corporation and was then developed by Xerox, DEC, and Intel. Ethernet was later formulated into the IEEE 802.3 standard.

Fast Ethernet

Based on the IEEE 802.3 standard, Fast Ethernet is a LAN technology that provides a data rate of 100 megabits per second.

Token Ring

Based on the IEEE 802.5 standard, Token Ring is LAN technology in which all of the network devices are connected in a ring format. IBM conducted the initial development of Token Ring.

Gigabit Ethernet

Gigabit Ethernet has been defined in the IEEE 802.3z standard and provides a data rate of 1000 megabits per second.

Fiber Distributed Data Interface (FDDI)

FDDI is a LAN access method that has been standardized by ANSI. FDDI provides data rates of 100 megabits per second.

Copper Distributed Data Interface (CDDI)

CDDI is an implementation of FDDI over UTP and STP cabling. CDDI works well at short distances (about 100 m).

10Base2

10Base2 is a thinwire coaxial cable with a maximum segment length of 185 meters and supports a data rate of 10Mbps.

10Base5

10Base5 is a thickwire coaxial cable with a maximum segment length of 500 meters and supports a data rate of 10Mbps.

10BaseT

10BaseT is an Ethernet standard that uses twisted-pair cables. 10BaseT is most widely used in campus LANs due to its lower cost and flexibility.

10BaseF

10BaseF is an Ethernet standard that uses optical fibers and provides a maximum segment length from 500 m to 2000 m.

Fiber-Optic Inter-Repeater Link (FOIRL)

FOIRL is an IEEE standard for fiber-optic Ethernet. FOIRL is a standard that is generally used to extend a backbone beyond the 328-foot limitation of 10BaseT.

100BaseT

100BaseT is a derivative of Ethernet that offers high speeds. 100BaseT provides a data rate of 100Mbps and is 10 times faster than Ethernet. 100BaseT is defined in the IEEE 802.3u standard.

100BaseFX

100BaseFX is a 100BaseT or Fast Ethernet specification that uses two strands of multi-mode fiber-optic cable per link.

100Base-T4

This specification of Fast Ethernet uses four pairs of Category 3, 4, or 5 UTP cable.

100BaseTX

This specification of Fast Ethernet uses two pairs of either UTP or STP cabling.

Source Route Bridging (SRB)

Source Route Bridging (SRB) is used to connect two or more Token Ring networks via bridges.

Source Route/Translational Bridging (SR/TLB)

SR/TLB is configured on bridges to enable communication between Ethernet and Token Ring hosts.

Inter-Switch Link (ISL)

ISL is a Cisco proprietary protocol that is used to maintain VLAN information between switches and routers.

American National Standards Institute (ANSI)

ANSI is a voluntary organization that coordinates standards-related activities in the United States.

High-Speed Token Ring (HSTR)

HSTR is an emerging technology that will provide data rates of 100Mbps on a Token Ring network.

Broadcast Domain

A broadcast domain is formed by a collection of network devices that share the same Ethernet segment. These are also known as bandwidth domains.

Collision Domain

Every broadcast domain consists of a number of collision domains that are separated by the use of either switches or bridges.

Data Terminal Equipment (DTE)

DTE is a device at the customer premises that controls data flowing to and from the network. A modem, for example, is a DTE.

Remote Monitoring (RMON)

Remote monitoring is a standard monitoring specification that enables various network monitors and console systems to exchange network-monitoring data. RMON can be used for network monitoring, troubleshooting problems, and reporting.

Webliography

Sales Tools Central—Tools Central:
`http://www.cisco.com/warp/public/779/smbiz/service/tools/index.html`
March 2000

Sales Tools Central—Product Central:
`http://www.cisco.com/warp/public/779/smbiz/service/pindex.html`
March 2000

Find a Product:
`http://www.cisco.com/pcgi-bin/front.x/corona/prodtool/select.pl`
March 2000

Designing Wide Area Networks (WANs)

Objectives Covered in This Chapter

1. Scalability constraints and issues for standard WAN technologies and performance budgets

2. Defining WAN and identifying the layers of the *Open Systems Interconnectivity* (OSI) reference model at which the WAN technologies operate

3. Defining and describing the operation of point-to-point, circuit-switched, and packet-switched links through a WAN

4. Defining PVC and SVC and identifying the key differences between them

5. Describing the operation of the DDR and dial-backup WAN implementations

6. Identifying and describing the basic functions of the devices that are commonly found in WANs

Introduction

With the *Local Area Network* (LAN) design complete, the next task is to design the WAN. Many of the concepts that were covered in the LAN design chapter do not apply to WANs, however. In general, the protocols and technologies are completely different in the WAN arena. The average link speed is generally slower on WANs than on LANs. The theoretical maximum speed of a WAN is greater than the maximum speed of a LAN, however. This statement might seem like an incorrect assumption; however, you should remember that the fastest LAN speed is currently 1 *gigabit per second* (Gbps) with Gigabit Ethernet. The fastest WAN circuit in operation is an OC-192, which is approximately 10Gbps.

WAN Circuits

There are two general types of WAN circuits: switched and permanent. Some WAN technologies fall within only one of these classifications. Other WAN technologies can be classified as both switched circuits and permanent circuits. These technologies—specifically Frame Relay and *Asynchronous Transfer Mode* (ATM)—are hybrid technologies. In general, there is not a preferred type of circuit. Both permanent and switched circuits have specific advantages and disadvantages.

Switched Circuits

Switched circuits are circuits that are set up when necessary and are disconnected when they are no longer needed. There are two primary types of switched circuits: analog circuits, which are also called *Plain Old Telephone Service* (POTS) lines, and ISDN circuits.

Analog   This circuit is the most common type of circuit that is in use today across the world. This circuit is a simple phone line—a single pair of copper wires that carries voice traffic in an analog, or non-digital, format. All call setup information is transmitted over the same line or channel as the voice traffic.

Call setup begins when the phone is lifted from the cradle. This action sends an off-hook signal to the central office. The central office is the phone company's local office that provides residential and business connections for a specific area. A central office is typically comprised of telephone switches and batteries. When the central office receives the off-hook signal, it provides a dial tone to the phone. Then, the numbers on the phone can be dialed. By pressing a number on the phone, a tone is generated. The central office recognizes these tones as call setup information. The office takes the call setup request and routes the call to the appropriate destination.

The area code and exchange of the phone number help these telephone switches route the call through the *Public Switched Telephone Network* (PSTN). For example, many years ago, all area codes had either a one or a zero as the second digit. No other local exchange had these numbers for a second digit. This situation enabled the central office switch to quickly determine whether a call was going to be a long-distance call by the time the second digit was dialed. If a long-distance call was being made, then an outbound long-distance trunk could be reserved for the call.

NOTE: *This description is a simplification of the process that is used to route calls through the PSTN. Signaling System 7 (SS7) is a complex protocol that enables calls to be quickly routed through the PSTN. In addition, SS7 enables additional phone services such as Caller ID, call return, and other services.*

Data is transmitted over analog lines via modems. Modems modulate a digital signal from a computer onto the analog line. Then, the other side of the connection demodulates the analog signal into a digital format for the receiving device. Analog modems are generally used for the following applications:

1. Dial-in access for telecommuters and mobile users (this application is depicted in Figure 9-1)

2. A backup for another type of circuit

NOTE: *Another popular application of analog lines is for out-of-band connections to routers. The auxiliary port of a router can be connected to an analog modem. With this connection, maintenance and troubleshooting can be performed on a remote router regardless of the WAN's circuit status.*

ISDN   ISDN was positioned as a replacement for standard analog phones. ISDN is a digital service that provides two separate channels for information. A third channel is used to carry signaling infor-

Figure 9-1
Analog modem connections for a telecommuter

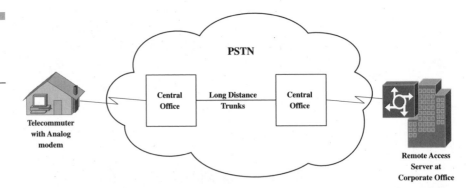

mation from the dialing station to the central office. Like analog calls, all ISDN calls are switched through the same PSTN.

There are two varieties of ISDN: basic rate and primary rate. There are respectively referred to as BRI and PRI. They are essentially the same, with the exception of maximum capacity. A BRI ISDN circuit is comprised of two data (or B) channels and one signaling (or D) channel. The B channels are also called bearer channels. Each B channel is 64 *kilobites* (Kb), and the D channel is 16Kb. This configuration is generally noted as 2B+1D.

An ISDN PRI circuit in North America is comprised of 23 B channels and 1 D channel. Each B channel can transmit 64Kb of data. The D channel is increased in size to 64Kb, however. This configuration is noted as 23B+1D.

Data is transmitted over ISDN lines with terminal adapters or routers. These devices simply set up a call over the D channel to another ISDN device. This device receives the setup call on its D channel and establishes the circuit. Then, authentication data is passed over the B channels. If this authentication fails, the circuit is disconnected via D-channel signaling. If the authentication is successful, data continues to pass along the B channels. ISDN circuits are generally used for the following applications:

1. Dial-in access for telecommuters where increased speed is required. This application is identical to the analog connection that is depicted in Figure 9-1. The only difference would be that the telecommuter would be using an ISDN terminal adapter or router.

2. A backup for another type of circuit

ISDN Configuration Examples   The following configuration examples will help the network designer understand the topics that we discussed in the previous section. The first example, depicted in Figure 9-2, is a basic ISDN BRI connection between two sites. Following the figure are the configurations for each router. No special authentication or configuration commands are used.

```
Trafalger Router Config
hostname Trafalger
!
```

```
!
isdn switch-type basic-ni1
!
interface BRI0
 ip address 172.16.2.1 255.255.255.0
 dialer string 18185559830
 dialer-group 1
 isdn spid1 81855589640101
 isdn spid2 81855589680101
!
interface Ethernet0
 ip address 172.16.1.1 255.255.255.0
!
ip classless
!
dialer-list 1 protocol ip permit

Midway Router Config
hostname France
!
!
isdn switch-type basic-ni1
!

interface BRI0
 ip address 172.16.2.2 255.255.255.0
 dialer string 18185558964
 dialer-group 1
 isdn spid1 81855598300101
 isdn spid2 81855598340101
!
interface Ethernet0
 ip address 172.16.4.1 255.255.255.0
!
ip classless
!
dialer-list 1 protocol ip permit
```

Figure 9-2
ISDN BRI
configuration
example

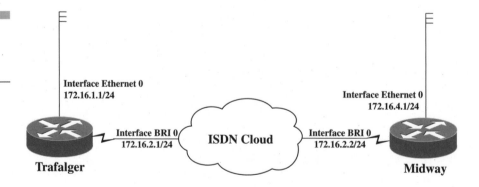

Interface Ethernet 0
172.16.1.1/24

Interface Ethernet 0
172.16.4.1/24

Interface BRI 0
172.16.2.1/24

ISDN Cloud

Interface BRI 0
172.16.2.2/24

Trafalger

Midway

NOTE: *Throughout this chapter, the configurations are used as examples only. They are not part of the CCDA exam.*

The next ISDN configuration example shows a primary-rate interface, or ISDN PRI. This example shows the possible configuration of an AS5200 that has two PRI lines connected to it. Figure 9-3 shows how the access server is connected to the remote user and to the network. The configuration for the access server follows the figure.

```
Trafalger Router Configuration
hostname trafalger
!
username erik password cisco
ip subnet-zero
async-bootp dns-server 172.16.128.2 172.16.128.1
async-bootp nbns-server 172.16.128.2 172.16.128.1
isdn switch-type primary-5ess
!
!
controller T1 0
 framing esf
 clock source line primary
 linecode b8zs
 pri-group timeslots 1-24
!
controller T1 1
 framing esf
 clock source line secondary
 linecode b8zs
```

Figure 9-3
ISDN PRI
configuration
example

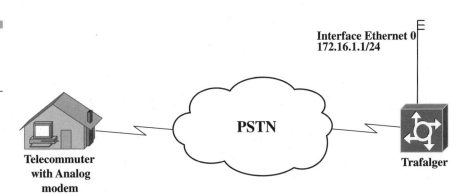

Interface Ethernet 0
172.16.1.1/24

PSTN

Telecommuter
with Analog
modem

Trafalger

```
  pri-group timeslots 1-24
 !
interface Loopback0
 ip address 10.10.10.1 255.255.255.0
 !
interface Ethernet0
 ip address 172.16.1.1 255.255.255.0
 !
interface Serial0:23
  ip unnumbered Ethernet0
 encapsulation ppp
 no ip route-cache
 dialer-group 1
 isdn switch-type primary-5ess
ppp authentication chap
 !
interface Serial1:23
 ip unnumbered Ethernet0
 encapsulation ppp
 no ip route-cache
 dialer-group 1
 isdn switch-type primary-5ess
ppp authentication pap chap
 !
interface Group-Async1
 ip unnumbered Ethernet0
 encapsulation ppp
 no ip route-cache
 no ip mroute-cache
 async mode interactive
ppp authentication chap pap
 group-range 1 48
 !
```

Permanent   Permanent circuits are circuits that are always active. Unlike switched circuits, permanent circuits do not require any signaling in order to set up a call to a destination. The connection must be in place and active; otherwise, no connection to the destination will occur. There is only one type of WAN circuit that is strictly permanent in nature: the leased line.

Leased Lines   A leased line is a circuit that is purchased from a service provider. The circuit begins at point A and ends at point B. This circuit is always active. Any data that leaves the router's connection to the leased line is transmitted through the service provider's network to the router at the other end. This circuit is also called a point-

Figure 9-4
A typical leased-line
WAN

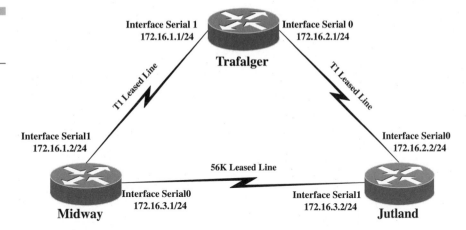

to-point circuit. Refer to Figure 9-2 to see a typical WAN that consists of leased lines.

The leased lines in Figure 9-4 have different speeds because the cost for leased lines is based on two factors: circuit speed and distance. The longer the distance, the greater the cost. This factor makes many long leased lines extraordinarily expensive and therefore rarely used. Following the figure are the configurations for each router.

```
Trafalgar Router Config

interface Serial0
 ip address 172.16.2.1 255.255.255.0
!
interface Serial1
 ip address 172.16.1.1 255.255.255.0
!

Jutland Router Config
interface Serial0
 ip address 172.16.2.2 255.255.255.0
!
interface Serial1
 ip address 172.16.3.2 255.255.255.0
 bandwidth 56
!

Midway Router Config
interface Serial0
```

```
 ip address 172.16.3.1 255.255.255.0
 bandwidth 56
!
interface Serial1
 ip address 172.16.1.2 255.255.255.0
!
```

Leased-line circuits are generally used in the following applications:

1. For a main WAN connection for two offices or a series of offices in a hub-and-spoke topology

2. As a backup for another type of circuit

Hybrid A hybrid WAN technology can exist as either permanent circuits or switched circuits, depending on the implementation. Rarely will a WAN be comprised of a hybrid technology that is acting in both permanent and switched capacities. The switched implementations of the following WAN technologies are used; however, the permanent circuit implementation is generally the more common. The reason is because most WANs are operated across service providers' networks. Even in the year 2000, most WAN service providers do not sell switched WAN services. There is no method available to price and account for the usage of these switched services. The three most commonly used WAN hybrid technologies are X.25, Frame Relay, and ATM.

X.25 X.25 is an older WAN technology. Although it is old, it is still in use throughout the world. X.25 is a WAN transport that provides a reliable transmission of packets. This reliability is an error-checking sequence that is built into X.25. As data moves from device to device, each packet is error checked and sequenced. If a packet is corrupt or is not received, the destined X.25 device requests retransmission of the missing or corrupt packet. In addition, X.25 is required in order to support many legacy applications. An X.25 network is depicted in Figure 9-5.

While this built-in error correction and the resulting reliability might seem to be a benefit, in actuality it slows the transmission of data when the data is sent over error-free links. Most links in North America are fiber optic and can be considered error free. In this situation, there is no reason for the added overhead that X.25 requires.

Figure 9-5
A typical X.25 WAN

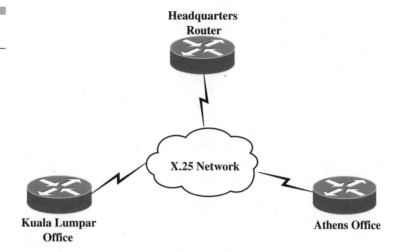

In many countries across the world, however, all data is passed over old copper lines. There might be an excessive amount of errors on these lines. In this scenario, X.25 will ensure that each packet is transmitted correctly from node to node—regardless of the errors on the circuit.

X.25 circuits are generally used for the following applications:

1. A reliable WAN backbone
2. Legacy application support

Frame Relay Frame Relay is a WAN technology that removes the overhead of X.25 and also provides a more cost-effective solution than leased lines for long-distance connections. Frame Relay networks are comprised of edge devices, routers (which connect to core devices), and Frame Relay switches. The routers send data to the Frame Relay switch. This switch then passes the data to other Frame Relay switches in the service provider's network until the destination router is reached. In some cases, it might be on the same Frame Relay switch; in other cases, it might have to traverse across the country.

Frame Relay is an unreliable WAN transport. Frame Relay provides best-effort services to all packets that traverse the network. It might be necessary to drop a packet because a specific Frame Relay switch is over-utilized. In this case, the sending device is responsible for resending the packet. This principle makes Frame Relay less reliable, but much faster. In Frame Relay, there are no inherent error-correction mechanisms. Packets are sent to the destination device. If errors are present, then the packet is dropped. Frame Relay relies on upper-layer protocols such as the *Transmission Control Protocol* (TCP) in order to initiate the retransmission of the missing packets.

The cost-effectiveness of Frame Relay is that a service provider can sell the use of the same Frame Relay switches to many customers. While leased lines use dedicated equipment, Frame Relay equipment is shared among the subscribers. This feature drastically lowers the cost of long Frame Relay circuits. A typical Frame Relay WAN is shown in Figure 9-6. The concept is exactly the same as X.25. A packet enters the Frame Relay cloud, moves through the cloud, and then exits at the destination.

While Figure 9-6 depicts the logical view of a Frame Relay network, there are several key items that have been omitted: the DLCI and the network address. Figure 9-7 depicts a more design-oriented diagram that includes this information. Following the figure are the

Figure 9-6
A typical Frame
Relay WAN

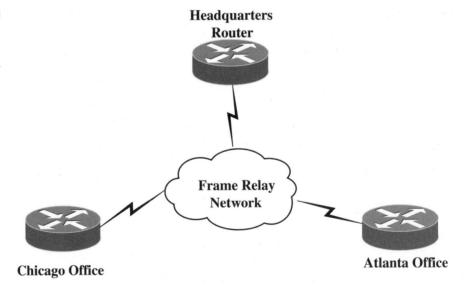

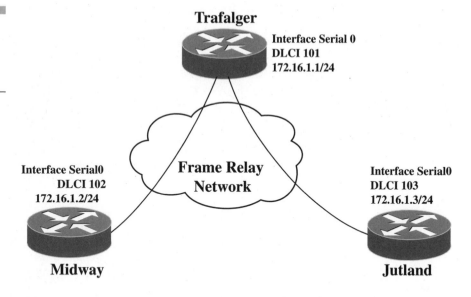

configurations for the routers.

```
Trafalgar Router Config

hostname Trafalger
interface Serial0
 ip address 172.16.1.1 255.255.255.0
 encapsulation frame-relay

Midway Router Config
hostname Midway
interface Serial0
 ip address 172.16.1.2 255.255.255.0
 encapsulation frame-relay

Jutland Router Config
hostname Jutland
interface Serial0
 ip address 172.16.1.3 255.255.255.0
 encapsulation frame-relay
```

Frame Relay circuits are generally used for the following applications:

1. High-speed WAN backbones
2. Low-cost long-distance WAN circuits

Asynchronous Transfer Mode (ATM) ATM is the most recently developed of all of the WAN technologies that we have discussed thus far. Because of its modernity, ATM is also the fastest and the most complex. ATM, unlike all of the previous technologies, uses fixed-length cells to transmit data instead of variable-length packets. This feature enables ATM devices to quickly pass traffic from source to destination.

Another feature of ATM is its capability to handle various types of traffic. ATM is capable of sending data, voice, and video across the same circuit. With the increase in network traffic, this flexibility is becoming increasingly important. In addition to this functionality, ATM enables a specific *quality of service* (QoS) to be associated with each traffic type. This feature enables voice traffic to reach its destination with little or no delay or jitter. On the other hand, data traffic—which can tolerate delay and jitter—uses bandwidth as it becomes available. Like Frame Relay, ATM is an unreliable transport mechanism. It will discard cells if an ATM switch is overloaded. Again, like a Frame Relay network, the upper-layer protocols will request retransmission of the missing information. A typical ATM WAN is shown in Figure 9-8. The concept is exactly the same as X.25

Figure 9-8
A typical ATM WAN

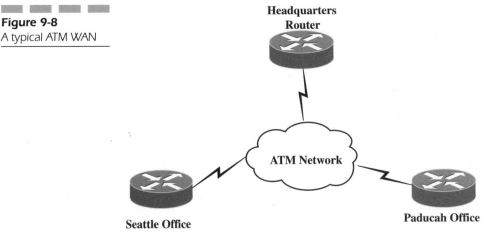

and Frame Relay. A cell enters the ATM cloud, moves through the cloud, and then exits at the destination.

ATM circuits are generally used for the following applications:

1. Very high-speed WAN backbones
2. Support for the simultaneous transmission of data, voice, and video

Circuit Provisioning Now that we have briefly explained the WAN technologies, the next step toward familiarization with WAN technologies is learning some of the terms and processes that are involved in actually ordering or provisioning a circuit. All circuit speeds are based on digital hierarchies. Once the speed and other characteristics have been determined, questions still remain about provisioning the circuit.

Digital Hierarchies WAN circuits and their associated speeds are based on digital hierarchies. A digital hierarchy is a group of WAN circuits where higher-speed circuits are actually comprised of multiple lower-rate circuits. The original North American digital hierarchy was the T Carrier system. The SONET digital hierarchy used today is based in part on the T Carrier system.

These hierarchies, which vary throughout the world, are roughly the same. All of these hierarchies are comprised of the same basic unit: the 64Kbps DS0. The DS stands for digital stream. T1s, DS1s, and DS3s are part of the North American digital hierarchy. E1s and E3s are part of the European digital hierarchy. Table 9-1 details some major components of digital hierarchies:

Table 9-1

Digital hierarchy circuit comparison

Circuit Type	Number of DS0s	Speed
DS0	n/a	64Kbps
DS1	24	1.544Mbps
DS3	672	44.736Mbps
E1	30	2.048Mbps
E3	480	34.064Mbps

In addition, higher-speed circuits that run over optical cables make up the SONET hierarchy of North America and the SDH hierarchy of Europe. Both systems are comprised of optical circuits (such as an OC-48). In the SONET system, an OC-48 optical signal is converted into a STS-48 electrical signal for processing. In the SDH system, the same OC-48 is converted into an STM-16 electrical signal for processing. See Table 9-2.

Provisioning Questions Answered   Provisioning a circuit can be a daunting task. There will be numerous questions that, if unfamiliar, can cause a network designer many lost hours. In the following section, only provisioning choices for 1.544Mbps DS1 circuits, T1s, will be covered. Other circuit speeds have similar choices.

DS1 versus T1   The first issue is what to call the circuit in question. The name T1 refers simply to the physical standards of the line. The signal itself, however, should be referred to as a DS1. It would be appropriate to say that a DS1 rides across a T1 line. Many in the industry still refer to these circuits as T1s.

Table 9-2

SONET and SDH comparisons

Optical Level	Electrical Level	Line Rate (Mbps)	SDH Equivalent
OC-1	STS-1	51.840	—
OC-3	STS-3	155.520	STM-1
OC-9	STS-9	466.560	STM-3
OC-12	STS-12	622.080	STM-4
OC-18	STS-18	933.120	STM-6
OC-24	STS-24	1244.160	STM-8
OC-36	STS-36	1866.240	STM-12
OC-48	STS-48	2488.320	STM-16
OC-96	STS-96	4976.640	STM-32
OC-192	STS-192	9953.280	STM-64

Channelized versus Unchannelized   These two terms refer to the composition of the DS1 frame itself. If the circuit is channelized, then 24 individual 64Kbps DS0 channels make up the DS1. In other words, in each DS1 frame there are 24 separate 64Kbps conversations taking place. Also, no one conversation can use more than 64Kbps. This setup is the standard implementation when a DS1 is used for voice traffic.

An unchannelized DS1 frame enables any one conversation to use as much of the circuit as possible. This setup is the standard implementation when a DS1 is used for data traffic (see Figure 9-9).

Framing and Line Coding   These options are specified at the ordering of the DS1 circuit. If the circuit is a new circuit, then the designer should use an *Extended Super Frame* (ESF) for framing and *Bipolar 8-Bit Zero Substitution* (B8ZS) for line coding.

Frame Relay CIR and Port Speed   Determining the required bandwidth for a Frame Relay network can be challenging. Not only do the spoke circuits have to be sized, but also the hub circuit is more complex than the spoke networks. In addition, the port speed of each connection must be ordered.

The *Committed Information Rate* (CIR) is the guaranteed speed that a circuit will always have available. CIR is the throughput that the Frame Relay network provider will guarantee. The CIR is equivalent to the California Highway Department guaranteeing that traffic will always move at 35 mph. Service providers also add that this CIR guarantee is based on an average over a few seconds.

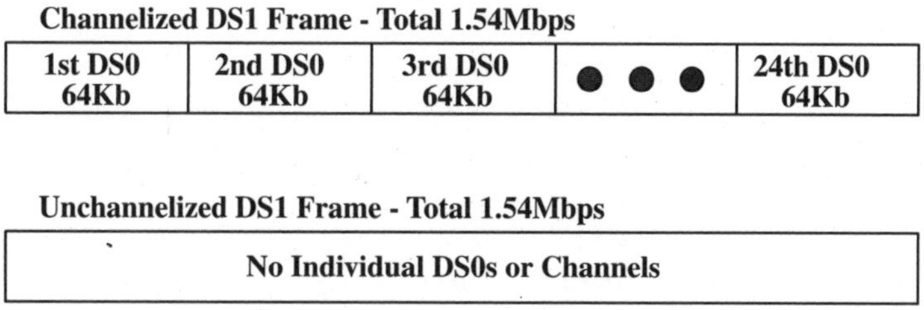

Figure 9-9
Channelized and
unchannelized DS1
frames

Channelized DS1 Frame - Total 1.54Mbps

1st DS0 64Kb	2nd DS0 64Kb	3rd DS0 64Kb	● ● ●	24th DS0 64Kb

Unchannelized DS1 Frame - Total 1.54Mbps

No Individual DS0s or Channels

The port speed or burst rate is the maximum amount of traffic that is provided. In most cases, the port speed is the actual speed of the circuit to the service provider. This amount, which is always equal to or greater than the CIR, can be used to move extra data across the Frame Relay network. Any traffic that is greater than the CIR, however, can be discarded by the Frame Relay network if there is excessive congestion on the Frame Relay backbone. In the same freeway analogy, the port speed would be the speed limit of 55 mph.

The steps toward provisioning a Frame Relay network are as follows:

1. Determine the CIR for the spoke networks. Based on the estimated utilization of a particular spoke office, the CIR should be sized in order to accommodate this traffic.

2. Determine the hub's CIR. Add the CIRs of all of the spokes. This total will determine the core bandwidth that is required at the hub site.

3. Determine the port speeds. The port speeds are based on price and required network bursts.

Platform Selection

Almost all routers that are in use today have some type of WAN connection. There are special instances of routers that do not have any type of WAN connections, but these situations are unusual. In general, there are four primary types of WAN connections: serial, integrated T1, ISDN, and auxiliary:

1. Serial ports are the primary WAN connection that is in use today. Almost all 2500 routers have a serial port. This serial port is connected to a CSU/DSU via a serial cable.

2. Integrated T1 ports are serial ports that have built-in CSU-DSUs. This feature enables the T1 or fractional T1 to be directly connected to the router.

3. ISDN ports can support either ISDN BRI or PRI circuits. They are not interchangeable. Depending on the port type, these ports

are connected to an NT1 or are directly connected to the ISDN network.

4. Auxiliary ports are connected to modems. This functionality enables users to dial into the router for access or enables the router to access other devices through this asynchronous connection.

Choosing the correct WAN connection can be quite difficult. First, there are numerous types of WAN modules. Next, these modules do not take the same type of cables. Even serial WAN connections use several different cable types. Finally, newer routers such as the 2600 and 3600 series use two types of interchangeable modules: WAN interface cards and network modules. These reasons make WAN platform selection more difficult that LAN platform selection.

Case Study

Widget Manufacturing has recently undergone some major corporate changes. The company has opened three separate manufacturing plants in order to increase the capacity of its existing facility. This drastic change has resulted in a new set of design requirements. The three additional sites are located as follows:

1. Two miles from the existing plant
2. In a neighboring city
3. On the opposite coast

The network staff of Widget Manufacturing has the following requirements for its WAN:

1. A permanent high-speed connection
2. A common WAN topology
3. Redundant WAN topology

By examining the WAN technologies in order, we can identify the right WAN solution for Widget Manufacturing:

- *Analog lines* By their very nature, analog lines are not persistent or reliable WAN connections. These circuits could be used for redundancy.

- *ISDN* These circuits are switched and are therefore not permanent. The redundancy that they offer for other circuits, however, will probably be required.

- *Leased lines* This option is a definite possibility. These are high-speed, permanent WAN circuits. The cost of a long-distance circuit will be excessive.

- *X.25* This option is a possibility. However, X.25 networks cannot reach high speeds.

- *ATM* This solution can also meet the requirements of the network staff. In general ATM is an expensive solution in terms of hardware and circuits.

- *Frame Relay* This solution is also a good possibility. This option meets the permanent high-speed requirement and can be effectively used in all locations.

For all of the listed requirements of Widget Manufacturing, the best WAN topology would be Frame Relay. Its low cost and its capabilities make it the best backbone technology for Widget Manufacturing. Also, in order to fulfill the redundant option of the requirements, some switched circuit would be required. That circuit choice would depend on the bandwidth that is required. If a fast Frame Relay circuit were used, the ISDN would be a suitable, redundant link. If the Frame Relay link were slow, however, an analog connection would be sufficient. Figure 9-10 depicts the new WAN of Widget Manufacturing.

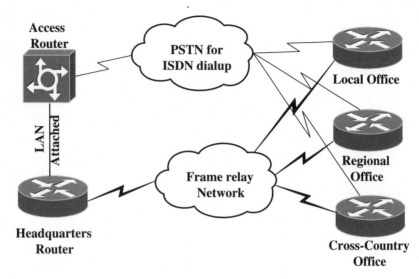

Figure 9-10
The proposed Widget
Manufacturing WAN

SUMMARY

WAN design is a difficult topic to condense into one chapter. The basic tenets that are required to design small to medium networks have been addressed. There were many technical details that were not covered in this text that will have a great impact on the final design of the WAN.

At this point in the design process, the LAN and the WAN designs are complete. New network maps have been drawn, and the equipment has been specified. The next step in the process is to determine the network addressing and naming specifications.

QUESTIONS ▦ ▦ ▦ ▦ ▦ ▦ ▦ ▦ ▦

Case Study: Limbo Medical Group

The Limbo Medical Group was on the cutting edge of network technology 10 years ago. It decided to implement a centralized computer system for all of its day-to-day operations. This system consists of an X.25 WAN that connects 50 small offices to a central hospital facility. This X.25 WAN carries legacy SNA traffic between hosts and a mainframe. Figure 9-11 is a representation of the existing network design.

Limbo Medical is now developing a new client/server application in order to replace this mainframe application. In addition, the legacy X.25 network will be replaced with a new network. The operations of the medical group run throughout the day. Any network down time would be detrimental to these operations. Therefore, the new network must be reliable and fault tolerant.

The new client/server application will be an IP-based application that is housed in an Oracle database. In order to keep client upgrades to a minimum, all client interaction will take place through a Web browser.

Figure 9-11
The existing Limbo
Medical network

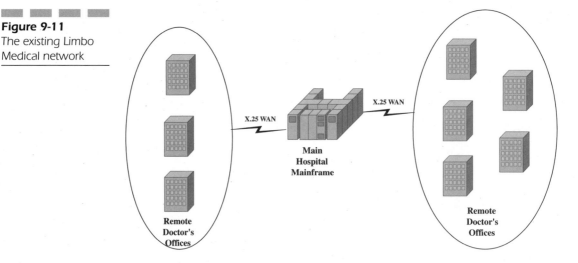

The *information technology* (IT) group of Limbo Medical realizes the need for the new application. Its focus, however, is on the new application. The staff is unsure of the network requirements. The idea for the new WAN was brought forward by a member of the Limbo LAN administration team. This project and concept has not yet been introduced to the executive management of Limbo Medical.

Performance of the new application is important to the Limbo IT group. The SNA application was sensitive to delays; therefore, the application response time was excellent. The LAN administrator is also concerned about security and manageability; however, he does not have any specific requirements.

1. What WAN technology would be a good fit for Limbo Medical?
   a. ATM
   b. Analog
   c. ISDN
   d. Frame Relay

2. Which of the following requirements is a basis for an ISDN DDR connection?
   a. Security
   b. Availability
   c. Manageability
   d. Throughput

3. What type of ISDN circuit would be used at the remote offices for DDR?
   a. BRI
   b. PRI
   c. 2B
   d. 23B

4. What type of DS circuit is comprised of 24 discrete DS0s?
   a. Channelized
   b. Unchannelized
   c. Bundled
   d. Unbundled

Case Study: Global Supplies Corporation

Global Supplies is a multi-national corporation that is comprised of approximately 15 separate facilities throughout North America. Each facility has an existing LAN that has been upgraded according to the needs of the specific facility. The LANs range from small 10Mb Ethernet networks to large Fast Ethernet networks with Gigabit backbones. Each LAN is administered by a department that does not normally interact with the corporate IT group.

The concern of the corporate IT group of Global Supplies is the WAN. The existing WAN is comprised of only leased lines. At least two leased lines connect each office to another office. In some cases, an individual office is connected via leased lines to three or four other offices. The multiple links ensure that the quickest path to the destination is selected and also ensure redundancy. The new WAN infrastructure must continue to support both voice and data traffic. The existing voice equipment cannot be changed at this time, however. Figure 9-12 shows a depiction of the existing network.

Currently, the only protocols that are in use across the WAN are IP, IPX, and SNA. SNA is used by some of the organizations for legacy mainframe connectivity. The existing leased lines are configured to use half of the bandwidth for voice and the other half for data. This split is performed by a multiplexer.

Figure 9-12
The existing Global Supplies Corporation network

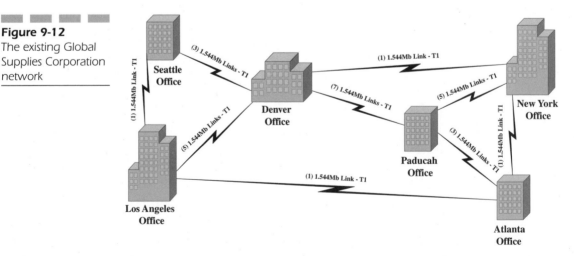

The IT department is concerned about monitoring the health and state of the network at all times. Because its responsibility is inter-company communication, the WAN must be up and error free.

A new application—a distance-learning application—has the most bandwidth requirements. This training is delivered in the form of intranet-based, streaming media presentations. It is imperative that this training be delivered in a timely manner.

5. What WAN technology can support the requirements of Global Supplies?
   a. Gigabit Ethernet
   b. X.25
   c. ATM
   d. Frame Relay

6. What feature enables voice traffic to be prioritized over an ATM circuit?
   a. *Virtual Private Network* (VPN)
   b. *Quality of Service* (QoS)
   c. NAT
   d. Traffic shaping

7. The disadvantage of proposing an ATM solution is:
   a. Scalability
   b. Fault tolerance
   c. Ease of installation
   d. Speed

Case Study: G&S Productions

Gimball Productions and Shapiro Productions have recently merged. The new company, G&S Productions, has become a major commercial production company. There are two main sites, each having about 250 users. In addition, each company has three to five smaller offices throughout the United States.

The two companies currently use an ISDN dialup connection in order to pass only e-mail traffic between each other. The e-mail server is a Windows NT-based system. The main company sites each

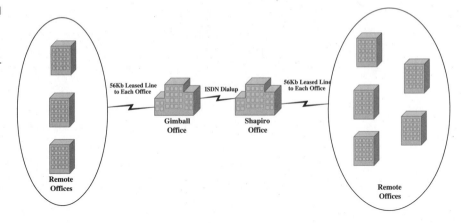

Figure 9-13
The existing G&S
Productions network

use leased lines to connect to the remote offices. The leased lines are only 56KB circuits. Figure 9-13 depicts the G&S Productions network after the merger.

The requirement from the newly formed IT department is to build a reliable, cost-effective WAN that will start the integration of the new network. Eventually, the financial and operational applications of both companies will be combined.

Though the IT departments have been "combined," they are still separate in their goals and requirements. The IT department from Gimball is interested in quickly linking the two main sites. The Shapiro IT department is more interested in a consolidated WAN between all of the offices. The Gimball department is interested in a simple configuration in which both IP and Appletalk protocols are sent across the WAN. The Shapiro IT group would prefer to see a more complex environment with IP as the only backbone protocol.

8. What would be the best type of circuit to connect the two offices?

    a. ATM

    b. ISDN

    c. Frame Relay

    d. Leased line

9. What is the speed of a T1 circuit?

   a. 64Kbps

   b. 1.54Mbps

   c. 2.04Mbps

   d. 45Mbps

10. What type of WAN circuit is X.25?

   a. Switched

   b. Permanent

   c. Both

ANSWERS

1. **d.** Frame Relay

   Frame Relay would probably be the best selection from all of these options. Analog and ISDN are not reliable. Finally, ATM would probably be too costly for Limbo Medical.

2. **b.** Availability

   This network operates 24 hours a day; therefore, reliability, up time, and fault tolerance are critical. ISDN would be an acceptable solution for DDR.

3. **a.** BRI

   A basic-rate interface, 2B+1D, would provide enough bandwidth. A PRI, 23B+1D, would be too much bandwidth.

4. **a.** channelized

   A channelized DS1 frame is comprised of 24 discrete DS0s. An unchannelized DS1 is not comprised of any discrete DS0s.

5. **c.** ATM

   ATM is the only solution that will be able to transport both voice and data over the same circuit.

6. **b.** Quality of Service

   QoS enables various types of traffic to be prioritized throughout a network.

7. **c.** Ease of installation

   ATM is a difficult and complex technology to implement.

8. **d.** Leased line

   Leased lines would be the best solution. The sites are close to each other. In addition, a single high-speed connection is needed between two discrete points.

9. **b.** T1

   A T1 circuit has a speed of 1.544Mbps.

10. **c.** both

    An X.25 network can be switched or permanent.

Designing Network Addressing

Objectives Covered in This Chapter

1. Identifying the difference between static address assignment, dynamic address assignment, and server address assignment

2. Identifying the key differences between names and addresses on an internetwork

3. Addressing the model for networks, subnetworks, and end stations that meet scalability requirements

4. Configuring addresses

5. Naming schemes for servers, routers, and user stations

Introduction

With the *Local Area Network* (LAN) and *Wide Area Network* (WAN) designs complete, the next task is to design the addressing structure for the new network. In many cases, the design of the network addressing can be a design project in itself. Unlike basic LAN and WAN design, this phase of network design requires an extensive knowledge of network-layer protocols such as the *Transmission Control Protocol / Internet Protocol* (TCP/IP) and IPX/SPX.

Each protocol that transits the network requires a separate addressing scheme. For example, if TCP/IP, IPX/SPX, and AppleTalk are all present in an environment, then three separate addressing designs are required. For the CCDA certification, you only need to know about TCP/IP and IPX/SPX network addressing design.

Network Addressing Principles

We covered the basics of IP and IPX addressing in Chapter 2, "Internetworking Technology Overview." For all network addressing (regardless of protocol), there are two key points to remember. First, the network address for all hosts on the same LAN must be identical. Second, each host on the same LAN must have a different host address. For example, in Figure 10-1, we see two networks: network

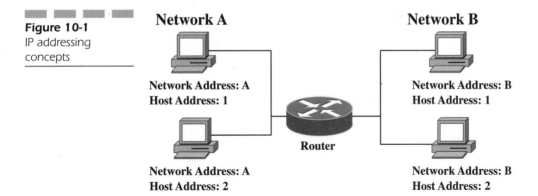

Figure 10-1
IP addressing
concepts

A and network B. There are two hosts on each network. Each host on network A must have a unique host address. The same rule applies for all hosts on network B. The uniqueness of the host number, however, only applies to hosts that are in the same network. Therefore, hosts on network A and network B can have the same host number.

IP Addressing

The next step toward a specific understanding of IP addressing is to adjust Figure 10-1 to represent an IP network. By replacing the network A and host 1 addressing format with IP addressing, you will find that the same rules are evident. The network numbers for network A and network B are now 192.168.1.0 and 192.168.2.0, respectively. Therefore, the network portions of the addresses for network A and network B are 192.168.1 and 192.168.2. The host portions can remain the same. Figure 10-2 depicts the usage of this IP addressing concept. The final IP address of each host is written as a combination of the network and host portion (for example, 192.168.1.1.1 or 192.168.2.1).

This figure shows an example of TCP/IP network addressing at its simplest. Each network number must be unique throughout the entire network. In this example, there is no specific reasoning for using these addresses. There are a few basic IP addressing concepts that will aid the designer in building network addressing schemes, however. These concepts are private IP addressing, variable-length subnet masking, address summarization, and network address translation. In

Figure 10-2
A basic IP addressing
scheme

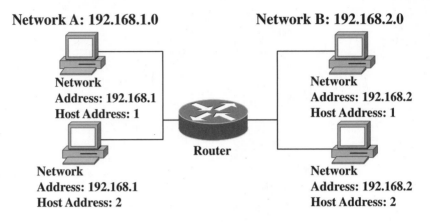

Network A: 192.168.1.0   Network B: 192.168.2.0

Network
Address: 192.168.1
Host Address: 1

Network
Address: 192.168.2
Host Address: 1

Router

Network
Address: 192.168.1
Host Address: 2

Network
Address: 192.168.2
Host Address: 2

addition to these concepts, part of an IP addressing design is the design of the *Domain Name Service* (DNS) and name resolution.

Public versus Private IP Addresses During the mid-1990s, a concern existed throughout the world about the shortage of IP addresses that were capable of communication over the Internet. One solution that helped alleviate this concern was the increased use of private IP address space according to RFC 1918. RFC 1918 set aside several IP address ranges that are never allowed on the Internet. This restriction enables many organizations to use these address ranges without inhibiting communication over select portions of the Internet. The ranges that RFC 1918 set aside are as follows:

Class A address range: 10.0.0.0 to 10.255.255.255

Class B address range: 172.16.0.0 to 172.31.255.255

Class C address range: 192.168.0.0 to 192.168.255.255

The advantage of using this restricted space is that it enables the organization to maintain a unique network addressing structure and enables communication over all parts of the Internet by using network address translation (discussed next). For example, if an organization selected 1.0.0.0 as its network number, it would be able to communicate with its other sites; however, the organization could not directly connect to the Internet with this addressing scheme. In addition, any traffic that is destined for any host on the true 1.0.0.0

network on the Internet might be routed incorrectly onto the organization's network.

Many organizations use addressing that falls within this private IP range. If an organization is using IP addresses that are outside these listed private IP ranges or that are public and do not belong to the organization, however, changing these IP addresses is difficult. Imagine the number of places in which these IP addresses could reside. DNS, host files, and UNIX scripts are just a few of the possibilities.

NOTE: *Changing the IP address range of an existing network is an almost impossible task. The best approach would be to run each piece of equipment with dual IP addresses for an extended amount of time. This procedure will provide the best amount of testing.*

A technology that is tightly coupled with the concept of private and public IP address ranges is *Network Address Translation* (NAT). NAT enables separate networks to communicate with one another without passing routing information from network to network.

NAT

As we stated, NAT enables the communication of two separate networks regardless of the IP addressing structure. NAT is a router function that converts the inside or local addresses to outside or global addresses. The local addresses are known to and understood by only the inside network. The outside addresses are known to and understood by only the outside or global interface. These local and global addresses are mapped to one another via several methods. First, the mappings can be statically mapped. In other words, a specific local address always maps to a specific global address. The other mapping method is dynamic mapping. This concept means that a pool of address space is defined, and addresses are used from the pool as needed. The mappings will not necessarily be the same from one day to the next. Figure 10-3 depicts this basic NAT principle.

One of the most common applications of NAT is connecting an organization to the Internet. When an organization purchases a connection

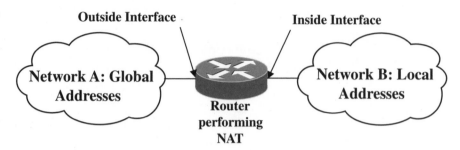

Figure 10-3
A basic NAT principle

with an *Internet Service Provider* (ISP), the organization receives a small block of registered, public IP addresses.

NOTE: *The number of addresses that are typically received depends on the speed of the connection that is purchased. In general, for each T1 purchased, a company would receive one Class C IP address range (or 254 addresses).*

This organization might have an existing IP addressing structure that is based on a private IP addressing scheme. Because these IP addresses are not permitted on the Internet, these addresses must be converted or translated into addresses that are public and registered. NAT converts the private IP addresses of the organization into public IP addresses that are acceptable for communication over the Internet. NAT uses a pool of addresses (in this case, addresses that are assigned by the ISP) to convert addresses from the inside network to the outside network. Figure 10-4 shows this NAT application, and Figure 10-5 shows the actual flow of IP addresses through the application.

Another common application of NAT is the connection of two separate networks. NAT is used to translate addresses that might be duplicated in the other network into addresses that are not duplicates. For example, two separate companies have recently merged. Each of their networks contains portions of the 10.0.0.0 network. If the networks are directly connected and routes are exchanged without planning, some sites might lose connectivity. For the short term, the best solution is to use NAT to pass traffic from one network to the other. The best long-term solution is to identify the network overlap and re-address the concern of duplicate networks.

Figure 10-4
A NAT application for
Internet connectivity

Outside Interface   Inside Interface

Network A: Global Addresses

Router performing NAT

Network B: Local Addresses

Figure 10-5
IP address flow
through NAT

NAT Table

Local Address	Global Address
10.1.1.1	200.0.0.1

Internet   New Source IP: 200.0.0.1   Source IP: 10.1.1.1

Figure 10-6
A NAT configuration
example

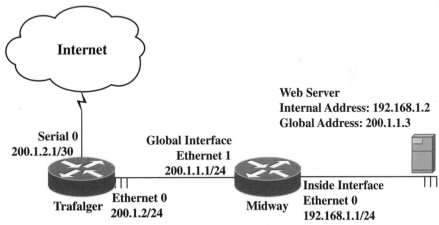

Internet

Web Server
Internal Address: 192.168.1.2
Global Address: 200.1.1.3

Serial 0
200.1.2.1/30

Global Interface
Ethernet 1
200.1.1.1/24

Trafalger
Ethernet 0
200.1.2/24

Midway

Inside Interface
Ethernet 0
192.168.1.1/24

NOTE: *The specifics of NAT implementation and configuration are beyond the scope of the* Designing Cisco Networks *(DCN) exam. The NAT principle is an integral part of IP addressing design, however. Studying Figure 10-6 and the following configuration might assist with understanding this topic.*

```
Trafalgar Router Config
interface Ethernet0
 ip address 200.1.1.2 255.255.255.0
!
interface Serial0
 ip address 200.1.2.1 255.255.255.252
!
ip route 0.0.0.0 0.0.0.0 Serial0
ip route 192.168.0.0 255.255.0.0 200.1.1.1

Midway Router Config
interface Ethernet0
 ip address 192.168.1.1 255.255.255.0
 ip nat inside
!
interface Erhernet1
 ip address 200.1.1.1 255.255.255.0
 ip nat outside
!
ip nat inside source static 192.168.1.2 200.1.1.3
ip route 0.0.0.0 0.0.0.0 200.1.1.2
```

Variable-Length Subnet Masks (VLSMs)

When networks are designed, there might be varying types of media and technologies. There might be both LAN and WAN segments of varying size and technology. As covered in Chapter 2, the subnet mask portion of the IP address specifies the maximum number of hosts that are permitted on the network.

For example, any IP address that has a subnet mask of 255.255.255.0 will always have 254 hosts available on the network. While this amount might be acceptable for a LAN segment, it is more hosts than can exist on a point-to-point circuit (and therefore is not an efficient use of the address space). Ideally, a point-to-point circuit would have a subnet mask of 255.255.255.252—which would enable two hosts on the network. There would be exactly one for each end of the circuit. Figure 10-7 depicts a router that is connected to two networks that have different subnet masks.

While it might seem prudent to assign the subnet mask for each network depending solely on the number of hosts, there could be serious repercussions. The first problem is the routing protocol that is in use. While routing design is not covered until Chapter 11, "Designing Routing Architecture," some routing protocols do not understand multiple subnet masks throughout a routing domain.

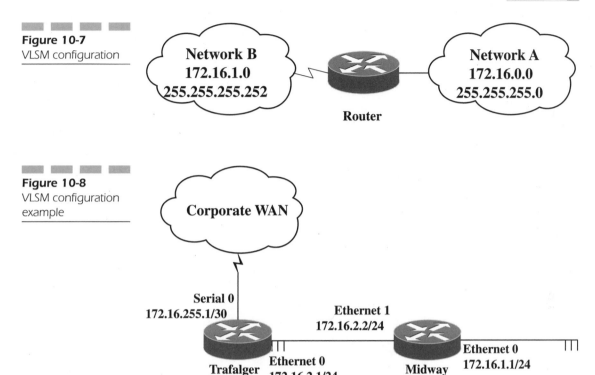

Figure 10-7
VLSM configuration

Figure 10-8
VLSM configuration
example

The second problem with various subnet masks is confusion. Imagine diagramming and explaining a network in which each network has a separate, unique subnet mask. Finally, there is no room for growth.

In VLSM, many subnet masks can be used throughout a network or even on the same router. Figure 10-8 depicts a small network that uses VLSM. The configuration for the routers follows. In this example, there are no routing protocols in use.

```
Trafalgar Router Config
interface Ethernet0
 ip address 172.16.2.1 255.255.255.0
!
interface Serial0
 ip address 172.16.255.1 255.255.255.252
!

Midway Router Config
interface Ethernet0
 ip address 172.16.1.1 255.255.255.0
!
```

```
interface Erhernet1
 ip address 172.16.2.2 255.255.255.0
 !
```

NOTE: *According to Cisco Systems, the suggested maximum number of subnet masks in a network at any time is two. The reason for this arbitrary limit is because more subnet masks might make network troubleshooting more complicated. This limit is only a recommendation.*

NOTE: *The specifics of VLSM implementation are beyond the scope of the DCN exam. The VLSM principle is an integral part of IP addressing design. Remember that the use of VLSM requires the routing protocol to understand the VLSM concept. This topic will be covered in Chapter 11.*

Address Summarization

As networks grow larger, the number of entries on routing tables grows as well. By logically designing IP addresses in a hierarchical manner, you can aggregate or summarize the many routes into a single route. This type of address summarization is depicted in Figure 10-9.

Figure 10-9
IP address summarization

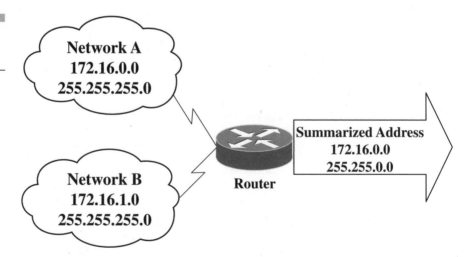

Network A
172.16.0.0
255.255.255.0

Network B
172.16.1.0
255.255.255.0

Router

Summarized Address
172.16.0.0
255.255.0.0

The concept of address summarization is complex and is not covered on the DCN exam. When IP addressing schemes are designed, however, it is imperative for possible summarization to be a factor in the design.

DNS   Part of designing an IP addressing scheme is designing the location of the DNS servers. These servers enable server names to be translated into IP addresses. For instance, which is easier to remember: www.cisco.com or 198.133.219.25? DNS enables users to remember only the common names for servers instead of complex IP addresses. DNS also enables administrators to change the addresses or the host in order to act as a virtual name for a series of servers that are located at various IP addresses.

The key to adding DNS services to any network is to ensure that these servers are centrally located on the network. You also must ensure that filters throughout the network are not blocking DNS requests.

Selecting Addresses   The selection of the actual IP addresses is quite straightforward. If an IP addressing scheme is not in place currently, then the designer has two choices: using public IP addresses or private IP addresses.

You should only use public IP addresses if an ISP has assigned a block of addresses to the organization. Never use a public IP address that has been chosen arbitrarily if the network will be connected to the Internet.

Private IP addresses are more commonly used now than public IP addresses. In addition, these addresses provide a much greater number of IP addresses and IP address blocks than traditional public IP address ranges that an ISP would assign. This additional space enables much more flexibility in subnetting and summarization. For private IP addresses, use the following address ranges. The actual range that is chosen will be based on the size of the organization, the theoretical number of hosts and networks, and the number of subnet masks on the network. Be sure to plan the addressing design.

There are no easy charts or tables for choosing which class of IP network to use, but here are some guidelines for each class:

Class A: 10.0.0.0—Offers the greatest number of hosts and subnets (can be configured into thousands of various configurations)

Class B: 172.16.0.0 to 172.31.0.0—Each Class B network can be used in an organization, or you can use only a single Class B network. For most organizations, a Class B address range provides more than enough hosts and more than enough subnets.

Class C: 192.168.0.0 to 192.168.255.0—Again, you can use each Class C network in an organization, or you can use only a single Class C network from this range. For small networks, this selection offers an acceptable number of hosts and networks.

IPX Addressing

Basics We covered the basics of IPX addressing in Chapter 2. Again, you should remember several key points. First, the network address for all hosts on the same LAN must be identical. Second, each host on the same LAN must have a different host address. These rules are identical to the IP addressing rules that we described earlier in this chapter. In addition to these rules, however, there is a third variable. On an IPX/SPX network, there are several different encapsulation types that you can configure on a router or on a Novell server. There can be up to four encapsulation types on each network, and each encapsulation type must have a unique network number.

The encapsulation types for Ethernet appear in Table 10-1. The Novell name is listed first, because when we discuss encapsulation

Table 10-1	**Novell Encapsulation**	**Cisco Encapsulation**	**IEEE Frame Type**
Novell Ethernet encapsulation types	Ethernet 802.3	Novell-Ethernet	"Raw" Ethernet
	Ethernet 802.2	SAP	802.3 Ethernet
	Ethernet II	ARPA	Ethernet II
	Ethernet SNAP	Snap	Ethernet Snap

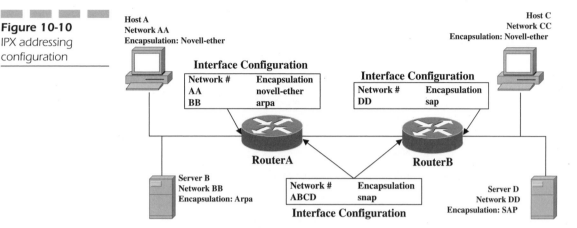

Figure 10-10
IPX addressing
configuration

types with server administrators, they will probably only understand the Novell references.

Figure 10-8 depicts a multi-router network with several encapsulations among all of the networks. Note that there are several encapsulations throughout the entire network. Communication between
hosts that have different encapsulations is required to pass through
a router. The hosts can reside on the same physical LAN, but they
are part of different logical networks and must pass through a router
in order to communicate. In Figure 10-10, you can see that Host A
can communicate with Server B by routing all traffic through Router
A. Host C cannot communicate with Server D or with any other
devices on other segments, however, because the local router does not
support the encapsulation for Host C. Host C can only communicate
with other hosts on the same physical segment that are configured
with the same network number and the same encapsulation.

Figure 10-11 shows an example of an IPX network that has various encapsulation types. The configuration of the routers follows.

```
Trafalgar Router Config
interface Ethernet0
 ipx network CC encapsulation arpa
!
interface Serial0
 ipx network AA
!

Midway Router Config
```

Figure 10-11
IPX addressing
configuration
example

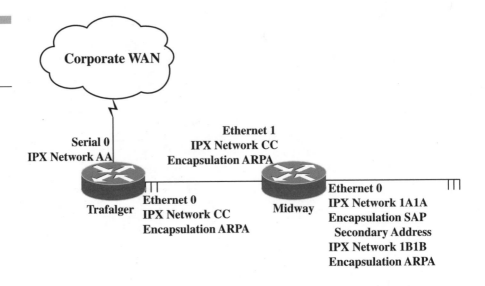

```
interface Ethernet0
 ipx network 1A1A encapsulation sap
 ipx network 1B1B encapsulation arpa secondary
!
interface Erhernet1
 ipx network CC encapsulation arpa
!
```

NOTE: *I have seen numerous Novell connectivity problems over the years. The problem is almost always a misconfiguration of the network number and encapsulation type. The automatic configuration of some machines generally can add to the confusion if more that one encapsulation is present on the network.*

Selecting Addresses

There are several ways to assign IPX addresses. Unlike IP addressing, there is no special range of IPX network numbers that are reserved. Any IPX network number is acceptable to use as long as it is unique.

If IP and IPX are both in use, one option for assigning IPX network addresses is to mirror the IP network address. IP addresses are four bytes long and are generally written in dotted decimal format

(10.0.0.0). IPX addresses are also four bytes long; however, they are always written in hexadecimal format. Therefore, because the IP network address will always be unique, the associated IPX network number will also be unique.

The main points that detract from this method of addressing are multiple encapsulations and Novell server addressing requirements. If more than one encapsulation type is in use, then additional network numbers are required for each encapsulation type. Also, every Novell server requires an internal network number. This network number identifies the server and must be unique throughout all networks and throughout all server internal networks. The best approach for internal network addresses is to use low numbers for all servers and to track their usage.

The only other option for assigning IPX addresses is to track the existing network numbers and ensure that new addresses do not duplicate existing network numbers.

Case Study

First, let's revisit the Widget Manufacturing case study. In the last chapter, Widget Manufacturing has opened three separate manufacturing plants in order to increase the capacity of its existing facility. This drastic change has resulted in a new set of design requirements. The three additional sites are located as follows:

1. Two miles from the existing plant
2. In a neighboring city
3. On the opposite coast

The network staff of Widget Manufacturing selected a Frame Relay WAN with ISDN backups. The next step of the design is to design an addressing scheme for the new LAN and WAN. Let's begin with the LAN.

Figure 10-12 depicts the new LAN design. This design is basically an upgrade of the old network. A switch router remains in the core of the network. In this scenario, we did not make any actual network addressing changes. All existing network segments remain intact, and the cable plant and equipment have changed based on these

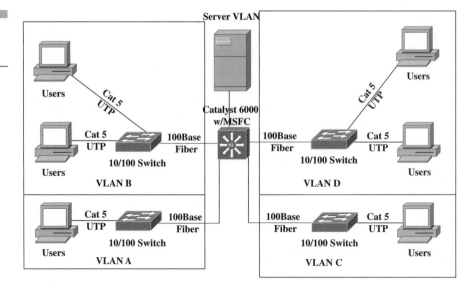

Figure 10-12
Proposed Widget
Manufacturing LAN

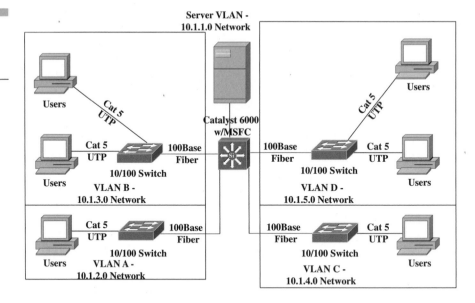

Figure 10-13
Proposed Widget
Manufacturing LAN
IP addressing

boundaries. Figure 10-13 represents the IP addressing structure of the LAN.

One reason for keeping the addressing structure is simply to avoid change. In general, any changes in a network or server—even with the most stringent precautions—can cause disastrous results. Therefore, by keeping all of the IP addresses intact, the designer and the Widget Manufacturing network operations groups can ensure that there will be no unforeseen connectivity issues that could result from an IP address change.

The next item that we must examine is the WAN IP addressing structure. Figure 10-14 represents the WAN design with a possible IP addressing scheme for the remote offices.

The basic IP addressing plan takes one important concept into account: summarization. All of the networks in the home office can be summarized as the 10.1.0.0 network. The other offices have been assigned to a large IP address range in order to aid in summarizing the network IP addresses. Subnet masks have not been assigned to the remote offices yet because the LANs in those offices have yet to be designed and installed.

The IP addressing plan is not complete, however, because the WAN itself has not been addressed yet. The initial diagram does not allow for an easy representation of the IP addressing for the Frame Relay and ISDN networks, so they have been depicted in Figure 10-15 and 10-16, respectively.

In this case, the high end of the 10.0.0.0 network was chosen. The network could have been any number, and it could even have been a

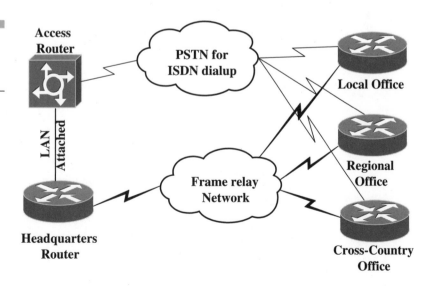

Figure 10-14
Proposed Widget
Manufacturing WAN
IP addressing

Figure 10-15
Proposed Widget
Manufacturing Frame
Relay IP addressing

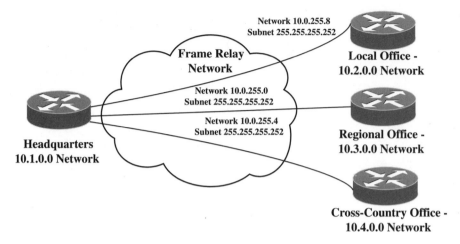

Figure 10-15
Proposed Widget
Manufacturing Frame
Relay IP addressing

Figure 10-16
Proposed Widget
Manufacturing ISDN
IP addressing

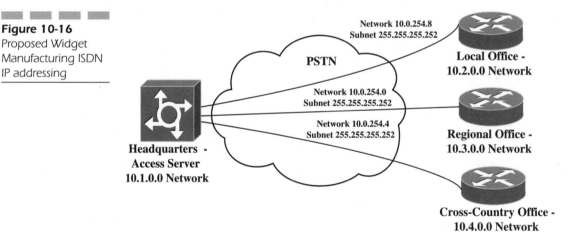

network other than 10.0.0.0. Remember that on the Widget network, IPX traffic is also in use. The IPX network numbers should remain the same on the existing network. If new IPX addresses are required for the remote WAN offices, the IP networks could be converted to an equivalent hexadecimal address in order to provide a mechanism for unique IPX network addresses.

SUMMARY

Network addressing is a topic that cannot be adequately covered in a text that is designed for the CCDA test. Entire books have been written about IP addressing architectures. The IP and IPX addressing information provided in this chapter applies to small and medium network designs.

The network addressing step of network design is the precursor of one of the most important design concepts: routing design. Because all networks have to communicate with one another, some type of routing protocol and routing design is almost always required. We will cover routing design next in Chapter 11.

QUESTIONS ▉ ▉ ▉ ▉ ▉ ▉ ▉ ▉ ▉

Case Study: Limbo Medical Group

Let's take another look at the case study of the Limbo Medical Group. The Limbo Medical Group was on the cutting edge of network technology 10 years ago. It decided to implement a centralized computer system for all of its day-to-day operations. This system consisted of an X.25 WAN that connected 50 small offices to a central hospital facility. This X.25 WAN carries legacy SNA traffic between hosts and a mainframe. In the previous chapters, there were several case study questions regarding LAN and WAN design. The following questions assume that Figure 10-17 is an accurate representation of a portion of the new WAN.

1. Why is an IP address design needed for the LANs?

   a. It is not needed; the same addresses will be used.

   b. The existing addresses will not work.

   c. The existing LANs are not running the IP protocol.

   d. Because of Frame Relay

Figure 10-17
New Limbo Medical
network design

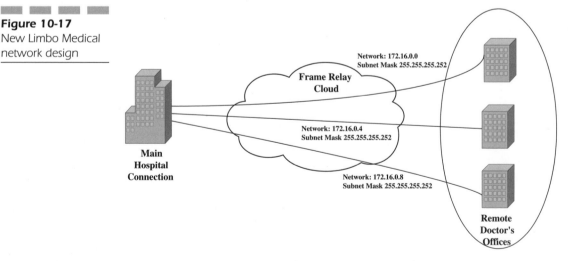

Network: 172.16.0.0
Subnet Mask 255.255.255.252

Frame Relay
Cloud

Network: 172.16.0.4
Subnet Mask 255.255.255.252

Main
Hospital
Connection

Network: 172.16.0.8
Subnet Mask 255.255.255.252

Remote
Doctor's
Offices

2. What IP addressing concepts should the designer plan to use?

   a. NAT

   b. VLSM

   c. Summarization

   d. SNMP

3. Why did Limbo Medical choose to use the 172.16.0.0 network addresses?

   a. They were assigned by ARIN.

   b. They were assigned by their ISP.

   c. They were existing numbers.

   d. This range is specified as a private IP address range by RFC 1918.

4. What addressing concept is required due to the varying number of hosts on the LANs?

   a. NAT

   b. VLSM

   c. Summarization

   d. SNMP

5. How will the IPX addresses for Limbo Medical be created?

   a. IPX is not required.

   b. By a hexadecimal conversion of IP addresses

   c. Natural selection

   d. Random generation

Case Study: Global Supplies Corporation

Again, to recap the situation of Global Supplies, this company is a multi-national corporation that is comprised of approximately 15 separate facilities throughout North America. Each facility has an existing LAN that has been upgraded according to the needs of the specific facility. The LANs range from small 10MB Ethernet networks to large Fast Ethernet networks that have Gigabit backbones.

At the previous step in the design process, the WAN transport was identified. The proposed solution for consolidating the T1s is an ATM

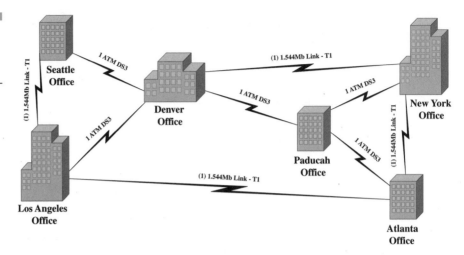

Figure 10-18
Global Supplies
network design
(proposed topology)

backbone. The proposed network topology is shown in Figure 10-18. All of the multiple T1 circuits have been replaced with an ATM network. The single T1s remain in order to provide data redundancy between sites.

The network currently has an IP addressing scheme in place. The company is using a public IP address Class B range and has not implemented VLSM or summarization.

6. Why must the IP addressing be redesigned for Global Supplies?

a. It uses a public address.

b. Because of VLSM

c. Because of summarization

d. It should not be redesigned.

7. IPX traffic is present on the WAN and LANs. What item relating to the IPX network can inhibit communication?

a. Default route

b. Encapsulation

c. Subnet mask

d. MAC address

8. How should the IPX network addresses be designed?

    a. Matching the IP addresses

    b. Chosen randomly

    c. Matching the MAC address

    d. It is already in place and should not be redesigned.

Case Study: G&S Productions

We will revisit the case study of Gimball Productions and Shapiro Productions. These two companies have recently merged. The new company, G&S Productions, has become a major commercial production company. There are two main sites, each with about 250 users. In addition, each company has three to five smaller offices throughout the United States.

After the WAN design portion of the project, the decision was made to connect the two offices via a leased line for the time being. One concern of the respective IT groups is IP addressing.

The Gimball office and WAN uses an IP addressing scheme of 192.168.1.0 to 192.168.3.0. The Shapiro office and WAN uses the same IP addressing scheme of 192.168.1.0.

9. Given the duplication of IP address ranges, what concept enables the interconnection of these networks?

    a. NAT

    b. VLSM

    c. Summarization

    d. They should *not* be connected.

10. What IP address should be chosen for the leased line?

    a. An address in the 192.168.0.0 range

    b. An address in the 198.162.0.0 range

    c. An address in any range except the 192.168.0.0 range

    d. An address in any range except the 198.162.0.0 range

ANSWERS

1. c. The existing LANs are not running the IP protocol.

The existing network is running SNA, not IP. Therefore, there is no existing IP address structure upon which to build.

2. b. and **c.** VLSM and summarization

VLSM would be the recommended approach for the point-to-point Frame Relay circuits and the other networks of various user counts. Summarization would ideally be designed into the addressing structure. Probably the only summarization would be the various networks at the central hospital location.

3. d. This range is specified as a private IP address range by RFC 1597.

The 172.16.0.0 is part of the Class B private IP address range set that is set aside by RFC 1918. It cannot be used by any organization on the Internet.

4. b. VLSM

VLSMs enable a network to have more than one subnet mask. If there are many various LAN sizes, then the best approach is VLSM in order to conserve addressing space.

5. a. IPX is not required on the network.

No IPX traffic is present on the network. The new application is 100 percent IP based.

6. d. It should not be redesigned.

While some benefits could be gained from summarization or from VLSM, there would be a greater probability of errors if the addresses were changed.

7. **b.** Encapsulation

   The IPX encapsulation type is an important component of the IPX network. The network/encapsulation pair must match in order for two devices to communicate.

8. **d.** It is already in place and should not be redesigned.

   Again, the IPX networks have already been addressed and should not be redesigned. Redesign can cause more problems for the design project.

9. **a.** NAT

   NAT will enable the network to be connected. A special configuration is required in order to ensure that information is transferred between the networks.

10. **c.** An address in any range except the 192.168.0.0 range.

    Because both networks use some of the same portions of this range, it would be advisable to select a network that does not exist within this range.

Designing Routing Architecture

Objectives Covered in This Chapter

1. Identifying scalability constraints and issues for IGRP, Enhanced IGRP, IP RIP, IPX RIP/SAP, NLSP, AppleTalk RTMP, static routing, and bridging protocols

2. Recommending routing and bridging protocols that meet a customer's requirements for performance, security, and capacity

Introduction

Anytime there is more than a single network in an organization, routing is required to pass information from network to network. Any network design project that has *Local Area Network* (LAN), *Wide Area Network* (WAN), and addressing designs is still incomplete without a routing design.

Routing designs can range from simple, single protocol designs to complex, multi-protocol designs that include route redistribution. In order to properly design routing architectures, however, the designer must understand the routing protocols.

In general, there are two fundamental categories of routing: static and dynamic. Static routing means that routes are coded into each router on a network. In addition, each router must have a coded route to each LAN and WAN in the network. Dynamic routes are further subdivided into three categories: distance-vector, link-state, and hybrid protocols. Each dynamic routing protocol type uses different mechanisms to dynamically build and change routing tables.

Static Routes

Static routing is similar to following directions. At every junction point (or router), a new route is given to a specific destination. For example, if someone was going from San Diego, California to Santa Monica, California, the static route would be as follows: Take the 5 freeway north. Upon reaching the junction of the 405 freeway, take 405 North. Eventually, you will reach Santa Monica.

With these directions, if the 405 North freeway was closed, there would not be an alternate route to Santa Monica. Static routes behave in the same manner. They dictate a specific route to a specific network. If the destination is not reachable, then the packets are dropped and will not be redirected around the problem.

Figure 11-1 depicts a network that is comprised of routes that use only static routes. The router configuration files from the three routers are also shown as follows. In this example, Trafalgar has static routes to the networks that are connected to the Jutland and Midway routers. The other routers, in turn, have static routes that direct traffic to the appropriate remote networks.

```
Trafalgar Router Config
interface Ethernet0
 ip address 172.16.1.1 255.255.255.0
!
interface Tokenring0
 ip address 172.16.2.1 255.255.255.0
!
ip route 172.16.3.0 255.255.255.252 172.16.2.2
ip route 172.16.4.0 255.255.255.0 172.16.2.2

Jutland Router Config
interface Serial0
 ip address 172.16.3.1 255.255.255.252
!
interface Tokenring0
 ip address 172.16.2.2 255.255.255.0
!
ip route 172.16.4.0 255.255.255.252 172.16.3.2
ip route 172.16.1.0 255.255.255.0 172.16.2.1
Midway Router Config
interface Ethernet0
 ip address 172.16.4.1 255.255.255.0
!
interface Serial0
```

Figure 11-1
Static routing example

Interface Ethernet 0
172.16.1.1/24

Interface Ethernet 0
172.16.4.1/24

Interface Token 0
172.16.2.1/24

Interface Token 0
172.16.2.2/24

Interface Serial 0
172.16.3.1/30

Interface Serial 0
172.16.3.2/30

Trafalger

Jutland

Midway

```
    ip address 172.16.3.2 255.255.255.252
    !
ip route 172.16.1.0 255.255.255.0 172.16.3.1
ip route 172.16.2.0 255.255.255.0 172.16.3.1
```

Static routing is beneficial in several scenarios. For example, it might not be possible for an external network to pass routing protocol information over the existing network. In this case, the best design solution is to place a static route in order to direct traffic to the distant network.

Static routes can be used in place of dynamic routing protocols. All routers would have to be configured with routes to all other networks then, however. Changes to the network—even changing router ports—would then become nearly impossible. As networks grow, the feasibility of using only static routes decreases. In order to successfully route information across these networks, dynamic routing is required.

Distance-Vector Protocols

The first type of dynamic routing protocols is distance-vector protocols. Distance-vector protocols maintain an entry in the routing table for each network that they have seen. This routing table generally lists the number of networks or hops away and the direction or next hop toward which to send the traffic. These factors help derive the name distance (or hops), vector, or direction. In general, all distance-vector protocols behave in a similar manner. Next, we will address the types, operation, and convergence of distance-vector protocols.

Examples Many types of distance-vector protocols are in use today. They are even used across multiple protocols. The most common form of the distance-vector protocol is the *Routing Information Protocol* (RIP).

IP RIP IP RIP, usually called RIP, is one of the most common distance-vector protocols that are in use today. It is only used for routing IP traffic. In addition, RIP is a standard, non-proprietary protocol. RIP broadcasts its routing table to its neighbors every 30 seconds by default. Upon receiving the update, the receiving router updates its routing table with any new or changed information. These RIP broadcasts are the primary method for transmitting network and route information across the network.

There are several limitations of IP RIP. The first limitation is that there can only be a maximum of 15 hops. In IP RIP, 16 hops is considered infinity or unreachable. Another limitation is that IP RIP is a classful routing protocol. In other words, IP RIP does not transmit the subnet information of the network that is being advertised. IP RIP assumes that the subnet mask is constant throughout the network. With classful routing protocols, the *Variable Length Subnet Mask* (VLSM) principle discussed in Chapter 10 cannot be used.

IP RIP Version 2 IP RIP version 2 is the second edition of classic RIP. It expands somewhat on the original protocol by attempting to correct the limitations of IP RIP version 1. First, the hop count limitation was increased from 15 to 32. This expansion enables the network to be dramatically larger than permitted in the previous version of RIP.

Second is the inclusion of the subnet mask for the advertised network. This feature makes IP RIP version 2 a classless routing protocol. A classless routing protocol bases the subnet mask of a network on the subnet mask that is received as part of the routing update. Finally, IP RIP version 2 is a protocol that is compatible across multiple vendors. Like IP RIP version 1, it is also a non-proprietary protocol.

IGRP IGRP is a Cisco proprietary protocol that was developed in order to address several of the limitations of IP RIP version 1. It is based on the same basic principle of broadcasting routing information to neighbors. The router then uses this information to update its own routing table. It makes one major improvement over basic IP RIP, however: the maximum hop count is raised from 15 networks to 254 networks. Another improvement is the addition of metrics (other than the hop count) for route selection. IGRP uses the following metrics in order to determine the best route:

1. Bandwidth
2. Delay
3. Reliability
4. Load
5. MTU

Once again, there are several limitations. First, like IP RIP, IGRP is a classful routing protocol. Again, no subnet mask information is transmitted with the advertised networks; instead, all networks are assumed to have the same subnet mask as the router. Second, IGRP is a proprietary protocol and will not interoperate with any device other than another Cisco router that is using IGRP.

IPX RIP First, do not confuse IPX RIP with IP RIP. They are separate routing protocols that operate over separate routed protocols. IPX RIP only works with the IPX protocol. IP RIP only works with the IP protocol. The similar name, however, correctly implies that they are similar in operation.

The classless and classful distinction is an IP-only classification and does not apply in an IPX environment. IPX RIP broadcasts are propagated throughout the network every 60 seconds. Like its IP counterpart, IPX RIP uses a time measurement called a tick, which is equal to one-sixteenth of a second, to determine the best route. In addition to ticks, however, IPX RIP also uses the hop count to break any ties.

In addition to IPX RIP, there is another IPX function that is often associated with IPX RIP. This associated function is the *Service Advertising Protocol* (SAP). While IPX RIP propagates routing and network information across the network, SAP propagates the available Netware services across the network. IPX RIP and SAP are inseparable; all clients use SAP to locate services and IPX RIP to route traffic to the service.

IPX RIP is easy to configure. When IPX networks are added, IPX RIP/SAP is automatically configured and enabled. When designing IPX networks, however, it is important to remember that these broadcasts can saturate a slow link if there are numerous services or networks. For instance, an IPX RIP packet is 432 bytes and can hold

50 routes. A SAP packet is 480 bytes and can hold seven services. Therefore, each router on a network that has 1,000 networks and 2,000 servers will send 20 IPX RIP packets and 286 SAP packets every 60 seconds. The total size of the IPX RIP traffic will be 8 Kbps each minute. The total size of the SAP traffic will be 124 Kbps every minute. This amount of traffic will take almost 2 seconds to transmit over a 64 Kbps line.

NOTE: *There are several options that will be discussed later for implementing large-scale IPX networks over slow-speed WANs.*

NOTE: *At the time of this writing (summer 2000), I was working on a large IPX environment. There were approximately 300 WAN sites connected to a 7513 router via Frame Relay. The WAN connections were comprised of both IPX and IP traffic. It was determined that some versions of Cisco IOS code can only support 200 directly connected IPX networks upon startup. More networks could be added after booting the routers, but this procedure would require many command entries after every router reboot. The eventual solution was to add another router and divide the WAN connection between the various routers.*

RTMP RTMP is the basic distance-vector routing protocol that AppleTalk uses. Like IP RIP, it broadcasts routing updates regularly. By default, the update interval is every 10 seconds. Also, because there is no concept of subnet masks in AppleTalk, there is no distinction in AppleTalk between classful and classless routing. Finally, RTMP is enabled by default once an AppleTalk address has been assigned to the interface (although it can be disabled if not needed).

The main limitation of RTMP is the update interval. The 10-second update intervals can put a large burden on slow WAN links in the same manner that IPX RIP and SAP advertisements can burden an IPX WAN circuit.

Operation The best way to classify the operation of distance-vector protocols is routing by rumor. The updates that a router receives are the rumors, and they can be classified as rumors because the routes in the routing table are learned from other routers. Many of the entries are second-hand, third-hand, or even worse. The router cannot validate the routes that are received; rather, it simply enters them into its routing table.

The main drawback to this operation is the problem of looping to infinity. For example, Figure 11-2 depicts the router trio with a simple IGRP configuration. For clarity, the configuration files are shown as follows.

```
Trafalgar Router Config
hostname Trafalgar
!
!
interface Ethernet0
 ip address 172.16.1.1 255.255.255.0
!
interface TokenRing0
 ip address 172.16.2.1 255.255.255.0
!
router igrp 1
network 172.16.0.0
!

Jutland Router Config
hostname Jutland
!
interface Serial0
ip address 172.16.3.1 255.255.255.252
!
interface TokenRing0
ip address 172.16.2.1 255.255.255.0
!
router igrp 1
```

Figure 11-2
Distance-vector
routing example

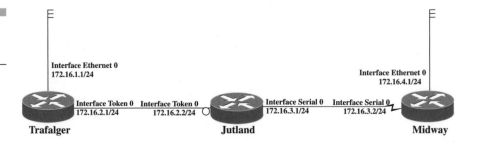

Interface Ethernet 0		Interface Ethernet 0
172.16.1.1/24		172.16.4.1/24

Interface Token 0   Interface Token 0   Interface Serial 0   Interface Serial 0
172.16.2.1/24   172.16.2.2/24   172.16.3.1/24   172.16.3.2/24

Trafalger   **Jutland**   **Midway**

```
network 172.16.0.0
!

Midway Router Config
hostname Midway
!
interface Ethernet0
ip address 172.16.4.1 255.255.255.0
!
interface Serial0
ip address 172.16.3.2 255.255.255.252
!
router igrp 1
network 172.16.0.0
```

In this example, we will concentrate on the Jutland router. The initial routing table for Jutland appears in Table 11-1.

Next, Jutland receives an update from the Midway router. This updates has a new network: 172.16.4.0. The hop count distance that is received in the routing advertisement for this network is 1. Then, Jutland adds the 172.16.4.0 network with a metric of 2 to the routing table. After this initial update, the new routing table is shown in Table 11-2.

In the next update, Jutland now propagates this table to all of the neighboring routers. Because Midway has a lower cost route to the 172.16.4.0 network, this update is dropped. The Trafalgar router

Table 11-1
Initial Jutland routes

Network	Metric	Next Hop
172.16.2.0	0	Directly Connected, Token Ring0
172.16.3.0	0	Directly Connected, Serial 0

Table 11-2
Updated Jutland routes

Network	Metric	Next Hop
172.16.2.0	0	Directly Connected, Token Ring0
172.16.3.0	0	Directly Connected, Serial 0
172.176.4.0	2	172.16.3.2

updates its route table with the new network. In addition, the Trafalgar router increments the hop count by 1 to 3.

In the next update received by Jutland, it receives the 172.16.4.0 network from two sources. Trafalgar advertises a hop count of 3, and Midway advertises a hop count of 1. The Midway route will continue to be stored in the routing table.

The limitation of distance-vector protocols is when a link fails. In this instance, the link between Jutland and Midway has failed. Jutland no longer receives updates for the 172.16.4.0 from Midway, and the route is cleared from the table after several seconds. Note that there is no route for the network. An update is received by Jutland from Trafalgar. Trafalgar can get to the 172.16.4.0 network with a hop count of 3. Jutland updates the route table, as shown in Table 11-3.

Remember, however, that the Trafalgar route to 172.16.4.0 was initially received from Jutland. So, when Jutland increases the hop count, Trafalgar increases the hop count by one as well. Several updates cycles later, the routing table of Jutland would look like Table 11-4.

Eventually, the metric will reach 16 (infinity), and both routers will remove the route from their tables entirely. This procedure might seem like a harmless problem; however, during this several-minute interval, packets that are destined for the lost network sim-

Table 11-3

Jutland routes after 3 exchanges

Network	Metric	Route
172.16.2.0	0	Directly Connected, Token Ring0
172.16.3.0	0	Directly Connected, Serial 0
172.16.4.0	4	172.16.2.1

Table 11-4

Jutland routes after 11 exchanges

Network	Metric	Route
172.16.2.0	0	Directly Connected, Token Ring0
172.16.3.0	0	Directly Connected, Serial 0
172.16.4.0	12	172.16.2.1

ply pass from router to router until they expire. If the routing table had the capability to remove the lost route sooner, the packets could quickly be marked as "destination net unreachable" and dropped.

This major limitation of distance-vector protocols initiated several mechanisms to prohibit counting to infinity. The mechanisms are split horizon and position reverse.

The rule of split horizon says that a router will not advertise a route out an interface if the router first learned that router from that interface. In the counting to infinity exercise, with split horizon enabled, Trafalgar would not advertise the 172.16.4.0 network back out its Token Ring 0 interface (to the Jutland router), because that route was originally learned from that interface.

The next mechanism is a modification of split horizon called poison reverse. In poison reverse, the route is advertised out the interface from which it was learned; however, the advertised network is given a metric of infinity (indicating that it is unreachable).

One or the other of these mechanisms is enabled by default in all implementations of a distance-vector protocol. It is possible to disable them; however, this action is inadvisable except in unique situations.

NOTE: *One instance in which split horizon or poison reverse might need to be disabled is on a multi-point Frame Relay network. With these mechanisms enabled, any routes that are learned from the Frame Relay interface would not be re-advertised on the Frame Relay interface. Due to the configuration of the frame circuit, this situation might mean that the routes are not exchanged between spoke Frame Relay sites.*

Figure 11-3 depicts a multi-protocol environment that uses distance-vector protocols. The configuration files for all of the routers are shown as follows.

```
Trafalgar Router Config
hostname Trafalgar
!
appletalk routing
ipx routing
!
!
interface Ethernet0
```

Figure 11-3
Multi-protocol
distance-vector
routing example

Interface Ethernet 0
172.16.1.1/24
IPX Network AA
AppleTalk Cable Range 10
AppleTalk Address 10.1
AppleTalk Zone French_Dept

Interface Token 0
172.16.2.2/24
IPX Network BB
AppleTalk Cable Range 20
AppleTalk Address 20.2
AppleTalk Zone English_Dept

Interface Serial 0
172.16.3.2/30
IPX Network CC
AppleTalk Cable Range 30
AppleTalk Address 30.2
AppleTalk Zone German_Dept

Interface Ethernet 0
172.16.4.1/24
IPX Network DD
AppleTalk Cable Range 40
AppleTalk Address 40.1
AppleTalk Zone Japanese_Dept

Trafalger

Interface Token 0
172.16.2.1/24
IPX Network BB
AppleTalk Cable Range 20
AppleTalk Address 20.1
AppleTalk Zone English_Dept

Jutland

Interface Serial 0
172.16.3.1/30
IPX Network CC
AppleTalk Cable Range 30
AppleTalk Address 30.1
AppleTalk Zone German_Dept

Midway

```
    ip address 172.16.1.1 255.255.255.0
    appletalk cable-range 10-10 10.1
    appletalk zone French_Dept
    ipx network AA
!
interface TokenRing0
    ip address 172.16.2.1 255.255.255.0
    appletalk cable-range 20-20 20.1
    appletalk zone English_Dept
    ipx network BB
!
router rip
network 172.16.0.0
!

Jutland Router Config
hostname Jutland
!
appletalk routing
ipx routing
!
interface Serial0
    ip address 172.16.3.1 255.255.255.252
    appletalk cable-range 30-30 30.1
    appletalk zone German_Dept
    ipx network CC
!
interface TokenRing0
    ip address 172.16.2.1 255.255.255.0
    appletalk cable-range 20-20 20.2
    appletalk zone English_Dept
    ipx network BB
!
router rip
network 172.16.0.0
!

Midway Router Config
hostname Midway
!
appletalk routing
```

```
ipx routing
!
interface Ethernet0
 ip address 172.16.4.1 255.255.255.0
 appletalk cable-range 40-40 40.1
 appletalk zone Japanese_Dept
 ipx network DD
!
interface Serial0
 ip address 172.16.3.2 255.255.255.252
 appletalk cable-range 30-30 30.2
 appletalk zone German_Dept
 ipx network CC
!
router rip
network 172.16.0.0
```

Convergence   Convergence is the network state when all changes have been assimilated. For example, refer again to Figure 11-3. In this example, the network is running the various distance-vector routing protocols. If the Midway router fails, convergence is the process that ensures that this change is propagated to all routers. If convergence takes a long time, like in the counting to infinity example, then many packets might float around the network until they expire. If convergence happens quickly, then the route is successfully flushed from each router and the packets are returned as unreachable.

In a small network that has split horizon and poison reverse enabled, convergence usually happens quickly. In a larger routing environment, convergence might take a long time. Remember that convergence for a distance-vector protocol relies upon periodic broadcasts in order to update neighbors. In a large network that has 10 hops, this process could take up to five minutes for RIP or 10 minutes for IGRP.

Overhead   Overheadis the amount of traffic that a protocol places on the network. As you can see from the IPX RIP example, distance-vector protocols—especially IPX RIP and RTMP—rely on sending many packets. Therefore, a lot of bandwidth must be dedicated for the overhead that these protocols require.

This overhead is negligible in a LAN environment. Even in a WAN that is composed of T1s, the overhead is minimal. The overhead of these protocols is evident in slow WAN links, however. Distance-vector protocols are generally a poor protocol to use on large networks for WAN links that are slower than 64Kbps.

Design Notes   Distance-vector routing protocols are fairly simple to design and implement. As long as the same protocol is used throughout the network and this protocol does not violate many of the rules that are associated with the protocol (such as hop count or subnet masks), then the protocols will work.

One caveat is that as a network grows and route updates become larger, the overhead burden on WAN links might cause saturation on these links. In this event, a new protocol would have to be implemented, or the bandwidth of the WAN links would have to be increased.

Link-State Protocols

Link-state routing protocols are based on the shortest-path algorithm that was developed by Edsger W. Dijkstra. This algorithm builds a series of paths through a network based on the cost that is associated with each route. Link-state protocols can also be identified because they form a special relationship, called an adjacency, with all neighboring routers. This special relationship enables each router to maintain a link state with each neighboring router.

In general, the operation of link-state protocols is more complex that distance-vector protocols. Although they are more complex, however, link-state protocols are often more stable and quicker to converge on a large network.

The metric that is used to select one route over another is referred to as the cost. When the shortest-path algorithm builds a route to a remote network, the cost is calculated for each step on the network. As a decision point is reached between two or more devices, the shortest-path algorithm will select the path that has the lowest cost. This process continues until the route to the network is complete and the final cost is tallied.

Examples   There are three major link-state protocols in use today. Two of these protocols, *Open Shortest Path First* (OSPF) and *Inter-*

mediate System-*to*-*Intermediate System* (IS-IS), are used for routing the IP protocols. The *Novell Link-State Protocol* (NLSP) is used to route IPX traffic.

OSPF The most popular link-state protocol that is in use today is OSPF. The OSPF protocol was developed to improve upon many of the limitations of IP RIP. A network that is running OSPF can support an almost unlimited number of hops. In addition, like RIP version 2, OSPF is a classless protocol and can support multiple subnet masks. OSPF is also an open routing protocol that can be used to connect routers from different vendors.

OSPF's operation is based on the concept of areas. An OSPF area is a group of routers that form adjacencies with each other in order to exchange local routing information and to create a common understanding of the network topology.

OSPF areas are connected so that routing information can be shared over a large organization. When connecting OSPF areas, however, the designer must begin with the backbone or transit OSPF area (area 0). All other OSPF areas should directly connect to area 0.

NOTE: *Cisco enables the use of virtual areas so that a non-area 0 OSPF area can be used as a transit communication between area 0 and the original area. This technique is generally considered a poor OSPF design and should only be used as an interim measure.*

Routers in an OSPF area, regardless of number, can always be categorized by the location and function in that area. The router names and categories are listed in Table 11-5.

There are two main types of routing communication that happen across an OSPF network: hellos and link-state advertisements. The hello packet is the mechanism that a router uses to establish a link-state session with all of its neighboring routers. If a hello packet is missed repeatedly, then the link becomes inactive. This situation will then force the router to dispatch a link-state packet that will update all area routers regarding the link failure. Then, the router will perform the shortest-path algorithm in order to re-determine the new best routes (if any).

Table 11-5

OSPF router types

Abbreviation	Name	Purpose
Int	Internal	Router with all interfaces on the same area
ABR	Area Border Router	Router with interfaces in multiple areas
ASBR	Autonomous System Boundary Router	Router with one interface in an OSPF area and another interface that interjects route information from another routing protocol, such as BGP or EIGRP

Table 11-6

OSPF Link-State Advertisements

Type	Name	Purpose
1	Router LSA	Generated by all routers; advertises the routers' links
2	Network LSA	Generated by the designated router of each network; advertises all attached routers
3	Summary LSA for *Area Border Routers* (ABRs)	Generated by ABRs; advertises destinations outside the area
4	Summary LSA for ASBRs	Generated by ABRs; advertises ASBRs
5	Autonomous System External LSA	Generated by ASBRs; advertises destinations that are external to an OSPF autonomous system

The second type of packet that is in use on an OSPF network is the *Link-State Advertisement* (LSA). LSAs alert the routers in an area of any changes or updates in the OSPF area. The types of LSAs are listed in Table 11-6.

Figure 11-4 depicts a multi-area OSPF network design. The configurations of the routers are shown as follows. In this case, there are three areas. The transit or backbone area 0 is the Token Ring segment between Trafalgar and Jutland. Area 1 is located on the serial links between Jutland and Midway as well as on the Ethernet segment of Midway. Area 2 is located on the Ethernet segment of Trafalgar. In this diagram, both Trafalgar and Jutland are *Area Border Routers* (ABRs). Midway is an internal router.

Figure 11-4
Multi-area OSPF
routing example

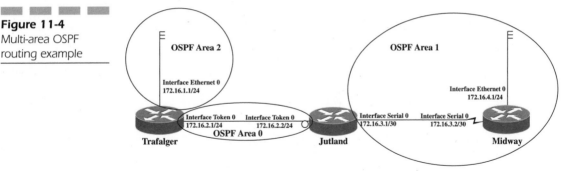

```
hostname Trafalgar
!
!
interface Ethernet0
 ip address 172.16.1.1 255.255.255.0
!
interface TokenRing0
 ip address 172.16.2.1 255.255.255.0

!
router ospf 100
 network 172.16.1.0 0.0.0.255 area 2
 network 172.16.2.0 0.0.0.255 area 0
!

hostname Jutland
!
interface Serial0
 ip address 172.16.3.1 255.255.255.252
!
interface TokenRing0
 ip address 172.16.2.2 255.255.255.0

router ospf 100
 network 172.16.2.0 0.0.0.255 area 0
 network 172.16.3.0 0.0.0.255 area 1
!

hostname Midway
!
interface Ethernet0
 ip address 172.16.4.1 255.255.255.0
!
interface Serial0
 ip address 172.16.3.2 255.255.255.252
!
router ospf 100
```

```
network 172.16.3.0 0.0.0.255 area 1
network 172.16.3.0 0.0.0.255 area 1
```

IS-IS   IS-IS is a complex link-state protocol that can be used to route IP traffic across a network. In addition, it was originally used to route ISO protocol (or Decnet Phase 5) traffic. IS-IS is used in the place of OSPF for one primary reason: it is the only link-state routing protocol that is endorsed by the *International Standards Organization* (ISO).

NOTE: IS-IS configurations are well beyond the scope of the CCDA. In fact, the only tests that include this protocol in the objectives are the CCIE written exam and CCIE lab.

Novell Link-State Protocol (NLSP)   NLSP is closely based on the IS-IS routing protocol. NLSP uses two types of routers: Level 1 and Level 2. Level 1 routers are similar to OSPF internal routers in that they only communicate with other routers in the same area. Level 2 routers are similar to OSPF ABRs because they communicate with intra-area Level 1 routers and inter-area Level 2 routers.

If NLSP is in use on the routers, you must also configure it for the Novell servers on the network. Cisco routers will redistribute routes automatically from IPX RIP networks into NLSP networks.

Operation   The operation of link-state protocols is a complex topic that is not part of the scope of the CCDA exam. The operation can be summarized as follows, however:

- Link-state protocols establish neighboring link-state relationships.
- Link-state protocol routers build a routing table based on these relationships.

- Internal link-state routers exchange route updates with all other routers in their own area.
- Only external routers communicate between areas.

Convergence   A network that is based on link-state protocols can quickly converge and reconfigure routing tables. The reason for this quick convergence is because link-state protocols do not wait for a broadcast interval to update other routers. As soon as a change is detected, an update is sent. This update is always propagated before new routes are determined. Because all routing updates are quickly flooded throughout the network, convergence tends to take place quickly. In other words, networks that are built on link-state protocols will converge quickly.

Overhead

There is little network overhead with link-state protocols. Hello packets, although sent as often as every five seconds, are small in size (64 bytes). These packets have barely any overhead at all. In addition, because route updates are only distributed in the event of a link failure, useless routing information is never broadcast over the network.

Design Notes

Beyond the general foundations that we have presented, the design of large-scale, link-state routing protocol networks is beyond the scope of this course. Most small to medium networks can be designed by using a small number of areas, however. One of the requirements of a network design that would necessitate the use of OSPF is the requirement of a protocol that will support interoperability between various vendors' routers.

In addition, the use of OSPF over Frame Relay and DDR implementations using ISDN can be especially difficult to the beginning designer/implementer. Several features of OSPF need to be reconfigured in order to ensure that OSPF will operate correctly across a Frame Relay network, and improper configurations can result in ISDN links flapping due to the exchange of hello packets and LSAs.

Hybrid Protocols

A hybrid protocol is a protocol that has similarities to both link-state and distance-vector protocols. The only protocol that currently fits this description is the Cisco proprietary protocol called *Enhanced Interior Gateway Routing Protocol* (EIGRP).

EIGRP EIGRP is not only an enhanced version of the distance-vector protocol IGRP, but it also uses a new algorithm—the Diffusing Update Algorithm—to build its routing table. In addition to being a routing protocol for IP, EIGRP can be used to route both IPX and AppleTalk protocols. Separate routing tables are used for each protocol.

Like OSPF, EIGRP uses a hello protocol to maintain a link-state relationship with its neighbors. Each router maintains a separate EIGRP neighbor database, however, and relies upon its neighbors to build that database. Also, like OSPF, EIGRP is a classless routing protocol that can support multiple subnet masks, and it can support an almost unlimited number of hops. EIGRP, like IGRP, uses the following metrics to select the best route:

1. Bandwidth
2. Delay
3. Reliability
4. Load
5. MTU

Figure 11-5 depicts an EIGRP network design. The configuration of the routers are shown as follows.

```
hostname Trafalgar
!
!
interface Ethernet0
```

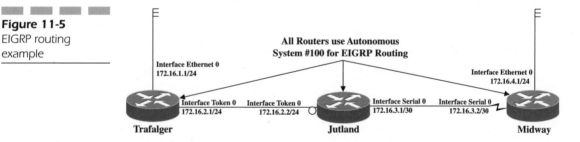

Figure 11-5
EIGRP routing
example

```
  ip address 172.16.1.1 255.255.255.0
 !
interface TokenRing0
  ip address 172.16.2.1 255.255.255.0

 !
router eigrp 100
  network 172.16.0.0 255.255.0.0
 !

hostname Jutland
 !
interface Serial0
  ip address 172.16.3.1 255.255.255.252
 !
interface TokenRing0
  ip address 172.16.2.2 255.255.255.0
 !
router eigrp 100
  network 172.16.0.0 255.255.0.0
 !

hostname Midway
 !
interface Ethernet0
  ip address 172.16.4.1 255.255.255.0
 !
interface Serial0
  ip address 172.16.3.2 255.255.255.252
 !
router eigrp 100
  network 172.16.0.0 255.255.0.0
```

Operation   EIGRP operations are comprised of four basic steps:

1. Building the neighboring link-state relationships

2. Discovering routes by replicating route tales with other neighboring routers

3. Choosing a primary route based on the five metrics listed previously (another backup route can be selected, as well)

4. Maintaining routes (the equivalent of the OPSF LSA process). If a neighboring link state is lost, then the route enters an active state and the router queries neighboring routers in order to update their tables and to determine whether a better path is available.

Convergence and Overhead

Like OSPF and other link-state protocols, the formalized neighbor state relationship in EIGRP enables fast convergence. In addition, the use of hello packets also means that the amount of network overhead that is used to maintain the protocol is minimal. Only changes in network configuration are communicated across the network.

Design Notes

EIGRP design for a small to medium network is almost as easy as designing a distance-vector protocol. One thing to remember is that an *Autonomous System* (AS) number takes care of all EIGRP protocol configurations. Even if the AS number is different between the routers, route information will still be exchanged. Different AS numbers might cause an unusual selection when determining the best route, however.

Bridging Protocols

There are no true bridging protocols; however, there are some protocols that cannot be routed. Therefore, these protocols must be bridged. Protocols cannot be routed if they do not carry a network-layer address. Two protocols that cannot be routed are *Systems Network Architecture* (SNA) and NetBEUI. In general, these two non-routed protocols run across two separate types of bridged networks.SNA is generally found on Token Ring networks that use source route bridging, and NetBEUI is found on Ethernet networks that use transparent bridging.

Operation

A bridge ensures that traffic remains on a specific segment unless it is destined for a remote segment. Depending on the bridging technology (transparent or source-route), this determination of local or remote segment is made in different ways.

Transparent Bridging

The name *transparent bridging* speaks a great deal about the operation of the protocol. This bridge is essentially transparent to the end device. The bridge maintains a table that matches a host and the interface on which that host is located. In Figure 11-6, a small transparent bridging scenario is depicted. In this case, if either Host A or B communicate with Host C, the bridge will forward the packets. If Host A communicates with Host B, the bridge will drop the packets. If the destination is Host D (which is unknown to the bridge at this time), the bridge will flood the broadcast out all ports—with the exception of the port on which the bridge received the packet in order to locate Host D.

Transparent bridging can be used with routers, as well. Figure 11-7 shows a network that is using bridging to pass NetBEUI traffic between several networks. The configuration for the routers is shown as follows.

Figure 11-6
Transparent bridge
forwarding example

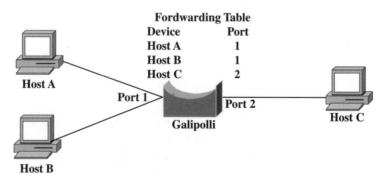

Fordwarding Table	
Device	Port
Host A	1
Host B	1
Host C	2

Figure 11-7
Transparent bridge
forwarding example

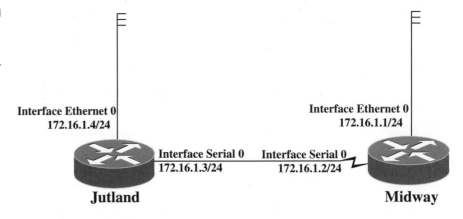

```
hostname Jutland
!
bridge 1 protocol ieee
!
interface Ethernet0
 ip address 172.16.1.4 255.255.255.0
 bridge-group 1
!
interface Serial0
 ip address 172.16.1.3 255.255.255.0
 bridge-group 1
!

hostname Midway
!
bridge 1 protocol ieee
!
interface Ethernet0
 ip address 172.16.1.1 255.255.255.0
 bridge-group 1
!
interface Serial0
 ip address 172.16.1.2 255.255.255.0
 bridge-group 1
!
```

Source-Route Bridging

Source-route bridging is generally seen in Token Ring environments
that are running SNA. The operation of a source route network is
quite different from transparent bridging. In transparent bridging,
the clients have no knowledge that any bridging is taking place. In a

source-route bridging environment, however, if the host does not know the location of a destination host, it must first determine the location of the host.

A Token Ring host begins the process by sending a local explorer frame to locate the destination on the local segment. If it cannot be found locally, the host then sends out an all-routes explorer that explores all possible routes in order to find the destination. Bridges receive the explorer frame and record the ring and bridge number inside the packet. The explorer packet continues through the ring/bridge combinations until the destination is located. The destination replies, and the packet follows the same route in reverse to return to the host, providing the host with a specific path to take for future packets that are traveling to the destination. Figure 11-8 depicts this process.

In Figure 11-8, Host A sends an explorer frame to locate Host C. This frame is passed across all of the bridges and rings. The traveled path is recorded in the frame. When Host C receives the frame, it is returned along the same path to Host A. Host A now has a specific path to Host C. If Host A receives several paths to Host C, it will always use the first explorer response that is received. In Figure 11-8, the path that could be selected would be as follows:

- Step 1: Ring 10
- Step 2: Bridge 1
- Step 3: Ring 11
- Step 4: Bridge 2

Figure 11-8
Source-route bridging example

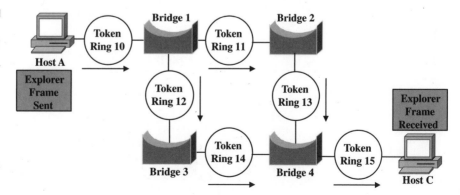

- Step 5: Ring 13
- Step 6: Bridge 4
- Step 7: Ring 15
- Step 8: Bridge 0 (Bridge 0 indicates that the destination has been reached)

This source-route information is then placed in the packets that are being sent between hosts. This information makes up a part of the packet called the *routing information field* (RIF). RIFs enable Token Ring packets to travel between hosts across multiple bridges.

Routers can also be used as source route bridges. Figure 11-9 depicts two Token Ring routers that are being used as bridges. The configuration of the routers is shown as follows.

```
hostname Jutland
!
!
interface TokenRing0
 ip address 172.16.1.4 255.255.255.0
 source-bridge 1 10 2
!
interface TokenRing1
 ip address 172.16.1.3 255.255.255.0
 source-bridge 2 10 1
!

hostname Midway
!
interface TokenRing0
 ip address 172.16.1.1 255.255.255.0
 source-bridge 3 11 2
```

Figure 11-9
Source-route bridging with routers

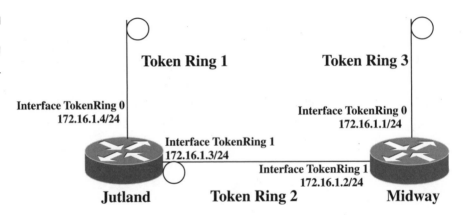

```
!
interface TokenRing1
 ip address 172.16.1.2 255.255.255.0
 source-bridge 2 11 3
!
```

Overhead

There is no additional overhead with these protocols except for the fact that a bridge will not restrict broadcasts from one segment to another. This additional broadcast traffic might be a tremendous burden on a slow WAN circuit. Be cautious when designing bridging over WAN circuits.

Design Notes

This type of design is still found; however, it is slowly being replaced by fully routed networks. More SNA networks are being encapsulated in TCP/IP, enabling the use of *Data Link Switching* (DLSw). Also, many Microsoft environments have also chosen to use TCP/IP instead of NetBEUI. The primary reason for this conversion is to carry a single protocol across the backbone and to ensure that Internet access is available to users.

Case Study

First, let's revisit the Widget Manufacturing case study. In the last chapter, the new network is addressed and the design is almost complete. One of the final items to design is the routing that will exist on the new LAN and WAN.

The existing LAN is being upgraded from a multi-network LAN to an almost identical LAN. The existing routing protocols that are in use today on the LAN are IP RIP and IPX RIP. Because the WAN is a new addition to the network, there is currently no routing design for the WAN. The WAN is depicted in Figure 11-10.

The first routing option to consider is IP routing. Because IP RIP is in use on the LAN, we can assume that the current staff is familiar

Figure 11-10
Widget
Manufacturing
WAN design

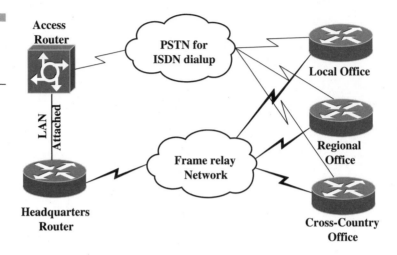

with IP RIP. Because the WAN is quite small, it would be acceptable to continue to use IP RIP as the routing protocol.

If the staff intended to use VLSMs, however, then RIP v2, OSPF, or EIGRP must be used. Also, because all of the LAN equipment is being replaced, implementing a new routing protocol would not be an additional change.

The next routing decision to make regards IPX routing. Because a WAN is involved, it might be advisable to use a protocol that has a low overhead. The possible selections are NLSP, EIGRP, or continuing to use IPX RIP. Currently, there are approximately 30 IPX routes and 10 IPX servers in the Widget environment. This small number of network and servers will not require an excessive amount of IPX RIP/SAP packets for operation. Therefore, using IPX RIP is the simplest and probably best solution.

SUMMARY

Books have been written about network routing. Books have even been written about the detailed operation of the OSPF and EIGRP routing protocols. Routing protocols are all complex technologies that cannot be truly covered in a short chapter. The design of routing protocols in a simple network is relatively straightforward; however, as networks grow and become complex, the cohabitation of multiple protocols is a difficult concept to master.

Now that the routing design is complete, there is one final step in the actual deign process. This step is finalizing the "little things." The little things can range from access lists to encryption. Once the final touches are complete, the design itself is complete.

QUESTIONS

Case Study: Limbo Medical Group

Let's take another look at the case study of the Limbo Medical Group. The Limbo Medical Group was on the cutting edge of network technology 10 years ago. The group decided to implement a centralized computer system for all of its day-to-day operations. This system consists of an X.25 WAN that connects 50 small offices to a central hospital facility. This X.25 WAN carries legacy SNA traffic between hosts and a mainframe. In the previous chapters, there were several case study questions regarding LAN and WAN design. The following questions will assume that Figure 11-11 is an accurate representation of a portion of the new network. According to the information that was provided in earlier chapters, the only protocol that will traverse the new WAN is IP.

1. If a requirement exists for interoperability between the new IP routing protocol and another vendor's router, what protocol should be selected?

   a. IPX RIP
   b. OSPF
   c. EIGRP
   d. IGRP

Figure 11-11
New Limbo Medical network design

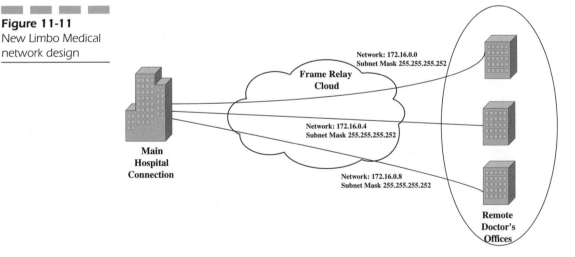

2. It has been proposed that IP RIP should be used as the routing protocol. If the intended subnet mask of the WAN links is 255.255.255.252, why is IP RIP a poor selection?

   a. It is a proprietary protocol.

   b. It is a classless protocol.

   c. It does not support a mask of 255.255.255.252.

   d. It is a classful protocol.

3. What type of bridging protocol was most likely used in the SNA environment?

   a. Transparent bridging

   b. Translational bridging

   c. Source-route bridging

   d. Source-route transparent bridging

Case Study: Global Supplies Corporation

Again, to revisit the situation of Global Supplies, this company is a multi-national corporation that is comprised of approximately 15 separate facilities throughout North America. Each facility has an existing LAN that has been upgraded according to the needs of the specific facility. The LANs range from small 10MB Ethernet networks to large Fast Ethernet networks that have Gigabit backbones.

At the previous step in the design process, the WAN transport was identified. The proposed solution to consolidate the T1s is an ATM backbone. The proposed network topology is shown in Figure 11-12. All of the multiple T1 circuits have been replaced with an ATM network. The single T1s remain in order to provide data redundancy between sites.

For the Global Supplies WAN, both IP and IPX protocols are in use. Routing at the individual LAN locations is handled by the local LAN administrators. In the past, a mix of protocols and route-redistribution schemes has been used. The existing WAN group would like to see a complete routing redesign.

Figure 11-12
Global Supplies
network design

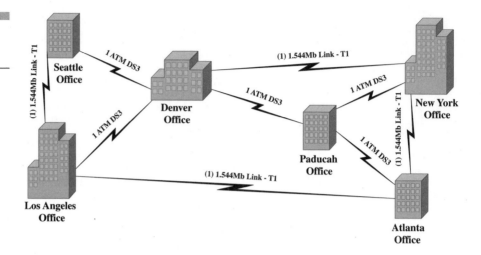

4. For the IPX protocol, what protocol would ensure that local administrators do not have to learn a new technology?

   a. NLSP

   b. EIGRP

   c. IPX RIP

5. For the IPX protocol, what protocol would ensure that local administrators do not have to learn a new technology and that there is not an excessive amount of redundant routing information being propagated?

   a. NLSP

   b. EIGRP

   c. IPX RIP

6. For the IP protocol, what protocol would ensure that all of the subnet masks that are in use can be accessed and can interoperate with the various devices at the LANs?

   a. IGRP

   b. RIP

   c. EIGRP

   d. RIP v2

7. If OSPF was selected as the routing protocol, then it would be reasonable that the WAN would become which area?

   a. Area 1

   b. Area 0

   c. The virtual area

   d. Area A

Case Study: G&S Productions

Again, we will revisit the case study of Gimball Productions and Shapiro Productions. They have recently merged. The new company, G&S Productions, has become a major commercial production company. There are two main sites, each having about 250 users. In addition, each company has three to five smaller offices throughout the United States.

After the WAN design portion of the project, the decision was made to connect the two offices via a leased line for the time being. One concern of the respective IT groups is IP addressing. Remember that the Gimball office and WAN uses an IP addressing scheme of 192.168.1.0 to 192.168.3.0 and that the Shapiro office and WAN uses the same IP addressing scheme of 192.168.1.0. Therefore, we decided that NAT would be used for the time being to connect the two sites. Figure 11-13 depicts the new G&S network.

8. What type of routing must be performed in order to connect the two networks?

   a. Static

   b. RIP

   c. IGRP

   d. EIGRP

9. If the original Gimball WAN uses RIP and the Shapiro WAN uses IGRP, what protocol should be used for the integrated network?

   a. OSPF

   b. EIGRP

   c. RIP v2

   d. It does not matter.

Figure 11-13
G&S Productions
network design

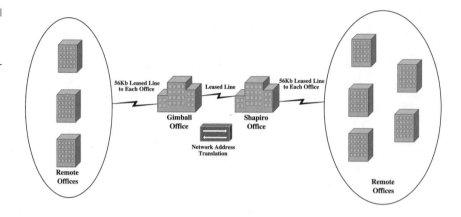

10. Earlier in the case study, we mentioned that AppleTalk is in use on the network. If the network must communicate via AppleTalk and the WAN links remain free of overhead traffic, what protocol would be the best selection?

a. AURP

b. EIGRP

c. RTMP

d. RIP

ANSWERS

1. b. OSPF

Only OSPF is a non-proprietary routing protocol. IPX RIP is used for IPX/SPX, and IGRP/EIGRP is a Cisco proprietary protocol.

2. d. It is a classful protocol.

A classful protocol can only understand one subnet mask. Therefore, either all of the LANs would have to have the same mask or the serial links would not be reachable.

3. c. Source route bridging

Source route bridging is most likely the protocol that is used with the SNA traffic.

4. c. IPX RIP

The IPX RIP protocol will not require any changes to the local network and is most familiar to the LAN administrators. NLSP is unacceptable because it must also be implemented on the local servers. EIGRP could work because it is implemented only on the WAN portion of the network.

5. b. EIGRP

EIGRP should be implemented on the WAN portion in order to reduce the amount of routing overhead. Because IPX RIP is implemented on the LAN portion and is automatically redistributed into the route tables, there are no changes on the LAN.

6. d. RIP v2

RIP version 2 is the only protocol listed that is classless and that is an open protocol. RIP and IGRP are classful, and EIGRP is a proprietary protocol.

7. b. Area 0

The backbone or transit area of an OSPF network is Area 0. Due to the centralized nature of the WAN, it would be advisable to design this area as Area 0.

8. a. Static routes

Because NAT is used, a static route would be used to direct all traffic that is destined for NAT traffic.

9. d. It does not matter.

It does not matter which protocol is run, because NAT makes the networks appear invisible to each other. Only static routes will enable traffic to be passed from one network to another.

10. b. EIGRP

EIGRP will enable the networks to interoperate. Both RTMP and AURP have an excessive amount of overhead and would not be an acceptable choice. Finally, RIP can only route IP, not AppleTalk.

The Finishing Touches

Objectives Covered in This Chapter

1. Scalability issues for various Cisco IOS software features, access lists, proxy services, encryption, compression, and queuing

Introduction

Finally, the last step of the design process itself has been reached. This step can best be described as the finishing touches of the design. These finishing touches are used to adjust the network design to fit the exact requirements of the customer.

These finishing touches are almost always present in the Cisco IOS code on the router. The IOS has a rich feature set that enables many different services to be implemented as part of a network design.

Router Software Features

All software features are enabled through the Cisco command line. A command is typed, and then other arguments are added as required. Some services require several commands to be implemented in full. The software features that can complete a network design are access lists, proxy services, encryption, compression, and queuing.

Access Lists

Access lists are used to control network traffic as it passes across a router. This traffic control can be blocking traffic to certain resources, or it could be used to improve network performance. Access lists can also be used as a basic security mechanism. An access list can block information from a specific network or host to a specific destination network or host.

An access list is comprised of a series of commands that build a criteria set for permitting or denying traffic. Each command can either permit or deny a specific type of traffic. A packet is matched with each line of an access list in order to determine whether the packet is permitted to continue or whether the packet will be denied and dropped.

There are two general types of access lists: standard and extended. Standard access lists are simple access lists that only enable basic criteria to be matched. Usually, standard access lists can only match the source address of the packet. Extended access lists can match a more complex set of criteria, such as destination address, TCP port, packet size, and upper-layer protocol. Each protocol also has a specific criteria set that can be matched in an extended access list.

Access List Operation   There are several steps to creating an access list. These steps are as follows:

1. Define the access list by name or number.

2. Enter commands in order to build the access list.

3. Apply the access list to an interface.

Define the Access List   The first step toward access list creation is to actually define the access lists. The common method for performing this task is to use a number that represents the type of access list. Table 12-1 shows the numbers that are reserved for access lists.

There is also second method for identifying IP and IPX standard and extended access lists. These types of access lists can be identified by a name. This method of identifying access lists has one distinct advantage over numbered IP addresses: building and changing the access list criteria.

Entering Commands to Build the Access List   The second step in access list creation is to define the selection criteria of the access lists. Each command specifies whether the listed selection criteria should permit a packet or deny a packet. A single access list can have multiple commands.

Table 12-1

Access list numbering

Type of Access List	Range
IP standard	1–99
IP extended	100–199
Bridge type code	200–299
DECnet standard and extended	300–399
XNS standard	400–499
XNS extended	500–599
AppleTalk	600–699
Bridge MAC	700–799
IPX standard	800–899
IPX extended	900–999
IPX SAP	1000–1099
Bridge extended	1100–1199
NLSP route aggregation	1200–1299

The most important factor in building access lists is the order in which the commands are entered. A packet is matched to the commands in the order that they were entered. Once a match (either a permit or a deny) is made, the packet is filtered. Even if a later command would have the opposite effect, the first match takes priority.

For example, imagine that there are several commands in an access list. The first command permits all packets from the 192.168.1.0 network. The second command denies all traffic that is destined to 192.168.2.10. The remaining commands are not important in this example. If a packet from the 192.168.3.0 network (destined for 192.168.2.10) enters the routers, the second command will deny the packet. If a packet from the 192.168.1.0 network is sent to the same device, 192.168.2.10, the first command will permit this packet. If the command order were reversed, then no packets that are destined for the host 192.168.2.10 would ever be permitted.

Finally, there is one last important concept to remember when building access lists. All access lists (regardless of protocol) always end with an implied command that denies all other packets. This concept is important to remember, because an access list will deny any traffic unless it is specifically permitted in a command.

Applying the Access List to an Interface   Without applying an access list to an interface, the access list commands are useless. The list has been built but not applied. The final step is to actually apply the list to an interface.

With most protocols, the access list can be applied to the interface as either inbound or outbound. An inbound access lists examines packets as they are received on the interface. If the packet matches a permit command, the packet is passed to the router. If the packet matches a deny command, then the packet is simply dropped.

An outbound access lists examines packets as they are sent on the interface. If the packet matches a permit command, the packet is sent out the interface. If the packet matches a deny command, then the packet is simply dropped.

NOTE: *In general, it is preferable to apply access lists in outbound mode. When an access list is applied in inbound mode, all packets (regardless of destination) must be examined. With an outbound-applied access list, only packets that are sent out the interface are examined. This process might reduce the* central processing unit *(CPU) overhead of the router.*

Access List Examples   The first access list example is a standard IP access list that uses numbers. The vendor network requires access to the 192.168.1.0 network only. An access list is being used to restrict all traffic from the vendor network of 172.16.0.0 to other destinations on the network. Figure 12-1 depicts the network and vendor connection in detail. The configuration for the routers is shown as follows.

```
Trafalgar Router Config
interface Ethernet0
 ip address 192.168.1.1 255.255.255.0
 !
interface Serial0
 ip address 172.16.1.1 255.255.255.252
```

Figure 12-1
Standard IP access list

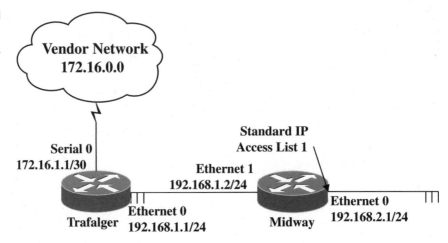

```
!
router eigrp 1
 network 192.168.1.0
!

Midway Router Config
interface Ethernet0
 ip address 192.168.2.1 255.255.255.0
 access-group 1 out
!
interface Ethernet1
 ip address 192.168.1.2 255.255.255.0
!
router eigrp 1
 network 192.168.1.0
 network 192.168.2.0
!
access-list 1 permit 192.168.1.0 0.0.0.255
```

This figure and the configuration only have one access list command. This command permits traffic from the 192.168.1.0 network. The implicit "deny all" denies all other packets.

The next access list example is an extended IP access list that uses numbers. Now, the vendor network requires access to the Web server on the 192.168.2.0 network and requires access to the 192.168.1.0 network. An access list is being used to restrict all traffic from the vendor network of 172.16.0.0 to other destinations on the network. Figure 12-2 depicts the network and vendor connection in detail. The configuration for the routers is shown as follows.

Figure 12-2
Extended IP
access list

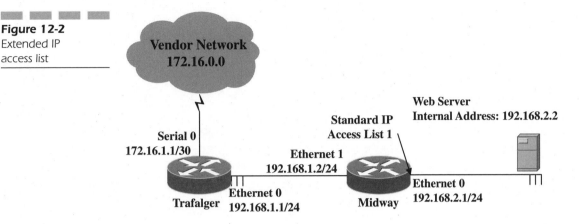

```
Trafalgar Router Config
interface Ethernet0
 ip address 192.168.1.1 255.255.255.0
!
interface Serial0
 ip address 172.16.1.1 255.255.255.252
!
router eigrp 1
 network 192.168.1.0
!

Midway Router Config
interface Ethernet0
 ip address 192.168.2.1 255.255.255.0
 access-group 100 out
!
interface Ethernet1
 ip address 192.168.1.2 255.255.255.0
!
router eigrp 1
 network 192.168.1.0
 network 192.168.2.0
!
access-list 100 permit 192.168.1.0 0.0.0.255
access-list 100 permit 172.16.0.0 0.0.255.255 host
192.168.2.2 eq www
```

The figure and configuration only have two access list commands. The first command permits traffic from the 192.168.1.0 network. The next line enables only Web access from the vendor network to the Web server. The implicit "deny all" denies all other packets.

Access List Design Notes   Access lists are efficient methods for securing networks and for improving performance. A popular use of IPX access lists is to inhibit the replication of many Novell services. In a large Novell server environment, it might be advisable to restrict all *Service Access Protocol* (SAP) traffic except for core servers.

Routers must examine each packet to determine whether access lists are in use. In other words, the router will match each packet against the access list until a match is found. If there are many lines in an access list and the packets match the last line, then the router will use a lot of processing power to match this access list. In general, the commands that have the most matches should be placed at the top of the list. The less commands to check, the less processing that will be required on the router.

Proxy Services

Proxyservices enable a router to act as a service that is not available locally. There are three main uses for proxy services: resource discovery, traffic reduction, and performance enhancement.

Resource Discovery   In some configurations, there are no resources on the local network. All connections to the network resources are discovered and provided through the router. In this case, there are several proxy services that the router provides:

1. A router can provide a response to a GetNearestServer request from an IPX/Netware client. This situation will only happen if there is no local server.

2. Some workstations do not understand the concept of subnet masks. In other words, a host that has an IP address of 172.16.1.1 would think that all of the hosts on the 172.16.0.0 network are locally attached. In this instance, a router would proxy the ARP request to the remote address. This concept is known as proxy ARP.

3. An IP helper-address enables a router to propagate a broadcast to remote hosts or networks. For instance, this process enables the use of centralized DHCP servers.

Traffic Reduction   Another facet of proxy services is reducing the amount of traffic over bridged networks and *Wide Area Networks* (WANs). By reducing the overhead traffic, the performance of the network increases. There are three main types of traffic reduction services:

1. A router acting as a source-route bridge will convert an all-routes explorer frame into a single-route explorer frame. This procedure will reduce the number of explorer frames on a network that has multiple paths.

2. Novell servers and Netware clients send keepalive messages every five minutes. The keepalives use the Netware Core Protocol. If a dialup or DDR WAN circuit is in use, these keepalives will not permit the circuit to disconnect. A router will "spoof" these keepalives for both the server and the client. This process is called watchdog spoofing.

3. Another Novell spoofing technique is SPX spoofing. Here, keepalives that use the SPX protocol are spoofed in the same manner as watchdog spoofs.

Performance Enhancement   The last proxy service is used to enhance the performance of SNA environments. SNA uses an LLC packet to transmit information. This packet requires an acknowledgment from the destination. In a large routed network, this acknowledgment might be delayed. This delay could cause the SNA session to time out.

The router provides a LLC local acknowledgment. This acknowledgment ensures that the client does not receive a late acknowledgment and prevents a session timeout.

Encryption

As data and packets more across the network, they are susceptible to many types of attacks. Data can be read or altered from any point between the source and the destination. An outside person could even forge packets that are sent between two devices.

Encryption provides a method to protect data as it travels between Cisco routers. This principle is shown in Figure 12-3.

Cisco encryption technology involves three steps. The first step is to configure the encryption keys on one peer router. The second step is to authenticate peer routers. The last step is to encrypt the actual data.

Encryption Key and Peer Router Configuration

Peer routers perform the actual encryption and decryption of packets. All routers between these routers do not perform any encryption function; rather, they route packets. Before peer routers can communicate with one another, each router must have the DSS public and private keys generated. Each peer router's public and private DSS keys are unique.

The DSS private key is never shared. The public key is given to the administrators of the peer routers. The remote peer router is then configured with the public key of the peer router. This process is shown in Figure 12-4.

Peer Router Authentication

Before two peer routers can send encrypted data, an encrypted session must be established. To establish an encrypted session, the peer routers exchange connection messages. These methods authenticate each router to one another and create a temporary *Data Encryption Standard* (DES), or session key.

Figure 12-3
Encryption principles

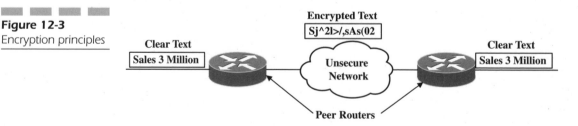

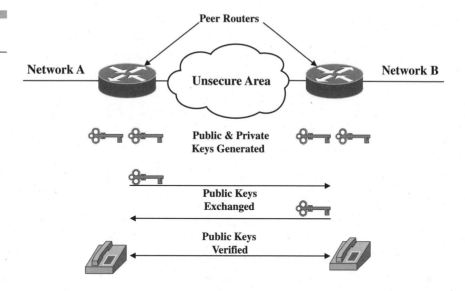

Figure 12-4
DSS key creation

Authentication between the peer routers is accomplished by attaching a character string, called a signature, to the message. This signature is derived from the routers' DSS private key and is authenticated by the public key on the peer router. A signature is unique to the sending device and cannot be spoofed.

The temporary DES key that is generated is the key that will be used to encrypt all of the traffic in the encrypted session. The DES key is computed by exchanging *Diffie-Hellman* (DH) numbers in the connection messages. Then, these DH numbers are used to compile the DES key that will be shared by the routers and that will be used in the encrypted session.

Actual Data Encryption

After the peer routers have been authenticated and have exchanged a DES or session key, data can be encrypted and exchanged. A DES encryption algorithm uses the DES or session key to encrypt IP packets during the session.

Only IP packets can be encrypted. Any other protocol that needs to be encrypted must be encapsulated in an IP packet. After encryption, the IP packets can be seen on the wire. The data or payload is encrypted, however, and cannot be read. The *Internet Protocol* (IP) and *Transmission Control Protocol* (TCP) or UDP headers are not encrypted and continue to be transmitted in clear text.

An encrypted session will be terminated if the session times out. When the session times out, both the DH numbers and the DES keys are discarded. The private and public keys remain the same. When a new encrypted session is required, new DH numbers and DES keys are created.

IPSec *Cisco Encryption Technology* (CET) is a Cisco proprietary protocol that will only operate between two Cisco routers. IPSec is a standards-based encryption technology that is almost identical to CET. IPSec enables Cisco routers to communicate over encrypted sessions with non-Cisco devices and with other IPSec-compliant clients.

IPSec also uses digital certificates—the *Internet Key Exchange* (IKE) protocol and *Certification Authorities* (CAs). A digital certificate is comprised of information that identifies the user or device, such as the name, IP address, and most importantly the public key. All devices register their certificates with a CA. The CA then signs the digital certification.

When the digital certifications are exchanged between peer routers, the routers accept the digital certificate as long as the router trusts the CA. This automatic exchange renders the manual exchange and verification of public keys obsolete.

Compression Compression basically reduces the size of a data frame to be transmitted over the network. All data-compression algorithms are based on two types of encoding techniques: statistical and dictionary.

Statistical Compression This compression mechanism uses a fixed encoding method to compress data. It is best used in single applications where the data is relatively consistent. Data network traffic is rarely consistent. Therefore, statistical compression is generally not used for router-based compression.

Dictionary Compression This compression mechanism uses a dynamically encoded dictionary to replace a string of continuous characters with code sequences. The codes and the associated symbols are stored in memory. This mechanism is the best approach to the variations in data networks.

Cisco Compression Algorithms Cisco uses two main compression algorithms. Both are based on dictionary compression. The compression algorithms are the Stacker and the Predictor algorithm.

STAC Electronics developed the Stacker algorithm, often called STAC. The Cisco IOS version of STAC provides good compression; however, it can be CPU intensive. The Predictor compression algorithm attempts to guess or predict the next characters in the data stream. When compared with STAC, the Predictor algorithm is less CPU intensive, but it requires more memory.

The Cisco IOS currently provides four primary data-compression solutions:

1. *TCP/IP header compression according to RFC 1144* This solution is designed to improve the bandwidth utilization of low-speed serial links. A TCP/IP packet includes a 40-byte header. Once a connection is established, the header information does not need to be repeated in every packet. A smaller header that identifies the connection and indicates the fields that changed is transmitted, and the compressed header averages 10 bytes.

2. WAN link compression is configured on the main interface only.

3. Payload compression is configured on point-to-point or multi-point interfaces or subinterfaces.

4. Hardware compression on the Compression Service Adapter of the Cisco 7200 and 7500 series routers

Software compression is a resource-intensive activity on a router (especially on the CPU). Because different router series have different CPU processing power, the amount of serial lines that can be compressed varies as well. Table 12-2 lists the router series and the maximum amount of serial line speeds that can be compressed. If the router is performing other CPU-intensive tasks (such as OSPF), the line rates listed in Table 12-2 should be reduced.

Again, remember that compression is a resource-intensive process. The best way to determine the actual effect of compression on the

Table 12-2

Maximum serial
line compression

Router Series	STAC Compression	Predictor Compression
Cisco 2500 Series	128Kbps	256Kbps
Cisco 4000 Series	256Kbps	500Kbps
Cisco 4500 Series	500Kbps	T1
Cisco 4700 Series	T1	(2) T1s
Cisco 7000 Series	256Kbps	500Kbps

CPU load is to compare the CPU usage of a pre-compression router with the CPU utilization of a post-compression router.

If the router CPU load is more than 40 percent, then Cisco recommends for all encryption and compression to be stopped. If compression or encryption is required, the best long-term solution would be to purchase a router that has more processing power.

Queuing

Regardless of the speed of a network WAN link, there will be occasions when the amount of information is more that the link can accommodate or when packets are received at the same time. When this situation happens, all of the information will be stored in a buffer. There are many methods for emptying this buffer. The method that is used to empty the buffer will determine the order in which to send the waiting packets. Cisco IOS software supports the following queuing methods:

1. *First in, first out* (FIFO) queuing
2. Priority queuing
3. Custom queuing
4. *Weighted Fair Queuing* (WFQ)

FIFO Queuing   FIFO queuing is the default queuing method for all links that are greater than 2Mbps. This method works just as the name implies and requires no configuration in order to operate on an interface. The first packet to arrive in the buffer is the first packet to be sent. There is no precedence given to any specific type of packet.

The only determining factor for the order in which the packets are sent is the order in which they are received.

FIFO does not provide any type of *Quality of Service* (QoS) guarantee. Also, it is possible that a single application might completely saturate the link and not enable any other applications to communicate. Because this method might cause unfair delays in application transmission, the remaining three queuing methods can provide better performance.

Priority Queuing   Priority queuing gives a specific type of packet priority over all other packets. This type of queuing was designed to give time-sensitive protocols (such as SNA) priority over other protocols. Packets can be prioritized based on protocol, source address, destination address, or size. If WAN links are sometimes congested, then priority queuing is an effective solution. If the congestion is near constant, however, the priority queuing will not solve the root cause of the problem.

Priority queuing requires extra CPU processing. Priority queuing has four priority queues: high, medium, normal, and low. The router will attempt to send a packet via the high queue. If no packet is there, it will send a packet from the medium queue. After each packet is sent, the high queue is again examined for a packet. In priority queuing, it is possible that packets in the low-priority queues might never be sent. The operation of priority queuing is seen in Figure 12-5.

Creating a priority queue on a router is a four-step process. The router commands are not part of the CCDA exam, but we provide information about them here to help explain the steps.

1. Create an output priority queuing list:

```
priority-list 1 protocol ip high tcp 23
priority-list 1 protocol ip medium
priority-list 1 interface ethernet 0 low
```

2. Assign a default queue:

```
priority-list 1 default normal
```

3. Specify the queue sizes (the number packets to hold in the queue; this specification is not required, however):

Figure 12-5
Priority queuing
operation

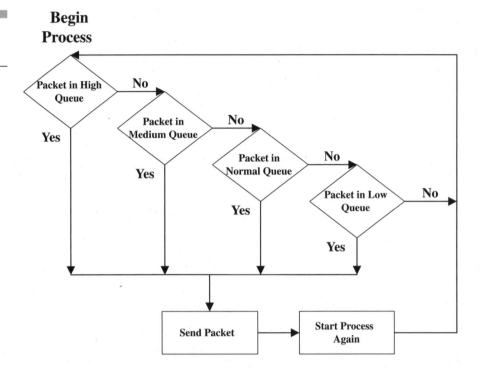

```
priority-list 1 queue-limit 15 20 20 50
```

4. Assign a priority list number to the interface:

```
Interface Serial0
priority-group 1
```

Custom Queuing   Custom queuing enables bandwidth to be shared among applications. Custom queuing assigns amounts of queue space to different protocols. Then, the queues are handled in a round-robin order. Custom queuing will send packets from all of the queues in order (unlike priority queuing, which will always send packets in the high-priority queue first).

Custom queuing provides guaranteed bandwidth at a congestion point. Custom queuing assures each specified traffic type a fixed portion of bandwidth. Custom queuing puts packets in 1 of 17 queues. The router services queues 1 through 16 in round-robin order. Queue 0 is the system queue and is always emptied first. Once the packets are transmitted from a queue and the queue exceeds the transmis-

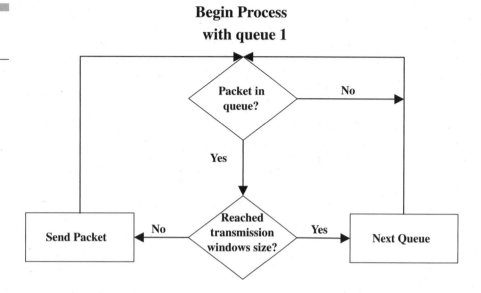

Figure 12-6
Custom queuing
operation

sion window size, the next queue is checked for packets to send. Custom queuing is shown in Figure 12-6.

Creating a custom queue on a router is a five-step process. The router commands are not part of the CCDA exam, but we provide information about them here to help explain the steps.

1. Create custom queue filtering for a protocol or interface:

```
queue-list 1 protocol ip 1
queue-list 1 protocol ipx 2
queue-list 1 interface ethernet0 3
```

2. Assign a default queue:

```
queue-list 1 default 5
```

3. Change the queue capacity (the number of packets to hold in the queue):

```
queue-list 1 queue1 limit 40
```

4. Configure the transfer rate per queue (not required):

```
queue-list 1 queue 1 byte-count 4500
```

5. Assign a queue list number to the interface:

```
Interface ethernet0
custom-queue-list 1
```

WFQ   WFQ is an algorithm that is designed to reduce delay. WFQ also provides apredictable response time for traffic flows. The purpose of WFQ is to ensure that low-volume applications are not overwhelmed by high-volume applications. For instance, Telnet traffic will not be delayed by large, high-volume *File Transfer Protocol* (FTP) transfers when WFQ is in use.

WFQ recognizes the traffic flows that are associated with the underlying packets. Because WFQ can recognize the traffic flows, low-volume traffic flows are prioritized over high-volume traffic flows.

WFQ adapts to changing network traffic automatically and requires almost no configuration. WFQ is the default queuing mode on most serial interfaces that are configured to run at or below E1 speeds (or 2.048Mbps). On interfaces where WFQ is not enabled by default, WFQ can be enabled with the command `fair-queue`.

Case Study

Now, let's revisit the Widget Manufacturing case study. In the last chapter, the new network now has a complete routing design. The final item to design is any software features that are required to meet the customer's requirements.

Before the requirements and features can be designed, you should examine Figure 12-7 (the Widget Manufacturing LAN design) and Figure 12-8 (the Widget Manufacturing WAN design).

There are two customer requirements that need to be addressed with the various software features. The requirements are as follows:

1. VLAN A is the accounting department. Because of the sensitive nature of its work, all access to its network must be restricted. Access to several devices is permitted on a case-by-case basis.

2. The Frame Relay connections to the remote offices are provisioned with relatively low-speed connections. For this reason, all Telnet traffic needs to be prioritized across this link

Figure 12-7
Widget Manufacturing LAN design

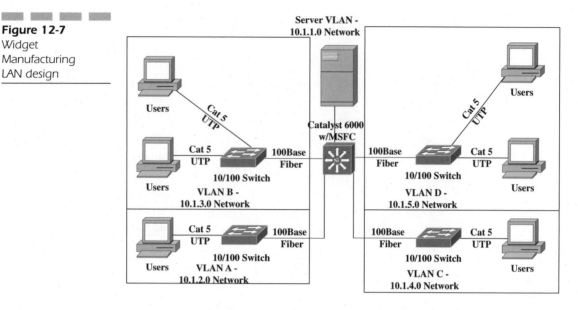

Figure 12-8
Widget Manufacturing WAN design

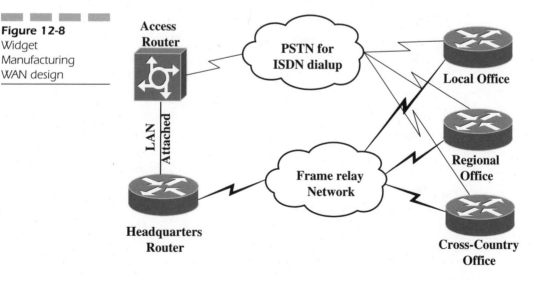

in order to ensure adequate performance of the manufacturing system.

The first requirement can be satisfied with an access list (specifically, an extended access list). A standard access list would not be an acceptable choice, because the security is based on more factors that just the source address. A standard access list can filter the source address only. An extended access list can be configured to filter traffic based on source address, destination address, and upper-layer protocol or application port.

Only queuing can meet the second requirement. Compression would make more bandwidth available on the links, but it would not ensure that Telnet traffic is prioritized. Both custom or priority queuing would meet the requirement of prioritizing Telnet traffic; however, they might restrict or inhibit other traffic flows. The best solution would be to use WFQ. This method would ensure that low-volume traffic such as Telnet is prioritized over other traffic flows. If the bandwidth congestion were excessive, then either custom or priority queuing would replace WFQ in order to ensure that Telnet traffic was prioritized to the destination.

SUMMARY

The finishing touches that we have discussed are what make the design truly come together. Many of the customer requirements that a designer will see can only be addressed with these software features. Also, there are many software features that are beyond the scope of the CCDA exam. These features, such as traffic shaping, RSVP, and tag switching, might be required to truly complete a design.

Now, the design itself is complete—but it still must be validated and proven. A design that is unproven is not worth the paper on which it is written. There are two steps to proving the design. The first step is developing a test plan, and the second step is actually proving the design.

QUESTIONS

Case Study: Limbo Medical Group

Let's take another look at the case study of the Limbo Medical Group. The Limbo Medical Group was on the cutting edge of network technology 10 years ago. The group decided to implement a centralized computer system for all of its day-to-day operations. This system consists of an X.25 WAN that connects 50 small offices to a central hospital facility. This X.25 WAN carries legacy SNA traffic between hosts and a mainframe. In the previous chapters, there were several case study questions regarding LAN and WAN design. The following questions will assume that Figure 12-9 is an accurate representation of a portion of the new network. According to the information that we provided in previous chapters, the only protocol that will traverse the new WAN is IP.

The customer requirements for the design are as follows:

The central hospital has many connections to other vendors. There must be some type of security in place in order to

Figure 12-9
New Limbo Medical
network design

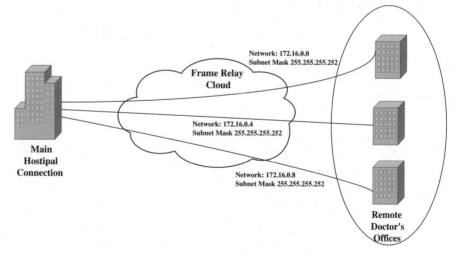

protect the internal network. In general, the vendors require access to several hosts on the network.

The WAN circuits are, in general, slower than 128Kbps. It is necessary to ensure that the maximum amount of bandwidth is used.

1. In the sever farm, there are several antiquated UNIX servers that do not recognize subnet masks. What software feature enables these servers to communicate with the rest of the network?

   a. Proxy services
   b. GNS proxy
   c. LLC local acknowledgement
   d. Proxy ARP

2. What software feature would solve the first requirement?

   The central hospital has many connections to other vendors. There must be some type of security in place in order to protect the internal network. In general, the vendors require access to several hosts on the network. What would you use?

   a. Standard access list
   b. Extended access list
   c. Encryption
   d. WFQ

3. What software feature should be used to fulfill the second requirement?

   The WAN circuits are, in general, slower than 128Kbps. It is necessary to ensure that the maximum amount of bandwidth is used. What would you use?

   a. Compression
   b. Custom queuing
   c. Priority queuing
   d. WFQ

Case Study: Global Supplies Corporation

Again, to revisit the situation of Global Supplies, this company is a multi-national corporation that is comprised of approximately 15 separate facilities throughout North America. Each facility has an existing LAN that has been upgraded according to the needs of the specific facility. The LANs range from small 10MB Ethernet networks to large Fast Ethernet networks with Gigabit backbones.

At the previous step in the design process, the WAN transport was identified. The proposed solution to consolidate the T1s is an ATM backbone. The proposed network topology is shown in Figure 12-10. All of the multiple T1 circuits have been replaced with an ATM network. The single T1s remain in order to provide data redundancy between sites.

For the Global Supplies WAN, both IP and IPX protocols are in use. The corporate WAN team has several requirements:

The number of Novell server advertisements must be kept at a manageable level.

One of the ATM links will be delayed in delivery. In the interim, an ATM circuit over a public carrier will be used instead. All traffic across this link must be protected.

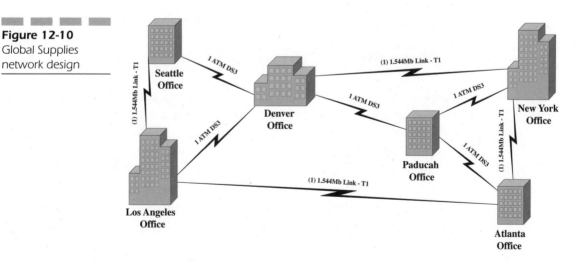

Figure 12-10
Global Supplies
network design

4. For the IPX protocol, what software feature service would ensure that local clients can always reach a Novell server—even if the local server is down?

   a. Proxy ARP
   b. Proxy IPX
   c. Watchdog spoofing
   d. Get nearest server response

5. What type of access list would fulfill the following requirement?

   The number of Novell server advertisements must be kept to a manageable level. What would you use?

   a. Standard IPX
   b. Extended IPX
   c. IPX SAP
   d. IPX RIP

6. What two services would ensure that the following requirement is fulfilled?

   One of the ATM links will be delayed in delivery. In the interim, an ATM circuit over a public carrier will be used instead. All traffic across this link must be protected. What would you use?

   a. Access Lists
   b. Encryption
   c. Compression
   d. Queuing

Case Study: The Bank of Pompeii

Next, we will revisit the Bank of Pompeii case study. The Bank of Pompeii has just completed a new corporate office tower in a prime downtown location. This office will enable the bank to consolidate six small offices into the new corporate tower. In addition to this move, all of the SNA traffic will be removed from the WAN.

All of the offices are connected via a Frame Relay WAN in a hub-and-spoke configuration. The hub of the Frame Relay network will be the new corporate tower. The remainder of the offices will remain

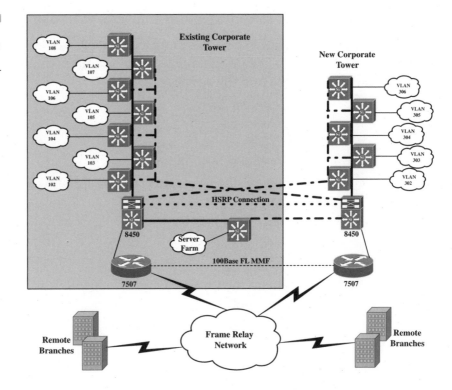

Figure 12-11
The Bank of Pompeii's
new network design

on the Frame Relay network. The new LAN and WAN network design is depicted in Figure 12-11.

As part of the customer requirements, the following items are needed for the upgrade: an IP addressing scheme, a routing plan, a network diagram, and a complete specification of all equipment that is required. One of the most important requirements for any installation at the Bank of Pompeii is security. A complete audit trail is required for all equipment that is placed on the network. This audit material is routinely scanned for any unusual activity.

In addition, there are several requirements that the design must meet:

All DHCP, BOOTP, and DNS servers are located in the server farm. The design must enable seamless communication between clients and the services.

In order to maximize the Frame Relay links, compression must be used.

7. What software feature fulfills the following requirement?

   All DHCP, BOOTP, and DNS servers are located in the server farm. The design must enable seamless communication between clients and the services.

   a. IP helper address
   b. Proxy ARP
   c. SPX spoofing
   d. Watchdog spoofing

8. What type of encryption is non-proprietary?

   a. CET
   b. STAC
   c. Predictor
   d. IPSec

9. What specific type of compression will fulfill the following requirement?

   In order to maximize the Frame Relay links, compression must be used.

   a. Hardware compression
   b. STAC
   c. Payload compression
   d. Statistical compression

10. Which queuing solution prioritizes one traffic type at the expense of other traffic types?

   a. Custom
   b. Priority
   c. FIFO
   d. WFQ

ANSWERS ▮ ▮ ▮ ▮ ▮ ▮ ▮ ▮

1. **d.** Proxy ARP

   Some workstations do not understand the concept of subnet masks. In other words, a host that has an IP address of 172.16.1.1 would think that all of the hosts on the 172.16.0.0 network are locally attached. In this instance, a router would proxy the ARP request to the remote address. This concept is known as proxy ARP.

2. **b.** Extended Access List

   Because a number of destinations and sources exist, the best security method would be an extended access list.

3. **a.** Compression

   The key requirement is to maximize the WAN bandwidth. Queuing will not maximize the bandwidth; instead, it will simply manage the existing bandwidth. Only compression will provide the maximum amount of bandwidth.

4. **d.** *Get nearest server* (GNS) response

   The GNS response enables a router to answer a `GetNearestServer` request from a Novell client and to provide an available server to the client.

5. **c.** IPX SAP

   The number of servers and services that are propagated through the network can only be managed by IPX SAP access lists. They occupy the 1000–1099 number range.

6. **a.** and **b.** Access lists and encryption

   Because a public network is in use, all traffic that is crossing this link must be encrypted. In addition, in order to ensure that no unauthorized people gain access through the router, access lists should be used on each end of the link.

7. **a.** IP helper address

   An IP helper address enables certain broadcasts (such as DHCP and BOOTP) to be propagated seamlessly through the network.

8. d. IPSec

CET is an encryption technology but is not an open standard. Only IPSec is an open standard.

9. c. Payload compression

Only payload compression is an actual compression solution.

10. b. Priority queuing

Priority queuing gives a specific type of packet priority over all other packets. This type of queuing was designed to give time-sensitive protocols (such as SNA) priority over other protocols.

Proving the Design

Objectives Covered in This Chapter

1. Prove that the network design meets the customer's needs.
2. Complete the tasks that are required to build a prototype that demonstrates the functionality of the network design.

Introduction

After much work, the new design is finally complete. There is still one major milestone left in the design cycle, however: testing. Your design must be tested in order to ensure that it meets the customer's requirements. These requirements form the basis for all of your design decisions; therefore, the design's testing must address each of these requirements.

When testing a design, you will rarely find it practical or cost effective to build the entire new network. A small-scale replica of the intended network needs to be designed and built in order to test the new design. There are two methods for performing this testing: pilots and prototypes.

Prototype versus Pilot

A prototype is an implementation of a portion of the network that is used to prove your design concept. A pilot is a smaller prototype that has more basic features and functions.

On average, prototypes cost more than pilots; however, they tend to derive more conclusive results. Pilots will not always prove all of the customer's requirements; however, the reduced cost often makes this method an attractive option. The way to determine the best option is to look closely at each option. Then, present to the customer the costs as well as the customer requirements that will be validated from both the pilot and the prototype.

The Prototype   A prototype is simply a small portion of the complete design that represents all of the design requirements that the solution meets. A prototype could be one small department in an

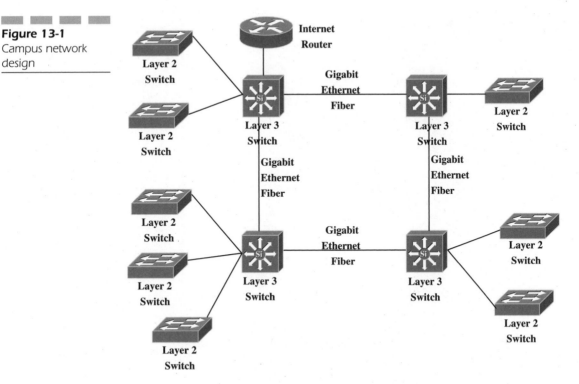

Figure 13-1
Campus network
design

entire corporation, or it could be one floor of a 21-story network redesign.

Figure 13-1 represents a network design that involves several sister companies that cohabitate on the same campus network. This network design is an upgrade of the existing network infrastructure. In this figure, each company contains one layer 3 switch and one or more layer 2 switches.

Although all of the requirements of the design have not been detailed, the main requirement is to ensure connectivity from any workgroup to another workgroup. The best way to prototype the solution is to install only two layer 3 switches and two layer 2 switches. Figure 13-2 represents a possible prototype for the network design represented in Figure 13-1.

The prototype in Figure 13-2 will enable the network design to prove the basic connectivity between layer 2 workgroups. Any workgroup switch on any layer 2 switch can be used. By selecting two adjacent layer 3 switches instead of two distant layer 3 switches, however, only two layer 3 switches are required for the test.

Figure 13-2
Campus network
design prototype

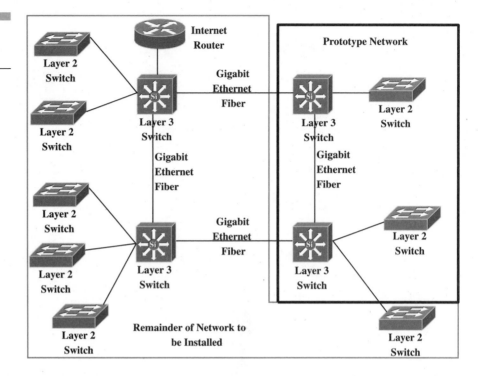

Building a network prototype is more than simply dividing the network into a small part. The designer needs to consider several items when selecting the prototype. The following steps are required for building a prototype:

1. Reviewing the requirements
2. Scaling the prototype
3. Detailing a test plan
4. Configuring the hardware
5. Testing the prototype

Step 1 involves reviewing the requirements. At this stage of the prototype development, you need to review the customer's requirements. Ensure that the requirements have not changed since your initial discovery. The requirements are crucial to your determination of the scale of the prototype. For instance, if one requirement is integration with the customer's existing network, then a larger-scale prototype might be in order so that you can test all facets of the integration.

In Figure 13-2, the requirement was connectivity between the various sister companies. This connectivity extends to all protocols. In other words, the devices must be configured for all protocols that are currently in use on the production network. Another possible requirement for this network would be a new gigabit fiber-optic backbone. This solution would entail testing this backbone as part of the prototype.

 NOTE: *Integration of the prototype with the existing network is probably one of the most challenging requirements that a customer can make. Remember, the existing network is a production network. The designer must ensure that the changes that are being made will not affect production traffic. This situation can have drastic consequences (besides invalidating the prototype or design).*

Step 2 involves scaling the prototype. Once the requirements are verified, you can determine the size of prototype that is required. For instance, if there are a few simple requirements, then the prototype will probably be smaller in scale. If there are many complex requirements, however, the size of the prototype might be close to the size of the actual implementation. In this case, the customer might have to forego testing of some of the requirements in order to reduce the scale of the prototype.

Step 3 involves detailing a test plan. Once the prototype scale has been determined, you are ready to develop a test plan for your prototype. This plan will detail the steps that are required to test all of the customer's requirements. For instance, if a customer requirement of a new network is faster Internet connectivity, you can specify several pings, *File Transfer Protocol* (FTP), and *Hypertext Transport Protocol* (HTTP) tests in order to verify this requirement. Probably the best way to validate a requirement is to take pre- and post-pilot measurements. This technique will show the effect of the proposed changes.

Step 4 involves configuring the hardware. Now, it is time to acquire the hardware and configure the prototype. Follow the test plans that you developed in Step 3 for connecting the equipment.

Step 5 involves testing the prototype. This step will be examined in greater detail in Chapter 14, "Testing the Design."

The Pilot   Pilots are similar to prototypes except that they are generally smaller in scope and size. Pilots are best used in projects that have few parts. In a 50-site *Wide Area Network* (WAN), a prototype would need about five sites in order to prove inter-site communication. In a five-site WAN, a prototype of five sites would complete the project without any testing. In this instance, a pilot of two sites would probably prove most of the inter-site communication requirements.

The following steps are required to build a pilot:

1. Develop a test plan.
2. Configure the hardware.
3. Test the pilot.

Step 1 involves detailing a test plan. This step is similar to the prototype-planning phase. Given the customer requirements, develop a plan that will best meet these specifications. For instance, if the design is for a *Voice over IP* (VoIP) network and the requirement is low latency, you might detail a small pilot using IP phones and two routers. This pilot would provide a proof of concept while still being low cost.

Step 2 involves configuring the hardware. Now, it is time to acquire the hardware and configure the pilot. Follow the test plans that you developed in Step 1 for connecting the equipment. Often, because a pilot is smaller in scope, it might be possible to use existing equipment or arrange to borrow the equipment for a short period of time. This action will further reduce the cost of the pilot method.

Step 3 involves testing the prototype. This step will be examined in greater detail in Chapter 14.

Case Study: Widget Manufacturing

Again, Widget Manufacturing can be used to explain the pilot and prototype processes. First, the new designs of the Widget *Local Area Network* (LAN) and WAN need to be reviewed. Figure 13-3 depicts the new design for the Widget LAN, and Figure 13-4 depicts the new Widget WAN.

Figure 13-3
New Widget
Manufacturing
LAN design

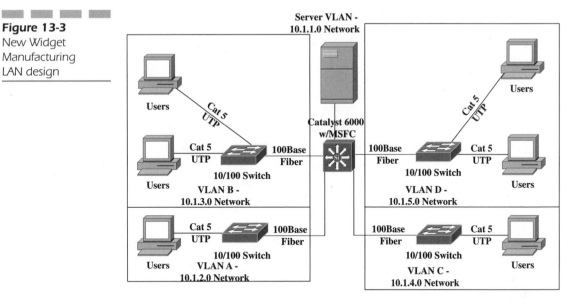

Figure 13-3
New Widget
Manufacturing
LAN design

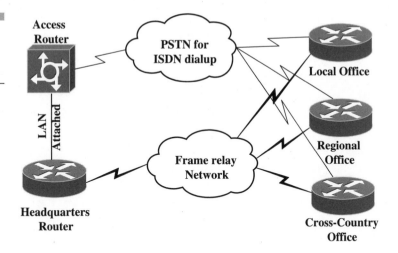

Figure 13-4
New Widget
Manufacturing
WAN design

Both the LAN and WAN design are excellent examples of where to use a prototype and pilot, respectively. The LAN design is complex and has several parts; therefore, it would be best suited for a prototype. A portion of the new network can be designed. This prototype will then enable the designer to prove the design concept. The WAN design is basic, and a full prototype would probably encompass the entire network. The best solution for the WAN design is a small pilot test of one site. First, the LAN design prototype will be examined on a step-by-step basis.

Step 1 involves reviewing the requirements. The following were some of the requirements of Widget Manufacturing:

1. The new network will be capable of supporting 24-hours-a-day, seven-days-a-week operation.

2. The network will have numerous fault-tolerant design points in order to ensure high availability.

3. The network will support management from one or more central stations. The level of management and integration with existing software has yet to be determined.

4. The existing network is thought to have performance problems. The requirement is for the new network not to inhibit performance in any way.

Step 2 involves scaling the prototype. This task is one of the most difficult steps in the prototype process. The scale of the design should be small enough to prove the design concepts and to fulfill the requirements, but it should not be overly expensive.

Looking at the LAN design, we can see that the network can be segmented into separate *Virtual Local Area Networks* (VLANs). The best way to implement a prototype would be to replace the old segments with new equipment. This approach would occur in two phases. The first phase would entail replacing the access-layer hubs with switches. These switches would connect to the legacy router, which will enable the designer to test the access-layer design. Next, the core Cisco 7000 router will be replaced with the new Catalyst switch router. This replacement will now validate the communication between access-layer switches and the core/ distribution layer router. Between these portions of the prototype, Steps 3 through 5 will take place for each portion of the prototype.

Step 3 involves detailing a test plan. For each prototype, a detailed list of tests to perform must be developed. This list will ensure that the designer and the customer have the same objectives. In this case, the same test plan can be used for the access switches and for the core router. The test plan is comprised of the following steps:

1. Testing intra-VLAN communication with PING
2. Testing inter-VLAN communication with PING
3. Verifying IPX connectivity by testing for a successful Novell login
4. Verifying e-mail operation of the host on the VLAN by sending an e-mail to another user on the corporate mail server
5. Verifying Novell operation of the host on the VLAN by opening a file on a Novell server

Step 4 involves configuring the hardware. Ensure that all portions of the device configuration are complete, including passwords and any management information.

NOTE: *Do not expect the configurations to be perfect the first time. There might be many changes as the configuration is refined. Make sure that all changes are documented in case some items need to be removed or reversed.*

Step 5 involves testing the prototype. This step will be covered in the next chapter.

The WAN design for Widget Manufacturing is a relatively small implementation. Only three sites are being added. By the time that the core router and one site are complete, approximately half of the project will be complete. This design would best be validated by using a pilot implementation.

Step 1 involves detailing a test plan. For each pilot, a detailed list of tests to perform must be developed. This step will ensure that the designer and the customer have the same objectives. In this case, the same test plan can be used for the remote routers and for the core router. The test plan consists of the following steps:

1. Testing the Frame Relay communication with the ping command
2. Verifying IPX connectivity by testing for a successful Novell login
3. Verifying e-mail operation of the host on the VLAN by sending an e-mail to another user on the corporate mail server
4. Verifying the Novell operation of the host on the VLAN by opening a file on a Novell server

Step 2 involves configuring the hardware. Ensure that all portions of the device configuration are complete, including passwords and any management information.

Step 3 involves testing the prototype. This step will be covered in the next chapter.

SUMMARY

One the design is complete, the design concept must be proven. A design without a proof of concept is simply a 90 percent complete design. Simply put, no design is ever complete without proving the design itself. Because most designs include tens or even hundreds of components, implementing all of the components would be costly—especially if all of the requirements were not met.

At this point, the types and requirements of prototypes and pilots have been covered. There is still one final point remaining, however: the actual testing of the prototype or pilot.

QUESTIONS ▬ ▬ ▬ ▬ ▬ ▬ ▬ ▬ ▬ ▬

Case Study: Limbo Medical Group

Again, let's revisit the scenario of the Limbo Medical Group. The company is now developing a new client/server application in order to replace this mainframe application. In addition, the legacy X.25 network will be replaced with a Frame Relay network. The operations of the medical group run throughout the day. Any network down time would be detrimental to these operations. Therefore, the new network must be reliable and fault tolerant. The new network design is depicted in Figure 13-5.

The new WAN consists of a Frame Relay WAN that connects 50 small offices that are connected to a central hospital facility. This WAN carries IP traffic between the client and the servers.

1. Why would a pilot be a poor choice to validate this design?

    a. Too many requirements

    b. Limited budget

    c. Too many sites

    d. Too many protocols

▬ ▬ ▬ ▬

Figure 13-5
Limbo Medical
WAN design

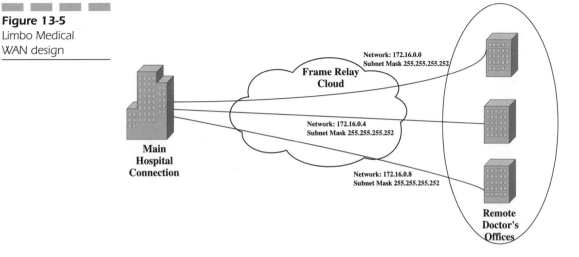

2. How many offices should be used in the prototype?

    a. One

    b. Two

    c. Five

    d. Ten

3. Which of the following would not be part of the test plan?

    a. Pinging the central office

    b. Testing the client/server application

    c. Pinging another remote office

    d. Testing connectivity to IPX severs

Case Study: Global Supplies Corporation

Again, Global Supplies is a multi-national corporation that consists of approximately 15 separate facilities throughout North America. Each facility has an existing LAN that has been upgraded according to the needs of the specific facility. The LANs range from small 10MB Ethernet networks to large Fast Ethernet networks with Gigabit backbones. Each LAN is administered by a department that does not normally interact with the corporate IT group.

The concern of the corporate IT group of Global Supplies is the WAN. The new WAN design is based on an ATM backbone. Figure 13-6 shows the new WAN design for Global Supplies.

Figure 13-6
Global Supplies
WAN design

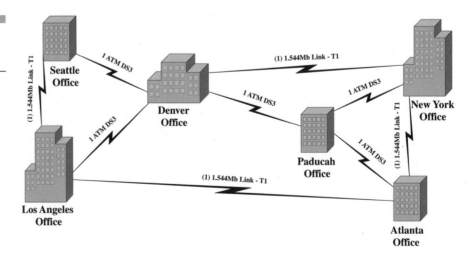

Therequirements of the IT department are covered in the following paragraph. The IT group is concerned about monitoring the health and state of the network at all times. Because its responsibility is inter-company communication, the WAN must be up and error free. A new application, a distance-learning application, has the most bandwidth requirements. This training is delivered in the form of intranet-based streaming media presentations. It is imperative that this training be delivered in a timely manner.

4. Why would a prototype not be a feasible selection for proving the design concept?

   a. ATM is too complex.

   b. ATM hardware is costly.

   c. Local LANs are not part of the design.

5. Which of the following would not be part of the test plan?

   a. Testing connectivity to the local LANs

   b. Testing the delivery of training material across the link

   c. Testing connectivity between servers on the LANs

Case Study: The Bank of Pompeii

Next, we revisit the Bank of Pompeii's case study. The Bank of Pompeii has just completed a new corporate office tower in a prime downtown location. This move will enable the bank to consolidate six small offices into the new corporate tower. In addition to this move, all of the SNA traffic will be removed from the WAN.

All of the offices are connected via a Frame Relay WAN in a hub-and-spoke configuration. The hub of the Frame Relay network will be the new corporate tower. The remainder of the offices will remain on the Frame Relay network. The new LAN and WAN network design is depicted in Figure 13-7.

One expectation for the IT department of the bank is that the design will be completed in time for budget reviews in one month. Another deadline is that the project must be in place before the offices move in three months. This network expansion is a necessary part of the relocation project and is supported by all levels of management.

Figure 13-7

Bank of Pompeii new
network design

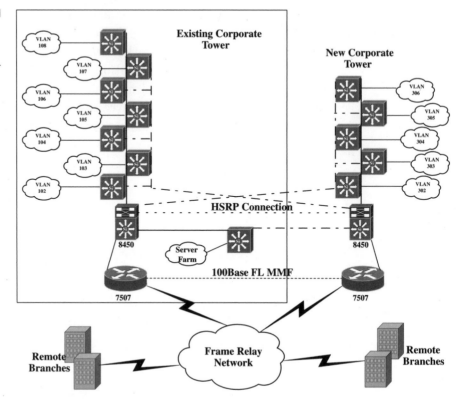

As part of the customer's requirements, the following items are needed for the upgrade: an IP addressing scheme, a routing plan, a network diagram, and complete specifications of all equipment that is required. One of the most important requirements for any installation at the Bank of Pompeii is security. A complete audit trail is required for all equipment that is placed on the network. This audit material is routinely scanned for any unusual activity.

6. Why is a pilot a poor choice for validating the design?

   a. The high-security requirement

   b. Too many requirements

   c. Limited budget

   d. Too many sites

7. What factor would cause the prototype step to be implemented quickly?

 a. The equipment that is in use

 b. Specification requirement

 c. Requirement for a routing and addressing design

 d. Relocation time frame

8. Which step would not be part of the test plan?

 a. Testing HSRP

 b. Testing network management

 c. Testing routing protocol updates

 d. Testing IP connectivity

Case Study: G&S Productions

Again, the specifics of the G&S Productions network design need to be reviewed. Gimball Productions and Shapiro Productions have recently merged. The new company, G&S Productions, has become a major commercial production company. There are two main sites, each of which has about 250 users. In addition, each company has three to five smaller offices throughout the United States.

The new design for the two companies will be a leased-line connection between the sites. The e-mail server is a Windows NT-based system. The main sites each use leased lines to connect to their remote offices. The leased lines are only 56KB circuits. The new network is shown in Figure 13-8.

9. Why would a prototype not be the appropriate selection to validate the design?

 a. There is only one circuit.

 b. Only e-mail is exchanged.

 c. Only 250 users are impacted.

 d. The leased lines are 56KB.

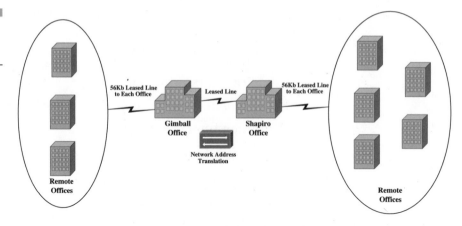

Figure 13-8
G&S Productions
new network design

10. Which of the following would not be part of the test plan?
    a. A connectivity test from the Shapiro WAN site to the Gimball main office
    b. A connectivity test from the Gimball WAN site to the Shapiro main office
    c. A connectivity test from the Gimball WAN site to the Gimball main office
    d. A connectivity test from the Gimball main office to the Shapiro main office

ANSWERS

1. **a.** Too many requirements

   The more requirements, the more likely that a pilot will not address all of the requirements.

2. **c.** Five

   This answer is somewhat arbitrary, but one or two sites is too few for an accurate test, and 10 would be too much (20 percent of the sites, which is too many).

3. **d.** Testing connectivity to IPX servers

   There are no Novell or IPX-based servers in the environment, so this step is not required.

4. **b.** ATM hardware is costly.

   ATM hardware is quite expensive. Implementing a full proto-type of ATM hardware would be costly, especially considering the few ATM circuits that are being installed.

5. **c.** Testing connectivity between servers on the LANs

   All intra-LAN communication is not the responsibility of the corporate IT group and will not be tested in this pilot.

6. **b.** Too many requirements

   Again, the more requirements, the more likely that a pilot will not address all of the requirements. The variety of the requirements means that a detailed prototype plan is required.

7. **d.** Relocation time frame

   The complete project must be completed before the relocation happens in two months. Therefore, the design must be validated in enough time for the remaining equipment to be ordered.

8. **b.** Testing network management

   With the information provided, there are no requirements for any network-management items.

9. **a.** There is only one circuit.

   After the circuit is installed and tested, the project is complete. There is no need for an involved prototype phase.

10. **c.** A connectivity test from the Gimball WAN site to the Gimball main office

    This circuit is not being changed or impacted, so it should not necessarily be a part of the test plan.

Testing the Design

Objectives Covered in This Chapter

1. Learning about the Cisco IOS software commands that you should use in order to determine whether a network structure meets the customer's performance and scalability goals

2. Demonstrating how the prototype meets the requirements for performance, security, capacity, and scalability and ensuring that the costs and risks are acceptable

Introduction

The final step in the prototype process is the actual testing of the prototype and the validation of the exam. The prototype has already been built, and the test plan has already been written.

The first step in testing the design is to identify the resources that will assist the designer with testing the prototype. The final step is to explain several points in presenting the design package to the customer.

Designing Testing Resources

There are two main resources that can be used to test the network design prototype. The first resource is actually built into the router: the Cisco IOS command set. Many IOS commands can verify that the customer's requirements have been achieved.

The next resource is a protocol analyzer. This resource will enable the designer to prove many facets of the customer requirements.

Showing Commands

Cisco IOS software commands can display everything from routing information to Novell servers. The various commands can prove almost any customer requirement. The following commands are some of the most popular commands that are used when testing a network design:

1. *Show interface*   This command will identify various layer 2 information and errors that are present on an interface.

2. *Show processes*   This command will identify the *central processing unit* (CPU) usage. This step might be especially necessary when using encryption or compression features.

3. *Ping*   This command will identify layer 3 connectivity for various protocols. In addition, the round trip time and performance can be measured.

4. *Traceroute*   This command is more detailed than ping and provides layer 3 connectivity and the route that is used.

5. *Show ip route*   This command will show the routing table for the specified protocol and will enable the designer to prove network reachability.

6. *Show access-lists*   This command will show any access lists that have been configured on the router. This command is valuable if there are security concerns. In addition to this test, it would also be advisable to test the access list with ping or with a protocol analyzer.

7. *Debug*   The best use of this command in a design scenario is to prove that the expected packet was received.

NOTE: *Using* show *commands to prove a customer requirement might not work in all circumstances. If the customer is not familiar with routers, he or she might be more conformable seeing the requirements proven on a client or server.*

Protocol Analyzers

Protocol analyzers can be useful devices when you are testing the network design. There are several instances where this tool can be of value. Protocol analyzers perform two important tasks: 1) they capture network traffic, and 2) they generate network traffic.

Capturing Network Traffic

One of the best ways to verify a customer requirement is to show him or her the specific requirement in packet form. Also, if a customer requirement is for increased performance and reduced error counts, then a protocol analyzer that has been active for many hours can provide the necessary statistics.

Generating Network Traffic

Many of the devices and hosts that are required for a network prototype might not be available. For example, it might be impossible to duplicate a critical UNIX server. A protocol analyzer can generate responses that emulate this critical server. In addition, a protocol analyzer can generate enough traffic to test the performance of a circuit or device.

Customer Presentation

In sales, nothing matters if the deal is not closed. In essence, there is the same pressure in this phase of the design process. Everything has been completed, and the requirements have been proven to the customer. The final step is to present the solution to the customer and gain final approval of the design. The presentation can take many forms. There will almost always be a written document and drawing. In addition, a slide or PowerPoint presentation might be required. This presentation can be given to the senior or executive management, to the customer, or simply to the IT department.

Requirements

One of the items that must be completely addressed in the documentation and presentation are the requirements. The requirements and how they were satisfied must be reviewed. The test process and results that validate the requirements should be covered in depth, as well.

Cost

The cost is always an important topic. The estimated project cost must be reviewed and validated with the customer. If there is any variance in the budget, it is imperative for this variance to be made evident as soon as possible.

NOTE: *When designing networks for a customer, you must ensure that you keep the customer aware of the costs and of any changes that will increase the costs. This notification will ensure that there are no surprises at the conclusion of the project.*

Risk

The final portion of the presentation should be a description of the risk that is involved. Any change in a network is risky. You take another risk if you do not perform the upgrade, however. For example, if a network is comprised of many old devices, there might be more risk in not performing the upgrade.

Customer Presentation Template

The actual design document should include the following sections at a minimum. Other sections can be added if necessary:

1. Executive summary
2. Design requirements
3. Design solution
4. Summary
5. Appendices

Part 1: Executive Summary   The executive summary is a brief summary of the rest of the document. This portion should contain a concise version of the design requirement and solutions, followed by a short summary. The executive summary should be read by the key decision makers and should never be more than two pages in length. The four keys points to make are as follows:

1. *Project purpose*   The project purpose and how it relates to the company's business or mission should be addressed.

2. *Design recommendations*   Outline the design in general and how it relates to the project's purpose.

3. *Project implementation considerations*   List issues such as time constraints or support requirements.

4. *Solution benefits*   Finally, recap the overall project benefits and determine how these relate to the company's goals and objectives.

Part 2: Design Requirements   The section summarizes the designer's findings from the network documentation section. This information was covered in Chapters 5 and 6. The important information to include is the characterization of the existing network and the customer's requirements.

Part 3: Design Solution   This portion of the document consists of all of the design work that was completed during the project. The keys points to make are as follows:

1. *Network topology*   A network topology map or series of maps must be included.

2. *Hardware review*   The proposed network hardware should be detailed. The reason(s) for the hardware selection should also be included.

3. *Addressing and naming model*   The addressing model and naming convention should be included in this section.

4. *Routing design*   The network routing design, or bridging design, should be included.

5. *Other design features*   Finally, any special design features, such as queuing or access lists, should be listed here.

Part 4: Summary   The summary should show the benefits of the design and the reason why the customer should accept the design proposal. Be sure that the design proposal not only meets the key requirements but that it also meets the company's overall business objectives.

Part 5: Appendix The appendix should include any information that needs to be included on the design portfolio but that is too detailed for the actual report. An example of this type of information is baselining or detailed protocol analysis results.

Case Study: Widget Manufacturing

Again, Widget Manufacturing can be used to explain the prototype testing processes. First, the new designs of the Widget LAN and WAN need to be reviewed. Figure 14-1 depicts the new design for the Widget LAN, and Figure 14-2 depicts the new Widget WAN.

The next step is to review the test plan. For each prototype, a detailed list of tests to perform must be developed. These tests will ensure that the designer and customer have the same objectives. In this case, the same test plan can be used for the access switches and for the core router. The test plan is comprised of the following steps:

1. Testing the intra-VLAN communication with the ping command
2. Testing the inter-VLAN communication with the ping command

Figure 14-1
New Widget
Manufacturing
LAN design

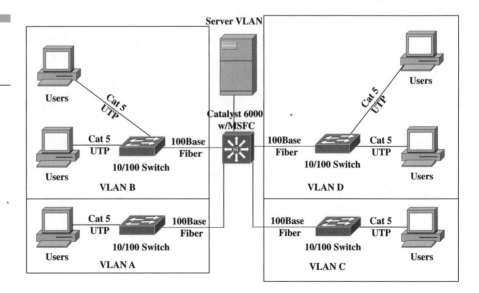

Figure 14-2
New Widget
Manufacturing
WAN design

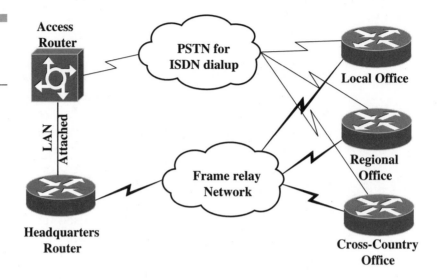

Figure 14-2
New Widget
Manufacturing
WAN design

3. Verifying IPX connectivity by testing for a successful Novell login

4. Verifying e-mail operation of the host on the VLAN by sending an e-mail to another user on the corporate mail server

5. Verify Novell operation of the host on the VLAN by opening a file on a Novell server

Finally, the prototype can be tested. In addition to these tests, there are several IOS commands that can assist with testing:

1. `Show interfaces` One of the original requirements was that the error rate, specifically collisions, should be rescued. This command will validate this requirement.

2. `Show ipx servers` This command displays all of the servers that are present on the network.

3. `Debug dialer` This command validates that the ISDN DDR connections are working correctly.

SUMMARY

With this testing cycle complete, the design process is complete. The design has been developed and then validated. If all of the requirements have been fulfilled, the risks assumed, and the costs budgeted, then the project will begin.

At this point, the actual implementation of the design can begin. Some designers do not take part in the implementation of their design. Other designers not only perform the actual implementation but also manage the entire project.

The next step for the fledgling design is the Internet and the bookstore. Then, you must increase your knowledge of routing and other networking principles. Advanced design is a combination of basic design principles learned here and advanced networking topics (which are learned by hours and hours of reading and studying).

QUESTIONS ▮▮ ▬ ▮▮ ▬ ▮▮ ▬ ▮▮ ▬ ▮▮ ▬ ▬

Case Study: Limbo Medical Group

Again, let's visit the scenario of the Limbo Medical Group. This company is now developing a new client/server application in order to replace its mainframe application. In addition, the legacy X.25 network will be replaced with a Frame Relay network. The operations of the medical group run throughout the day. Any network down time would be detrimental to these operations. Therefore, the new network must be reliable and fault tolerant. The new network design is depicted in Figure 14-3.

The new WAN consists of a Frame Relay WAN that connects 50 small offices that are connected to a central hospital facility. This WAN carries IP traffic between the client and the servers.

1. Given everything that is known about the Limbo Medical Group, which IOS command would not be a part of the testing?

   a. Show ipx servers
   b. Show ip route
   c. Show interface
   d. Show processes

▬▬ ▬▬ ▬▬ ▬▬

Figure 14-3
Limbo Medical
WAN design

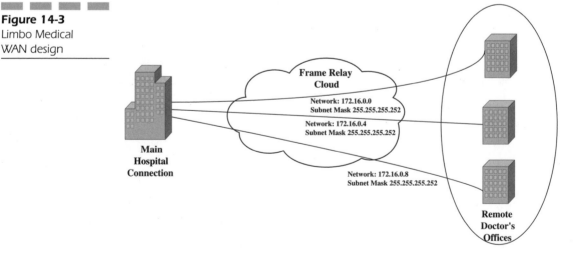

2. What IOS command is used to display the CPU utilization of a router?

   a. Show memory

   b. Show CPU

   c. Show utilization

   d. Show processes

3. Which of the following scenarios would require a protocol analyzer in order to generate traffic?

   a. Routing protocol convergence

   b. Frame Relay congestion avoidance

   c. Encryption

   d. Inter-VLAN routing

Case Study: Global Supplies Corporation

Again, Global Supplies is a multi-national corporation that consists of approximately 15 separate facilities throughout North America. Each facility has an existing LAN that has been upgraded according to the needs of the specific facility. The LANs range from small 10MB Ethernet networks to large Fast Ethernet networks with Gigabit backbones. Each LAN is administered by a department that does not normally interact with the corporate IT group.

The concern of the corporate IT group of Global Supplies is the WAN. The new WAN design is based on an ATM backbone. Figure 14-4 shows the new WAN design for Global Supplies.

4. Given all of the prior case study materials, which two IOS commands will provide the best validation of the design?

   a. Show interface

   b. Show ipx servers

   c. Traceroute

   d. Show interface

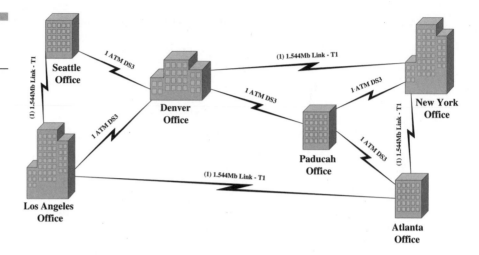

Figure 14-4
Global Supplies
WAN design

5. Which IOS command shows the individual commands of all access lists?

   a. Show ip access list
   b. Show access-list
   c. Show ip access-list
   d. Show access list

Case Study: The Bank of Pompeii

Next, another visit to the Bank of Pompeii case study is required. The Bank of Pompeii has just completed a new corporate office tower in a prime downtown location. This move will enable the bank to consolidate six small offices into the new corporate tower. In addition to this move, all of the SNA traffic will be removed from the WAN.

All of the offices are connected via a Frame Relay WAN in a hub-and-spoke configuration. The hub of the Frame Relay network will be the new corporate tower. The remainder of the offices will remain on the Frame Relay network. The new LAN and WAN network design is depicted in Figure 14-5.

Figure 14-5

The Bank of Pompeii's
new network design

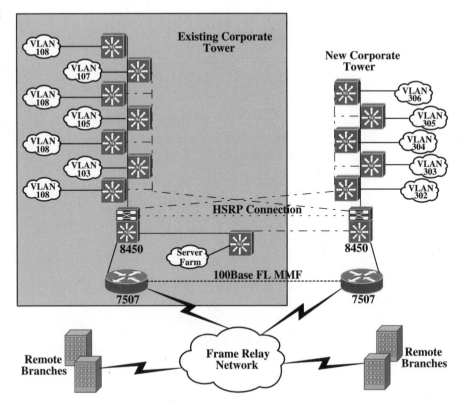

6. Given all of the prior case study material, which IOS command
   will not provide any validation of the design?

   a. Show ip route
   b. Ping
   c. traceroute
   d. show ipx route

7. What portion of the customer documentation is intended for
   senior management?

   a. Executive summary
   b. Design requirements
   c. Design solution
   d. Summary

8. What type of IOS commands can be used to validate that a specific packet was received?

    a. `Show commands`
    b. `Debug commands`
    c. `Set commands`
    d. `Packet commands`

9. What two tasks would a protocol analyzer be used for when testing a network validation?

    a. Capturing network traffic
    b. Testing network connectivity
    c. Verifying routing tables
    d. Generating network traffic

10. What portion of the customer documentation is comprised of the addressing and naming model?

    a. Executive summary
    b. Design requirements
    c. Design solution
    d. Summary

ANSWERS

1. a. show ipx servers

The IPX/SPC protocol is not in use on Limbo Medical's network.

2. d. show processes

This command is the only legitimate command listed that actually shows the CPU utilization.

3. b. Frame Relay congestion avoidance

Although it has not been specifically addressed, it is the only selection that actually requires a tremendous amount of generated traffic.

4. b. and **c.** show ipx servers and traceroute

Both of these commands will validate the operation of TCP/IP and IPX/SPX.

5. b. show access-list

The other commands are either not valid or only show IP access lists, not all access lists.

6. d. show ipx route

Again, there is no IPX traffic present on the network; therefore, no IPX routes are present.

7. a. Executive summary

The executive summary is a brief summary of the rest of the document. It should contain a concise version of the design requirement and solutions, followed by a short summary. The executive summary is intended to be read by the key decision makers.

8. b. Debug commands

Debug commands are used to show detailed router events (including packet receipt and transmission).

9. a. and **d.** Capturing and generating network traffic

The best use of a protocol analyzer in the testing phase is for capturing and generating network traffic.

10. c. Design solution

The design solution is comprised of the topology, addressing design, routing design, and hardware overview.

APPENDIX A

10Base2

10Base2 is 10Mbps, base-band Ethernet that is deployed in 185-meter segments. It is the IEEE 802.3 substandard for ThinWire, coaxial cable.

10Base-2A

10Base-2A is a 10Mbit base-band network that uses thin Ethernet coaxial cable.

10Base5

The original IEEE 802.3 cabling standard for Ethernet that uses coaxial cables (type RG-8). The name derives from the fact that the maximum data transfer speed is 10Mbps. It uses base-band transmission, and the maximum length of cables is 500 meters (1,640 feet) with a maximum of 100 MAUs. The maximum end-to-end propagation delay for a coaxial segment is 2165ns. Maximum attenuation for the segment cannot exceed 8.5dB (17dB/km) for each 500m segment. 10Base5 is also known as thick Ethernet, ThickWire, or ThickNet.

10Base-5A

10Mbit/s base-band network that uses thick Ethernet coaxial cable

10BaseF

A 10Mbps base-band network over fiber-optic cabling; the IEEE 802.3 substandard for fiber-optic Ethernet that refers to the 10BaseFB, 10BaseFL, and 10BaseFP standards for Ethernet over fiber-optic cabling

10Base-FB

Part of the IEEE 10Base-F specification that provides a synchronous signaling backbone that enables additional segments and repeaters to be connected to the network

10Base-FL

IEEE 10Base-Fiber specification that is designed to replace the *Fiber Optic Inter-Repeater Link* (FOIRL) standard that provides Ethernet over fiber-optic cabling. Interoperability is provided between the old and new standards. 10BaseFL is part of the IEEE 10BaseF specification, and although it is capable of interoperating with FOIRL, it is designed to replace the FOIRL specification. 10BaseFL segments can be up to 3,280 feet (1,000 meters) long if used with FOIRL and up to 1.24 miles (2,000 meters) if 10BaseFL is used exclusively in the deployment.

10Base-FP

Part of the IEEE 10Base-F specification that enables the organization of a number of end nodes into a star topology without the use of repeaters. *See 10Base-FB and 10Base-FL.*

10Base-FT

The IEEE specification for base-band Ethernet over fiber-optic cabling. *See 10Base-FB, 10Base-FL, and 10Base-FP.*

10Base-T

An IEEE 802.3 physical layer specification that enables telephone UTP cable to be used for 10Mbps Ethernet over two pairs of UTP wiring. This technology is one of several adaptations of the Ethernet (IEEE 802.3) standard for LANs. The purpose of the 10Base-T standard was to provide a simple, inexpensive, and flexible means of attaching devices to the ubiquitous twisted-pair cable. 10Base-T is a multi-segment 10Mbps base-band network that operates as a single collision domain.

10Broad36

A 10Mbps Ethernet specification that uses broad-band coaxial cable and is part of the IEEE802.3 standard. 10Broad36 has a distance limitation of 3,600 meters. *See Ethernet and IEEE 802.3.*

100Base-F/100Base-FX

Standard for fiber optic cabling used with Fast Ethernet; often used to mean Fast Ethernet with fiber-optic cabling

The 100Base-FX system is designed to enable fiber-optic segments of up to 412 meters in length. The 100Base-FX specification requires one pair of *Multi-Mode Fiber* (MMF) cable per link. The typical fiber-optic cable that is used for a fiber link segment is a graded index MMF cable with a 62.5-micron core and 125-micron cladding. The wavelength specified is 1,350 nanometers with an 11 *decibel* (dB) loss budget per link.

100Base-T

100Base-T refers to Fast Ethernet, or an IEEE 802.3 physical layer specification for 100Mbps Ethernet over different grades of *Unshielded Twisted-Pair* (UTP) wiring. Fast Ethernet offers a natural migration from traditional 10Mbps Ethernet because it uses the same CSMA/CD access mechanism. Officially, the 100Base-T standard is IEEE 802.3u. There are several different cabling schemes that can be used with 100Base-T, including the following:

- 100Base-TX   Two pairs of high-quality twisted-pair wires
- 100Base-T4   Four pairs of normal-quality twisted-pair wires
- 100Base-FX   Fiber-optic cables

The physical medium for 10Base-T is twisted-pair wiring. 10Base-T networks are typically installed and utilize existing unshielded telephone wiring and typical telephony installation practices. Thus, the end-to-end path might include different types of wiring, cable connectors, and cross-connects. Typically, a DTE connects to a wall outlet by using a twisted-pair patch cord. Wall outlets are connected through building wiring and to a cross-connect to the repeater hub in a wiring closet. This term is also known as UTP, twisted pair, and twisted sister.

100Base-T4

100Base-T4 refers to an IEEE 802.3 specification for base-band Fast Ethernet over four pairs of Category 3, 4, or 5 UTP wire. Physical segments are limited to 100 meters in length in order to ensure that the round trip timing specifications are met. The 100Base-T4 standard operates over four pairs of wires with a signaling system that makes it possible to provide 100Mbps Ethernet signals over standard voice-grade cabling systems. This signaling method uses three wire pairs for transmitting and receiving, whereas the fourth pair is used to listen for collisions. 100Base-T4 specifies a segment of up to 100 meters in length, but two 100-meter 100Base-T4 segments can be connected together through a single Class I or Class II repeater. A system that has a total maximum diameter of 200 meters between any two DTEs is therefore provided. 100Base-T4 requires a transmit/receive signal crossover. The standard recommends that buildings are cabled straight through and ports on the hub/repeater perform the crossover internally. If two stations are linked with a single 100Base-T4 segment (or if the repeater hub does not implement the signal crossover internally), then a crossover cable must be provided for proper operation.

100Base-TX

100Base-TX is an IEEE 802.3 specification for Fast Ethernet over two pairs of Category 5 UTP wire or Type 1 *Shielded Twisted-Pair* (STP) wire. The first pair of wires is used to receive data; the second pair is used to transmit data. The maximum distance for a segment is 100 meters. Two 100-meter transmission segments can be connected together through a single Class I or Class II repeater, thereby providing up to 200 meters between DTE devices.

100Base-VG

100Base-VG is a joint AT&T and Hewlett-Packard proposal for a 100Mbps, four-pair, Category 3 Ethernet. This system is being standardized by the IEEE 802.12 working group.

100Base-X

100Base-X is a Grand Junction Networks proposal for 100Mbps Ethernet by using two pairs of Category 5 wire and CSMA/CD. It is being standardized by the IEEE 802.13 working group.

100VG-AnyLAN

100VG-AnyLAN is a new 100Mbps *Local Area Network* (LAN) technology that was originally developed by Hewlett-Packard. This technology is currently refined and described in the IEEE 802.12 standard. 100VG-AnyLAN departs from traditional Ethernet in that it uses a centrally controlled Demand Priority access protocol instead of CSMA/CD. It builds on the positive aspects of both Token Ring and Ethernet to run at 100Mbits/s with resilience and a high realization of its potential. This technology is generally considered technically better than Fast Ethernet (the alternative), but it has been less than successful in the marketplace.

110 type block

A wire block that terminates 100 to 300 pairs of wire; has excellent electrical characteristics and a relatively small physical footprint; organizes pairs horizontally in order to connect them

802.1d

IEEE standard for spanning a tree

802.1p

The IEEE standard that adds important filtering controls to the 802.1d standard; designed with VLANs in mind

802.1Q

The IEEE encapsulation standard that calls for adding four bytes to a packet in order to tag it for virtual LAN purposes. *See VLAN-Tagged Frame.*

802.10

IEEE standard for packet tagging for security within LANs; also used by some companies (such as Cisco Systems) to tag packets for virtual LANs

802.11

IEEE standard for wireless LANs that use Ethernet bridges with roaming to join them to the network

802.11b

The IEEE standard for wireless LANs that use Ethernet bridges with roaming to join them to the network; specifies a carrier-sense media access control and physical layer specifications for 1Mbit/s and 2Mbit/s wireless LANs

802.12

IEEE standard that specifies the physical layer and the MAC sublayer of the data link layer of the seven-layer OSI reference model

802.2

IEEE standard for the control of the lower part of layer 2 LLC of the seven-layer OSI reference model

802.3

IEEE broadband bus networking system that uses the CSMA/CD protocol; Ethernet has become the commonly used name, although it is one trademarked version of 802.3

802.4

IEEE standard for the token bus medium access method

802.4I

IEEE standard that governs broad-band bus and broad-band token bus; usually used in industrial applications

802.5

IEEE standard that governs the characteristics and operation of Token Ring networks

802.6

IEEE standard that governs *Metropolitan Area Networks* (MANs)

802.9

Integrated voice and data LAN IEEE standard

802.x

The set of IEEE standards for the definition of LAN protocols

A

AAA

See authentication, authorization, and accounting.

Access Control List (ACL)

A list defining the kinds of access granted or denied to users of an object

Acknowledgment (ACK)

A positive response message sent by a protocol, such as TCP, which acknowledges the reception of a transmitted packet from the receiving end station. ACKs can be separate packets or piggybacked on reverse-traffic packets.

Acronym

Technically, a word that is formed by combining some parts (usually the first letters) of other terms. For example, *modem* is the acronym that is derived from the proper title *modulator/demodulator*. Various cultural groups, newsgroups, chat rooms, and e-mail users have spawned a rich set of acronyms and abbreviations for common phrases. A few common ones are listed as follows.

Acronym	Meaning
ASAP	As Soon As Possible
BTW	By The Way
FWIW	For What It's Worth
FYI	For Your Information
IMHO	In My Humble Opinion
IMO	In My Opinion

Adapter Address

Twelve hexadecimal digits that identify a LAN adapter

Adapter Card

A hardware card that provides the interface between the computer (DTE) and the physical network circuit. *See Network Interface Card.*

Adaptive Routing

A method of routing packets of data or data messages in which the system's intelligence selects the best path; this path might change with traffic patterns or link failures

Address Mapping

Address mapping is a technique that enables different protocols to interoperate by translating addresses from one format to another. For example, when routing IP over X.25, the IP addresses must be mapped to the X.25 addresses so that the IP packets can be transmitted by the X.25 network. *See address resolution.*

Address Mask

The address mask is a bit combination that is used to describe which portion of an address refers to the network or subnet and which part refers to the host. Sometimes, this term is referred to simply as the mask. Each class of IP address has a default mask. *See IP addressing.*

Address Resolution

A means for mapping different OSI layer addresses to another layer; for example, network-layer (Layer 3) addresses to data link layer (Layer 2) media-specific addresses

Address Resolution Protocol (ARP)

ARP is the TCP/IP protocol that is used to dynamically bind a high-level IP address to low-level physical *Media Access Control*

(MAC) hardware addresses. ARP works across single physical networks and is limited to networks that support hardware broadcasts. *See RARP.*

Adjacency

A relationship formed between neighboring OSPF routers for the purpose of exchanging link-state information. *See OSPF.*

Adjacent

In an internetwork, devices, nodes, or domains that are directly connected by a physical connection.

Administrative Distance

A rating of the trustworthiness of the route to a destination; typically, the best route is the route that has the lowest administrative distance. The higher the value, the lower the trustworthiness rating.

ADSL

See Asymmetric Digital Subscriber Line.

Advanced Research Projects Agency Network (ARPANET)

A large WAN that was created by the United States Defense Advanced Research Project Agency and the precursor to the Internet, which was established in 1969

American National Standards Institute (ANSI)

A voluntary organization that creates standards in programming languages, electrical specifications, communications protocols, and many other issues affecting the computer industry

Analog

Almost everything in the electronic world can be described or represented in one of two forms: analog or digital. The principal feature of analog representations is that they are continuous in form and appearance. In contrast, digital representations consist of values that are measured at discrete intervals, such as on and off or one and zero. When an analog signal is transmitted over wires or through the air, the transmission conveys information through a variation of some combination of signal amplitude, frequency, and phase.

Anonymous File Transfer Protocol (FTP)

One of the earliest methods of Internet file transfer, anonymous FTP uses FTP along with some simple conventions. FTP was designed to enable a user to connect a remote system on which he or she had an account, to authenticate by using a user ID/password combination, and then to navigate a directory hierarchy and retrieve files. Anonymous FTP extends this idea by enabling users who do not have accounts to use FTP for retrieving public data. To perform this task, a user connects to an anonymous FTP server via a normal FTP client, offering anonymous as a user ID and sending an identifying string (typically an e-mail address) as the password. Servers that are configured for anonymous FTP will accept almost anything as a password, so this information is really based on an honor code. Once connected in this manner, the user can examine the server's file repository and download anything of interest by using FTP's standard capabilities. Anonymous FTP servers typically implement various security measures in order to prevent anonymous users from gaining access to anything but an area that is designated for public information.

ANSI

See American National Standards Institute.

Application Layer

The seventh and highest layer of *Systems Network Architecture* (SNA) and *Open Systems Interconnection* (OSI); it supplies functions to applications or nodes, enabling them to communicate with other applications or nodes

Application Service Provider (ASP)

A service provider that provides hosted Internet-based application solutions, such as e-commerce and enterprise resource planning, to businesses for a monthly subscriber fee. The ASP provides the hardware (servers) that run the desired application for the customer, thus relieving the customer of having to dedicate resources in support of the application (people, time, more hardware, and so on). ASPs enable access to their servers via the Internet through VPNs or collocate their servers on a customer's network, depending on the needs.

Application Specific Integrated Circuit (ASIC)

A chip that is designed for a particular application

Area Border Router (ABR)

The name given to a router that is running OSPF and that is located on the border of one or more OSPF areas that are connected to the OSPF backbone (commonly known as Area 0). As a result, ABRs are considered members of both the OSPF backbone and the attached areas. ABRs maintain routing tables that describe both the backbone topology and the topology of the other OSPF areas. *See OSPF.*

ARPANET

See Advanced Research Projects Agency Network.

Asymmetric Digital Subscriber Line (ADSL)

ADSL is a method for moving data over regular phone lines. Currently, ADSL is not widely deployed, but telecommunications companies are promising quick expansions within many metropolitan areas. Although ADSL is deployed over regular phone lines, it is much faster than a regular phone connection—and the wires coming into the subscriber's premises are the same (copper) wires that are used for regular phone service. This feature enables easy installation at the customer's premises. An ADSL circuit must be configured to connect two specific locations, and as a result, it is similar to a leased line in its operation. ADSL supports data rates of 1.5Mbps to 9Mbps when receiving data (known as the downstream rate) and from 16Kbps to 640Kbps when sending data (known as the upstream rate). ADSL is often discussed as an alternative to ISDN, enabling higher speeds in cases where the connection is always to the same place. *See XDSL.*

Asynchronous Transfer Mode (ATM)

ATM is a telecommunications concept that was defined by ANSI and CCITT standards committees for the transport of a broad range of user information (including voice, data, and video communication) on any *User-to-Network Interface* (UNI). ATM might well be positioned to be the high-speed networking tool of the next century. ATM can be used to aggregate user traffic from multiple existing applications onto a single UNI. The ATM concept aggregates a myriad of services onto a single access arrangement.

ATM Adaptation Layer (AAL)

AAL is a collection of standardized ATM-based protocols that provides services to higher layers by adapting user traffic to a cell format. The AAL is divided into the *Convergence Sublayer* (CS) and the *Segmentation and Reassembly* (SAR) sublayers. At present, the four types of AALs that are recommended by the ITU-T are AAL1, AAL2, AAL3/4 , and AAL5. AAL is the first type. An ATM protocol standard that is used for the transport of *Constant Bit Rate* (CBR) traffic (such as audio and video) and for emulating TDM-based circuits (such as DS1 and E1). AAL is the second type—an ATM protocol standard for supporting *Time-Dependent Variable Bit Rate* (VBR-RT) of connection-oriented traffic (such as packetized video and audio). AAL type 3 and 4 is an ATM protocol standard for supporting both connectionless and connection-oriented *Variable Bit Rate* (VBR) traffic. AAL is also used to support SMDS.

AURP Tunnel

An AURP tunnel is a logical connection that is created in an AURP-based WAN, which contains two discontiguous AppleTalk internetworks. An AURP tunnel functions as a single, virtual data link between the two AppleTalk internetworks that are physically separated by a foreign network (such as a TCP/IP network).

Authentication

Authentication is a process of establishing identity.

Authentication, Authorization, and Accounting (AAA)

AAA is a security method that enables you to implement three unique aspects of security into a cohesive whole. These unique aspects are authentication, authorization, and accounting. AAA uses protocols such as RADIUS, TACACS+, and Kerberos to administer and control its security functions.

Autonomous System (AS)

An autonomous system is an internetwork that is part of the Internet. An AS has a single routing policy. Each autonomous system is assigned an autonomous system number.

Autonomous System Boundary Router (ASBR)

An ASBR is a router that is located between an OSPF autonomous system in a non-stub area and a non-OSPF network, such as a network that is running RIP or BGP. ASBRs will run both OSPF and another routing protocol (such as RIP). *See OSPF.*

Auxiliary Port (AUX)

The logical name in DOS systems for the standard communications port; usually the same as COM1

Available Bit Rate (ABR)

A best-effort service type where the network makes no absolute guarantee of cell delivery. The available bit rate provides only best effort delivery.

Average Cell Rate

The mean number of cells that the source can inject into a network over a given *Virtual Connection* (VC)

Average Cell Transfer Delay

The arithmetic average of a number of *Cell Transfer Delays* (CTD).

B

Back Pressure

Back pressure is the propagation of network congestion information upstream through an internetwork. A good example is an Ethernet switch that signals the end station on a port by raising the carrier signal in order to prevent further transmissions until the congestion within the switch drops to an acceptable level. This back pressure on the end stations minimizes retransmissions due to pack loss within the switch.

Backward Error Correction (BEC)

BEC is an error-correction scheme where the sender retransmits any data that is found in error, based on the feedback from the receiver.

Backward Explicit Congestion Notification (BECN)

BECN is a bit set by a Frame Relay network in frames that are traveling in the opposite direction of frames that are encountering a congested path. The DTE that is receiving frames with the BECN bit set can request higher-level protocols to take flow control action as appropriate. *See FECN.*

Bandwidth (BW)

Bandwidth is the transmission capacity of a communications medium (the amount of data that can be transmitted in a fixed amount of time). Bandwidth is usually expressed in bits per second or bytes per second for digital devices. For analog devices, bandwidth is expressed in cycles per second or *Hertz* (Hz). A subtle difference should be noted with the definition of bandwidth: the number of bits that a communications line can transmit might not be the total bandwidth for data, because some bits might be used for control signals. This situation leaves a lesser amount as real bandwidth for the user. For example, an OC3 SONET line in ATM, which is rated at 155Mbits, really only has 149.76 of real data bits that are available to the user.

Big Endian

Big endian is the historical name of a technique that identifies the most significant bytes in multi-byte data types. In systems that support big-endian architectures such as mainframes, the leftmost bytes are the most significant. In little-endian supported architectures (such as personal computers, or PCs), the rightmost bytes are most significant. For example, consider the number 1,025 (two to the 10th power plus one) represented in a four-byte integer:

```
00000000  00000000  00000100  00000001
```

Big Endian Representation of 1,025	Little Endian Representation of 1,025
00	0000000000000001
01	0000000000000100

02	0000010000000000
03	0000000100000000

Note that this example shows only big- and little-endian byte orders. The bit ordering within each byte can also be big- or little-endian, and some architectures actually use big-endian ordering for bits and little-endian ordering for bytes (or vice-versa). Converting data between the two numbering systems is sometimes referred to as the NUXI problem. Imagine the word UNIX stored in two two-byte words. In a big-endian system, it would be stored as UNIX. In a little-endian system, it would be stored as NUXI.

The terms big endian and little endian are derived from the Lilliputians in the book *Gulliver's Travels*. The Lilliputians' major political issue was whether soft-boiled eggs should be opened on the big side or on the little side. Likewise, the big-/little-endian computer debate has much more to do with political issues than technological merits.

Bootstrap Protocol (BOOTP)

BOOTP is an *Internet Protocol* (IP) that is documented in RFC951, and it enables a diskless workstation to determine its own IP address, the IP address of the BOOTP server, and which file to be loaded into memory in order for the workstation to boot.

Border Gateway Protocol (BGP)

The BGP is the dynamic routing protocol that is used between *Internet Service Providers* (ISPs) in order to manage extremely large routing tables. BGP enables groups of routers (called autonomous systems) to share routing information so that efficient, loop-free routes can be established. BGP is commonly used within and between ISPs. The protocol is defined in RFC 1771.

BPDU

See Bridge Protocol Data Unit.

Bridge

A bridge is a) an interface connecting two similar or dissimilar LAN-media types, or b) a device that connects two LANs. A bridge performs its functions at the *Data Link Control* (DLC) layer.

Bridge Forwarding

Bridge forwarding is a process that uses entries in a filtering database to determine whether frames with a given *Media Access Control* (MAC) destination address can be forwarded to a given port or ports. Bridge forwarding is described in the IEEE 802.1 standard. *See IEEE 802.1.*

Bridge ID

To create the bridge ID, the bridge label is combined with the address of the adapter connecting the bridge to the LAN segment with the lowest LAN segment number.

Bridge Label

The bridge label is a two-byte hexadecimal number that the user can assign to each bridge.

Bridge Number

The bridge number is the bridge identifier that the user specifies in the bridge program configuration file. The bridge number distinguishes between parallel bridges.

Bridge Protocol Data Unit (BPDU)

A BPDU is a spanning-tree protocol hello packet that is sent at regular intervals in order to exchange information among switches/bridges on the network. *See bridging.*

Bridge Static Filtering

Bridge static filtering is a process by which a bridge maintains a filtering database that consists of static entries. Each static entry equates a MAC destination address with a port that can receive frames with this MAC destination address and a set of ports on which the frames can be transmitted. This concept is defined in the IEEE802.1 standard. *See IEEE 802.1.*

Bridging

Bridging is a method of path selection (contrast routing). On a bridged network, no correspondence is required between addresses and paths. Put another way, addresses do not imply anything about where hosts are physically attached to the network. Any address can appear at any location. In contrast, routing requires more thoughtful address assignment (corresponding to physical placement). Bridging relies heavily on broadcasting. Because a packet might contain no information other than the destination address (and that implies nothing about the path that should be used), the only option might be to send the packet everywhere. This function is one of bridging's most severe limitations, because this method is very inefficient and can trigger broadcast storms. In networks that have low-speed links, this situation can introduce crippling overhead.

Broadcast Domain

The broadcast domain is the part of a network that receives the same broadcasts.

Broadcast Storm

A broadcast storm is a state in which a message that has been broadcast across a network results in even more responses. Each response then results in more responses, producing a snowball effect. A severe broadcast storm can block all other network traffic, resulting in a network meltdown. Broadcast storms can usually be prevented by carefully configuring a network to block illegal broadcast messages.

Byte

A byte is a set of eight bits that represents a single character.

C

Carrier-Sense Multiple Access with Collision Avoidance (CSMA/CA)

CSMA/CA is a wireless LAN media access method, as specified by the IEEE 802.11 specification.

Carrier-Sense Multiple Access with Collision Detection (CSMA/CD)

CSMA/CD is a protocol that utilizes equipment that is capable of detecting a carrier, which permits multiple access to a common medium. This protocol also has the capability to detect a collision (because this type of technology is broadcast-oriented). *See Ethernet.*

Central Office (CO)

The central office is a facility that contains the lowest node in the hierarchy of switches that comprises the public telephone network. The CO is also any place where the phone company has located telephone switching equipment. The premises of a carrier's service provider are where customer lines (such as telephone lines) are multiplexed and switched to other COs.

Central Processing Unit (CPU)

The CPU is the circuitry that executes instructions. It is sometimes called the brain of the computer.

Certification for Information System Security Professional (CISSP)

CISSP is a certification that reflects the qualifications of information systems security practitioners. The CISSP examination consists of multiple-choice questions that cover topics such as access control systems, cryptography, and security management practices. This exam is administered by the *International Information Systems Security Certification Consortium* (ISC²). The ISC² promotes the CISSP as an aid to evaluating personnel who are performing information security functions. The certification was first available in 1989.

Challenge Handshake Authentication Protocol (CHAP)

CHAP is a high-security method of authentication that is used in *Point-to-Point Protocol* (PPP).

Cisco Connection Online (CCO)

According to Cisco Systems, CCO is the foundation of the Cisco Connection Web site (essentially, this site is www.cisco.com). CCO also provides registered users with a suite of interactive, networked services that provide immediate and open access to Cisco's information, resources, and systems. CCO is one of the most valuable resources for anyone who is seeking information about Cisco and networking. It is a true marvel that contains a wealth of information. While a good portion of the information is available to the general public, the true power and knowledge is available to those who are registered users of CCO. Cisco has defined the following four different types of registered users:

1. *Cisco customers* Cisco customers who have a SMARTnet or comprehensive support contract with Cisco (www.cisco.com/public/regben_pica.html)

2. *Cisco PICA customers* Cisco customers who receive service from an authorized Cisco partnet (www.cisco.com/public/regben_pica.html)

3. *Cisco partners* Cisco sales partners who have a reseller, distributor, or OEM service agreement with Cisco (www.cisco.com/public/regben_part.html)

4. *Premier resellers* Authorized resellers who have a reseller service agreement with Cisco (www.cisco.com/public/regben_cpropart.html)

Cisco Discovery Protocol (CDP)

CDP is a proprietary Cisco network protocol that is used by Cisco routers to discover other Cisco networking devices on the network.

Cisco Group Management Protocol (CGMP)

CGMP is a specialized protocol that was developed by Cisco Systems to integrate with the Cisco *Internetwork Operating System* (IOS). The Cisco IOS enables switches to more efficiently handle layer 3 IP multicast traffic. CGMP provides switches with the capability to map the layer multicast group address and to map it to the equivalent layer 2 MAC address. Once the address becomes layer 2, the switch can act on it (because a switch is a layer 2 device).

Cisco Systems

According to its Web site, Cisco provides the following marketing information for public consumption; however, the real story (discussed later in this entry) is that Cisco Systems is the worldwide leader in networking for the Internet. Cisco's networking solutions connect people, computing devices, and computer networks—enabling people to access or transfer information without regard for differences in time, place, or type of computer system. Cisco provides end-to-end networking solutions that customers use to build a unified information infrastructure of their own in order to connect to someone else's network. An end-to-end networking solution is one that provides a common architecture that delivers consistent network services to all users. The broader the range of network services, the more capabilities that a network can provide to users.

CISSP

See Certification for Information System Security Personnel.

Class A IP Address

This address is a type of unicast IP address that segments the address space into many network addresses and few host addresses.

Class B IP Address

This address is a type of unicast IP address that segments the address space into a medium number of network and host addresses.

Class of Service (COS)

COS is a designation of the transport network characteristics (such as route security, transmission priority, and bandwidth) that are needed for a particular session. The class of service is derived from a mode name specified by the initiator of a session. In SNA, this term defines explicit routes, virtual routes, and priority and is used to provide a variety of services within the network.

Classless Inter-Domain Routing (CIDR)

CIDR is an IP addressing scheme that replaces the older system based on classes A, B, and C. With CIDR, a single IP address can be used to designate many unique IP addresses. Faced with the exhaustion of class B address space and the explosion of routing table growth triggered by a flood of new class C addresses, the *Internet Engineering Task Force* (IETF) began implementing CIDR in the early 1990s. CIDR is documented in RFC 1518 and RFC 1519.

The primary requirement for CIDR is the use of routing protocols that support it, such as RIP version 2, OSPF version 2, and BGP version 4. The subnetting mask becomes an integral part of routing tables and protocols. A route is no longer an IP address that is broken down into network and host bits according to its class. A route is now a combination of an address and a mask. Networks can be broken down into subnets and also combined into supernets as long as they have a common network prefix. CIDR defines address assignment and aggregation strategies that are designed to minimize the size of top-level Internet routing tables. A CIDR IP address looks like a normal IP address, except that it ends with a slash followed by a number (called the IP prefix). For example, `172.200.0.0/16` is a CIDR IP address. The IP prefix specifies how many addresses are covered by the CIDR address, with lower numbers covering more addresses. An IP prefix of `/12`, for example, can be used to address 4,096 former Class C addresses. CIDR addresses reduce the size of routing tables and make more IP addresses available within organizations.

Committed Information Rate (CIR)

In Frame Relay, the CIR is the information rate that the network is committed to provide the user under any network conditions.

Competitive Local Exchange Carrier (CLEC)

A CLEC is a telephone company that competes with an *Incumbent Local Exchange Carrier* (ILEC), such as a *Regional Bell Operating*

Company (RBOC), GTE, ALLNET, and so on. With the passage of the Telecommunications Act of 1996, there has been an explosion in the number of CLECs.

Compressed Serial Link Internet Protocol (CSLIP)

CSLIP is an extension of SLIP that enables just header information to be sent across a SLIP connection, reducing overhead and increasing packet throughput on SLIP lines when appropriate. *See SLIP.*

Congestion

Congestion refers to a) a network state caused by one or more overloaded network devices, leading to datagram loss, and b) a stable condition where a network becomes flooded with retransmissions. *See Congestion Control.*

Congestion Control

A resource and traffic-management mechanism to avoid and/or prevent excessive situations (buffer overflow, insufficient bandwidth) that can cause the network to collapse; various congestion-control methods exist.

Congestion Indication (CI)

CI is a bit in the RM cell that indicates congestion. It is set by the destination if the last cell received was marked.

Copper Distributed Data Interface (CDDI)

CDDI is a 100Mbps FDDI LAN standard based on Token Ring arbitration protocols and is used over UTP copper cable of lengths of up to 100 meters. Like all Token Ring implementations, redundancy is provided by using a dual-ring architecture. CDDI was a trade name of Crescendo Communications (acquired by Cisco Systems in 1993) and was commonly used instead of the general term *Twisted-Pair Physical Layer Medium* (TP-PMD).

Core Gateway

The primary routers on the Internet

Core Network

A combination of switching offices and the transmission plant that connects the switching offices; in the United States local exchange, core networks are linked by several competing interexchange networks (in the rest of the world, core networks extend to national boundaries)

Core Router

A router that is part of the backbone in a packet-switched star topology and that serves as the single pipe through which all traffic from peripheral networks must pass on its way to other peripheral networks

Core-Based Trees (CBT) Routing Protocol

A routing protocol characterized by a single tree shared by all nodes. The CBT routing protocol is characterized by a single tree that is shared by all members of the group. Group members receive multicast traffic over this shared tree regardless of the source of the message. A small number of core routers constructs the tree, and routers can join the tree by sending a join message to the core.

Corporate Network

An internetwork, a WAN, or an enterprise network; a network of networks that connects most or all of a corporation's LANs (connections between networks and LANs are made with bridges and routers)

Count to Infinity

A problem that can occur in routing algorithms that have slow convergence in which routers continuously increment the hop count to particular networks, thus counting up to infinity. Typically, some arbitrary hop-count limit is imposed in order to prevent this problem.

D

D Channel or Data Channel

The D channel refers to a) a channel in ISDN lines that is used to set up calls and to carry out-of-band information about the calls, and b) an IBM term that is used as a synonym for an input/output channel.

Data Encryption Standard (DES)

In computer security, the *National Institute of Standards and Technology* (NIST) DES, adopted by the U.S. government as *Federal Information Processing Standard* (FIPS) publication 46, enables only hardware implementations of the data encryption algorithm. A popular symmetric-key encryption method, it was developed in 1975 and was standardized by ANSI in 1981 as ANSI X.3.92. It was a widely used method of providing secure connections through data encryption until it was broken in July 1998. DES uses a 56-bit key and is illegal to export out of the United States or Canada if the exporter does not meet BXA requirements.

Data Link Connection Identifier (DLCI)

Used to indicate a Frame Relay port connection to and from a Frame Relay network; DLCIs are associated with virtual circuits, and a pair of DLCIs (one at either end) mapped across a Frame Relay network becomes a *Virtual Circuit* (VC)

Data Link Layer

Layer 2 of the OSI reference model; synchronizes transmission and handles error correction for a data link

Data Link Switching Plus (DLSW+)

A legacy networking protocol; a type of serial device connection (for example, a dumb terminal)

Data Service Unit or Digital Service Unit (DSU)

A DSU is a device that is used in digital transmission that connects end-user equipment, such as a router, to a digital transmission circuit or service. DSUs terminate a digital circuit, such as T1, at the customer's site. For example, to bring Frame Relay service into a building, you could connect the incoming digital leased line (fractional T1) to the building's DSU, which in turn could be connected to the building's router via a serial media by using the Frame Relay protocol. For Frame Relay service, DSUs range in speed from 56Kbps to T3 (51Mbps).

Datagram

In IP networks, a datagram is a packet—a way of sending data in which a data message is randomly broken into parts and the parts are correctly reassembled by the receiving machine. Each message part contains information about itself, including its destination and source. Datagrams are small pieces of data, often in the 256- to 2,000-byte range. Datagrams are completely self-contained. They have a source and a destination, but they have nothing that could be called a connection. A datagram has no relationship to any other datagrams that came before or after it. Although most networking communication uses data streams, all Internet transfers are in the form of datagrams. Internet streams are actually emulated by the TCP protocol by using datagrams. To diagnose Internet operation, a packet decoder such as TCPdump is used to view individual packets. This tool, along with a knowledge of TCP operation, enables the Internet engineer to assemble a mental picture of network operation.

Datagram Delivery Protocol (DDP)

In AppleTalk networks, a protocol that provides socket-to-socket delivery of data packets

Daughtercard

A daughtercard is a printed circuit board that plugs into another circuit board (usually the motherboard). A daughtercard is similar to an expansion board, but it accesses the motherboard components (memory and CPU) directly instead of sending data through the slower expansion bus. A daughtercard is also called a daughterboard.

DB-9

A physical connector that has nine pins

DB-15

Connector used for data-connectivity applications; has 15 pins and can be configured for several protocols, including the popular RS-232

DB-25

A connector that is used for data-connectivity applications; has 25 pins and can be configured for several protocols, including the popular RS-232

De Facto Standard

A standard that results from technology that has been developed, widely used, and that has achieved some level of popularity; a standard that exists by nature of its widespread use (compare with de jure standard).

De Jure Standard

A standard that is set by a body or official consensus; a standard that exists because of its approval by an official standards body (compare with de facto standard).

Decimal

Decimals are numbers in base 10 (the numbers that we use in everyday life). The numbers 9, 100345000, and D256 are all decimal numbers. Note that a decimal number is not necessarily a number with a decimal point in it. Numbers that have decimal points (that is, numbers that have a fractional part) are called fixed-point or floating-point numbers. In addition to the decimal format, computer data is often represented in binary, octal, and hexadecimal formats.

Dense Wave-Division Multiplexing (DWDM)

A transmission technique for transmitting eight or more different light frequencies on a single fiber, thereby enabling an increase in its capacity to carry information

Digital Subscriber Line (DSL)

DSL is an always-on Internet connection that is typically billed monthly, usually for a fixed price and unlimited usage. DSL, when installed in a socket on your wall, looks much like a phone socket. At least in the United States, the wall socket is, in fact, a phone socket—and for the popular residential-type DSL (ADSL), the same wiring carries voice and data. The key advantage of DSL over a modem is speed. DSL is from several to dozens of times faster than a modem connection. DSL is also a great way to save money, compared to paying per minute for ISDN data (or expensive T1 lines).

Digital Versatile Disc or Digital Video Disc (DVD)

A DVD is a type of CD-ROM that holds a minimum of 4.7GB, which is enough for a full-length movie. Many experts believe that DVD disks, called DVD-ROMs, will eventually replace CD-ROMs as well as VHS video cassettes and laser discs. Unlike DVD-ROMs, however, the digital video format includes a *Content Scrambling System* (CSS) to prevent users from copying discs. In other words, today's DVD-ROM players cannot play DVD video discs without a software or hardware upgrade in order to decode the encrypted discs.

Distance Vector Multicast Routing Protocol (DVMRP)

An internetwork gateway protocol that is largely based on RIP and that implements a typical dense-mode IP multicast scheme. DVMR uses IGMP to exchange routing datagrams with its neighbors. *See IGMP.*

DIX Ethernet

A version of Ethernet developed by Digital, Intel, and Xerox

DoD Four-Layer Model

The *Department of Defense* (DOD) Four-Layer Model was developed in the 1970s for the DARPA Internetwork Project that eventually grew into the Internet. The core Internet protocols adhere to this model, although the OSI Seven-Layer Model is justly preferred for new designs. The four layers in the DoD model, from bottom to top, are as follows:

1. The network access layer, which is responsible for delivering data over the particular hardware media that are in use. Different protocols are selected from this layer, depending on the type of physical network.

2. The Internet layer, which is responsible for delivering data across a series of different physical networks that interconnect a source machine and a destination machine. Routing protocols are most closely associated with this layer, as is the IP protocol (the Internet's fundamental protocol).

3. The host-to-host layer, which handles connection rendezvous, flow control, the retransmission of lost data, and other generic data-flow management. The mutually exclusive TCP and UDP protocols are this layer's most important members.

4. The process layer, which contains protocols that implement user-level functions such as mail delivery, file transfer, and remote login

Domain

A domain is a) a group of computers and devices on a network that are administered as a unit that has common rules and procedures. Within the Internet, domains are defined by the IP address. All devices that are sharing a common part of the IP address are said to be in the same domain. A domain also refers to b) a part of the DNS naming hierarchy.

Domain Name

A domain name is the unique name that identifies an Internet site. It is an English language standard for a computer system's TCP/IP numeric address (for example, 10.10.12.1). Domain names always have two or more parts separated by dots (for example, `netcerts.com`). The part on the left is the most specific, and the part on the right is the most general. A given machine might have more than one domain name, but a given domain name points to only one machine. For example, the domain names `netcerts.com`, `mail.netcerts.com`, and `ftp.netcerts.com` can all refer to the same machine, but each domain name can refer to no more than one machine. Usually, all of the machines on a given network have the same right-hand portion of their domain names. It is also possible for a domain name to exist but to not be connected to an actual machine. This procedure is often done so that a group or business can have an Internet e-mail address without having to establish a real Internet site. In these cases, some real Internet machine must handle the mail on behalf of the listed domain name. As documented in RFC 1591, top-level domain names take one of two forms. First, they can be generic domains, all of which are populated by predominantly American domains. Alternately, a top-level domain can be a United Nations two-digit country code listed in ISO-3166—the most common form for non-American domains. To be used, domain names must be converted into 32-bit IP addresses by using the DNS protocol. Domain name registration should be handled by the InterNIC in North America, RIPE in Europe, and APNIC in Asia. Domain name assignment is completely distinct from IP address assignment.

Generic Domains Country Domains (partial list)	
.com	commercial
.uk	United Kingdom
.edu	educational (colleges and universities included)
.fr	France
.org	nonprofit organizations
.de	Germany
.net	networking providers
.nl	Netherlands
.mil	U.S. military
.us	United States
.gov	U.S. government
.au	Australia
.int	international organizations
.ax	Antarctica

Domain Name Server

In TCP/IP environments, a protocol for matching object names and network addresses; designed to replace the need to update /etc/hosts files of participating entities throughout a network

Domain Name System (or Service) (DNS)

A DNS is an Internet service that translates domain names into IP addresses. Because domain names are alphabetic, they are easier to remember. The Internet, however, is really based on IP addresses. Every time you use a domain name, therefore, a DNS service must translate the name into the corresponding IP address. For example, the domain name `www.example.com` might translate to 19.15.32.4. The DNS system is, in fact, its own network. If one DNS server does not know how to translate a particular domain name, it asks another one (and so on) until the correct IP address is returned. DNS uses a distributed database protocol to delegate control of domain name hierarchies among zones, each of which is managed by a group of name servers. For example, `*.NetCerts.com`, where * is anything, is completely the responsibility of NETCERTS. NETCERTS is responsible for constructing name servers to handle any domain name ending in `NetCerts.com` (referred to as their *Zone of Authority* [ZOA]). A zone takes its name from its highest point, so this zone is simply called `NetCerts.com`. NETCERTS registers its zone with InterNIC, which loads the name server IP addresses into the root name servers (which makes this information available to the global Internet). NETCERTS can also make subdelegations, which is much like delegating news (`NetCerts.com` to its news division). This process can be as simple as creating new name server entries with the longer names, but mechanisms exist if the delegate wants to operate an independent name server (RFC 1034).

DS0

A data circuit carrying 56Kbps or 64Kbps of information; might be its own line or one channel in a DS1 (T1/E1); can also be referred to as a 56Kbps or 64Kbps leased line

DTE/DCE

The interface between *data terminal equipment* (DTE) and *data circuit-terminating equipment* (DCE); one of the most common interfaces in networking

E

E-1

European Digital Signal 1; the European standard for digital physical interface at 2.048Mbps; consists of 32 64Kbps channels (channels can be ordered as needed from the phone company)

E-2

European Digital Signal 2; the European standard for digital physical interface at 8.448Mbps; can simultaneously support four E-1 circuits

E-3

European Digital Signal 3; the European standard for a digital physical interface at 34.368Mbps; can simultaneously support 16 E-1 circuits (compare with T3).

E-4

European Digital Signal 4; European standard for digital physical interface at 139.264Mbps

EIA/TIA 32E

EIA/TIA 32E stands for Interface between Data Terminal Equipment and Data Circuit-Terminating Equipment Employing Serial

Binary Data Interchange (July, 1991). EIA/TIA 32E is a common physical-layer interface standard that was developed by EIA and TIA. It supports unbalanced circuits at signal speeds of up to 64kbps. EIA/TIA 232 E closely resembles the V.24 specification and was formerly called RS-232. This standard is applicable to the interconnection of DTE and DCE, employing serial binary data interchanges.

EIA/TIA-232

Common physical layer interface standard developed by EIA and TIA that supports unbalanced circuits at signal speeds of up to 64Kbps; closely resembles the V.24 specification (formerly known as RS-232)

EIA-232D

Electronics Industries Association-232D; the official designation for RS-232 (Recommended Standard-232), an Electronics Industries Association standard asynchronous serial line that is used commonly for modems, computer terminals, and serial printers

EIA-530

Two electrical implementations of EIA/TIA-449: RS-422 (for balanced transmission) and RS-423 (for unbalanced transmission). *See RS-422 and RS-423.*

Enhanced Interior Gateway Routing Protocol (EIGRP)

A Cisco proprietary dynamic routing protocol

Ethernet

Ethernet is a common method of networking computers on a LAN. Ethernet is a data link-level protocol. Version 2.0 was defined by the

Digital Equipment Corporation, the Intel Corporation, and the Xerox Corporation in 1982. The Ethernet specification serves as the basis for the IEEE 802.3 standard, which specifies the physical and lower software layers. Ethernet handles about 10,000,000 bits per second and can be used with almost any kind of computer. It specifies a data rate of 10Mbits/s, a maximum station distance of 2.8 km, a maximum number of stations (1,024), a shielded coaxial cable using baseband signaling, functionality of CSMA/CD, and a best-effort delivery system. *See Bandwidth.*

Ethernet Meltdown

When the Ethernet protocol is used as the data link layer protocol in a network, it is called an Ethernet meltdown. It is an event that causes saturation or near-saturation on an Ethernet data link. This scenario usually results from illegal or misrouted packets and lasts a short time.

Explicit Route (ER)

In SNA, a series of one or more transmission groups that connect two subarea nodes; identified by an origin subarea address, a destination subarea address, an explicit route number, and a reverse explicit route number

Explicit Routing

A type of routing used in MPLS that eliminates hop-related routing (and, as a result, routing efficiency by controlling the direction that the packet takes to its destination). Explicit routing can also assist on an IP network that is using VPNs because it does not have to encrypt the traffic (because the traffic is kept within the *Label Switch Path* [LSP]). This feature also reduces the process overhead on the router.

Extended ASCII

Extended ASCII is a set of codes that extends the basic ASCII set. The basic ASCII set uses seven bits for each character, giving it a total of 128 unique symbols. The extended ASCII character set uses eight bits, which gives it an additional 128 characters. The extra characters represent characters from foreign languages and special symbols for drawing pictures.

Extended Binary-Coded Decimal Interchange Code (EBCDIC)

IBM's basic character set that is used to represent data within the SNA environment; consists of 256 eight-bit characters and control functions

Extended Superframe Format (ESF)

ESF is a T1 framing standard that is used for frame synchronization and to locate signaling bits. ESF consists of 24 bits instead of the previous standard 12 bits. ESF enables easy error data storage and retrieval, thus facilitating network maintenance and performance monitoring.

F

Fast Ethernet

Fast Ethernet is the 100Mbps version of IEEE 802.3. Fast Ethernet offers a speed increase of 10 times the 10BaseT Ethernet specification while preserving qualities such as frame format, MAC mechanisms, and MTU. These similarities enable the use of existing 10BaseT applications and network management tools on Fast Ethernet networks. Fast Ethernet is based on an extension of the IEEE802.3

specifi-cation. Compare Fast Ethernet with Ethernet. *See 100BaseFX, 100BaseT, 100BaseT4, 100BaseTX, 100BaseX, and IEEE 802.3.*

Forward Explicit Congestion Notification (FECN)

FECN is a bit that is set by a Frame Relay network in order to inform the DTE that is receiving the frame that congestion was experienced in the path from the source to the destination. DTE-receiving frames with the FECN bit set can request higher-level protocols to take flow-control actions as appropriate. *See Backward Explicit Congestion Notification.* For more information, visit www. frforum.com.

G

Generic Cell-Rate Algorithm (GCRA)

The GCRA is a reference model proposed by the ATM Forum for defining cell-rate conformance in terms of certain traffic parameters. It is usually referred to as the leaky-bucket algorithm.

Generic Flow Control (GFC)

GFC is a four-bit field in the ATM cell header that is used to support multiplexing functions. Its default value is 0000 when the GFC protocol is not enforced. The GFC mechanism is intended to support simple flow control in ATM connections.

Generic Routing Encapsulation (GRE)

GRE is a tunneling protocol developed by Cisco Systems that can encapsulate a wide variety of protocol packet types inside IP tunnels, creating a virtual point-to-point link between Cisco routers at remote

points over an IP internetwork. By connecting multi-protocol subnetworks in a single-protocol backbone environment, IP tunneling
via GRE enables network expansion across a single-protocol backbone environment.

Get Nearest Server (GNS)

GNS is an IPX request packet that is sent by a client on an IPX network in order to locate the nearest active server of a particular type.
An IPX network client issues a GNS request to solicit either a direct
response from a connected server or a response from a router that
tells it where on the internetwork the service can be located. GNS is
part of the IPX SAP. *See Internet Packet Exchange.*

Gigabit Ethernet

Gigabit Ethernet is a high-speed version of Ethernet (a billion bits
per second) and is under development by the IEEE.

H

Hello Packet

A hello packet is a multicast packet that is used by routers for neighbor discovery and recovery. Hello packets also indicate that a client
is still operating and is network ready. Hello packets are also used in
ATM networks with the PNNI protocol in order to discover adjacent
switches.

Hello Protocol

The hello protocol is the protocol used by OSPF systems to establish
and maintain neighbor relationships. Do not confuse the hello protocol with the hello routing protocol.

Hierarchical Network

A hierarchical network is a multi-segment network configuration that provides only one path through intermediate segments between source segments and destination segments. One of the prime benefits of arranging a network in a hierarchical fashion is that it greatly simplifies network address searches. Prefix addresses can be used to help accelerate the routing through the network to the destination address.

Hierarchical Routing

In TCP/IP, hierarchical routing is based on a hierarchical addressing scheme. Most TCP/IP routing is based on a two- or three-level hierarchy in which an IP address is divided into a network portion until the datagram reaches a gateway that can deliver it directly. The concept of subnets introduces additional levels of hierarchical routing.

High-Level Data Link Control (HDLC)

HDLC is a group of protocols or rules for transmitting data between network points (sometimes called nodes). HDLC is a method of WAN data encapsulation in which data is organized into a unit (called a frame) and is sent across a network to a destination that verifies its successful arrival. The HDLC protocol also manages the flow or pace at which data is sent and supports several modes of operation, including a simple sliding window mode for reliable delivery. HDLC is an ISO standard developed from the *Synchronous Data Link Control* (SDLC) standard proposed by IBM in the 1970s and documented in ISO 3309. For any HDLC communications session, one station is designated as primary, and the other is deemed secondary. A session can use one of the following connection modes that determine how the primary and secondary stations interact:

- *Normal unbalanced*   The secondary station responds only to the primary station.

- *Asynchronous*   The secondary station can initiate a message.

- *Asynchronous balanced*   Both stations send and receive over their part of a duplex line. This mode is used for X.25 packet-switching networks. The *Link Access Procedure-Balanced* (LAP-B) and *Link Access Procedure D-Channel* (LAP-D) protocols are subsets of HDLC. Many variants of HDLC have been developed. Both PPP and SLIP use a subnet of HDLC's functionality. ISDN's D channel uses a slightly modified version of HDLC. The Cisco routers' default serial link encapsulation is HDLC.

High-Speed Serial Interface (HSSI)

HSSI is a high-speed WAN connection supporting speeds of up to 54Mbps.

Highest Potentiality OpenView (HP OpenView)

HP OpenView is a network discovery engine developed by Hewlett-Packard. HP OpenView provides integrated network, system, application, and database management for multi-vendor distributed computing environments. HP OpenView can probe IP-, IPX-, or SMS-based networks.

Hot Standby Router Protocol (HSRP)

HSRP is a protocol that was developed by Cisco Systems and provides high network availability and transparent network topology changes. HSRP creates a hot standby router group with a lead router that uses a virtual IP address that services all packets that are sent to the hot standby (virtual) address. The lead router's operation is monitored by other routers in the group, and if it fails, one of these standby routers inherits the lead position and the hot standby (virtual) group address.

HSRP

See Hot Standby Router Protocol.

Hypertext Markup Language (HTML)

HTML is coding language that is used to create hypertext documents for use on the World Wide Web. HTML resembles typesetting code, where a block of text is surrounded with codes that indicate how the text should appear. Using HTML, a word or block of text can be linked to another file on the Internet. HTML files are meant to be viewed by using a World Wide Web client program, such as Netscape or Mosaic. For more information about HTML, also see books by Laura Lamay.

Hypertext Transfer Protocol (HTTP)

HTTP is the protocol for moving hypertext files across the Internet. HTTP requires an HTTP client program on one end and an HTTP server program on the other end. HTTP is the most important protocol used on the World Wide Web.

I

IEEE 802

The IEEE committee overseeing standards for LANs

IEEE 802.1

The IEEE specification that describes an algorithm that prevents bridging loops by creating a spanning tree. The algorithm was invented by the Digital Equipment Corporation. The digital algorithm and the IEEE 802.1 algorithm are not exactly the same, nor are they compatible. *See Spanning-Tree Algorithm and Spanning-Tree Protocol.*

IEEE 802.12

The IEEE LAN standard that specifies the physical layer and the MAC sublayer of the data link layer; IEEE 802.12 uses the demand priority media-access scheme at 100Mbps over a variety of physical media. *See 100VG-AnyLAN.*

IEEE 802.12VG

IEEE 802.12VG is a 100 Base VG AnyLAN standard approved by the IEEE. 100 VG AnyLAN is a 100Mbps high-speed networking standard that was originally developed to transmit Ethernet or Token Ring packets on existing wiring. The VG in 100 VG AnyLAN stands for voice grade, meaning that the 100 VG technology will run standard Ethernet frames at 100Mbps—utilizing voice-grade Category 3, 4, and 5 UTP wire. Data packets are transferred from node to node by a hub, based on the address of the data packet. This process ensures orderly transmission and eliminates collisions. Because of this managed transfer of data, 100 VG AnyLAN can transmit data at peak speeds of 96Mbps, compared to four to six Mbps on Ethernet. 100 VG AnyLAN is easily implemented either standalone or in existing Ethernet networks. Additionally, 100 VG AnyLAN provides high-speed migration paths for Token Ring users and can be bridged to ATM backbones when necessary.

IEEE 802.2

IEEE 802.2 is the IEEE LAN protocol that specifies an implementation of the LLC sublayer of the data link layer. IEEE 802.2 handles error framing, flow control, and the network-layer (layer 3) service interface. It is used in IEEE 802.3 and IEEE 802.5 LANs.

IEEE 802.3

IEEE 802.3 is the IEEE LAN protocol defining an implementation of the physical layer and MAC sublayer of the data link layer. IEEE 802.3 uses the CSMA/CD access method at a variety of speeds over several different media transmission types, such as UTP. IEEE 802.3 is the basis of the Ethernet standard. Extensions to the IEEE 802.3 standard specify implementations for Fast Ethernet. Physical variations of the original IEEE 802.3 specification include 10Base-2, 10Base-5, 10Base-F, 10Base-T, and 10Broad36. Physical variations for Fast Ethernet include 100Base-T, 100Base-T4, 100BaseX, and 802.3Z Gigabit.

IEEE 802.3Z

This standard is the IEEE 802.3z standard that was created to extend the 802.3 protocol to an operating speed of 1,000Mbps in order to provide a significant increase in bandwidth while maintaining maximum compatibility with the installed base of CSMA/CD nodes, previous investment in research and development, and principles of network operation and management. It defines CSMA/CD, MAC parameters, and minimal augmentation of its operation, physical layer characteristics, repeater functions, and management parameters for the transfer of 802.3 and Ethernet format frames at 1,000Mbps.

IEEE 802.4

The IEEE physical layer standard that specifies a LAN with a token-passing access method on a bus topology; used with *Manufac-*

turing Automation Protocol (MAP) LANs; typical transmission speed is 10Mbps

IEEE 802.5

The IEEE LAN protocol defining an implementation of the physical layer and MAC sublayer of the link layer; 802.5 uses the token-passing access method at 4Mbps or 16Mbps over STP cabling.

IEEE 802.6

The IEEE *Metropolitan-Area Network* (MAN) specification based on DQDB technology; supports data rates of 1.5Mbps to 155Mbps.

IEEE 1394

IEEE 1394 is an external bus standard that supports data transfer rates of up to 400Mbps (400 million bits per second). Products supporting the 1394 standard go under different names, depending on their manufacturer. Apple, which originally developed the technology, uses the trademarked name FireWire. Other companies use other names, such as I-link and Lynx, to describe their 1394 products. A single 1394 port can be used to connect up to 63 external devices. In addition to its high speed, 1394 also supports isochronous data-delivering data at a guaranteed rate. This feature makes it ideal for devices that need to transfer high levels of data in real time, such as video devices.

IETF

See Internet Engineering Task Force.

IGMP

See Internet Group Management Protocol.

IGRP

See Interior Gateway Routing Protocol.

Institute of Electrical and Electronics Engineers (IEEE)

IEEE is pronounced "I-triple-E." Founded in 1884, the IEEE is an organization composed of engineers, scientists, and students. The IEEE is best known for developing standards for the computer and electronics industry. In particular, the IEEE 802 standards for LANs are widely followed, as well as 802.11 (the standard for wireless LANs). For more information, see www.ieee.org.

Integrated IS-IS

Integrated IS-IS is a routing protocol based on the OSI routing protocol IS-IS, but it has support for IP and other protocols. Integrated IS-IS implementations send only one set of routing updates, making it more efficient than two separate implementations. Integrated IS-IS was formerly referred to as dual IS-IS.

Interior BGP

A subset of the *Border Gateway Protocol* (BGP) that only exchanges routing updates within an *Autonomous System* (AS) as a single network domain

Interior Gateway Routing Protocol (IGRP)

IGRP is a proprietary dynamic routing protocol developed by Cisco to address the problems associated with routing on large, heterogeneous networks. *See Enhanced IGRP, OSPF, and RIP.*

Interior Routing

Interior routing is a type of routing that occurs within an AS. Most common routing protocols, such as RIP and OSPF, are interior routing protocols. The basic routable element is the IP network or subnetwork (or CIDR prefix for newer protocols).

International Organization for Standardization

The ISO is an organization of national standards-making bodies from various countries and was established to promote the developmental standards to facilitate the international exchange of goods and services, and develop cooperation in intellectual, scientific, technological, and economic activity. One such standard is *Open Systems Interconnection* (OSI).

International Standardization for Organization

The ISO is a special agency of the United Nations that is charged with the development of communications standards for computers. Membership in the ISO consists of representatives from international standards organizations throughout the world. Note that ISO is not an acronym; instead, the name derives from the Greek word *iso*, which means equal.

International Telecommunication Union (ITU)

The ITU is an inter-governmental organization through which public and private organizations develop telecommunications. The ITU was founded in 1865 and became a United Nations agency in 1947. It is responsible for adopting international treaties, regulations, and standards governing telecommunications. The standardization functions were formerly performed by a group within the ITU called CCITT, but after a 1992 reorganization, the CCITT no longer exists as a separate body.

International Telecommunications Union-Telecommunications Standards Sector (ITU-T)

The ITU-T is a formal international standards, specifications, and recommendations body (formerly known as CCITT-ITU-T) and is part of the ITU, which was founded in 1948. ITU-T is sponsored by the United Nations and promotes telephone and telegraphy issues.

Internet Assigned Number Authority (IANA)

Many protocol specifications include numbers, keywords, and other parameters that must be uniquely assigned. Examples include version numbers, protocol numbers, port numbers, and MIB numbers. The IAB has delegated to the IANA the task of assigning such protocol parameters for the Internet. The IANA publishes tables of all currently assigned numbers and parameters in RFCs titled "Assigned Numbers" (RFC 1602). *See NIC.* For more information, the IANA maintains a Web page at `www.isi.edu/iana/` and can be contacted at `iana@isi.edu`.

Internet Engineering Steering Group (IESG)

The IESG is the organization that is responsible for the technical management of IETF activities and the Internet standards process. As part of the ISOC, it administers the process according to the rules and procedures that have been ratified by the ISOC trustees. The IESG is directly responsible for the actions associated with entry into and movement along the Internet standards track, including final approval of specifications as Internet standards. The IESG can be contacted at `iesg@cnri.reston.va.us`. *See IETF.*

Internet Engineering Task Force (IETF)

The IETF is the main standards organization of the Internet—a loosely self-organized group of network designers, operators, vendors, and researchers who make technical and other contributions to the engineering and evolution of the Internet and its technologies. It is the principal body that is engaged in the development of new Internet-standard specifications. Its mission includes identifying and proposing solutions to pressing operational and technical problems with the Internet; specifying the development or usage of protocols and the near-term architecture to solve such technical problems for the Internet; making recommendations to the *Internet Engineering Steering Group* (IESG) regarding the standardization of protocols and protocol usage on the Internet; facilitating technology transfer from the IRTF to the wider Internet community; and providing a forum for the exchange of information within the Internet community between vendors, users, researchers, agency contractors, and network managers. The IETF is divided into eight functional areas: Applications, Internet, Network Management, Operational Requirements, Routing, Security, Transport, and User Services. Each area has one or two area directors. The area directors, along with the IETF/IESG chair, form the IESG. Each area has several working groups. The individuals belonging to the working group work under a charter to achieve a certain goal. That goal might be the creation of an informational document, the creation of a protocol specification, or the resolution of problems in the Internet. Most working groups have a finite lifetime. That is, once a working group has achieved its goal, it disbands. As in the IETF, there is no official membership for a working group. Unofficially, a working group member is somebody who is on that working group's mailing list; however, anyone can attend a working group meeting (RFC 1718). The IETF and its various working groups maintain numerous mailing lists. To join the IETF announcement list, send a request to `ietf-announce-request@cnri.reston.va.us`. To join the IETF discussion list, send a request to `ietf-request@cnri.reston.va.us`. For more information, see `www.ietf.org`.

Internet Gateway Routing Protocol (IGRP)

A proprietary protocol designed for Cisco routers

Internet Group Management Protocol (IGMP)

IGMP is a protocol documented in Appendix I of RFC 1112 that enables Internet hosts to participate in multicasting. RFC 1112 describes the basics of multicasting IP traffic, including the format of multicast IP addresses, multicast Ethernet encapsulation, and the concept of a host group, which is the set of hosts interested in traffic for a particular multicast address. Important multicast addresses are documented in the most recent Assigned Numbers RFC, currently RFC 1700. IGMP allows a router to determine which host groups have members on a given network segment. The exchange of multicast packets between routers is not addressed by IGMP. Important multicast addresses are documented as the most recent assigned numbers RFC, currently RFC 1700.

Internet Packet Exchange (IPX)

IPX is a Novell protocol that operates at OSI layer 3. It is used in the NetWare protocols and is similar to IP in TCP/IP.

Internet Protocol (IP)

IP is a protocol that is used to route data from its source to its destination (part of TCP/IP protocol).

IP address

The IP address is the 32-bit dotted-decimal address assigned to hosts as an identifier for a computer or device on a TCP/IP network that wants to participate in a local TCP/IP internet or the central (connected) Internet. IP addresses are software addresses. An IP address consists of a network portion and a host portion. The partition makes routing efficient. Networks using the TCP/IP protocol route messages based on the IP address of the destination. The format of an IP address is a 32-bit numeric address written as four numbers separated by periods. Each number can be 0 to 255. For example, 1.160. 10.240 is an IP address. These numbers are placed in the IP packet header and are used to route packets to their destination. Within an isolated network, you can assign IP addresses at random as long as each one is unique. However, connecting a private network to the Internet requires using registered IP addresses (called Internet addresses) to avoid duplication. The four numbers in an IP address are used in different ways to identify a particular network and a host on that network. An IP address has five classes, three of which (A, B, and C) are primary. The InterNIC Registration Service assigns Internet addresses from the following three classes:

- Class A   Supports 16 million hosts on each of 127 networks
- Class B   Supports 65,000 hosts on each of 16,000 networks
- Class C   Supports 254 hosts on each of 2 million networks

The number of unassigned Internet addresses is running out, so a new classless scheme called *Classless Interdomain Routing* (CIDR) is gradually replacing the system based on classes A, B, and C and is tied to adoption of IPv6. *See domain name, and TCP/IP.*

IP Datagram

In TCP/IP networks, an IP datagram is a basic unit of information passed across a TCP/IP Internet. An IP datagram is to an Internet as a hardware packet is to a physical network. It contains a source address and a destination address along with data.

IP Multicast

A one-to-many transmission described in RFC 1112. The RFC describes IP multicasting as: "the transmission of an IP datagram to a host group, a set of zero or more hosts identified by a single IP destination address. A multicast datagram is delivered to all members of its destination host group with the same best-efforts reliability as regular unicast IP datagrams. The membership of a host group is dynamic; that is, hosts may join and leave groups at any time. There is no restriction on the location or number of members in a host group. A host may be a member of more than one group at a time."

IP Multicast Datagram

A datagram delivered to all members of the multicast host group; such datagrams are delivered with the same best-effort reliability as regular unicast IP datagrams

IP Multicast Router

A router supporting IGMP and one or more of the multicast routing protocols, including distance DVMRP, MOSPF, PIM-DM, CBT, and PIM-SM

IPng

IPng stands for Internet Protocol Next Generation. A new version of the *Internet Protocol* (IP) currently being reviewed in IETF standards committees. The official name of IPng is IPv6, or Internet Protocol version 6. The current version of IP is version 4 (IPv4). IPng is designed as an evolutionary upgrade to the Internet Protocol and will, in fact, coexist with the older IPv4 for some time. IPng is designed to allow the Internet to grow steadily, both in terms of the number of hosts connected and the total amount of data traffic transmitted.

IPv6

See IPng.

K

Kilobits (Kbits)

One thousand bits; the measurement of kilobits per second (kbits/s) is used to designate a data transfer rate of one thousand bits per second.

Kilobits per Second (Kbps)

A measure of data transfer speed

Kilobyte (KB)

In the metric system, 1,000 bytes; however, KB can also represent 1,024 bytes when used to describe data storage because the binary value closest to 1,000 bytes is 1,024

L

Link-Access Procedure or Protocol (LAP)

According to DEC documentation, a set of procedures used for link control on a packet-switched data network. X.25 defines two sets of procedures: LAP and the DTE-DCE interface, defined as operating in two-way simultaneous, asynchronous response mode with the DTE and DCE containing both a primary and secondary function. LAPB is the DTE/DCE interface, defined as operating in two-way asynchronous balanced mode. According to Apple documentation, an AppleTalk protocol that controls the access of a node to the network hardware. A link-access protocol makes it possible for many nodes to share the same communication hardware.

Link-Access Procedure Balanced (LAPB)

Balanced mode, bit-oriented protocols; an enhanced version of HDLC; a method of WAN data encapsulation used on X.25 packet-switching networks

Link-Access Procedure D-Channel (LAPD)

An ISDN protocol that operates at the data-link layer (level 2) of OSI 7 layer model. LAPD was derived from the LAPB protocol and is designed primarily to satisfy the signaling requirements of ISDN basic access (ISDN BRI). The D channel carries signaling information for circuit switching. ITU-T Recommendations Q.920 and Q.921 define LAPD.

Logical Link Control (LLC)

A protocol developed by the IEEE 802 committee, common to all of its LAN standards, for data-link-level transmission control that governs the transmission of frames between data stations independently of how the transmission medium is shared; the upper sublayer of the IEEE layer 2 (OSI) protocol that further defines the MAC protocol (IEEE standard 802.2) The LLC layer provides the basis for an unacknowledged connectionless service or connection-oriented service on the LAN such as error control, broadcasting, multiplexing, and flow control functions.

Loop

a) A situation that occurs when network devices have multiple circular paths to a destination, when in fact no path ever reaches the destination. b) In programming, a series of instructions that is repeated until a certain condition is met. Each pass through the loop is called an iteration. Loops constitute one of the most basic and powerful programming concepts.

Loopback Address

An address used for communications between clients and servers that reside on the same host. For example, the address 127.0.0.1 is a commonly acknowledged loopback address. When the Ping command is issued, this address will always return the name of the computer from which the Ping command was issued.

M

MAC Address

Also known as an Ethernet address, hardware address, station address, burned-in address, or physical address. It uniquely identifies each node in a network. A set of 6 two-digit hexadecimal numbers burned into an Ethernet product by its manufacturer. This is a data-link layer address associated with a particular network device; it is often called a hardware address or physical address because of its device association. This is in contrast to an IP protocol address, which is a network-layer address that defines a network connection. In IEEE 802 networks, the *Data Link Control* (DLC) layer of the OSI Reference Model is divided into two sublayers: the *Logical Link Control* (LLC) layer and the *Media Access Control* (MAC) layer. The MAC layer interfaces directly with the network media. Consequently, each different type of network media requires a different MAC layer. On networks that do not conform to the IEEE 802 standards, but do conform to the OSI Reference Model, the node address is called the *Data Link Control* (DLC) address. *See Network Address.*

Management Information Base (MIB)

A collection of managed objects. A term used with the concept of SNMP-based network management. A database of objects for referencing variables such as integers and strings. In general, it contains information regarding a network's management and performance, i.e., traffic parameters that can be monitored by a network management system. Both SNMP and RMON use standardized MIB formats that allow any SNMP and RMON tools to monitor any device defined by a MIB. An individual equipment manufacturer may develop an MIB extension to the standard to uniquely define variables that apply to its implementation (that cannot be defined by the variables already in the base MIB standard). *See SNMP.*

MIB Browser

An MIB browser is an application that has been built to enable a network engineer to access the information that is stored within any SNMP-compliant device that is running SNMP (and thus uses abstract syntax notation).

Millisecond (ms)

One thousandth of a second. Access times of hard disk drives are measured in milliseconds.

Minimum Cell Rate (MCR)

A parameter that gives the minimum rate that cells can be transmitted by a source over a *Virtual Connection* (VC).

Multi-Chassis Multi-Link Point-to-Point Protocol (MMP)

A Cisco protocol that enables multiple connections from a single site to terminate in multiple access servers while still looking like one single, larger connection

Multi-Homing

Addressing scheme in IS-IS routing that supports the assignment of multiple area addresses

Multi-Layer Switch

Switch that filters and forwards packets based on MAC addresses and network addresses; a subset of LAN switch; compare with the LAN switch

Multi-Link Point-to-Point Protocol (MP)

An extension to the PPP protocol that allows multiple physical connections between two points to be combined into a single logical connection. The combined connections, called a bundle, provide greater bandwidth than a single connection. Unlike channel bonding, which usually combines two channels for the duration of a connection, MP supports dynamic bandwidth allocation, which means that physical links can be added or removed from the bundle as needed. MP works with a number of technologies, including ISDN, X.25, and frame relay. It is an open standard, specified in RFC 1990.

Multi-Link PPP (MPPP)

Method of extending PPP so that multiple connections can be added together for higher bandwidth and lower latency; must be supported at both ends of the connection

Multi-Mode

The transmission of multiple modes of light

Multi-Protocol Label Switching (MPLS)

MPLS is an emerging high-performance IETF standard for forwarding packets (frames) through a network. The main concept is to include a label on each packet by enabling edge routers to apply simple labels to packets (frames). ATM switches or existing routers in the network's core can then switch these packets according to the label with minimal lookup overhead. This labeling of packets enables full mesh connectivity across a public network without the added complexity of creating and managing virtual circuits. MPLS combines layer 2 performance and virtual circuit capabilities with the scalability of layer 3 routing. The MPLS label is formatted as follows:

```
|-20bits Label-|-3bits CoS-|-1bit Stack-|-8bits TTL-|
```

The 32-bit MPLS label is located after the layer 2 header and before the IP header. The MPLS label contains the following fields:

- *The* label *field (20 bits)*   Carries the actual value of the MPLS label
- *The* CoS *field (three bits)*   Can affect the queuing and discard algorithms that are applied to the packet as it is transmitted through the network
- *The* Stack *(S) field (one bit)*   Supports a hierarchical label stack
- *The* TTL *(time to live) field (eight bits)*   Provides conventional IP TTL functionality (also called a "shim" header)

Multicast

Method of transmitting messages from a host using a singe transmission to a selected subset of all the hosts that can receive the messages; also a message that is sent out to multiple devices on the network by a host. A simple example of multicasting is sending an e-mail message to a mailing list. Teleconferencing and videoconferencing also use multicasting, but require more robust protocols and networks. Standards are being developed to support multicasting over a TCP/IP network such as the Internet. These standards, IP Multicast and Mbone, will allow users to easily join multicast groups. *See IP.*

Multicast Address-Resolution Server (MARS)

A program used to support IP Multicast over ATM. It contains tables of IP multicast addresses and associated ATM addresses.

Multicast Group

A group set up to receive messages from a source. These groups can be established based on frame relay or IP in the TCP/IP protocol suite, as well as in other networks.

Multicast OSPF (MOSPF)

A series of extensions applied to the OSPF intradomain routing protocol for all OSPF to support IP multicast routing

Multicast Router

Router running a multicast enabled routing protocol, like MOSPF, that is used to route IGMP query messages on its attached local networks

Multicast Server

A specialized server that establishes a one-to-many connection to each device in a VLAN, thus establishing a broadcast domain for each VLAN segment. The multicast server forwards incoming broadcasts only to the multicast address that maps to the broadcast address.

Multicast Source Discovery Protocol (MSDP)

MSDP is also being considered by the IETF to become a standard. It allows for the connecting of multiple PIM sparse mode domains while enabling them to use their own rendezvous points. The benefit is that the node for sharing of routes between providers is removed.

Multicast Transport Protocol (MTP)

This protocol gives application programs guarantees of reliability. The MTP protocol could be useful when developing some types of applications, for example with distributed databases that need to be certain that all members of a multicast group agree on which packets have been received.

Multicasting

A directory service agent uses this mode to chain a request to many other directory service agents.

Multimedia

A way of presenting to the user a combination of different forms of information such as text, data, images, video, audio, and graphics (i.e., videoconference). Nearly all PCs are capable of displaying video, although the resolution available depends on the power of the computer's video adapter and CPU. Because of the storage demands of multimedia applications, the most effective media are CD-ROMs.

N

Nagle's Algorithm

The Nagle algorithm was introduced in TCP to reduce the number of small TCP segments by delaying their transmission, in hopes of further data becoming available, as commonly occurs in Telnet or rlogin traffic. It's actually two separate congestion control algorithms, which can be used in TCP-based networks. One algorithm reduces the sending window; the other limits small datagrams. For example, when someone types in a Telnet session, one character is sent in as packet. (The transmission of a single-character message originating at a keyboard typically results in a 41-byte packet [one byte of data, plus 40 bytes of header] being transmitted for each byte). This is very wasteful of bandwidth. Instead, if the source waits some finite time before sending another short packet, then a couple of characters accumulate in the next packet. The ratio of overhead to real data goes down and network efficiency goes up.

Network Control Program (NCP)

An interactive utility program that enables a manager to control and monitor a network. Also a switch or network node; software designed to store and forward frames between nodes. An NCP may be used in LANs or larger networks. In IBM systems, the main software component in a 37xx communication controller. NCP is generated from a library of IBM-supplied modules and controls communication controller operations.

Network Element (NE)

In integrated services digital networks, a piece of telecommunications equipment that provides support or services to the user. An example of a network element is a router, switch, or hub on the network.

Network Interface Card (NIC)

A *Network Interface Device* (NID) in the form of a circuit card that is installed in an expansion slot of a computer to provide network access. Examples of NICs are cards that interface a computer with an Ethernet LAN and cards that interface a computer with an FDDI ring network.

Network Layer

Layer 3 of the seven-layer *Open Systems Interconnection* (OSI) stack. It is responsible for data transfer across the network. It functions independently of network media and topology. There are seven network layers in the *Open Systems Interconnection Reference Model* (OSI-RM), which is an abstract description of the digital communications between application processes running in distinct systems. The model employs a hierarchical structure. Each layer performs value-added service at the request of the adjacent higher layer and, in turn, requests more basic services from the adjacent lower layer:

1. The Physical Layer (Layer 1), is the lowest of the seven hierarchical layers. The Physical layer performs services requested by the Data Link Layer. The major functions and services performed by the physical layer are: a) establishment and termination of a connection to a communications medium; b) participation in the process whereby the communication resources are effectively shared among multiple users, e.g., contention resolution and flow control; and c) conversion between the representation of digital data in user equipment and the corresponding signals transmitted over a communications channel.

2. The Data Link Layer (Layer 2) responds to service requests from the Network Layer and issues service requests to the Physical Layer. The Data Link Layer provides the functional and procedural means to transfer data between network entities and to detect and possibly correct errors that may occur in the Physical Layer. Examples of data link protocols are HDLC and ADCCP for point-to-point or packet-switched networks and LLC for local area networks.

3. The Network Layer (Layer 3) responds to service requests from the Transport Layer and issues service requests to the Data Link Layer. The Network Layer provides the functional and procedural means of transferring variable length data sequences from a source to a destination via one or more networks while maintaining the quality of service requested by the Transport Layer. The Network Layer performs network

routing, flow control, segmentation/desegmentation, and error control functions.

4. The Transport Layer (Layer 4) responds to service requests from the Session Layer and issues service requests to the Network Layer. The Transport Layer provides transparent transfer of data between end users, thus relieving the upper layers from any concern with providing reliable and cost-effective data transfer.

5. The Session Layer (Layer 5) responds to service requests from the Presentation Layer and issues service requests to the Transport Layer. The Session Layer provides the mechanism for managing the dialogue between end-user application processes. It provides for either duplex or half-duplex operation and establishes checkpointing, adjournment, termination, and restart procedures.

6. The Presentation Layer (Layer 6) responds to service requests from the Application Layer and issues service requests to the Session Layer. The Presentation Layer relieves the Application Layer of concern regarding syntactical differences in data representation within end-user systems. An example of a presentation service would be the conversion of an EBCDIC-coded text file to an ASCII-coded file.

7. The Application Layer (Layer 7) is the highest layer; it interfaces directly to and performs common application services for application processes; it also issues requests to the Presentation Layer. The common application services provide semantic conversion between associated application processes. Examples of common application services of general interest include the virtual file, virtual terminal, and job transfer and manipulation protocols.

Network Time Protocol (NTP)

A protocol that is used to synchronize date and time for computers and routers

NIC

See Network Interface Card.

Nonbroadcast Multi-Access (NBMA)

One of the new WAN technologies; a type of network broadcast service that is found in Frame Relay and ATM

O

Octothorpe

The proper name for the symbol # (pound sign)

Open Shortest Path First (OSPF)

A routing protocol developed for IP networks based on the shortest path first or link-state algorithm. OSPF uses the Djikstra or Shortest Path Algorithm to calculate the shortest path between routers in an internetwork. Each router running OSPF will send the "links" it is aware of and their status to its neighboring routers. From this link-state database, a routing table is calculated using the shortest path first algorithm. Routers use link-state algorithms to send routing information to all nodes in an internetwork by calculating the shortest path to each node based on a topography of the Internet constructed by each node. Each router sends that portion of the routing table (keeps track of routes to particular network destinations) that describes the state of its own links, and it also sends the complete routing structure (topography). The advantage of shortest path first algorithms is that they result in smaller, more frequent updates everywhere. They converge quickly, thus preventing such problems as routing loops and count-to-infinity (when routers continuously increment the hop count to a particular network). This makes for a stable network. The disadvantage of shortest path first algorithms is that they require a lot of CPU power and memory. In the end, the advantages out weigh the disadvantages. OSPF Version 2 is defined in RFC 1583.

Open System Interconnection (OSI)

Also known as the OSI Reference Model or OSI Model. In the 1980s, the *International Standards Organization* (ISO), began to develop the *Open Systems Interconnection* (OSI) networking suite. The result was an ISO standard for worldwide communications that defines a networking framework for implementing protocols in seven layers.

P

Packet Switching

A WAN transmission method where a network device shares a single synchronous serial point-to-point link to transport packets from source to destination. Examples of a packet-switched network include Frame Relay and X.25. Packets within this type of network can vary in length, whereas cell switching uses fixed-length packets.

Password Authentication Protocol (PAP)

The most basic form of authentication used in PPP, in which a user's name and password are transmitted in clear (unencrypted) text. *See CHAP.*

Permanent Virtual Circuit (PVC)

A virtual connection established by network management between an origin and a destination that can be left up permanently (used in X.25, Frame Relay, and ATM protocols). Generally, it is a permanent logical association between two DTEs, analogous to a leased line. Packets are routed directly by the network from one DTE to the other. This concept is in contrast to *Switched Virtual Circuits* (SVCs), which are initiated by the calling party and are torn down at the end of the call or session.

Physical Address

Standardized data-link layer address required for every port or device that connects to a LAN. Other devices in the network use these addresses to locate specific ports in the network and to create and update routing tables and data structures. MAC addresses are 6 bytes long and are controlled by the IEEE. Also known as a hardware address, MAC-layer address, and physical address. *See MAC Address.*

Physical Layer

Layer 1 of the OSI model, the lowest of seven hierarchical layers. The physical layer performs services requested by the data-link layer. The major functions and services performed by the physical layer are: a) establishment and termination of a connection to a communications medium; b) participation in the process whereby the communication resources are effectively shared among multiple users, e.g., contention resolution and flow control; and c) conversion between the representation of digital data in user equipment and the corresponding signals transmitted over a communications channel. As the first layer of the ATM protocol reference model, it is subdivided into two sublayers, the *Transmission Convergence* (TC) and the *Physical Medium* (PM) sublayers. It provides to ATM cells transmission over the physical interfaces that interconnect ATM devices. It is also one of the first two sublayers of the FDDI physical layer.

Plain Old Telephone Service (POTS)

The standard analog telephone service used in most homes. Data transmission over a POTS system is usually accomplished via a modulator/demodulator (modem). POTS is restricted to about 52 Kbps (52,000 bits per second) and is also known as the *Public Switched Telephone Network* (PSTN).

Point-of-Presence (POP)

A physical access point to a long distance carrier's network, typically found in a city or location where customers can connect to it, often with dial up phone lines.

Point-to-Point Protocol (PPP)

The successor to SLIP is documented in RFC 1661, PPP is currently the best solution for dial-up Internet connections, including ISDN. PPP is a layered protocol, starting with a *Link Control Protocol* (LCP) for link establishment, configuration and testing. Once the LCP is initialized, one or more of several *Network Control Protocols* (NCPs) can be used to transport traffic for a particular protocol suite. Each NCP is documented in its own RFC. The *IP Control Protocol* (IPCP), documented in RFC 1332, permits the transport of IP packets over a PPP link. Other NCPs exist for AppleTalk (RFC 1378), OSI (RFC 1377), DECnet Phase IV (RFC 1762), Vines (RFC 1763), XNS (RFC 1764), and transparent Ethernet bridging (RFC 1638).

Point-to-Point Tunneling Protocol (PPTP)

A protocol that is used to ensure transmission between VPN nodes. Developed jointly by Microsoft Corporation, U.S. Robotics, and several remote-access vendor companies, known collectively as the PPTP Forum. It is defined in RFC 2637. PPTP has also been embedded in Windows 95, Windows 98, and Windows NT.

Point-to-Multipoint Optical Network (PON)

A high-bandwidth fiber network based on ATM

Poison Reverse Updates

Routing updates that explicitly indicate a network or subnet is unreachable, rather than implying that a network is unreachable by not including it in updates. Poison reverse is a technique used to prevent routing loops.

Private Automatic Branch Exchange (PABX)

a) A subscriber-owned telecommunications exchange that usually includes access to the public switched network. b) A switch that serves a selected group of users and that is subordinate to a switch at a higher level military establishment. c) A private telephone switchboard that provides on-premises dial service and may provide connections to local and trunked communications networks. A PBX operates with only a manual switchboard; a *Private Automatic Exchange* (PAX) does not have a switchboard, a *Private Automatic Branch Exchange* (PABX) may or may not have a switchboard. Use of the term PBX is far more common than PABX, regardless of automation.

Private Branch Exchange (PBX)

A private telephone network, used within an enterprise, which relays telephones, terminals, or other equipment, and provides access to the public telephone system

Protocol Data Unit (PDU)

A general term used to refer to that which is exchanged between peer-layer entities. Originally used in the OSI model to describe what passed across two adjoining layers. It contains header, data, and trailer information.

Protocol Independent Multicast (PIM)

Multicast routing architecture that enables the addition of IP multicast routing on existing IP networks. PIM is unicast routing protocol independent and can be operated in dense or sparse mode. Briefly dense mode is driven by data and closely resembles typical multicast routing, whereas sparse mode limits the number of receiving devices.

Q

Q.2110

ITU-T recommendation for specifying the UNI SSCOP

Q.2130

ITU-T recommendation for specifying the UNI SSCF

Q.2931

ITU-T recommendation derived from both Q.931 and Q.933 to provide SVC specifications and standards; an ATM signaling specification

Q.920/Q.921

ITU-T specifications for the ISDN UNI data link layer.

Q.921

Also referred to as *Link Access Protocol-D Channel* (LAPD) and a close cousin of HDLC, Q.921 is the data link protocol that is used over ISDN's D channel.

Q.922A

ITU-T specification for Frame Relay encapsulation

Q.931

ITU-T recommendation for specifying the UNI signaling protocol in N-ISDN. ISDN's connection control protocol, roughly comparable to TCP in the Internet protocol stack. Q.931 doesn't provide flow control or perform retransmission, because the underlying layers are assumed to be reliable and the circuit-oriented nature of ISDN allocates bandwidth in fixed increments of 64 kbps. Q.931 manages connection setup and breakdown. Like TCP, Q.931 documents both the protocol itself and a protocol state machine. In accordance with the conventions of ITU standards, bits are numbered from *Least Significant Bit* (LSB) to *Most Significant Bit* (MSB), 1 to 8 (Internet standards use MSB to LSB, 0 to 7). The general format of a Q.931 message includes a single-byte protocol discriminator (8 for Q.931 messages), a call reference value to distinguish between different calls being managed over the same D channel, a message type, and various *Information Elements* (IEs) as required by the message type in question.

Q.933

ITU-T recommendation for specifying the UNI signaling protocol in Frame Relay

Q.93B

Currently called Q.2931

Quality of Service (QoS)

A guaranteed throughput level for critical network applications, such as *Voice over IP* (VoIP). One of the biggest advantages of ATM over competing technologies such as Frame Relay and Fast Ethernet, is that it supports QoS levels. This allows ATM providers to guarantee to their customers that end-to-end latency will not exceed a specified level. These parameters include the CLR, CER, CMR, CDV, CTD, and the average cell transfer delay. Simply stated, QoS parameters are used in traffic engineering to state the level of loss (inverse of throughput), latency, and jitter that a traffic stream will be guaranteed in a network. For more information, see www.ietf.org/html.charters/qosr-charter.html.

QoS Classes

Five service classes defined by the ATM Forum in terms of the QoS parameters:

- Class 0: Refers to best-effort service
- Class 1: Specifies the parameters for circuit emulation, CBR (uncompressed) video and for VPN. AAL1 supports this kind of connection-oriented service.
- Class 2: Specifies the parameters for VBR audio and video. AAL2 supports this delay-dependent, connection-oriented class.
- Class 3: Specifies the parameters for connection-oriented data transfer. AAL3/4 and mostly AAL5 support this delay-independent class of service.

R

RARP

See Reverse Address Resolution Protocol.

Real-Time Streaming Protocol (RTSP)

A proposed standard for controlling streaming data over the World Wide Web. A session involves the complete RTSP transaction; in other words, the viewing of a movie. A session typically consists of a client setting up a transport mechanism for the continuous media stream, starting the stream with Play or Record, and closing the stream with a tear down.

Remote Access Services (RAS)

A feature that is built into Windows NT that enables users to log into an NT-based LAN using a modem, X.25 connection, or WAN link. RAS works with several major network protocols, including TCP/IP, IPX, and NetBEUI. To use RAS from a remote node, a user needs a RAS client program, which is built into most versions of Windows, or any PPP client software. For example, most remote control programs work with RAS.

Remote Authentication Dial-In User Service (RADIUS)

A protocol invented by Livingston Enterprises (recently acquired by Lucent) for authenticating dial-in users across multiple dial-in servers. Used by many *Internet Service Providers* (ISPs). When a user dials in to the ISP, they enter a username and password. This information is passed to a RADIUS server, which checks that the information is correct, and then authorizes access to the ISP system. Though not an official standard, the RADIUS specification is maintained by a working group of the IETF.

Remote Copy Protocol (RCP)

Protocol that enables users to copy files to and from a file system residing on a remote host or server on the network. The RCP protocol uses TCP to ensure the reliable delivery of data. An RCP server is a router or other device that acts as a server for RCP.

Request for Comments (RFCs)

A series of notes about the Internet, started in 1969 (when the Internet was the ARPANET). An RFC can be submitted by anyone to the IETF. The Internet Engineering Task Force is a consensus-building body that facilitates discussion, and eventually establishes new standards. The reference number/name for the standard retains the acronym RFC; for example, the official standard for e-mail is RFC 822. Each RFC is designated by an RFC number. Once published, an RFC never changes. Modifications to an original RFC are assigned a new RFC number.

Resource Reservation Setup Protocol (RSVP)

An Internet protocol that enables the Internet to support specified *Quality of Service* (QoS) classes in IP applications (such as videoconference, multimedia).Using RSVP, an application is able to reserve resources along a route from source to destination. RSVP-enabled routers then schedule and prioritize packets to fulfill the QoS. RSVP is a chief component of a new type of Internet being developed, known broadly as an integrated services Internet. The general idea is to enhance the Internet to support transmission of real-time data.

Reverse Address Resolution Protocol (RARP)

A TCP/IP protocol for mapping Ethernet addresses to IP addresses. It is typically used by diskless workstations that do not know their IP addresses. RARP enables a computer to discover its IP address by broadcasting a request on a network. In essence, it asks the question, "Who am I?" Normally, a response is provided by a RARP server and is cached in the host.

RIF

See Routing Information Field.

Ring Latency

The time required for a signal to propagate once around a ring on a Token Ring or IEEE 802.5 network

Ring Monitor

A centralized management tool for Token Ring networks based on the IEEE 802.5 specification.

Ring Topology

One of the three principal topologies used in LANs. All devices are connected to one another in the shape of a closed loop, so that each device is connected directly to two other devices, one on either side of it. Ring topologies are relatively expensive and difficult to install, but they are robust (one failed device does not usually make the entire network fail).

RIP

See Routing Information Protocol.

Route

An ordered sequence between origin and destination stations that represents a path in a network between the stations.

Route Extension

A path from the destination in SNA subarea node through the peripheral equipment to an NAU

Route Map

Method of controlling the redistribution of routes between routing domains

Route Reflectors

Route reflectors reduce BGP traffic within an AS by limiting the amount of necessary neighboring connections. This task is performed by enabling an IBGP router to advertise another neighbor's advertisement. In this way, a certain hierarchy can be introduced where BGP routers talk to a single router that passes information to other routers. This specific router is known as the route reflector. An AS can have multiple route reflectors, each managing their own group of routers and talking to each other. Thus, these groupings and dependencies introduce a hierarchy-like structure within your BGP network.

Routing

Process usually performed by a dedicated device called a router. In internetworking, the process of moving a packet of data from source to destination. Routing is a key feature of the Internet because it enables messages to pass from one computer to another and eventually reach the target machine. Each intermediary computer performs routing by passing along the message to the next computer. Part of this process involves analyzing a routing table to determine the best path. Routing assumes that addresses have been assigned to facilitate data delivery. In particular, routing assumes that addresses convey at least partial information about where a host is located. This permits routers to forward packets without having to rely on either broadcasting or a complete listing of all possible destinations. At the IP level, routing is used almost exclusively, primarily because the Internet was designed to construct large networks in which heavy broadcasting or huge routing tables are not feasible. Routing is often confused with bridging, which performs a similar function. The principal difference between the two is that bridging occurs at a lower level and is therefore more of a hardware function, whereas routing occurs at a higher level where the software component is more important. Because routing occurs at a higher level, it can perform more complex analysis to determine the optimal path for the packet.

Routing Information Field (RIF)

Field in the IEEE802.5 header that is used by a source-route bridge to determine through which token ring network segments a packet must transit. A RIF is made up of ring and bridge numbers as well as other information.

Routing Information Identifier (RII)

Bit used by *Source Route Transparent* (SRT) bridges to distinguish between frames that should be transparently bridged and frames that should be passed to the *Source Route Bridging* (SRB) device for handling.

Routing Information Protocol (RIP)

An early BSD UNIX dynamic routing protocol that has become an industry standard; often used because WIN NT and UNIX systems can understand it. RIP is considered an outdated router protocol. *See OSPF and EIGRP.*

Routing Table Maintenance Protocol (RTMP)

A protocol that enables an AppleTalk router to obtain and keep information about routes to the various AppleTalk networks.

Routing Table Protocol (RTP)

VINES routing protocol based on RIP. Distributes network topology information and aids VINES servers in finding neighboring clients, servers, and routers. Uses delay as a routing metric.

Routing Tables

In Internet routing, each entry in a routing table has at least two fields the IP Address Prefix and Next Hop. The Next Hop is the IP address of another host or router that is directly reachable via an Ethernet, serial link, or some other physical connection. The IP Address Prefix specifies a set of destinations for which the routing entry is valid. To be in this set, the beginning of the destination IP address must match the IP Address Prefix, which can have from 0 to 32 significant bits. For example, a IP Address Prefix of 128.8.0.0/16 would match any IP Destination Address of the form 128.8.X.X. If no routing table entries match a packet's destination address, the packet is discarded as undeliverable (possibly with an ICMP notification to the sender). If multiple routing table entries match, the longest match is preferred. The longest match is the entry with the most 1 bits in its subnet mask.

Routing Update

A message sent from a router indicates a network reachability and associated cost information. Routing updates are typically sent at regular intervals and after a change in network topology.

RS-232C

A standard interface approved by the *Electronic Industries Association* (EIA) for connecting serial devices. In 1987, the EIA released a new version of the standard and changed the name to EIA-232-D.

In 1991, the EIA teamed up with *Telecommunications Industry Association* (TIA) and issued a new version of the standard called EIA/TIA-232-E. Many people, however, still refer to the standard as RS-232C, or just RS-232. Almost all modems conform to the EIA-232 standard and most personal computers have an EIA-232 port for connecting a modem or other device. In addition to modems, many display screens, mice, and serial printers are designed to connect to a EIA-232 port. In EIA-232 parlance, the device that connects to the interface is called *Data Communications Equipment* (DCE) and the device to which it connects (e.g., the computer) is called a *Data Terminal Equipment* (DTE). The EIA-232 standard supports two types of connectors—a 25-pin D-type connector (DB-25) and a 9-pin D-type connector (DB-9). The type of serial communications used by PCs requires only 9 pins so either type of connector works equally well. Although EIA-232 is still the most common standard for serial communication, the EIA has recently defined successors to EIA-232 called RS-422 and RS-423. The new standards are backward compatible so that RS-232 devices can connect to an RS-422 port.

RS-422

Balanced electrical implementation of EIA/TIA-449 for high-speed data transmission. Now referred to collectively with RS-423 as EIA-530. *See EIA-530 and RS-423.*

RS-423

Unbalanced electrical implementation of EIA/TIA-449 for EIA/TIA-232 compatibility. Now referred to collectively with RS-422 as EIA-530. *See EIA-530 and RS-422.*

RS-449

Popular physical-layer interface now known as EIA/TIA-449.

S

Session Layer

Layer 5 of the OSI reference model. The session layer coordinates the dialog between two communicating application processes by establishing, managing, and terminating sessions between applications; it manages data exchange between presentation layer entities. It corresponds to the data-flow control layer of the SNA model. *See Application Layer, Data Link Layer, Network Layer, and Physical Layer.*

Shortest Path First Algorithm (SPF)

Sometimes called Dijkstra's algorithm. SPF is commonly used in link-state routing algorithms such as OSPF.

Simple Mail Transfer Protocol (SMTP)

The protocol standard developed to support the exchange of *Electronic Mail* (e-mail) services. The SMTP protocol specifies how two mail systems interact and the format of control messages.

Simple Network Management Protocol (SNMP)

Originally developed for the Department of Defense in the early '80s. SNMP has since evolved into the IETF-defined standard management protocol for managing TCP/IP networks. SNMP is normally found as an application on top of the *User Datagram Protocol* (UDP), and is essentially a request-reply protocol running over UDP (ports 161 and 162), though TCP operation is possible. The agent is the device being managed; all that its software has to do is implement a few simple packet types and a generic get-or-set function on its MIB variables. The management station presents the user interface. Examples of these devices include routers, hubs, and switches. A device is said to be "SNMP compatible" if it can be monitored and/or controlled using SNMP messages. SNMP Version 1 is documented in RFC 1157. SNMP Version 2 is documented in several RFCs: RFC 1902 (MIB Structure), RFC 1903 (Textual Conventions), RFC 1904 (Conformance Statements), RFC 1905 (Protocol Operations), RFC 1906 (Transport Mappings), and RFC 1907 (MIB). SNMP's packet formats are described using abstract syntax notation 1 (ASN.1), one of ISO's "Open" protocols. ASN.1 basically fills the role of XDR, but does so differently. ASN.1, like all OSI standard documents, is not freely available on-line. An SNMP operation takes the form of a *Protocol Data Unit* (PDU), basically a fancy word for packet. Version 1 SNMP supports five possible PDUs:

- GetRequest/SetRequest supplies a list of objects and, possibly, values they are to be set to (SetRequest). In either case, the agent returns a GetResponse.

- GetResponse informs the management station of the results of a GetRequest or SetRequest by returning an error indication and a list of variable/value bindings.

- GetNextRequest is used to perform table transversal, and in other cases where the management station does not know the exact MIB name of the object it desires. GetNextRequest does not require an exact name to be specified; if no object exists of the specified name, the next object in the MIB is returned. Note that to support this, MIBs must be strictly ordered sets (and are).

- Trap is the only PDU sent by an agent on its own initiative. It is used to notify the management station of an unusual event that may demand further attention (like a link going down). In version 2, traps are named in MIB space. Newer MIBs specify management objects that control how traps are sent.

- SNMP communities is the only security architecture found in SNMP that enables an intelligent network device to validate SNMP requests from sources such as the NMS. *See SNMP.*

Small Office/Home Office (SOHO)

A small, remote office with a WAN or MAN connection back to a larger corporate network or to the Internet

SNMP

See Simple Network Management Protocol.

Source Route

A route determined by the source; TCP/IP implements source routing by using an option field in an IP datagram

Source-Route Translational Bridging (SR/TLB)

A method of bridging where source-route stations can communicate with transparent bridge stations with the help of an intermediate bridge that translates between the two bridge protocols. *See Source-Route Transparent Bridging.*

Source-Route Transparent (SRT) Bridging

An IBM bridging scheme that merges the two most prevalent bridging strategies, source route bridging and transparent bridging. Source-route transparent bridging employs both technologies in one device to satisfy the needs of all end stations. No translation between bridging protocols is necessary. *See Source-Route Translational Bridging.*

Source Routing

A method used by a bridge for moving data between LAN segments. The routing information is embedded in the token.

Spanning-Tree Algorithm (STA)

An algorithm used to create a logical topology that connects all network segments, and ensures that only one path exists between any two nodes. A spanning tree is loop free and is a subset of a network. Multicast routers construct a spanning tree from the multicast source located at the root of the tree to all the members of the multicast group.

Spanning-Tree Protocol (STP)

Bridge protocol developed by Radia Perlman. It utilizes the spanning-tree algorithm, and enables a switch or learning bridge to dynamically work around loops in a network topology by creating a spanning tree. Switches exchange BPDU messages with other switches to detect loops, and then remove the loops by blocking traffic on selected switch interfaces/ports.

Static Route

A route that is explicitly (statically) configured and entered into the router's routing table. Static routes will commonly take precedence over routes chosen by dynamic routing protocols.

Symmetric Digital Subscriber Line (SDSL)

Technology that enables more data to be sent over existing copper telephone lines. SDSL supports data rates up to 3 Mbps. SDSL is called symmetric because it supports the same data rates for upstream and downstream traffic. SDSL works by sending digital pulses in the high-frequency area of telephone wires. Because these high frequencies are not used by normal voice communications, SDSL can operate simultaneously with voice connections over the same wires.

Synchronous Transfer Mode (STM)

A packet-switching approach where time is divided into specific portions or slots, each assigned to a single channels. During its allowed time slot, users can transmit data on each channel. Basically, time slots denote allocated (fixed) parts of the total available bandwidth.

Synchronous Transport Module-1 (STM-1)

An ITU-T-defined SDH physical interface for digital transmission in ATM at the rate of 155.52Mbps

Synchronous Transport Module-n (STM-n)

An ITU-T-defined SDH physical interface for digital transmission in ATM at n times the basic STM-1 rate. There is a direct equivalence between the STM-n and the SONET STS-3n transmission rates.

Synchronous Transport Signal-1 (STS-1)

SONET signal standard for optical transmission at 51.84Mbps

Synchronous Transport Signal-n (STS-n)

SONET signal format for transmission at n times the basic STS-1 signal (in other words, STS-3 is at 155.52Mbps)

T

T-1

Digital line consisting of 24, 64-Kbps channels, with a total of 1.544Mbps of throughput available per second. Each channel can be configured to carry voice or data traffic. Most providers will allow you to buy just some of these individual channels, known as fractional T-1 access.

T-3

A leased-line connection capable of carrying data at 44.736Mbps (44,736,000 bits per second). T-3 lines are sometimes referred to as DS3 lines and can be multiplexed into 28 T-1 signals. A T-3 line actually consists of 672 individual channels, each of which supports 64Kbps. *See Bandwidth, Byte, Ethernet, and T-1.*

Telnet

An asynchronous, virtual terminal emulation program and protocol documented in RFC 854. It is used in TCP/IP networks, like the Internet, to allow remote access to the network. Telnet operates using the TCP Protocol, and depends heavily on option negotiation. Telnet options are documented in their own RFCs. The organization of these RFCs, and instructions for registering new Telnet options, is found in RFC 855. Many Telnet options exist; a complete, current list can be found in the Internet Official Standards RFC, currently RFC 2400.

Terminal Access Controller Access Control System (TACACS)

An authentication protocol that provides remote access authentication and related services, such as event logging. User passwords are administered in a central database rather than in individual routers, providing an easily scaleable network security solution.

Threshold

A percentage value that is set for a resource, usually to limit a process or action

Throughput

The rate of data transferred from one place to another and/or processed in a specified amount of time within a network. Throughput is measured in Kbps, Mbps, and Gbps. It is one of three basic service-level agreement parameters:

- THT
- TI RPC
- TIA

Trace

A record of events that is captured and used to troubleshoot hardware and/or software

Traceroute

Network debugging utility that is documented in RFC792 and attempts to trace the path a packet takes through the network from source to destination by its route. Traceroute utilities work by sending packets with low *Time-to-Live* (TTL) fields. When a packet can't reach its destination because the TTL value has expired, the last host returns the packet and identifies itself to the sender. By sending a series of packets and incrementing the TTL value with each successive packet, traceroute finds out who all the intermediary hosts are. Traceroute has a variety of options you can use to customize its operation to your networking environment. Here's a short list of common traceroute options:

- `-m max-ttl` max-ttl (default 30) sets a limit on how long traceroute keeps trying. If the target host is farther than 30 hops away, you'll need to increase this value.

- `-n` Numerical output only. Use this if you're having nameserver problems and traceroute hangs trying to do inverse DNS lookups.

- `-p port` Base UDP port. Port is the UDP port number that traceroute uses on its first packet, and increments by one for each subsequent packet.

- `-q queries` How many packets should be sent for each TTL value. The default is 3, which is fine for finding out the route.

- `-w wait` Wait is the number of seconds packets have to generate replies before traceroute assumes they never will and moves on. The default is 3.

Transmission Control Protocol (TCP)

Documented in RFC 793 as a standardized transport protocol developed for interconnecting IP-based networks. Operating on top of IP, it is responsible for multiplexing sessions, error recovery, end-to-end reliable delivery, and flow control; it guarantees delivery of data and that packets will be delivered in the same order in which they were sent. The IP protocol deals only with packets, TCP enables two hosts to establish a connection and exchange streams of data. TCP adds a great deal of functionality to the IP service it is layered over:

- *Streams* TCP data is organized as a stream of bytes, much like a file. The datagram nature of the network is concealed. A mechanism (the Urgent Pointer) exists to let out-of-band data be specially flagged. Important features of TCP are:

  - *Reliable delivery* Sequence numbers are used to coordinate which data has been transmitted and received. TCP will arrange for retransmission if it determines that data has been lost.

- *Network adaptation* TCP will dynamically learn the delay characteristics of a network and adjust its operation to maximize throughput without overloading the network.

- *Flow control* TCP manages data buffers, and coordinates traffic so its buffers will never overflow. Fast senders will be stopped periodically to keep up with slower receivers.

- *Full-duplex operation* TCP usually operates full duplex. The algorithms described operate in both directions, in an almost completely independent manner. It's helpful to think of a TCP session as two independent byte streams, traveling in opposite directions.

- *Sequence numbers* TCP uses a 32-bit sequence number that counts bytes in the data stream. Each TCP packet contains the starting sequence number of the data in that packet and the sequence number (called the acknowledgment number) of the last byte received from the remote peer. With this information, a sliding-window protocol is implemented. Forward and reverse sequence numbers are completely independent, and each TCP peer must track both its own sequence numbering and the numbering being used by the remote peer. TCP uses a number of control flags to manage the connection. Some of these flags pertain to a single packet, such as the URG flag indicating valid data in the Urgent Pointer field, but two flags (SYN and FIN), require reliable delivery as they mark the beginning and end of the data stream. In order to insure reliable delivery of these two flags, they are assigned spots in the sequence number space. Each flag occupies a single byte.

- *Window size and buffering* Each endpoint of a TCP connection will have a buffer for storing data transmitted over the network before the application is ready to read the data. This lets network transfers take place while applications are busy with other processing, improving overall performance. To avoid overflowing the buffer, TCP sets a Window Size field in each packet it transmits. This field contains the amount of data that may be transmitted into the buffer. If this number falls to zero, the remote TCP can send no more data. It must wait until buffer space becomes available and it receives a packet announcing a non-zero window size.

■ *Round-trip time estimation*   When a host transmits a TCP packet to its peer, it must wait a period of time for an acknowledgment. If the reply does not come within the expected period, the packet is assumed to have been lost and the data is retransmitted. The obvious question is, how long to wait? All modern TCP implementations seek to answer this question by monitoring the normal exchange of data packets and developing an estimate of how long is "too long."

Transmission Control Protocol/ Internet Protocol (TCP/IP)

A set of protocols that enables cooperating computers to share resources across a heterogeneous network. The combined main protocol was developed by the Department of Defense for the Internet. Originally designed for the UNIX operating system, TCP/IP uses several protocols, the two main ones being TCP and IP, mistakenly thought of as one protocol. TCP provides for the reliable transmission of data. IP provides connectionless datagram service. *See IP and TCP.*

U

User Datagram Protocol (UDP)

A connectionless transport protocol defined in RFC768. It provides no guarantee of packet sequence or delivery and is thus termed an unreliable protocol. It functions directly on top of IP and does not provide error-recovery services. Instead it offers a direct method of sending and receiving datagrams over an IP Network, while making no provision for acknowledgment or guarantee of packets received. This requires that error processing and retransmission be handled by other protocols.

Uniform Resource Locator (URL)

Strins that specifies how to access network resources, such as HTML documents. Part of the more general class of *Universal Resource Identifiers* (URIs). The most important use of URLs is in HTML documents, to identify the targets of hyperlinks. When using a Web browser, every highlighted region has a URL associated with it; this URL is accessed when the link is activated by a mouse click. Relative URLs specify only a portion of the full URL—the missing information is inferred though the context of the source document. URLs are documented in RFC 1738. Relative URLs are documented in RFC 1808. URIs are documented in RFC 1630.

Universal Serial Bus (USB)

An external bus standard for plug-and-play interfaces between a computer and add-on devices such as mice, modems, keyboards, audio players, joysticks, telephones, scanners, and printers. USBs support data transfer rates of 12Mbps (12 million bits per second). A single USB port can connect up to 127 devices.

UNIX

An operating system developed in 1969 at Bell Laboratories by Ken Thompson and Dennis Ritchie. UNIX became the first operating system written in the C language and was designed to be a small, flexible system used exclusively by programmers.

Unshielded Twisted Pair (UTP)

The most common kind of copper telephone wiring, consisting of two unshielded copper wires twisted around each other. Because the cost is so low, UTP cabling is widely used for LANs and telephone connections that require short-distance wiring. Even though UTP is inexpensive and easy to work with, it does not offer as high bandwidth or as good protection from interference as coaxial or fiber optic cables.

V

Virtual Channel (VC)

The unidirectional flow of ATM cells between connecting (switching or end-user) points that share a common identifier number (VCI). This number is unique and has significant meaning to the two endpoints of an ATM connection. *See Virtual Circuit.*

Virtual Channel Identifier (VCI)

A 16-bit value in the ATM cell header that provides a unique identifier for the VC that carries that particular cell

Virtual Channel Link (VCL)

Connection between two ATM devices. A *Virtual Channel Connection* (VCC) is made up of one or more VCLs.

Virtual Circuit

A connection set up across the network between a source and a destination. A fixed route is chosen for the entire session and bandwidth is dynamically allocated. These are logical circuits created to ensure reliable communication between two network devices. A virtual circuit is defined by a VPI/VCI pair, and can be either a *Permanent Virtual Circuit* (PVC) or a *Switched Virtual Circuit* (SVC). Virtual circuits are used in frame relay and X.25. In ATM, a virtual circuit is called a virtual channel. Sometimes abbreviated VC. *See VCI.*

Virtual Private Network (VPN)

Network resources provided to users, on demand, by public carriers (via the Internet for example) so that users view this partition of the network as a private network. The advantage of the VPNs over the dedicated private networks is that the former allow a dynamic allocation of network resources through encrypted network connections so the entire network is "virtually" private.

VLAN-Tagged Frame

A tagged frame whose tag header carries VLAN identification information

VLAN Membership Resolution Protocol (VMRP)

A protocol that uses GARP to provide a mechanism for dynamic maintenance of the contents of the port egress lists for each port of a bridge, and for propagating the information they contain to other bridges

VLAN Trunk Protocol (VTP)

A protocol that enables each device (router or LAN-switch) to transmit advertisements in frames on its trunk ports. These advertisement frames are sent to a multicast address to be received by all neighboring devices. However, they are not forwarded according to normal bridging procedures. These advertisement frames list the sending device's management domain, its configuration revision number, the VLANs, which it knows about, and certain parameters for each known VLAN. Once a device receives these advertisement frames, all devices in its same management domain learn about any new VLANs now configured in the transmitting device. This allows a new VLAN to be created or to have its configuration altered on only one device within a domain. The resulting changes are automatically advertised throughout the domain.

Voice-over-IP (VoIP)

A feature that carries voice traffic, such as telephone calls and faxes, over an IP network simultaneously with data traffic

W

Well-Known Port

A designated port assigned to TCP/IP applications and the programs that reside on top of TCP and UDP

Whois

An Internet directory service that returns information about a domain name or IP address. It is used to look up records in InterNIC's main database for second-level domains. Whois can be used as a program, by telneting to `ds.internic.net` or by going to `http://rs.internic.net/cgi-bin/whois`. Whois performs generic, string-based searches on several databases maintained by InterNIC, the most important of these being the domain registration database. Whois provides information about who owns an Internet host or domain and whom you can contact regarding that host or domain. A Whois request displays a contact name, mailing address, telephone number, and network mailbox for all users and organizations that are registered with one of the official Whois servers, such as the

Internet Network Information Center (InterNIC) database. You can go directly to the Network Solutions Whois web interface at `www.network solutions.com/cgi-bin/whois/whois`.

Wildcard Mask

An address mask specified when setting up access lists. It is used in conjunction with an IP address to determine which bits in an IP address should be ignored when comparing that address with another IP address.

X

X.25

For packet-switched WAN technology, a standard approved by the CCITT (now the ITU), which defines Layers 1, 2, and 3 in the OSI reference model and is based on an IBM product called *Synchronous Data Link Control* (SDLC). ISO further modified it to become *High Level Data Link Control* (HDLC). HDLC was adopted by CCITT as part of its X.25 network access standard, where it is known as *Link Access Protocol* (LAP); a later version known as LAPB. X.25 level 3 is an extension of X.25 level 2 to provide networking functions.

XDSL

A technology for bringing high-bandwidth information to homes and small businesses over ordinary copper telephone lines. It can be synchronous or asynchronous; the X represents the various forms of *Digital Subscriber Line* (DSL) technologies, which includes ADSL, R-ADSL, HDSL, SDSL, or VDSL. All DSL technologies run on existing copper phone lines and use modulation to boost transmission rates, whereas the different approaches (ADSL, RADSL, HDSL, SDSL, and VDSL) are best suited to different applications. *See Digital Subscriber Line.*

Z

Zone Information Protocol (ZIP)

An AppleTalk protocol that maintains a table in each router (called the *Zone Information Table* [ZIT]) that lists the relationship between zone names and networks

Zone of Authority

In the domain name system, the group of names authorized by a given name server

APPENDIX B

Firewalls and DMZ Design

Objectives

Upon completion of this chapter, you will be able to do the following tasks:

■ Identify the different types of attacks.

■ Identify the different types of *Denial of Service* (DoS) attacks.

■ Explain the steps that are necessary to combat specific attacks.

■ Recommend the appropriate firewall design based on the network infrastructure.

■ Identify the key components in a firewall design.

This chapter gives the reader the necessary knowledge to recommend and design an appropriate security solution for a network infrastructure. We will present different firewall designs along with the advantages and disadvantages of each design. Additionally, this chapter will present the most popular attacks that can be initiated against a network and will describe each attack in detail. The reader will then learn the knowledge that is necessary in order to combat each attack and to protect the internal network. By the end of the chapter, the reader should have a solid understanding of the most common attacks used against networks (along with the different methods of prevention for each attack.)

Attacks

Many different types of attacks can be orchestrated against a network or host in order to deny services or compromise systems. This section will discuss each attack. There are other types of attacks (such as trojans or worms) that are not specific to networks, however, and we will not discuss them in this chapter. While this chapter does cover many of the more popular types of attacks that are used today, it does not list every type of attack—because there are new applications being developed every day to exploit specific vulnerabilities of networks. This section is divided into two parts: *Denial of Service* (DoS) attacks and non-DoS attacks. DoS attacks are becoming more prevalent on today's Internet. Therefore, this section will discuss the different types of DoS attacks, and the following section will describe the different methods of preventing DoS and non-DoS attacks.

Packet Sniffing

Attackers can use a packet sniffer to obtain confidential information that resides on the company's internal network. A packet sniffer generally needs to be placed on a segment on the internal network in order to capture the majority of sensitive information. Flat networks, such as those that use hubs, are also easier to capture data because the sniffer will capture all data on the segment. The packet sniffer can capture information such as username/password combinations and can determine which types of applications and protocols that the network is running. Using a packet sniffer on a switched segment becomes difficult due to the nature of switches. Different vendors, however, have been known to have problems with layer 2 address tables reaching their limits and then flooding the traffic out all ports or have experienced software bugs (features) that present the same symptoms. In this situation, you can glean login and password information.

Another type of eavesdropping can take place if the attacker gains access to your system and uses this access to monitor the traffic that is passing by. On all Unix platforms, tools such as Snoop, tcpdump, and others are used to perform packet analysis.

NOTE: *Packet sniffing is not an attack; rather, it is data gathering or reconnaissance in preparation for a later attack.*

IP Address Spoofing

Spoofing is the art of manipulating packet headers in order to make the source address appear as if the packet is originating from a different source machine, such as the internal network or a trusted network. Spoofing can be used in several different types of attacks. First, you can use it to fool a firewall into believing that the packet can be trusted and that the packet should be passed to the internal network. Spoofing can also be used to hide the real source address of a DoS attack. A spoofed source address can also be used to target a victim in a smurf attack, where massive amounts of traffic are sent as a reply to the spoofed source address.

Port Scans

Port scans are not an attack by themselves; rather, they are considered reconnaissance. Port scanning is usually considered an unfriendly activity. A port scan is the process of sending packets to a host or range of *Internet Protocol* (IP) addresses in order to determine the *Transmission Control Protocol* (TCP) or UDP ports to which they are listening. This process is known as port scanning, and the host that they probe first is typically the firewall. Specific applications, services, or trojans run on predetermined ports. By determining which ports are active, an attacker can take advantage of the services that are running on these ports by using applications that will exploit those services. A port scan is typically the first action that an attacker will take when attempting to break into a network. There are many different types of port scans, and this next section will discuss four types.

Port Scan   The typical port scan uses the TCP three-way handshake to determine which ports on a device are listening. A custom-made application, usually developed by a white-hat hacker and distributed freely, is used to initiate the scanning. The application will transmit a TCP SYN packet with the destination port specified (for example, port 25 for the *Simple Mail Transfer Protocol* [SMTP]).

The destination host will reply with a SYN, ACK packet if port 25 is listening or will respond with an ACK, RST if the port is not listening. The ACK, RST resets the session and indicates that the port is not listening. If the destination host replies, the application will reply with an ACK packet followed immediately by an ACK, FIN packet in order to terminate the session. The hacker will now know that the port is listening and can often determine which services and operating systems the devices are running.

The biggest drawback to this type of attack is that firewalls will log the attack. The security administrator will notice that a port scan has occurred and will take the necessary steps to deny that IP address. The security administrator can also take higher measures by tracking down the culprit's upstream *Internet Service Provider* (ISP) and denying the IP address at the source.

SYN Scan   A SYN scan, or TCP half scanning, consists of using a custom-made application but slightly altering its primary function. The application that performs SYN scanning will only use the first part of the TCP three-way handshake. The application will send a SYN packet along with a destination port that is specified to the destination host. If the destination host is listening on the port that is specified in the SYN packet, it will reply with a SYN, ACK—and the hacker will know that the port is listening. The application will immediately transmit an RST packet in order to terminate the session.

The biggest advantage of this type of port scan is that many firewalls do not log half-open sessions, and the security administrator will never know that the network was scanned.

FIN Scan   A FIN scan is nearly identical to a SYN scan except that a FIN scan sends only ACK, FIN packets to the destination host. As noted previously, most firewalls are configured to deny SYN packets. Most firewalls are not configured to deny FIN packets, however, and this situation is convenient for the hacker. The hacker will use a custom-made application as with other attacks, but the application will be configured to send ACK, FIN packets. Often, firewalls will enable FIN packets to pass through the firewall. This situation enables the hacker to port-scan devices on the internal network. The destination device will respond to the ACK, FIN packet with an ACK, RST if the port is "not listening." If the destination device does not respond, it means that the port is listening. The reason is because the destination host does not have a session to terminate.

You should note that Microsoft devices will respond with an ACK, RST for all ports (whether they are listening or not). The ACK, RST will indicate that the destination host is running a Microsoft operating system but will not establish which ports are active and listening.

A FIN scan is the most effective type of port scan. Its primary advantage is that it is extremely difficult to track and to log. Most security administrators will never know that they have been scanned, and it is extremely difficult to stop these attacks. FIN packets cannot be blocked like SYN packets can. SYN packets can be blocked if the security policy does not enable incoming connections. If FIN packets were blocked, however, internal hosts would never receive the necessary packet in order to terminate a session—and all outgoing traffic would ultimately be hindered.

RingZero Scan   This type of scan is run from a trojan application that is delivered to your server and that infects your server. This application scans for proxies on ports 8080 and 3128. When it finds out what you have, it then calls home and delivers the information to the receiving system. The way to identify this type of scanning is by noticing an abnormal amount of outbound traffic on ports 80, 8080, and 3128. You want to examine the system that sources these requests for files that are called `its.exe`, `ring0.vxd`, and/or `pst.exe`. The `pst.exe` file is responsible for scanning your system for the proxy servers and for sending the results to the remote host that is gathering this data.

Small Servers

Portscanning can identify the following services. Many of these are vulnerable to abuse or hacking.

Cisco's IOS includes small servers that can be used for diagnostics on a router. These servers include both TCP and UDP small servers. Enabling these small servers, however, can cause the router to crash

TCP Small Servers

Echo: Echoes back whatever you type. Type the command `telnet x.x.x.x echo`.

Chargen: Generates a stream of ASCII data. Type the command `telnet x.x.x.x chargen`.

Discard: Throws away whatever you type. Type the command `telnet x.x.x.x discard`.

Daytime: Returns the system date and time (if correct). The date and time are correct if you are running NTP or have set the date and time manually from the exec level. Type the command `telnet x.x.x.x daytime`.

UDP Small Servers

Echo: Echoes the payload of the datagram that you send

Discard: Silently pitches the datagram that you send

Chargen: Pitches the datagram that you send and responds with a 72-character string of ASCII characters that is terminated with `CR+LF`

if the appropriate Telnet command is run while the router is active. Table B-1 lists the different types of small servers.

NOTE: *In the command* `telnet x.x.x.x`, *the* `x.x.x.x` *should be replaced with the IP address of the router.*

DoS Attacks

DoS attacks do not actually attempt to gain access to a network; rather, they cause a service to be denied to legitimate users by utilizing all of the system's resources. There are many different types of DoS attacks, and most of them are initiated by *script kiddies*. Script kiddies are usually defined as beginner crackers who use ready-made applications to generate DoS attacks against an unsuspecting party. These ready-made applications are usually developed by white-hat hackers and are created to exploit the vulnerabilities of systems. Security professionals can perform vulnerability assessments on client network infrastructures and identify potential vulnerabilities by using these tools. This process will give the client the necessary information to address security risks so that the client can take appropriate counter-measures. While there is no way to eliminate the possibility of a DoS attack, a network can be prepared to deal with such an attack quickly.

Examples of DoS attacks include *Synchronous Sequence Numbers* (SYN) flood, FIN flood, land, teardrop, and smurf. Each of these types of DoS attacks are described in this section. We will give examples of how attackers orchestrate these attacks as well as the effects that they have on networks and hosts. The following section will describe the different methods of preventing each different kind of attack.

Teardrop

Teardrop is a popular attack that is done from a Unix shell or Linux PC. The teardrop attack sends an invalid packet header to a Windows-based PC. The packet header will report the packet size as one size, but the actual packet will be a different size. Windows machines that do not have the appropriate patches will wait for the correct-size packet to be received. Of course, the correct-size packet is not going to show up and Windows cannot run other services during this time. The Windows-based machine will eventually display a blue screen, and the operating system will be unusable until restarted.

Another example of a teardrop attack is initiated by sending oversized packets that exceed 65535 bytes to a Windows-based machine. Windows machines contain a Microsoft TCP/IP stack that is not *Request for Comment* (RFC) compliant. Earlier Microsoft TCP/IP stacks have been known to cause Windows machines to display a blue screen when they receive packets that exceed 65535 bytes. This situation is caused by creating a buffer overflow (because the earlier

· Microsoft TCP/IP stacks could not process any packet that exceeded the maximum packet size of 65535 bytes).

Land.c

The land attack, also known as Land.c (named after the program that is used to initiate the attack), is a TCP loopback DoS attack and is used to deny service to legitimate users and administrators. Land works by sending a TCP SYN packet (a connection initiation) that uses the target host's address in both the source and destination address fields and the target host's port in both the source and destination port fields. This attack has been known to cause router failures in previous versions of IOS. The router has to be rebooted before it can be brought back online.

SYN Flood

The normal TCP connection sequence is called the TCP three-way handshake (see Figure B-1). This handshake consists of the source host sending a SYN packet to the destination host in order to initiate a session. The destination host will respond with a SYN, ACK

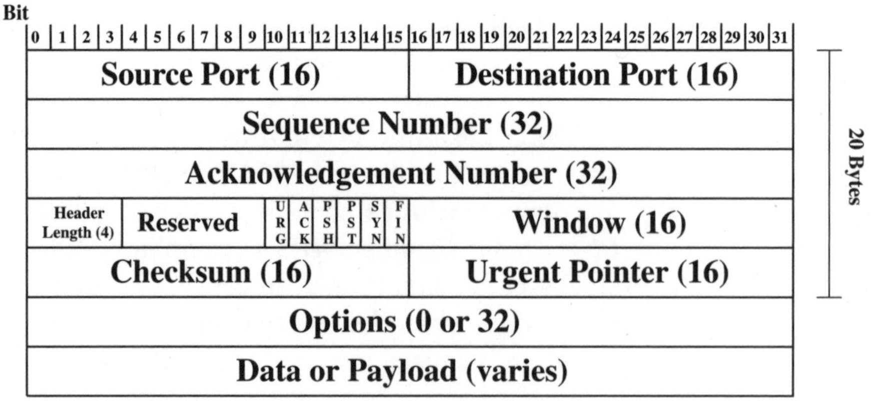

Figure B-1
TCP three-way handshake

Bit		
0 1 2 3 4 5 6 7 8 9 10 11 12 13 14 15	16 17 18 19 20 21 22 23 24 25 26 27 28 29 30 31	
Source Port (16)	**Destination Port (16)**	
Sequence Number (32)		
Acknowledgement Number (32)		
Header Length (4)	**Reserved**	U R G / A C K / P S H / P S T / S Y N / F I N	**Window (16)**
Checksum (16)	**Urgent Pointer (16)**	
Options (0 or 32)		
Data or Payload (varies)		

20 Bytes

packet, indicating that it received the request. The source host then responds with an ACK followed by data. The two hosts now continue exchanging information until the TCP session ends. The TCP session ends when the source sends a FIN packet. The FIN bit is part of the TCP header and is set to indicate that the source has reached the end of its byte stream. Figure B-2 illustrates the TCP header.

The SYN flood, or TCP SYN attack, uses the TCP three-way hand-shake to attack network devices. The TCP SYN attack works by flooding a network resource, such as a Web server, to exhaustion by sending SYN packets. By sending a SYN packet, the Web server creates a half-open connection by sending a SYN, ACK packet and awaits a response from the host that initiated the response. The Web server has a connection queue that keeps track of all open TCP sessions. This queue is normally emptied quickly, because ACKs are usually received within milliseconds. Because the source host is not responding with an ACK, however, the connection queue keeps the half-open sessions in its queue for a longer period of time. The attacker will continue to flood the Web server with SYN packets that are spoofed with different source IP addresses. The Web server's connection queue will continue growing and eventually will use all of the system's memory resources—thus preventing it from servicing legitimate requests.

FIN flood

A FIN flood is similar to a SYN flood except that it floods the destination host with TCP ACK, FIN packets instead of TCP SYN packets. Most firewalls do not deny FIN packets because they are

Figure B-2
TCP segment format

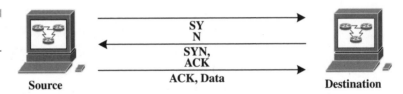

Source   Destination

necessary for internal hosts to communicate with outside devices. Therefore, FIN floods are generally more effective than SYN floods and are difficult to log.

Smurf Attack

One of the more popular DoS attacks is known as the smurf attack. The smurf attack is also one of the easiest DoS attacks to perform. This attack is initiated by using the *Packet Internet Grouper* (Ping) utility to send a stream of *Internet Control Message Protocol* (ICMP) packets to an entire subnet that can perform IP-directed broadcasts. Cisco routers have the capability to frame layer 3 IP broadcasts (for example, 172.16.255.255) into layer 2 broadcast frames (FF:FF:FF: FF:FF:FF for Ethernet). This concept is called IP-directed broadcasts. In the case of a smurf attack, the attacker sends a continuous ping to the subnet range of a site that is enabling IP-directed broadcasts (for example, 172.16.255.255) with the source IP address spoofed to be the victim's IP address. The router then forwards these packets to all of the hosts on the specified network. Every host that is turned on and that has an enabled TCP/IP stack will respond to the ping. The following example shows the steps that an attacker takes when performing a smurf attack (also see Figure B-3).

In this example, the hacker is looking to shut down Corporation A's Web server. First, a *Domain Name Service* (DNS) lookup is performed in order to find the IP address of the Web server. Once the IP address is found (for example, 172.31.58.11), the hacker inputs the IP address into the smurf program. The smurf program manipulates the IP packets so that the source address is the Web server's (victim's) IP address of 192.168.58.11. The application is then run so that a continuous stream of ICMP echo requests are sent to a network that is known to have IP-directed broadcasts enabled and that is generally known to contain a large amount of hosts that will reply. It is also extremely useful to find networks that have extremely large pipes to the Internet. This way, the flood of ICMP echo replies from the reflector network will overwhelm the smaller pipe of the victim's network. These networks are usually known throughout the hacker circle (in hacker chat rooms, Web sites, newsgroups, and so

Figure B-3
Smurf attack

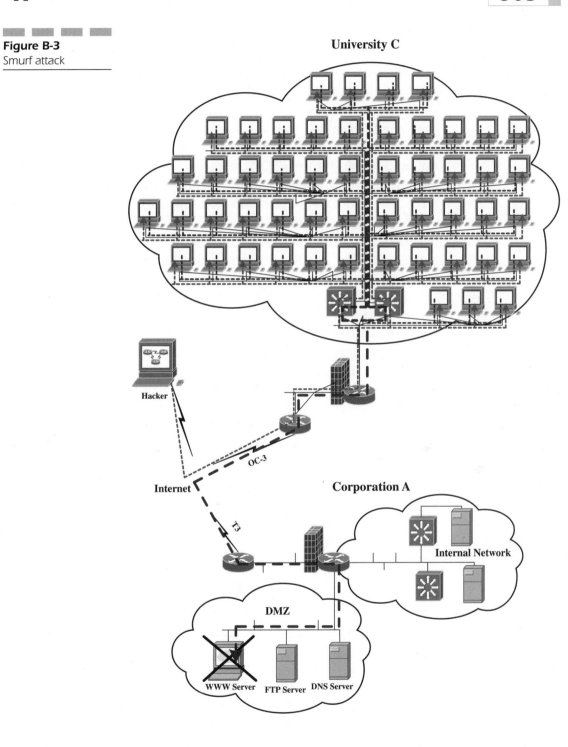

on). In this example, University C is known to be vulnerable and has an *Optical Circuit 3* (OC-3) 155.52Mbps connection to the Internet. This university will be used as the reflector of this attack. University C owns an IP address of 192.168.0.0, leaving a possible 65,534 usable IP addresses for hosts. (Note: 192.168.0.0 is a private address space that is not permitted over the Internet. It is only used in this discussion as an example.) University C is also known to have approximately 1,800 hosts with TCP/IP stacks enabled and is online at any given time, which makes this network an excellent resource to use as a reflector. Once the application is running and is sending the continuous stream of ICMP echo requests to 192.168.255.255, the perimeter router of University C's network receives these ICMP packets and frames them into layer 2 broadcast frames. These broadcasts are then distributed to all hosts on the 192.168.0.0 network segment. All hosts that are online with an enabled TCP/IP stack now respond with an ICMP echo reply to the 172.31.58.11 IP address of Corporation A's Web server. This continuous stream of ICMP echo requests is coming into University C at a rate of 50Kbps over the hacker's *Digital Subscriber Line* (DSL) from home. This 50Kbps stream of ICMP packets is duplicated by all 1,800 hosts on University C's network and is being distributed to Corporation A's Web server. This new stream of ICMP echo replies is now coming from University C and is hitting Corporation A's Web server at a rate of 90Mbps. This rate is more than twice the bandwidth of Corporation A's T3 connection to the Internet. These attacks will not only shut down the Web server but will also deny all other inbound connections to Corporation A (as well as any outbound connections from the internal network).

Distributed Denial of Service Attack (DDoS)

There are three main components of a DDoS attack: the client, the handler, and the agent. The client is the hacker's own machine to which he or she is connecting (and that he or she is using to compromise other hosts). The hacker will find hosts on the Internet, such as Sun, Unix, Linux, or NT machines that have security holes. The hacker will then exploit these security holes by installing programs on the machines so that he or she can control additional machines.

This situation makes it much more difficult for a victim to track down a hacker. These machines are called handlers and are illustrated in Figure B-4.

The last step that a hacker takes in creating a DDoS attack is to use a handler to find additional machines that will be used as *agents* or *zombies*, as illustrated in Figure B-5. The hacker installs programs on these compromised hosts so that the program can be used to initiate the attack against the victim. Once this process is complete, the hacker can set up the handlers to run the installed program at a specific time. The program will then instruct the agents to start their own program against the victim. The program on the agent usually consists of running a SYN flood or "Ping of Death" for the victim, as illustrated in Figure B-6. Because the source of the attack is coming from multiple hosts, it is much more difficult for the victim to identify and block access to the appropriate host.

Firewalls and university network systems tend to have a lower level of security than most enterprise networks. Hackers will often exploit these vulnerabilities by using devices on these networks as the handlers and agents. Universities generally do not have the budget of other enterprise networks and therefore do not have the necessary security infrastructure in place or the resources that are needed to support such an infrastructure. Hackers will also install handlers and agents on other networks that are known throughout the hacker circle to have vulnerabilities.

Some of the more common programs that are used to initiate a DDoS attack include Trinoo, TFN, Stacheldraht, and TFN2K.

NOTE: *It is important to note that implementing any DDoS attack of any kind is strictly illegal and can result in a lengthy prison term. Because DDoS attacks have become more prevalent, companies have stepped up their security policies and security infrastructure. Companies are now using more advanced firewall designs and intrusion detection systems to catch DDoS attacks while they are happening and to dynamically shut them down. It is also interesting to note that an entire new field called network forensics is starting to breed. Security consultants who specialize in network forensics are often able to track down the attacker through a series of tests and investigations.*

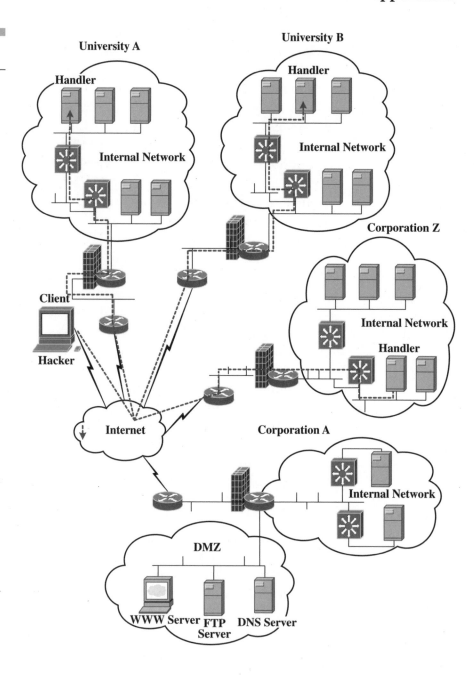

University A

University B

Handler

Handler

Internal Network

Internal Network

Corporation Z

Internal Network

Handler

Client

Hacker

Corporation A

Internal Network

Internet

DMZ

WWW Server FTP DNS Server
Server

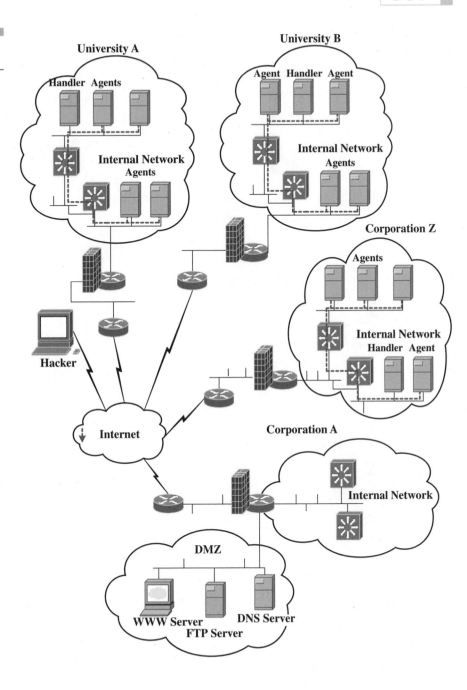

Figure B-6
DDos attack

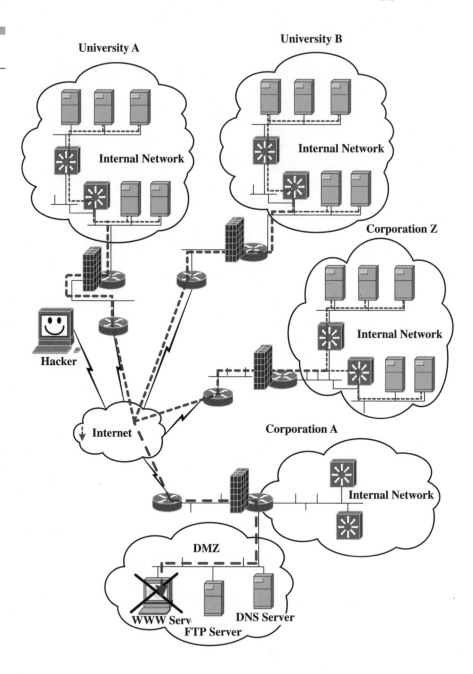

Prevention Methods

This section focuses on ways to prevent an attack. We describe these steps so that you can avoid becoming a victim, a handler, or an agent in which your systems are responsible for an attack against another company.

Context-Based Access Control (CBAC)

CBAC is a stateful application-layer filtering mechanism that is used within Cisco's IOS Firewall Feature Set.

One of the benefits of CBAC, as well as one of the main reasons for a firewall, is the capability to provide internal users with access to the Internet while preventing external users from accessing the internal network. CBAC is available on a per-interface basis, enabling administrators to apply it to the interfaces that need protection from outside threats. CBAC works by dynamically creating temporary access lists that are used in conjunction with existing access lists. These dynamic access lists only enable inbound traffic that is associated with a particular user session. For example, in Figure B-7, Host A wants to communicate with www.cisco.com. Host A will attempt to initiate a session with Cisco's Web page by entering www.cisco.com in the *Uniform Resource Locator* (URL) section of an Internet browser window. Once the name is resolved by a DNS server, Host A will send a connection initiation sequence to Cisco's Web server. The firewall will capture this connection-initiation sequence and will store it in a state table (sometimes referred to as a *connection table*). The firewall will then receive the acknowledgment sequence from Cisco's Web server and will reference the state table to determine whether the packet is a response from an internal request. Once the firewall verifies that the packet *is* a response to a valid internal request, the packet will be granted access by dynamically and temporarily creating an access list to enable the specified traffic to pass through the firewall.

If an outside user were to attempt to make a connection to an internal device without a request originating from the internal network, the packet would be denied because the firewall would not be capable

Figure B-7
CBAC example

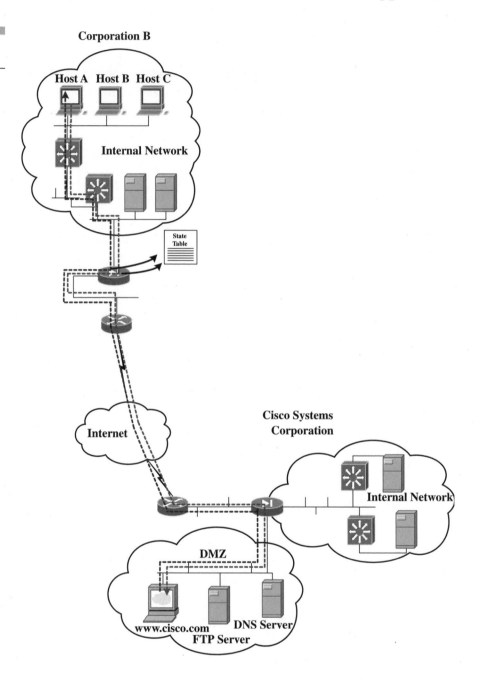

of finding an open connection in the state table. Because every packet is inspected by the firewall, the packets that are sent during an attack will be discarded because they are not replies to internal requests.

One of the more efficient ways to prevent a TCP SYN attack is with the use of CBAC (included with Cisco's IOS Firewall Feature Set). CBAC inspects all incoming traffic and will drop TCP SYN packets that have not received an ACK from the source host after the default of 500 is reached. This amount can be changed with the command `ip inspect max-incomplete high <number>`. CBAC will continue to delete incoming TCP SYN packets until the threshold is met with the command `ip inspect max-incomplete low` and defaults to 400. This feature enables the number of TCP SYN packets to be reduced to a low enough level so that legitimate requests can be serviced. You should note that these numbers represent the total amount of TCP SYN packets that the router or firewall has received for all destination hosts. These numbers also reflect only TCP SYN packets that have not received a response (also known as half-open connections).

It is also possible to adjust the number of half-open sessions for destination hosts. This task is accomplished with the command `ip inspect tcp max-incomplete host <number>`, and the default is 50. Once this threshold is met, CBAC will continue to drop the oldest half-open connection for every new half-open connection that is received. An additional feature of this command is the option to block all incoming TCP SYN packets that are sent to a host for a specified amount of time. This length of time can be adjusted with the command `ip inspect tcp max-incomplete host 50 block-time <number>`. This feature enables CBAC to drop all incoming TCP SYN packets that are destined for a host that has reached the threshold of 50 half-open sessions until the amount in minutes has expired under the `<number>` syntax.

CBAC will also drop half-open connections that have not received an ACK after a default of 30 seconds. This time period is adjusted by the command `ip inspect tcp synwait-time`.

NOTE: *Although CBAC is an extremely useful tool for slowing down the effects of a DoS attack, the firewall could still be saturated with open connections—thus flooding the state table with validations. This situation would ultimately cause legitimate requests to be denied.*

Refer to Table B-2 for a list of protocols that CBAC currently supports.

TCP Proxy

Although it is difficult to prevent a TCP SYN attack from happening, there are ways to slow an attack. As described previously, a TCP SYN attack consists of sending half-open connections to an internal host. The internal hosts can be protected with a firewall that is set up as a TCP proxy on behalf of the internal hosts. The firewall will respond to all incoming TCP initiations and will ensure that the session is valid before it passes the traffic to the internal host. The next paragraph illustrates how the firewall validates an incoming TCP session and passes the session to the internal host (see Figure B-8).

In this example, Host A is attempting to communicate with the internal host, Host B. In the first step, Host A starts by sending a TCP SYN to Host B, which is intercepted by the firewall. The firewall will then respond with a TCP SYN ACK to Host A on behalf of Host B to determine whether the TCP session is valid. If the session is valid, Host A will respond with an ACK (plus data) with the established bit set. Now that the firewall knows that this session is valid, it will pass along the ACK (plus data) packet to the internal Host B. This process is Step 4. The next step consists of Host B responding to Host A. After this step, Host A can communicate directly to Host B via the firewall. The firewall will now enable all packets originating from Host A that are destined to Host B until the TCP session is over (in which case Host A will have to repeat this process for the next TCP session).

An additional method of prevention for a TCP SYN attacks is to configure the server to clear out old connections after a specified amount of time. This procedure might work if the attacker is not sending the attack for a long period of time or if the server is on a low-speed link. For high-speed links, we suggest configuring the server to deny all incoming TCP SYN requests once a certain threshold is met.

Table B-2

CBAC-supported protocols

Protocol	Description
Audio/Video Streaming	
CU-SeeMe by White Pine	Application that supports live audio/videoconferencing and text chat across the Internet
H.323	New standard in audio/videoconferencing
Internet Phone by Intel	Voice communication application above the H.323 protocol stack
NetMeeting by Microsoft	Audio, video, and application sharing implemented over T.120 and H.323
RealAudio and RealVideo by Progressive Networks	Protocol for the transmission of high-quality streaming sound and video on the Internet
StreamWorks by Xing	Protocol for the transmission of high-quality streaming sound and video over the Internet
VDOLive by VDOnet	Application for transmitting high-quality video over the Internet

Information Seeking	
Archie	Standard tool for searching Internet file servers
Gopher	Application that provides a menu-driven front end to Internet services
HTTP	Primary protocol used to implement the *World Wide Web* (WWW)
Network News Transfer Protocol (NNTP)	Protocol that is used to transmit and receive network news
Pointcast by Pointcast (HTTP)	Protocol for viewing news in a TV-like fashion
Wide Area Information Servers (WAIS)	Tool for keyword searches, based on database content, of databases on the Internet

Security and Authentication	
HTTPS	Secured (that is, encrypted) HTTP; an implementation of the *Secure Sockets Layer* (SSL)
TACACS+	Authentication protocol

(continues)

Protocol	Description
Security and Authentication	
Kerberos	Authentication service
LDAP	Lightweight Directory Access Protocol; standard for Internet directory services
RADIUS	A widely adopted authentication protocol
Secure ID	Protocol used by an authentication service; product of Security Dynamics Technologies, Inc.
Databases	
Lotus Notes	Proprietary protocol developed by Lotus to implement its Notes application
SQL Server by Microsoft	A data replication server
SQLNet version 1	Oracle protocol for the transmission of *Structured Query Language* (SQL) queries
SQLNet version 2	Extension of SQLNet Version 1, which adds support for port redirection
Mail	
Comsat	Mail notification protocol
IMAP	Internet Mail Access Protocol
POP Version 2	Mail protocol that enables a remote mail client to read mail from a server
POP Version 3	Modified version of POP Version 2
SMTP	Simple Mail Transfer Protocol; protocol that is widely used for the transmission of e-mail
Other TCP and UDP Services	
Chargen	TCP chargen server sends a continual stream of characters until the client terminates the connection; UDP chargen servers send a datagram containing a random number of characters in response to each datagram that a client sends
Daytime	Daytime server returns the date and the time of day in text format and can be run over TCP or UDP

Table B-2

Continued.

Protocol	Description
Other TCP and UDP Services	
Chargen	TCP chargen server sends a continual stream of characters until the client terminates the connection; UDP chargen servers send a datagram containing a random number of characters in response to each datagram that a client sends
Daytime	Daytime server returns the date and the time of day in text format and can be run over TCP or UDP
Discard	Discard server discards whatever is sent to it by a client and can be run over TCP or UDP
DNS	Distributed database used by TCP/IP to map names to IP addresses
Finger	Protocol that provides information about users on a specified host
FTP	File Transfer Protocol; protocol for copying files between hosts
Identd (auth)	Protocol used for user identification
Internet Relay Chat (IRC)	Protocol for online chat conversations over the Internet
NetBIOS over TCP/IP (NBT)	NetBIOS name, datagram, and session services encapsulated within TCP/IP
Network Time Protocol (NTP)	Protocol that provides time synchronization across a network by using precise clocks that are implemented over TCP and UDP
RAS	Remote Access Service
Rexec	Protocol that provides remote execution facilities
Rlogin	Protocol that enables a remote login between hosts
Rsh	Protocol that enables commands to be executed on another system
Simple Network Management Protocol (SNMP)	Protocol used for managing network resources
SNMP Trap	Notification by an SNMP to the manager of some event of interest
Syslog	Protocol that enables a computer to send logs to another computer
Telnet	Telecommunications Network Protocol; remote terminal protocol enabling any terminal to log in to any host
TFTP	Small, simple FTP used primarily for booting diskless systems
Time	Service that returns the time of day as a binary number

(continues)

Protocol	Description
Other TCP and UDP Services	
UNIX-to-UNIX Copy Program (UUCP)	A Unix file-copying protocol
Who	Service that uses local broadcasts to provide information about who is logged on to the local network
X11	Windowing system protocol
Remote Procedure Call Services	
Lockmanager (nlockmgr)	Protocol used for the transmission of lock requests
Mountd	Protocol used for the transmission of file mount requests
Network File System (NFS)	Protocol that provides transparent file access over a network
Network Information Service (NIS)	Protocol that provides a network-accessible system-administration database, widely known as the Yellow Pages
Rstat	Protocol used to obtain performance data from a remote kernel
Rwall	Protocol used to write to all users on a network

Unicast Reverse Path Forwarding

One way to thwart a DDoS attack is to implement unicast reverse path forwarding by using the `ip verify unicast reverse-path` command on a Cisco router. This command, when used in conjunction with *Cisco Express Forwarding* (CEF), enables the router to verify that each packet received has a route in the CEF table. If the source IP address of the packet does not have a route in the CEF table that points back to the same interface on which the packet is received, the router will drop the packet. Installing Unicast RPF on the router will stop smurf attacks and other attacks that depend on the source IP address to be spoofed, because the router is verifying the path back to the source.

The following configuration example enables Serial Interface 0 to perform Unicast RPF:

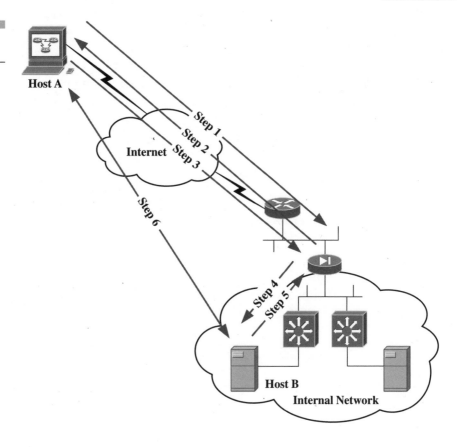

Figure B-8
TCP proxy example

```
Router(config)#interface serial0
Router(config-if)aip verfiy unicast reverse-path
```

TCP Intercept

The TCP Intercept feature is available in PIX software versions 5.2 and later. TCP Intercept enables the PIX to monitor half-open connections (also called embryonic connections) and to prevent TCP SYN attacks from disabling the servers. Once the predetermined limit of embryonic connections is reached, the PIX will intercept the SYN packets that are destined for the specific server and reply with an empty SYN, ACK packet. It will continue this process until the embryonic connection falls below the threshold.

Additional Prevention Methods

There are many lines of configuration that need to be standard on a perimeter router in order to provide a more secure environment. The following list describes these important commands that should be implemented on Cisco routers:

`No ip directed broadcast`

This command is an absolute must to protect your network from becoming a reflector for a smurf attack against another site. If every router had IP-directed broadcasts enabled, the smurf would quickly become obsolete. There are networks on the Internet, however, that do not have a competent staff to configure the router correctly to disable the framing of layer 3 IP broadcasts into layer 2 broadcast frames. Cisco realized this fact and disabled IP-directed broadcasts as of IOS version 12.0.

`No service tcp-small-servers`
`No service udp-small-servers`

Both of these commands can cause a router to crash simply by telneting to the router's IP address with the corresponding protocol appended to the end. Refer to the Small Servers section of this book for a list of the commands. Small servers must be disabled on all routers to reduce the risk of a router failure.

`No cdp enable`

Many companies disable CDP. If an attacker gains access to a switch on the internal network, he or she can find all of the other CDP-enabled devices and can usually plot out the network—creating an easier path to hack into the systems.

`No service finger`

Finger is a service that is run by the Unix client and server and is used to finger a user account by name so that data about that user can be collected. The finger service can be used to monitor Telnet sessions and to capture username/password combinations. This service should be disabled on Cisco routers.

```
No ip bootp server
```

This command should be disabled if possible so that a hacker does not attempt to redirect DHCP requests to a hacked machine that is capable of disseminating false information to users.

Another useful way to limit the impact of ICMP-based DoS attacks is by the use of *Committed Access Rate* (CAR), *Generic Traffic Shaping* (GTS), or custom queuing. The discussion of these applications is out of the scope of this book; however, it is important to note that any of these applications can be implemented in order to slow the amount of ICMP packets that are received by the router.

Firewall Types

A firewall can be defined as a system (or group of systems) that is used to enforce an access control policy. The access control policy can be anything from a simple set of *Access Control Lists* (ACLs) on a router to a more advanced stateful packet filter or content filter.

Firewalls can be used for internal traffic by restricting access to restricted networks or Web sites, or they can be used for external traffic by restricting inbound traffic from unauthorized networks. Firewalls are typically placed between a trusted network (internal) and an untrusted network (external, such as the Internet). In more secure environments, multiple firewalls can be used in a multi-tier fashion in order to protect specific resources.

This section will discuss two of the primary types of firewalls. The advantages and disadvantages of each type will be discussed, and the following section will use both of these types of firewalls in the designs.

Stateful Packet Filter (SPF)

This firewall is often referred to as an SPF firewall. SPF firewalls inspect traffic based on a rules set. The rules set is put in place by the security administrator and is based on the security policy. In a PIX firewall, the rules set would consist of a combination of access lists and conduit statements. In other firewalls, the rules set might consist of *Graphical User Interface* (GUI)-based entries of the networks or hosts that need to be permitted or denied. An SPF firewall is also set up to perform stateful packet filtering. This setup would consist of using CBAC for the PIX. CBAC is used to keep track of session information for the packets that are traversing through the firewall. CBAC can be configured to only enable traffic from external networks (that is, a reply to an outgoing user session).

The main advantage of an SPF firewall is the speed in which it can process packets. An SPF firewall does not have to initiate a new TCP/IP stack for each packet like a proxy firewall does; rather, it verifies the packet against a predefined rules set and forwards the packet to the destination.

Examples of SPF firewalls are Cisco's PIX firewall and Checkpoint's Firewall-1.

Proxy Firewall

The second type of firewall is the proxy firewall. A proxy firewall usually consists of a GUI-based firewall (such as Network Associate Inc.'s Gauntlet firewall or Axent's Raptor firewall). They also contain a rules set that is implemented by the security administrator. The main difference between an SPF firewall and a proxy firewall is that the proxy firewall initiates a new TCP/IP stack for every packet that traverses through the firewall. A proxy establishes its own sessions on the inside and outside. The originator only talks to the proxy, and the receiver only replies to the proxy. Because the proxy runs all messages up its own TCP stacks and back down again, malformed packets are rejected and session states are maintained. This feature prevents any external hosts from gaining access to the internal host's TCP/IP stack.

One of the biggest disadvantages of proxy firewalls is the speed in which they process the inbound and outbound packets. The proxy firewall takes the packet to the application layer and identifies the rule that enables this type of communication to occur. The firewall then recreates the packet and establishes a proxied session for the inbound or outbound source. Some firewall vendors are trying to combine the speed of an SPF with the application inspection process of a proxy firewall. This type of firewall would, upon first receiving an initiating session packet, validate it through the application proxy and then subsequently process the remaining session packets through an SPF engine—thus reducing the overhead of proxying and increasing the performance of the firewall. This process is a compromise of price for performance and security.

Both of these firewall types can be configured to perform NAT, which is used to keep the internal address space private and addresses issues such as address depletion. NAT works by mapping public (external) IP addresses to private (internal) IP addresses. NAT is discussed in detail later in this chapter.

Firewall and DMZ Design

There are many different firewall designs that can be implemented to protect the internal network. These designs vary depending on the amount of money that is budgeted for such a design and the extent to which the internal network needs to be protected. For a small network, a single router with firewall capabilities could be sufficient. For a large enterprise network that has multiple database servers containing sensitive information, however, the network will need to be protected with a multi-tier firewall design. This next section discusses some of the benefits and drawbacks of each design.

A Single Router

The simplest and least-expensive firewall design consists of a single router. This router is used on the perimeter of the internal network and is used to access the external network or the Internet. This router will have firewall capabilities such as the IOS Firewall Feature Set. ACLs should be set up to prevent unauthorized access to the internal network. One of the most important types of ACLs to install on a router is anti-spoofing ACLs. Anti-spoofing ACLs deny the private IP address space or RFC1918 addresses. These addresses consist of the following components:

- 10.0.0.0/8 or 10.0.0.0–10.255.255.255 with a subnet mask of 255.0.0.0

- 172.16.0.0/12 or 172.16.0.0–172.31.255.255 with a subnet mask of 255.240.0.0

- 192.168.0.0/16 or 192.168.0.0–192.168.255.255 with a subnet mask of 255.255.0.0

These addresses are called *private* because they have been specified by an *Internet Engineering Task Force* (IETF) standard, RFC1918, and cannot be used across the Internet. Therefore, it is the responsibility of all ISPs, as well as all other companies, to prevent these addresses from routing across their backbone. Many companies use a private address space on their internal network and perform NAT on a public address pool in order to gain access to the Internet. This procedure adds a level of security to the design, because internal hosts do not have a registered public IP address. The following code is an example configuration that denies the RFC1918 private address space:

```
Router(config)#access-list 101 deny 10.0.0.0 0.255.255.255 any
Router(config)#access-list 101 deny 172.16.0.0 0.15.255.255 any
Router(config)#access-list 101 deny 192.168.0.0 0.0.255.255 any
Router(config)#access-list 101 permit ip any any
Router(config)#interface ethernet 0/0
Router(config-if)#ip access-group 101 in
```

This design is typically used for small networks that do not offer public services (such as HTTP, DNS, and FTP). A third interface can be added to the perimeter router in order enable access to public services. If the perimeter router is compromised, however, the entire internal network is now open to an attack. This design enables a single point of failure. Figure B-9 illustrates an example of this design.

Dedicated Firewall

To provide a more secure network but still remain cost effective, a dedicated firewall could be added to the previously mentioned

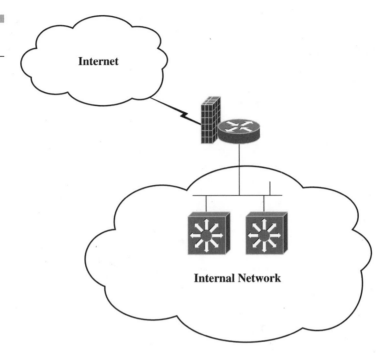

design. This design steps away from the single point of failure and enables a more secure design by placing a dedicated firewall behind the perimeter router. The router will perform traffic filtering and will be the network's first line of defense. Extended ACLs can be placed on the router to five specific hosts or networks access to the internal network. They will also be used to give internal hosts access to the Internet. The firewall contains more extensive packet-filtering capabilities, such as the use of CBAC on a PIX firewall. CBAC inspects traffic on a per-packet basis to determine whether the packet can pass through to the internal network. CBAC is discussed in detail later in this chapter. Such extensive filtering forces the firewall to be much more *central processing unit* (CPU) process intensive than a normal router. Most routers do not have the CPU capabilities to route traffic while maintaining a high percentage of packet filtering. Large networks that have a need for a security policy generally rely on a dedicated firewall. The firewall ensures that the security policy

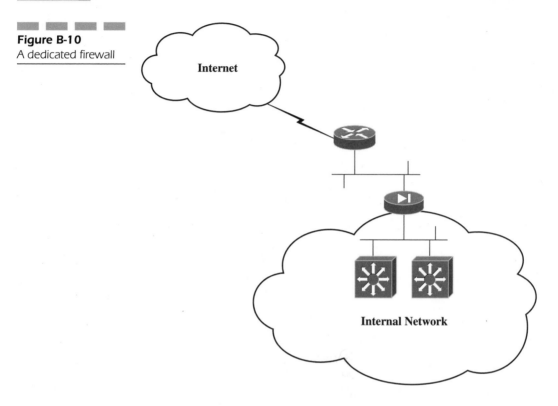

is adhered to by granting or denying packets through the firewall. Figure B-10 illustrates a dedicated firewall design.

Dedicated Firewall with DMZ

This design can also provide an additional network segment that is separate from the internal or external network. This segment is configured off a third interface on the firewall, and this network is referred to as the *Demilitarized Zone* (DMZ). Figure B-11 illustrates a firewall design with a DMZ.

DMZs are networks that run between the internal (trusted) and external (nontrusted) networks. They are more secure than the Internet (nontrusted) and less secure than the internal network. DMZs are generally placed behind a perimeter router and in front of a firewall (or in series between two firewalls). Some firewalls, such as

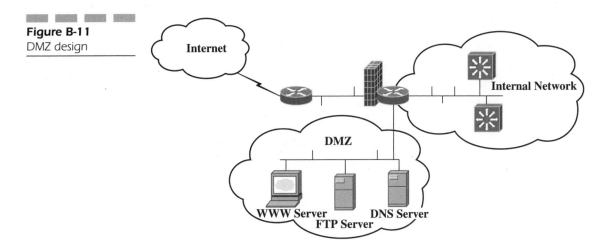

Figure B-11
DMZ design

Cisco's PIX firewall, enable a third interface that can be used as a DMZ interface. The Cisco DMZ is equivalent to placing the server between two firewalls. Each side of the DMZ can have its own independent rules set. Another alternative is to put the DMZ on its own firewall and to put the internal users on a separate firewall that is used only for outgoing connections. This design is illustrated in Figure B-12.

Multi-Tier Firewall Design

The most elaborate and security-centric design is the multi-tier firewall. This design places two different types of firewalls in a hierarchical structure in order to implement different security levels based on the application. This section will first discuss these two different types of firewalls and will then discuss the advantages and disadvantages of the design. Refer to Figure B-13 for an illustration of the examples in this next section.

The multi-tier firewall design uses the advantages of both of these types of firewalls. SPF firewalls are generally faster than proxy firewalls. Therefore, SPF firewalls are deployed at the perimeter of the network. There, they inspect all traffic that is inbound from the external network and match the traffic with an access list. They also

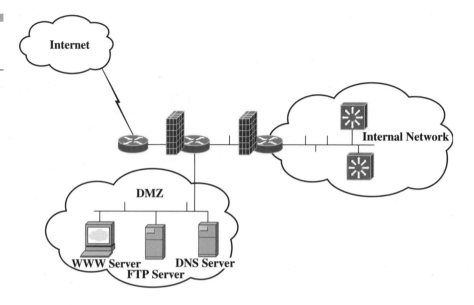

verify whether the packet is a response from an existing session that was initiated by an internal host. If the traffic originates from an explicitly allowed external network or host and is destined for a Web server, the traffic will pass through the SPF firewall and to the Web servers that are located within the first DMZ. If the traffic originates from an external network and is destined for a database server, the traffic must first be permitted by the SPF firewall and then permitted by the proxy firewall. The external host will be hitting an external IP address for the database server (such as 204.128.10.5), and the proxy firewall will map that IP address to an internal IP address that is configured on the database server (such as 10.65.127.1). The static translation, or external-to-internal IP address mapping, is done on the proxy firewall. The firewall on the edge of the internal network is used to enable internal traffic to travel outbound and should be configured to deny all external traffic. If possible, no external hosts should be given access to the internal network. This feature is the primary benefit of DMZs. Devices in which the public or any external entities need access to are placed within DMZs, which enables a more secure network and prevents any external hosts gaining access to the internal network.

Figure B-13
Multi-tier firewall
design

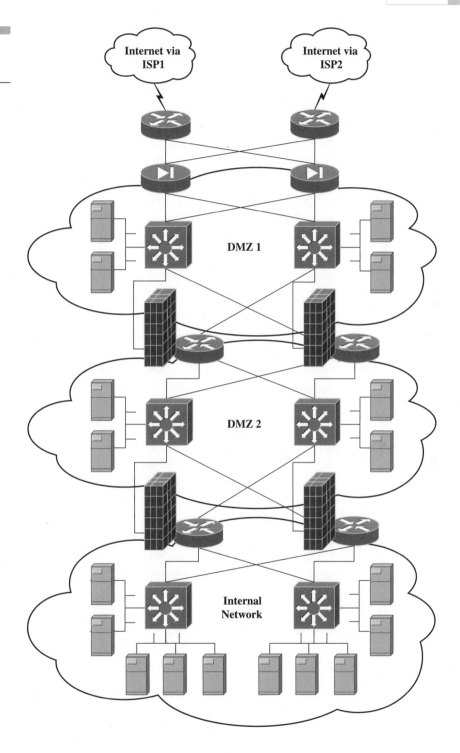

The multi-tier firewall design can contain multiple DMZs. Each DMZ will have its own unique security level. The DMZs that are closest to the internal network will have the highest security levels, whereas the DMZs that are located next to the perimeter of the network will have the lowest security level. The reason for the different security levels is because the amount of the firewalls' external traffic must traverse. The more firewalls that the traffic has to traverse, the higher the security level.

You should also note the amount of redundancy that this design provides. Notice that the perimeter routers are connected to dual ISPs and are connected to dual SPF firewalls on the internal side. From there, the traffic is split off to dual multi-layer switches and to dual proxy firewalls. This setup continues through the design to the internal network. This design does not have a single point of failure like the rest of the designs that we have presented thus far. Additional protocols such as BGP can be run to the ISPs and HSRP internally in order to enable additional redundancy and load balancing.

At the SPF firewall level, the PIXs have the capability to perform stateful failover as of version 5.2 of the PIX IOS. Stateful failover retains session information, so if a PIX loses connectivity or goes down, it can transfer the session to the standby PIX and continue with the session without losing any data.

To add even greater security, the servers could be dual homed, breaking them up on the switch by using *Virtual Local Area Networks* (VLANs). This setup would increase the protection and slow down the would-be hacker because you could then relegate the less-secure protocols (such as SunRFC port mapping) to the inside servers and reduce outside access to this exploitable process. There are issues to contend with when deploying a dual connected server (bastion host), however, such as proper routing and binding the right services to the right interfaces. Additional consideration for the application fail-over process can be looked at with multiple Web server, application server, and database server farms that offer the same services.

The addition of an out-of-band management network or side-band network to serve network management functions can benefit an organization as well. This type of network can offer potentially insecure processes such as DNS, NTP, and others so that the firewalls that are protecting the servers do not have to permit these ports to pass through.

Bastion Host

The DMZ is used to enable public-accessible services such as WWW, SMTP, DNS, and so on. Servers that run these public services are called *bastion hosts*. Bastion hosts are machines that run a general-purpose operating system (such as Windows NT or UNIX) and that are placed within the DMZ. These servers must be highly fortified, or hardened, by installing the correct service packs and by locking down the machines (only enabling open ports to access the specific services that the server is meant to provide). The problem with public-accessible servers, however, is that they are wide open to attack. It is much more difficult to secure a Web server or any other server that is open to the public, because the entire Internet has access to the server in one way or another (depending on the services that it is running). For example, Web servers must be highly secured —only enabling access to HTTP and to other Web-related protocols such as CGI and Java (if applicable). These servers are placed into the DMZ so that the general public can gain access to them and pull down HTTP Web pages. Most cases of DoS attacks take place on Web servers because of their vulnerability.

NOTE: *Bastion hosts are often referred to as sacrificial hosts because of the fact that they are wide open to the Internet and are most susceptible to DoS attacks. The name* bastion *host originates from the highly fortified protections on the outer walls of medieval castles.*

Figure B-14 illustrates the design, and the next section will discuss an example of traffic flow through this design.

In this example, the hacker is attempting to gain access to Corporation A's network.

The hacker must first find the public address space for Corporation A. He or she can perform this task in a few ways. One, he or she can perform a DNS lookup of Corporation A's Web site and find the IP address to which it resolves. The hacker can then perform a port scan on the subnet range to find any open holes/vulnerabilities on the company's systems and network devices.

Figure B-14
A hacker's path

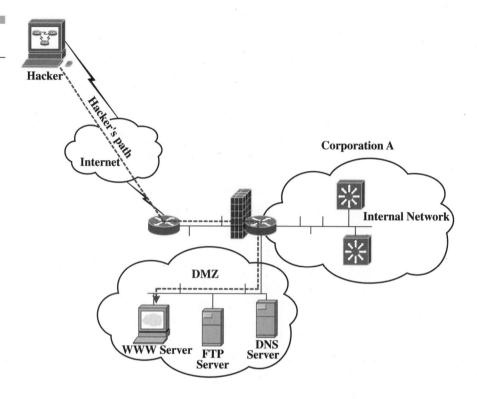

Figure B-14
A hacker's path

Most often, the hacker will use a custom-made application to exploit the vulnerabilities that are found by the port scanner and to run an attack against the Web server. Once the hacker can compromise the Web server, he or she can exploit the attack by changing the content of the Web pages or by performing other malicious acts against the server.

Additional Firewall Features

Firewalls can perform other functions to add additional security features to the network. These features can include intrusion detection and auditing capabilities. Intrusion detection is the process of monitoring a network segment to detect whether any unauthorized intruders have gained access (or have attempted to gain access) to the internal network. Auditing enables the firewall to log any suspicious activity or any violations of the security policy or rules set. An administrator can then view these firewall logs to determine whether there were any threats to the network. This method is more of a reactive approach, whereas intrusion detection is more of a pro-active approach. Intrusion detection can be set up to e-mail an alert to the administrator if the security policy is violated. This feature can sometimes give the administrator enough advance notice to track down the hacker and to take any necessary precautions (such as statically blocking access, or in extreme cases, shutting down the server that is being attacked).

NAT

NAT (RFC 1631) was introduced in May of 1994 to deal with two very real issues: IP address depletion and scalable routing. NAT works by setting up an internal translation table of all inside IP addresses that will be sending packets through the NAT-enabled device. Then, the device sets up a table of port numbers to use on the outside IP addresses. When the inside network sends packets to the outside network, the NAT device performs the following actions:

1. The device records the source IP address and source port number in the appropriate translation table.
2. The device replaces the IP address of the packet with its own untrusted interface IP address.
3. The device then assigns a specific port number to the outgoing packet, places this information into the translation table, and replaces the source port number with the selected port.
4. The device recalculates the IP and TCP checksums and verifies them for integrity.
5. In addition, the device must convert any application packet that contains references to the inside IP address with the untrusted IP address.

When the response comes back to the NAT-enabled device, it checks the packet's destination port number. If there is a match to a source port that is assigned in the translation table, the packet is rewritten with the originating information and is transmitted to the intended host on the inside network.

There are two modes associated with NAT: dynamic and static. The previous description dealt mainly with dynamic mode. Static NAT employs the same mechanisms, except the inside IP addresses are statically represented by an outside IP address in a one-to-one relationship. This feature enables users and systems from the outside network to connect to specific systems on the inside network through the NAT-enabled device while taking advantage of filtering and rules-based processing.

SUMMARY

This chapter has covered a lot of ground on the different types of attacks to be aware of and the appropriate methods of prevention. It is important to remember that there are many different types of attacks, and it is up to you to keep up to date on new vulnerabilities of your systems and network devices. The content in this chapter also provides the framework for assessing a security architecture and recommending an appropriate firewall design. Keep in mind the costs of the associated devices and the budget that has been scoped for the project.

From the Real World

Security is a major concern for all of us. Even if you do not have any systems that you care to protect, it is still your duty to lock down your network devices to keep yourself from becoming a reflector or handler in an attack against another company. Negligence is not an excuse. There might come a time when companies fall victim to an attack because of other networks not securing their devices appropriately. These companies will pursue legal action against these companies to compensate for their loss. In other cases, if an attack results in a significant financial loss to the company, the stockholders could hold the corporate officers legally responsible.

The following Web sites contain information relating to security, hacking, and attacks. Many of these sites are updated constantly to keep people aware of the latest viruses and attacks. As a security administrator (or anyone who is responsible for any security aspects in an organization), you need to keep up to date on new exploits and attacks and take the appropriate measures to protect your network.

```
www.sans.org
www.cert.org
www.ciac.org
www.securtiyfocus.com
www.attrition.org
www.insecure.org
www.dsi.com
www.eeye.com
```

The attacks that are listed in this book are very real and are used every day. Ensure that your network is safe by applying the appropriate methods to your systems and network devices.

APPENDIX C

Desktop Protocol Design

This chapter describes both the AppleTalk and IPX/SPX protocol suites and the underlying protocols and functions that operate within them. We will explain the operation of AppleTalk and IPX and the routing protocols that route AppleTalk and IPX over a *Wide Area Network* (WAN). This chapter will also describe the steps to configure AppleTalk and IPX on Cisco routers. Additionally, we will give a routing protocol design and a description for both of these protocols.

Objectives

Upon completing this chapter, you will be able to perform the following tasks:

- Describe basic AppleTalk operation.
- Describe basic IPX operation.
- Identify the advantages and disadvantages of different routing protocols.
- Configure the AppleTalk protocol in an internetwork environment.
- Configure the IPX/SPX protocol in an internetwork environment.

Introduction to AppleTalk Protocols

AppleTalk, also known as AppleShare, is a protocol suite that was developed by Apple Computer in the early 1980s. This application was primarily created as an afterthought, enabling a community of users to share resources such as disk space and printing services.

When Apple engineers developed this protocol, their intent was to create a protocol that was adaptive to the environment in which it resided, lining up with the standards when possible but providing a simple, open architecture that was seamless and easy to operate. This protocol was delivered in an inexpensive way, integrated into the Macintosh computer system, and only required the user to connect the terminator and network cable. The operating system would then locate and process all of the network negotiations behind the scenes while the user was unaware. AppleTalk systems operate in a client-server environment, where they assign a node ID to each device. The node IDs are broken into two ranges. The address range 1 through 127 is assigned to the client or workstation, and the range 128 to 254 (253 in phase 2) is assigned to the server. This address is known as the protocol address, and it is set into the network card during boot time. AppleTalk was first deployed by using LocalTalk as its network access method. AppleTalk is a very chatty protocol and is not efficient for large-scale networks. Apple Computer later released support for TCP/IP to support larger environments and to enable access to the Internet.

This section will discuss the various AppleTalk protocols that make up the AppleTalk protocol suite. Refer to Figure C-1 to view how these protocols map to the OSI model.

AARP, DDP, NBP, ATP, ASP, AFP, AEP, ADSP, ZIP, and PAP

The following paragraphs will describe some important protocols.

- *AppleTalk Address-Resolution Protocol* (AARP) works in much the same way as TCP/IP's version of the *Address Resolution Protocol* (ARP). AARP is a network-layer protocol that is used to map an AppleTalk network address—which consists of 16 bits for the network address and 8 bits for the node ID—to a 48-bit Ethernet or Token Ring hardware address. A device specifies the destination network address and relies on AARP to resolve this address to a hardware address. Each AppleTalk node maintains

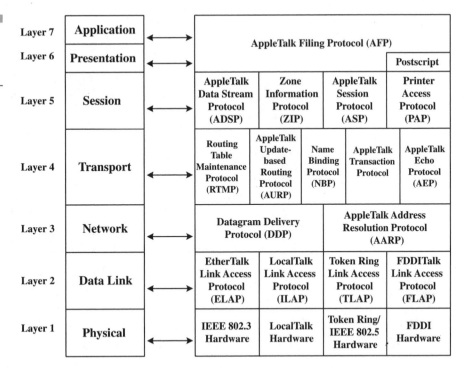

Figure C-1
AppleTalk protocol suite mapped to the OSI model

	OSI Layer				
Layer 7	Application	AppleTalk Filing Protocol (AFP)			
Layer 6	Presentation				Postscript
Layer 5	Session	AppleTalk Data Stream Protocol (ADSP)	Zone Information Protocol (ZIP)	AppleTalk Session Protocol (ASP)	Printer Access Protocol (PAP)
Layer 4	Transport	Routing Table Maintenance Protocol (RTMP)	AppleTalk Update-based Routing Protocol (AURP) — Name Binding Protocol (NBP)	AppleTalk Transaction Protocol	AppleTalk Echo Protocol (AEP)
Layer 3	Network	Datagram Delivery Protocol (DDP)		AppleTalk Address Resolution Protocol (AARP)	
Layer 2	Data Link	EtherTalk Link Access Protocol (ELAP)	LocalTalk Link Access Protocol (ILAP)	Token Ring Link Access Protocol (TLAP)	FDDITalk Link Access Protocol (FLAP)
Layer 1	Physical	IEEE 802.3 Hardware	LocalTalk Hardware	Token Ring/ IEEE 802.5 Hardware	FDDI Hardware

an *Address Mapping Table* (AMT) to translate the AppleTalk address to a hardware address.

There are three types of AARP packets: request, response, and probe. The request packet is used to find another node's AppleTalk address or MAC address if the data is not located in the AMT. The response packet is used to carry the AppleTalk or MAC address back to the requesting node. The probe packet is used to secure an AppleTalk protocol address and to verify that no other system on the local network is using the same address. This type of packet is sent up to 10 times with a maximum transmission latency of two seconds.

■ *Datagram Delivery Protocol* (DDP) is AppleTalk's network-layer protocol that is used to provide connectionless datagram service between AppleTalk sockets. DDP relies on the upper layers of the AppleTalk protocol suite and is similar to IP in the TCP/IP protocol suite.

DDP sends packets by receiving data from socket clients, creating a DDP header with the destination address and passing the packet to the appropriate data link layer protocol. DDP receives packets by receiving data link layer frames and routing them to the destination socket based on the destination address that is located in the DDP header.

■ *Name Binding Protocol* (NBP) is an AppleTalk transport-layer protocol that is used to map lower-layer addresses to AppleTalk names. Node services that are available over an AppleTalk network are referred to as *Network Visible Entities* (NVEs). An example of an NVE is a file service that is located remotely on an AppleTalk network. NVEs are often referred to by an entity name. These names consist of an ASCII string that contains three fields: object, type, and zone. The format for an entity name is `object:type@zone`. The object field is the name of the device (for example, `Mac`). The type field is associated with the entity (for example, `Workstation`). The zone field is the actual location of the entity (for example, `HR Zone`). Therefore, this entire entity would be named `Mac:Workstation@HR Zone`. The process that is used to map these NVE entity names with network addresses is referred to as name binding. Every AppleTalk node on the network will map its own NVEs to its network address and store these mappings in a names table. All of the names tables together create the names directory, which is a distributed database of all name-to-address mappings on the network.

NBP performs four primary functions:

1. Name lookup is used to find the network address of the NVE that needs to be accessed. This function is performed before the NVE is accessed.
2. Name recognition is used to create the names table. This function verifies that the name is not already in use by another node on the network and then creates the name-to-address mapping in the names table.
3. Name confirmation is used to verify that the mapping that was learned by using a name lookup is still accurate.
4. Name deletion is used in cases such as powering off a device. It will delete the name-to-address mapping from the names table.

The DDP packet format consists of two types: short and extended.

- *Short*   The short DDP packet is used to communicate between two nodes on the same network segment on a non-extended network only.

- *Extended*   The extended DDP packet is used to communicate between two nodes that have different network numbers in a non-extended network and is used for any transmissions on an extended network.

Figure C-2 illustrates an extended DDP packet.

- *AppleTalk Transaction Protocol* (ATP) is a transport-layer protocol that is used to provide reliable transactions between socket clients. ATP works similarly to TCP in the TCP/IP protocol suite. ATP provides acknowledgment and retransmission of packets as well as packet sequencing, segmentation, and reassembly.

  ATP uses three types of transactions: *transaction requests* (TReq), *transaction responses* (TResp), and *transaction release* (TRel). When ATP initiates a request, a transaction identifier is assigned—and the TReq is sent to the destination node (where it is processed). The destination node then responds with the data via a TResp packet, and the initiating station replies with a TRel packet. In TCP/IP, this process is known as the three-way handshake.

  Two protocols in the AppleTalk suite run over ATP. These protocols are *AppleTalk Session Protocol* (ASP) and *Printer Access Protocol* (PAP):

- ASP is a session-layer protocol that is used to provide sessions between Apple clients and servers. This protocol does not care

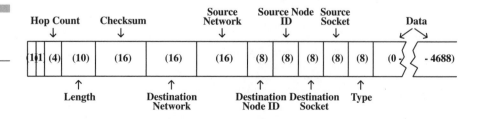

Figure C-2
An extended
DDP packet

about the delivery of the data. An Apple client can have multiple sessions open to the server, and ASP handles the sending of commands to the server. ASP uses services of other lower-level protocols (such as ATP) for sequencing and NBP for name resolution.

■ AFP performs exactly as it sounds. AFP is used to provide file sharing between Apple clients across a network. AFP works at the presentation and application layers of the AppleTalk protocol suite. Apple clients can access remote shares just like they would local shares, thus enabling the process to be transparent to the user.

■ *AppleTalk Echo Protocol* (AEP) is a transport-layer protocol that is used to test the reachability of another host across the network. This protocol works similarly to *Packet Internet Grouper* (PING) of the TCP/IP protocol suite. AEP uses socket number four (called the echoer socket).

If connectivity between hosts needs to be verified in an IP environment, the PING application is used. PING will send ICMP echo-request packets and will receive ICMP echo-reply packets from an active and reachable node. PING operates similarly in an AppleTalk environment, except that it uses AEP packets instead of ICMP. AEP works by passing an AEP request packet to the DDP source. DDP addresses the packet as an AEP request in the type field of the packet header and passes it on to the destination. The destination device receives the packet, and DDP finds that the packet is an AEP request. DDP will copy the packet and change it to an AEP reply. This packet will then be sent back to the source host to verify connectivity between the two hosts.

The following code is an example of an AppleTalk PING to the device on network 110 and node 89 (or 110.89):

```
Protocol [ip]: appletalk
Target Appletalk address: 110.89
Repeat count [5]:
Datagram size [100]:
Timeout in seconds [2]:
Verbose [n]:
Sweep range of sizes [n]:
Type escape sequence to abort.
```

```
Sending 5, 100-byte AppleTalk Echos to 110.89, timeout is 2
seconds:
!!!!!
Success rate is 100 percent, round-trip min/avg/max =
4/4/8 ms
```

Table C-1 gives a description of the possible AppleTalk PING characters.

■ *AppleTalk Data Stream Protocol* (ADSP) is a session-layer, connection-oriented protocol that is used to maintain full-duplex connectivity between two AppleTalk nodes. Although it is a session-layer protocol, ADSP works similarly to TCP in the TCP/IP protocol suite. ADSP provides data sequencing and ensures that packets are not duplicated. ADSP also provides a flow control mechanism that is similar to TCP in that the receiver can advertise a smaller receive window to slow incoming packets from the source. ADSP runs over DDP.

■ *Zone Information Protocol* (ZIP) is another session-layer protocol in the AppleTalk protocol suite and is used to maintain network number-to-zone name mappings in AppleTalk routers. AppleTalk nodes also use ZIP services to choose their zone during startup. ZIP maintains a *Zone Information Table* (ZIT) in each AppleTalk router. A ZIT is a list that maps network numbers to one or more zone names. Every ZIT contains a network number-to-zone name mapping for every network on the entire AppleTalk

Table C-1 AppleTalk PING character description	Character	Meaning
	!	The packet was echoed successfully from the target address.
	.	The timeout period expired before an echo was received from the target address.
	B	A bad or malformed echo was received from the target address.
	C	An echo was received with a bad DDP checksum.
	E	Transmission of the echo packet to the target address
	R	The transmission of the echo packet to the target address failed for lack of a route to the target address.

Figure C-3
A ZIT

ZIT Table

Network Number	Zone Name
20	Engineering
50	Marketing
100 - 110	Sales
120 - 140	HR
180	Executive

network. NBP also uses ZIP to determine which nodes belong to a given network. Figure C-3 illustrates a ZIT.

■ PAP is a session-layer protocol that is used by client workstations to establish connections to a server or printer. PAP is a connection-oriented protocol that requires a connection to the server before transmitting data. PAP uses NBP to find the network address of the server to which the user wishes to connect. PAP then opens a connection between the client and the server. ATP is then used to transfer data between devices, and PAP is used again to end the session. PAP supports multiple sessions. PAP has five basic functions: opening and closing connections to the destination, transferring data to the destination, checking the status of a print job, and filtering duplicate packets. An example would be a print server that can handle multiple requests from numerous clients.

EtherTalk, FDDITalk, LocalTalk, and TokenTalk

AppleTalk was designed to be a link-layer, independent protocol. In other words, it was designed to run over any type of link-layer implementations (such as Token Ring and Ethernet). This section will discuss the four different AppleTalk specifications that can be run over a link-layer implementation.

- *EtherTalk* AppleTalk over Ethernet is referred to as EtherTalk. This system is probably the most common implementation of AppleTalk on today's networks. EtherTalk enables AppleTalk to run over the standard 802.3 implementation. In turn, that enables AppleTalk to be deployed over any of the many Ethernet networks that are in existence today. This way, it can adhere to the same limitations, which include the same speeds, segment lengths, and active nodes that apply to 802.3 networks. The protocol that handles the communication between the upper-layer protocols of AppleTalk and the Ethernet protocols is called the *EtherTalk Link-Access Protocol* (ELAP).

- *ELAP* ELAP handles the communication between the upper-layer protocols in the AppleTalk protocol suite and the IEEE 802.3 data link layer. ELAP encapsulates the upper-layer data into three levels of encapsulation:

  - *Subnetwork Access Protocol* (SNAP) header
  - IEEE 802.2 *Logical Link-Control* (LLC) header
  - IEEE 802.3 header

AppleTalk protocols do not understand standard IEEE 802.3 hardware addresses. Therefore, ELAP is used to address the transmissions by referencing the *Address Mapping Table* (AMT) that is used by AARP.

The ELAP data transmission process works as follows:

1. ELAP receives a DDP packet.

2. ELAP finds the protocol address specified in the DDP header and references the AMT in order to find the corresponding IEEE 802.3 hardware address.

3. ELAP prepends the three different headers listed previously. First, the SNAP and IEEE 802.2 LLC headers are prepended, then the IEEE 802.3 header is prepended.

4. The IEEE 802.3 hardware address learned from the AMT is placed in the destination address field of the IEEE 802.3 header.

5. The IEEE 802.3 frame is then placed on the physical medium for transmission.

- *FDDITalk*   FDDITalk is used to enable AppleTalk to operate over an ANSI FDDI implementation. FDDITalk networks adhere to all of the same limitations of a standard FDDI network (including the same speeds and number of active nodes on a network).

- FDDITalk Link-Access Protocol *(FLAP)*   FLAP is used to communicate between the upper-layer AppleTalk protocols and the standard FDDI data link layer. As with 802.3 addresses, AppleTalk does not recognize FDDI hardware addresses. Therefore, FLAP is used to address the transmissions by referencing the AMT that is used by the AARP. FLAP also uses three levels of encapsulation when transmitting DDP packets:

  - SNAP header
  - IEEE 802.2 LLC header
  - FDDI header

  The FLAP data transmission process works as follows:

  1. FLAP receives a DDP packet.

  2. FLAP finds the protocol address specified in the DDP header and references the AMT in order to find the corresponding FDDI hardware address.

  3. FLAP prepends the three different headers listed previously. First, it prepends the SNAP and IEEE 802.2 LLC headers; then, the FDDI header is prepended.

  4. The FDDI hardware address that is learned from the AMT is placed in the destination address field of the FDDI header.

  5. The FDDI frame is then placed on the physical medium for transmission.

- *LocalTalk*   LocalTalk was developed by Apple Computer as a proprietary media-access system. Implementing LocalTalk is a cost-effective way to connect local workgroups, because it is built into Apple products and only requires the devices to be connected by inexpensive twisted-pair cabling (which supports a speed of 230.4Kbps). LocalTalk networks use a bus topology where devices are connected in a series and segments can be up to 300 meters in length (supporting a maximum of 32 nodes). The number of nodes can be expanded by using routers to interconnect the segments. The physical interface is EIA/TIA-422 (formerly known as RS-422). LocalTalk is only supported in non-extended networks.

■ LocalTalk Link-Access Protocol *(LLAP)* The protocol that LocalTalk uses to communicate with the lower data link layers is called LLAP. LLAP provides a best-effort, error-free delivery of frames between AppleTalk nodes. LLAP does not provide a guaranteed delivery of frames, however, because this function is handled by higher-layer AppleTalk protocols.

Unlike EtherTalk, which uses the hardware address of the network card as its data link layer address, LocalTalk uses LLAP to acquire a data link layer address dynamically. This process assigns a unique address to the node without permanently assigning the address. The address is known as the node ID, which is a random number assigned by LLAP. LLAP sends a special packet with the destination address of the newly assigned node ID. If the node receives a response, a new node ID is assigned. This process is repeated until the node receives no response, in which time it will resend the packet with the same destination address. After a number of subsequent attempts with no reply, the address is temporarily assigned until the node is shut down.

LLAP uses a media-access scheme known as *Carrier-Sense Multiple Access, Collision Avoidance* (CSMA/CA). This scheme instructs the active nodes to listen to the link before sending data. The link must be idle for a certain random amount of time before the node can begin transmitting. If two nodes transmit at exactly the same time, a collision will occur and the packets will be discarded. To recover from this situation, LLAP uses data exchanges called handshakes. The sending nodes will not receive a handshake from their respective destination nodes. They will both retransmit their data after remaining idle for a random amount of time. Because both nodes are waiting for a random amount of time before retransmitting their respective data, the chances that another collision will occur decrease dramatically.

- *TokenTalk*   TokenTalk is used to enable AppleTalk to communicate over standard IEEE 802.5/Token Ring implementations. TokenTalk networks adhere to the same limitations of IEEE 802.5/Token Ring networks (including speeds, active number of nodes, and so on).

- TokenTalk Link-Access Protocol *(TLAP)*   As with the other link access protocols described in this chapter, TLAP is used to provide the communication between the upper-layer AppleTalk protocols and the IEEE 802.5 data link layer. TLAP uses the AMT to address transmissions, because AppleTalk does not recognize IEEE 802.5 hardware addresses. TLAP performs three levels of encapsulation when transmitting DDP packets:

  - SNAP header
  - IEEE 802.2 LLC header
  - IEEE 802.5 header

  The TLAP data transmission process works as follows:

  1. TLAP receives a DDP packet.
  2. TLAP finds the protocol address that is specified in the DDP header and references the AMT to find the corresponding IEEE 802.5/Token Ring hardware address.
  3. TLAP prepends the three different headers listed previously. First, it prepends the SNAP and IEEE 802.2 LLC headers; then, the IEEE 802.5/Token Ring header is prepended.
  4. The IEEE 802.5/Token Ring hardware address that is learned from the AMT is placed in the destination address field of the IEEE 802.5/Token Ring header.
  5. The IEEE 802.5/Token Ring frame is then placed on the physical medium for transmission.

AppleTalk Phases

There are currently two versions of AppleTalk:

- AppleTalk Phase 1
- AppleTalk Phase 2

This section discusses the differences between the two AppleTalk phases.

AppleTalk Phase 1   AppleTalk Phase 1 was the first implementation of the AppleTalk protocol. Phase 1 was designed to support network segments that contained up to 127 clients and 127 servers. Phase 1 also supports only one network number in a single zone.

AppleTalk Phase 2   AppleTalk Phase 2 was developed with new enhancements in order to address some of the limitations of AppleTalk Phase 1. Phase 2 is designed for larger networks and is enhanced with greater routing capabilities. Phase 2 also supports up to 253 hosts and supports multiple logical networks on a single physical network in a zone. These hosts can be any number of clients or servers (up to 253). Phase 2 also supports both extended and non-extended networks, whereas Phase 1 only supports non-extended networks. Both extended and non-extended networks will be discussed later in this chapter.
Table C-2 outlines some of the main differences between non-extended and extended networks.

AppleTalk Network Types

There are currently two types of AppleTalk networks: non-extended and extended. This section will discuss the difference between the two AppleTalk network types.

Non-Extended Networks   The first network type discussed is the non-extended AppleTalk network. A non-extended AppleTalk network was the first type of AppleTalk network. Non-extended networks are single physical networks that are assigned a single

Table C-2

AppleTalk Phase 1
and Phase 2

Capability	AppleTalk Phase 1	AppleTalk Phase 2
Networks, Nodes, and Zones		
Number of logical networks (cable segments)	1	65,279[1]
Maximum number of devices	254[2]	253[3]
Maximum number of end nodes	127	Does not apply[4]
Maximum number of servers	127	Does not apply
Number of zones in which a network can be extended	1[5]	1 (non-extended)
Media-Level Encapsulation		
Non-extended network	Does not apply	Yes
Extended network	Does not apply	Yes
Cable addressing	Does not apply; uses network numbers	Single network number (non-extended)
		Cable range of one or more (extended)

[1] The 65,279 value is per AppleTalk specifications.

[2] The node addresses 0 and 255 are reserved.

[3] The node addresses 0, 254, and 255 are reserved.

[4] There is no restriction on the types of devices. There can be a total of 253 end nodes and servers.

[5] In terms of zones, an AppleTalk Phase 1 network can be thought of as a non-extended AppleTalk Phase 2 network.

network number. They cannot contain more than one network number, and only one AppleTalk zone can be configured per non-extended network. The network number can range from 1 to 1,024. Every AppleTalk node in a non-extended network must be unique. Non-extended networks only support a single AppleTalk zone per network segment and only run over a LocalTalk media access system. Phase 1 only supports non-extended AppleTalk networks; however, non-extended networks have become obsolete with the introduction of AppleTalk extended networks. Apple explicitly removed support for non-extended networks, but these types of networks are still sup-

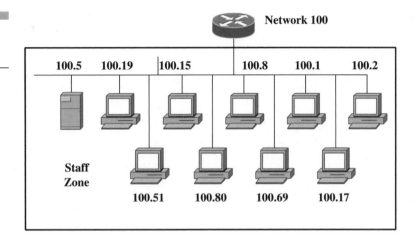

Figure C-4
Non-extended
network

ported by Cisco. Figure C-4 illustrates an example of a non-extended AppleTalk network.

Extended Networks Extended networks are physical network segments that can be assigned multiple network numbers. This assignment is referred to as a cable range. Cable ranges enable greater flexibility in that they can be configured to support single or multiple consecutive network numbers. Every address has a network number and host number, and this combination must be unique on an extended network. Multiple hosts can possess the same host addresses, however, as long as they each have a separate network number. Extended networks can also have multiple AppleTalk zones configured on a single network segment.

Extended AppleTalk networks can be configured on Ethernet (EtherTalk 2.0), FDDI, and Token Ring media. Extended AppleTalk networks were designed to overcome the many shortcomings of non-extended networks. Extended networks have more efficient algorithms to choose the best routers for traffic and are designed to limit the amount of broadcast traffic sent by routing updates. Figure C-5 illustrates an example of an extended AppleTalk network.

Table C-3 outlines some of the main differences between non-extended and extended networks.

Figure C-5

Extended AppleTalk network

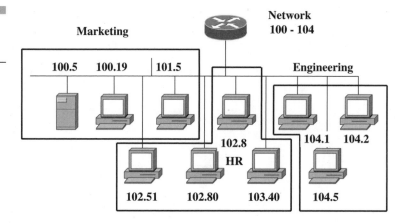

Table C-3

Non-extended AppleTalk and Extended AppleTalk networks

Attribute	Non-Extended	Extended
Media-level encapsulation method	Encapsulation of the 3-byte LocalTalk packet in an Ethernet frame	ISO-type encapsulations only (no encapsulation of the 3-byte LocalTalk packets)
Physical media that supports media-level encapsulation methods	LocalTalk	All physical media except for LocalTalk
Node addressing method	Each node number is unique.	Each `network.node` combination is unique.
Cable addressing method	A single number per cable	A number range corresponding to one or more logical networks

AppleTalk Zones

An AppleTalk zone is a logical group of networks, and these networks can be contiguous or noncontiguous. Zones are identified by zone names, which can be up to 32 characters long. These characters can consist of standard characters and AppleTalk special characters. A special character is included by typing a colon followed by the two hexadecimal characters that represent the special character in the Macintosh character set. In AppleTalk Phase 2, an extended network can have up to 255 zones; a non-extended network can have only one zone.

One advantage of creating zones is to simplify the process of locating and selecting network devices. Another benefit is that zones have the capability to group several networks that might contain devices from the same department. This functionality simplifies the process for the user.

Zones are not limited by geographical location and can contain networks from throughout the entire internetwork. Zones are logical groups and are not restricted by physical boundaries.

The following illustrations show examples of AppleTalk networks. One network is configured without zones, and the other is configured with zones. The benefit of zones in an AppleTalk environment will be discussed.

The first illustration shown in Figure C-6 is an example of a typical AppleTalk network with no configured zones. In this example, a

Figure C-6
No zones

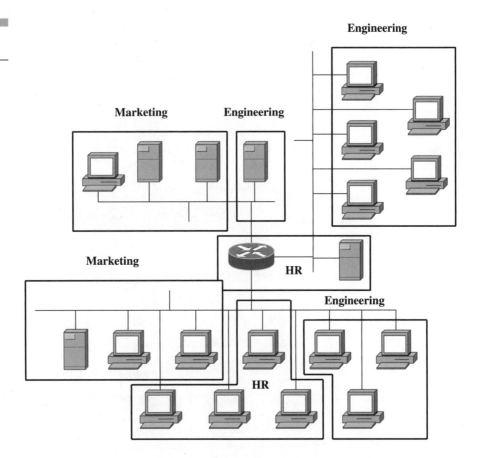

user is attempting to search for a server in the Engineering department by using the Chooser. The Chooser is an application on Macintosh machines that is used to browse and search for particular resources. The servers that represent the Engineering department are located in five different networks along with other resources. The user must search through all of the resource names in the Chooser and find the correct server. This process can take a long time if there are hundreds or thousands of resource names through which the user must scroll in order to find the device.

In the next example (see Figure C-7), zones are configured to simplify the user intervention that is needed when searching for a particular resource. Because there is now an Engineering zone, the

Figure C-7
Zones

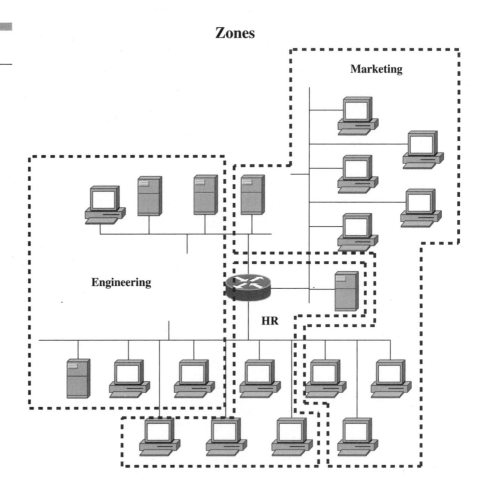

Zones

process for the user is greatly simplified. The user can now quickly browse the Engineering zone to find the correct server.

Zones are configured on the router. At least one zone must be configured for every interface that is AppleTalk enabled for non-extended networks. Extended networks must have at least one zone but can contain more. AppleTalk routing is not officially enabled on an interface until a zone is configured.

AppleTalk Addresses

AppleTalk addresses are 24 bits long and represent a `network. node` format. These addresses use decimal numbers in both the network and node fields. An example of an AppleTalk address on network 11 and node 50 would be represented as `11.50`. The network portion of the address is 16 bits long, and the node portion consists of 8 bits. Refer to Figure C-8. AppleTalk addresses are similar to the addresses that are used by TCP/IP and IPX in that they also use socket numbers to identify a specific process on the device. Socket numbers are prepended to the end of the AppleTalk address and consist of 8 bits. Figure C-9 illustrates the address packet format with a socket number.

AppleTalk address assignment is done dynamically. A node receives a provisional network-layer address upon startup. The network portion of the provisional address is taken from a startup range —a specific range of network addresses that are reserved for provisional assignments. This range of network addresses is 65,280 to 65,534. The node will also choose a provisional node address, which will be a random number. The node will then use the ZIP to find the

Figure C-8
Network address

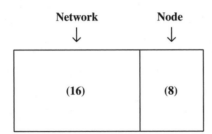

Network ↓	Node ↓
(16)	(8)

Figure C-9
Network address
with socket

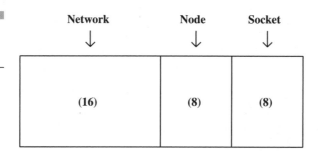

router that is attached to the network. The node will then pick a network number based on the valid cable range specified by the router. Once the network address is assigned, the node will then randomly assign itself a node number and will send a broadcast message to determine whether it is in use by any other node. If another node replies that it has that specific node number, a new node number will be randomly chosen. Then, this process will be repeated. The node will continue to repeat this process until it receives no reply from another node on the network. It will then assign itself the particular node address. See Figure C-10 for an illustration of this process.

Phase 1 Addresses AppleTalk Phase 1 uses a single network number that corresponds to the physical network. Phase 1 can only use a single network number per network segment. The network number 0 is reserved in AppleTalk Phase 1 networks.

AppleTalk node numbers are eight-bit decimal numbers (as described previously). These addresses must be unique per network segment. AppleTalk Phase 1 only enables 254 addresses and uses node numbers 1 through 127 for user nodes and node numbers 128 through 254 for server and printer nodes. Node numbers 0 and 255 are reserved.

Phase 2 Addresses AppleTalk Phase 2 has the capability of supporting multiple network numbers. Networks are identified by a cable range that corresponds to one or more logical networks. Cable ranges can vary from a single network number to a contiguous sequence of networks and can use the format `start-end`. A cable range consisting of a single network number of 1,200 would be represented as `1200-1200`. A cable range consisting of networks 50, 51,

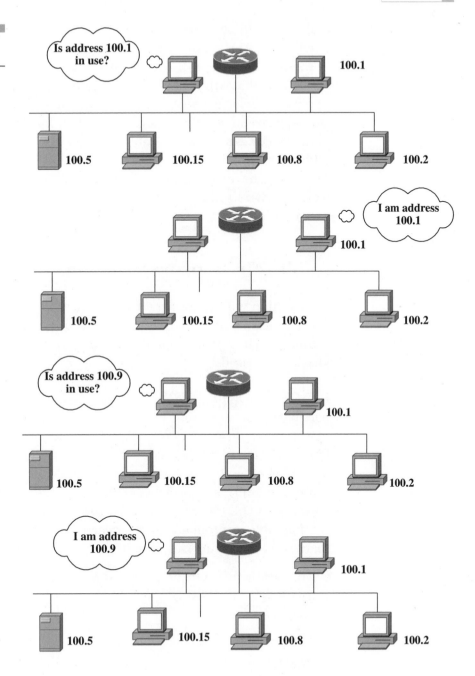

Figure C-10
Address assignment

and 52 would be represented as 50-52. The network number 0 is reserved in AppleTalk Phase 2 networks.

In AppleTalk Phase 2, node numbers 1 through 253 can be used for any nodes that are attached to the network. These node addresses apply to each logical network, meaning that duplicate node addresses can appear on a cable range but must have a unique network address. For example, on a cable range of 10–12, a node can have an address of 10.15 and another node can have an address of 11.15. They each have the same node number (15) but use different network numbers within the cable range. Node numbers 0, 254, and 255 are reserved.

AppleTalk Routing Protocols

This section will discuss the three routing protocols for AppleTalk. Each protocol will be discussed, and we will also show configuration examples. The advantages and disadvantages of each protocol will also be discussed.

RTMP   The *Routing Table Maintenance Protocol* (RTMP) is a transport-layer routing protocol for AppleTalk. RTMP establishes and maintains routing tables in an AppleTalk network and is based upon RIP (using the same method for determining routes). This method is known as a hop count. A hop count is determined by the number of routers or intermediary devices that the packet must pass during its travel from the source network to the destination network. RTMP routing tables contain an entry for each network that a datagram can reach. RTMP routing tables contain the following information:

- The number of hops to the destination network
- The port on the router that is used to reach the destination network
- The node ID of the next-hop router
- The network cable range of the destination network
- The current state of the entry (the state of the entry can be defined as either good, suspect, or bad)

Figure C-11
RTMP routing table

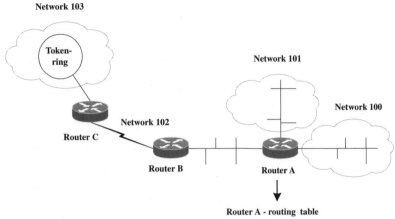

Router A - routing table

Network	Distance	Port	Next Router	Entry State
100	0	1	0	Good
101	0	2	0	Good
102	1	3	Router B	Good
103	2	3	Router B	Good

Figure C-11 illustrates an example of an RTMP routing table in an RTMP architecture.

AppleTalk routing is disabled by default. The following steps are required to explicitly enable AppleTalk routing:

1. AppleTalk routing can be enabled by entering the following line:

```
Router(config)#appletalk routing
```

This command enables RTMP, which is AppleTalk's default routing protocol.

2. The next step is to configure an interface. An AppleTalk address needs to be assigned to the interface, and an AppleTalk zone needs to be configured as well. The following are the commands that are needed:

```
Router(config-if)#appletalk address network.node
Router(config-if)#appletalk zone zone-name
```

After an address and a zone name are configured on the interface, the router will search for another router on the network in order to verify that there are no conflicts. If the router does not find another router, it will assume that the information is correct.

3. To manually configure an interface for extended addressing, a cable range must be specified. The following command configures the interface with a cable range:

```
Router(config)#appletalk cable-range cable-range
[network.node]
```

Dynamic Address Assignment

AppleTalk routers can be configured to dynamically address their interfaces and to obtain zone and cable information from another router. The first router is manually configured and defined as the seed router. This router is used to configure other routers that are set up for dynamic discovery. Dynamic discovery cannot be done over serial lines. Routers that are attached to other routers via a LAN segment can be configured for dynamic discovery, however.

Seed routers verify their configuration when they are started. If the configuration is valid, they will start functioning. To become a seed router, these configurations must be implemented. Non-seed routers will attempt to communicate with a seed router upon startup. They can get part of their configuration from the seed router, and the configuration is verified. The following commands are used to enable a router for discovery mode in a non-extended network:

```
Router(config-if)#appletalk address 0.0
```

This command enables the interface to search for a valid network number. The router will search for a seed router and will get the correct network number of the segment.

If the network number is known, the interface can be configured with the network number—and dynamic discovery can be configured to find the rest of the configuration (such as zones). The following command configures the interface with a network number and enables the router to find a seed router for all other network information:

```
Router(config-if)#appletalk address network.node
Router(config-if)#appletalk discovery
```

To enable routers for dynamic discovery on an extended network, the following command can be used:

```
Router(config-if)#appletalk cable-range 0.0
```

This command enables the router to search for the cable range to which it is attached. It will search for a seed router to find this range.

As with non-extended networks, interfaces in extended networks can also be configured with an address and can dynamically find other network information from the seed router. The following commands enable the interface to perform this task:

```
Router(config-if)#appletalk cable-range cable-range
[network.node]
Router(config-if)#appletalk discovery
```

The following diagram (see Figure C-12) illustrates the dynamic discovery process. Router A is a non-seed router. Router A is configured to receive network configurations from Router B and Router D via serial interfaces 0 and 1, respectively.

Figure C-12
Dynamic discovery

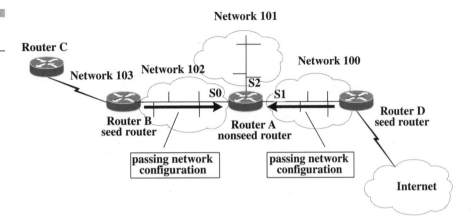

AppleTalk Update Routing Protocol (AURP)

AURP is a transport-layer AppleTalk routing protocol that is used to connect two non-contiguous AppleTalk networks over a foreign network (such as TCP/IP). AURP actually encapsulates AppleTalk packets (such as RTMP and ZIP) into UDP headers to be transported over a TCP/IP network. The exterior routers are routers that are on the edge of an AppleTalk network. These routers encapsulate AppleTalk packets into UDP headers and transfer them to the destination router. The destination router receives the UDP packet, strips off the UDP headers, and passes the AppleTalk packets along to their destination. The process of encapsulating a protocol and passing it over a foreign network is referred to as tunneling. The exterior routers create tunnels to the destination routers. If the exterior router is connected to only one destination router, the tunnel is referred to as a point-to-point tunnel. If the exterior router is connected to multiple-destination routers, the tunnel is referred to as a multi-point tunnel. This tunnel is also referred to as a fully connected tunnel if all exterior routers know about the tunnel. If there are any exterior routers that do not know about the tunnel, it is referred to as a partially connected tunnel. See Figure C-13 for an example of an AURP network.

Figure C-13 is an example of a fully connected tunnel, because all routers on this network know about the exterior routers. These routers encapsulate the AppleTalk data that is received from their LAN segments and encapsulate that data into UDP packets to be sent across the TCP/IP network.

AURP abides by the rule of split horizon. In other words, it does not send routing updates out of interfaces from which the update was learned. Therefore, because AURP uses point-to-point and multi-point tunnels, it will only broadcast routing updates about information regarding its locally attached networks. AURP broadcasts routing updates when one of the following events occurs:

- An exterior router is attached to the tunnel. All exterior routers will exchange network numbers and zone information with the newly attached router.
- Distance to a network has changed.

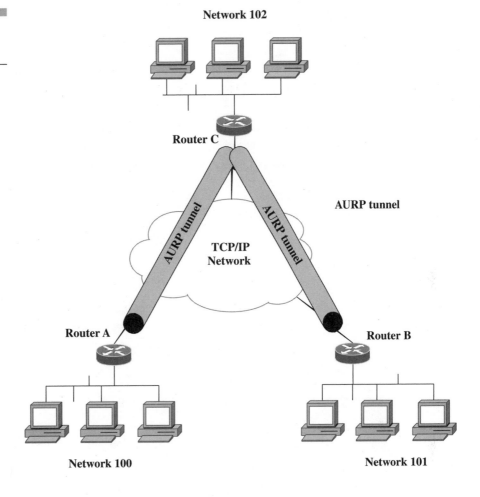

- A new network is added to the routing table.
- A network is removed from the routing table.

The following are items that must be configured in order to enable AURP:

1. The following command enables route redistribution on the router:

```
Router(config)#appletalk route redistribution
```

2. The interface that is to be used to connect to the destination router must have an IP address specified. The following command configures an IP address on that interface:

```
Router(config)#interface type number
Router(config-if)#ip address ip-address subnet-mask
```

3. Creating a tunnel interface enables AppleTalk to be encapsulated into IP packets (specifically, UDP headers). The following command creates a tunnel interface:

```
Router(config-if)#interface tunnel number
```

4. AURP must be explicitly enabled on an interface. The following command accomplishes this task:

```
Router(config-if)#appletalk protocol aurp
```

5. The tunnel source and destination must be specified. This information tells the router which physical interfaces it will use for the tunnel source and destination. The following commands accomplish this task:

```
Router(config-if)#tunnel source {ip-address | type number}
Router(config-if)#tunnel destination {hostname | ip-address}
```

6. The routing protocol for the tunnel must be specified after the tunnel is created. In this case, AURP is assigned to the tunnel:

```
Router(config-if)#tunnel mode aurp
```

AppleTalk Enhanced Interior Gateway Protocol (EIGRP)

EIGRP is a hybrid protocol that uses the advantages of both link-state and distance-vector protocols. EIGRP supports AppleTalk as well as IPX and IP. This functionality makes EIGRP an appealing routing protocol, because it can be used as the sole routing protocol on the network (thus saving the overhead and complexities of additional routing protocols).

Using EIGRP for AppleTalk saves bandwidth, because RTMP and AURP both create more broadcast traffic. EIGRP can be configured on an interface along with RTMP. If one destination router is only running RTMP, the router will exchange routing updates via RTMP. If another destination router is running EIGRP or RTMP as well, however, the routers will use EIGRP for the routing updates because EIGRP supercedes RTMP. RTMP should be disabled on interfaces that have EIGRP running and that are connected to destination routers that are running EIGRP, because RTMP will continue to send routing updates although they will not be used. Remember that RTMP is enabled by default when AppleTalk routing is enabled. Therefore, it must be explicitly disabled. The following configuration in interface configuration mode will disable RTMP on the interface:

```
Router(config-if)#no appletalk protocol rtmp
```

To enable AppleTalk EIGRP, the following configuration must be entered:

```
Router(config)#appletalk routing eigrp router-number
Router(config-if)#appletalk protocol eigrp
```

The `router-number` for this configuration must be a unique router number and not the autonomous system number.

Split horizon controls AppleTalk EIGRP update and query packets. To reduce the chance of routing loops, you will find that split horizon is enabled by default on all interfaces. This solution does not work well in some cases of *Non-Broadcast Multi-Access* (NBMA) networks, however, because routing updates might not be passed to any destination routers. Split horizon can be disabled on specific interfaces with the following command:

```
Router(config-if)#no appletalk eigrp-splithorizon
```

Introduction to IPX Protocols

IPX is part of the IPX/SPX suite—a proprietary suite of protocols from Novell. The IPX/SPX suite is derived from the *Xerox Network Systems* (XNS) protocol suite. The IPX/SPX protocol suite is similar to the TCP/IP protocol suite in that many other protocols coexist and interact within the suite.

NetWare is a network operating system that was developed by Novell to enable seamless file and print services as well as database access and e-mail services to workstations that use the Novell client. NetWare uses IPX as its default protocol. Therefore, IPX has a large prevalence in today's LANs because many of them run Novell NetWare servers. IPX/SPX is not as efficient as TCP/IP. With the ever-increasing use of the Internet and the efficient use on networks, TCP/IP is the de facto standard protocol for use on today's networks. Novell has realized this fact and has made TCP/IP the default protocol in NetWare 5.0.

IPX, SPX, SAP, NCP, and NetBIOS

The following paragraphs describe these different protocols and systems.

■ IPX works at layer 3 of the OSI model. It was derived from XNS's *Internet Datagram Protocol* (IDP). IPX provides network-layer addresses that are assigned to nodes. These addresses are represented as hexadecimal numbers and are 80 bits long. They consist of both the network number and the node number. IPX provides connectionless datagram delivery that is similar to UDP in the TCP/IP protocol suite. It does not require an acknowledgment from the end device. IPX uses sockets to communicate with the upper-layer protocols, much like TCP/IP ports do. Sockets enable IPX to handle multiple sessions on the same machine. The minimum IPX packet size is 30 bytes, and the maximum packet size is 65,535 bytes. Each IPX packet has a 30-byte packet header, as illustrated in Figure C-14. The numbers in brackets are represented as bytes.

This section will describe each field in the IPX header.

The Checksum field contains a two-byte value that is used to verify packet integrity. The checksum was not used in NetWare systems until the release of NetWare 4.x. NetWare 4.x enables the use of the Checksum field (if desired). The reason why the checksum field is not

Figure C-14
IPX header

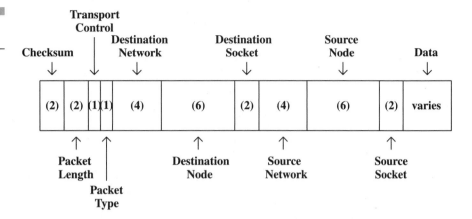

required is because a CRC check is already performed on the entire frame and data. The Checksum field only verifies the IPX header. The Checksum field cannot be used with the Novell Ethernet_802.3 frame type because the checksum field is used to indicate that the frame is a NetWare packet.

The Packet Length field contains a two-byte value defining the length of the entire packet. This length includes the IPX header, which is 30 bytes.

The Transport Control field is a one-byte field that indicates the number of routers (hops) that a packet has traversed in order to reach its destination. This value starts at zero and can be as high as 15 in IPX RIP-enabled networks. Each router that receives the packet will increment this value by one. After the packet has reached its 16th hop, the router will discard the packet. The use of NLSP enables the hop count to reach as high as 127 hops.

The Packet Type field is a one-byte field indicating the type of service that the packet will use. Table C-4 lists the optional packet types.

The Destination Network field contains the four-byte network address of the destination node. This field is set to 0x00-00-00-00 if the packet is destined for the same network as the source node and will not be passed on by a router. A special situation occurs, however, when the workstation first initializes and sends out SAP Get Nearest Server and RIP Get Local Target broadcast requests. The workstation sets its Source and Destination Network fields to 0 (0x00-00-00-00) because it does not yet know which network to which it

Table C-4

Packet type
descriptions

Packet Type	Field Value (Hexadecimal)	Purpose
NLSP	0x00	NLSP Packets
Routing information	0x01	RIP Packets
Service advertising	0x04	SAP Packets
Sequenced	0x05	SPX Packets
NCP	0x11	NCP Packets
Propagated	0x14	NetBIOS and other propagated packets

belongs. The router will receive this request and will reply directly to the workstation, filling in the Source and Destination Network fields.

The Destination Node field is a six-byte field that contains the node address of the destination node. A workstation can broadcast to all nodes on the local network by setting its Destination Node field to 0xFF-FF-FF-FF. This field will contain a value of 0x00-00-00-00 if the packet is destined for a NetWare 3.x or 4.x server. The destination server's actual hardware address will be in the Destination Address field of the Ethernet or Token Ring frame.

The Destination Socket field is a two-byte field defining the socket address of the packet destination process. Sockets are used to route packets to different processes within a single node. Table C-5 lists some processes with their corresponding socket numbers.

The Source Network field contains a four-byte field that defines the source network address to which the source node is attached. The source node will set this field to zero (0x00-00-00-00) if the source network is unknown. If the source node is a NetWare 3.x or 4.x server, it will set this field to the internal IPX address.

The Source Node field is a six-byte field containing the address of the source node. This field cannot contain a broadcast address (0xFF-FF-FF-FF-FF-FF).

The Source Socket field contains a two-byte field defining the socket number of the process from the source node that is transmitting the packet. Servers will reply from defined socket numbers,

Table C-5

Socket numbers and their associated processes

Socket Number	Process
0x451	NCP
0x452	SAP
0x453	RIP
0x455	Novell NetBIOS
0x456	Novell Diagnostics
0x457	Serialization packet
0x9001	NLSP
0x9004	IPXWAN protocol

whereas workstations will use dynamically assigned socket numbers ranging from 0x4000 to 0x8000.

The Data field is of variable length and contains the data portion of the packet. This field is not included as part of the IPX header.

■ *Sequenced Packet Exchange* (SPX), derived from the *Sequenced Packet Protocol* (SPP) of the XNS protocol, works at layer 4 of the OSI model and provides connection-oriented services to network applications that require a connection-oriented session. Novell's *Remote Console* (RCONSOLE), *Print Server* (PSERVER), and *Remote Printer* (RPRINTER) are all examples of programs that use SPX communications. SPX uses virtual circuits to establish sessions between nodes. Each virtual circuit is identified by a connection ID in the SPX header. An SPX header contains all of the same fields as an IPX header (with an additional 12 bytes). These 12 bytes contain sequence and acknowledgment fields to support the connection-oriented services that SPX provides. The SPX header is 42 bytes long, as illustrated in Figure C-15. The numbers in brackets are represented as bytes.

The Connection Control field contains a one-byte value that controls the bidirectional flow of data. Table C-6 lists the possible values for this field.

The Datastream Type field contains a one-byte value that indicates the type of data that is stored in the packet. The value can be

Figure C-15
SPX header

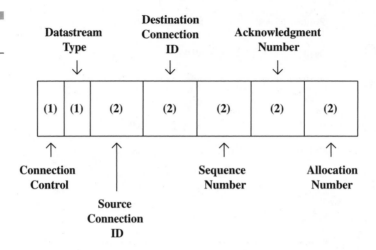

Table C-6	Value	Name	Description
Connection control field values, names, and descriptions	0x04 (Introduced in SPX II)	Size	Negotiation size request/response
	0x08 (Introduced in SPX II)	SPX2	SPX II type packet
	0x10	End-of-Message	Indicates that the client has requested to end the session
	0x20	Attention	This field is not presently in use.
	0x40	Acknowledgment Required	The data has been sent, and acknowledgment is required.
	0x80	System Packet	Acknowledgement packet; this value is only used internally

defined by the client or can contain one of the following values listed in Table C-7.

The Source Connection ID field contains a two-byte number defined by the source node. SPX can have multiple sessions running on a single machine (using the same socket numbers). To distinguish between each session, a virtual connection is identified with a num-

Value	Name	Description
0xFC	Orderly release request	(Introduced in SPX II)
0xFD	Orderly release acknowledgement	(Introduced in SPX II)
0xFE	End-of-Connection	Indicates that the client has requested to end the session
0xFF	End-of-Connection Acknowledgment	Transmitted after an end-of-connection request is received

Table C-7

Datastream type field values, names, and descriptions

ber. The source node will use this number in the Source Connection ID field, and the receiving station will use this same number in its Destination Connection ID field.

The Destination Connection ID field was described briefly in the last paragraph. It also contains a two-byte connection ID number of the destination node. This field is set to 0xFFFF during the initial connection establishment because the sending node does not yet know what number the destination node will use.

The Sequence Number field contains a two-byte value for the number of data packets that are sent by a single node. This value is incremented after receiving an acknowledgement for a data packet that has been transmitted. This value does not increase after sending an acknowledgement packet.

The Acknowledge Number field contains a two-byte sequence number that is expected in the next SPX packet from the responding SPX node. This field is similar to the Acknowledgment number in TCP/IP. If the sequence number is incorrect, the receiving node assumes that an error occurred during the packet transmission and will request a retransmission.

The Allocation Number field contains a two-byte value indicating the number of receive buffers at a workstation. The value starts at zero, which means that a value of four would equal five packet-receive buffers. Each time the receiving station receives a packet, it increments this value. These buffers are then freed up each time a receiving device processes information.

NOTE: Novell created an enhanced version of SPX called SPX II. SPX II was first implemented in NetWare 4.x. Enhancements include packet sizes up to the MTU of the network and more efficient windowing features. With the original SPX, packet size was limited to 576 bytes, including the 42-byte header. The original SPX also only allowed one packet to be sent at a time before receiving an acknowledgement. SPX II enables multiple packets to be sent before receiving an acknowledgement, thus greatly improving efficiency.

- SAP enables an end device to locate network services and enables servers to advertise their services and addresses to other servers and routers. SAP is a broadcast-type packet, and when a NetWare server is configured, it will send SAP broadcasts every 60 seconds.

The three types of SAP packets are as follows:

1. *Periodic updates*   Periodic updates are used by NetWare servers to advertise a list of their services and addresses to the local network for other servers and routers to store. They are sent every 60 seconds and can contain up to seven entries (with a maximum packet size of 576 bytes). The servers and routers store the updates in their own *server information tables* (SITs). The SIT at each server or router will store a complete list of the available services on the network. The periodic updates are not sent across router boundaries; however, routers will build their own SAP table and will forward the complete SAP table to other routers. By default, this process happens every 60 seconds. The interval at which routers forward the SAP table is configurable, however. This process enables clients to find remote services across the *Wide Area Network* (WAN). Each SAP update contains a hexadecimal number identifying the type of server that is broadcasting its services. Table C-8 lists some examples of the different SAP updates.

2. *Service queries*   Clients do not receive SAP broadcasts. Instead, a client will send a service query SAP when it wants to know about services that are available on the network. There are two types of service queries: general service queries and nearest service queries. The most popular type of service

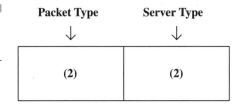

Figure C-16

SAP service query
packet format

query is the *Get Nearest Server* (GNS) request, which is used
to find the nearest server depending on the type of service
that is required. The service query packets define which type
of server they are requesting. Figure C-16 illustrates the
service query packet format. The numbers in brackets are
represented as bytes.

The service query packet follows the IPX header and defines both
the packet type and server type that is requested.

The Packet Type field is a two-byte value defining whether the
packet is a general service query with a value of 0x0001 or a nearest service query with a value of 0x0003.

The Service Type field is a two-byte field defining the type of service required in the request. Table C-8 lists some of the possible
server types that are available (as defined by Novell).

1. *Service responses*   The third type of SAP packet is a service
   response packet. Service responses are used to reply to service
   queries. There are two types of service response packets:
   general service responses and nearest service responses.
   General service responses are used for service information
   broadcasts. Each general service response packet can contain
   information about a maximum of seven servers. If the server
   needs to respond with additional servers that are available
   for the request, an additional general service response will
   have to be sent.

The nearest service response, also known as GNS responses,
contains information about only one server. The server that is
listed in the response will be the closest (in hops away) from the
requester.

Table C-8

SAP service
type options

Type	Service
0X0001	User
0X0002	User group
0X0003	Print server queue
0X0004	File server
0X0005	Job server
0x0007	Print server
0x0009	Archive server
0x000A	Job server queue
0x002E	Dynamic SAP
0x0047	Advertising print server
0X004B	Btrieve VAP 5.0
0X004C	SQL VAP
0X007A	TES—NetWare for VMS
0x0098	Access server
0x009A	Named pipes server
0X009E	Portable NetWare—UNIX
0X0102	RCONSOLE
0x0111	Test server
0x0166	*NetWare Management* (NMS)
0x026A	NMS console
0x026B	Time synchronization (NetWare 4.x and later)
0x0278	Directory services (NetWare 4.x and later)

Figure C-17 illustrates a service response packet. The numbers in brackets are represented as bytes.

The Packet/Response Type field is a two-byte field identifying the type of service response. The two possible values are 0x0002 for SAP general service responses or 0x0004 for nearest service responses.

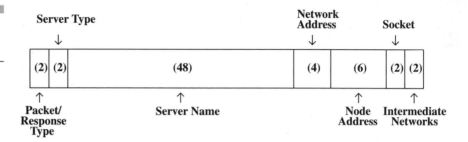

Figure C-17

SAP service response packet

The Server Type field is a two-byte field identifying the type of service that is available. The list of possible server types is listed in the previous table (possible server types for service queries).

The Server Name field is a 48-byte field containing the object name of the server. The server name must be unique per server type. For example, a file server (0x0004) can have the same name as a job server (0x0005). Two file servers (0x0004) cannot use the same name. If a server's name is fewer than 48 bytes long, however, the field will be padded with zeros following the server name in order to maintain the 48-byte field length.

The Network Address field is a four-byte field identifying the network address of the server.

The Node Address field is a six-byte field identifying the node address of the server. This field will contain a value of 0x00-00-00-00-00-01 for NetWare 3.x and 4.x servers.

The Socket field contains a two-byte value identifying the socket number that the server will use to receive service requests for the server type.

- *NetWare Core Protocol* (NCP) is the protocol that is used for client and server communication. Clients send NCP requests to the server for file access and transfers, drive mappings, searching the directories, the print queue status, and more. NetWare servers reply to these requests with NCP replies. Once the server has processed and completed the request, the workstation will terminate the connection by sending a Destroy Service Connection request to the server.

An NCP header follows the frame and IPX/SPX header. An NCP Request header defines the service warranted by the sending workstation. The header is used in all communication from the client to

Figure C-18
NCP Request header

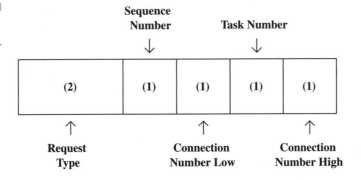

Sequence Number		Task Number	

Request Type — (2)
Connection Number Low — (1)
Connection Number High — (1)

Table C-9	Value	Description
NCP Request types	1111	Create Service Connection
	2222	Service Request
	5555	Destroy Service Connection
	7777	Burst Mode Transfer

the server and is six bytes long, followed by other NCP information defining the client's request. Figure C-18 illustrates an NCP Request header. The numbers in brackets are represented as bytes.

The Request Type field contains a two-byte value indicating the type of request that is sent from the client to the server. Table C-9 lists the possible Request type values.

Clients use the Create Service Connection and specify 1111 in the Request Type field in order to connect to a server. The client will then send a Destroy Service Connection and specify 5555 in the Request Type field in order to detach from a server. Clients will specify 2222 in the Request Type field in order to request general services and will specify 7777 when using the Burst Mode protocol.

The Sequence Number field contains a one-byte value that is used to track the sequence of communication between the client and the server. The client will add 1 to the last sequence number and place that value in this field.

The Connection Number Low field is a one-byte value containing the service connection number assigned to the client, by the server, upon login.

The Task Number field contains a one-byte value indicating which client task is making the request. The client will set this value to zero when all tasks have been executed.

The Connection Number High field is used in 1,000 user versions of NetWare. All other NetWare versions will have a value of 0x00 in this field.

NCP Reply is used by the server to respond to NCP requests. The NCP Reply header follows the frame and IPX/SPX header. It also adds two additional fields to the NCP Request header. Figure C-19 illustrates an NCP Reply header. The numbers in brackets are represented as bytes.

The Reply Type field is a two-byte field containing the type of reply that the server is using to respond to the NCP Request. Table C-10 lists the possible NCP Reply types.

Figure C-19
NCP Reply header

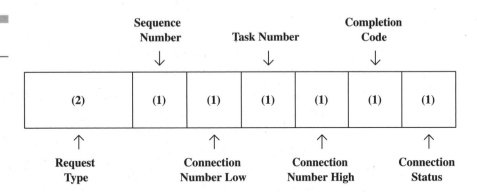

Table C-10	Value	Description
NCP Reply types	3333	Service Reply
	7777	Burst Mode Connection
	9999	Request Being Processed

The server will respond to most requests with a Service Reply by using 3333 as the value in the Reply Type field. If a workstation sends an NCP Request and does not receive a response within a specified amount of time, it will send another NCP request. The server will receive the request and will respond with a Request Being Processed NCP Reply by using 9999 in the Reply Type field. The Burst Mode Connection with the 7777 value is used when using Burst Mode to transfer files.

The Completion Code field is a one-byte field added for the NCP Reply header. The Completion Code is used to indicate that the request was processed correctly. If an error occurs on the server while processing the request, it will use a number in this field to indicate that there was an error during the process. If the server completes the request successfully, it will use a zero in this field.

The Connection Status Flags field is a one-byte value indicating the connection status between the client and the server. The server will mark the fourth bit in this byte as 1 when the Down command is issued at the server.

NCP also uses a term called *function codes*. These function codes work in conjunction with the NCP Reply and Request headers to specify specific functions that the client is requesting, such as opening a file. Some functions apply to a range of functions and require subfunction codes.

■ NetBIOS is a non-routable protocol that can be used over IPX to obtain information about the named nodes on the network. NetBIOS is a broadcast type protocol that uses type-20 broadcast packets to flood the network. Routers do not forward broadcasts, so to propagate the type-20 broadcasts to external networks, the router's IPX interfaces (either Ethernet or Token Ring and Serial) must be configured to enable the type-20 broadcasts to be forwarded.

NetBIOS uses a type 20 (0x14) IPX packet with a socket number of 0x455 to identify itself as a NetBIOS packet. The Destination Node field in the IPX header is set to 0xFF-FF-FF-FF-FF-FF.

Figure C-20 shows how routers must be configured in order to forward IPX NetBIOS packets.

Figure C-20
IPX NetBIOS example

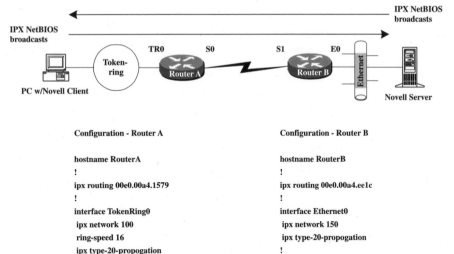

```
Configuration - Router A

hostname RouterA
!
ipx routing 00e0.00a4.1579
!
interface TokenRing0
 ipx network 100
 ring-speed 16
 ipx type-20-propogation
!
interface Serial0
 bandwidth 128
 ipx network 200
 ipx type-20-propogation
```

```
Configuration - Router B

hostname RouterB
!
ipx routing 00e0.00a4.ee1c
!
interface Ethernet0
 ipx network 150
 ipx type-20-propogation
!
interface Serial1
 bandwidth 128
 ipx network 200
 ipx type-20-propogation
```

Routing IPX with RIP, NLSP, and EIGRP

The following paragraphs describe how to route IPX with RIP, NLSP, and EIGRP.

■ RIP is a distance-vector routing protocol derived from XNS and used route IPX over the WAN. RIP exchanges IPX routing information to neighboring IPX routers. As soon as new routing information is learned, an IPX RIP router will immediately broadcast its entire routing table to its neighboring routers. Those routers will then broadcast their routing tables to their neighboring routers until all IPX RIP routers in the WAN have been updated with the new routing information. The time that it takes to complete this entire process is called the *convergence time*. IPX RIP will also send periodic routing updates every 60 seconds to its neighboring routers. This situation happens even if there are no new changes in the network. These broadcasts can often cause excessive overhead traffic in the network, leading to oversubscribed circuits and latency delays for other types of traffic trying to traverse the network.

IPX RIP uses two metrics during its routing decision process. These metrics are ticks (delay) and hop count (the number of routers a packet traverses to get to its destination). One tick is equal to 1/18 of a second. The router will first look at the tick count of the route to determine which path to take. The route with the lowest tick count, or delay, will be chosen as the best path to the destination. If two routes exist with the same tick count, the router will chose the route with the lowest hop count to the destination. The hop count is determined by counting the number of routers that the packet will traverse to reach the destination router. The maximum hop count used by IPX RIP is 15. In other words, the packet will be discarded after it has reached its 16th hop. The hop count is incremented and counted in the Transport Control field of the IPX header. The reason for the maximum hop count used by RIP is to alleviate routing loops in the network. Figure C-21 is used to reference as an example for the following section.

San Jose needs to send data to New York. The example shows that San Jose has a 56K connection to Chicago and a T1 connection to Dallas. New York has T1 connections to both Miami and Chicago. IPX RIP will first look at the tick information to decide which path it will take to reach New York. Although there are fewer hops (two) from San Jose to New York via the Chicago router, the 56K connec-

Figure C-21
RIP example

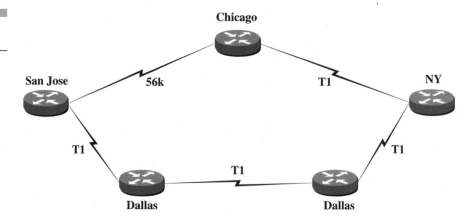

tion is much less desirable than a T1 connection. The cumulative ticks from the source to the destination calculate the tick count. This cumulative tick count is passed via IPX RIP updates. So, assuming that the 56K link is being saturated with a large amount of traffic, the tick count for the path over the 56K link to New York will be higher than the tick count for the path through Dallas and Miami. Therefore, IPX RIP will find that the tick count is less via the route to Dallas and Miami to get to New York, and this is the best route that will be chosen by the San Jose router. If it was decided to upgrade the 56K connection to a T1, then the San Jose router would chose the path to New York via the Chicago router because of a lower tick value.

Circumstances might occur, however, where the route through the 56K link will be chosen. This situation might occur if there is little to no traffic traversing the link. This situation will cause the delay time to be low and the router will maintain a low tick count across this link. This would ultimately result in the San Jose router sending packets across the 56k link to Chicago to get to New York. To alleviate this problem, the tick count can be inflated so that the San Jose router will never chose the route through the 56k link over the route through Dallas and Miami.

The example also shows the configuration of the San Jose router. The tick count can be manually adjusted by using the following command in interface configuration mode:

```
Router(config-if)#ipx delay tick
```

The `tick` portion of the command will be replaced with a number to define the tick count. By default, all LAN interfaces have a RIP delay of one, and all WAN interfaces have a delay of six. The higher the tick count, the less desirable the link becomes.

■ EIGRP is a hybrid routing protocol, using some of the advantages of a link-state routing protocol and distance-vector routing protocol. EIGRP is a more efficient protocol with faster convergence time over the use of IPX RIP. The only drawback is that EIGRP can only be used on the WAN links. In other words, IPX RIP will be used on the LAN, and static routes will have to

Figure C-22
IPX EIGRP example

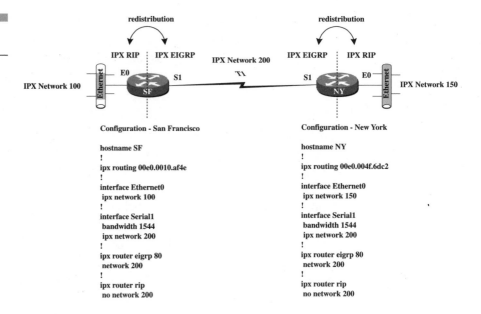

```
Configuration - San Francisco

hostname SF
!
ipx routing 00e0.0010.af4e
!
interface Ethernet0
 ipx network 100
!
interface Serial1
 bandwidth 1544
 ipx network 200
!
ipx router eigrp 80
 network 200
!
ipx router rip
 no network 200
```

```
Configuration - New York

hostname NY
!
ipx routing 00e0.004f.6dc2
!
interface Ethernet0
 ipx network 150
!
interface Serial1
 bandwidth 1544
 ipx network 200
!
ipx router eigrp 80
 network 200
!
ipx router rip
 no network 200
```

be entered for the NetWare servers to access routers across the WAN or redistribution must be done at the router. By default, EIGRP redistributes IPX RIP internal routes into EIGRP external routes and EIGRP routes into IPX RIP. Figure C-22 shows a basic IPX EIGRP configuration.

Going through the configurations, each of the relevant commands will be discussed.

The first command is `ipx routing`. This command starts the IPX routing process and will take the MAC address of the router for the node address unless a node address is specifically defined. This command is entered in global configuration mode:

```
Router(config)#ipx routing [node]
```

This command enables IPX RIP and SAP services on the router. The `node` part of the command is optional; a four-digit hexadecimal number can be entered (xxxx.xxxx.xxxx).

If a node is not specified, the router will use the MAC address of the first Ethernet, Token Ring, or FDDI interface card.

The `ipx network` commands are entered on each interface defining the IPX network number for that specific interface. Notice that both routers share the same IPX network number on their respective serial interfaces. The link between both routers is considered to be a single network (similar to operation in a TCP/IP environment):

```
Router(config)#interface Ethernet0
Router(config-if)#ipx network network
```

The `network` portion of this command is the IPX network number that is used on the interface. The `ipx router eigrp` command is used to enable the Enhanced IGRP protocol on the router. This command is entered in global configuration mode:

```
Router(config)#ipx router eigrp autonomous-system-number
Router(config-router)#network network
```

The `autonomous-system-number` argument is the EIGRP autonomous system number. This number can range from 1 to 65,535. The EIGRP autonomous system number must be the same for each network. In this example, the number 80 is used.

The `network` statement after the `ipx router eigrp` command is used to list all of the networks for which EIGRP will be routing. In the example, network 200 was used because that is the IPX network that is running on the WAN interfaces (where EIGRP is routing).

The last command discussed in the configuration is the `ipx router rip` command. This command is also entered in global configuration mode:

```
Router(config)#ipx router rip
Router(config-router)#no network network
```

The `ipx router rip` command is used to enable IPX RIP. IPX RIP is enabled by default once the `ipx routing` command is entered.

The no network command is used to deny IPX RIP from routing this network. Because IPX RIP is enabled by default, it will route all IPX networks listed on the interfaces. In this scenario, the command no network is used so that IPX RIP does not route for IPX network 200 and rather leaves the routing to EIGRP. IPX RIP will route for the internal IPX network 100 on the San Francisco router and the internal IPX network 150 on the New York router, although these networks are not explicitly defined under the IPX router rip process. It is important to remember to deny all IPX networks that EIGRP will be routing under the IPX router rip process.

EIGRP uses hello packets to establish neighbor relationships with its directly connected routers. Hello packets also allow the router to dynamically learn about new routers on directly connected networks. They are also used to identify when a neighbor becomes unreachable. Hello packets are sent to all neighbor routers every 5 seconds, by default (60 seconds default for low speed NBMA links). If a router does not receive hello packets for a specified interval, called the hold down timer, it believes that the neighbor has become unreachable. The hold down timer is three times the hello packet interval, or 15 seconds. Hello packets do not have a priority higher than any other packet. In other words, if a circuit becomes oversubscribed and packets are being dropped, the hello packets could be discarded, causing the router to lose its neighbor relationships and basically dropping from the network. Hello packets also cause an increase in WAN bandwidth utilization because of the rate at which they are sent. Increasing the interval in which hello packets are sent can alleviate these problems. The hold down timer will also have to be increased to compensate for the delay in hello packets. The recommended setting for the hold down timer is three times the hello interval. The following example shows the configuration steps that are necessary to increase the hello interval and the hold-down timer:

```
Router(config)#ipx hello-interval eigrp autonomous-system-
number seconds
Router(config)#ipx hold-time eigrp autonomous-system-number
seconds
```

The autonomous-system-number argument is the EIGRP autonomous system number used for the network. The seconds statement in the `ipx hello-interval` command is the interval between hello packets (in seconds). The default hello interval is five seconds for T1 links and higher. The `seconds` statement in the `ipx hold-time eigrp` is the hold time (in seconds). The hold time is advertised in hello packets and indicates to neighbors the length of time they should consider the sender valid. The default hold time is 15 seconds for T1 links and higher, which is three times the hello interval.

Some additional enhancements that EIGRP has over IPX RIP include the following:

■ *The support of incremental SAP updates.* NetWare servers send out SAP updates every 60 seconds regardless of whether any changes have occurred. EIGRP can be configured to send out SAP updates only when changes have occurred and will send only the changed SAP information instead of the entire SAP table.

The following command is used to configure EIGRP so that it supports this feature:

```
Router(config)#interface Serial1
Router(config-if)#ipx sap-incremental eigrp autonomouns-
system-number [rsup-only]
```

This command enables SAP updates to be sent out of Serial Interface 1 incrementally only when changes occur, instead of periodically every 60 seconds. The command is entered in interface configuration mode and the interface specified should be the interface to which the router is sending the SAP updates.

The `autonomous-system-number` argument is the EIGRP autonomous system number that is used for the network. The `[rsup-only]` is a option that allows the router to use IPX RIP for the routing updates and will only use EIGRP to transport incremental SAP updates.

■ EIGRP IPX networks support up to 224 hops, instead of the limited 15 hops of IPX RIP.

■ EIGRP IPX determines the best path to a destination by performing a calculation including the bandwidth and delay of a link. This is a much more optimal solution to determining the best path than IPX RIP's ticks and hop count.

- NLSP is a link-state routing protocol from Novell designed to overcome some of the limitations of IPX RIP and SAP. NLSP is based upon the OSI IS-IS and is similar to other link-state protocols such as OSPF for IP. The main difference between NLSP and other link-state protocols is that NLSP does not support the use of areas. Using NLSP is similar to having all routers in an OSPF network in area 0.

NLSP provides many benefits over the use of RIP and SAP. NLSP allows for better efficiency, improved routing, and greater scalability. As with other link-state protocols, every router in a NLSP network maintains an identical copy of the link-state database containing the entire topology of the network. Routers in a NLSP network send routing updates only when there is a topology change in the network. This is in contrast to routers in a RIP environment that send routing updates every 60 seconds. In addition, routers will send service-information updates only when services change, not every 60 seconds as SAP does. NLSP also provides improved routing by guaranteeing delivery using a reliable delivery protocol. NLSP can also scale up to 127 hops compared to RIP, which supports only 15 hops.

Adjacencies, similar to neighbor relationships in EIGRP, are established between routers with the use of hello packets. These adjacencies contain information regarding the link to the neighboring routers as well as attributes of the neighboring routers. Each router will then build an Adjacency database that will store the adjacency information. Adjacency-establishment can be accomplished over a WAN or a LAN. Establishing adjacencies over a WAN requires that the routers first exchange identities. This task is done with the use of IPXWAN. IPXWAN is a connection startup protocol that enables a router that is running IPX routing to connect via a serial link. IPXWAN must be configured on the serial interfaces that will be using NLSP. Once this is accomplished the routers will then send hello packets to establish their adjacency databases. Once the adjacency database is built, the routers will send *link-state packets* (LSPs) to each other to establish their link-state database. LSPs are flooded to all other NLSP devices on the network to inform them of a topology change. Each router would then update its respective link-state database. LSPs are flooded through the network to all NLSP devices every time a link state changes. LSPs are refreshed every two hours.

Besides the Adjacency database and Link-state database, NLSP also uses a Forwarding database. The Forwarding database is simply a computation calculated from the Adjacency and Link-state databases using Dijkstra's *Shortest Path First* (SPF) algorithm.

NLSP also uses a *designated router* (DR). This DR is a router that is elected to represent a network.

SAP Updates

This section describes how SAP updates work on an IPX network.

NetWare servers send SAP updates to all other servers on the network to inform them of the services they offer. Once a server receives a SAP update from another server, it will update its own SAP table and send out that new information in the next SAP update. The local router will also receive these SAP updates. The router does not forward broadcasts, so it builds its own SAP table and sends its SAP table to all of its neighbor routers. These neighbor routers will now update their SAP tables. This process allows a remote client to learn about NetWare services on a remote network. Figure C-23 steps through this process.

As show in the example, the NetWare servers send SAP updates carrying information about all of the services they have learned from other servers as well as their own services. The arrows represent the NetWare servers sending their SAP updates to the other NetWare servers as well as the router. The Los Angeles router will then send its entire SAP table to the San Jose router. The San Jose router will then update its own SAP table and the clients attached to its Token Ring segment will be able to learn about the NetWare services in Los Angeles via the San Jose router.

Where IPX Protocols Fit into the OSI Model

Figure C-24 shows how IPX/SPX and its underlying protocols map to the OSI Model. A description follows on how the protocols map to their associated OSI layer.

Figure C-23
SAP update example

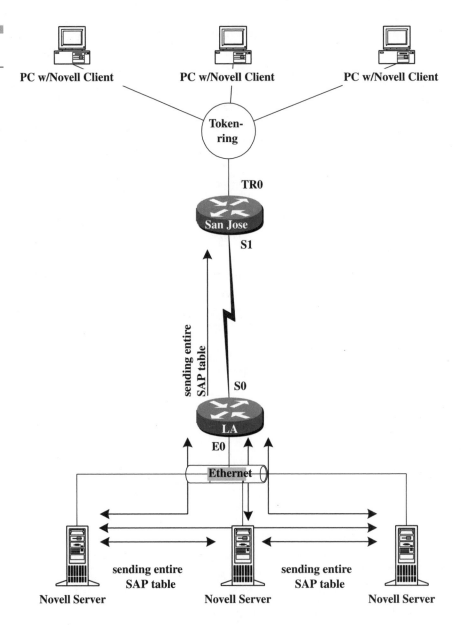

The IPX/SPX protocol suite, much like the TCP/IP protocol suite, has many underlying protocols that interact and work with each other to allow communication in an IPX/SPX environment. The MAC protocols along with IPX handle the addressing of the nodes, allowing packets to be delivered to the correct destinations. RIP, SAP, and NLSP all provide routing capabilities, storing routing information

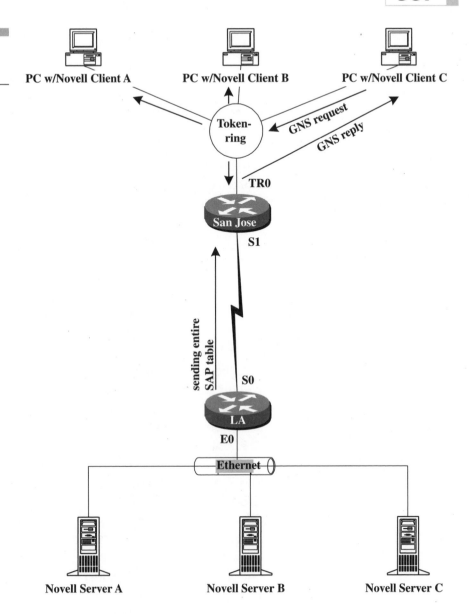

Figure C-24
IPX/SPX mapped to
the OSI model

about the network and handling the delivery process to the individual nodes. NCP is an upper-layer protocol used to handle the client-to-server interaction working with the individual processes between nodes. NCP also provides session control and packet-level error checking between NetWare workstations and the routers. SPX is a connection-oriented transport layer protocol that provides a guaranteed delivery of packets.

NetWare Addresses

NetWare uses a layer 3 IPX address to assign to nodes on the network. Each address is represented as a hexadecimal address. In other words, each digit in the address can be a value from 0–9 or A–F. The hexadecimal address is represented in the format `network.` `node`. The network number of the address is 4-bytes long (32-bits) and identifies a physical network. Each IPX network is assigned a globally unique network number. The network number is represented as eight hexadecimal numbers (for example, `C0.A8.33.00`). IPX network numbers are often represented as fewer numbers than eight because the leading zeros are not shown in the address. For example, a network number of 00.00.00.12 could be shown simply as `12`. The network administrator assigns the IPX network number to routers and servers. The clients will learn the network number dynamically upon startup of the workstation.

The node number of the IPX address consists of a 6-byte (48-bit) number. It is represented as 12 hexadecimal numbers (for example, `00.00.62.65.A3.7F`). The node number is taken from the device's MAC address. This feature enables IPX to know the MAC address of the end station it needs to communicate with when it already knows the device's IPX address. This eliminates the need to use ARP to find the MAC address. IPX requires that each node number be unique per IPX network. In other words, a node on network 10 can have a node number of 00.00.10.AF.AA.11, and a node on network 11 can have the same node number of 00.00.10.AF.AA.11. Each address is considered unique because they have different network numbers.

IPX also uses a socket number. The socket number is a 2-byte hexadecimal number that is appended after the node number to create a complete 12-byte IPX address. The socket number identifies the server process, or ultimate destination of an IPX packet. IPX uses different processes and each process has a unique socket number. A process that needs to communicate on the network will request that a socket number be assigned to the IPX packet. Once

Table C-11	Socket Number	Process
IPX socket numbers	0x451	NCP
	0x452	SAP
	0x453	RIP
	0x455	Novell NetBIOS
	0x456	Novell Diagnostics
	0x457	Serialization packet
	0x9001	NLSP
	0x9004	IPXWAN protocol

the IPX packet is received, it will pass it directly to the process. Table C-11 lists some processes with their corresponding socket numbers.

Socket numbers are dynamically used by the process and are not configured on the router. Therefore, an IPX address that is configured on a router or server will be a 10-byte (80-bit) address. The IPX address changes to the 12-byte (96-bit) length when sockets are used.

Basic NetWare Operation

The following section discusses some of the basic operations in a NetWare environment. The use of GNS as well as the interaction between RIP and SAP is thoroughly discussed.

GNS

GNS is a SAP service query to find the closest server. Clients use GNS requests when they are first booted, to find a server to login to. The client will send a GNS request and all local NetWare servers will respond with a GNS reply. The client will then choose the closest server or the first to respond to the request. Once the client is logged in to the server, it can start using resources from additional servers. If there are no local servers to log into, the router will reference its SIT, also known as a SAP table, and reply with a GNS reply specifying the IPX address of the closest remote server.

Figure C-25 steps through this process.

In the example, Workstation C gets booted and sends out a GNS request broadcast to all nodes on the Token Ring segment. There are

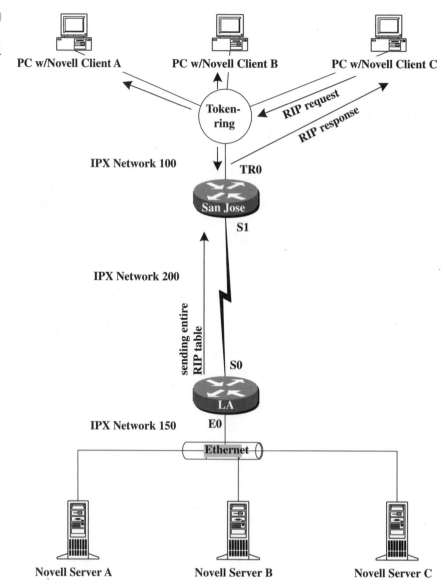

Figure C-25
GNS request example

no servers on the local segment to respond to the GNS request. Therefore, the router will respond with a GNS reply telling Workstation C about Novell Server A in Los Angeles and including the IPX address of the server.

RIP

This section discusses the operation of IPX RIP in an IPX environment.

Continuing with the previous discussion, Workstation C now knows about Novell Server A and has the associated IPX address. Workstation C does not have a route to Novell Server A, however. Therefore, a RIP broadcast will be sent from Workstation C asking for the route to network 150, in which Novell Server A resides. The San Jose router is able to process this request and send a RIP response packet indicating that it knows a route to IPX network 150. The San Jose router knows of this route because it exchanges RITs with the Los Angeles router. Figure C-26 illustrates this process.

Workstation C can now send packets to Novell Server A in order to log in and use server resources.

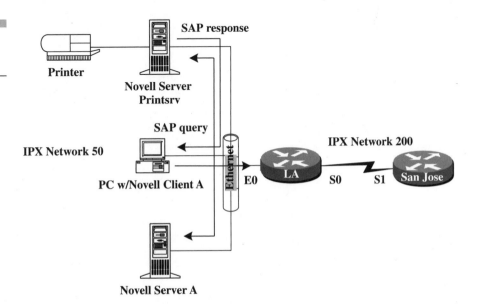

Figure C-26
IPX RIP update example

NOTE: *IPX RIP can be configured to send out RIP updates less frequently, creating less overhead and utilizing a smaller percentage of bandwidth. The command to initiate this feature is listed as follows:*

```
Router(config)#interface Serial0
Router(config-if)#ipx update interval rip 120
```

This command enabled IPX RIP updates to be sent out of Serial Interface 0 every 120 seconds.

SAP

A previous example earlier in this chapter discussed the use of SAP updates in an IPX network. This section will instead focus on how the SAP query and response is used in an IPX environment. Figure C-27 shows an example of how an SAP query and response is used.

In this scenario, the Los Angeles router has already built up its routing tables from the SAP updates of the NetWare servers. Workstation A needs to be able to print a document. Therefore, it will send out a SAP query with a packet type of 0x0001, indicating that this query is a General Service query. It will also add 0x0007 in the server type field, indicating that it is requesting print services. This SAP query is broadcast on to the local network. The local router, Los Angeles, will respond to the SAP query with a SAP response packet. The SAP response packet will include the IPX address of the Novell Server Printsrv. Workstation A now has the IPX address of the server with the requested services and will send packets directly to the server.

It is important to remember that SAPs are used prevalently in NetWare 3.x networks. With the release of NetWare 4.x, Novell servers went to a directory services structure where a client will reference an NDS server to locate services. SAP requests are still required, in the form of GNS requests, to locate an NDS server, during bootup.

■■ ■■ ■■ ■■

Figure C-27
SAP query and
response example

Ethernet II

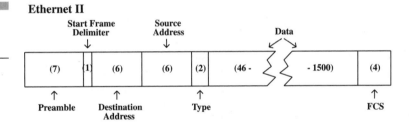

802.3

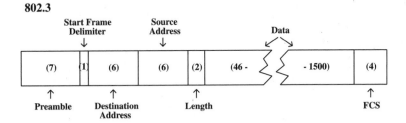

802.2

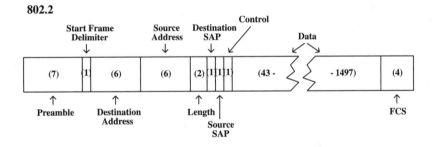

802.2 SNAP

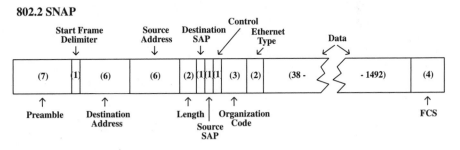

■■ ■■ ■■ ■■ ■■ ■■ ■■ ■■ ■■ ■■ ■■ ■■ ■■ ■■ ■■ ■■ ■■ ■■

NOTE: *SAP updates are sent periodically, every 60 seconds, just as RIP updates are. A problem occurs when a remote router receives a SAP update containing new services, but has yet to receive a RIP update that defines the path to this new service. The following command configures the router to send SAP updates immediately* *after RIP updates, enabling remote networks to always have a path to new network services:*

```
Router(config)#interface Serial1
Router(config-if)#ipx update sap-after-rip
```

This command enabled SAP periodic updates to be synchronized with IPX RIP updates and be sent out of Serial Interface 1.

Encapsulations of IPX

IPX can run on Ethernet, Token Ring and FDDI. Novell supports four different encapsulation types for use over these layer 2 protocols. Novell uses these encapsulation settings to package upper-layer protocol information and data into a frame. Each of these encapsulation types uses a different MAC frame. If a workstation is configured for one of these encapsulation settings and uses a certain MAC frame, it will not be able to communicate with other workstations on the same LAN, that are using a different type of MAC frame, without first going through a router.

NetWare supports the following four encapsulation types:

- 802.2—Referred to as SAP encapsulation by Cisco. This encapsulation type includes an IEEE 802.3 length field followed by a IEEE 802.2 (LLC) header.

- 802.3—Referred to as Novell-Ether encapsulation by Cisco. It is also called 802.3 raw or Novell Ethernet_802.3. This is the initial encapsulation scheme used by Novell and is also the default encapsulation on a Cisco Ethernet interface.

- Ethernet II—Referred to as ARPA encapsulation by Cisco. Ethernet II consists of an Ethernet II including Source and Destination Address fields followed by an EtherType field.

- SNAP—Referred to as SNAP encapsulation by Cisco. This encapsulation type is also referred to as Ethernet_SNAP. SNAP extends the 802.2 (LLC) header to include a type code similar to the type code in Ethernet II.

Figure C-28 illustrates the different IPX encapsulation types.

Figure C-28
IPX encapsulation types

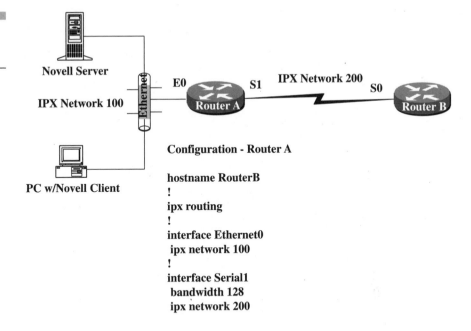

Configuration - Router A

hostname RouterB
!
ipx routing
!
interface Ethernet0
 ipx network 100
!
interface Serial1
 bandwidth 128
 ipx network 200

   Table C-12 lists the encapsulation types supported for Ethernet, Token Ring and FDDI.

Configuring IPX on Cisco Routers

This next section will show the steps that are necessary to configure IPX on a Cisco router. Secondary addresses as well as subinterfaces will be discussed.

IPX Routing   The first step to enable IPX on a Cisco router, is to enter the command `ipx routing`. This command enables the IPX routing process and allows IPX networks to be entered on the interfaces. This command also enables IPX RIP and SAP services on all interfaces with an IPX address. This command is entered in global configuration mode:

```
Router(config)#ipx routing
```

Table C-12

Encapsulation
types supported on
different interface
types

Interface Type	Encapsulation Type	IPX Frame Type
Ethernet	Novell-Ether (default)	
ARPA		
SAP		
SNAP	Ethernet_802.3	
Ethernet_II		
Ethernet_802.2		
Ethernet_Snap		
Token Ring	SAP (default)	Token-Ring
Token-Ring_Snap		
FDDI	SNAP (default)	
SAP		
Novell_FDDI	FDDI_Snap	
FDDI_802.2		
FDDI_Raw		

As described in an earlier section, a `node` can be specified and is
an optional command. In this example, the router will use the MAC
address of its Ethernet 0 card.

IPX Addresses on Interfaces

The next step to take is to enter networks for the interfaces that will
be using IPX. In this example, Ethernet Interface 0 and Serial Interface 1 on Router A will be configured:

```
RouterA(config)#interface Ethernet0
RouterA(config-if)#ipx network 100
```

```
RouterA(config)#interface Serial1
RouterA(config-if)#ipx network 200
```

In this example, Ethernet 0 is configured to use an IPX network number of 10. Serial 1 is configured to use an IPX network number of 20.

These steps are all that is required for basic IPX routing. Refer to Figure C-29.

Figure C-29
Illustrates the preceding configuration

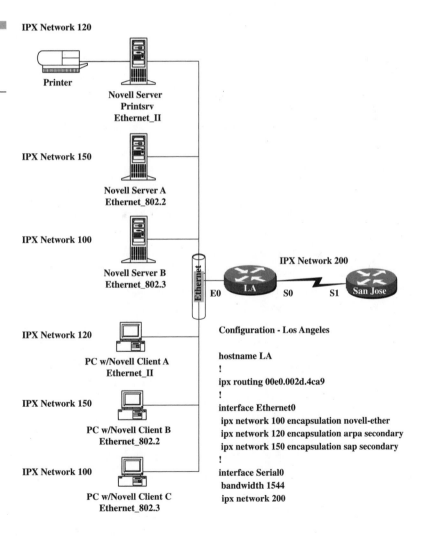

Configuration - Los Angeles

hostname LA
!
ipx routing 00e0.002d.4ca9
!
interface Ethernet0
  ipx network 100 encapsulation novell-ether
  ipx network 120 encapsulation arpa secondary
  ipx network 150 encapsulation sap secondary
!
interface Serial0
  bandwidth 1544
  ipx network 200

Multiple Networks and Encapsulation Types on One Interface

IPX enables multiple networks to be configured on a single interface. It is also possible to define different types of encapsulation settings on a single interface. The following example configures a secondary network address on an Ethernet interface:

```
Router(config)#interface Ethernet0
Router(config-if)#ipx network 150 secondary
```

The `secondary` option sets IPX network 150 as a secondary network on Ethernet 0. Multiple networks can be configured by duplicating the previous steps and entering a different IPX network number.

This next example will define a primary and multiple secondary networks that have different encapsulation settings:

```
Router(config)#interface Ethernet0
Router(config-if)#ipx network 100 encapsulation novell-ether
Router(config-if)#ipx network 120 encapsulation arpa
secondary
Router(config-if)#ipx network 150 encapsulation sap
secondary
```

Three different encapsulation settings are used on this single Ethernet interface.

The IPX networks are listed next to each workstation and server. Each encapsulation type has its own network, both on the router and the workstations and servers.

Now, in this scenario, Workstation C can communicate only with Novell Server B. They are both using the same type of encapsulation. If Workstation C needed to use Printsrv, it would have to first go through the router. Since the router is configured to support the Ethernet 802.3/Novell-Ether encapsulation, it will route the packet to Printsrv. If the router was not configured for Novell-Ether it would not be capable of forwarding the packet, and Workstation C would only be capable of communicating with Novell Server B. This principle applies to all workstations and servers.

SUMMARY

This appendix has broken down the IPX and AppleTalk protocol and described each in detail. Example designs and configurations were given for the associated routing protocols as well as the advantages and disadvantages of each. The information in this chapter is designed to give the reader a solid understanding of these protocols so that they can feel comfortable designing and implementing desktop protocols in an internetwork environment. Many Cisco certification tests include many questions regarding desktop protocols. This chapter covers the details of each protocol so that the reader can confidently answer these questions.

From the Real World

Legacy protocols still reside in many of the larger enterprise networks in the world. Although we keep thinking that some day we will get rid of them and standardize on TCP/IP it seems every network you see has a few subnets running legacy protocols. Many state and government run organizations run on legacy protocols. It is extremely valuable to understand these protocols so that you can feel comfortable working in such an environment.

APPENDIX D

Windows NT Networks

Introduction

Some of the topics that we cover in this appendix are covered in great detail, and others are not covered as much. Basic terms such as *Dynamic Host Configuration Protocol* (DHCP), *Domain Name System* (DNS), and *Windows Internet Name Resolution* (WINS) are covered. This appendix will delve into each concept and determine how each interoperates within the *Local Area Network* (LAN) environment. Then, this appendix will press on into LAN protocols such as *Transmission Control Protocol / Internet Protocol* (TCP/IP) and IPX/SPX to different LAN topologies (Ethernet, Token Ring, and FDDI). Following that, a brief rundown of Cisco routers, switches, and hubs and their functionality and adaptability will be covered to help you prepare for the Cisco *Designing Cisco Networks* (DCN) test. To put the finishing touches on this appendix, some of the more elusive aspects of the networking environment will be covered, such as remote access, managing your Windows NT/Windows 2000 LAN and Cisco hardware, and migrating your Windows NT 4.0 internetwork to Windows 2000.

What you should come away with from this appendix is a basic understanding of the key concepts and components of designing your network—whether related to a LAN or to a *Wide Area Network* (WAN) —and the ability to take those concepts and put them into practice.

Section I: Basic Terms and Definitions

Before delving into the meat and potatoes of this appendix, this section will go over some basic networking terms and how they are applied when designing your network:

- DHCP and its many components
- Static and dynamic mappings for name resolution

DHCP

DHCP is used to automate the assignment of TCP/IP addressing over the network. DHCP can also be used to provide additional configuration information to workstations, printers, and other IP devices (such as the default gateway, DNS server, and WINS server). DHCP uses UDP port 67 when the client is sending to the server and UDP port 68 when the server is sending to the client. DHCP relies on a central database and address lease assignment to hand this additional TCP/IP information to the clients. This process minimizes wasted addresses and reduces the amount of duplicate IP addresses that are issued. The alternative to a DHCP server would be to physically go to each machine on your network and hard-code them.

The DHCP system consists of three components:

- A DHCP server
- DHCP clients
- DHCP relay agents

The DHCP server can run on either Windows NT 4.0 or Windows 2000, and it must have a static IP address. DHCP servers on a Windows NT 4.0 system are managed through the DHCP Manager; on Windows 2000, however, they are managed through a DHCP MMC snap-in. Various operating systems can interact with a Windows-based DHCP server in order to include Linux and Unix. Some other operating systems that can interoperate with a Windows DHCP server are Network Client 3.0 for MS-DOS and LAN Manager versions 2.2c. Typically, you want to have at least two DHCP servers on your network for redundancy.

The DHCP clients are individual workstations, printers, or other hardware devices that are configured to obtain their IP address from the DHCP server(s).

The difficulty with DHCP comes into play when you have multiple subnets and your DHCP clients have to breach a router in order to obtain their IP address and all of the appropriate TCP/IP information (refer to the previous example). The problem lies in the protocol from which DHCP originated: BootP. BootP is a broadcast-type protocol. Routers do not pass BootP because it is a broadcast packet. In order for the DHCP process to work, you will need to configure the router to be a DHCP relay agent. To establish your router as a DHCP replay agent, the router will need to be configured to enable the forwarding of DHCP broadcast packets through the router. To perform this task, you have to place a command in the interface configuration that is closest to the client(s) who needs the address.

Let's take a look at the process as a whole before getting into the configuration of your routers. The next section of this chapter deals with the IP lease and how the DHCP server gives out the IP address. Then, the DHCP relay agent is revealed, and we will explore some of the solutions that Cisco has for supporting DHCP service.

IP Address Lease Acquisition Steps

Figure D-1 shows an example of DHCP lease steps between a DHCP client and DHCP server.

Step 1: The first time that a DHCP client boots up, it sends out a broadcast message asking for an address. This procedure is known as a DHCPDISCOVERY broadcast.

NOTE: *If the client previously had a DHCP-assigned IP address and it is restarted, the client will ask for the previously leased IP address specifically in a special DHCPREQUEST packet. At this point, the sever might or might not respond. If the server determines that the client has a valid address, it will either remain silent or ACK the DHCPREQUEST. If the server determines that the IP address is invalid, it will send a NACK. The client will then begin the discover process, but the DHCPDISCOVERY packet will still attempt to lease the same address. This situation can be a problem unless your routers are configured as DHCP relay agents. This situation is illustrated in Figure D-1.*

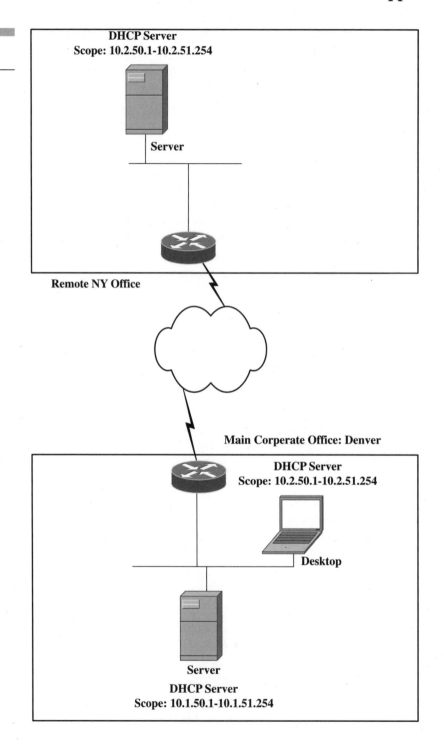

DHCP Server
Scope: 10.2.50.1-10.2.51.254

Server

Remote NY Office

Main Corperate Office: Denver

DHCP Server
Scope: 10.2.50.1-10.2.51.254

Desktop

Server

DHCP Server
Scope: 10.1.50.1-10.1.51.254

When our mobile client is in his home office in New York City, he asks for and receives an IP address from his DHCP server. That server releases a 10.2.51.17 address. When our client comes to the corporate office for a meeting and plugs in, he will automatically look to renew his 10.2.51.17 address from the local DHCP server. The local DHCP server will respond with a NACK, because the segment 10.2.x.x is not on this network and therefore is an invalid address. The mobile client will then end up attempting to renew his address with a DHCPDISCOVERY packet. If the router is not set up to forward the DHCP broadcasts across the WAN link to the sister DHCP server, the broadcast dies. The processes have errors, and the mobile client retains his 10.2.51.17 address (which of course will not work on the Denver network). Your client ends up frustrated, and your *Information Technology* (IT) department looks as if it does not understand the technology that it is using.

Step 2: Any DHCP servers on that segment respond to the request with a DHCPOFFER. The DHCP server offers an IP address. Accompanying this offer are other global options that are established at the DHCP server level and are handed out by that DHCP server, such as subnet mask, default gateway (router), lease time, WINS server address (NetBIOS name service), and the NetBIOS node type.

Step 3: The client accepts the first offer that it gets and responds with another broadcast called a DHCPREQUEST. This process confirms that the client has the IP address. The DHCPREQUEST is another broadcast packet; it is sent to everyone on the wire in order to notify all of the DHCP servers that the client is responding to the offer with an address. More than one DHCP server might have responded to the DHCPDISCOVERY with an offer and might be holding a reservation for an offer made to the client. This DHCPREQUEST enables those other DHCP servers to know that they can release their offered addresses and return them to their available pools.

Step 4: When the DHCP server's offer is accepted, it responds with a DHCP *acknowledge* (ACK) message. The offer includes the lease time and other configuration information that the DHCP server has been configured to hand to the client. Refer to Figure D-2 for a representation of this process.

Figure D-2
IP address lease steps

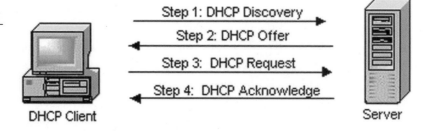

NOTE: *If the lease period expires while a client is offline and the IP address was given to another client, the DHCP server responds to the DHCPREQUEST with a* negative acknowledgment (NACK). *Once the client receives the NACK, it will send a DHCPDISCOVERY broadcast—and the process will begin again.*

DHCP Relay Agents

Because the DHCP protocol relies on network broadcast traffic for initial client configuration, a DHCP server can only service a network that is local to it. To overcome the hurdle systems, routers can be configured to forward client DHCP requests from remote subnets to a DHCP server for action.

DHCP Design Questions

Q. How many DHCP servers is enough?

A. There are many ways to configure a network; therefore, there are many answers to this simple question. But simply stated, if you have a single LAN environment that is not routed, one DHCP server is sufficient. On the other hand, if you have a LAN environment in which you have multiple routers but want WAN capability, you would want two servers. Be sure to separate your DHCP servers into different subnets to provide redundancy. Also, you will have to configure the router to act as a DHCP relay agent. If you are routed and have a WAN link, placing a DHCP server on either side of a slow WAN link is good practice.

Q. What is the DHCP scope?

A. The DHCP scope is a repository of concurrent IP addresses that are handed to the clients. The addresses are handed out by the DHCP server starting at the bottom of the scope's range and working toward the top of the range. The DHCP server will not give out previously used and expired addresses to a new client until all the unused IP addresses have been used. The scope also contains information such as the IP address of the DNS server, WINS server, and the default gateway. It also includes the lease time of the IP address within that particular scope.

Q. Are there other means to set up DHCP on my network without a server?

A. The answer is yes. Cisco offers various routers and management tools to aid in DHCP support:

- Cisco 700 series (DHCP server)
- Cisco IOS routers (BootP forwarder)
- Cisco Server Suite 1000 and DNS/DHCP Manager (DHCP server)

700 Series Router DHCP Commands

Refer to Table D-1 for a description of 700 Series router commands for DHCP.

Configuring an IOS Router to Forward DHCP (BootP) To configure the Cisco IOS to be the BootP forwarder, the command ip helper-address needs to be configured on the interface that will be forwarding the request. The general rule is to configure the command on the interface that is closest to the client. The address that is used in the ip helper-address command can be a specific

Table D-1

700 Series router
commands for
DHCP

IOS Command	Description
set dhcp address ip_address [count|all]	Configures the range of IP addresses that are served from the router's DHCP server pool. In our example, the command Set dhcp address 10.2.50.1 100 in New York's router configuration creates a pool of 100 IP addresses that the router will assign to DHCP clients. The router begins with 10.2.50.1 and sequentially serves address until the pool is exhausted.
set dhcp dns primary | secondary server_address	Specifies the IP address of the DNS that the router assigns the DHCP client to use. Up to two different addresses can be specified.
set dhcp gateway primary | secondary ip_address	Specifies the IP address of the default gateway that the router assigns the DHCP client to use. Up to two different addresses can be specified.
set dhcp netmask xxx.xxx.xxx.xxx	Specifies the IP netmask that the router assigns to the DHCP clients
set dhcp [server|relay ip_address|off]	This command enables/disables the router to act as either a DHCP server or as a DHCP relay agent. When configured as a DHCP server, the router responds to DHCP client requests directly. The router can dynamically assign the following items: IP address, subnet mask, default gateway, and DNS server. If configured as a DHCP relay agent, the router relays DHCP client requests to a separate DHCP server with the specified address.

server IP, or it can be the network address if other DHCP servers are on the destination network:

```
ip helper-address ip_address
```

Conclusion

Delving into the installation and configuration of a DHCP server is not the scope of this book or its purpose. The objective was instead to give you an overview of the basics of DHCP. After reading this section, you should have learned about 1) DHCP servers and clients using broadcast traffic to talk to one another (therefore, they must be within the same segment unless a DHCP relay agent has been established to enable the routing of the broadcast traffic) and 2) the scope, which contains general network information such as DNS, WINS, and the default gateway.

Name Resolution

Name resolution is the process by which a user-friendly name is translated, or resolved, to an IP address. To translate the NetBIOS or host name into an IP address, the server needs to have a mapping. This mapping is then stored in either a static or dynamic table. In a static table, mappings are stored in one of two text files: the Hosts file or the LMHosts file. With a dynamic table, the mappings are stored in the DNS or WINS servers. Currently, applications in Windows 2000 use the host name to resolve the IP address, and some older software packages (such as Windows NT and Windows 9x) still use NetBIOS names.

Static IP Mapping

Static mappings are stored locally on each computer, and each is customizable. Each user can create any amount of entries. It is difficult to maintain and update static tables if the tables change often, however, or if they contain a large number of IP addresses. The two static files are the Hosts file and the Lmhosts file.

Hosts File   The Hosts file is a text document that you can find at `c:\winnt\system32\drivers\etc` (in both Windows NT and Windows 2000). This file contains IP address-to-host name mappings. When configuring the Hosts file, you should remember a few key points:

- Multiple host names can be assigned to the same IP address.

- Entries are case sensitive (depending on the platform). Hosts file entries that are running on Windows 2000 or Windows NT version 4.0 are not case sensitive.

Lmhosts File   The Lmhosts file is also a text file, and it too can be found at `c:\winnt\system32\drivers\etc` (in both Windows NT and Windows 2000). This file contains IP address-to-NetBIOS mappings. A portion of the Lmhosts file is preloaded into memory and is referred to as the NetBIOS name cache.

Dynamic IP Mapping   Dynamic tables have one major advantage over static tables: they are updated automatically. To accomplish this automatic update, the dynamic tables use two services: DNS and WINS.

These two tables provide the same functionality as the Hosts and Lmhosts file but without the added hassle of manually updating them.

DNS   DNS is used by the applications on the client workstations, hosts/servers, routers, and other devices to resolve the dotted-decimal format of the IP address into an easy-to-remember, people-friendly phrase (for example, 198.133.219.25 is the same as `www.cisco.com`, and remembering `www.cisco.com` is easier for most people).

Can an IP network survive without a DNS server? The answer is yes. Each client would need to know every other client's address on the network, however. If something were changed afterward, all clients would have to be updated. So yes, your network can survive without the aid and benefit of a DNS server. Does this author recommend it? The answer is, "Absolutely not!" With the added benefit of DNS, clients can be relocated and keep their same names.

DNS Domains   To aid computers in talking to each other, computers are given names with a name space. DNS is composed of many components that interoperate to provide the end user with seamless name resolution. The specific name space defines the rules for naming the computer and indicates how those names will be resolved into IP addresses. This resolution is accomplished through a name-resolution service.

There are two different kinds of name spaces and name-resolution methods used in Microsoft Windows NT 4.0 and Windows 2000. In Windows NT, NetBIOS names are resolved through the use of WINS and/or DNS (also, Hosts and/or LMHosts files were used). In Windows 2000, NetBIOS names are still used to identify your computer; however, instead of using WINS or Hosts files, you are using DNS exclusively.

First, understand that a DNS domain and a Microsoft administrative domain are not synonymous. Microsoft domains, such as Windows NT 4.0 and Windows 2000, are there to primarily share resources, to implement security procedures, and to provide centralized user administration. DNS domains operate more on the organizational level. The DNS namespace functions much like a file system. There is a root level (the file cabinet, if you will) with subdomains beneath it. Each domain functions like a drawer in the file cabinet in that the domain might hold individual files and subfolders. A diagram of the hierarchy looks like an inverted tree, as illustrated in Figure D-3.

The *Internet Assigned Numbers Authority* (IANA) controls the domains at the top of the tree, such as .com and .edu. The IANA delegates the task of providing second-level domain names to those who

Figure D-3
DNS domain model

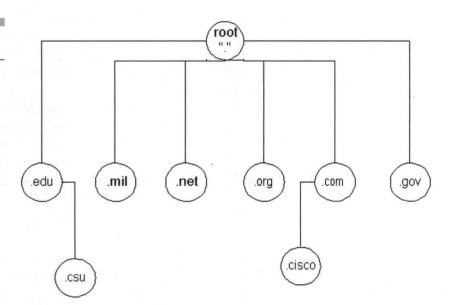

request them. Second-level domain names are granted to individual organizations on a first-come, first-served basis. After a second-level domain name has been granted, subdomains are created within the name space of the second-level domain. If the accounting department at CSU had its own Web server, for example, it might look like `www.accounting.csu.edu`. A DNS path that includes both the host and the intervening domains up to the root is known as the *Fully Qualified Domain Name* (FQDN).

DNS Components

A zone is an area that has one or more domains and/or subdomains for which a DNS name server can resolve addresses. When you boil it down, the essence of a zone is a file that is stored on the DNS server. This file is known as the zone file, and it contains information about a portion of the domain namespace. The server that contains the master zone file for a domain is known as the primary DNS server. For each windows domain, only one DNS server acts as the primary name server. Other DNS servers are referred to as secondary name servers. The primary name server has absolute authority over the zone information; it has the final say-so on address-to-domain name mapping. Secondary name servers store a copy of the primary name server's zone and can be configured to receive a periodic zone transfer from the primary name server. Also, the secondary name server can act as an authoritative source for name-resolution requests for any DNS client.

Resource records are the smallest unit in the DNS database. They are what make up the zone files, and each individual record performs some IP address/host-name mapping, sets DNS functionality parameters, or provides information about advertised services. Table D-2 contains some of the more common resource records.

Name Resolution

Name resolution is what DNS is all about. Any DNS client can query a DNS host by using three types of queries: recursive, iterative, and inverse:

Table D-2

DNS record types

DNS Record Type (Abbreviation)	Description
Host (A)	Supports iterative requests; contains a host name and corresponding IP address
Name server (NS)	Identifies a server that can respond to DNS queries for the zone
Canonical name (Cname)	Identifies another name as an alias for a server
Mail exchange (MX)	Contains a list of one or more e-mail servers that are configured to receive e-mail for a specific domain
Pointer record (PTR)	Contains IP addresses and hosts and supports reverse lookups
Start of Authority (SOA)	Identifies the primary server that is responsible for the zone

- *Recursive queries* These queries are the most common type. This query is sent from a DNS client to the DNS name server, requesting that the DNS name server translate a host name to an IP address.

- *Iterative queries* This query is sent between DNS hosts and is used when either the primary or one of the secondary name servers is incapable of servicing a DNS client request.

- *Inverse queries (or reverse lookup)* This situation occurs when a DNS client inquires to a DNS host to resolve an IP address to a host name.

WINS

WINS is similar to DNS in that it is a naming service that maps host names to IP addresses. The names that it maps, however, are not host names (like DNS). Rather, they are NetBIOS names. Granted, they should be one in the same (for example, your host name should reflect your NetBIOS names, and vice-versa). In some cases, however, this situation is not true. WINS keeps a dynamically changing database that gives the client the capability to register a name space and to resolve the names of other systems within the network. WINS uses the Microsoft jet database engine to provide this functionality.

The main difference is that WINS does its job to reduce and/or eliminate the need for broadcast traffic that is generated by NetBIOS-based networks. Because NetBIOS was originally designed to run on bridged networks, there was no system in place to support its use on routed networks. WINS was designed as the DNS of NetBIOS. WINS serves as a central repository for the NetBIOS names and IP addresses. Using WINS a client can enable you to look up a particular node by name and receive its IP address without a broadcast being transmitted across the network.

Database Maintenance

Because records are added to the WINS database dynamically, it follows that records would be capable of being removed dynamically, also. Each record that enters the database is given certain properties that will determine the length of time that particular record will remain within the database. This situation is like a *time to live* (TTL) for WINS records. Table D-3 covers these properties.

There are several very important tasks that need to be accomplished in order to keep your WINS servers functioning properly:

- *Scavenging* In a multi-WINS server infrastructure, records that reference released and removed clients that were originally

Table D-3

WINS record properties

Property	Function
Renew interval	Determines how often a client will reregister its name in the database (six days is the default)
Extinction interval	Sets the amount of time between when a record is marked as Released and when it is marked as Extinct in the database. Again, the default is six days.
Extinction timeout	Determines how long a record is extinct before it is eligible for scavenging (the default for this property is six days, as well)
Verification interval	Determines how long a WINS server will keep a record that was replicated to it before it queries the other WINS servers (if any) to verify that the record is still valid (default is 24 hours)

registered at other WINS servers accumulate in the database of each WINS server. At regular intervals, the current database should be scavenged to remove information that is not current. Scavenging should happen automatically according to an interval that is established in the server properties; however, should you need to scavenge more often (or on a special occasion), choose Scavenge from the action menu in WINS Server Manager.

- *Deleting and tombstoning entries in the WINS database* There might be times when waiting for the expiration of a WINS entry is not an option (for instance, if a system changes an IP address and is then turned off without the opportunity to release its name from the WINS database). Upon rebooting, the system comes up with a new IP address and the same name and then tries to register itself. The WINS server denies the registration, because it already has an entry for that name but has a different IP address. To repair this situation, you need to delete the record or change the IP address back to what is reflected in the WINS server database.

- *Checking database consistency* Part of maintaining the database is regularly checking it for consistency. This process compares the records that it receives via replication in its database with the original records that are being stored on other WINS servers.

Section II: Planning Your Network

Windows 2000 uses TCP/IP by default. If you plan on working in native mode (in other words, all domain controllers are Windows 2000), then Active Directory requires the use of TCP/IP as well. There are other protocols supported by Windows 2000, such as NWLink (IPX/SPX), NetBEUI, and AppleTalk; however, because TCP/IP is the most widely used LAN protocol and is the default with Windows 2000, we will focus our attentions there.

There are three steps involved with the initial planning of your physical network and its needs:

- *Take stock of your current situation*   In other words, determine what you currently have in place (such as the number of segments and hosts, which protocols your company is using in the infrastructure, and what hardware is used to separate the company into VLANs and/or broadcast domains such as routers, switches, hubs, and so on). At this point in your survey of current business capacity, you need to ask yourself two questions:

  - Does our current infrastructure support the company's current business requirements?
  - Will it support future growth and expansion?

  When you have answered both of these questions, you can go forward with Step 2:

- Determine what network capabilities are needed to support current and future business requirements. Will you need Internet access and/or a remote dial-in? Will you need support for other LAN protocols, such as NetBEUI or IPX/SPX?

- If you plan on running Windows 2000 in native mode, you will need to determine how your subnets will be used to divide your network into physical sites. A site is defined as a collection of TCP/IP subnets that share a high-bandwidth connection. Active Directory uses sites in your network to control logon traffic, replication traffic, and access to network resources. Please note that when you plan your Windows 2000 domain, it is not as straightforward as it was with Windows NT.

Networking Fundamentals

LAN Topologies

There are three types of LAN topologies: Ethernet, Token Ring, and FDDI. Each of these protocols has it own unique advantages and disadvantages and each has different aspects to add to your networking environment. All three will be covered because it is useful to have at least a basic understanding of these topologies when you're designing and building your network.

Ethernet The Ethernet was originally designed to move data at speeds of up to 10Mbps. All of the devices on an Ethernet segment are unaware of each other or of their intentions to use the media. Therefore, it is possible for two devices to send data at the same time on the same wire. To avoid this situation, Ethernet uses a *Carrier Sense Multiple Access with Collision Detection* (CSMA/CD) protocol. The basic algorithm for CSMA/CD follows these basic steps:

1. Listen to find out whether a frame is being received.
2. If no other frame is on the Ethernet, send the information.
3. If another frame is on the Ethernet, wait and then listen again.
4. While sending, if a collision occurs, stop, wait, and listen again.

Ethernet media is the next hurdle. Table D-4 summarizes the various kinds of Ethernet cabling media.

Fast Ethernet or 100BaseT Fast Ethernet is similar to standard Ethernet because it utilizes CSMA/CD over Category 5 UTP. As with basic Ethernet, Fast Ethernet interconnects by using hubs, switches, and repeaters. The major difference is that 100BaseT transmits data

Table D-4

Ethernet cabling media

Standard	Maximum Cable Length	Type of Cable
10B5	500m[1]	50 Ohm thick coaxial cable
10B2	185m[1]	50 Ohm thin coaxial cable
10BT	100m[1]	UTP
10BFL	2000m[2]	Fiber
100BTx	100m[2]	UTP/STP
100BT4	100m[2]	UTP/4 pair
100BFx	400m[2]	Fiber
1000BT	100m[2]	UTP/STP (4 pair)
100BFx	400m[2]	Fiber

[1] For entire bus.

[2] From device to hub/switch.

at 100Mbps. There are various kinds of 100BaseT. Fast Ethernet that runs over Category 3 cabling by using four pairs of wires is called 100BaseT4. Fast Ethernet that runs over fiber is called 100BaseFx. Refer to Table D-4 for cable lengths and types. Ethernet can be run over a backbone technology or over a star topology. You will need networking gear that supports 100Base T standard in order to take advantage of the higher speed. Refer to Figure D-4 for information about LAN topologies.

Token Ring   Token Ring uses a token-passing protocol to regulate the flow of data onto the ring. All devices are logically configured in a ring, and a frame, called a token, is passed around that ring. Token Ring runs on either 4Mbps or 16Mbps. A basic Token Ring network consists of ring stations that are connected to a concentrator that uses Category 5 UTP or STP cabling that is located centrally in a wiring closet. Larger rings can be built by connecting multiple Token Ring hubs by using specifically designed ports called *Ring In* (RI) and *Ring Out* (RO) ports. Figure D-5 shows the basic layout of a token ring network.

There are three frame types used by Token Ring networks: token, *Media Access Control* (MAC), and *Logical Link Control* (LLC):

- Tokens are used to control the transmission of data onto the ring. There is only one token on a ring at a time. If a ring station needs to transmit data, it must first claim the free token (and then it can transmit).
- MAC frames are used by the ring stations to communicate with other ring stations. These frames are used to control the operation of the ring and to report errors.
- LLC frames are the frames that contain the user's data. LLC frames use protocols such as TCP/IP and IPX/SPX to transmit the user data.

Because only one ring station can transmit data at a time, there is no need for a contention protocol such as CSMA/CD. There is always the chance that a clumsy user, a bad *Network Interface Card* (NIC), or broken cable can cause errors and/or packet loss. To combat these eventualities, Token Ring has a troubleshooting method called bea-

Figure D-4
LAN topologies

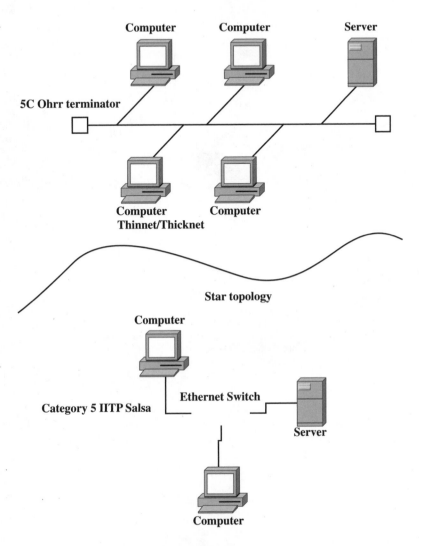

coning that attempts to identify and correct hardware errors. When a ring station sees a loss of signal on the ring, it sends a beacon frame containing its address and the address of its *Nearest Addressable Upstream Neighbor* (NAUN). When a beacon occurs, the network tries to reconfigure itself by sending the traffic in the opposite direction. If the beacon frame travels the entire ring and reaches the NAUN, that

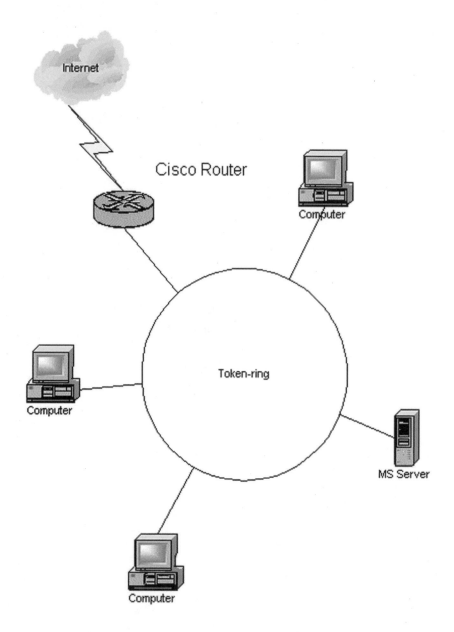

NAUN station will remove the frame and try to reinsert it onto the ring. The theory behind the beaconing frame and the NAUN is that if the frame gets all the way back to the NAUN, the problem must then reside with the NAUN. The reinsertion process includes a self-test that should cause the faulty station to remain off the network.

FDDI   FDDI is a token-passing protocol that uses fiber cabling to transmit data at 100Mbps. There are several major differences between Token Ring and FDDI:

1. FDDI is faster than Token Ring (100Mbps as opposed to 16Mbps).
2. FDDI outdistances Token Ring networks. With fiber, you can run many kilometers before needing a repeater.
3. FDDI is comprised of two parallel rings—the primary and secondary rings—which connect each station to its neighbors via two links. Each ring transmits data in the opposite direction. Only one ring is operational at a time. During normal operations, the secondary ring sits idle until the primary ring breaks.

Distance capabilities and fault tolerance make FDDI an ideal media for network backbones. See Figure D-6 for a logical FDDI diagram.

Open Systems Interconnectivity (OSI) Reference Model

Before preceding to the next section, the OSI reference model should be covered briefly. OSI is a well-defined set of protocol specifications that has many options for accomplishing the same task. The OSI reference model was developed in 1978 by the *International Standardization Organization* (ISO) in order to specify a standard that could be used for the development of open systems and for a comparative measure against other communication systems. The computer network systems that are designed according to the OSI framework speak the same language and use similar or compatible methods of communication. The OSI model consists of seven layers, as shown in Table D-5. The layers (working from the bottom up) are as follows: physical, data link, network, transport, session, presentation, and application.

Lower-Level Protocols

The lower-level protocols are comprised of layers 1 and 2 of the OSI reference model (the physical and data link layer). These two layers

Figure D-6
Logical FDDI diagram

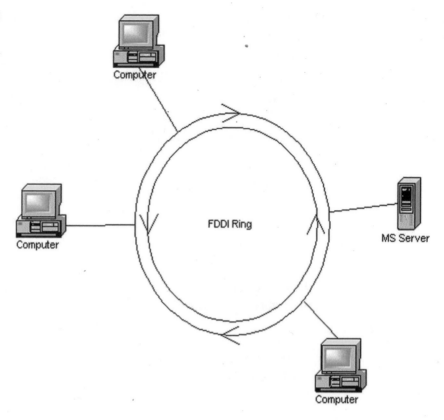

Table D-5

The seven-layer
OSI model

Physical

Data link

Network

Transport

Session

Presentation

Application

define much of the physical network. The physical layer determines the cabling type (either fiber, twisted pair, or coaxial). The data link layer, layer 2, determines which topology will be used (refer to the LAN Topologies section of this book).

Upper-Level Protocols

What are upper-level protocols? They are the lower-level protocols (for instance, the media that you are using and the topology that you have chosen) that form the foundation upon which the upper-level protocols run. They are comprised of TCP/IP, IPX/SPX, and NetBEUI, and they typically run from layer 3 (the network layer) upward. Table D-6 shows where they sit on the OSI framework. From this table, you can see that IP and IPX both reside at layer 3 of the OSI reference model (which is used for addressing), and TCP and SPX sit on layer 4 for end-to-end transport.

TCP/IP

TCP/IP is a protocol suite (a group of protocols working together). TCP/IP operates at the upper five layers of the OSI reference model. The lowest level that it ever sees is layer 3, which is the network layer. Table D-7 shows some of the major protocols in the TCP/IP suite and at which layer of the OSI reference model they operate.

Table D-6

Upper-level
protocols and
corresponding
OSI layers

Protocol	Layer of the OSI Reference Model
TCP	Layer 4—transport
IP	Layer 3—network
IPX	Layer 3—network
SPX	Layer 4—transport

Table D-7

Examples of other
protocols in the
TCP/IP suite

Protocol	Name	Layer
FTP	File Transfer Protocol	layer 7
HTTP	Hypertext Transfer Protocol	layer 7
IP	Internet Protocol	layer 3
NFS	Network File System	layer 7
SMTP	Simple Mail Transfer Protocol	layer 7
SNMP	Simple Network Management Protocol	layer 7
TCP	Transmission Control Protocol	layer 4
UDP	User Datagram Protocol	layer 4

Due to its popularity and widespread acceptance on the Internet
and in enterprise computing, it is no wonder that all Cisco hardware
—which makes up more than 90 percent of the Internet backbone—
includes support for the TCP/IP suite. Along with Cisco, Microsoft
has joined in praising TCP/IP. Windows 2000 installs TCP/IP as the
default protocol when you install networking.

IPX/SPX

Inter-Network Packet Exchange/Sequenced Packet Exchange (IPX/
SPX) was developed by Novell, Inc. for use with Netware. IPX/SPX
was derived from Xerox's XNS protocol.

IPX operates at the network layer and handles the addressing of
the network devices and keeps track of the routes within the IPX
network. SPX resides on the transport layer and provides for the
reliability of the end-to-end communication between stations.

IPX/SPX shares information about the network via the *Service
Advertising Protocol* (SAP). Services use SAP to advertise themselves onto the network. Workstations use the information that is
contained within the SAP packet to obtain information about the
network address of the servers. By default, SAP is broadcast every
60 to 90 seconds.

NetBEUI

NetBIOS Extended User Interface (NetBEUI) is a broadcast-based, non-routable protocol that requires no configuration. All name resolution over NetBEUI is accomplished by NetBIOS. IBM developed NetBIOS in the mid-1980s as a common *Application Programming Interface* (API). An API is a set of functions or procedures for a programming language that enables the application to use services that other software provides.

NetBEUI was developed by Microsoft to communicate within a LAN environment. NetBEUI locates other devices on the LAN by using NetBIOS machine names. To locate another device on the network, the sending device broadcasts onto the network—looking for a specific NetBIOS name. Every device on the LAN looks at the broadcast packet to see whether it is intended for them. The device with the broadcast name responds to the source device, and the sending device then sends the data onto the LAN with a specific address.

NetBEUI is a simple, quick, and efficient protocol if it is used on smaller networks. Most of the network overhead is consumed by the NetBIOS announcement broadcasts. As your network (and the number of nodes) increases, the constant broadcasts will severely hinder your network by increasing latency and delaying response times.

IP Routing Protocols

We have talked about LAN protocols such as TCP/IP and IPX/SPX. Following that discussion, a brief overview of the routing protocols and their advantages and disadvantages will follow.

At its most basic definition, routing is the process of moving data between LANs in order to facilitate communication across the street or across the nation. To accomplish this task, you need to connect your LANs with routers. Routers use a routing table to determine what path a packet should take to its destination. Routing tables can either be updated manually or dynamically (if you have them configured to use either routing protocols). Routing protocols are used by routers to encapsulate the network protocol (TCP/IP and IPX/SPX) and to send it over the WAN link. There are two different types of routing protocols: distance-vector protocols and link-state protocols.

Distance-Vector Protocols With distance-vector routing protocols, the routes are advertised as vectors of direction and hop count. The hop count is usually limited to 15 hops. The direction is the next-hop router to which the packet will be forwarded.

These distance-vector routing protocols use algorithms that require each router to send the entire routing table or partial routing table updates to its neighbors. Based on this information, the router builds a new routing table and sends it to its neighbors.

The following list shows the distance-vector protocols. In a Microsoft Windows environment (or IP environment), you will not use the some of the protocols that are listed here (such as IPX RIP or RMTP, to name a few):

- IP RIP
- Cisco's *Interior Gateway Routing Protocol* (IGRP)
- IPX RIP
- AppleTalk *Router Table Maintenance Protocol* (RMTP)
- DEC DNA Phase IV
- Xerox's *XNS Routing Information Protocol* (XNS RIP)

A router that uses the distance-vector protocol will broadcast packets to its immediate neighbors concerning the network topology about every 60 to 90 seconds. Table D-8 lists the advantages and disadvantages of using distance-vector protocols.

Link-State Protocols When a router is configured to use a link-state routing protocol, the router gathers information about the pro-

Table D-8	Advantages	Disadvantages
Advantages/ disadvantages of distance-vector protocols	Easy to configure	Slow to converge
	Widely accepted	15 hop count limit
	Low resource requirement on the router	No VLSM capabilities

tocol (such as the IP address, their connected links, and the state of each of those links). That information is then forwarded from router to router within the network via a packet called a *Link-State Adver-tisement* (LSA). With the information garnered from this LSA, all routers note the change and immediately recompute their routes by using their link-state algorithm. The following list describes the link-state routing protocols:

- IP *Open Shortest Path First* (OSPF)
- CLNS and IP *Intermediate System to Intermediate System* (IS-IS)
- DEC DNA Phase V
- IPX *Netware Link-Service Protocol* (NLSP)

Table D-9 summarizes the advantages and disadvantages of using link-state routing protocols.

IP Routing Protocols from a Design Perspective

The main items that you should be concerned with when it comes to designing your network are as follows:

- How the routing tables are updated
- How quickly those updates are propagated throughout the network in order to maintain proper data flow

It was briefly mentioned in the beginning of this section that rout-ing tables can either be updated manually or dynamically. To update them manually, you need personnel who have time to spare. For dynamic updates, you need to configure the router to use one of the

Table D-9	Advantages	Disadvantages
Advantages/ disadvantages of link-state protocols	Faster convergence	Higher CPU and memory requirements
	No hop-count limit	Difficult to configure
	VLSM	Reduced bandwidth consumption

various types of routing protocols. Another thing to consider when deciding to update manually or dynamically is that when updating manually, you need to be aware that a problem has occurred and then have the staff on hand update the routing tables on all of the routers within your company. If you are a small company, this situation might not be an issue for you; however, if you are part of a global company, this situation can be a requirement that is impossible to maintain. Alternatively, you can ease router management by implementing either distance-vector protocols or link-state protocols.

Section III: What to Use

After determining the basic LAN topology and wiring scheme for your organization, you need to be able to make an educated decision as to the various components that you will have to purchase (such as routers, switches, hubs, Remote Access Services, and so on). This chapter will give insight as to the benefits of each hardware component and will list several of its capabilities.

Hardware

The goal of any network designer is to have a network that is configured to perform effectively and at its highest level. You will want to get your network hardware to fit within the following parameters:

- Features
- Functionality
- Scalability
- Cost

To reach this goal, you need to be able to choose the correct tool for the job. Cisco offers a wide variety of tools that will satisfy all situations. You should check and double-check the features, functionality, and scalability of the hardware that you are about to purchase. Many times, MIS managers purchase a switch that fits their current budget and has the required functionality but is not scalable. Then, six months later, they have to trade it in and get more hardware that fits the company's goals. Think long-term when purchasing the hardware for your company. The next session will cover tools such as routers, switches, and hubs and their functionality and adaptability.

Routers   Routers make forwarding decisions based on the network layer address. In addition to forwarding packets, routers control collision domains and broadcast domains. Each router has at least two interfaces: one Ethernet and one serial. Each interface is a separate broadcast domain that is defined by a subnet and a subnet mask.

In addition to segmenting network traffic into collision and broadcast domains, routers are capable of forwarding packets of routed protocols such as IP, IPX, Decnet, and AppleTalk.

Routers provide the following benefits:

■ They enable communication across WAN links.

■ They enable communication via various protocols.

■ They enable the partitioning of broadcast domains.

■ They have some security features, such as IP access lists.

We now present an easy-to-read reference table for various Cisco routers and their functionalities:

Product	Features
Cisco 700 Series	ISDN router
	■ Cisco 76x models: one Ethernet port (10BaseT) and a one-port BRI (NT1 models available)
	■ Cisco 77x models: four Ethernet ports (10BaseT) and two analog telephone ports (NT1 models available)
	■ Supports up to 30 users
Cisco 800 Series	ISDN, IDSL, and serial routers with Cisco IOS technologies
	■ One-port BRI (optional NT1), IDSL, or one-port serial
	■ Optional four-port Ethernet hub with two analog telephone ports (ISDN models)
	■ Advanced security features

(continues)

Cisco 1000 Series	Fixed-configuration desktop access router
	▪ One-port Ethernet
	▪ One-port BRI (optional NT1) or one-port sync or async serial
Cisco 1400 Series	ADSL routers
	▪ Either one-port Ethernet (10BaseT) and one-port ATM-25 (1401) or one-port Ethernet (10BaseT)
	▪ Designed for DSL access up to 8Mbps
	▪ Part of Cisco's end-to-end DSL solutions
Cisco 1600 Series	Modular desktop access router
	▪ One- or two-port Ethernet (10BaseT)
	▪ One-port BRI (optional NT1) or one-port sync or async serial
	▪ One *WAN Interface Card* (WIC) slot
Cisco 1700 Series	Flexible, secure, modular-access routers
	▪ One-port autosensing 10/100 Fast Ethernet LAN
	▪ Modular slots support a wide variety of WAN and analog voice interface cards.
	▪ Supports secure Internet, intranet, and extranet access as well as new WAN applications (including VPNs, integrated voice/data such as *Voice-over-IP* (VoIP), and broad-band services)
Cisco 2500 Series	Fixed and modular configuration access routers and servers
	▪ Single or dual LAN; Ethernet or Token Ring
	▪ Router/hub or access server
	▪ Single, dual serial, or high-density serial models
Cisco 2600 Series	Modular access router, voice-data gateway, and dial access server
	▪ Single or dual LAN (Ethernet, 10/100 Mbps Ethernet, Token Ring and mixed Ethernet, and Token Ring options)
	▪ Shares WAN interface cards and network modules with Cisco 1600, 1700, and 3600 series
	▪ Wide variety of media support, including async and sync serial, ISDN, fractional and channelized T1/E1, Ethernet, analog modems, and ATM

Cisco 3300 Series	Carrier-Class SONET Access Device
	▪ Fully redundant platform
	▪ Combines SONET reliability and layer 3 awareness
	▪ Ethernet interfaces support a variety of service interfaces that can be configured for bridging or routing and that can connect to a local LAN via analog modems and ATM.
Cisco 3600 Series	Modular, High-Density Access Router
	▪ Two-, four-, and six-slot models
	▪ Wide variety of media support, including async, sync serial, ISDN channelized T1/E1, Ethernet, Fast Ethernet, Token Ring, digital modems, and ATM
	▪ Voice/fax-over-IP or Frame Relay
Cisco MC3810	Compact, Low-Cost, Multi-Service Access Router
	▪ One-port Ethernet and two-port serial
	▪ Six-port analog or 24/30 port digital voice
	▪ Data, voice, and video integration
Cisco 4000 Series	Modular, High-Density Router
	▪ Three slots for all models
	▪ Choice of 100Mhz or 133Mhz processor
	▪ Wide variety of media support, including async, sync serial, ISDN channelized T1/E1, Ethernet, Fast Ethernet, Token Ring, FDDI, HSSI, and ATM
Cisco AS5300 Series	Hybrid Async and ISDN Access Servers
	▪ Three NIC slots
	▪ Four-port and eight-port PRI (T1/E1) and four-port serial
	▪ Up to 240 integrated modems
Cisco AS5300/Voice	High-Performance T1/E1 VoIP Gateway
	▪ Four T1/E1 ports (96/120 /voice/fax channels) and four-port serial
	▪ One 10/100 Fast Ethernet and one 10BaseT Ethernet
	▪ G.711, G.729, G.729a, G.723.1, G.726, and G.728 voice codecs and 14.4Kbps Group III fax relay

(continues)

Cisco AS5800 Series	High-End Dial Products
	▪ Hybrid, asynchronous, and ISDN termination
	▪ Accommodate both mobile and high-bandwidth requirements

Cisco 6400 Series	A Carrier-Class Aggregation Device for Termination of a Large Number of Subscribers and Multi-Domain Services in a POP or Central Office
	▪ Up to 14,000 subscribers terminated per platform
	▪ L2TP, LAC/LNS, multi-domain services
	▪ Full ATM capability

Cisco 6700 Series	Integrated Access Platform for Circuit-Switched and Packet-Based Voice/Data Traffic
	▪ Modular, scalable, high platform that delivers end-to-end integrated voice and data services
	▪ Five-line card slots for RT and CPE applications (Cisco 6705)
	▪ 32-line card slots for CO and RT applications (Cisco 6732)

Cisco 7100 Series	Large Branch and Central Site VPN Router
	▪ Comprehensive suite of VPN services, including encryption, tunneling, and firewall and bandwidth management
	▪ Embedded I/O for ease of deployment
	▪ Service modules slots for IPSec and PPTP encryption coprocessing

Cisco 7200 Series	WAN-Edge Router for Intelligent Services, Modularity, High Performance, and Scalability
	▪ Fully modular, chassis-based
	▪ Four- or six-slot models and choice of three system processors
	▪ Wide variety of LAN and WAN options, including Ethernet, Fast Ethernet, 100VG-AnyLAN, Token Ring, FDDI, serial, ISDN, HSSI, ATM, and packet over DS3/E3

Cisco 7500 Series	Premier High-End Services-Enabled Core and WAN Aggregation Router for Voice, Video, and Data in Enterprise and Service Provider Applications
	▪ Five-, seven-, and 13-slot models
	▪ One-, two-, or four-bus models offering 1Gbps, 2Gbps, or 4Gbps backplanes

■ Wide variety of LAN and WAN options, including Ethernet, Fast Ethernet, Gigabit Ethernet, Token Ring, FDDI, serial, ISDN, HSSI, ATM, and packet over DS3/E3

Cisco 12000 Series	Scalable *Gigabit Switch Router* (GSR)
	■ 8-, 12-, or 16-slot models
	■ 40, 60, or 80Gbps switching fabric, depending on the model
	■ Optimized for IP
	■ Carrier class

Switches

There are two types of switches: layer 2 and layer 3. A layer 2 switch is an alternative to a hub. This type of switch alleviates congestion on your network by segmenting your network into collision domains.

Layer 3 switches are a hybrid between a switch and a router. In other words, they have the functionality of performing as a data link layer switch and as a network router. Layer 3 switches are capable of running routing protocols and passing information to neighboring switches and routers. The individual ports can be configured into their own collision domains, and each interface can be grouped into subnets for VLANs.

Switches provide the following benefits:

■ Reduction of collisions

■ Control of broadcast and flooding

■ Segmentation of traffic by using VLANs

The Cisco 1548 Series Micro Switch has one important characteristic: eight 10/100 auto-sensing ports.

The Cisco 1900 Series has the following benefits:

■ 10- or 24-port 10BaseT; 2-port 100BaseTX; or 1-port 100BaseFX and 1-port 100BaseTX

■ Manageable

■ Supports VLANs

■ Some security features

The Cisco 2900 Series has the following features:

- 8-, 12-, or 24-port 10/100 auto-sensing; two-port 100BaseTX or two-port 100 BaseFX
- Two modules (2916M XL and 2924M XL only)
- Advanced security
- High density supports VLANs

The Cisco 4000 Series has the following features:

- No fixed ports
- Three-slot chassis (one slot for the supervisor engine and the remaining two slots for switched port modules); one chassis can support up to 96 10/100 Fast Ethernet or up to 36 Gigabit Ethernet
- Provides a wide range of port densities from 10/100 to 1000Mbps
- Supports layer 2 switching

The Cisco 5000 Series has the following features:

- No fixed ports
- 2, 5, 9, or 13 modules (depending on the model)
- Supports up to 384 user ports
- High performance
- Full system redundancy

The Cisco 6000 Series has the following features:

- No fixed ports
- Six- and nine- slot versions; support for up to 384 10/100 Ethernet, 192 100FX Fast Ethernet, and up to 130 Gigabit Ethernet ports
- Provides layer 3 functionality to include QoS, security, and traffic management

The Cisco 8000 Series has the following features:

- One-port Ethernet; two-port serial
- 5 to 13 modular slots

- Provides layer 2 and layer 3 functionality
- Aggregates throughput of up to six million *parts per second* (pps)

Hubs

A hub aggregates connections from nodes and forwards the traffic to a layer 3 device (either a layer 3 switch or a router). A hub is a great low-cost solution for small to medium networks; however, for larger and higher traffic networks, a switch is a more appropriate choice. Hubs cannot segment network traffic into broadcast and/or collision domains. Cisco makes several models of hubs, which gives your organization economical and scalable solutions when creating LANs.

The Cisco 1500 Series Micro Hub has the following features:

- Eight 10/100 auto-sensing fixed ports
- No modules
- Manageable
- Up to five hubs can be stacked.

The Cisco HP 10BaseT Hub-16M has the following features:

- 16-port 10BaseT; 1 AUI (fixed ports)
- No modules
- Cascaded up to 58 users
- Manageable via SNMP, Telnet, or a terminal

The Cisco 1528 Micro Hub has the following features:

- Eight 10/100 auto-sensing fixed ports
- No modules
- Not manageable

The Cisco FastHub has the following features:

- 12-, 15-, 16-, or 24-port Ethernet 10/100 Base TX (depends on the model that you purchase)
- Two modules (316T and 316C); one switched uplink module (400)

- Manageable and unmanaged (depends on the model that you purchase)
- Stackable and unstackable (again, it depends on the model that you purchase)

Remote Access and Authentication (RAS)

RAS is a method of extending your network across dial-up lines to your remote sales force and to other mobile clients. This concept is similar to taking a piece of home with you. To connect (reliably), you will need to have a team of hardware components to include Cisco remote-access servers and/or a Windows RAS server.

What Are My Options?   From a Windows NT or Windows 2000 point of view, the options are limited to a *Remote Access Server* (RAS). From a Cisco point of view, there are a myriad of options: Cisco AS5200/AS5300 server, Cisco AS5800, AccessPath, or Access Server. All of these will provide some form of remote access to your mobile clients.

Microsoft RAS: An Overview

If you have a small to medium-sized company and your budget does not allow for Cisco hardware at the cost of a constant connection (such as a T1 or Frame Relay line), your answer to the remote access question is a Windows NT or Windows 2000 RAS server.

Through the life cycle of Windows NT, we have seen the evolution of RAS: Windows NT 3.1 RAS-supported IP, IPX, NetBEUI, compression, and basic encryption. With the advent of Windows NT 4.0, Microsoft included PPP and PPTP. Now, with the latest release of the Microsoft server OS, Windows 2000, there is support for protocols such as L2TP, IPSec, EAP, and RADIUS. Along with this new functionality, Windows 2000 supports fully integrated routing API availability for developers, networks, and dial-up connection interfaces that are intuitive for the remote client to utilize and an MMC snap-in for centralized management. Furthermore, whereas Windows NT was limited to 256 concurrent connections, Windows 2000 is limited only by your hardware.

RAS can communicate across the *Public Switched Telephone Network* (PSTN), ISDN, or X.25 packet-switched networks. Once the link has been established, you can use standard LAN protocols such as TCP/IP, IPX/SPX, or NetBEUI. The RAS client—the person who is dialing in—acts just like he or she was connected to the network. The only difference is the speed of the data transfer. There are a few key points that you should keep in mind when considering a Microsoft Windows RAS server as opposed to a Cisco RAS solution:

- Windows NT only supports PPP clients.
- Windows RAS supports both IP and IPX routing.
- Windows RAS supports NetBIOS and Windows Sockets applications.
- Windows NT and Windows 2000 support PPTP, making it possible for clients who are using either operating system to communicate securely over the Internet.

Installing MS Windows 2000 Routing and Remote Access Services (RRAS)

RRAS is fully integrated with Windows 2000. You use the RRAS snap-in to set up and manage your server (See Figure D-7).

Once you have it open, right click the server status to add the RRAS server (unless the RRAS server is the one at which you are sitting currently). From there, you can choose a specific machine (all RRAS servers) or search the Active Directory for the specific server.

Configuration Parameters Once you have the MMC open, you will need to configure the RRAS server. To perform this task, highlight the server in the MMC console and click Action, then click Configure and Enable Routing and Remote Access. This action will start the RRAS Configuration Wizards, which will give you five choices:

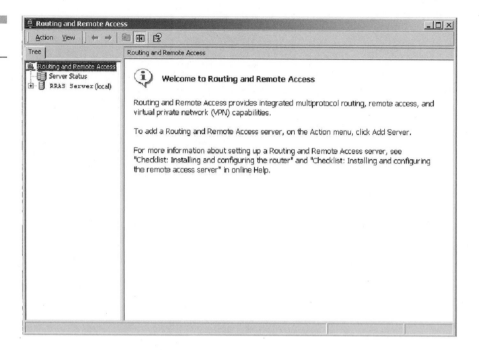

- *Internet Connection Server*   Enables all of the computers on the network to connect to the Internet through RRAS
- *RAS Server*   Enables remote clients to dial in to your network
- *VPN Server*   Enables remote clients to connect to your network through the Internet
- *Network Router*   Enables the RRAS server to communicate with other networks
- *Manually Configure*   Enables you to start the server with default settings

The RRAS server properties sheet has the following items:

- Whether the server is a router and/or an RAS
- The authentication providers, methods, and accounting providers
- Authentication and accounting providers (either Windows or RADIUS)
- Authentication methods: PAP, CHAP, and *Extensible Authentication Protocol* (EAP)

- How to assign an IP and or IPX address
- The protocol tabs (they appear only if the protocol is configured on the server)
- Default PPP options for multi-link, LCO extensions, and software compression
- Logging preferences

What Does RRAS Have to Offer?

RAS offers several benefits such as multi-link and encryption methods. Multi-link is the capability to combine multiple physical links into a single, wider logical connection. Windows 2000 offers four different encryption methods, as viewed in Table D-10.

Cisco Remote Access Servers

There are several means by which a remote client can gain entry to the network. Cisco has several options that enable you to accomplish this task and enable you to provide the end users and remote client enough bandwidth to choke a horse.

The Cisco AS5200/AS5300 Series server offers asynchronous serial connection and ISDN line service. This functionality is good for

Table D-10	**Encryption Method**	**Description**
Encryption methods for RRAS	No encryption	Used only to enable unencrypted connections
	Basic	For dial-up and PPTP-based connections, *Microsoft Point-to-Point Encryption* (MPPE) with a 40-bit key for L2TP over IPSec-based VPN or a 56-bit DES encryption is used.
	Strong	For dial-up and PPTP-based connections, MPPE with a 56-bit key for L2TP over IPSec-based VPN or a 56-bit DES encryption is used.
	Strongest	For dial-up and PPTP-based connections, MPPE with a 128-bit key for L2TP over IPSec-based VPN or a triple DES encryption is used (only in North America).

small- to medium-sized companies that have few people on the road. The Cisco AS5800 is a little bigger and offers ISDN line service, a bank of modems, and up to 48 channelized T1/E1/PRI or two channelized T3 interfaces. The AS5800 is great for medium to large companies that have several remoter clients. Better yet is the AccessPath server. The AccessPath server has the capability to terminate more than 2,500 concurrent calls, and it can terminate up to 84 channelized T1/E1/PRI or three channelized T3 interfaces.

For further specifications of these remote-access servers, refer to the hardware router section in this book or visit `www.cisco.com/warp/public/779/servpro/solutions/remote/`.

Cisco's Authentication, Authorization, and Accounting (AAA) Services

Although AAA is referred to as one entity, it actually consists of three independent security services. Cisco has conveniently grouped them together to form a tri-security model to help provide consistent and better protection for your network and its architecture. The benefits of AAA are as follows:

■ Scalability

■ Standardized authentication methods

■ Increased flexibility and control

■ Redundancy

To accomplish its goal of constant and better protection, AAA uses one of two different protocols: RADIUS and/or TACACS+. These protocols can be applied to a server whose entire purpose is to act as the security server. AAA uses a router or access server acting as a *Network Access Server* (NAS) to establish communication with the security server.

From a design perspective, your customers will need the capability of connecting to your network and feeling secure about the data that they are moving back and forth between the dial-up links. At the same time, however, you must prevent spoofers and hackers from getting to your company's vital data. One of the most important things is to have the ability to dial in and check your e-mail, get important files off the file server, or push important files back to the file server to share. The road warriors of your organization will attest to that. But in this requirement lies the catalyst of another requirement for the ever-vigilant network administrator: network security. Cisco has several means by which you can implement network security without a lot of overhead and configuration time. We will cover these topics later:

- *Remote-Access Dial-In User Service* (RADIUS)
- TACACS+
- CiscoSecure *Access Control Server* (ACS)

RADIUS

RADIUS is a protocol that is used for centralized access control and is supported on IOS releases 11.1 and higher. RADIUS is also supported in CiscoSecure *Access Control Server* (ACS) and is built on the principles of the client/server model. Figure D-8 shows the basic NAS-RADIUS server architecture. The clients are the NASs, and the server is the RADIUS server. To accomplish authentication, the NAS box sends user information to the RADIUS server. The RADIUS server authenticates the user (if valid) and then returns all of the

Figure D-8
NAS-RADIUS
logical path

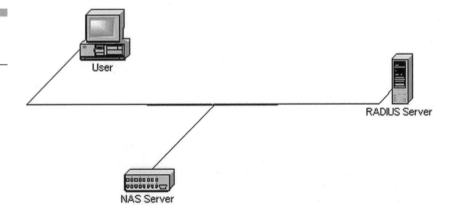

User

RADIUS Server

NAS Server

configuration information of that user back to the NAS box to provide the user with the appropriate service. RADIUS can use the Windows *Security Account Manager* (SAM) or a local flat-file database for authentication.

1. The client requests access to the network. This request is sent to the RADIUS server via the NAS server with information such as
   a. The username and encrypted password
   b. The network access IP address
   c. The network access IP port
2. The RADIUS security server searches the database for the user credentials (the database can either be Windows SAM or a flat-database file that you created):
   a. Username
   b. Password
3. If it is accepted, the RADUIS server returns an ACCESS ACCEPT packet. This packet contains items such as the following:
   a. Service type
   b. Protocol type
   c. IP address

Communication between the NAS and RADIUS servers is accomplished via UDP. The RADIUS protocol combines the process of authentication and authorization. The ACCESS ACCEPT packets that are sent by the RADIUS server to the client contain all of the information that the client needs to gain access to resources on the network.

Terminal Access Controller Access Control System (TACACS1)

TACACS+ simplifies access management by providing the means to manage accounts for authentication, authorization, and accounting centrally. TACACS uses TCP as its transport protocol, whereas RADIUS uses UDP. This feature enables immediate identification of a server that is down or unreachable. Further benefits of TACACS+ are as follows:

1. Secure login
2. Allows for multiple levels of user privileges
3. Central control over user accounts and privileges
4. Redundancy
5. Accounting records
6. Encrypted authentication traffic

CiscoSecure ACS v2.1

The software is installed on a Windows NT box to support centralized access control and accounting for dial-up access services. ACS can access the SAM database on Windows NT for the AAA request; therefore, user accounts do not need to be duplicated on both the AAA server and on the NT domain. ACS provides for global control of the AAA and assists in controlling users' logins to the network and their privileges. Key features and benefits include the following:

- Simultaneous TACACS+ and RADIUS support
- HTML/JAVA GUI, which provides an administrator-friendly interface
- Group assignments for administrators in order to simplify changes in security policies
- Domain stripping and authentication forwarding
- Automatic replication
- CHAP, PAP, and ARA password support
- Time-of-day and day-of-week access restrictions
- Administrator's capability to configure permitted failed attempts before accounts are disabled
- Administrator capability to view active sessions
- Windows NT performance-monitoring support for real-time statistics

Requirements (Hardware and Software)   To utilize the functionality of CiscoSecure ACS, you will need to have the following hardware:

- Intel-call Pentium 133Mhz
- CD-ROM
- 800-by-600 screen resolution or better
- 32MB of *Random Access Memory* (RAM)
- 10MB of hard drive space

  You will also need the following software:

- Microsoft NT 4.0
- Internet Explorer (v5.5 is the latest version)
- Cisco IOS 11.1 or later for TACACS+ or version 11.2 or later for RADIUS

Virtual Private Networks (VPNs)

This term refers to the creation of a VPN over the public Internet or over a public IP-based network. VPN is used to connect users, computers, or networks to other users, computers, or networks through the use of various tunneling protocols (PPTP, L2TP, and IPSec, to name a few). Through the use of these protocols, the security of the RAS connection increases. But let's face it: When it comes right down to it, the important things about VPNs are cost effectiveness and security. If you are looking to increase your raw performance, look elsewhere. To access the VPN, users can utilize dial-up modems, ISDN, xDSL, Frame Relay, and ATM. VPNs are implemented for any combination of application scenarios, remote access (most popular), intranet, and/or extranet.

VPN Application Scenarios

The application scenarios cover how VPN is implemented in different situations that you might encounter as the network engineer. The application scenarios include the following:

- Remote access
- Intranets
- Extranets

Remote-Access VPNs The cost-benefit analysis of a remote-access VPN is favorable—especially for remote users. The downside would be that the remote user has to have access to the Internet or to other IP-based networks over a dial-up line in order to establish the pipe between his or her laptop and the network. Also, he or she needs to load client software in order to ensure IPSec connections. Taking that situation into consideration, also consider that the amount of bandwidth that he or she will have will depend on the link to the Internet. So yes, he or she might be able to establish a secure pipe to the network, but what good will it do him or her if the bandwidth is 56K? In addition to this potential "white elephant," every remote user will have to have the laptop configured with the applicable operating system and software for the tunneling protocol.

Intranet VPNs Intranet VPNs are used to link branch offices, regional offices, and geographically separated offices with the home office. In other words, if you have a main insurance office in Pierre, South Dakota, you could use an intranet VPN to connect the satellite sites in Rapid City and in Sioux Falls to the main office. Normally, this access to the VPN would require dedicated circuits, usually in the form of an unchannelized T-carrier (which might run the Frame Relay protocol or perhaps ATM).

Extranet VPNs Extranet VPNs are used to connect vendors, customers, and affiliates to the main corporate office through the use of various access techniques and security measures.

Tunneling Protocols Tunneling is the process of encapsulating an encrypted packet in an IP packet for secure transmission across the Internet. We will cover three of the more popular tunneling protocols:

- *Point-to-Point Tunneling Protocol* (PPTP)
- *Layer 2 Tunneling Protocol* (L2TP)
- *IP Security* (IPSec)

PPTP PPTP is available on all platforms (Windows 9x, Windows NT 3.x and 4.0, and Windows 2000). PPTP supports client-to-server and server-to-server connections. PPTP cannot be used in conjunction with IPSec; however, it can be used with MPPE—a lower-level encryption capability offered by Microsoft. PPTP will encrypt all of the following network-layer protocols: IP, IPX, and NetBEUI. The benefits of PPTP are three-fold:

- Lower administrative costs by simplifying and reducing the cost of deploying an enterprise-wide, remote-access solution for remote users

- Decreased transmission cost by providing secure and encrypted communication over public telephone lines and the Internet

- Lower hardware costs by eliminating the need for expensive, leased-line or private enterprise-dedicated communication servers (because you use PPTP over PSTN)

Typically, there are three computers involved in every PPTP deployment: the PPTP client, a network access server, and a PPTP server.

A PPTP Connection Scenario Normally, the deployment of PPTP starts with a mobile PPTP client who wants to gain access to your private LAN by using his or her ISP. The client uses dial-up networking and the remote access protocol PPP to connect to an NAS at the ISP. Once he or she has established a connection, a second dial-up networking call is made over the existing PPP connection. This second call creates the VPN connection to a PPTP server on the Internal LAN (called a tunnel) and is shown in Figure D-9.

Client Requirements Your clients should be running Windows NT 4.0, Windows Professional, or Windows 98 as their operating systems. The box should be at least a 200Mhz Pentium class machine with 64MB of RAM and 110MB of free space on the hard disk.

Figure D-9
PPTP connection

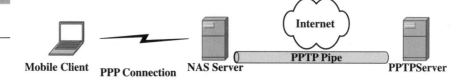

Mobile Client   PPP Connection   NAS Server   Internet   PPTP Pipe   PPTPServer

Server Requirements   Your PPTP server should have the basic equipment of the client (such as the same hard drive space, RAM, and speed requirements). The operating system should be Windows NT 4.0, Windows 2000 Server, or Advanced Server.

L2TP

Like PPTP, L2TP is available on all Microsoft platforms for client-to-server connections (except for Windows 2000, where it only supports server-to-server connections). It can be used with IPSec encryption to establish secure transport connections. L2TP encrypts IP, IPX, and NetBEUI within an IP header that is similar to PPTP.

IPSec (IP Security)

IPSec enables complete, standards-based encryption. IPSec uses advanced authentication techniques to identify a user. It has two different modes: IPSec transport and IPSec tunnel. IPSec operates by negotiating between a sender and a receiver about how to encrypt the data portion of the IP packet. To enable IPSec on your Windows 2000 RRAS server, you use the IP Security Management MMC.

From a network design point of view, this functionality enables those members who are higher up on the corporate food chain to encrypt the data that is being transmitted across the network so that it cannot be intercepted, viewed, or captured while en route.

Section IV: Managing Your Cisco Hardware

As your company grows, so does your network. Nodes multiply, and applications need bigger servers, databases, and throughput. Trying to keep this system tied together is the network administrator. The buzzword is *proactive*. If you do anything proactively, you have to know about the problems beforehand and fix them before they become problems. Ideally, this technique is the way that things should be done. Most of the time, however, things are more of a fire drill—a knee-jerk reaction to something that has been building for a long time. With the help of Cisco's managing software packages, however, you can keep the word *proactive* on your resume and feel good about yourself. There are three kinds of managing software packages: CiscoWorks for Windows, CiscoWorks 2000, and NTManage. These software packages ease the network administrator's nightmares by providing ease of administration with a user-friendly GUI.

CiscoWorks for Switched Internetworks for Windows

CiscoWorks for Windows is a GUI-based suite of applications that runs on the Windows 9x and Windows NT platforms. In addition to the OS, your server needs to be running Resource Manager. CiscoWorks for Windows is best used by small- to medium-sized companies. The applications that are used within CiscoWorks for Windows use SNMP to communicate with the Cisco routers, switches, and hubs. Those applications and a brief description are listed as follows:

- *Threshold Manager*   Establishes the thresholds on RMON-enabled devices
- StackMaker   Manages switches and hubs when they are configured to be members of a stack
- Flash File System   Used to edit and display functionality for high-end router configuration files

CiscoWorks for Windows can be integrated with the following network-management applications:

- Castle Rock Computing SNMP
- HP Openview Network Node Manager for Windows NT
- HP Openview Professional Suite for Windows

Hardware Requirements for CiscoWorks

You will need to have a box configured to these minimum specs in order to get CiscoWorks for Windows to function properly:

- Windows 9x or Windows NT 4.0
- Pentium 90
- 1024-by-768 screen resolution
- 32MB of RAM
- 327MB of free space for installation and 50MB to 80MB thereafter
- An NIC

CiscoWorks2000

As with everything this year, CiscoWorks for Windows is being replaced by a new version: CiscoWorks2000. We highly recommend that you do not collocate, or run simultaneously, CiscoWorks2000 and CiscoWorks for Windows. In fact, do not even put them on the same network. Like its predecessor, CW2000 is a suite of software applications. These applications, however, are divided into two subcategories: Resource Manager Essentials and *CiscoWorks for Switched Internetworks* (CWSI). Table D-11 breaks down the various software applications and indicates where they can be found.

Hardware and Software Requirements for CiscoWorks2000

You will need to have a box configured to these minimum specs in order to get CiscoWorks2000 to function properly. This software package is a bit meatier than its predecessor, so your requirements should be higher to reflect this fact. Keep in mind that this list is a bare-bones minimum:

Table D-11

CiscoWorks 2000
application suite

Resource Manager Essential Applications	CWSI Application
Availability Manager	CWSI Discovery
Device Configuration Manager	VLANDirector
Software Manager	UserTracker
Inventory Manager	CiscoView
Change Audit Service	TrafficDirector
Syslog Analyzer	ATMDirector
Cisco Connection Online (CCO) Service Tools	

- Pentium 300Mhz
- 256MB RAM
- 4GB of free space on an NTFS partition

Here are the software requirements (all of these requirements must be met or the software package will not function properly):

- Windows NT 4.0 with Service Pack 3 or higher
- Despite its name, it is not compatible with Windows 2000 yet.
- Furthermore, although the most recent service pack for Windows NT 4.0 is 6a, nothing higher than Service Pack 3 has been tested. I do not recommend using anything higher than Service Pack 3 without first checking with your Cisco representative or with Cisco's Web site, www.cisco.com.
- Do not run from a *Primary Domain Controller* (PDC) or from a *Backup Domain Controller* (BDC).
- Internet Explorer 4.01 with Service Pack 1
- Do not install active desktop.
- Option Pack installed with the following components:
  - Data Access Component v1.5
  - MMC
  - *Internet Information System* (IIS) 4.0
  - Windows Scripting Host

NTManage

NTManage is a network management and troubleshooting application that runs on the Windows NT platform (on both the workstation and the server). NTManage has auto-discovery functions as well as real-time reporting. This feature enables quick fault detection and device management.

Requirements   NTManage does not have as many stringent requirements as the previous two management applications. The only requirement for you is to make sure that you have the SNMP service already running before you install NTManage.

Section V: Managing Your Windows Environment

I was told once that my title should be network custodian, not network administrator, because as the network administrator, I went around maintaining the network like a superintendent maintains an apartment complex. In truth, the person who told me this opinion was right. The tasks that I accomplished on a daily basis never afforded me the time to devote to taking a long view of the company needs and/or the long-term strategies that would help the company reach its goals. I spend my time performing the following tasks:

- Creating and modifying user accounts
- Managing printer queues and resolving printer problems
- Maintaining routers and switches
- Troubleshooting network connectivity issues
- Supporting remote users

With the tools that are inherent in Windows NT (and now in Windows 2000), monitoring the network and maintaining a happy balance between knee-jerk reactions and proactive maintenance has become easier. It is just a matter of knowing where the tools are located and how to use them to your benefit. We will briefly go through four of the network-management tools and describe each of them.

When troubleshooting problems in Windows NT or Windows 2000, you can use the following tools/utilities to help you:

- Diagnostic network utilities such as ping, ipconfig, nslookup, and tracert
- Event Viewer
- Performance Monitor
- Network Monitor

Diagnostic Network Utilities

Before you begin any troubleshooting problem solving, always start with the basics. Table D-12 lists some basic IP utilities that can help you test the various layers of the network architecture.

Event Viewer

This utility is used to inspect three different log files: Application, Security, and System. The Application log records information and alerts you to NT's internal processes. The Security Log records

Table D-12	**Utility**	**Used For**
Basic network diagnostic utilities	ipconfig	Verifies the current TCP/IP configuration; releases and renews the current IP configuration from a DHCP server; registers the host name and IP address with a DNS server
	nslookup	Verifies whether DNS is running on a particular DNS server; verifies the IP addresses provided by DNS for a host-name lookup; verifies the registration of service records by domain controllers; verifies whether DNS used WINS to resolve the IP address of a specific host
	ping	Tests the connectivity between two IP hosts
	tracert	Displays the path taken by packets from your computer to another host; helps identify routing problems

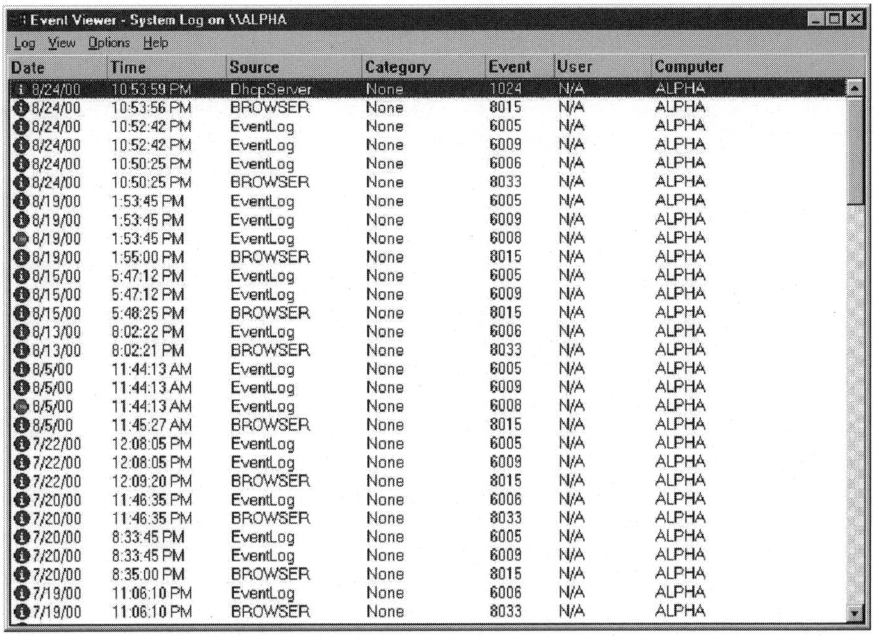
Event Viewer - System Log on \\ALPHA

Log View Options Help

Date	Time	Source	Category	Event	User	Computer
8/24/00	10:53:59 PM	DhcpServer	None	1024	N/A	ALPHA
8/24/00	10:53:56 PM	BROWSER	None	8015	N/A	ALPHA
8/24/00	10:52:42 PM	EventLog	None	6005	N/A	ALPHA
8/24/00	10:52:42 PM	EventLog	None	6009	N/A	ALPHA
8/24/00	10:50:25 PM	EventLog	None	6006	N/A	ALPHA
8/24/00	10:50:25 PM	BROWSER	None	8033	N/A	ALPHA
8/19/00	1:53:45 PM	EventLog	None	6005	N/A	ALPHA
8/19/00	1:53:45 PM	EventLog	None	6009	N/A	ALPHA
8/19/00	1:53:45 PM	EventLog	None	6008	N/A	ALPHA
8/19/00	1:55:00 PM	BROWSER	None	8015	N/A	ALPHA
8/15/00	5:47:12 PM	EventLog	None	6005	N/A	ALPHA
8/15/00	5:47:12 PM	EventLog	None	6009	N/A	ALPHA
8/15/00	5:48:25 PM	BROWSER	None	8015	N/A	ALPHA
8/13/00	8:02:22 PM	EventLog	None	6006	N/A	ALPHA
8/13/00	8:02:21 PM	BROWSER	None	8033	N/A	ALPHA
8/5/00	11:44:13 AM	EventLog	None	6005	N/A	ALPHA
8/5/00	11:44:13 AM	EventLog	None	6009	N/A	ALPHA
8/5/00	11:44:13 AM	EventLog	None	6008	N/A	ALPHA
8/5/00	11:45:27 AM	BROWSER	None	8015	N/A	ALPHA
7/22/00	12:08:05 PM	EventLog	None	6005	N/A	ALPHA
7/22/00	12:08:05 PM	EventLog	None	6009	N/A	ALPHA
7/22/00	12:09:20 PM	BROWSER	None	8015	N/A	ALPHA
7/20/00	11:46:35 PM	EventLog	None	6006	N/A	ALPHA
7/20/00	11:46:35 PM	BROWSER	None	8033	N/A	ALPHA
7/20/00	8:33:45 PM	EventLog	None	6005	N/A	ALPHA
7/20/00	8:33:45 PM	EventLog	None	6009	N/A	ALPHA
7/20/00	8:35:00 PM	BROWSER	None	8015	N/A	ALPHA
7/19/00	11:06:10 PM	EventLog	None	6006	N/A	ALPHA
7/19/00	11:06:10 PM	BROWSER	None	8033	N/A	ALPHA

Figure D-10 Screen shot of event Viewer

security-related events, and the system log records NT application events, alerts, and system messages. Refer to Figure D-10 for a screen shot of Event Viewer.

Figure D-10 shows an example of the system log from my home computer, a Windows NT server. Each log contains the date and time of the error (the errors are the red stop signs), the source of the error (I have a DHCP problem that I must fix), and the event ID. The event ID is most important for looking through TechNet or Microsoft's knowledge base on the Web site `www.microsoft.com/knowledgebase`. Just search for the event ID and find the KB entry that matches your solution.

To open the event logs on a Windows 2000 box, you can either double click Event Viewer in the Administrative Tools program group, Start Manage Computer and then navigate to System Tools\Event Viewer, or you can type `EVENTVWR` at the command prompt.

There are five different event types that can be recorded in Event Viewer:

- *Information*   An event that is logged for information purposes only (does not require action)
- *Warning*   An event that indicates some significant condition that might require action
- *Critical*   An event that indicates a failure or a significant problem
- *Success audit*   An event that records information about a successful access attempt on a resource
- *Failure audit*   An event that records information about an unsuccessful access attempt on a resource

Performance Monitor (PERFMON)

PERFMON is a utility that is used to inspect the performance and activity of processes, resources, physical components, networks, and remote machines. Opening PERFMON and getting inside is the easy part. Knowing what metrics and counters to watch and knowing what to do about them if they are too high or too low is the difficult part.

Performance monitor has four views (see Table D-13).

Common Objects and Counters

Listed next are just a few of the main counters. In reality, you should be more familiar with the various counters and what they actually mean. Fortunately, if you do not quite understand a counter, you can

Table D-13

Performance monitor views

View	Description
Chart View	Enables users to view real-time data in a line graph or histogram
Alert View	Enables users to set and view alerts and alert statistics
Log View	Enables users to create and save a log of a system performance
Report View	Enables users to create custom reports of performance monitor data

Table D-14

Common objects
and counters in
performance
monitor

Object	Counter	Description
Processor	%Processor Time	If the processor counter measures 80 percent or more for an extended period, this situation could indicate that the processor is in need of an upgrade.
System Length	Processor Queue	If the number of threads waiting to be processed is greater than two, the processor might be a bottleneck for the system.
Processor	Interrupts/Sec	If this counter increases and the processor time does not, a hardware device might be sending false interrupts to the processor.
Memory	Cache Faults, Page Faults, and Pages/Sec	These counters indicate how frequently your system needs to swap pages with the hard drive swap space.
PhysicalDisk/LogicalDisk	%Disk Time	This counter shows how much processor time is being spent servicing disk requests.
PhysicalDisk/LogicalDisk	Disk Bytes/Transfer	When you need to see how fast your hard disks are transferring data, use this counter.
PhyscialDisk/LogicalDisk Length	Current Disk Queue	This counter shows how much data is waiting to be transferred to the hard disk.

highlight it in the Add To dialog box and click the Explain button to get more information. Some of the more common objects and their counters are listed in Table D-14.

For a screen shot of Performance Monitor, see Figure D-11.

These are just some of the many objects and counters within PERFMON. Trying to look at all of them at the same time will cause you to be quickly overwhelmed at what is being displayed and will only provide you with a large jumble of information that will end up meaning very little. The counters that are available in PERFMON will give you the information that you are looking for, provided that you choose the right combinations of counters. Your best bet is to find

Figure D-11

Performance Monitor
screen shot

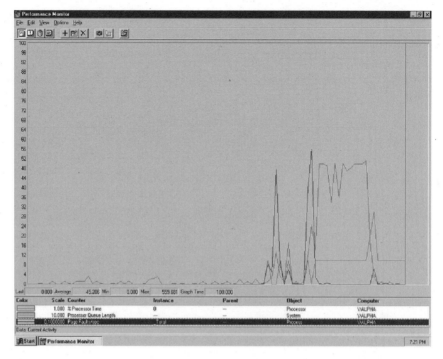

about five or six major processes and watch those. They are indicator processes. If these processes peak, then there is something wrong and you should spend time checking it out.

In Windows 2000, Performance Monitor is an MMC snap-in. You can either double click Performance in the Administrative Tools program group or run PERFMON at the command line.

Network Monitor

Network Monitor is a tool that is used for capturing and analyzing network traffic. It is comprised of a Kernal mode driver called Network Monitor Driver and a user-mode application that is located in the Administrative Tools program group (Windows 2000) called Network Monitor. In Windows NT, you will have to add the service by going to Network Neighborhood . . . Properties . . . Services tab . . . Add. You can use Network Monitor in either operating system to perform the following tasks:

- Troubleshooting communications problems
- Viewing which devices on the network are sending and receiving the most traffic
- Monitoring for specific events
- Actually viewing conversations between applications on the network. (You might think that I am crazy, but it was a real joy to watch the ARP broadcasts as computers tried to resolve IP addresses to MAC addresses, and witnessing the DHCP traffic was really interesting.)

Section VI: Migrating NT 4.0 Domains to Windows 2000

This description is not all-inclusive of migrating your current Windows NT domains to Windows 2000 by any means. This text is a highlighted, broad-stroked overview of the main points. Designing a viable and stable Active Directory will require careful planning of the three Active Duty components: domains, *Organizational Units* (OUs), and sites.

Planning the Domain

There has been a drastic change in the operating system (from Windows NT to Windows 2000)—so much that the majority of the NT domain designs are obsolete. For example, in the majority of internetworks, only a single domain controller will comprise your Active Directory structure. Now, with Windows NT, the domain is comprised of several domains that have individual PDCs and subservient BDCs.

To begin the long process of planning your environment, you should follow these three steps:

1. Evaluate the current environment.
2. Decide where Windows 2000 domains are appropriate.
3. Determine the proper placing of the domain within the tree or forest.

Evaluating the Current Environment

To determine the scope of the current environment, you must first ask yourself three questions:

1. What is the current organizational structure, and how is it expected to grow/change within the next three to five years?
2. How is your current network infrastructure set up? What is the LAN speed? Is there a WAN structure? What subnets are being used?
3. How much time do you spend administrating the domain?

Deciding Where Windows 2000 Domains Are Appropriate

Begin by planning to have only one domain. Current Windows NT 4.0 domain models will not be completely accurate when it comes to designing your Windows 2000 domain structure. Table D-15 summarizes the migration of Windows NT domains into what will be a workable solution in Windows 2000.

There are four reasons why a multi-domain model might be necessary:

1. Political pressure
2. Domain replication traffic
3. Domain policies
4. International differences

Table D-15

Microsoft Windows domain conversions

Current Domain Model	Windows 2000 Domain Model
Single Domain	Single Domain
Master-resource domain	Single domain (possible multi-domain)
Multi-master domain	Multi-domain models are likely; however, a single domain model with child domains will work.
Complete trust	Multi-domain model

Political pressure is the most common reason why multi-domain models are prevalent. People tend to cite autonomy and/or privacy as reasons for their separate domain request. Keep in mind that OUs will solve this problem without the potential headache when it comes to domain management.

Replication traffic can be an issue in a single-domain model. A multi-domain model isolates the replication traffic from all other domains. In other words, it acts as a load-balancing service to the organization's backbone.

Domain policies are the third reason for creating a multi-domain model. For example, if two or more groups require different values for a domain-level setting (such as password length or account lockouts), it is beneficial to create a separate domain to provide less politics in the workplace and more ease of administration.

The final reason for multi-domain models is international differences. Each country has its own currency symbols, languages, and business requirements. For these reasons, it is always best to separate each country into its own domain.

Determining Proper Placing of the Domain within the Tree or Forest

That phrase is odd—like you are actually planting a tree. Well, in a lot of ways, you are. A tree is a living thing that is constantly changing. If it does not have adequate light or water, it will die. Well, your domain changes constantly (is added to and is pruned), and like a tree, if there is not enough room for the root system to thrive, the domain will die and you will have to start over. So, after you have determined which model you will be using, you have to define the Active Directory. If you are in a single domain model, it is as simple as attaching your domain to the single tree. If you are in a multi-domain model, you will have to consider whether a forest or tree design is preferable.

A forest is best suited for large corporations that are made up of several sites or business units. Navigation and administration of forests, however, are much more difficult than in a single-tree environment. You must remember, though, that 99.9 percent of the time, users will not need access to anything outside of their site and therefore will not have a need to navigate through the forest.

DNS is another concern. Take care when choosing your domain name. Changing it once everything has been established can be a taunting task.

Planning the OU Structure

After you have determined the domain model, you need to populate your domain with OUs. OUs are used for segmenting administrative tasks and users that have differing group policy requirements.

There are a few things that you need to consider when determining your OUs:

- A shallow OU structure performs better than a deeper hierarchy.
- OUs should represent static business units or *lines of business* (LOB).
- OUs should be organized by location, function, or both.
- Inheritance from parent containers can be leveraged in order to simplify security.

Your objective when designing the OU structure for your company is two-fold. First, you want to avoid (at all costs) OU reorganization. Second, if you make a great analysis of your organization's structure, it will help create the best design. See Figure D-12 for a representation of the Windows 2000 domain structure.

Restructuring Your Windows NT Domain Model

After you have completed the Active Directory structure design, you will need to restructure your NT domain. Once this process has begun, you might notice that previous NT domain models and the future Windows 2000 domain model do not mesh. Many domain models differ so much that a common strategy is to reorganize your NT domain structure before continuing with the migration. This process is time consuming and difficult and should not be taken

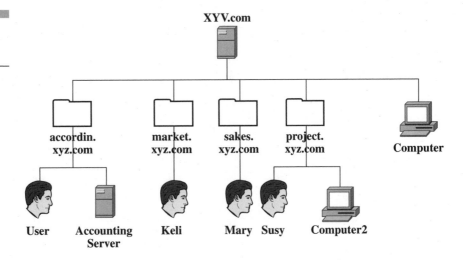

Figure D-12
Windows 2000
domain structure

lightly. See Table D-16, which contains some aspects of migration that you will want to consider.

There are two thoughts on consolidating domains. The first is to migrate prior to deploying Windows 2000, and the second is to migrate as part of your deployment (or after the deployment is complete).

Pre-Migration Restructuring

Pre-migration restructuring should happen when 30 percent or more of your current domain will be collapsed in on itself to facilitate the migration process. Microsoft has created a suite of migration tools called SIDWalker. SIDWalker can set the access control lists on objects previously owned by accounts that were moved, orphaned, or deleted. It can be found in the Windows 2000 Resource Kit. Do not consolidate domains if the combined size of the SAM database will be larger than 40MB. It is not that Active Directory cannot handle it; rather, once combined and prior to migration, Windows NT will not be capable of handling it. Also, if the main reason for consolidating the domains is for ease of administration, consolidate after the migration. It is not worth the headache.

Table D-16

Domain
restructuring
considerations

Consideration	Action(s)
User and machine accounts	Migrated to the destination domain
Groups	Global groups need to be migrated; local groups have to be recreated
Permissions	All types of permissions; file, share, and registry rights need to be remapped to accounts in the destination domain
User rights	User rights, domain security policies, and system policies have to be transferred to the destination domain.
Services	Services that use user credentials for logon rather than the LocalSystem account have to be remapped to use accounts in the destination domain.
Applications	Many applications might require reconfiguration or reinstallation in order to move to a new domain. Wherever possible, server applications that are installed on domain controllers should be relocated to member servers.
Member servers	Have to join the destination domain
Workstations	Moved to the destination domain
Domain controllers	Non-2000 domain controllers should have any services that they provide moved to other servers. Then, the domain controllers of the source domain should be taken offline.

Migration Gotchas

Be forewarned—companies that have chosen to migrate have run into a few political and technical roadblocks:

1. Time
2. Politics
3. Desktop lockdown
4. Knowing and understanding why the company is migrating (do not lose sight of the objective)
5. Planning

Time   It will take a great deal of time to properly plan your Active Directory structure and test your applications. Also, you're going to want to take some time to thoroughly test your third party applications. It would be very beneficial to create a "test-bed" environment within your company. This lab environment can incorporate a Cisco switch in utilizing VLANs, which will segment the traffic and simulate a distributed LAN environment.

Political Concerns   Although not part and parcel of this writing, a brief coverage of this touchy subject is needed. Inter-office politics is a tinderbox anyway, but now with the centralized network infrastructure management power contained in Windows 2000 it becomes more of a problem. Active Directory and group policies provide more power to a centralized IT Department and removes it from branch office and business units. Many companies have gone to a decentralized IT department. For instance, if you have your main corporate headquarters in Dallas and sub-offices in San Francisco, Denver, and Boston, each site would have an IT department of two or three members answering to the MIS Director in Dallas. Now with Windows 2000, the headcount can be cut in half, because the group policies can be forced directly to the Organizational Unit.

To start the creation of the AD tree:

- First, understand that the tree is the basis for computing infrastructure, security, and desktop management.
- Secondly designing your AD tree requires input from all business units. This process of properly designing an AD tree can last any from six to nine months. Many companies have taken to hiring an outside contractor to be the project manager on their Windows NT to 2000 migration project. This manages to take the edge off the politics and allow for a smoother transition.

There is no stopping the political posturing the migration will encourage. For example attempting to wrest control of your companies DNS server from the Unix side of the house (where it resides in most companies) and assigning it to the Active Directory will be a chore. Group policies also add another element of complexity.

■ Desktop "Lockdown"

IT departments can utilize Windows 2000 group policies to centrally control desktops. If your end-users are anything like mine you'll find they take it very personally when you attempt to control what they can load or add to their PCs. We just remind them—delicately—that their desktop computers are property of the company and not their personal computers. In addition, in new employee orientation we inform them that we do control access to their PCs to alleviate them installing unapproved applications. Some firms go even further and lock out the Internet Explorer, and access to the command prompt.

On the bright side, little to no training is required when upgrading your end-users from Windows 95/98 or NT to Windows 2000. The OS is intuitive and easy to use.

■ Avoiding Scope Creep with Proper Planning

Take the time to formally document the total-cost-of-ownership goals before rushing headlong into the mire that is migration. Once a decision to go forward and a migration is warranted, establish a test bed, and make sure your third party software and drivers will run in a Windows 2000 environment by checking the Hardware compatibility list. You can find it online at `http://www.microsoft.com/hcl/default.asp` or if you have Windows NT you can find the updated Windows NT Hardware Compatibility List is available in the MS Windows NT Workstation Technical Notes directory on your CD-ROM.

Migration Summary

When migrating from a Windows NT domain environment to a Windows 2000 with a single domain, you will need to accomplish the following steps:

1. Define the domain type.
2. Define the Active Directory structure.
   ■ Determine the OUs.
3. Perform any pre-migration consolidation.

4. Make a complete copy of all servers.

5. Synchronize and power down a *Backup Domain Controller* (BDC).

6. Migrate a *Primary Domain Controller* (PDC).

7. Follow-up with migrating the BDCs.

8. Finish up with the member servers and workstations.

When migrating from a Master-Resource and/or multi-master domain, perform the following tasks:

1. Define the domain type.

2. Define the Active Directory structure.

   ▪ Determine the OUs.

3. Perform any pre-migration consolidation.

4. Make a complete copy of all servers.

5. Migrate the master domain first by following Steps 6 through 8.

6. Synchronize and power down a BDC.

7. Migrate a PDC.

8. Follow up with migrating the BDCs.

9. Finish up with the member servers and workstations.

Leave each Windows 2000 domain in mixed mode until all domain controllers have been converted. Once all domain controllers use Windows 2000, you can utilize universal groups and group nesting.

SUMMARY ▬ ▬ ▬ ▬ ▬ ▬ ▬ ▬ ▬

The basic concepts needed to help build and design your network should have been given to you in this brief overview of Cisco and Windows. Covered in this short appendix were DHCP, DNS, and WINS, LAN topologies and the protocols used within your network, followed up by routing protocols, remote access, and VPN connectivity. Basic tools needed to maintain your hardware and software, such as CiscoWorks and NTManage on the Cisco side, were covered. In closing, we followed up by the Windows Management tools (such as Performance Monitor and Event Viewer).

This appendix was not meant as a means to bring you up to speed on designing networks—that is what the meat of the book is for. Instead, it was meant to stir your memory of the major components and concepts that are used in designing your Windows/Cisco-meshed network.

APPENDIX E

OSI Model

The OSI Model is used to describe how information from one application on one computer can move to an application on another computer. Developed by the *International Organization for Standardization* (ISO) in 1984, it is the primary architectural model for internetworking communications. The OSI Model has seven layers:

- Physical layer
- Data link layer
- Network layer
- Transport layer
- Session layer
- Presentation layer
- Application layer

We will now take a look at their purposes within the OSI Model and give an example of a technology that correlates to that particular layer.

Layer 1: The Physical Layer

The definition of the physical layer is that it is Layer 1 of the OSI Reference Model. The physical layer defines the electrical, mechanical, procedural, and functional specifications for activating, maintaining, and deactivating the physical link between end systems. It is comprised of three components. These components, in some instances, are the same in *Local Area Network* (LAN) and *Wide Area Network* (WAN) environments. They are cables or wires, connectors, and encoding.

Cables and Wires

The majority of the cable in place today falls into three types: *Unshielded Twisted Pair* (UTP), coaxial, and fiber optic. The majority of modern internal cable plant wiring is UTP. However, coaxial cable is still used today for specific LAN applications as well as for some high-speed WAN applications. Finally, the high-speed cable of choice is fiber. Fiber is used as the backbone for all high-speed LAN and WAN connections today.

Unshielded Twisted Pair (UTP)   UTP has many uses. It is used for voice communication, key card readers, alarm systems, and data communications. The first distinction in the type of UTP that can be used is the rating of the cable. UTP cable is rated for *either* or *plenum* use. If an area is a plenum or air return space, plenum rated cable must be used. Otherwise, standard cable is acceptable for use.

NOTE: *Plenum-rated cable is approximately twice the cost of standard UTP cable.*

The next distinction, and probably most important, is the category designator. The category, often abbreviated as CAT, levels officially run from Category 1 to Category 5:

- *CAT 1*   Here cable performance is intended for basic communications and power-limited circuit cable. No performance criteria exist for cable at this level.

- *CAT 2*   Low performance UTP. Typical applications are voice and low-speed data. This is not specified in the *Electronic Industries Association / Telecommunications Industry Association* (EIA/TIA) 568A for data use.

- *CAT 3*   This is data cable that complies with the transmission requirements in the EIA/TIA 568A. It has a maximum transmission speed of 16Mbps. In current installations, this is the grade most often used for voice cabling.

- *CAT 4*   An infrequently used category. It has a maximum transmission speed of 20Mbps.

- *CAT 5*   The most commonly used UTP category. Its maximum transmission speed is 100Mbps.

Coaxial Cable   The coaxial cable used in networks is a relative of the coax cable used in many households for cable TV reception. Just like UTP, there can be both PVC and plenum-rated varieties for each variation. Many variations of this cable exist, but only three are used for data communications. The impedance or resistance of the cable is the item that differentiates the specific cables. RG58, RG59, and RG62 have approximately the same diameter, but each cable has a different amount of impedance. Table E-1 summarizes the coax categories, as follows:

- *RG58*   Also called ThinNet. Rated for 10MHz transmissions over a distance of 185 meters

- *RG8*   Also called ThickNet. Rated for 10MHz transmissions over a distance of 500 meters

- *RG62*   Used for IBM controller cabling

- *RG59*   Not used for data transmissions. Used primarily for video transmissions and household cable TV

Fiber Optic Cable   Fiber optic cable is the cable of choice for high-speed, long-distance communications. Simply put, a light source such as a low-powered laser is used to generate the optical or light signals down this type of cable. These cables are constructed out of small, thin strands of glass that look like fibers. The distance limitation of fiber is often measured in kilometers. Fiber optic cable, like UTP and

Table E-1

Coaxial cable
variations

Type of Coaxial Cable	Impedance	Cable Diameter	Usage
RG8	50 Ohm	10mm	10Base5, Thick Ethernet
RG58	50 Ohm	5mm	10 Base2, Thin Ethernet
RG59	75 Ohm	6mm	Video
RG62	93 Ohm	6mm	IBM 3270, Arcnet

coax, is rated either for PVC or plenum use. Two different types of fiber optic cable exist:

- Multimode Fiber *(MMF)*   Multimode fiber enables light to travel over one of many possible paths. Light, for example, could bounce under various angles in the core of the multimode cable. Because of the larger diameter of the core, it is much easier to get the light within it, allowing for less expensive electronics and connectors. The maximum distance for MMF is 2 km.

- Single Mode Fiber *(SMF)*   This offers the light only one route to travel through. SMF has a much smaller core than MMF (eight microns for SMF versus 50 or 62.5 microns for MMF). The smaller core enables much longer distances than MMF. Telephone companies interconnect their network equipment with SMF. The typical distance is between five and 1,000 miles. Simply put, if you want more distance, use a stronger laser.

NOTE: *SMF equipment is much more expensive than the equipment for MMF.*

Physical Terminations and Connectors

Without connectors and terminations, cables would have to be "hardwired" to the end device. This would make quick disconnects and reconnects impossible. Connectors usually vary depending on the media type.

UTP   Four basic modular jack styles are used in UTP. Figure E-1 shows the eight-position and eight-position keyed modular jacks. These jacks are commonly and incorrectly referred to as RJ45 and keyed RJ45 respectively.

The six-position modular jack is commonly referred to as RJ11. Using these terms can sometimes lead to confusion since the RJ des-

Figure E-1
UTP jacks

8-position

8-position
keyed

6-position

6-position
modified

ignations actually refer to specific wiring configurations called *Universal Service Ordering Codes* (USOC).

The designation RJ means "registered jack." Each of these three basic jack styles can be wired for different RJ configurations. For example, the six-position jack can be wired as an RJ11C (one-pair), RJ14C (two-pair), or RJ25C (three-pair) configuration. An eight-position jack can be wired for configurations such as RJ61C (four-pair) and RJ48C. The keyed eight-position jack can be wired for RJ45S, RJ46S, and RJ47S.

The fourth modular jack style is a modified version of the six-position jack (modified modular jack or MMJ). It was designed by *Digital Equipment Corporation*® (DEC) along with the *modified modular plug* (MMP) to eliminate the possibility of connecting DEC data equipment to voice lines and vice versa.

Cable Termination Practices for UTP   Two primary wiring standards exist. One set of standards is set by the EIA/TIA; the other is set by the USOC. The various pinouts are detailed in Figure E-2.

Two wiring schemes have been adopted by the EIA/TIA 568-A standard. They are nearly identical, except that pairs two and three are reversed. T568A is the preferred scheme because it is compatible with one or two-pair USOC systems. Either configuration can be used for *Integrated Services Digital Network* (ISDN) and high-speed data applications.

USOC wiring is available for one-, two-, three-, or four-pair systems. Pair 1 occupies the center conductors; pair 2 occupies the next two contacts out, and so on. One advantage to this scheme is that a

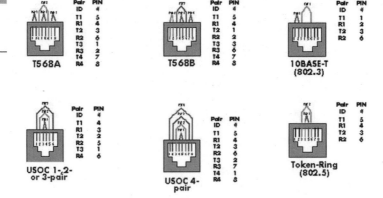

six-position plug configured with one or two pairs can be inserted into an eight-position jack and maintain pair continuity.

Ethernet uses either of the EIA/TIA standards in an eight-position jack. However, only two pairs are used. On the other hand, Token Ring wiring uses either an eight-position or six-position jack. The eight-position format is compatible with T568A, T568B, and USOC wiring schemes. The six-position format is compatible with one- or two-pair USOC wiring.

Coaxial Connectors   Coaxial cables use two different connectors. One type is used specifically for ThickNet. All other types of coax use the same type of connector.

All ThinNet and other coax cables, except RG8 (ThickNet), use the *Bayonet Neil-Concelman* (BNC) connector, shown in Figure E-3. The acronym BNC has also been purported to mean British Naval Connector and Bayonet Nut Connector, but those references are incorrect.

NOTE: *If the connector is not firmly connected to the cable, the connection will have intermittent connection issues. This is not acceptable for DS3 WAN circuits.*

Figure E-3
BNC connector for
coaxial cable

	AUI Pin #	Ethernet V2.0	IEEE 802.3	RJ45 (EIA/TIA568A) Pin #
Table E-2	1	Shield	Control in Shield	
AUI and RJ45	2	Collision Presence +	Control in A	
pinouts	3	Transmit +	Data out A	1
	4	Reserved	Data in Shield	
	5	Receive +	Data in A	3
	6	Power Return	Voltage Common	
	7	Reserved	Control out A	
	8	Reserved	Control out Shield	
	9	Collision Presence −	Control in B	
	10	Transmit −	Data out B	2
	11	Reserved	Data out Shield	
	12	Receive −	Data in B	6
	13	Power	Voltage	
	14	Reserved	Voltage Shield	
	15	Reserved	Control out B	
	Connector Shield ———————————————			Protective Ground

ThickNet (RG8) uses an *Attachment Unit Interface* (AUI) connector to connect devices to the cable. The AUI connector itself is a standard male DB-15M with studs instead of mounting screws; the
female is a DB-15F with a slide-clip that attempts to lock onto the
studs. Table E-2 lists the pinouts for an AUI connector as well as an
RJ45-pinned connector.

A) ST Connector   B) SC Connector

C) MIC Connector

Fiber Optic Connectors   Five popular types of fiber connectors exist. They can be used for both MMF and SMF. The most common types of connectors, ST, SC, and MIC, are pictured in Figure E-4. The less common connector types are ESCON and MT-RJ. The following is a brief description of each of the connectors:

- *ST*   A commonly used connector in the earlier days of fiber installations

- *SC*   The most commonly used connector type today. Almost every connector on Cisco equipment uses an SC connector.

- *MIC/FSD*   The *Medium Interface Connector/Fiber Shroud Duplex* (MIC/FSD) connector is used for fiber-based *Fiber Distributed Data Interfaces* (FDDI) connections. It is polarized so that TX/RX are always correct.

- *ESCON*   This is used to connect to IBM equipment as well as channel interface processors.

- *MT-RJ*   A new fiber connector that is able to fit into a standard 110 patch panel. It almost doubles the port capacity of an SC module.

Physical Encoding Methods

An encoding method is the method that a device uses to put data on the media. Although the media and connectors for LANs and WANs are similar, the encoding variations for LANs and WANs are different.

LAN Encoding   Four basic LAN encoding schemes exist. The first encoding scheme is the foundation for all the other encoding schemes. Thus, it is important that you understand the basic encod-

Figure E-5
Common encoding methods

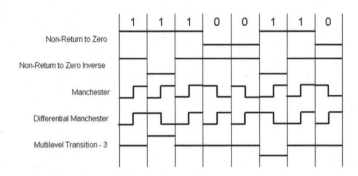

ing scheme that everything is based on, the *Non-Return To Zero-Level* (NRZ-L). Figure E-5 shows how the various encoding methods reduce the binary numbers to electrical or optical signals.

The common encoding methods are as follows:

- Non-Return to Zero-Level *(NRZ-L)* This is the basic type of encoding upon which all others are based. A *one* is positive voltage; a *zero* is no voltage. The problem with this is that timing information cannot be retrieved from a string of zeros. Thus, other encoding methods have been developed to overcome this problem.

- Non-Return to Zero Inverted *(NRZI)* Used in 100Base-Fx fiber networks, NRZI uses a change in signal to represent a one.

- *Manchester* Used in Ethernet, this encoding is based on the signal transition in the middle of the bit. An upward transition is a one. A downward transition represents a zero.

- *Differential Manchester* Used in Token Ring networks, this always has a transition in the middle. However, the encoding is based on the transition at the bit boundaries. A transition indicates a zero. No transition indicates a one.

- *MLT-3* Used in Fast Ethernet Networks. Instead of two voltage levels (voltage and no voltage), MLT-3 uses three layers: positive voltage, no voltage, and negative voltage. Changing the voltage represents a one. For instance, a series of ones would be represented as $0,1,0,-1,0,1,0.-1$.

Table E-3

The Pinouts of T1
and E1 lines

Eight Position Jack Pinouts	T1/EI
1	Receive (tip)
2	Receive (ring)
3	Not used
4	Transmit (tip)
5	Transmit (ring)
6	Not used
7	Not used
8	Not used

WAN Connectors   Remember that the same types of media are used in WANs as LANs. However, the connectors used in WANs differ depending upon their use. Too many WAN connectors exist for us to cover every type, but the most common WAN connectors terminate T1 and E1 lines. Table E-3 displays the pinouts of T1 and E1 Lines.

NOTE: *The use of the terms tip and ring are typically not used today. Their usage is historical in perspective when testing was done with a tone tester. This test would allow a different tone to be present depending on which tip or ring was tested.*

WAN Encoding   Before the topic of WAN encoding can be addressed, the concept of the digital hierarchy must be familiar to the reader. The digital hierarchy is a classification of circuit speeds. In North America, it is called the North American Digital Hierarchy. In Europe and the majority of the world, it is called the CCITT Digital Hierarchy. Both begin at the DS0 level with a single 64Kbps circuit. Then differences appear in the two systems.

In the North American Digital Hierarchy, this DS0 circuit is multiplied 24 times into a DS1 circuit with a speed of 1.544Mbps. This

DS1 is then multiplied 28 times into a DS3 circuit with a speed of over 44Mbps.

The CCITT Digital Hierarchy combines 30 DS0s into an E1 circuit with a speed of 2.048Mbps. Next, 16 E1 circuits are combined to form an E3 circuit with a speed of over 34Mbps.

The WAN media type used depends on the circuit speed. T1 and E1 circuits generally use UTP. DS3 and E3 circuits use coax. However, all speeds above DS3/E3 require the use of fiber optic cables. The terms *North American Synchronous Optical Network* (SONET) and *International Synchronous Digital Network* (SDH) identify the circuits in this range. Table E-4 denotes the various circuit names and speeds.

The variations in WAN encoding first occur at the DS1 level. When a DS1 line is ordered, it is necessary to specify the framing and line coding. These settings must match the *Channel Service Unit / Data Service Unit* (CSU/ DSU) and the other end of the circuit.

NOTE: *One of the most difficult issues to troubleshoot is the incorrect encoding of a circuit. More that once, I have seen a service provider finally determine that the cause of a line fault is improper encoding at one end of the circuit.*

The two frame types available for DS1s are *D4 / Super Frame* (SF) and *Extended Super Frame* (ESF). The two frame types for E1s are CRC4 and no CRC4.

Table E-4

Various circuit names and speeds

Optical Circuit	Speed
OC-1	51.8Mbps
OC-3	155.5Mbps
OC-12	622.1Mbps
OC-48	2488.3Mbps

The available line codings for DS1s are *Alternate Mark Inversion* (AMI) and *Bipolar Eight-Zero Substitution* (B8ZS). The only available line codings for E1s are AMI and *High-Density Bipolar 3* (HDB3).

Conclusion

The physical layer may be seen as the most trivial or least important of the seven layers. After all, no fancy things like routing or switching happen at this layer. No addresses are used at the physical layer. However, many of the issues faced in the networking world are solved at the physical layer. A UTP cable might run too close to a fluorescent light or an OC-3 fiber patch cord might get accidentally crushed. When troubleshooting network problems, one of the most effective methods is to follow the OSI Model and troubleshoot by layers. Thus, you would start at the physical layer and move up once you have determined each layer is operating correctly.

Layer 2: The Data Link Layer

Layer 2 of the OSI Reference Model is the data link layer. Figure E-6 shows the placement of the network layer in the OSI Reference Model.

The data link layer is responsible for describing the specifications for topology and communication between local systems. Many examples of data link layer technology exist:

- Ethernet
- Fast Ethernet
- Token Ring
- Frame Relay
- HDLC
- *Point-to-Point Protocol* (PPP)
- *Serial Line Interface Protocol* (SLIP)

Figure E-6
The data link layer in the OSI Reference Model

7	Application Layer
6	Presentation Layer
5	Session Layer
4	Transport Layer
3	Network Layer
2	**Data Link Layer**
1	Physical Layer

Figure E-7
An example of data link layer conversations

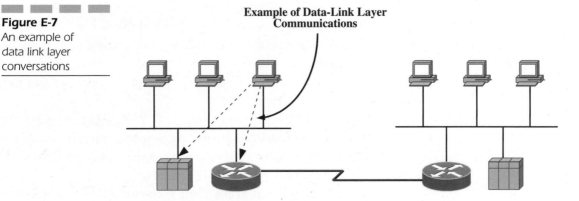

Example of Data-Link Layer Communications

All of these services describe how conversations take place between two devices on the same media. Remember that the data link layer implementation used is independent of the physical layer. For example, Ethernet can use UTP or coaxial cable. It does not matter which physical layer media it uses; the rules that govern the technology are the same. This is the beauty of the OSI Model: any layer can be replaced without concerns about the lower or upper layers.

Communication at the data link layer is between two hosts on the same network. Those two hosts can be a desktop computer communicating with a local file server or a local host sending data to a router that is destined for a remote host (see Figure E-7).

Data Link Layer Example

The following section focuses on Ethernet, one of the most commonly used data link layer standards. If we look at the frame format of an Ethernet frame, we can get a better understanding of each component's purpose. In Figure E-8, we see a standard IEEE 802.3 Ethernet frame format. If we look at each component, we can easily see its purpose.

Preamble The preamble is an alternating pattern of ones and zeros. It tells the other stations on the media that a frame is coming. The IEEE 802.3 preamble ends with two consecutive ones, which serves to synchronize the frame reception of all stations on the LAN.

Data Link Layer Addressing (Destination and Source Address)
The capability to distinguish one host from another is critical when multiple hosts have access to the same media. Compare that to point-to-point connections in which the capability to distinguish the end point is irrelevant because there is only one other node on the network that can hear the data.

The address used by end hosts to identify each other is called the *Media Access Control* (MAC) address. It is often referred to as the physical address, burned-in address, or hardware address. The MAC address of each Ethernet *Network Interface Card* (NIC) is by definition unique. It is a 48-bit address built into the NIC that uniquely identifies the station. It is generally represented in one of three formats:

Figure E-8
Ethernet frame
format

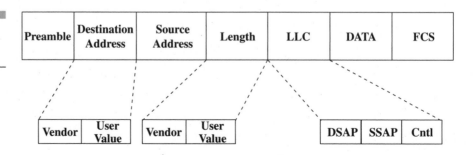

- 00-60-94-EB-41-9F
- 00:60:94:EB:41:9F
- 0060.94EB.419F

If we look closely at the MAC address, we will see that it can be broken down into two distinct components: the vendor's address and a unique host identifier. The first three octets (24 bits) identify the vendor. Using the example listed previously, we can look up 00-60-94 at `http://standards. ieee.org/regauth/oui/oui.txt`.

We can see that this NIC was manufactured by IBM. This can be useful when attempting to locate a device on the network that is malfunctioning.

Length   The Length field indicates the number of bytes contained in the Data field. Although all of the other fields are of a predetermined length (the Destination and Source addresses are six bytes) the Data field can be up to 1,500 bytes. If the data in the frame is insufficient to fill the frame to a minimum 64-byte size, the frame is padded to ensure at least a 64-byte frame.

Logical Link Control (LLC)   The IEEE 802.2 *Logical Link Control* (LLC) header is used to specify which upper layer protocol is contained in the data. Without the capability to distinguish which upper layer protocol a packet belongs to, it is impossible to carry multiple network layer protocols over a data link layer implementation. For example, because Novell's 802.3 RAW frame format does not have a method to distinguish between network layer protocols, it could only carry a single network layer protocol. This is one of the reasons why Novell's 802.3 frame format is generally not employed.

Another example of a data link layer technology not using a type field is SLIP. Even though it enjoyed some success in the late '80s and early '90s as a dialup protocol, its incapability to distinguish between different network layer protocols has allowed PPP to become the standard dialup protocol.

The following fields all play a part in LLC identification:

- *DSAP*   The *Destination Service Access Point* (DSAP) is a one-byte field that acts like a pointer in the receiving station. It tells the receiving NIC which buffer to put this information in. This function is critical when users are running multiple network layer protocols.

■ *SSAP* The *Source Service Access Point* (SSAP) is identical to the DSAP, except that it indicates the source of the sending application.

■ *Control* This one-byte field is used to indicate the type of LLC frame of this data frame. Three different types of LLC frames exist:

  ▪ *LLC1* An unacknowledged connectionless service. It uses unsequenced information to set up communication between two network stations. This type of LLC is generally used with Novell's *Internetwork Packet Exchange* (IPX), TCP/IP, and Vines IP.

  ▪ *LLC2* A connection-oriented service between two network stations. This type of service is generally used in SNA and NetBIOS sessions.

  ▪ *LLC3* A connectionless but acknowledged-oriented service between two different stations. This type of service can be used by SDLC.

Data The Data field in an IEEE 802.3 frame can be between 43 and 1,497 bytes. However, depending upon the type of frame being used, this size can vary. For example, an Ethernet II frame can hold between 46 and 1,497 bytes of data, while a frame using Novell's RAW 802.3 frame format can hold between 46 and 1,500 bytes of data.

Frame Check Sequence (FCS) The last four bytes of a IEEE 802.3 frame are used to verify that the frame is not corrupt. By using a complex polynomial, the NIC can detect errors in the frame. If errors are detected, then the frame is discarded and it never reaches the memory buffers.

Now that we understand the frame format of an IEEE 802.3 frame, we need to discuss how those frames get on the wire.

Carrier Sense Media Access with Collision Detection (CSMA/CD) Ethernet is one of the most common network topologies. The basic rule behind Ethernet communication is called *Car-*

rier Sense Multiple Access with Collision Detection (CSMA/CD). If we break down each phrase, we can interpret its meaning:

- *Carrier Sense* All Ethernet stations are required to listen to the network to see if any other devices are sending data. This serves two purposes: one, it keeps the station from sending data when someone else is sending data and, two, it enables the station to be ready when another station wants to send it data.

- *Multiple Access* This means more than two stations can be connected to the same network at the same time and that all stations can transmit data whenever the network is free. In order for data to be transmitted, the station must wait until the Ethernet channel is idle. Once the channel is idle, the station can transmit a frame, but it must listen to see if there is a collision.

- *Collision Detection* If there is a collision, then both stations must immediately back off and use a backoff algorithm to randomly determine how long they should wait before trying to transmit again. It is important that a random number be generated for this timer, because if some standard number were used, then both stations would wait the same length of time and then attempt to transmit again, thus causing another collision.

NOTE: *A collision is the simultaneous transmitting of a frame by two different stations. A station can detect a collision within the first 64 bytes of the transmission.*

Conclusion

Many different types of data link layer technologies exist, and Ethernet is one of those technologies. Although a data link layer technology can theoretically use any physical layer implementation, generally the actual implementation of a data link layer technology goes hand in hand with the physical layer implementation. For example, PPP is generally used over dialup networks or WAN networks, while Ethernet and Token Ring are used in LAN environments. This means that you probably won't see very many implementations of PPP using CAT 5 cable for its wiring infrastructure. Likewise, you probably won't see Token Ring being deployed from a corporate office to a telecommuter's home using the Telco's wiring infrastructure.

Layer 3: Network Layer

Layer 3 of the OSI Reference Model is the network layer. Figure E-9 shows the placement of the network layer in the OSI Reference Model.

This layer is responsible for providing routing for the network. Routing, in a generic sense, is simply finding a path to a destination. In the context of the network layer, routing means finding a path to a destination that is a member of a different Layer 2 network than the source. Physical networks can be connected together with bridges to form larger Layer 2 networks. Unfortunately, Layer 2 networks cannot scale to an infinite size. As these networks grow, more bandwidth is used to transmit broadcast packets that flood the entire

Figure E-9
The network layer
and the OSI
Reference Model

7	Application Layer
6	Presentation Layer
5	Session Layer
4	Transport Layer
3	**Network Layer**
2	Data Link Layer
1	Physical Layer

Layer 2 network. These broadcast packets are used to find the destination host.

Routing enables Layer 2 networks to be broken into smaller segments, enabling the network to grow to support more hosts. Figure E-10 shows the concept of routing.

The data link control layer passes packets up to the network layer. These packets have headers to define the source and destination addresses and other network layer parameters of the data in the packet. The network layer only uses the data in the network layer packet header for information to perform its functions. This maintains the modularity of the network layer. Therefore, there is no dependency on the information from the data link control layer headers and the transport layer headers.

Network layer communication is not guaranteed. This means that there is no mechanism to determine if the destination node received the network layer packets. Guaranteed delivery is maintained at

Figure E-10
Routing between
Layer 2 networks

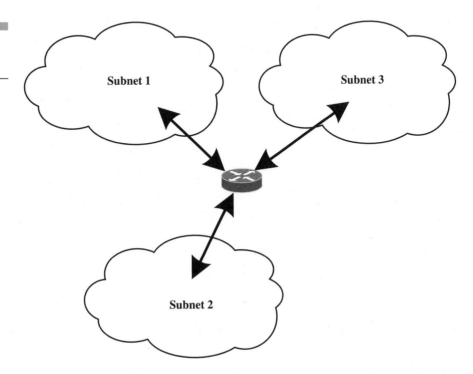

other layers in the OSI Reference Model. The most obvious reason for not implementing guaranteed delivery at the network layer is because this layer has no concept of end-to-end delivery. It would be more appropriate for upper layer protocols that implement more connection-oriented services to make sure that the data reaches its destination. The network layer routes data on a packet-by-packet basis.

Only one network layer process exists for each network node. Several data link control layer processes may be found below the network layer, depending on the number of physical interfaces in the node, and several transport layer processes may be found above the network layer, depending on the number of connection-oriented streams terminating at the node. Several network layer protocols may be running on a node, but each of these protocols corresponds to a separate logical internetwork and they do not intercommunicate.

A special node called a *gateway* connects logical networks formed by network layer addressing schemes. Gateways have a special sublayer in the upper portion of the network layer called the *Internet sublayer*. This sublayer handles the intercommunication between subnets. When a packet arrives from one subnet that is destined for another, the packet will be passed from the network layer to the Internet sublayer. The Internet sublayer in turn determines the destination subnet and forwards the packet back down to the lower portion of the network layer to the destination subnet. This is the basic idea behind routing. Figure E-11 illustrates the concept of a network node.

Each network layer process at each node is a peer process. These peer processes work together to implement distributed algorithms. These distributed algorithms are the routing algorithms corre-

Figure E-11
Network node model

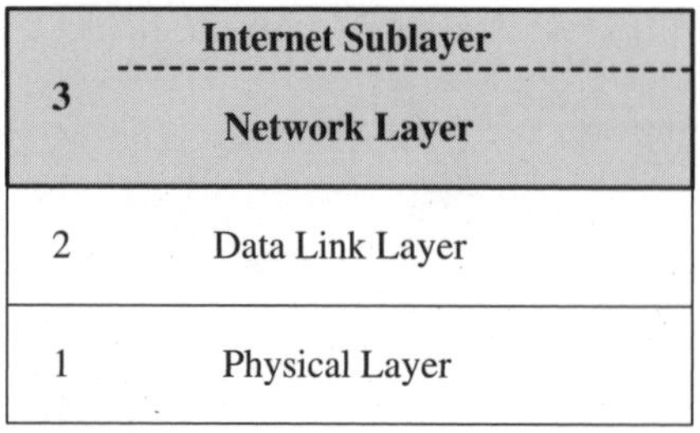

3	**Internet Sublayer**
	Network Layer
2	Data Link Layer
1	Physical Layer

sponding to various routing protocols. These protocols provide a means to automatically discover and transmit routing information between gateways.

The Internet Protocol (IP)

The most familiar protocol that operates at the network layer is the *Internet Protocol* (IP). IP is by far the most widely deployed network layer protocol due to the success of the Internet. This protocol is the foundation of the Internet in terms of addressing and packet routing. The Internet employs multiple protocols in the other OSI Reference Model layers, but it only uses IP in the network layer.

Another example of a network protocol is Novell's *Internet Packet Exchange* (IPX). Novell has since refined NetWare to use IP as the native network layer protocol instead of IPX.

IP Node Operation

If an IP host wants to communicate with another IP host, the transmitting IP source must determine if the destination IP address is in the same subnet or not. If the destination is in the same subnet, the host must send an *Address Resolution Protocol* (ARP) request packet to obtain the MAC address of the destination, assuming the destination MAC address isn't already in its ARP table. If the destination is not in the same subnet as the source, the source must send the packet to the MAC address of the gateway for that subnet. Most IP hosts have one IP address to send their packets to if they are destined for any subnet other than their own. This is called the *default gateway* or *default router address*. The user configures the default gateway address.

Once the default gateway (router) gets the packet and sees that the packet is destined for its own MAC address and at the same time destined for another IP host, the router knows that it must forward the packet to another interface to move the packet closer to its destination.

The mechanism for determining if the destination IP host is in the same subnet is as follows. The subnet mask is bitwise ANDed with both the source IP address and the destination IP address. The logic table for the AND operation is shown in Table E-5.

The result of these two functions is *exclusively ORed* (XORed). If this final result is not zero, then the destination IP address is in another subnet. The logic table for the XOR operation is shown in Table E-6.

Here is an example of determining if the destination address is in the same subnet as the host:

Source IP address:

$(100.1.43.1)_{\text{dotted-decimal}}$ $(01100100.00000001.00101011.00000001)_{\text{binary}}$

Subnet mask:

$(255.255.255.0)_{\text{dotted-decimal}}$
$(11111111.11111111.11111111.00000000)_{\text{binary}}$

Destination IP address:

$(100.1.44.2)_{\text{dotted-decimal}}$ $(01100100.00000001.00101100.00000010)_{\text{binary}}$

Table E-5

Logic table for AND operations

	1	0
1	1	0
0	0	0

Table E-6

Logic table for OR operations

	1	0
1	0	1
0	1	0

Source IP address ANDed with subnet mask:

01100100.00000001.00101011.00000001
<u>11111111.11111111.11111111.00000000</u>
01100100.00000001.00101011.00000000

Destination IP address ANDed with subnet mask:

01100100.00000001.00101100.00000010
<u>11111111.11111111.11111111.00000000</u>
01100100.00000001.00101100.00000000

The two results XORed:

01100100.00000001.00101011.00000000
<u>01100100.00000001.00101100.00000000</u>
00000000.00000000.00000111.00000000

The result of the XOR function is not zero. Therefore, the destination IP address is in another subnet than the source and the packet must be sent to the default gateway to be routed to the destination subnet.

When the router gets a packet to be forwarded to another subnet, the router must manipulate the MAC and IP header fields to ensure that the packet is forwarded toward its destination.

Three things must happen when the router forwards the packet at the network layer:

- The interface to forward the packet to must be determined.
- The destination MAC address must be updated with the MAC address of the next-hop router or destination host.
- The *Time to Live* (TTL) field must be decremented in the IP header.

The interface that the packet is forwarded out of is determined by looking through the route table that the router maintains. This route table associates a route to a destination with a physical interface.

The destination MAC address must be updated with the MAC address of the destination IP host if the host is directly connected to the router. If the destination host is not directly connected to one of the ports of the router, the router must forward the packet to the next router to move the packet toward the destination IP host. In either case, if the router doesn't know the MAC address of the next hop toward the destination, it must ARP for the MAC address.

The TTL field is then decremented. This field provides a mechanism for the packet to be removed from the network if it gets caught in a loop. Without such a mechanism, the packet may be forwarded for as long as the routing loop is active. The packet is removed by a router if its TTL field is zero.

Internetwork Packet Exchange (IPX) Operation

Another example of a Layer 3 protocol is the IPX protocol. The IPX protocol was developed by Novell NetWare. Novell NetWare is a *Network Operating System* (NOS) that provides network file and print services. IPX is quickly being replaced by IP since NetWare now provides native IP support, but there remains a large installed base of IPX networks in campus networks.

Unlike IP, IPX has no concept of multiple subnets per the Layer 2 network. Instead, IPX has only one address per physical network called a *network number*. The full network layer address for a network device is made of two parts: the 32-bit network number and the node's 48-bit MAC address.

Some argue that the combination of Layer 2 and Layer 3 addresses to form a Layer 3 address undermines the modularity of the OSI Reference Model. This is due to the fact that IPX (Layer 3) network numbers depend on the Layer 2 addressing scheme. This argument is purely academic since the MAC address scheme is so prevalent. The real limitation to IPX is its inability to logically subnet hosts on the same physical network.

Layer 4: Transport Layer

Layer 4 of the OSI Reference Model is the transport layer. Figure E-12 shows the placement of the network layer in the OSI Reference Model.

Figure E-12
The transport layer
and the OSI
Reference Model

7	Application Layer
6	Presentation Layer
5	Session Layer
4	**Transport Layer**
3	Network Layer
2	Data Link Layer
1	Physical Layer

Figure E-13
The transport layer
differentiating
between
conversations

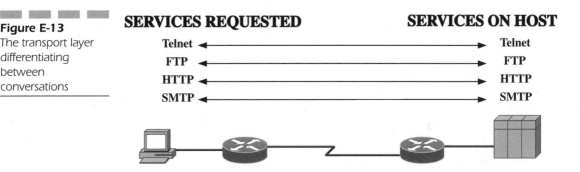

The transport layer is responsible for data transfer issues such as reliability of the connection, establishing error detections, recovery, and flow control. In addition, this layer is responsible for delivering packets from the network layer to the upper layers of the OSI Model.

If we think of the network layer as responsible for delivering packets from one host to another, the transport layer is responsible for identifying the conversations between two hosts. For example, Figure E-13 shows an example of how the transport layer keeps the conversations between the different applications separate.

Two different variants of transport layer protocols are used. The first provides a reliable, connection-oriented service, while the second method is a best-effort delivery. The difference between these two protocols dictates the paradigm in which they operate. When using TCP/IP, the two different protocols are TCP and UDP. Inside an IP packet is a protocol number that enables the host to identify whether the packet contains a TCP message or a UDP message. The TCP protocol value is 6 and for UDP it is 17. Many other (~130) protocols types exist, but these two are commonly used to transport user messages from one host to another.

Transport Layer Protocol Examples

In this section, we'll examine some examples of transport layer protocols.

Transmission Control Protocol (TCP) The TCP described in RFC 793 provides applications with a reliable connection-oriented service. Three basic instruments are used to make TCP a connection-oriented service:

- Sequence numbers
- Acknowledgments
- Windowing

In order for data to be handed down to the network layer, the data must be broken down into messages. These messages are then given a sequence number by TCP before being handed off to the network layer. The purpose of the sequence number is so that in case the packets arrive out of order the remote host can reassemble the data using the sequence numbers. This only guarantees that the data is reassembled correctly.

In addition to sequence numbers, acknowledgements are used by the remote host to tell the local host that the data was received, guaranteeing the delivery of data. If, for whatever reason, a packet gets dropped along the way, the remote host can see that it is missing a message and request it again, as shown in Figure E-14.

Although windowing enables TCP to regulate the flow of packets between two hosts, this minimizes the chances of packets being dropped because the buffers are full in the remote host.

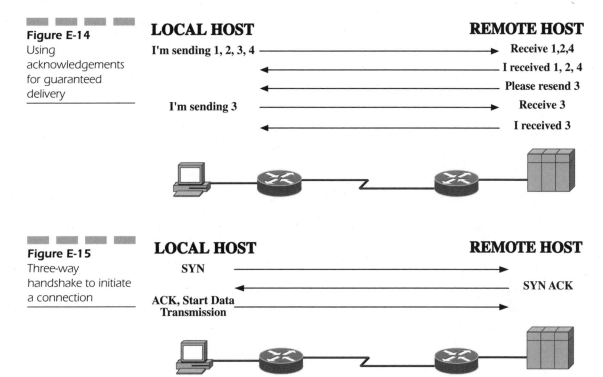

Figure E-14
Using
acknowledgements
for guaranteed
delivery

LOCAL HOST

I'm sending 1, 2, 3, 4 ————————→ Receive 1,2,4

←———————— I received 1, 2, 4

←———————— Please resend 3

I'm sending 3 ————————→ Receive 3

←———————— I received 3

REMOTE HOST

Figure E-15
Three-way
handshake to initiate
a connection

LOCAL HOST

SYN ————————→

←———————— SYN ACK

ACK, Start Data ————————→
Transmission

REMOTE HOST

In order for a TCP connection to be established, a three-step handshake is exchanged between the local host and the remote host. This three-way handshake starts with the local host initiating a conversation by sending a *Synchronize Sequence Numbers* (SYN) packet to the remote host, as shown in Figure E-15.

The remote host acknowledges the SYN and sends an SYN acknowledgement back to the local host. The local host responds by sending an acknowledgement and then starts sending data. The purpose of this handshake is to synchronize the sequence numbers that identify the proper order used to reconstruct the messages throughout the conversation.

User Datagram Protocol (UDP) The UDP, as described in RFC 768, provides applications with a connectionless best-effort delivery service. Because there is no time wasted setting up a connection, applications that utilize UDP are very fast. Applications that send short bursts of data can take advantage of UDP's speed, but if the messages get delivered out of order or a message gets dropped, then the entire message fails.

Well-known Ports   We've seen how we can guarantee the delivery of a packet through the use of TCP and how we can improve throughput by using a connectionless delivery service, but how are discrete conversations between two hosts handled? Both TCP and UDP utilize a mechanism called a port (also known as a socket). By utilizing a source port and a destination port, two hosts can distinguish between multiple conversations.

In order to provide services to unknown callers, a host will use a well-known port number. Well-known port numbers are assigned by the *Internet Assigned Numbers Authority* (IANA). By adhering to the well-known port numbers published by the IANA, we can make sure that various services do not utilize the same port. Both TCP and UDP use port numbers and when a service can utilize both TCP and UDP, the port number is identical. Table E-7 shows us a sampling of the well-known port numbers.

Until recently, the assigned port range was from 0 to 255. However, the range has been expanded from 0 to 1,023.

Conclusion

The transport layer protocol helps end devices distinguish between simultaneous conversations between the same two hosts. The proto-

Table E-7

Well-known port numbers

Port Number	Service
20	FTP (Data)
21	FTP (Control)
23	Telnet
25	SMTP
42	Host Name Server
53	Domain Name Service
80	HTTP

col that is used, connection-oriented or connectionless, is dependent upon the needs of the upper layer application. Some applications want the speed of UDP and will implement their own form of reliability-checking in an effort to speed up the transmission of the data. Although this obviously adds a lot of overhead to the programmer's job, it can be worth it, depending upon the applications requirements.

Layer 5: Session Layer

Layer 5 of the OSI Reference Model is the session layer. Figure E-16 shows the placement of the session layer in the OSI Reference Model.

The session layer is responsible for providing such functions as directory service and access rights. The session layer has a defined role in the OSI Reference Model, but its functions are not as critical as the lower layers to all networks. For example, a network without the physical layer, the data link layer, network layer, or the transport layer would be lacking basic functionality that would make the network useful. Until recently, the session layer has been ignored or at least not seen as absolutely necessary in data networks. Session layer functionality has been seen as a host responsibility, not a network function. As networks become larger and more secure, functions such as directory services and access rights become more necessary.

Figure E-16
The session layer and the OSI Reference Model

7	Application Layer
6	Presentation Layer
5	**Session Layer**
4	Transport Layer
3	Network Layer
2	Data Link Layer
1	Physical Layer

Access rights functionality deals with a user's access to various network resources such as computer access and authentication, file access, and printer access. Devices providing the service such as file and print servers have typically implemented access rights. There has been a shift in responsibility for these functions in recent years. Authentication can now be distributed using authentication services such as Kerberos. File and print service access control is moving to network directory services such as Novell's *Network Directory Service* (NDS) or Microsoft's *Active Directory Services* (ADS). These services control what resources a host may access.

Directory services are services that find resources on the network. Typically, a user would have to have prior knowledge of a service to gain access to the service. Some services have the capability of broadcasting their presence, but that methodology does not scale well in a large network with many hosts and many services. True directory services act as a redirection point for hosts to be given addressing information to find a particular resource. Novell's NDS or Microsoft's ADS can act as directory services as well as define a user's access rights, as previously mentioned.

The session layer has no hard and fast rules for interfacing with the presentation layer since the presentation layer is optional in many cases. The session layer services are typically accessed via TCP or UDP port numbers, therefore defining the interface to the transport layer.

Layer 6: Presentation Layer

Layer 6 of the OSI Reference Model is the presentation layer. Figure E-17 shows the placement of the network layer in the OSI Reference Model.

The presentation layer is responsible for providing data encryption, data compression, and code conversion. The functions in this layer have not been considered a function of the network and have been handled by various applications. In recent years, data encryption, compression, and code conversion have moved into the mainstream of the network protocol functionality.

7	Application Layer
6	**Presentation Layer**
5	Session Layer
4	Transport Layer
3	Network Layer
2	Data Link Layer
1	Physical Layer

Data encryption is moving to the forefront of networking since networks are carrying more sensitive data. Encryption can be handled in a number of ways. The easiest and most secure method for encrypting data is to encrypt all the data on a particular link. This requires a device on both ends of a path to encrypt and decrypt the payload of each packet that passes over the link. This requires that sensitive data always pass over a path installed with an encryption device. This does not scale well for a large network. The more scalable method for encryption is for the applications at both ends of a session to set up a means for encrypting the data. This method of encryption requires that a device have more processing power to handle the application and the data encryption in real time.

Data compression conserves bandwidth over a link. Like data encryption, data compression can be done on both ends of a path through a network. This requires an external device to compress the network data. This method does not scale well in large networks where there can be many paths through a network. A more scalable method for data compression is to allow the application at both ends of a session to compress the data. The tradeoff in this method is more processing power is required on the host to support the application and real-time compression/decompression.

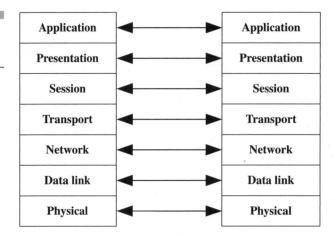

Code conversion involves converting a set of data or a data stream from one format to another. Data formats can be for character sets, video formats, graphics formats, and presentation formats. Examples of character set formats are ASCII and EBCDIC, video formats are MPEG and MJPEG, graphics formats are GIF, TIFF, JPEG, and bitmap, and presentation formats are HTML, XML, and SHTML.

No hard and fast rules define the interface between the presentation layer and the session layer since the session layer may be optional for a particular network. The presentation layer communicates to the application layer by addressing the application with an appropriate transport layer (session) address such as a TCP port number.

Layer 7: Application Layer

The final layer, Layer 7, of the OSI Model is the application layer. This section will define the application layer and examine in moderate detail what takes place at Layer 7.

The application layer consists of an application that requires the use of a network to perform its task. Communication between applications takes place at Layer 7. As with the previous layers, Layer 7 exchanges messages with Layer 7 only. Restated, an application communicates with only a peer application. Figure E-18 depicts this layer-to-layer communication.

An example application could be something as simple as a *chat* program. The application connects to its peer application and sends characters that are entered on the keyboard. It also displays characters received from the peer application. The applications communicating at Layer 7 use the lower layers and the services they provide to send and receive application-specific information.

Furthermore, it is common for applications to further define the contents of the data that is being exchanged. Even with the simple chat program, a protocol is defined: "Each message received from a peer application contains a single character." This creates a challenge for troubleshooting network-related problems.

Although only a handful of protocols are used at the lower layers, the protocols are usually well specified. As you can see, anyone can define a new protocol for his or her specific application. This makes it difficult for vendors that develop network analyzers to provide the capability of troubleshooting application, or Layer 7, problems.

As you can see, this layer can be any application that requires network communication. The application communicates with its peer application at Layer 7, and an application may arbitrarily define a protocol that specifies application-to-application communication.

Conclusion

It is important to remember that the OSI Model is only for reference. Not all protocols and technologies have a direct correlation to one of the seven layers. Frequently, a protocol may straddle different layers, such as ARP, which is used when a computer knows the IP address it needs to communicate with (network layer) but it doesn't know its MAC address (data link layer). ARP enables a computer to map an IP address to a MAC address. So is ARP a data link layer-protocol or a network-layer protocol? Technically, it straddles both layers, so it doesn't really fit the OSI Model, but without it IP communication on a LAN couldn't happen.

BIBLIOGRAPHY

Bibliographic Chapter References

Berkowitz, Howard. *Designing Addressing Architectures for Routing and Switching*. Macmillan Technical Publishing, 1998.

Berkowitz, Howard. *Network Architecture and Development Series: Designing Routing and Switching Architectures*. Macmillan Technical Publishing, 1999.

Cisco CCIE Fundamentals: Network Design and Case Study, 2nd Edition. Cisco Press, 1999

Clark, Kennedy, and Kevin Hamilton. CCIE Professional Development: Cisco LAN Switching. Cisco Press, 1999.

Comer, Douglas E. *Internetworking with TCP/IP, Volume I, Third Edition*. Englewood Cliffs, NJ: Prentice Hall, 1995.

Held, Gilbert. *Cisco Router Performance Guide*. McGraw-Hill, 2000

Oppenheimer, Priscilla. *Top Down Network Design*. Indianapolis: Cisco Press, 1999.

Pepelnjak, Ivan. *EIGRP Network Design Solutions*. Cisco Press, 2000.

Perlman, Radia. *Interconnections: Bridges, Routers, Switches, and Internetworking Protocols*. Reading, MA: Addison Wesley, 1999.

Stevens, W. Richard. *TCP/IP Illustrated, Volume 1: The Protocols*. Addison-Wesley Publishing, 1994.

Thomas, Thomas. OSPF Network Design Solutions. Cisco Press, 1998.

WEBLIOGRAPHY

ATM Forum, February 2000.
http://www.atmforum.com

Approved ATM Technical Specifications, February 2000.
http://atmforum.com/atmforum/specs/approved.html

Charles Spurgeon's Ethernet Web Site, February 2000.
http://www.bellereti.com/ethernet/ethernet.html

Cisco Intelligent Networking
www.cisco.com/warp/public/cc/sol/mkt/ent/
cmps/netsr_wp.htm

Cisco Internetworking Technology Overview, February 2000.
http://www.cisco.com/univercd/cc/td/doc/cisintwk/
ito_doc/index.htm

Cisco Product Catalog, February 2000.
http://www.cisco.com/univercd/cc/td/doc/pcat/
index.htm

Cisco Product Documentation, February 2000.
http://www.cisco.com/univercd/cc/td/doc/product/
index.htm

Cisco Router Tunnel Lab, February 2000.
http://www.ocio.usda.gov/tso/ian/tunnllab.html

Designing the Next-Generation Campus Network
www.cisco.com/warp/public/784/packet/apr99/9.html

Faqs.org, February 2000.
http://www.faqs.org

Internetworking Design Basics
www.cisco.com/univercd/cc/td/doc/
cisintwk/idg4/nd2002.htm

Internet RFC Archive, February 2000.
http://www.faqs.org/rfcs/

MRTG, May 2000.
http://eestaff.ethz.ch/>oetiker/webtools/mrtg/
mrtg.html

PMG NetAnalyst, Network Analysis Training and Services, May
2000. `http://www.pmg.com`

Protocols for WANs and LANs, February 2000.
`http://www.protocols.com/`

RFC Editor Home Page, February 2000.
`http://www.rfc-editor.org`

Sniffer Technologies, A Protocol Analyzer, May 2000.
`http://www.sniffer.com`

Understanding IP Addressing, February 2000.
`http://www.3com.com/nsc/501302.html`

INDEX

10Base5 networks, 238
  coaxial cable, 202
10BaseF standard, 238
10Base-FL networks
  fiber optic cable, 202
10BaseT networks, 34, 207, 238
  UTP cable, 202
10Mbps, 201–202
100Base-FX
  Fast Ethernet, 206, 239
100BaseT specification, 239
100Base-T4
  Fast Ethernet, 206, 239
100Base-TX
  Fast Ethernet, 206, 239
  ports, 207
100Mbps (Fast Ethernet), 201, 206
1000Base-CX (Gigabit Ethernet), 208
1000Base-LX (Gigabit Ethernet), 208
1000Base-SX (Gigabit Ethernet), 208
1000Base-T (Gigabit Ethernet), 208
1000Base-X (Gigabit Ethernet), 208
16/4 standards
  Token Ring, 212
1600 series routers, 58
2500 series routers, 57
  AUI ports, 58
2600 series routers, 58
3600 series routers, 59
4000 series routers, 59
5-4-3 rule
  LAN design, 222–224
700 series routers, 64
7000 series routers, 60
7500 series routers, 60
80-20 rule
  LAN design, 222
800 series routers, 64

A

AAA (Authentication, Authorization, and Accounting), 6
AARP (AppleTalk Address-Resolution Protocol), 32
acceptance criteria
  documenting, 144
access layer
  hierarchical network model, 88, 170
access lists

router software, 334–335
  design notes, 340
  examples, 337–339
  operation, 335–337
active monitors (Token Ring), 42
adapter cards (Token Ring), 213
addresses
  AppleTalk, 33
  IP, 26
  IPX, 31
addressing (network), 272
  G&S Productions case study, 293
  Global Supplies Corporation case study, 291
  IP, 273
    public vs. private, 274–275
  IPX, 282–283
    selecting addresses, 284–285
  Limbo Medical Group case study, 290
  NAT, 275–276
  selecting addresses, 281
  summarization, 280
    DNS, 281
  VLSMs, 278–280
  Widget Manufacturing case study, 285–287
algorithms (Ethernet), 203
American National Standards Institute, See ANSI
analog switched WAN circuits, 245
ANSI, 240
ANSI X3T11 Fiber Channel specification, 208
AppleTalk, 31–33
  addresses, 33
  application layer, 33
  network layer, 32
  routing protocols, 33
  session layer, 32
  transport layer, 32
AppleTalk Transaction Protocol, See ATP
application layer
  AppleTalk, 33
  IPX/SPX, 30
  TCP/IP, 24
application requirements, documenting, 146
application usage, 107–108
ARP, 24
AS5xxx series routers, 65
ATM (Asynchronous Transfer Mode), 21, 209
  cells, 21
  switches, 66
ATP (AppleTalk Transaction Protocol), 32
AUI (Attachment Unit Interface) ports, 58
  2500 series routers, 58

authentication
peer router, 342
author notes, 4
availability statistics, documentation process, 114

B

bandwidth
EIGRP, 316
IGRP, 302
Bank of Pompeii case study, 356–358
design test, 373, 390
baseband signaling, 34
bastion hosts, 188
BGP, 25
bridges, 37
bridging protocols, routing architecture, 318
broadband signaling, 34
broadcast domains, 240
LAN design, 220–221
broadcast storms, Ethernet, 40
business constraints, documenting, 141
business goals, documenting, 140–141
business issues, documenting, 137–138

C

cabling, Ethernet, 34–35
Carrier Sense Multiple Access and Collission Detection, *See*
    CSMA/CD
case studies, 5
    Bank of Pompeii, 356–358
    design testing
        Bank of Pompeii, 373, 390
        Global Supplies Corporation, 372–373, 389
        Limbo Medical Group, 371–372, 388
        Widget Manufacturing, 366–369, 385–386
    G&S Productions
        documentation standards, 160–162
        routing architecture design, 329
    Global Supplies Corporation, 354–356
        documentation standards, 156–160
        routing architecture design, 327
    LAN design, 224–226
    Limbo Medical Group, 353–354
        documentation standards, 154–155
        routing architecture design, 326
    Widget Manufacturing, 350–352
        documentation standards, 148–153
        routing architecture design, 323
Catalyst 5000, 208–210
    switches, 63

Catalyst 6000, 222
    switches, 63
Catalyst 8500
    switches, 64
CCDA certification
    exams, 8, 13
    requirements, 8–12
CDDI, 238
cells, ATM, 21
certifications, CCDA
    requirements, 8–12
    study tips, 8
    taking the exam, 13
Charles Spurgeon's Ethernet Web site, 241
circuits, WAN, 244–245
    G&S Productions case study, 267
    Global Supplies Corporation case study, 266
    Limbo Medical Group case study, 264–265
    platform selection, 260
    switched, 245–259
    Widget Manufacturing case study, 261–262
Cisco
    700 series routers, 64
    800 series routers, 64
    1600 series routers, 58
    2500 series routers, 57
    2600 series routers, 58
    2900 switches, 208
    3600 series routers, 59
    4000 series routers, 59
    7000 series routers, 60
    7500 series routers, 60
    12000 GSRs (Gigabit Switch Router), 61
    AS5xxx series routers, 65
    Catalyst 5000 switches, 63
    Catalyst 6000 switches, 63
    Catalyst 6500 switches, 63
    Catalyst 8500 switches, 64
    compression algorithms, data encryption, 345–346
    framework triangle, 80–83
        media problems, 82
        protocol problems, 81–82
        transport problems, 83
    IOS Firewall Feature Set, 185
    Secure Integrated Software, 184
CiscoSecure, 68
CiscoWorks, 111
CiscoWorks 2000, 69
classes, IP addresses, 26
Clustering switches, 62
coaxial cable
    Ethernet, 35
    networks used for, 202
collision domains, 240
    Ethernet, 37
    LAN design, 218–219

commands, showing design tests, 380–381
company policies, documenting, 142–143
compression, data encrypton, 344
   Cisco compression algorithms, 345–346
   dictionary, 344
   statistical, 344
configurations, router, standards used in book, 4
constraints, business, documenting, 141
convergence
   EIGRP, 318
   link-state protocols, 315
copper distributed data interface, *See* CDDI
core layer
   hierarchical network model, 86–87, 169
costs, design tests, 383
counter rotation, FDDI, 42
CRC, 236
   Ethernet, 203
CSMA/CD (Carrier Sense Multiple Access/Collision
      Detection), 19
   10Mbps Ethernet, 201
CSRs (Campus Switch Routers)
   8500 series routers, 64
customer presentation templates, 382
   design testing, 383–384
customers, project requirements, 144
custom queuing
   data encryption, 348–349
CWSI (CiscoWorks for Switched Internetworks), 69
cyclic redundancy check, *See* CRC

D

DAS (dual attached station), 217
   FDDI, 43
data encryption, 343–350
   compression, 344–346
   IPSec, 344
   queuing, 346–349
   WFQ, 350
Data Link Switching, *See* DLSw
Data Terminal Equipment, *See* DTE
data-link layer technologies, 200
   Ethernet functions, 201
DDP (Datagram Delivery Protocol), 32
delay
   EIGRP, 316
   IGRP, 302
design
   access lists (router software), 340
   project requirements, documenting, 145
   testing, 362, 380
      case studies, 366–373, 385–390
      commands, showing, 380–381

      costs, 383
      customer presentation, 382–384
      network traffic, capturing, 382
      network traffic, generating, 382
      pilots, 366
      protocol analyzers, 381
      prototypes, 363–365
      risk, 383
desktop modular access routers, 58
dictionary compression
   data encryption, 344
distance vector routing, 40
distance-vector protocols, 300–308
   convergence, 309
   link failure, 306
   overhead, 309
distribution layer
   hierarchical network model, 87–88, 170
DIX Ethernet, 201
DLCIs (Data Link Connection Identifiers), 21
DLSw, 323
DMZ (demilitarized zone), 187
DNS
   address summarization, 281
documentation checklists, 102–103
   application usage, 107–108
   availability statistics, 114
   network management, 118
   network maps, 103
   performance statistics, 116
   protocol analyzers, 110–111
   protocol usage, 109
   reliability statistics, 115–116
   router/switch load statistics, 117
   server/user maps, 106
   topology maps, 104
   utilization statistics, 112–113
documenting existing networks, 102–103
   application usage, 107–108
   availability statistics, 114
   network management, 118
   network maps, 103
   performance statistics, 116
   protocol analyzers, 110–111
   protocol usage, 109
   reliability statistics, 115–116
   router/switch load statistics, 117
   server/user maps, 106
   topology maps, 104
   utilization statistics, 112–113
documenting
   acceptance criteria, 144
   application requirements, 146
   business constraints, 141
   business goals, 140–141
   business issues, 137–138

case studies
  G&S Productions, 160–162
  Global Supplies Corporation, 156–160
  Limbo Medical Group, 154–155
  Widget Manufacturing, 148–153
company policies, 142–143
design requirements, 145
documentation checklist, 136
manageability requirements, 145
performance requirements, 146
problems
  identification, 138–139
project scope, 144
requirements
  project, 144
security requirements, 145
traffic-pattern predictions, 147
usage requirements, 147
drop action
  MACs, 220
DSL routers, 64
DTE, 218, 241
Dual Attached Station, *See* DAS
dynamic routing
  distance-vector protocols, 300–308
    convergence, 309
    overhead, 309
  hybrid protocols
    EIGRP, 316–318
  link-state protocols, 310
    NLSP, 314
    convergence, 315
    IS-IS, 314
    OSPF, 311–312
    overhead, 315

E

Early Token Release, *See* ETC
EIGRP, 25, 31, 316
  convergence, 318
  metrics, 316
  overhead, 318
encryption
  data, 343–350
    compression, 344–346
    IPSec, 344
    queuing, 346–349
    WFQ, 350
  keys, 342
  traffic reduction, 341
Enhanced Interior Gateway Routing Protocol, *See* EIGRP
Ethernet, 19, 237
  algorithim flows, 203

bridges, 37
broadcast storms, 40
cabling, 34–35
collision domains, 37
CRC field, 203
data-link layer, 201
healthy, 203
hubs, 36
jams, 202
layers of, 203
LLC2, 203
media types, 34
MSAUs, 41
operation, 202
routers, 40
signaling types, 34
speeds, 34
standards, 238
STP, 36
switches, 38
types, 34
Ethernet: The Definitive Guide, book by Charles Spurgeon, 205
ETR, 212
examples, access lists (router software), 337–339
exams, CCDA certification
  study tips, 8
  taking the exam, 13

F

FAQs, 70
Fast Ethernet, 19, 201, 206, 237
  100Base-FX, 206
  100Base-T4, 206
  100Base-TX, 206
  specifications, 239
Fast Ethernet Interface Processor, *See* FEIP
Fast Link Pulse, *See* FLP
FDDI (Fiber Distributed Data Interface), 20, 42, 201, 216–217, 237
  counter rotation, 42
  DASs (dual attached stations), 43
  DLCIs (Data Link Connection Identifiers), 21
  media problems, 83
  SASs (single attached stations), 43
  secondary rings, 43
FEIP, 207
fiber distributed data inteface, *See* FDDI
fiber optic cable
  Ethernet, 35
  networks used for, 202
  Token Ring, 213
Fiber Optics White Paper Web site, 241

fiber-optic inter-repeater link, *See* FOIRL
FIFO queuing, data encryption, 346
Find a Product Web site, 242
firewalls, 186–188
    DMZ, 187
    PIX options, 65
fixed-port switches, 61
flat network designs, 170–171
flood action, MACs, 220
FLP, 207
FOIRL, 238
    fiber optic cable, 202
forward action, MACs, 220
Frame Relay, 20
    hierarchical network model, 89–92
Frame Relay CIR
    switched WAN circuits, 259
framing
    switched WAN circuits, 259
FTP, 25

G

G&S Productions case study
    documentation standards, 160–162
    network addresses, 293
    routing architecture, 329
    switched WAN circuits, 267
Gigabit Ethernet, 19, 201, 208–210, 237
Gigabit Ethernet Alliance, 210
Gigabit Ethernet Alliance Web site, 241
Gigabit NICs, 209
Global Supplies Corporation case study, 354–356
    design test, 372–373, 389
    documentation standards, 156–160
    network addresses, 291
    routing architecture, 327
    switched WAN circuits, 266
goals, business, 140–141
GRPs (Gigabit Route Processors), 61

H

HDLC, 20
Healthy Ethernet, 203
hierarchical network model, 169
    access layer, 88, 170
    core layer, 86–87, 169
    distribution layer, 87–88, 170
    Frame Relay WANs, 89–92
high-end routers, 60
High-Speed Token Ring Alliance Web site, 241

high-speed Token Ring, *See* HSTR
hosts
    redundancy, 182–183
HSTR, 216, 240
HTTP, 25
hubs, 36
hybrid protocols, EIGRP, 316
    convergence, 318
    metrics, 316
    overhead, 318
hybrid switched WAN circuits, 252–256

I

ICMP, 24
IEEE, 802.3 standard, 201
IEEE, 802.3u standard, 206
IEEE, 802.3z standard, 208
IEEE, 802.5 standard, 211
IEEE Standards Web site, 241
IGRP, 25, 301
    metrics, 302
inter-switch link, *See* ISL, 240
Interconnections, book by Perlman, 203
IOS (Internetworking Operating System), 68
IP, 23
    addresses, 26
        classes, 26
        octets, 26
    addressing, 273
        public vs. private, 274–275
    subnet masks, 27
    subnets, 26
IP RIP, 300
IP RIP version 2, 301
IPSec, data encrypton, 344
IPX
    addresses, 31, 282–283
    addressing
        selecting addresses, 284–285
    network layer, 29
    routing protocols, 30
    transport layer, 30
IPX RIP, 30, 302–303
IPX/SPX, 29
    application layer, 30
IS-IS protocol, 314
    link-state protocol, 314
ISDN (Integrated Services Digital Network), 21
    routers, 64
    switched WAN circuits, 246–249
ISL, 240
    ports, Ethernet, 207

J–L

jams
  Ethernet, 202
LAN design, 200–226
  100Mbps (Fast Ethernet), 201–202, 206
  5-4-3 rule, 222–224
  80-20 rule, 222
  broadcast domains, 220–221
  case study, 224–226
  collission domains, 218–219
  FDDI, 201, 216–217
  Gigabit Ethernet, 201, 208–210
  guidelines, 222–224
  QoS, 224
  SRB, 213–215
  Token Ring, 201, 211–213
LAN protocols, 19
LAN technologies
  Ethernet, 237
  Fast Ethernet, 237
LANs
  Ethernet
    bridges, 37
    hubs, 36
    routers, 40
    switches, 38
  FDDI, 42
  hierarchical network model, 169
  switches, 61
  Token Ring, 41
layer 2, OSI model, 220
layer 3 switches, 63
layers
  OSI model, 17
    See also Appendix C
LightStream, 1010 switches, 66
Limbo Medical Group case study, 353–354
  design test, 371–372, 388
  documentation standards, 154–155
  network addresses, 290
  routing architecture, 326
  switched WAN circuits, 264–265
line coding
  switched WAN circuits, 259
link state routing, 41
link-state protocols, 310
  convergence, 315
  IS-IS, 314
  NLSP, 314
  OSPF, 311–312
  overhead, 315
LLC2, Ethernet, 203
load balancing options, 67
load

EIGRP, 316
IGRP, 302
lobe cable
  Token Ring, 206, 213
Local area networks, See LANs
LocalDirector, 67

M

MAC protocol, 218
MACs
  drop action, 220
  flood action, 220
  forward action, 220
managing network performance, 69
managing projects
  documenting requirements, 145
MAU, 236
  ring in ports, 213
  ring out ports, 213
  Token Ring, 213
Media Access Conrol protocol, See MAC protocol
media problems, Cisco framework triangle, 82
media types, Ethernet, 34
Metcalfe, Bob, 201
MHS (Message Handling System), NetWare, 30
microsegmenting, 82
mid-range routers, 59
MLS (multilayer switching), 63
modular switches, 62–63
monitoring probes, 67
MPOA network model
  (Multiprotocol over ATM), 174–175
MRTG (Multi-Router Traffic Grapher), 111
MSAU (MultiStation Access Unit)
  Ethernet, 41
  Token Ring, 213
MSRs (Multiprotocol Switch Routers)
  8500 series routers, 64
MTU
  EIGRP, 316
  IGRP, 302
multistation access unit, See MAU

N

Nagule, Matthew G., 203, 242
NAT, network addressing, 275–276
NBP (Name Binding Protocol), 32
NCPs (NetWare Core Protocols), 30
NetBEUI, 318
NetFlow switching, 63

Netsys, 69
NETSYS, protocol analyzer, 111
NetWare
   MHS (Message Handling System), 30
Network Interface Cards, *See* NICs
network layer
   AppleTalk, 32
   IPX, 29
   TCP/IP, 23
network management
   documentation process, 118
network maps, 103
network performance management, 69
Network Protocol Handbook, book by Matthew G.
      Nagule, 203
networks, *See also* LANs
   addressing, 272
      G&S Productions case study, 293
      Global Supplies Corporation case study, 291
      IP, 273–275
      IPX, 282–285
      Limbo Medical Group case study, 290
      NAT, 275–276
      selecting addresses, 281
      summarization, 280–281
      VLSMs, 278–280
      Widget Manufacturing case study, 285–287
   documenting, 102–103
      application usage, 107–108
      availability statistics, 114
      management, 118
      network maps, 103
      performance statistics, 116
      protocol analyzers, 110–111
      protocol usage, 109
      reliability statistics, 115–116
      router/switch load statistics, 117
      topology maps, 104
      user/server maps, 106
      utilization statistics, 112–113
   firewalls, 186–188
   MPOA model, 174–175
   physical redundancy, 178
   redundant model, 177
   router-hub model, 170–171
   secure model, 183–184
   three layer, 84
   topologies, Ethernet, 34
   traffic
      capturing, 382
      generating, 382
   VLAN model, 172–174
   VPNs, 189
NICs, Gigabit Ethernet, 209
NLP (Normal Link Pulse), 207

NLSP (NetWare Link-Service Protocol), 31
   link-state protocol, 314
NT1s (Network Termination Type, 1 devices)
   ISDN routers, 64

O

octets, IP addresses, 26
Open Shortest Path First, See OSPF
OSI (Open Systems Interconnect) model, 17
   layer 2, 220
   layers, 17
      See also Appendix C
OSPF, 25
   link-state protocol, 311–312
overhead
   EIGRP, 318
   link-state protocols, 315
   source-route bridging, 323

P

PAMs (Port Adapter Modules), 60
PCs, first, 200
peer router authentication, 342
performance
   management, networks, 69
   requirements, documenting, 146
   statistics, documentation process, 116
Perlman, Radia, 203
permanent switched WAN circuits, 250–251
personal computers, first, 200
physical network redundancy, 178
pilots, design testing, 366
PIX firewalls, 65
platforms, switched WAN circuits, 260
poison reverse, disabling, 307
port speed, switched WAN circuits, 259
ports, 100Base-TX, 207
priority queuing, data encryption, 347
private IP addresses, 274–275
problems, identifying, documentation, 138–139
protocols
   AARP, 32
   analyzers
      design tests, 381
      documentation process, 110–111
   AppleTalk, 31
   ARP, 24
   ATP, 32
   BGP, 25
   DDP, 32

EIGRP, 25
FTP, 25
HTTP, 25
ICMP, 24
IGRP, 25
IP, 23
    addressing, 273–275
IPX/SPX, 29
IPX addresses, 282–285
LAN-based, 19
NBP, 32
NCP, 30
NLSP, 31
OSPF, 25
problems, Cisco framework triangle, 81–82
RIP, 25
routed, 22
routing, 22
RTMP, 33
SAP, 31
Telnet, 25
UDP, 24
usage, 109
WAN-based, 20
prototypes, design testing, 363–365
provisioning, switched WAN circuits, 257–258
proxy services, 340
public IP addresses, 274–275

Q

QoS, LAN design, 224
queuing
    data encrypton, 346
        custom, 348–349
        FIFO, 346
        priority, 347

R

RADIUS (Remote Dial-in User Service), 68
redundant network model, 177
redundant routers/switches, 179–181
redundant servers, 182–183
reliability
    EIGRP, 316
    IGRP, 302
    statistics, documentation process, 115–116
remote access routers, 65
remote monitoring probes, 67
remote monitoring, *See* RMON
repeaters, *See* hubs

RIF, 213
    Token Ring, 236
ring in (RI) ports, MAU, 213
ring out (RO) ports, MAU, 213
RIP, 25, 300
    broadcasts, protocol problems, 82
risk, design tests, 383
RME (Resource Manager Essentials), 69
RMON, 241
routed protocols, 22
router-hub network model, 170–171
router/switch load statistics, documentation process, 117
routers
    700 series, 64
    800 series, 64
    1600 series, 58
    2500 series, 57
    2600 series, 58
    3600 series, 59
    4000 series, 59
    7000 series, 60
    7500 series, 60
    AS5xxx series, 65
    configurations, standards used in book, 4
    DSL, 64
    Ethernet, 40
    high-end, 60
    ISDN, 64
    mid-range, 59
    redundancy, 179–181
    remote access, 65
    small-office, 57
    software features, 334
        access lists, 334–340
        data encryption, 343–350
        peer router autthentication, 342
        proxy services, 340
        traffic reduction, 341
routing architecture
    bridging protocols, 318
    case studies
        G&S Productions, 329
        Global Supplies Corporation, 327
        Limbo Medical Group, 326
        Widget Manufacturing, 323
    design, 298–330
    dynamic, 300–310
        convergence, 309
        overhead, 309
    source-route bridging, 320, 323
        overhead, 323
    static, 298–300
    transparent bridging, 319–320
routing by rumor, 40
Routing Information Field, *See* RIF
routing protocols, 22

AppleTalk, 33
IPX, 30
TCP/IP, 25
RSMs (Route Switch Modules), 63, 173
RTMP (Route Table Maintenance Protocol), 33, 303

S

S/T interfaces, ISDN routers, 64
Sales Tools Central[mdProduct Central Web site, 242
SAP (Service Advertisement Protocol), 31
    broadcasts, protocol problems, 82
SAS (single attached station), 217
        FDDI, 43
scope of project, documenting, 144
secondary rings, FDDI, 43
secure network model, 183–184
security, documenting requirements, 145
Server maps, 106
servers, redundancy, 182–183
session layer, AppleTalk, 32
shielded twisted pair, *See* STP
signaling types, Ethernet, 34
Single Attached Station, *See* SAS
small-office routers, 57
SNA, 318
soft errors, Token Ring, 211
software
    router, 334
        access lists, 334–340
        data encryption, 343–350
        peer router authentication, 342
        proxy services, 340
        traffic reduction, 341
source route bridging, *See* SRB
source route/translational bridging, *See* SR/TLB
speeds of Ethernet, 34
split-horizon, disabling, 307
Spurgeon, Charles, 205
SRB, 39, 213–215, 239
    routing architecture, 320, 323
        overhead, 323
SR/TLB, 39, 239
stackable switches, 61
static routing, 298–300
statistical compression, data encryption, 344
statistics tracking, network documentation, 112
STP (shielded twisted pair), 237
    Ethernet, 36
    Token Ring, 213
subnet masks, IP, 27
subnets, IP, 26
summarization, network addressing, 280
    DNS, 281

switch clustering, 62
switch load statistics, network documentation, 117
switched circuits, WAN, 245
    analog, 245
    circuit provisioning, 257–258
    Frame Relay CIR and Port Speed, 259
    framing and line coding, 259
    G&S Productions case study, 267
    Global Supplies Corporation case study, 266
    hybrid, 252–256
    ISDN, 246–249
    Limbo Medical Group case study, 264–265
    permanent, 250–251
    platform selection, 260
    Widget Manufacturing case study, 261–262
switches
    ATM, 66
    Catalyst 5000, 63
    Catalyst 6000, 63
    Catalyst 6500, 63
    Catalyst 8500, 64
    fixed-port, 61
    LightStream 1010, 66
    modular, 62–63
    redundancy, 179–181
switching routers, 63
switching, NetFlow, 63
SwitchProbe series, 67
System Network Architecture, *See* SNA

T

TACACS+ (Terminal Access Controller Access Control
        System Plus), 68
TCP/IP
    application layer, 24
    network layer, 23
    routing protocols, 25
    transport layer, 24
Telnet, 25
templates, customer presentation, 383–384
testing designs, 362, 380
        case studies, 366–373, 385–390
        commands, showing, 380–381
        costs, 383
        customer presentation, 382–384
        network traffic, capturing, 382
        network traffic, generating, 382
        pilots, 366
        protocol analyzers, 381
        prototypes, 363–365
        risk, 383
three layer networks, 84
Token Ring, 20, 41, 201, 211–213, 237

16/4 standards, 212
active monitors, 42
adapter cards, 213
lobe cable, 206, 213
MAU, 213
media problems, 83
MSAU, 213
soft errors, 211
switches, 215–216
translational bridges, 213
topologies of networks, Ethernet, 34
topology maps, 104
traffic pattern predictions
documenting, 147
traffic reduction, router software, 341
encryption, 341
performance enhancement, 341
translational bridges, Token Ring, 213
transparent bridging, 38
routing architecture, 319–320
transport layer
AppleTalk, 32
IPX, 30
TCP/IP, 24
Cisco framework triangle, 83
twisted pair, 236
types of Ethernet, 34

U

U interfaces, ISDN routers, 64
UDP (User Datagram Protocol), 24
unshielded twisted pair, See UTP
usage documentation, 107
usage requirements, documenting, 147
user maps, 106
utilization statistics, documentation process, 112–113
UTP (Unshielded Twisted Pair), 35, 236
Ethernet, 35
networks used for, 202
Token Ring, 213

V

Variable Length Subnet Masks, See VLSMs
VIPs (Versatile Interface Processors), 60
VLAN (Virtual LANs) network model, 172–174, 215
VLSMs (Variable Length Subnet Masks)
network addressing, 278–280
protocol problems, 81
VoIP (Voice over IP), 223
VPNs (Virtual Private Networks), 189

W

WAN protocols, 20
WANs circuits, 244–245
G&S Productions case study, 267
Global Supplies Corporation case study, 266
Limbo Medical Group case study, 264–265
platform selection, 260
switched, 245–259
Widget Manufacturing case study, 261–262
Web sites
Charles Spurgeon's Ethernet, 241
Fiber Optics White Paper, 241
Find a Product, 242
Gigabit Ethernet Alliance, 241
High-Speed Token Ring Alliance, 241
IEEE Standards, 241
Sales Tools Central—Product Central, 242
WFQ, data encrypton, 350
Widget Manufacturing case study, 350–352
documentation standards, 148–153
network addresses, 285–287
routing architecture, 323
switched WAN circuits, 261–262
design test, 366–369, 385–386
wire speed routers, 63
witches, 38
workgroup switches, 61
Xerox Corporation, 201

SOFTWARE AND INFORMATION LICENSE

The software and information on this diskette (collectively referred to as the "Product") are the property of The McGraw-Hill Companies, Inc. ("McGraw-Hill") and are protected by both United States copyright law and international copyright treaty provision. You must treat this Product just like a book, except that you may copy it into a computer to be used and you may make archival copies of the Products for the sole purpose of backing up our software and protecting your investment from loss.

By saying "just like a book," McGraw-Hill means, for example, that the Product may be used by any number of people and may be freely moved from one computer location to another, so long as there is no possibility of the Product (or any part of the Product) being used at one location or on one computer while it is being used at another. Just as a book cannot be read by two different people in two different places at the same time, neither can the Product be used by two different people in two different places at the same time (unless, of course, McGraw-Hill's rights are being violated).

McGraw-Hill reserves the right to alter or modify the contents of the Product at any time.

This agreement is effective until terminated. The Agreement will terminate automatically without notice if you fail to comply with any provisions of this Agreement. In the event of termination by reason of your breach, you will destroy or erase all copies of the Product installed on any computer system or made for backup purposes and shall expunge the Product from your data storage facilities.

LIMITED WARRANTY

McGraw-Hill warrants the physical diskette(s) enclosed herein to be free of defects in materials and workmanship for a period of sixty days from the purchase date. If McGraw-Hill receives written notification within the warranty period of defects in materials or workmanship, and such notification is determined by McGraw-Hill to be correct, McGraw-Hill will replace the defective diskette(s). Send request to:

Customer Service
McGraw-Hill
Gahanna Industrial Park
860 Taylor Station Road
Blacklick, OH 43004-9615

The entire and exclusive liability and remedy for breach of this Limited Warranty shall be limited to replacement of defective diskette(s) and shall not include or extend any claim for or right to cover any other damages, including but not limited to, loss of profit, data, or use of the software, or special, incidental, or consequential damages or other similar claims, even if McGraw-Hill has been specifically advised as to the possibility of such damages. In no event will McGraw-Hill's liability for any damages to you or any other person ever exceed the lower of suggested list price or actual price paid for the license to use the Product, regardless of any form of the claim.

THE McGRAW-HILL COMPANIES, INC. SPECIFICALLY DISCLAIMS ALL OTHER WARRANTIES, EXPRESS OR IMPLIED, INCLUDING BUT NOT LIMITED TO, ANY IMPLIED WARRANTY OF MERCHANTABILITY OR FITNESS FOR A PARTICULAR PURPOSE. Specifically, McGraw-Hill makes no representation or warranty that the Product is fit for any particular purpose and any implied warranty of merchantability is limited to the sixty day duration of the Limited Warranty covering the physical diskette(s) only (and not the software or information) and is otherwise expressly and specifically disclaimed.

This Limited Warranty gives you specific legal rights; you may have others which may vary from state to state. Some states do not allow the exclusion of incidental or consequential damages, or the limitation on how long an implied warranty lasts, so some of the above may not apply to you.

This Agreement constitutes the entire agreement between the parties relating to use of the Product. The terms of any purchase order shall have no effect on the terms of this Agreement. Failure of McGraw-Hill to insist at any time on strict compliance with this Agreement shall not constitute a waiver of any rights under this Agreement. This Agreement shall be construed and governed in accordance with the laws of New York. If any provision of this Agreement is held to be contrary to law, that provision will be enforced to the maximum extent permissible and the remaining provisions will remain in force and effect.